Essays in Economics

THE PAPERS OF JAMES TOBIN

Volume 1 *Essays in Economics: Macroeconomics,* New York: North-Holland, 1971; MIT Press 1987

Volume 2 *Essays in Economics: Consumption and Econometrics,* New York: North-Holland, 1975

Volume 3 *Essays in Economics: Theory and Policy,* Cambridge, MA: MIT Press, 1982

Essays in Economics
Macroeconomics

James Tobin

The MIT Press, Cambridge, Massachusetts, and London, England

Second printing, 1988

First MIT Press Edition 1987

Library of Congress Cataloging-in-Publication Data

Tobin, James, 1918–
  Essays in economics.

  (The Papers of James Tobin ; v. 1)
  Reprint. Originally published: Amsterdam ; New York :
North-Holland, 1971.
  Includes bibliographies and index.
  1. Economics   2. Macroeconomics.   I. Title
II. Series: Tobin, James, 1918–   Essays.
Selections ; v. 1.
HB34.T622   1987   339   86-21157
ISBN 0-262-20062-7

PREFACE

This volume is a collection of professional papers I have written in macroeconomics over the past thirty years. A subsequent volume will include papers on other subjects, principally consumer behavior and econometrics. These collections do not include less scholarly essays on economic policy intended for a popular audience. I have previously published a collection of such papers in *National Economic Policy* (Yale University Press, 1966).

The essays in this volume are arranged by topic; within each topic they are generally in chronological sequence except when a different order seems to provide a more logical exposition of the subject matter. The papers are not reprinted here exactly as they were originally published. To the best of my ability I have corrected typographical errors and other slips. More important, I have deleted material that would be repetitive of other chapters; and in some cases I have deleted material that today appears to me irrelevant or wrong. I have also provided new footnotes to help the reader see the connection between one chapter and another and in some instances to point out changes in my views or to make other comments. The introductions to the topical sections attempt to provide some perspective and structure for the essays that follow.

In spite of these efforts at updating and integration, the volume remains a collection of separate papers written at different times rather than a coherent statement of macroeconomics as I might expound it today. Whatever unity it has derives from the quest it represents. I have been trying over these years to piece together for myself a reasonably systematic understanding of the related phenomena ,of short-run economic fluctuation and long-run growth.

Koen Suryatmodjo faithfully and skillfully read the articles to spot errors and repetitions, and to suggest editorial changes appropriate for this collection. Stephen Webb also gave able assistance in preparing the articles for republication. I am grateful to both of them. For help in this project, as in so many other of my endeavors, I am deeply indebted to Mrs. Laura Harrison, my secretary.

Some of the papers in this volume were written with collaborators. I would like to thank William Brainard, F.T. Dolbear, Jr., H.S. Houthakker, Robert M. Solow, Harold W. Watts, Christian von Weizsäcker, and Menahem

v

Yaari for graciously consenting to the inclusion here of articles of which they were joint authors, and Mrs. Challis Hall for permitting me to republish here a series of three papers written jointly with her late husband, my friend and colleague.

Finally, I acknowledge with gratitude the permission of the original publishers of the articles:

American Economic Review
Econometrica
Economia International
Richard D. Irwin, Inc.
Journal of Money, Credit, and Banking
Journal of Political Economy

Alfred Knopf, Inc.
Prentice-Hall, Inc.
Quarterly Journal of Economics
Review of Economic Studies
Review of Economics and
Statistics

INTRODUCTION

MACROECONOMICS

Macroeconomics concerns the determinants of the performance of entire economies: nations, groups of nations, the whole world. The theoretical concepts and statistical measures involved are generally economy-wide aggregates or averages, such as national income, total employment, or a national cost-of-living index. The objective is to explain ups and downs of these magnitudes and their interrelations. The basic assumption is that this can be done without much attention to the constituents of the aggregates, that is, to the behavior and fortunes of particular households, business firms, industries, or regions. As usual in economics, the strategy is to build models that lay bare the essentials of the phenomena under study; the art is to find those simplifying abstractions that clarify and do not distort. Macroeconomics is based on the faith that economies are subject to laws of motion which are largely independent of the details of their internal structure.

This faith, in turn, rests on a fact of common observation centuries old. Economies — at least the decentralized, market economies of the western world — are subject to pervasive tides of prosperity and depression, inflation and deflation, that dominate the experiences of their members. These waves give a strong component of common and shared experience even to individuals, firms, regions, and nations whose skills, resources, and luck are otherwise very different. Times were hard for virtually everybody during the Great Depression. In contrast, the climate of steady overall prosperity and rapid growth in western industrial countries since World War II has advanced the fortunes of almost everyone. It is much more plausible to attribute the differences in individual experiences before and after the war to differences in the overall climate, which individuals had no control over, than to attribute the economy-wide contrast between the two periods to a massive coincidence of individual failures or successes.

Reprinted from *Economics*, Nancy D. Ruggles, ed. (Englewood Cliffs, N.J.: Prentice-Hall, Inc., 1970) pp. 44–54.

Since it is concerned with tides and trends in general business activity, macroeconomics has a strong and direct orientation to public policy. Ever since the Great Depression, overall economic performance has been an acknowledged governmental responsibility in all industrialized market economies. The party in power is blamed if unemployment is too high, or price inflation too rapid, or the balance of payments too unfavorable. Macroeconomics contributed some of the intellectual justification for this historic expansion of the span of government responsibility; the political and moral steam came from a general resolution that the Great Depression never be allowed to happen again. In any event, one preoccupation of macroeconomics has been to show how the fiscal and monetary tools of the central government can be used to stabilize the economy. Macroeconomics has been heavily involved in public policy, both at the level of popular and parliamentary debate of the great issues of fiscal and monetary policy and at the more technical levels of operations of the government agencies charged with economic stabilization.

This policy orientation is one reason that the nation has been the customary unit of analysis. The instruments of policy are in the hands of national governments. Of course, foreign trade and other international transactions are an essential part of the analysis of most national economies. From a broader standpoint, a true international macroeconomics must treat simultaneously several national economies and the transactions among them. As at the national level, analysis is developing parallel with the development of policy-making institutions, in this case intergovernmental collaborations. The European Economic Community is the main example of such machinery, but consultation in the interests of "harmonizing" national policies occurs also in wider and looser groupings of countries. (The Organization of Economic Cooperation and Development, the International Monetary Fund, and the Group of Ten major monetary powers are examples.)

Although macroeconomic models do not pay explicit attention to the internal composition of the aggregates, the relationships among aggregate variables that make up the models are intended to be consistent with theoretical and empirical knowledge of the behavior of individual economic units and particular markets. Aggregate consumption spending is the sum of the consumption outlays of 60 million households, and the explanation of total consumption in terms of national income and other variables in an aggregative model should conform with what is known about the behavior of individual households. Similarly, an important relationship in aggregative models is a production function linking national output to the economy-wide inputs of labor and other resources. This relationship should be consistent with what is known of input-output technology in the units – plants, firms, industries – where production occurs.

Unfortunately it is seldom true that an exact relationship among aggregate variables, independent of their composition, can be built up from the basic microeconomic relationships. The usual procedure is simple analogy, but it is not clear that this is always the best approximation. Although there is a theory of aggregation, so far it gives little guide to the optimal specification of aggregate variables and relationships. Fortunately this logical gap does not seem to be of decisive practical importance. Economists have long known that there is no best way of averaging individual price changes; for example, to construct a price index. But the insolubility of the "index number problem" has not prevented useful index numbers from being constructed.

There are two persistent grand themes in macroeconomics. One is the explanation of short-run fluctuations – some would call them cycles – in business activity, the year-to-year or month-to-month changes that add up to prosperity or recession, inflation or deflation. The other is the explanation of long-run economic trends, the rate of progress of an economy over the decades.

The difference between the two themes is not completely captured by the difference in time horizon. By and large, the short-run fluctuations are not changes in the productive capacity of an economy but in the degree of utilization of capacity, due in turn to changes in aggregate *demand* for goods and services. But long-run trends – the Great Depression excepted – are generally dominated by changes in productive capacity, somehow, in the long-run demand adapts so that over the decades changes in the degree of utilization of resources are small relative to changes in the supply and productivity of the resources. The theory of long-run growth is essentially a theory of aggregate *supply*.

In one sense it is true to say that both these branches of macroeconomics have a long history. Most of the great names of the history of economic thought have been concerned with one or both of these problems: Hume, Ricardo, Malthus, Marx, Fisher, Wicksell, Schumpeter. But in another and more important sense, macroeconomics is a new field. In its modern form, it is a development of the last forty years. The continuity that links modern microeconomic theory – the theories of value, general equilibrium, and welfare – to its pioneers in the nineteenth century does not exist in macroeconomics.

Four distinct but related developments established the foundations of modern macroeconomics:

1. In the 1920s and 1930s Simon Kuznets, the National Bureau of Economic Research, and the U.S. Department of Commerce laid the conceptual and statistical groundwork of national income accounts. National income and its components and related measures are the basic theoretically meaningful variables of macroeconomics. They provide comprehensive summary measures of the results and uses of economic activity in a nation. They provide, for example, estimates of saving, investment, and consumption and make it possible to study the processes of capital accumulation that play so central a role in both short-run and long-run macroeconomics. Similar national accounts have been estimated for virtually all developed and many undeveloped countries.

Moreover, in the United States and elsewhere, auxiliary statistical information has been improved and expanded: employment and unemployment data, price indexes, wages and hours data, financial and monetary data, national balance sheets and flows of funds, international trade and balance of payments figures, and so on. Although the statistical base is still by no means adequate, current empirical macroeconomics would have been inconceivable without the national income accounts and the other statistical innovations and improvements of the past forty years.

2. Keynes' *General Theory* (1936) was the theoretical *magna charta* for macroeconomics (just as, according to Schumpeter, Walras' work was the magna charta for general equilibrium theory). Keynes set out to build a model to explain the persistence of general involuntary unemployment in the Great Depression, a fact that existing modes of thought in economics had great difficulty in accommodating. One of Keynes' objectives, and eventual triumphs, was to liberate economists and statesmen from misplaced inhibitions on pragmatic measures to relieve unemployment, inhibitions supported by orthodox modes of economic analysis.

But for our present purpose, the specific content of Keynes' message is less important than the fact that he effectively inaugurated explicit macroeconomic model-building. He showed, at least by example, how the equilibrium of the economy as a whole could be described as the solution of a system of equations, and how "comparative statics" results (like the famous "multiplier") could be derived by examining the effects on the solution of varying the parameters of the system. The techniques were not novel. That their application to this subject was relatively novel, however, is indicated by the fact that Keynes had to reconstruct imaginatively the "classical" macroeconomic models he was opposing. At any rate Keynes' example, and the more elegant mathematization of his theory by Hicks and others, unleashed a vast quantity of latent model-building energy. This is the medium in which macroeconomics has been discussed, debated, taught, and advanced ever since.

3. The national income accounting revolution in statistical data and the Keynesian revolution in theory combined to stimulate econometric testing and estimation of economy-wide models. Keynesian and post-Keynesian theory dealt in variables for which national income accounting and related statistical developments provided good numerical counterparts.

Fortunately a considerable development in the power and sophistication of statistical and econometric technique occurred in the 1940s. This development concerned particularly the estimation of systems of simultaneous equations from time series. Subsequently the computer revolution has made it possible to apply techniques and tests previously beyond the limits of practical application.

4. Finally, macroeconomics has shared the benefits of accelerated application of mathematical techniques to economic theory. The use of difference and differential equations in business cycle models was beginning before Keynes, but the substantive economic content of such models was improved by the Keynesian discussion. Subsequently both short-run and long-run macroeconomics have undergone extensive mathematical development. The static equilibrium models of Keynes have given way to dynamic sequential models of both growth and fluctuations. Large-scale computers have made it possible to handle theoretical or empirical models that are too complex for explicit analysis.

The achievements of this combination of developments have been considerable. At the simplest level intellectually, but possibly the most important practically, general understanding of macroeconomic mechanisms has greatly increased. It is inconceivable that policymakers today, aided by their theoretical understanding of the mechanisms and by the statistical information at their disposal, would begin to make the serious errors committed by governments in 1929–32. Nor is this change just a one-shot result of the Keynesian revolution. As Chapter 9 indicates, the intelligence and skill of stabilization policy have improved steadily since World War II.

One reason is that short-run economic forecasting has improved. There are several sources of this improvement. One is the availability of better and more timely data, of which a notable example is the useful surveys of anticipated investment expenditures. Another is the use of more sophisticated and theoretically better-grounded forecasting models. Purely statistical techniques – looking for barometric indicators of future fluctuations of business activity without worrying about the causal mechanisms involved – have largely given way to fully specified models. These may be highly aggregative and simple, susceptible of manipulation and solution by pencil or desk calculation. Or they may be very complex, involving many equations and requiring large-scale computation. Finally, the improvement of forecasting is due to the accumulation of experience and data from the postwar economy, interpreted with the help of modern techniques of statistical and econometric inference.

One advantage of the use of fully specified consistent models of causal mechanisms in forecasting is that the same models can be used in policy-making. The models foretell not only the probable course of the economy but how the course would be altered by changes in policy, such as changes in taxes, government spending, or federal reserve actions.

Empirical estimation of multiequation aggregative models of the United States economy began with Tinbergen (1932) and was given a major new impetus by Klein (1950). The postwar development of models of this kind has culminated in the Brookings model, involving nearly five hundred variables and over three hundred equations. This is the result of collaborative effort by a large team of economists. It is too early to appraise its success and usefulness. It seems clear, however, that computerized models of this kind will play an increasing role in economic research, forecasting, and policy-making.

The monetary side of macroeconomics deserves a special word. Before the Great Depression and Keynes, monetary economics was about the only aggregative economics there was. Monetary policy was similarly the only tool of economic stabilization that was considered and used. The depression led to considerable skepticism regarding the effectiveness and utility of monetary policy, and Keynesian theory provided an intellectual basis for believing that there were times when monetary and financial events had little importance in shaping the course of economic activity. Since World War II, both monetary policy and monetary economics have enjoyed a renaissance. Economists and practical men now agree that "money matters," and this has stimulated a substantial amount of theoretical and empirical research.

Monetary and financial data, so far as they are based on institutional balance sheets and prices in organized markets, are abundant. Modern machines have made it possible to improve, refine, and expand the compilation of these data, and also to seek empirical regularities in financial behavior in the multitude of individual observations. On the aggregative level, the Federal Reserve Board has developed a financial accounting framework, the "flow of funds," for systematic and consistent organization of the data, classified both by sector of the economy (households, nonfinancial business, governments, financial institutions, and so on) and by type of asset or debt (currency, deposits, bonds, mortgages, and so on). Although many people hope that this organization of data will prove to be as powerful an aid to economic understanding as the national income accounts, this hope has not yet been fulfilled. Perhaps the deficiency is conceptual and theoretical; as some have said, the Keynes of "flow of funds" has yet to appear.

One important strand of current monetary economics emphasizes very strongly the central importance of the commercial banking system and the central bank's control of the quantity of commercial bank deposits. The approach is similar in emphasis and spirit to predepression monetary and aggregative economics. That is, the quantity of money – the stock of bank deposits plus currency outside banks – is regarded as the most important determinant of aggregate money income. However, the modern "quantity theory" is supported by more sophisticated theoretical analysis and more extensive empirical research. In any event, the equality of supply and demand for money is considered the basic equation of aggregative economics, and the focus of research is on the functions describing the two sides of this equality. The policy conclusions of this approach – that the rate of change of the quantity of money is the fundamental determinant (although with a long and variable lag) of the course of money national income, that fiscal policy is of negligible significance in this regard, that the best stabilization policy is a steady rate of growth in the quantity of money without reference to the current or projected state of the economy – have attracted widespread support, interest, and controversy.

Other strands of postwar monetary economics are more diverse, eclectic, and uncertain in their conclusions and policy recommendations. They are generally characterized by one or more of the following features:

(a) Emphasis on a general multiequation equilibrium of the entire spectrum of assets and debts; all financial markets, and all financial institutions replace the narrower traditional concentration on the quantity of money and the commercial banking system. No one equation – not even equality of demand and supply of money – is regarded as the determining equation for macroeconomics.

(b) Mechanistic views of the workings of the banking and monetary system and of other financial intermediaries give way to a more behavioristic approach to the functions of the institutions and markets involved. On the conceptual plane, considerable use is made of advances in the theory of decision-making under uncertainty and in inventory theory. The key questions are the linkages of financial variables to real investment and to other spending on goods and services. This is at the same time the area of greatest practical importance for monetary policy, the area of greatest ignorance, and the focus of an increasing amount of empirical research. In recent attempts to estimate econometric models of the economy, notably the model designed and estimated by economists at the Federal Reserve Board and at the Massachusetts Institute of Technology, the financial-real links are formulated in a more explicit and sophisticated manner, and their estimation is regarded as the central task.

CONTENTS

MACROECONOMIC THEORY

Part I contains several theoretical articles on the determination of aggregate employment, income, and prices in the short run. The first two articles concern the effects on employment of a general change in money wage rates, an issue at the center of the debate between Keynes and the classical economists. The question was whether unemployment could persist in equilibrium. The orthodox answer, typified by Pigou, was negative: excess supply of any commodity, including labor, causes its price to fall until the excess supply is eliminated. Keynes attempted to explain why, in the case of labor, the money wage need not fall in the face of unemployment and why a money wage decline, even if it did occur, might not affect the volume of employment. While I accepted, in these articles, the realism of Keynes' observation that money wages are sticky, I pointed out that the very same features of individual and institutional behavior were likely to make employment responsive to any changes in money wages that could be contrived.

In retrospect I think that Pigou and Leontief were theoretically right in denying that unemployment could exist in a competitive equilibrium. Keynes was unsuccessful in providing an *equilibrium* theory of involuntary unemployment. Pragmatically he was right, however, in urging policies other than wage cuts to remedy the mass unemployment of the thirties. Many of his orthodox predecessors and contemporaries were guilty of "misplaced concreteness" in applying equilibrium theory to short-run movements of wages and employment.

My two articles suffer in not distinguishing clearly among the reasons why a proportionate change in all current money wages and prices may affect real behavior. One reason would be "money illusion" proper. But it is hard to believe in indefinite persistence of irrationality that would lead people to behave differently after what amounts merely to a change of monetary unit, as from old francs to new francs. In the absence of true "money illusion," a uniform change in all *current* prices has real consequences when other determining variables denominated in the monetary unit do not change in the

1

same proportion. These other variables include assets, debts, and expected future prices. In general it will take some time for these variables to adjust to a change in current prices, and meanwhile there is nothing irrational or "illusory" in changes in labor supply, consumption, and other real behavior.

Chapter 3 is at least as timely now as in 1947. Clark Warburton was a "monetarist" before his time; the quantity theory of money, which he espoused, has lately enjoyed a new vogue under the persuasive leadership of Milton Friedman. Surprisingly and unfortunately, current discussions of monetary and fiscal policies still exhibit widespread misunderstanding of the theoretical conditions under which either policy or both policies can affect national income. It is as true now as in 1947 that the interest-elasticity of the demand for money is a crucial factor. It is as true now as in 1947 that the statistical evidence is against the zero elasticity on which the monetarist position depends. These issues are further discussed in Chapters 23 and 24.

Chapter 4 is an analysis of the short-run macroeconomic effects of income taxation, but its interest lies as much in its methodology and in its general exposition of Keynesian, classical, and neoclassical theory as in its specific conclusions. In this essay I had the benefit and pleasure of collaborating with my long-time friend and colleague Challis Hall, whose untimely death in 1968 deprived the profession of a leading scholar of public finance.

A recurring question in postwar economic theory, and particularly in this volume, is the role of the size and composition of wealth in the determination of economic activity. The fifth essay of Part I is a critical and, I hope, clarifying examination of various propositions on this subject.

One feature of this article is its skepticism as to the inclusion of interest-bearing deadweight public debt in private wealth, on the now familiar ground that the future taxes to pay the interest are an offsetting private liability. Over the years I have vacillated on this point. Today I believe that the calculus of total wealth is less important than the change in the composition of private balance sheets that the government engineers by borrowing from the public – forcing on taxpayers a long-term debt of some uncertainty while providing bond-holders highly liquid and safe assets. Since no one else can perform the same intermediation, the government's debt issues probably do, within limits, augment private wealth. Another way to make the point is to observe that future tax liabilities are likely to be capitalized at a higher discount rate than claims against the government.

In every period of inflation, proposals are made to provide tax incentives for saving and to make saving compulsory. The weaknesses of these proposals are discussed in Chapter 6, which also explains how to design an effective anti-inflationary saving scheme.

Chapter 7 is an irreverent spoof of a distribution theory advanced by Nicholas Kaldor and others. Perhaps it belongs in Part II, because it is a footnote to the running controversy between neoclassical growth theory and its opponents. Neoclassical theory would have the division of full employment output between investment and consumption depend on the society's propensity to save. If property owners and wage earners differ in their saving behavior, the distribution of income between them would help to determine the share of investment in national output. The income distribution, in turn, depends, in neoclassical theory, on the marginal productivities of capital and labor. Kaldor rejected marginal productivity theory and needed an explanation of factor shares in its place. He regarded the investment share of total output as independently determined by technology and entrepreneurship — something to which the national saving propensity must adapt, rather than vice versa. This is the background for the theory described and attacked in my short note. I would like to record here my judgment, which the reading lists of my courses confirm, that Mr. Kaldor has made many outstanding contributions to economic theory. He should be excused this aberration.

CHAPTER 1

A NOTE ON THE MONEY WAGE PROBLEM

Is the money wage rate an independent determinant of the volume of employment, or does a general change in the money wage alter the level of employment only if it happens to affect some other variable in the system, such as the rate of interest? According to Keynesian theory, the money wage is not an independent determinant of employment; abstracting from effects due to the specific situation, which general theory cannot predict, a change in the money wage will not by itself affect the level of employment. By influencing the demand for money balances for transactions purposes, a rise or fall in the money wage may raise or lower the rate of interest; and a change in the interest rate may induce more or less investment, and accordingly change the volume of employment. But this shaky line of causation is the only channel through which general wage policy can influence the volume of employment. This note will examine some assumptions which underlie the Keynesian theory of the effects on employment of a change in the money wage rate, and their relations to the assumptions of Keynes' general theory, of which this wage theory is supposed to be a part. It will be shown (1) that Keynes' conclusions concerning wages and the employment of labor depend upon the assumption of behavior on the part of those supplying other factors of production exactly contrary to the behavior which Keynes assumes for the factor labor, and (2) that Keynes' conclusions concerning wages and employment depend upon the assumption that individuals as consumers react towards money values in a way which is exactly contrary to their assumed behavior as wage earners.

I

The exposition of money wage doctrine in the *General Theory* [1] and the Pigou–Kaldor discussion of the problem in the *Economic Journal* [2] were

Reprinted from *Quarterly Journal of Economics* (May 1941), 508-16.

carried on within the framework of a model which assumed, among other things, that labor is the sole prime factor. This model rules out the possibility of substitution between other factors and labor as a result of the change in the money wage rate. This fact has led some economists to dismiss the Keynesian money wage doctrine on the ground that it is incompatible with the theory of substitution between factors, with marginal productivity analysis. [3] As Lerner has shown, [4] however, recognition of the possibility of substitution does not alter the Keynesian conclusions, provided that one assumption is added to the usual Keynesian assumptions for the problem. This additional assumption is the crucial thing: it is that all factors other than labor are fully employed and their prices completely flexible. In order to demonstrate how crucial this assumption is, it will be well to rehearse the process by which a change in the wage rate is absorbed into the system. In this section we shall accept all the Keynesian assumptions, including the "crucial" one we have just listed; the Keynesian results will follow smoothly. This account will incidentally show that, given the necessary assumptions, Keynesian money wage doctrine is perfectly reconcilable with marginal productivity theory. In section II we shall show that the Keynesian doctrine breaks down if the "crucial" assumption is removed, and we shall consider the validity of the assumption. And in section III we shall examine the crucial nature and the validity of another of the Keynesian assumptions.

From the standpoint of theory it makes no difference whether the argument is expounded in terms of a money wage rise or a money wage cut The two cases are symmetrical, and translation from one to the other is easy Each case, moreover, has practical importance, since each is frequently proposed as a remedy for unemployment. Out of deference to the tradition in discussion of this problem, the argument here presented is in terms of a money wage cut; but it is equally applicable to a money wage rise.

Consider, then, the case of a general cut in the money wage rate. Consider it first solely from the point of view of marginal productivity theory, which takes no account of reactions on the demand side. Faced with reduced labor costs and unchanged demand curves, businessmen will naturally expand output. This will be one reason for an increase in the employment of labor. Further, marginal productivity theory tells us that the impulse of entrepreneurs who find that wages have been lowered will be to hire more labor relatively to other factors whose prices are unchanged. None of these other factors will in fact be dismissed, since by assumption the prices of these factors are perfectly flexible and will be lowered sufficiently to keep them fully employed. This process will continue until these prices are so low that there is no longer any inducement to try to substitute labor for other factors.

This point will occur when the ratio of the price to the marginal product for each of these other factors is once again equal to the corresponding ratio for labor. This will not restore the prices of the various factors to their former relation to each other; for the hiring of labor, the expansion of output, have altered the relation of their marginal products. In the new equilibrium there will be expanded output, increased employment of labor, and the same employment of other factors.

This is the story which marginal productivity analysis tells us, but it is not the whole story. For we cannot continue to assume unchanged demand curves. With more labor employed than before and with no less of other factors, the real income of the community must be greater. According to Keynes' psychological law of consumption, with a larger real income the community will try to save more. [5] Let us assume investment to be constant, in real terms, at some level k. If the system was formerly in equilibrium, then the rate of saving at the former level of real income must have been k. Now, however, real income has been increased; therefore, saving must be greater than k. This excess of saving over investment will continue so long as consumers' real income is not exactly as large as it was before. For so long entrepreneurs will be receiving less than they pay out as costs, they will be forced to contract output until they are producing the same amount as before. This amount they cannot produce except by restoring the previous level of employment of labor, because the prices of other factors are always adjusted so that these factors are fully employed. [6]

This result is not at all inconsistent with marginal productivity theory. As the demand for their products diminishes, entrepreneurs will attempt to dismiss both laborers and other factors. Since the tendency to dismiss other factors will result in a lowering of their prices, while the wage rate remains constant, they will dismiss labor. The rise in the marginal product of labor relative to that of other factors during this process must be just offset by the fall in the prices of other factors. Otherwise it would be profitable, at each level of demand, to substitute labor for other factors or other factors for labor. This means that when the former total output and total employment are reached, the price of labor must be in the same proportion to the prices of other factors as before the original wage cut. The net result is that all prices are reduced in proportion to the wage cut, and employment and output are the same in the new equilibrium as in the old. (In order to isolate the effects of wage policy, we neglect the possible effect on the rate of interest of this reduction in prices, and assume that the supply of money is perfectly elastic.)

The same argument applies, *mutatis mutandis*, to a rise in the money wage rate. It will step up all prices proportionally, and leave employment and output unchanged.

II

It is easy to see the crucial nature of the assumption that all factors other than labor are fully employed and that their prices are perfectly flexible. If the persons who supply these factors acted differently, they would not always adjust their money rates of remuneration so that they are fully employed. If entrepreneurs' demand for them fell off, their prices would not fall sufficiently to keep some of these factors from becoming unemployed and being replaced by labor. This would be the result in case of a cut in the wage rate. Consequently, even granting that the original level of output is restored, it would be produced more by labor and less by other factors. There would be in the new equilibrium more employment of labor than before. Conversely, a wage rise would under these circumstances result in decreased employment of labor. For if other factors were not fully employed to begin with, it would be possible for entrepreneurs to obtain more of them, at the same rate or at a higher rate if necessary. They would be substituted for labor, and in the end the same output would be produced less by labor and more by other factors.

It is clear, therefore, that this assumption is crucial to the Keynesian money wage doctrine. But this assumption means that the persons who supply these other factors are expected to behave differently from the persons who supply the factor labor. Wage earners, according to Keynes, are interested in the money wage, and they will supply more labor at a given real wage the higher is the money wage. The consequence of this attitude of wage earners is that the money wage is likely to be rigid. The persons who supply the other factors in the Keynesian society act quite differently. They are not at all interested in their money rate of remuneration, and always adjust it so that the factors they supply are fully employed.

Professor Leontief has shown that Keynes' propositions in regard to the supply of labor amount to a denial, for the supply of labor, of what Leontief calls the "homogeneity postulate," namely, that all supply and demand functions, with prices taken as independent variables, are homogeneous functions of the zero degree. [7] Keynes, however, does not deny the homogeneity postulate in regard to the supply of any other factor. The retention of the postulate for these other factors is one of the reasons that Keynes is able to come to the special conclusions he reaches concerning the one factor for which he denies the postulate. Certainly Keynes could not reach the same conclusions for any other factor, e.g. executive personnel, as he does for labor; for one of his data would be that the money wage rate is fixed, not perfectly flexible.

Keynes presents no reasons for this all-important distinction of treatment between labor and other factors. Lerner, however, asserts that it "is plausible and in conformity with the assumption of rationality of entrepreneurs and capital-owners who would rather get something for the use of their property than let it be idle, while labor has non-rational money-wage demands." [8] It seems doubtful, however, that "nonrational" money price demands are confined to labor. Executive and professional personnel may well have "nonrational" money salary demands; salaried classes probably do not look upon a halving of the price level as equivalent to a doubling of money income. And they may often be financially more able than labor to afford the luxury of such "nonrationality." Nor is this attitude completely irrational, as a matter of fact; their taxes, their debts and interest obligations, their insurance premiums, remain constant in money terms. These same considerations apply, though perhaps with less force, to the behavior of landlords. Moreover, raw materials and intermediate products belong on the list of "other factors." And the entrepreneurs who control their supply very often pursue, sometimes with the aid of government, policies designed to stabilize money prices. Here is a case of money price demands on the part of entrepreneurs analogous in effect to the "nonrational" money wage demands of labor. (Whether these price and wage policies are in fact rational or not need not be discussed here.) The conclusion is that the money prices, salaries, and rents of "other factors" are likely to be rigid, just like the money wages of labor. There is a possibility of fluctuation in the use of these other factors, just as there is a possibility of less than full employment of labor. If the existence of price rigidity in all sectors of the economy is recognized, if the denial of the homogeneity postulate is generalized, the Keynesian money wage doctrine cannot be maintained. The money wage rate becomes once again an independent determinant of the volume of employment.

III

So far it has been shown that Keynes' failure to generalize his denial of the homogeneity postulate to the supply of factors other than labor is responsible for his peculiar doctrine on money wages. We now must note that there is an even more important place where he failed to generalize his denial of the homogeneity postulate, with even more serious results. For Keynes assumes that, given the broad forces which mold consumption habits, consumption is a function of the size and distribution of real income alone, to the exclusion of money income. In other words, at any level of money income the same amount of goods will be consumed – and the same amount saved – out of a given real income. This assumption Keynes adopts by defining income, consumption, and saving in terms of wage units and asserting that consumption so defined is uniquely determined by income. [9] Whereas Keynes' wage earners are concerned with their money wages and are not at all conscious of the price level, Keynes' consumers keep an eagle eye on the price level and are solely concerned with their real incomes. But wage earners, after all, form a large part of the consuming public; if it is realistic to believe that they have "nonrational money-wage demands," surely it is just as realistic to believe that they are equally nonrational in their consumption decisions. (The same holds for non-wage-earners if, as we have contended, their attitude towards money values is likely to be the same as that of wage earners.) At any rate, no reasons have been presented in support of the proposition that their personalities are split.

It is easy to see that this assumption, too, is essential for the process described in section I above. For let us assume instead that, given the distribution of income, a greater sum will be saved from a given real income the higher the money income, and a greater sum from a given money income the higher the real income. This would be the natural behavior of members of a money dominated economy; they would consider themselves worse off simply because of a decline in money income, and would save less accordingly. Then it is clear that if money incomes were to fall enough following a wage cut so that the former levels of real income and employment were restored, saving would be not equal to but less than investment. Saving, in real terms, would be less than before the wage cut. Saving would be equal to investment at some higher money income and real income, and employment would be greater in the new equilibrium than in the old. Likewise, a wage rise would regain its independent power of causing a decrease in employment.

By denying the homogeneity postulate in regard to the supply of labor, Keynes introduces the possibility of involuntary unemployment of labor at a given money wage; that is, more laborers could and would go to work at this wage if the price level were raised. Then he proceeds to show that this involuntary unemployment cannot be remedied by reducing the money wage. This demonstration succeeds only because Keynes assumes that to the supply of all other factors and to the supply of saving the homogeneity postulate does apply. In short, Keynes carries his denial of the homogeneity postulate, his recognition of monetary realities, far enough and just far enough so that he can (1) prove the existence of involuntary unemployment of labor and (2) prove that altering the wage rate does not affect employment.

Thus the Keynesian doctrine that the money wage is not an independent determinant of the volume of employment rests on two assumptions which are both shaky in factual basis and inconsistent with other parts of the Keynesian schema. One is that the persons supplying factors other than labor behave so that these factors are always fully employed and their prices perfectly flexible. The other is that consumers behave so that saving is a function of real income to the exclusion of money income. By dropping the former, we find that a wage cut can increase employment (or a wage rise reduce it) by causing substitution, even if it does not alter the level of real income. By dropping the latter, we find that a wage cut will increase employment and real income (or a wage rise reduce them), substitution or no substitution. When the two effects are superimposed, the rise (or drop) in employment becomes all the greater. The removal of these two assumptions — or of either one of them alone — reinstates the money wage rate as an independent determinant of the volume of employment.

Notes

[1] Keynes, *General Theory of Employment, Interest and Money* (New York: Harcourt, Brace and World, 1936), Chapter 19.

[2] *Economic Journal,* September 1937, 405; December 1937, 745; March 1938, 134.

[3] It might be thought that since Keynesian doctrine concerns the short run, and marginal productivity theory principally the long run, their compatibility was of no consequence. It is true that the ultimate adjustments described by marginal productivity theory — adjustments of the employment of labor relative to the employment of capital — are long-run results. With these results Keynesian theory, which concerns the short run when the amount of capital equipment is fixed, need not be reconciled. But marginal productivity analysis applies also to the short run, just as truly as the profit motive operates in the short run. For business firms, even with a fixed plant, must choose between various possible combinations of prime factors. Marginal productivity theory describes this short-run choice; hence it is important to reconcile Keynesian money wage doctrine with this analysis.

[4] A.P. Lerner, "Mr. Keynes' General Theory of Employment, Interest, and Money," *International Labor Review,* October 1936, 435; "The Relation of Wage Policies and Price Policies," *American Economic Review,* March 1939, Supplement, 158.

[5] I recognize, of course, that the rate of saving is influenced by the distribution of income, as well as by its aggregate amount. But it is unlikely that, aside from government policy, a change in distribution will occur which in direction and extent will counteract the expected relation of saving to the amount of real income. The greatest part of saving is done by non-wage-earners and by business firms, and there is no doubt that their income moves in the same direction as aggregate income. In the present case business faces wage costs which are lower in relation to demand curves than before. The incomes of business firms and of non-wage-earners will surely be greater than before, no matter what has happened to their relative shares. Accordingly, they will save more than before. The change in this portion of total saving is reenforced by what happens to the saving of

wage earners. Some wage earners, it is true, have suffered small decreases in real income, and they will tend to save slightly less. But other wage earners have become newly employed; their real incomes have risen greatly. They will probably save on a larger scale or cease to dissave, more than counteracting the decrease in saving by workmen previously employed. For these reasons, the possibility that the influence on saving of the distribution of income will offset the effect of the aggregate amount of income can be safely disregarded.

[6] In any complete analysis of this process, the possibility of a change in investment due to the wage cut cannot be ruled out. But the purpose of this paper is to focus attention on the significance of the two assumptions to be discussed; hence the assumption of constancy of investment, which is usually made by writers on this subject, is also made here. In defense of this assumption it may be argued that a wage cut can stimulate an increase in investment greater than the increase in saving it induces only if the system is unstable. If the system is stable, the increase in saving will be the greater; the result will be the same as if investment were constant. But this question cannot be discussed here. (Cf. Lerner, "Relation of Wage Policies and Price Policies," p. 161.)

[7] W. Leontief, "The Fundamental Assumption of Mr. Keynes' Monetary Theory of Unemployment," *Quarterly Journal of Economics*, November 1936, 192.

[8] "The Relation of Wage Policies and Price Policies," *American Economic Review*, March 1939 Supplement, 163.

[9] *General Theory*, pp. 91–92.

CHAPTER 2

MONEY WAGE RATES AND EMPLOYMENT

What is the effect of a general change in money wage rates on aggregate employment and output? [1] To this question, crucial both for theory and for policy, the answers of economists are as unsatisfactory as they are divergent. A decade of Keynesian economics has not solved the problem, but it has made clearer the assumptions concerning economic behavior on which the answer depends. In this field, perhaps even more than in other aspects of the *General Theory*, Keynes' contribution lies in clarifying the theoretical issues at stake rather than in providing an ultimate solution.

1. Pre-Keynesian Solutions to the Money Wage Problem

How considerable this contribution is can be appreciated from a brief review of pre-Keynesian attempts to solve the problem. [2] These solutions rested on one of the following assumptions: (a) that the price level is unchanged. [3] (b) that aggregate money demand (MV) is unchanged, [4] or (c) that some component of aggregate money demand, e.g., non-wage-earners' expenditure, is unchanged. [5] Naturally, if money demand is assumed to be maintained in any of these ways, the conclusion follows easily that a money wage cut will increase, and a money wage rise diminish, total employment and output. These assumptions, or any variant of them, beg the central question raised by the fact that money wage-rate changes are double-edged. They change money costs, but they change at the same time money incomes and hence money expenditures. Even the money expenditures of non-wage-earners cannot be assumed unchanged, for their incomes depend in part on the expenditures of wage earners.

From *The New Economics*, edited by Seymour E. Harris. Copyright 1947 by Alfred A. Knopf, Inc. Reprinted by permission of the publisher.

2. The Role of the Consumption Function in Keynes' Solution

Keynes replaced these assumptions with a proposition which, whatever its shortcomings, is certainly a more plausible description of actual economic behavior. This proposition is his consumption function: that *real* consumption expenditure is a unique function of *real* income, with the marginal propensity to consume positive but less than unity. So far as consumption expenditure alone is concerned, therefore, Keynes concluded that a change in money wage rates could not affect the volume of employment and output. Because the marginal propensity to consume is less than unity, any increase in output and real income would fail to generate enough of an increase in real consumption expenditure to purchase the additional output. Any decrease in output and real income would cause, for the same reason, an excess of aggregate real demand over supply. The result of a change in money wage rates would be, still considering only reactions via consumption expenditure, a proportionate change in prices and money incomes and no change in employment, output, real incomes, or real wage rates.

These are the implications of Keynes' systematic theory. In the course of remarks which are, from the standpoint of his systematic theory, *obiter dicta*, Keynes considered two possible effects of a money wage cut on the propensity to consume: "redistribution of real income (a) from wage earners to other factors entering into marginal prime cost whose remuneration has not been reduced, and (b) from entrepreneurs to rentiers to whom a certain income fixed in terms of money has been guaranteed." [6] The effects on consumption of the second type of transfer, (b), Keynes thought doubtful and apparently unimportant. The first type of transfer, (a), from wage earners to other prime factors, would, if it occurred, be likely to diminish the propensity to consume; it would, therefore, be unfavorable to employment. However, Keynes overestimated the likelihood of such a redistribution of income. Maintenance of the prices of other variable factors in the face of a wage cut would encourage substitution of labor for these factors; such substitution would not only be directly favorable to employment of labor but would also diminish or reverse the transfer of income from labor to non-wage-earners. On the other hand, if the owners of other variable factors sought to avoid such substitution, they would, as Lerner has shown, reduce their prices in the same proportion as the wage rate and consequently would not gain income at the expense of labor. [7]

3. Effects of Money-Wage Rate Changes on Investment

The possibility remains that a change in money wage rates may induce a change in the other component of Keynes' effective demand, real investment. So far as real investment is itself dependent on the level of real income or the volume of real consumption expenditure, there is clearly no reason for such a change. Likewise, the marginal efficiency of capital, so far as it is objectively determined by the amount of additional output which can result from an increment of capital, is not altered by a change in money wage rates. Three types of reactions on the rate of real investment are left:

1. Conceivably, a change in money wage rates may affect that delicate phenomenon, the state of business confidence. However, the direction of this influence cannot be predicted in a general theory. [8] Individual businessmen making investment decisions may be impressed chiefly by the fact that a money wage cut reduces their costs. On the other hand, a fall in wages and prices embarrasses entrepreneurs by increasing the real burden of their debt. Without underrating the importance of these types of reactions, therefore, Keynes had to exclude them from his theoretical structure. [9]

2. In an open economy, a change in the general wage rate and price level will affect the balance of trade. A reduction of money wage rates and prices will stimulate demand for exports and shift domestic demand to home goods in preference to imports. Such a change in the balance of trade is equivalent to an increase in real investment and has a multiplied effect on home real income and employment. This effect may be strengthened by a worsening of the terms of trade, which increases the employment necessary to obtain the equilibrium level of real income and real saving. A rise in money wage rates would have the opposite effects. On this score there is little dispute. These effects may be nullified, however, by similar wage adjustments in other countries or by changes in exchange rates.

3. A change in the level of money wage rates, prices, and money incomes alters in the same direction the demand for cash balances for transactions purposes. With an unchanged quantity of money, a reduction of money wage rates leaves a larger supply of money to satisfy the demand for cash balances from precautionary and speculative motives. The result is a reduction in the real investment. It was only by this circuitous route that Keynes found any generally valid theoretical reason for expecting in a closed economy a relationship between money wage rates and employment.

4. The Central Thesis of the General Theory

Such is the Keynesian solution to the money wage problem. It is important to view it in the broad setting of the *General Theory*. Keynes set himself the goal of establishing, first, that there may be involuntary unemployment of labor and, second, that there may be no method open to labor to remove such unemployment by making new money wage bargains. There may be involuntary unemployment because additional labor would be offered at the going money wage rate at the same or lower real wage rates. [10] Labor, beset by a "money illusion," will permit its real wage to be reduced by price rises without leaving the market, even when it will not accede to the same reduction in its real wage by a money wage cut. At the same time, labor is powerless to take advantage of the potential demand for its services at lower real wage rates, because a reduction in the money wage may not lead to a reduction in the real wage.

The linkage between money wage rates and employment via the rate of interest appears to destroy the second half of this central thesis. For, if money wage rates were flexible, they could presumably fall enough to lower the rate of interest to a level which would induce the volume of investment necessary to maintain full employment. This linkage is, however, extremely tenuous. It can be broken at either of the following points: (a) The interest elasticity of the demand for cash balances may be infinite; (b) the interest elasticity of the demand for investment may be zero. [11] Condition (a) is likely to be approximated at low interest rates, and condition (b) is supported by the evidence that interest calculations play an insignificant part in business investment decisions. The Keynesian thesis that labor cannot erase unemployment by revising its money wage bargains is, therefore, not seriously damaged by admitting the effect of money wage rates on the demand for cash balances.

5. Assumptions of Keynesian Money Wage Theory

It is damaged, however, by removal of certain of the restrictive assumptions of the Keynesian model; and their removal is logically necessary because they clash with other basic assumptions. To demonstrate this, the main assumptions of Keynesian money wage theory will be examined. They are: (1) that real wages are a decreasing function of the volume of employment, (2) that labor is the only variable factor of production, (3) that pure competition exists throughout the economy or that the degree of monopoly is constant, (4) that "money illusion" affects the supply function for labor, and (5) that "money illusion" does not occur in other supply and demand functions.

5.1. Diminishing Marginal Productivity

Adopting the traditional postulate of diminishing marginal productivity, Keynes assumed that real wage rates and employment are inversely related. Consequently, an increase in employment at the same money wage can occur only if there is a rise in prices sufficient to compensate business firms for the increase in marginal costs associated with an expansion of output. For this reason, the question whether labor will accept increased employment at a reduced real wage brought about by such a price rise becomes Keynes' criterion for the existence of involuntary unemployment. Keynes ventured the guess that real wages and money wages would usually be found to move in opposite directions, since money wages usually rise in periods of increasing employment and fall when employment is decreasing. [12] This conjecture provoked several statistical investigations designed to check the traditional postulate. [13] Statistically these investigations were inconclusive; [14] in any case the issue, though of great interest in itself, is not crucial for Keynes' central thesis. Equilibrium with decreasing marginal costs throughout most of the economy is conceivable in a world of monopolies. In such an economy, the involuntary nature of unemployment at a given money wage would be even clearer than on Keynes' definition. Increased employment would not be purchased at the expense of a higher cost of living but would yield higher real wages. The question raised by the second proposition of Keynes' central thesis — can unemployment be removed by a money wage cut? — remains the same whether increasing or decreasing marginal productivity prevails.

5.2. No Variable Factors Other than Labor

The assumption that labor is the only variable factor is more serious. By this simplification, Keynes rules out the possibility of substitution as a result of money wage rate changes. If the possibility of substitution between labor and other factors is admitted, the Keynesian solution of the money wage problem can be saved only by introducing another assumption. Paradoxically, this postulate is that all factors other than labor are fully employed and that their prices are completely flexible. Then their prices will always change in the same direction and proportion as the money wage rate. [15] If the money wage rate increases, business firms will attempt to economize on labor by substituting other factors. But since these other factors are already fully employed, attempted substitution can only result in bidding their prices up until the incentive to substitute vanishes. Likewise, if there is a cut in the money wage rate, business firms will attempt to substitute labor and reduce the employment of other factors. But since the prices of these factors are perfectly flexible, this substitution will be prevented by a lowering of the prices of these factors to keep them fully employed. If the price of any other factor were rigid, a change in the money wage rate would cause substitution between labor and that factor. A money wage cut would increase the employment of labor and a money wage rise reduce it.

5.3. Pure Competition or Constant Degree of Monopoly

Under conditions of pure competition, prices would be free to move up or down in the same ratio as the money wage rate, as Keynesian theory requires. Under monopolistic conditions, these proportionate price movements can occur only if the degree of monopoly — the ratio of the difference between price and marginal cost to price — remains the same. Monopolistic conditions lead to price rigidity and stickiness. Consequently a cut in the money wage rate will increase the degree of monopoly. Disregarding other results of the money wage cut, the increase in the degree of monopoly will increase the relative share of the national income going to non-wage-earners. Since non-wage-earners may be assumed to have a lower marginal propensity to consume than wage earners, this redistribution of income reduces the real demand for consumption goods. In this respect, a money wage cut is detrimental to employment and output. A money wage rise has the opposite effect. This is presumably the *rationale* of the arguments of proponents of raising wages as an antidepression policy. [16]

Rigidities in the prices of other factors of production, including unfinished goods and services, also lead to the substitution effects discussed in the previous section. The substitution effects of a money wage cut not only tend to increase employment directly, but also limit or prevent entirely the adverse effects on consumption expenditure from redistribution of income. Even though the degree of monopoly is increased, the increase in employment due to substitution tends to maintain labor's relative share. Monopolists in the finished and near-finished goods markets gain, possibly at the expense of labor but certainly at the expense of the sellers of factors with rigid prices, including the monopolists of unfinished products. Between the marginal propensities to consume of these two groups of non-wage-earners — monopolists in the final stages of production and monopolists in the early stages plus landlords and other property owners — there is little to choose. Taking substitution effects into account weakens the argument that because of price rigidities a money wage cut redistributes income adversely to consumption expenditure. Indeed, if the elasticity of substitution is high enough, the redistribution of income may be favorable to consumption.

5.4. *"Money Illusion" in the Supply of Labor*

Economic theory is usually predicated on the premise that, given their schedules of preferences for goods and services and leisure, individuals behave consistently and "rationally." A consumer is not supposed to alter his expenditure pattern when his income doubles, if the prices of the things he buys all double at the same time. Nor is a business firm expected to change its output, if the price of its product and the prices of all factors it employs change in the same proportion. Generalized, this premise is what Leontief calls the "homogeneity postulate," namely, that all supply and demand functions, with prices taken as independent variables, are homogeneous functions of the zero degree. [17] Applied to the supply of labor, this postulate means that a proportionate change in the money wage and in all current prices will leave the supply of labor unchanged. Considering the real wage rate as the ratio between the money wage rate and the current price level of goods consumed by wage earners, the postulate means that a given real wage rate will bring forth the same amount of labor whatever the level of the money wage rate — that labor will react in the same way towards a 10 percent cut in its real wage whether this cut is accomplished by a reduction of its money wage rate or by a rise in current prices. Any other behavior seems inconsistent and "nonrational," based on a "money illusion" attributing importance to dollars per se rather than on an understanding of their real value.

Clearly one of Keynes' basic assumptions — Leontief calls it *the* fundamental assumption — is that "money illusion" occurs in the labor supply function. [18] Labor does attach importance to the money wage rate per se, and more labor will be supplied at the same real wage the higher the money wage. This assertion concerning the behavior of wage earners is indispensable to Keynes in establishing the existence of involuntary unemployment.

What are the reasons for such "nonrational" behavior on the part of labor? First, high money wage rates are a concrete and immediate accomplishment of the leadership of individual unions. The object of individual labor groups in wage bargaining is to protect and if possible to advance their wages relative to other groups. Each union will resist a cut in money wages in order to avoid a relative reduction in real wages. The cost of living is a remote phenomenon, apparently beyond the control of organized labor, certainly beyond the control of any single bargaining unit. Money wage bargains must be made for periods during which the cost of living may frequently change. Second, wage earners have obligations fixed in terms of money: debts, taxes, contractual payments such as insurance premiums. These obligations are a greater burden when money wage rates are cut, even though all current prices may fall proportionately. Third, labor may have inelastic price expectations; a certain "normal" price level, or range of price levels, may be expected to prevail in the future, regardless of the level of current prices. [19] With such price expectations, it is clearly to the advantage of wage earners to have, with the same current real income, the highest possible current money income. For the higher their money incomes the greater will be their money savings and, therefore, their expected command over future goods. Wage earners with inelastic price expectations will resist money wage cuts even when prices are falling, not only because they fear that wages will not rise again when prices rise but also because the expected price rise would reduce the real value of their current saving. Fourth, labor may be genuinely ignorant of the course of prices or naively deceived by the "money illusion." Judged by labor's consciousness of the cost of living in the United States in 1946, this explanation, if it ever was important, is not now significant. Altogether, the support for Keynes' assumption in regard to the supply of labor is convincing; his denial of the "homogeneity postulate" for the labor supply function constitutes a belated theoretical recognition of the facts of economic life.

5.5. Absence of "Money Illusion" Elsewhere in the Economy

Wage earners are the only inhabitants of the Keynesian economy who are so foolish or so smart as the case may be, as to act under the spell of the "money illusion." They are under its spell only in their capacity as suppliers of labor. The "homogeneity postulate" is denied for the labor supply function; for all other demand and supply functions it is retained. Without the retention of the "homogeneity postulate" for all supply and demand functions except the labor supply function, the Keynesian money wage doctrine cannot be maintained. The dependence of the doctrine on this procedure and the justification for the procedure will be considered for (a) the supply functions of other factors, and (b) the consumption function.

5.5.1. Supply of Other Factors

When the existence of variable factors other than labor is admitted, Keynesian theory requires that these factors be fully employed and that their prices be perfectly flexible. [20] This is where the "homogeneity postulate" – the assumption of "rational" behavior – enters with respect to the supply functions of these factors. If the sellers of these factors were, like the sellers of labor, influenced by the "money illusion," their prices would be rigid like wages and there could be unemployment of these factors. A change in the money wage rate could then alter the employment of labor by causing substitution between labor and other factors.

Keynes, since he assumes away the existence of other factors, presents no reasons for this distinction between labor and other factors. Lerner, however, asserts that it is "plausible and in conformity with the assumption of rationality of entrepreneurs and capital owners, who would rather get something for the use of their property than let it be idle, while labor has non-rational money wage demands." [21] It is important to note what is included in "other factors": not only the services of land, other natural agents, and existing items of capital equipment, but also services and unfinished goods which are the products of some firms but serve as inputs for other firms. The sellers of these factors have much the same reasons as wage earners for having "nonrational" money price demands. Perhaps to a greater extent than labor, they have obligations fixed in terms of money. If their price expectations are inelastic, they have the same interest in high money rates of remuneration, whatever their current real returns, to protect their current savings against future price rises. They too must make money bargains for the sale of their services, contracts which will last over a period of many possible price level changes. Business firms which control the supply of intermediate goods and services often attempt to stabilize money prices, letting their output and sales fluctuate widely. Such price rigidities are money price demands on the part of entrepreneurs analogous in effect to the "nonrational" money wage demands of labor.

The "money illusion" will frequently influence the suppliers of other factors. Consequently there can be price rigidities in all markets and fluctuations in the use of all factors of production. In such an economy the money wage rate is an independent determinant of the volume of employment.

5.5.2. Consumption Decisions

The Keynesian consumption function, which is crucial to the Keynesian solution to the money wage problem, [22] is framed in real terms: real consumption expenditure is uniquely determined by real income. [23] It is not affected, for example, by a doubling of money income and of all prices. This is the application of the "homogeneity postulate" to the consumption function. If "money illusion" occurred in consumption and saving decisions, real consumption expenditure would depend on the level of money income as well as on the level of real income, just as the supply of labor depends on the money wage rate as well as on the real wage. A change in the money wage rate, changing the level of money incomes and prices, would alter the real demand for consumption goods and therefore affect the volume of both output and employment. Here again, therefore, retention of the "homogeneity postulate" is an essential assumption for Keynesian money wage doctrine.

But if wage earners are victims of a "money illusion" when they act as sellers of labor, why should they be expected to become "rational" when they come in to the market as consumers? Most of the reasons which compel them to behave "nonrationally" in making money wage bargains would logically compel them to act "nonrationally" as consumers. And if, as argued above, labor has no corner on such nonrationality, the whole body of consumers would be influenced by the "money illusion."

In which direction would the "money illusion" be expected to operate on the consumption function? With real income given, will an increase in money income cause an increase or a decrease in real consumption expenditure? The logic of the other assumptions of Keynesian theory leads to an inverse relationship between money income and real consumption expenditure, with real income constant. For wage earners are assumed to feel worse off when their money wages are cut; and when consumers feel worse off, they are supposed to devote a greater part of their real incomes to consumption and less to saving.

Consistency with other Keynesian assumptions is not, however, the most weighty argument in favor of such a relationship. One reason for non-homogeneous behavior in the supply of labor, we have seen, is the holding of inelastic price expectations. Such price expectations will also influence current consumption expenditure. If current prices are below the "normal" level expected to prevail in the future, consumers will substitute present purchases for future purchases, save less now and plan to save more in the future. If current prices are above expected future prices, consumers will reduce present consumption expenditure in favor of future expenditure, increase current saving at the expense of future saving. From the same real income, real consumption expenditure will be less the higher the current level of money incomes and prices. Inelasticity of price expectations is, therefore, one source of an inverse relationship between money income and real consumption expenditure out of a given real income.

If price expectations are not inelastic, a different but equally effective reason for the same relationship comes into operation. It is now widely recognized that the volume of accumulated savings held by consumers affects their propensity to consume. [24] The greater the volume of such holdings, the more consumers have already satisfied their desire to save, the greater the part of a given current income which will be spent for consumption. These assets are, except for equities, fixed or very nearly fixed in money value. Now if current price changes are expected to persist, a general decline in money prices and incomes will increase the real value of accumulated savings, and a general rise in money prices and incomes will reduce their real value. An increase in the real value of these assets should increase the propensity to consume, and a decrease in their value reduce it. [25] Such behavior on the part of consumers is quite consistent and rational; it appears to be the consequence of a "money illusion" only when current prices and incomes are taken as the sole variables relevant to consumption decisions.

Assuming that real consumption expenditure is, for these reasons, an inverse function of the level of money income, as well as a direct function of real income à la Keynes, a decrease in money wage rates must lead to an expansion of output and employment, and an increase in money wage rates to a curtailment of output and employment. A money wage cut, for example, will cause a general decline in prices and money incomes. This decline will stimulate an increase in the real demand for consumption goods and thereby cause a general expansion of output, real income, and employment. In the new equilibrium, prices will be lower; they will fall less than the money wage if increasing marginal costs prevail, and more than the money wage if decreasing marginal costs predominate. In the latter case, the expansion of output and employment will be greater either because more substitution of present for future consumption is induced or because the increase in real value of accumulated savings is larger. A rise in the money wage rate, of course, has the opposite effects.

These effects of changes in the money wage rate are superimposed on the substitution effects already discussed and act on the employment of labor in the same direction.

6. Conclusion

The central thesis of the *General Theory* contains two complementary propositions: first, that because labor has "nonrational" money wage demands, involuntary unemployment of labor is possible; second, that labor is in any case powerless to remedy this unemployment by altering its money wage bargains. (The second proposition Keynes qualifies by admitting the possibilities of reactions on employment via the rate of interest, but this qualification, for reasons given above, is of limited practical importance.) The second proposition of the central thesis rests on assumptions logically inconsistent with the assumption contained in the first; and the premises of the second proposition are as unrealistic as the assumption underlying Keynes' labor supply function is realistic. If Keynes' denial of the "homogeneity postulate" is extended to supply and demand functions other than the labor supply function – if, in other words, "money illusion" operates elsewhere than on the sellers' side of the labor market – then employment is inversely affected by money wage rate changes. Labor is not powerless to reduce unemployment by reducing its money wage demands. Changes in employment follow from changes in the money wage because of substitution between labor and other factors and because of the effects of "money illusion" on real consumption expenditure. The substitution effect can be avoided only by assuming, as in the *General Theory,* that labor is the only variable factor or, if other factors are considered, by assuming that the suppliers of these factors, unlike labor, have no "nonrational" money price demands. The consumption effect can be avoided only by assuming that wage earners – and the suppliers of other factors if they are admitted to behave like wage earners – act "rationally" as buyers even though they are "nonrational" as sellers, and by neglecting the effect of inelastic price expectations or accumulated savings on the propensity to consume. These two effects, or either one of them alone, make the money wage rate a determinant of the volume of employment. The consumption effect makes it also a determinant of the level of output and real income.

To summarize, a change in the money wage rate may alter the level of employment in the following ways:

1. By its effect on business confidence, which is not theoretically predictable, a change in the money wage rate may alter the volume of real investment.

2. In an open economy, a wage cut will have an effect equivalent to an expansion of investment by increasing the balance of trade. A wage rise will have the opposite results and affect employment adversely.

3. By reducing the demand for cash balances, a wage cut *may* reduce the rate of interest; reduction of the interest rate *may* stimulate investment and employment. A wage rise may have the opposite effects.

4. A wage cut may induce substitution of labor for other factors, and a wage rise may diminish employment by causing substitution of other factors for labor.

5. A wage cut may cause an increase in the real demand for consumption goods and therefore in both output and employment. Increased consumption demand would result either from substitution of present consumption for future consumption, when price expectations are inelastic, or from the increased real value of accumulated savings. A wage rise would have the contrary effect.

6. An effect contrary in direction to the four preceding possibilities is that a money wage cut will, because of price rigidities, redistribute income adversely to labor and thereby reduce the propensity to consume. For similar reasons, a money wage rise would be favorable to employment. This effect will be the stronger the weaker is the substitution effect; if substitution is considerable, it may be entirely absent.

Solution of the money wage problem was greatly advanced by replacing arbitrary assumptions concerning the price level or the level of money expenditure with Keynes' analysis of effective demand. Further progress towards a solution, and ultimately towards a quantitative solution, depends on refinement and extension, both theoretical and statistical, of the basic Keynesian system. What are the variables other than real rates of remuneration affecting the supply of labor and of other factors of production, and what effects do these variables have? What variables other than real income determine real consumption expenditure, and how? What variables lie behind the marginal efficiency of capital, and how do they enter business investment calculations? Only when economists have more satisfactory answers to these broader questions will they be able to give an acceptable solution to the money wage problem.

Notes

[1] This question concerns the effects of a general change in money wage rates which is expected to be permanent. A fall in money wage rates which is expected to be followed by further reductions will discourage output and employment, and a rise which is expected to continue will stimulate output and employment. On these propositions there is no disagreement.

[2] It should be noted that R.F. Harrod ("Review of Professor Pigou's *Theory of Unemployment*", *Economic Journal* 44 [March 1934], 19) anticipated the Keynesian solution.

[3] J.R. Hicks, *The Theory of Wages* (London: Macmillan, 1936), pp. 211–12.

[4] Cf. Hicks, "Mr. Keynes and the Classics: A Suggested Interpretation," *Econometrica* 5 (April 1937), 147.

[5] Smithies, "Wage Policy in the Depression," *Economic Record* (December 1935), 249; A.C. Pigou, *Theory of Unemployment* (London: Macmillan, 1933), pp. 100–106. In "Real and Money Wage Rates in Relation to Unemployment," *Economic Journal* 47 (September 1937), 405, Pigou relaxed this assumption to provide in effect that non-wage-earners' money expenditure, although not constant, is uniquely determined by the volume of employment. This variant has the same significance as the three assumptions discussed in the text. Later, under the prodding of Nicholas Kaldor ("Professor Pigou on Money Wages in Relation to Unemployment," *Economic Journal*, 47 [December 1937], 745), Pigou in "Money Wages and Unemployment" (*Economic Journal*, 48 [March 1938], 134), accepted in essence the Keynesian position.

[6] *General Theory*, p. 262.

[7] Problems raised by the existence of variable factors other than labor are discussed below.

[8] Except in the case discussed in note 1 above, or in the opposite case when wage expectations are inelastic.

[9] He considered the various possibilities in detail. *General Theory*, Chapter 19, especially pp. 262–64.

[10] *General Theory*, Chapter 2. See note 18 below.

[11] F. Modigliani ("Liquidity Preference and the Theory of Interest and Money," *Econometrica*, 12 [January 1944], 45-89) emphasizes that except when condition (a) which he calls the "Keynesian case," is satisfied, unemployment is attributable to an improper relationship between the quantity of money and the money wage rate, i.e., to rigid wages. He does not mention that condition (b) would constitute another and very important exception to the wage rigidity explanation of unemployment.

[12] *General Theory*, pp. 9-10.

[13] J.T. Dunlop ("The Movement of Real and Money Wages," *Economic Journal*, 48 [September 1938], 413) and L. Tarshis ("Changes in Real and Money Wages," *Economic Journal*, 49 [March 1939], 150) concluded, from English and U.S. experience respectively, that Keynes was wrong in his conjecture and that real and money wage rates generally moved in the same direction. J.H. Richardson ("Real Wage Movements," *Economic Journal*, 49 [September 1939], 425) supported the traditional, here also the Keynesian, position. M. Kalecki (*Essays in the Theory of Economic Fluctuations* [London: Allen and Unwin, 1939]) held that approximately constant marginal costs prevail.

[14] Cf. R. Ruggles, "Relative Movements of Real and Money Wage Rates," *Quarterly Journal of Economics*, 54 (November 1940), 130-49.

[15] Cf. A.P. Lerner, "Mr. Keynes' *General Theory of Employment, Interest, and Money*," *International Labor Review*, 34 (October 1936), 435; "The Relation of Wage Policies and Price Policies," *American Economic Review, Supplement* (March 1939), 158; *The Economics of Control* (New York: Macmillan, 1946), Chapter 23, especially pp. 287–88.

[16] Kalecki, *Essays*, Chapter 3, especially pp. 80-86.

[17] W. Leontief, "The Fundamental Assumption of Mr. Keynes' Monetary Theory of Unemployment," *Quarterly Journal of Economics*, 51 (November 1936), 192.

[18] Leontief, "The Fundamental Assumption," pointed out also that the wording of Keynes' definition of involuntary unemployment does not necessarily repudiate the "homogeneity postulate." ("Men are involuntarily unemployed if, in the event of a small rise in the price of wage-goods relatively to the money wage, both the aggregate supply of labor willing to work for the current money wage and the aggregate demand for it at that wage would be greater than the existing volume of employment." *General Theory*, p. 15.) It could be interpreted to mean merely that the supply schedule for labor with respect to its real wage is negatively inclined. To Keynes' definition should be added the condition that the amount of labor demanded at the lower real wage must be greater than or equal to the amount supplied.

[19] Hicks, *Value and Capital* (Oxford, 1939), pp. 269–72.

[20] p. 16 above.

[21] "Relation of Wage Policies and Price Policies," *American Economic Review, Supplement* (March 1939), 163.

[22] p. 13 above.

[23] This is the significance of Keynes' use of wage units.

[24] Cf., for example, A.P. Lerner, "Functional Finance and the Federal Debt," *Social Research,* 10 (February 1943), 49.

[25] Since the assets held by consumers are the debts of other economic units, price changes affecting the real value of consumers' assets will also affect the real burden of debt. Changes in the real burden of debt may influence business investment decisions. The resulting changes in investment will act in the opposite direction from the changes in consumption described in the text. (Keynes [*General Theory,* p. 264] and Hicks [*Value and Capital,* p. 264] both considered the possible depressing influence of price and wage reduction in increasing the burden of debt without mentioning the favorable effects of the increased real wealth of creditors.) But only part of consumers' assets are, directly or indirectly, business debts: the assets of private economic units exceed private debt by the total of public debt, the monetary gold reserve, and the supply of government issued currency. Hence, a given price change will cause a greater change in the real value of consumers' assets than in the burden of business debt.

CHAPTER 3

LIQUIDITY PREFERENCE AND MONETARY POLICY

The contention of this paper is that the demand for cash balances is unlikely to be perfectly inelastic with respect to the rate of interest, and that policy conclusions which depend on the assumption that the demand for cash balances is interest inelastic are therefore likely to be incorrect. First, the relationship between monetary and fiscal policy recommendations and assumptions concerning the interest elasticity of the demand for cash balances will be examined. Second, the argument of Dr. Clark Warburton, whose "Monetary Theory of Deficit Spending" implicitly depends on the interest inelasticity of the demand for cash balances, will be considered. Third, the position of Professor William Fellner, who explicitly makes and defends the same assumption, will be reviewed. It will be held that this assumption leads Professor Fellner into a theoretical dilemma which can be escaped only by abandoning the assumption, and that Professor Fellner's reasons for believing the demand for cash balances to be interest inelastic are inadequate. Finally, a statistical relationship between the demand for cash balances and the rate of interest will be presented; this relationship, though admittedly not conclusive, is difficult to reconcile with the hypothesis that the demand for cash balances is interest inelastic.

1. Relationship between Assumptions and Policies

Questions of policy often serve to expose with clarity differences in theory. In the field of monetary theory and policy, two crucial test questions are:

Reprinted from *Review of Economics and Statistics,* 29 (May 1947), 124–31; 30 (November 1948), 314–17. Part 5 of this article was originally published separately, at the later date, as a rejoinder to Clark Warburton's reply to the article here reprinted as Parts 1–4.

1. Will expansion of the money supply by methods which do not directly generate income − e.g., open market purchases − lead to an expansion of money national income?

2. Will expansion of income-generating expenditures financed by methods which do not increase the money supply succeed in increasing money national income?

At the level of static aggregative theory, the answers to these questions of policy depend on the views held with regard to the shapes of three functions: the L function, expressing the demand for cash balances as a function of the rate of interest; the I function, expressing investment demand as a function of the interest rate; and the S function, expressing the supply of current saving as a function of the interest rate. Naturally, the demand for cash balances, investment, and saving are functions of variables other than the interest rate; most important, the demand for cash balances, saving, and perhaps also investment are functions of the level of money income. But it is the nature of their partial elasticities with respect to the rate of interest which is the major issue.

The relationship between views on the interest elasticities of these functions and views on the two test questions of monetary policy are summarized in Table 3.1.

Table 3.1

Interest elasticities	Effectiveness of monetary policy alone (question 1)	Effectiveness of income generating expenditures alone (question 2)
(A) L function perfectly elastic, implying either I function not perfectly inelastic, or S function of positive elasticity, or both	Effective (constant velocity of money)	Ineffective
(B) L function elasticity between 0 and ∞, *and* either I function not perfectly inelastic or S function of positive elasticity or both	Effective, but less than (A)	Effective, but less than (C)
(C) (a) L function perfectly elastic, regardless of other elasticities, or (b) I and S functions perfectly inelastic, regardless of L function	Ineffective	Effective (complete leverage effect)

A. To assume that the L function is perfectly inelastic means that no change in the price of securities, i.e., in the interest rate, will induce substitution of money for securities, or vice versa. Changes in the money supply must therefore be absorbed entirely by substitution between goods and money. An addition to the money supply must result in an equivalent increase in the demand for cash balances, so that the additional money will be willingly held. Since no additional money will be willingly held as idle balances, i.e., in place of securities, the demand for cash for working balances must increase enough to absorb all of the additional supply. Money national income, which determines the demand for working balances, must rise until the cash required to handle it has increased as much as the money supply. There are two explanations of the process by which money national income is thus increased, one naive and the other sophisticated.

The naive explanation merely notes that if M is increased the community will have unwanted cash holdings and will seek to spend them until increased spending has restored the desired relationship between their incomes and their cash balances. The implicit proposition in regard to the community's decisions to spend money on goods is simply that whether total spending, including investment and consumption, exceeds, equals, or falls short of current money income depends directly on whether actual cash balances exceed, equal, or fall short of required cash balances.

The sophisticated explanation arrives at the same result, but does not rely on a doubtful direct relationship between consumption and investment decisions and the size of cash balances. Instead, investment and consumption expenditures are assumed to depend on the level of income and on the interest rate. Adding to the quantity of money creates unwanted cash balances which will be used to bid up the price of securities and lower the interest rate. Reduction of the interest rate induces an increase in spending, by encouraging investment or by discouraging saving. The expansion of income proceeds until all the additional money is required for working balances, since the decline in the interest rate cannot induce the public to hold larger idle balances. It is clear from this explanation that since the L function is perfectly inelastic with respect to the interest rate, then either the I function or the S function must not be interest-inelastic. Otherwise there would be no mechanism to restore equilibrium between the demand and supply of money.

On either explanation, the conclusion is that an increase in the quantity of money is a sufficient condition for the expansion of money national income. How great this expansion is depends only on the relationship between money national income and requirements for working cash balances. This relationship is usually taken to be a constant ratio, changing only slowly over time. The ratio is determined by the degree of ·synchronization of income and expenditure periods, the extent of business integration, and other institutional or customary arrangements. The velocity of money, the reciprocal of this ratio, is consequently a constant.

An increase in the quantity of money is also a necessary condition for an expansion of money national income. There can be no increase in money national income unless additional money is made available to support the higher value of transactions. It follows that added business investment (an upward shift in the I function) or government spending, financed by means which do not expand the money supply, cannot expand money national income. For the additional transactions involved in such spending will decrease the ratio of cash balances to money national income, and the community will endeavor to restore the desired ratio by reducing its other spending in order to acquire larger balances. Since the supply of money has not increased, this process will continue until the reduction of spending has cut income to its original level. The initial addition to business or government spending is offset by equal reductions in other spending. The sophisticated explanation of the same process would be that the attempt to obtain additional balances to support the initial increase in spending raises the rate of interest. But, since no rise in the interest rate will induce dishoarding, no addition to working balances can be obtained in this way. Therefore the rise in the interest rate must continue until enough consumption and investment expenditure is discouraged to offset completely the initial increase in spending, leaving the level of money income unchanged.

B. If the demand for cash balances is not completely inelastic with respect to the rate of interest, part of an addition to M will end up in idle balances. The added money will be used to bid down the rate of interest, and the lowering of the rate of interest will make the community willing to hold larger idle balances. So long as either investment or the propensity to consume is favorably affected by a lowering of the interest rate, there will also be an increase in money income. But since there is some increase in idle balances, the increase in money national income cannot be proportional to the increase in M; V cannot be considered a constant. On this set of assumptions, monetary expansion alone can increase money national income but not so effectively as under (A).

Similarly, on this set of assumptions, an increase in spending without any increase in M can succeed in expanding income. The additional transactions demand for money will raise the interest rate, and this rise in the interest rate will induce the community to hold smaller idle balances. Greater working balances are thereby made available to support a higher money national income. The increase in spending will increase national income, but not by the full leverage effect because the rise in the interest rate will cause a partially offsetting decline in other spending.

C. Under the third set of assumptions, purely monetary policy is impotent. An increase in the quantity of money merely piles up in idle balances; it requires no reduction in the rate of interest to induce the public to hold them. Or, if the rate of interest is reduced, investment and consumption expenditure are both insensitive to the reduction. In either event, there is no expansion of income. On the other hand, an increase in spending can be supported entirely by balances otherwise idle. Either these balances can be obtained for transactions purposes without a rise in the rate of interest, or, if a rise in the interest rate occurs, it has no effect on other spending. The initial increase in spending, therefore, will increase national income by the full amount of its leverage effect.

2. Warburton's Monetary Theory of Deficit Spending [1]

Dr. Warburton does not explicitly recognize that his "Monetary Theory of Deficit Spending" depends on the special assumption that the demand for cash balances is perfectly inelastic with respect to the rate of interest. But a mere statement of his propositions will suffice to show that they belong in category (A) discussed above. His main contentions can be summarized as follows:

1. The value of the gross national product is the product of the quantity of money and a circular velocity of money. For various reasons, outlined in the article, the circular velocity is gradually decreasing. Aside from this secular trend, V is a fairly stable quantity determined by the habits of payments of the community. [2] Therefore, fluctuations in GNP can be explained largely by changes in M.

2. Deficit spending is one of a number of techniques by which M may be increased. Deficit spending, like the other techniques, increases GNP by the amount of the increase in M associated with it times the circular velocity of money.

3. Net increases or decreases in total debt, whether public or private, need not imply changes in GNP if only the monetary authority keeps M increasing at a rate which just offsets the secular decline in V. [3]

It might be expected that such propositions would be buttressed by arguments in favor of the assumption that the demand for cash balances is perfectly inelastic with respect to the interest rate. No such arguments are presented. Dr. Warburton does present a correlation of gross national product with the quantity of money, after the quantity of money is corrected for his geometric secular decline in velocity. But this "secular" decline in velocity can be interpreted in a manner completely contradictory to Dr. Warburton's thesis. During most of the period, interest rates were declining; and at the extremely low rates of the 1930's the demand for cash balances may be so elastic with respect to the rate of interest that almost indefinite quantities of cash will be willingly held idle. This is what seems to have happened to the additions to the money supply during that decade. If this interpretation is correct, the only result of following Dr. Warburton's advice to keep the quantity of money increasing fast enough to offset the "secular" decline in velocity would have been to accelerate the decline in velocity itself.

3. Fellner's *Monetary Policies and Full Employment* [4]

Professor Fellner examines thoroughly and supports ably the theoretical assumptions on which his policy conclusions are based. Indeed his ultimate recommendation, with which adherents of any of our three positions could agree, is a combination of fiscal and monetary measures. The surest method to expand national income is government deficit spending financed directly or indirectly by borrowing from the central bank.

Professor Fellner believes that the L function is inelastic with respect to the rate of interest; consequently he is pessimistic concerning the results of deficit spending unaccompanied by an increase in the quantity of money. In fact, he is one degree more pessimistic concerning deficit spending than Dr. Warburton. For he suspects also that banks' demand for reserve balances as a percentage of their deposits is inelastic with respect to the rate of interest. [5] This means that no rise in the interest rate will suffice to induce banks to permit their deposits to increase unless their reserves are increased. For this reason, Professor Fellner has hope only for policies which increase bank reserves at the same time that they increase the quantity of money.

The chief issue remains the elasticity of the L function. Even if banks behave in the manner Professor Fellner fears, this would prevent deficit spending financed by methods which do not increase bank reserves from being effective only if the L function is perfectly inelastic. Banks' insistence on a certain reserve ratio merely places selling bonds to commercial banks as a means of deficit financing on the same footing as selling bonds to individuals. Both become methods of increasing income-generating expenditures without changing the quantity of money. They will fail, as shown in section I, only if the demand for cash balances is perfectly inelastic with respect to the interest rate.

For different reasons, Professor Fellner is less optimistic than Dr. Warburton concerning the effectiveness of monetary policy alone. He believes that the L function is inelastic and he concurs with the usual agnostic assumption that the S function is perfectly inelastic with respect to the interest rate. The I function he takes to be interest-elastic; he is logically compelled to do this, because at least one of these three functions must be interest-elastic. But in times of underemployment he fears that the I function has shifted so far to the left that even at a zero interest rate the volume of investment would be insufficient to restore full employment. This is the "Fellner impasse." [6] Deficit spending alone — without monetary expansion — cannot break through it. Because the L function is inelastic, increased demand for transactions balances will raise the rate of interest until an equal amount of private investment is discouraged. Monetary expansion alone cannot break through it. The rate of interest will fall, but even if it falls to zero it will not stimulate enough investment to bring full employment. The only escape Professor Fellner can find is the combination of fiscal and monetary expansion which is his chief recommendation.

The "Fellner impasse" is a position of disequilibrium. The supply of money exceeds the demand. Equality of the money supply and demand is supposed to be restored, after an increase in the supply, by an increase in the demand for idle balances due to a reduction in the interest rate or by an increase in requirements for working balances due to an expansion of money income. Professor Fellner permits neither of these equilibrating factors to operate. There is no increase in demand for idle balances because the L function is perfectly inelastic. There is little increase in the requirements for working balances because the I function is insufficiently elastic. The pertinent question to ask Professor Fellner at this point is: Why does not the excess supply of money drive the interest rate down far enough — to zero or below if necessary — to stimulate sufficient investment to absorb the excess money into working balances? This is the way out of the impasse which his own theory indicates, provided he sticks to the bitter end with the assumption that the L function is inelastic. The implausibility of that assumption could not be better dramatized. For surely at zero interest rates no one would be willing to hold securities rather than idle money balances. As the interest rate approached zero, more and more securities would be sold. In other words, the demand for cash balances would become elastic.

If it is admitted that the rate of interest cannot, for these reasons, fall to

zero no matter how much money is poured into the system, then the postulate that the L function is perfectly inelastic has been discarded in favor of
the Keynesian doctrine that at low positive rates the demand for cash balances approaches perfect elasticity. The "Fellner impasse" becomes the
"Keynesian impasse," case (C) in Table 3.1. The "Keynesian impasse" is,
unlike the Fellner version, a position of equilibrium; the demand for money is
equal to the supply because at the minimum rate of interest an indefinite
amount of cash will be held in idle balances. The "Keynesian impasse" can of
course be escaped by deficit spending, with or without monetary expansion.

If Professor Fellner sticks to the assumption that the demand for cash
balances is interest inelastic, his "impasse" can be avoided simply by expanding the quantity of money. He cannot then stick to his conclusion that
monetary expansion will be unsuccessful in raising the national income. If he
abandons the assumption, the way out of his "impasse" is deficit spending,
whether or not it is accompanied by monetary expansion. He cannot, in this
case, maintain that deficit spending, unless it is financed by the central bank,
will fail to increase national income.

Professor Fellner is led into this dilemma by his theory of interest. [7] Just
as his "impasse" is a condition of disequilibrium, his theory does not determine an equilibrium rate of interest. The interest rate, in his theory, is determined by the equation of the demand and supply of loanable funds. The
demand schedule is the sum of the I function, which is interest elastic, and
the L function, which is interest inelastic. The supply schedule is the sum of
the S function, current saving, and M, new money, both of which are taken as
interest inelastic. The interest rate is determined, then, by the condition that
$I + L = S + M$. [8] This is not a sufficient condition for equilibrium of the
system or of the interest rate. Equilibrium requires the additional condition
that $I = S$, (or, what amounts to the same thing, that $L = M$). So long as this
condition is not satisfied also, the level of income will change. Change in the
level of income will influence at least two of the determinants of the interest
rate: saving (S) and the demand for additional cash balances (L), and therefore change the interest rate.

On Professor Fellner's assumption, the equilibrium interest rate would be
determined as shown in Figure 3.1. In part A of Figure 3.1, S and L are
represented as functions of income (Y). New money (M) is given by the
decisions of the monetary authority. The level of income Y_0 is determined by
the equality of L and M_0; it must be such a level that all the new money is
absorbed into new working balances. At income Y_0 an amount S_0 will be
saved. In part B of Figure 3.1, S_0 is shown, and I gives the schedule of
investment with respect to the interest rate. The interest rate i_0 is determined

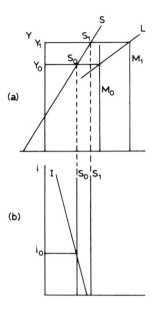

Fig. 3.1

by $I = S_0$. This presentation makes it clear that any level of Y can be achieved by creating enough new money. Professor Fellner's "impasse" arises when the amount of saving – e.g., S_1 from income Y_1 based on new money M_1 – exceeds the amount of investment which will be forthcoming even at zero interest rates. Here, on Professor Fellner's assumptions concerning the functions, equilibrium requires a negative interest rate. The failure of monetary policy to produce zero and negative interest rates can be explained only by departing from the assumption that the L function is perfectly inelastic with respect to the interest rate and, indeed, attributing to the L function perfect or near perfect interest elasticity at very low rates.

Professor Fellner's reasons for believing that the L function is inelastic with respect to the interest rate follow:

1. In Keynesian theory, the reason given for the high (negative) elasticity of the demand for money at low rates of interest is that "speculators" believe that the rate of interest will rise and therefore prefer to hold cash rather than securities. According to Fellner, "it is not convincing to argue that the expectation of a 'return to normalcy' of interest rates produces substantially increased hoarding at lower than normal rates. If the expectation of a return to

normalcy is strong enough to produce significant phenomena it is likely to produce a recovery to previous levels of the main economic variables. . . ." [9]

2. Therefore, idle balances should be regarded as being mainly contingency (or precautionary) balances rather than speculative balances. But contingency balances, according to the *communis opinio* of economists including Keynes, are insensitive to interest rate changes. [10]

3. "Moreover, the occurrence of (unfavorable) contingencies itself may appear to be more probable if interest rates rise, and it may appear to be less probable if interest rates decline, because interest rates enter into the costs of enterprise. Consequently, it is not only true that the interest elasticity of contingency hoarding is likely to be small, but the algebraic sign of this elasticity could sometimes even be 'inverse'." [11]

These points will be discussed in turn:

1. It is true that Keynesian theory emphasizes "that the demand for liquidity rises when interest rates decline because (a) the likelihood of a rise in interest rates . . . increases; and (b) at the same time, the compensation for bearing the risk of declining capital values is reduced." [12] Professor Fellner finds the first of these two reasons unconvincing. But either one of them alone is sufficient to justify an L function of negative elasticity and of high elasticity at low interest rates. Even if the risk of a rise in interest rates is no greater at low rates than at high, the compensation for bearing that risk approaches zero as the interest rate declines. Keynes, it is true, emphasizes strongly the increased liquidity preference of speculators at interest rates below what they consider normal and safe. Their psychology in this regard is quite compatible with the holding by a different set of individuals of pessimistic views concerning the profitability of real investment. But the case for a highly elastic L function at low interest rates does not depend on that psychology.

2. Keynes included precautionary balances in his M_1 (working balances), dependent not on the interest rate but on income. Professor Fellner correctly points out that precautionary balances have more in common with speculative balances (Keynes' M_2). For if there were no uncertainty in regard to future interest rates, contingency reserves would be held in interest-bearing assets rather than in cash. So long as there is a possibility of a rise in interest rates, even though such a rise is not expected more strongly than a fall, the interest rate is a relevant factor in determining the allocation of contingency reserves between cash and securities. Some skepticism is justified, therefore, regarding the *communis opinio* of economists that the demand for contingency cash balances is inelastic with respect to the interest rate. The effect of the reduction in the compensation for illiquidity applies here just as in the

case of speculative balances. In addition, individuals or firms holding contingency reserves differ from speculators in their attitude toward risk; in the case of contingency reserves, the disutility of the chance of a loss from a rise in interest rates is more likely to overbalance the utility of the chance of an equal capital gain. Even if the holder of a contingency reserve views a rise and fall in interest rates as equally likely, the chance of a rise may impress him more seriously. The lower the interest rate, the smaller the rise in it which will decrease the capital value of an asset enough to wipe out the yield. Uncertainty concerning the future of interest rates, whether or not a rise is considered more probable than a fall, is sufficient to make the risk of illiquidity seem greater the lower the rate.

3. Professor Fellner's ingenious argument for an inverse relationship between the demand for money and the rate of interest relies on the effects of higher interest rates as higher costs to the entrepreneur. The reasons for doubting that interest is a significant factor in cost calculations are familiar from discussions of the role of the interest rate in investment decisions.

4. Relationship of "Idle" Balances to Short-Term Interest Rate, 1922–45

Theories cannot be proved or disproved by statistics, but the statistical evidence at least suggests that the demand for cash balances is not perfectly inelastic with respect to the interest rate. In an attempt to discover the statistical relationship between idle deposits and the short-term interest rate, estimates of average "idle" deposits were computed for every year from 1922 to 1941 inclusive, and for subsequent years where comparable figures were available. Separate calculations were made for all commercial banks, for New York City banks only, for banks in 100 centers outside New York, and for Chicago banks only. In all cases the highest transactions velocity of deposits occurred in 1929. [13] To estimate the deposits in each year required for transactions purposes, total debits to demand deposits for each year were divided by the 1929 velocity. The result was subtracted from the actual average demand deposits for the year to obtain "idle" deposits, money which was not necessary to support the volume of transactions. This procedure results in arbitrarily defining "idle" deposits for 1929 as zero. Average "idle" deposits so computed are plotted against the average rate on prime commercial paper in Figures 3.2, 3.3, 3.4, and 3.5. The simple relationships shown can, on the whole, be improved by elimination of a downward secular trend in the commercial paper rate, but this has not been done. Even without such improvement, the relationships are of the general form postulated by liquidity preference theory. [14]

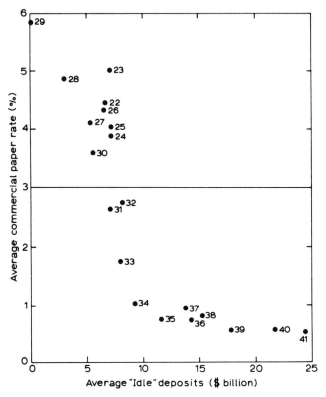

Fig. 3.2

5. A Rejoinder to Dr. Warburton [15]

The relevant broad facts of United States monetary experience since the first world war can be summarized as follows:

1. The quantity of money, however defined, has been larger in the late 1930's and in the 1940's than in the 1920's.

2. The velocity of money, however it is measured, has been lower throughout the 1930's and 1940's than in the preceding decade.

3. Interest rates have been lower in the 1930's and 1940's than in the 1920's.

4. The low levels of velocity and of interest rates have proved not to be merely depression phenomena; they have continued in a period of full employment and of incomes greatly exceeding those of the 1920's.

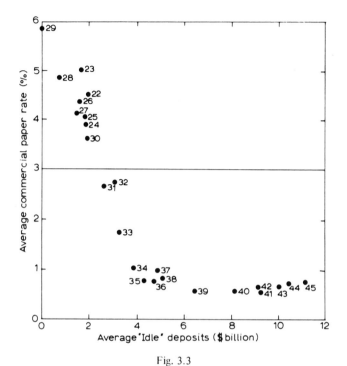

Fig. 3.3

Dr. Warburton interprets these phenomena — the increase in money supply, the decline in velocity, and the lowering of interest rates — as the results
of three unrelated secular trends. The alternative interpretation which I suggested is that the phenomena are interrelated; Keynesian theory provides an
explanation of why an increase in the money supply, a lowering of interest
rates, and a reduction in money velocity should occur together.

To illustrate the consistency of this interpretation with the facts, I presented the statistical record graphically in a manner suggested by Keynes' exposition of liquidity preference. Dr. Warburton contends that my results depend
on the particular data used and that the use of what he considers more
pertinent data would not confirm the consistency of the Keynesian interpretation with the facts. Specifically, he objects to (1) exclusion of time
deposits from the quantity of money, (2) use of bank debits rather than some
variant of national income as an index of the transactions demand for cash,
and (3) use of the short-term interest rate instead of a long-term rate. "Had
Mr. Tobin chosen the data relevant to his examination of the Keynesian

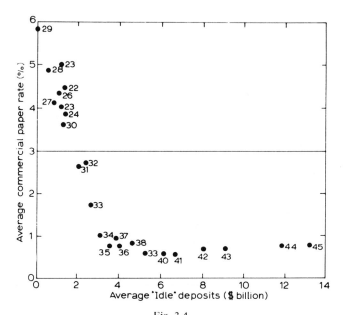

Fig. 3.4

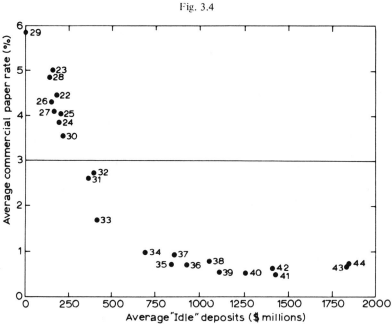

Fig. 3.5

hypothesis," he says, "and selected circuit velocity in 1929 as a base from which to measure 'idle' money in other years, he would have obtained a vastly different set of estimates, and would have found that these estimates bear little relationship to the rate of interest."

The results of the experiment which Dr. Warburton suggests are presented in Figure 3.6 which is based on his own data for payments for final products and for the quantity of money held by business and individuals. "Idle" balances are computed by subtracting from actual balances in any year the quotient of aggregate payments in that year by 1929 circuit velocity. "Idle" balances so computed are plotted against the long-term rate of interest. Contrary to Dr. Warburton's assertion, the results are not markedly different from those presented in my original article.

Figure 3.7 plots the results of the same calculation excluding time deposits, and further refutes Dr. Warburton's contention that my results reflected merely the erratic behavior of the bank debits series.

Dr. Warburton claims that, in contrast to the ratio between debits and demand deposits, the "circuit velocity of money ... shows very little relationship to the rate of interest." On Figures 3.8 and 3.9, therefore, I plot his own data.

Figures 3.6–3.9, which use Dr. Warburton's data, are submitted to show

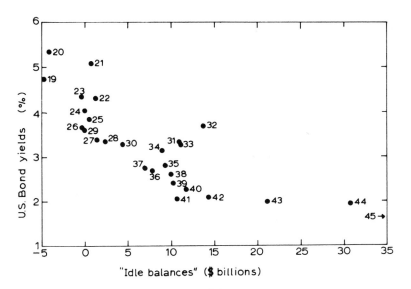

Fig. 3.6

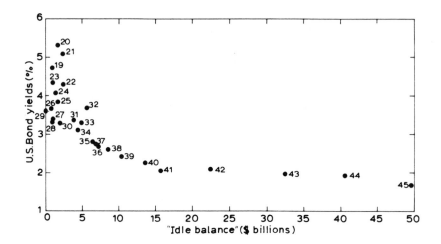

Fig. 3.7

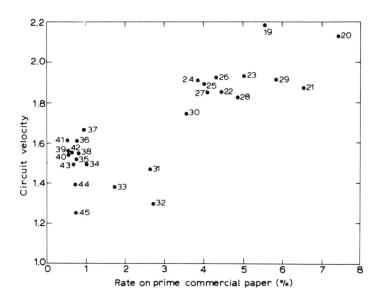

Fig. 3.8

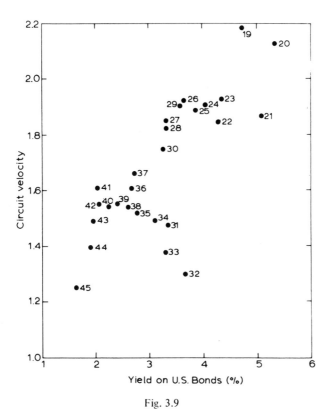

Fig. 3.9

that my results did not depend on the particular series originally used. This is more important than a defense of the relevance of those series. However, I am not convinced that Dr. Warburton's choices are more suitable, for the following reasons:

1. Inclusion of time deposits in the quantity of money conceals a phenomenon which the concept of liquidity preference illuminates. Demand deposits have increased much more rapidly than time deposits since 1929. At the same time the gain from holding time rather than demand accounts has been reduced, even if allowance is made for the former practice of paying interest on demand deposits. It is in conformity with Keynesian theory, therefore, to find that the circuit velocity of demand deposits plus currency shows a closer relationship to the rate of interest in the 1930's than Dr. Warburton's circuit velocity. (Compare my Figures 3.6 and 3.7.)

2. Neither bank debits nor any variant of national income is entirely

appropriate as a measure of the transactions demand for cash. The difficulties arise from what Dr. Warburton, following Copeland, calls transactions "outside the main money circuit," principally transactions in securities. The total dollar value of these transactions is not closely correlated with income; and "outside" transactions require a smaller ratio of cash holdings than those within the main money circuit. Income is a faulty index of transactions requirements because it omits the cash requirements for "outside" transactions. The series of bank debits is a faulty measure because it lumps "outside" transactions with those inside the income stream. Dr. Warburton emphasizes the distortions involved in the use of bank debits due to the erratically changing volume of security speculation. He ignores the fact that my findings are not changed by omission of New York City banks. (See Figure 3.4.) He does not face the fact that his circuit velocity makes no allowance for cash requirements for "outside" transactions, which, as he emphasized, do not move in correspondence with income.

3. The reason for using the short-term rate of interest in an examination of the holdings of demand deposits is that it applies, better than the long-term rate, to assets which are just below currency and demand deposits in the hierarchy of liquidity.

I agree with Dr. Warburton that the total value of the community's wealth is a variable relevant to the demand for cash balances. The logic of the liquidity-preference argument indicates the likelihood that, other things being equal, the demand for cash will vary directly with the value of the community's accumulated savings. Keynes' omission of this variable from his formal statement of the liquidity function is explained by the assumption made throughout the *General Theory* that the stock of capital is constant. The theory concerns a short run in which additions to accumulated savings are insignificant in comparison with the existing stock. Analysis of the demand for money over a longer run should reckon with changes in the total money value of wealth, but in practice a satisfactory series of wealth estimates is not available. It is possible, as Dr. Warburton suggests in his footnote 11, that accumulation of wealth may be responsible for a falling trend in circuit velocity independent of the rate of interest. However, this explanation cannot be used for the decline in velocity in the 1930's. Because of capital decumulation in the depression and the fall in valuation of existing wealth, the money value of the national wealth was not so large in the 1930's as ten years earlier. [16]

Dr. Warburton must use some other rationale for his trend in circuit velocity. The rationale should be consistent with evidence which sharply differentiates the period since 1929 from the previous forty years:

1. Currency plus all deposits grew as a percentage of national income from 51.4 per cent to 64.2 per cent in the 39 years 1890–1929. In 1940 the percentage had reached 85.3 and in 1946, 96. The average geometric rate of increase was in the first period less than 0.6 per cent per year, compared with 2.4 per cent since 1929. [17]

2. The income velocity of money, excluding time deposits, showed no downward trend from 1899 to 1929 but fluctuated about the value of 3.00. In the 1930's, however, income velocity fell to 2.00. [18]

The ambiguities which Dr. Warburton finds in the liquidity-preference analysis of the demand for cash vanish as soon as it is realized that the dependent variable in the L function is not a ratio, but an absolute amount measurable in dollars. The function can easily be amended to take account of the effects of the stock of wealth and of transactions not tied to income. It then takes the form $L = L(Y, r, W, T)$ where W is the money value of the community's wealth and T is the annual rate of transactions "outside the main money circuit," in dollars.

Dr. Warburton says that he has made no assumption one way or the other concerning the interest elasticity of the demand for cash balances. It was precisely his failure to make an explicit assumption which I originally criticized. The theoretical issue cannot be dodged by appealing to the secular trends, even if Dr. Warburton's interpretation of the trends is accepted. For Dr. Warburton's policy conclusions rest on the belief that at any given time the circuit velocity of money is a constant, in the following sense: its value for any date can be found from its time trend, and this value will hold whatever the interest rate may be on that date. Only such a belief can justify Dr. Warburton's confidence in the efficacy of expanding the quantity of money merely by transferring existing assets from the public to the banks. Only such a belief can explain his view of deficit spending as just another method of enlarging the money supply. And this belief depends, as I demonstrated in my original article, on the assumption that the demand for cash balances is independent of the interest rate.

Incidentally, Dr. Warburton misrepresents the *General Theory* when he attributes to Keynes the view that $v\ (= Y/M)$ "may be taken as constant for short periods." Keynes considered this to be a tolerable assumption for $V\ (= Y/M_1)$, but not for v. [19] Dr. Warburton distinguishes between v and V in the first part of his paper and then proceeds to ignore the distinction. From this confusion stems his statement that my interpretation of the downward trend in v as related to the interest rate is a departure from Keynes.

Notes

[1] *Review of Economics and Statistics,* 27 (1945), 74–84.

[2] This view of the stability of V is emphatically reaffirmed by Dr. Warburton in his Reply to H.W. Arndt's Comment, *Review of Economics and Statistics,* 28 (1946), 92.

[3] These propositions raise the incidental problem of controlling the quantity of money independently of the volume of public and private debt and of public and private deficit spending. In particular, M must be expanded at a rate sufficient to compensate for the decline in its rate of use, while total debt either remains unchanged or indeed is retired. Although Dr. Warburton emphasizes the breadth of his conception of monetary policy, most methods of monetary control would be unavailable to him since they involve direct or induced changes in public or private debt.

[4] Berkeley: University of California Press, 1946. Only Part Three, pp. 137–235, is considered here, and in particular Chapters 5 and 6. This excellent book covers a wide range of other topics.

[5] Fellner, pp. 183, 200–206.

[6] Fellner, pp. 180–86.

[7] Fellner, Chapter 5, especially pp. 140–52 and 166–73.

[8] Fellner, pp. 168–71; Figure 22, p. 170.

[9] Fellner, p. 149.

[10] Fellner, pp. 146–51.

[11] Fellner, p. 148.

[12] Fellner, p. 141.

[13] Board of Governors of the Federal Reserve System, *Banking and Monetary Statistics* (1943), Table 55, p. 254.

[14] The same conclusions can be reached by direct correlation of the transactions velocity with the short-term rate of interest. This has been done for English statistics by Kalecki, "The Short-Term Rate of Interest and the Velocity of Cash Circulation," *Review of Economics and Statistics,* 23 (1941), 97.

[15] Reprinted with minor omission from *Review of Economics and Statistics,* 30 (November 1948), 314–17. Figures and footnotes have been renumbered. Footnote 19 is new.

[16] Doane's estimates are 428.1 billion dollars in 1930 and 388.4 billion in 1938. (From J.P. Wernette, *Financing Full Employment,* Table 4, pp. 36–37.) The National Industrial Conference Board estimate for 1938 is below that for any year from 1924 through 1931. (*Economic Almanac for 1948,* p. 315.)

[17] Wernette, Table 8, p. 46. My calculation for 1946.

[18] J.W. Angell, *Investment and Business Cycles,* Appendix II, column (3), pp. 337–38.

[19] Here M refers to the total quantity of money and M_1 to that part of it held as working balances. The difference, M_2, represents idle or "speculative" holdings of money.

CHAPTER 4

INCOME TAXATION, OUTPUT AND PRICES

1. Impact Effects

One subject on which economists have displayed a confident consensus is the short run effects of income taxation. Given the amount of government outlays, it is widely and confidently agreed that an increase in income taxes will reduce real output, employment, and prices and that a reduction of income taxes will have the opposite effects. [1] The expansionary or deflationary consequences of changes in the tax are divided between effects on output and employment and effects on prices in proportions depending on the level of unemployment and the flexibility of prices and money wages. These conclusions are, for the most part, the fruits of applying a very simple theory of income and employment determination. The theory is the theory of the multiplier, or of the equilibrium of saving and investment, adapted to allow for taxes and other government transactions. The theory of the multiplier is an important part of a wider theory of income determination. But it is only a part, and it is a striking fact that taxes have not been assimilated into the complete theory. Economists are not content to analyze the consequences of, say, monetary policy or wage flexibility in the narrow theoretical framework of multiplier theory. But they have been content, for the most part, to ignore the implications of government finance for relationships other than the consumption function and the investment-saving identity.

This essay is an attempt to remedy that neglect, at least for one simple kind of tax, a proportional income tax. The conclusion is that, when all consequences of the tax are allowed for in a complete aggregative model, it is no longer possible to be confident of the generally accepted doctrine stated

"Income Taxation, Output and Prices" was prepared with Challis A. Hall, and is reprinted here from *Economia Internazionale* (August 1955), 522-42; (November 1955), 742-61; and (February 1956), 1-8. Footnotes, tables and figures have been renumbered.

We are indebted to Richard A. Musgrave for suggestions based upon an earlier and expanded version of this analysis.

above. Whatever contribution is made by the essay does not lie in this negative "anything can happen" conclusion but in calling attention to the characteristics of economic behavior that combine to determine the total effects of the tax.

There are two parts to this analysis. The first task is to examine the consequences of the tax for the various equations of a complete aggregative model. The identities and functional relationships, both behavioral and technological, that constitute the models of aggregative economic theory have been developed for an economy without government finance. (We shall call such models "anarchic," without going into the question whether it makes sense to assume that an economic system of this kind could exist at all in the absence of certain government financial transactions.) It is necessary, therefore, to modify and to supplement these anarchic equations to allow for government spending and taxation. This is a task both more difficult and more instructive than may at first appear. Teachers of partial equilibrium analysis have long known that one of the best ways to impart and to test understanding of the basic behavioral and technological assumptions that lie behind demand, cost, and supply curves is to consider the effects of taxation. So it is in aggregative theory. Consideration of the effects of a tax on an aggregative relationship forces the analyst back to the most primitive assumptions about economic behavior on which the relationship is based. It is not possible to say how taxation modifies, for example, a liquidity preference function without being clear why there is a liquidity preference function with certain characteristics in an anarchic model in the first place. In sections 1, 2 and 3 we have attempted the task of assimilating spending and taxation into an aggregative model in a manner consistent with the assumptions on which we conceive the anarchic relationships of the model to be based.

Once this first task is accomplished, the remainder of the analysis is an exercise in comparative statics, tracing the interactions of the impacts of spending and taxation on the separate equations of the model to determine the ultimate effects of taxation on the equilibrium solution of the complete system. [2]

1.1. Direct and Total Effects

The nature of direct or impact effects and total or economic effects of government financial transactions can be indicated by the formal properties of theoretical models. These models consist of systems of explicit functional relations or structural equations connecting the variables to be explained (dependent or endogenous) and those regarded as autonomous (independent or exogenous). Given the forms of the structural equations, equilibrium values of the dependent variables and derived relations between the dependent and independent variables may be determined. By altering the value of one or more independent variables and ascertaining the new equilibrium values of the dependent variables — the method of comparative statics — the total effects of a variation in the independent variables can be determined.

In comparison with anarchic aggregative systems, models allowing for taxation and other government transactions have a larger number of variables and equations, and structural equations of different form. For example, a flat-rate personal income tax adds the tax rate and total tax collections as variables, alters the function relating consumption to interest rate and income as well as other explicit functional relations, and adds the structural equation relating tax collections to the tax rate. These changes will in turn produce alterations in the derived relations of the system and in the equilibrium values of the dependent variables.

We define the *impact effects* of government finance to be the changes it produces in the structural equations and in the roster of variables. The *total effects* we define to be the changes it produces in the equilibrium of the whole system. For many purposes it may be useful to concentrate upon one aspect of each of these types. Thus, primary interest in an impact effect may focus on a particular equation, and in a total effect on one or two variables, such as real income and prices or wage income and property income. These concepts apply, of course, both to introduction of a government transaction and to change in the magnitude of an existing type of transaction.

1.2. *Method of Analysis*

The mutual interdependence of the variables in a macroeconomic system makes it necessary to examine the nature of other concurrent government transactions before the effects of a tax are analyzed. In particular, it is necessary to specify what kinds of current and capital transactions of government are being undertaken both before and after the imposition of the tax and what effects are produced by them.

Government current transactions prevailing before the imposition of the tax are assumed to include the payment of interest on the outstanding government debt and payments for currently-produced goods and services, used in the provision of basic government functions. Government expenditures on goods and services are assumed to be constant in real terms, and interest payments on the debt, which are regarded as transfer payments, to be fixed in terms of money. All other current government transactions, including receipts from taxes other than the income tax, are disregarded.

The income tax imposed is a permanent tax on income, levied at a flat rate, with full offsets for business losses. Income is conceived to be true economic net income, the whole of which is available for disposition by the owners of resources. According to these conceptions, depreciation allowances are corrected for price changes, and all property income, including corporate profits, is included in the tax base.[3] Finally, capital gains, which are excluded from true net income, are not taxed.

Before the imposition of the income tax, the prevailing system equilibrium and the forms of the structural relations will reflect the effects of government transfers (interest) and expenditures (payments for current goods and services); the total of these outlays is equal to the deficit and is financed by borrowing or by depletion of government cash balances. After the introduction of the tax, the new system equilibrium will reflect the effects of the tax collections, which are used to finance these outlays, retire government debt, or increase government cash balances.

For our analysis of the alterations in system equilibrium occasioned either by the tax or by the government spending, changes over time in government debt and money supply resulting from deficits or surpluses in the current budget are immaterial. These changes are dynamic phenomena, the influence of which depends upon the length of time a given budget balance has prevailed. The method employed in our analysis is static rather than dynamic; like any static analysis, it cannot take account of forces that depend upon time. This restriction is not important with respect to the short run, where the debt and money supply can be assumed to be large relative to the changes in them arising from budgetary unbalance over a short period. The restriction is analogous to the customary assumption, also implicit in the subsequent analysis, that the stock of physical capital is fixed even though the equilibrium of the system implies positive or negative investment. Consequently, when we speak of situations "before" and "after" a tax, we are not referring to a temporal sequence of events. The situations we are comparing both refer to the same point in time. We wish to see what difference it makes whether at that point in time a tax is being collected at a certain rate or not. In making such a comparison we must hold "other things equal," among them the government debt and the money supply. For comparative static analysis, therefore, the debt and the money supply are parameters unaffected by budget policy.

1.3. *Variables and Structural Equations*

Variables and their classification as independent or dependent are listed in Table 4.1.

The structural equations relating these variables are shown in Table 4.2 both for the anarchic model and for the final model, which allows for govern-

Table 4.1
Variables

Dependent variables		Independent variables	
p	price level of final output	M	quantity of money
C/p	real consumption	t	income tax rate *
I/p	real investment	B	government interest payments *
S/p	real savings	G/p	real government expenditures *
Y/p	real income		
r	long term interest rate		
N	employment		
w/p	real wage rate		
R/p	real income from wealth		
T/p	real tax collections *		

* These variables are excluded from the general anarchic model.

ment spending and proportional income taxation. In subsequent sections, the reasons for the modifications shown here are discussed in detail for each equation other than the first two. The necessary modifications for these two are obvious.

Saving Function

$$\frac{S}{p} = S\left[\frac{Y}{p}, r, \frac{R}{pr} + \frac{M}{p}\right] \tag{3A}$$

$$\frac{S}{p} = S\left[\frac{Y+B-T}{p}, r(1-t), \frac{R}{pr} + \frac{B}{pr} + \frac{M}{p}\right] \tag{3F}$$

Equation (3A) embodies familiar relationships: the propensity to save in relation to income, the "time preference" effect of interest on saving, and the dependence of saving on net private wealth. All variables, except of course the interest rate, are expressed in real terms in accordance with the postulate of rational behavior.

Net private wealth is represented by the sum of two components: the capitalized value of property income and the quantity of money. The appropriate monetary component of net private wealth is that portion of the money supply not offset by private liabilities to banks. [4] For convenience, we assume a monetary system, e.g., a 100 per cent reserve scheme, in which the whole quantity of money has this characteristic.

Government spending requires the addition of real government transfers

Table 4.2
Structural equations *

Anarchic model		Final model	
Income identity	(1A) $\dfrac{Y}{p} = \dfrac{C}{p} + \dfrac{I}{p}$	$\dfrac{Y}{p} = \dfrac{C}{p} + \dfrac{I}{p} + \dfrac{G}{p}$	(1F)
Saving invest-ment identity	(2A) $\dfrac{I}{p} = \dfrac{S}{p}$	$\dfrac{I}{p} + \dfrac{G}{p} = \dfrac{S}{p} - \dfrac{B}{p} + \dfrac{T}{p}$	(2F)
Saving function	(3A) $\dfrac{S}{p} = S\left[\dfrac{Y}{p}, r, \dfrac{R}{pr} + \dfrac{M}{p}\right]$	$\dfrac{S}{p} = S\left[\dfrac{Y+B-T}{p}, r(1-t), \dfrac{R}{pr} + \dfrac{B}{pr} + \dfrac{M}{p}\right]$	(3F)
Money demand-supply function	(4A) $M = k(Y) + L[r]$	$M = k(Y+B) + L[r,(1-t)]$	(4F)
Investment function	(5A) $\dfrac{I}{p} = I\left[\dfrac{Y}{p}, r\right]$	$\dfrac{I}{p} = I\left[\dfrac{Y}{p}, r\right]$	(5F)
Production function	(6A) $\dfrac{Y}{p} = f[N]$	$\dfrac{Y}{p} = f[N]$	(6F)
Wage rate pro-ductivity func-tion	(7A) $\dfrac{w}{p} = f'[N]$	$\dfrac{w}{p} = f'[N]$	(7F)
Labor supply function	(8A) $N = N\left[\dfrac{w}{p}, w\right]$	$N = N\left[\dfrac{w}{p}, w, (1-t)\right]$	(8F)
Wealth income identity	(9A) $\dfrac{R}{p} = \dfrac{Y}{p} - \dfrac{w}{p}N$	$\dfrac{R}{p} = \dfrac{Y}{p} - \dfrac{w}{p}N$	(9F)
Tax function	. . . .	$\dfrac{T}{p} = t\left(\dfrac{Y}{p} + \dfrac{B}{p}\right)$	(10F)

* Brackets prefixed with a letter are used as a symbol of a functional relation, the prefix (S in the third pair of equations, for example) denoting a function, not a variable.

B/p to the income variable. Likewise, the real value of the public debt must be added to the wealth variable; on the assumption that the debt is entirely in perpetuities, its real value is B/pr. Government expenditure on goods and services does not appear in (3F) because it is assumed that government out-lays do not provide households with goods and services substitutable for those for which households would otherwise spend or save.

Income taxation reduces the income relevant to savings decisions by T/p, the amount of real taxes collected. Similarly, the tax reduces the income return on saving from r to r $(1 - t)$, where t is the proportional tax rate. The wealth variable is not affected by the tax. Income taxation reduces in the same proportion the stream of net income from an asset and, given the market rate of interest, the effective rate of interest at which it is capitalized, leaving the capital value unchanged. For example, each item in the permanent stream of government interest payments is reduced to $B(1-t)$, and the capitalization rate, to $r(1-t)$, and their ratio remains B/r. The tax may induce a change in the market rate of interest, which will alter the value of assets, but this effect is already provided for in the saving function. It is an indirect effect of the tax, not a direct effect. Given the values of real income before taxes, the rate of interest, and net private assets, what is the net effect of the tax on consumption? On the one hand, the tax tends to lower consumption by reducing disposable income. On the other hand the tax may increase consumption by lowering the effective rate of return for saving. It is of course possible that saving is unrelated or negatively related to the rate of interest; in these cases, the interest-reducing effect of the tax is either absent or reinforces the income-reducing effect. But if saving is positively related to the rate of interest, it is conceivable that the net effect of the tax is to increase consumption. The result depends on the elasticity of substitution between present and future consumption and the marginal propensity to consume. The higher the elasticity of substitution in relation to the marginal propensity to consume, the more likely it is that the tax will expand consumption.

Money Demand-Supply Relation

$$M = k(Y) + L[r] \qquad (4A)$$

$$M = k(Y+B) + L[r,(1-t)] \qquad (4F)$$

Two relationships, one relating the demand for money to its determinants and the other equating the demand for money with the fixed supply of money, are summarized in (4A). [5] Various complex aspects of the demand for money — in particular its relation to the amount of wealth — could be taken into account, but their incorporation in the function would complicate the analysis without significantly altering it. The relation between income and the demand for money represents the transactions demand for money, and that between the interest rate and the demand for money, the speculative demand for money, liquidity preference proper.

1.3.1. Transactions Demand

In order to determine requirements for transactions balances in an economy with government transactions, it is necessary first to specify the assumptions that lead to the description of transactions requirements in an anarchic system as proportional to income (kY). There are many possible sets of assumptions that would lead to this result. One simple set is as follows: Let us divide the anarchic economy into two sectors, households and producers, and assume that each sector requires transactions balances equal to $k/2$ times its outpayments. Assume the following simple structure of payments:

From/To	Households	Producers	Total Outpayments
Households	0	$C+S$	$C+S$
Producers	$C+I$	0	$C+I$
Total receipts	Y	Y	$2Y$

Since total outpayments are $2Y$, transactions requirements are kY. Households' payments to producers are assumed to include both consumption expenditure and purchases of business securities with their savings. In this simple payments structure intrasector transactions are ignored.

The government is a third sector. We include its transactions requirements in the demand for money, and its holdings in the supply M. We assume that, like the private sectors, the government's demand for balances is $k/2$ times its outpayments. The structure of payments is as follows when the government budget is balanced or shows a deficit. Here it is assumed that households divide their savings between purchases of business securities S_1 and government securities S_2, where S_2 is the government deficit $(G + B - T)$. Government buys all its services directly from households, and all taxes are paid by households. On these assumptions, total outlays are $2(Y + B)$ and total transactions demand is $k(Y + B)$. Government interest transfers B are not counted as income, but they increase the need for cash balances. [6]

Clearly alternative, and more complex and realistic, assumptions about the payments structure and about the requirements of each sector could lead to different results in (4F). It is not important to pursue such refinements here, because they would make little difference in the final analysis of the effects of income taxation. But this discussion will serve to illustrate the method and to show that modification of a structural equation to allow for government transactions requires clarity and precision both in regard to the assumptions behind the anarchic version of the equation and in regard to the nature of government transactions.

From/To	Households	Producers	Government	Total Outpayments
Households	0	$C+S_1$	$T+S_2$	$C+S+T$
Producers	$C+I$	0	0	$C+I$
Government	$B+G$	0	0	$B+G$
Total receipts	$Y+B$	$C+S_1$	$T+S_2$	$2(Y+B)$

1.3.2. Liquidity Preference

There are at least two possible rationales for the inverse relationship between asset cash holdings and the rate of interest. One is based on the assumption of inelastic and divergent expectation of the future rate of interest by owners of wealth. This is our interpretation of Keynes' explanation of liquidity preference. The second is to base liquidity preference on individual uncertainty regarding future rates of interest without assuming inelastic expectations. [7] Both approaches lead to the conclusion that a proportional income tax which does not apply to capital gains and losses will increase the speculative demand for cash at a given market rate of interest.

On our interpretation of the Keynesian theory, each individual has a certain critical rate of interest such that he holds all his wealth in the form of money (other than transactions balances) if the current market rate is below the critical rate and in earning assets if the market rate is above the critical rate. These critical rates are assumed to differ among individuals. Consequently, the lower the current rate, the more critical rates it falls below, and the larger the number of individuals who hold their wealth entirely in cash. At the same time, the lower the current market rate by which future income streams are capitalized, the greater is the value of the wealth that the community has to allocate between money and earning assets. From these considerations may be derived the familiar shape of the liquidity preference curve, downward sloping and becoming perfectly elastic at the lowest critical rate.

The critical rate of interest for an individual is below his expectation of the future rate. It is that current rate at which the yield of an earning asset is exactly offset by a prospective capital loss. A proportional income tax reduces the yield of an earning asset at any current market rate r to $r(1-t)$, but assuming that the tax does not apply to capital gains and losses and does not affect expectations of future market rates, it does not change the expected capital gain or loss associated with any current rate. Consequently, its net effect is to raise the critical rate. [8] This increase in critical rates means that the tax shifts the liquidity preference curve up, as shown in Figure 4.1.

The alternative approach is to base the demand for money in excess of transactions requirements not on inelastic expectations of the future rate of interest but on aversion to the risks of a change in the rate. Suppose that each individual regards both capital gains and losses on earning assets as possible, but has an expectation, in the probability sense, of zero capital gain or loss. Suppose, moreover, that his subjective probability distribution of capital gains and losses remains the same, with zero expected value, regardless of the current rate of interest. This assumption avoids the inelasticity of interest rate

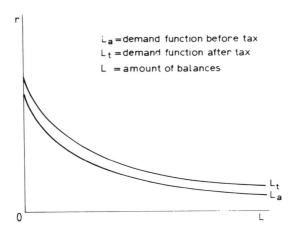

Fig. 4.1. Direct effect of income taxation on demand for speculative balances.

expectations required for the Keynesian explanation of liquidity preference. [9]

Suppose that an individual dislikes risk in the sense that he prefers $100
for certain to a game of chance with expected value of $100, e.g., $150 with
probability 1/2 and $50 with probability 1/2, and prefers in turn the
$150-$50 game to one in which the two equally likely outcomes are $200
and $0. Such an aversion to risk can be explained, if one believes in cardinal
utility, by diminishing marginal utility of income. The more of his wealth an
individual holds in earning assets, the greater his expected return but also the
greater his risk. He will divide his wealth between money and earning assets so
that the expected return just compensates him for the risk. A reduction in the
expected rate of return on earning assets, due either to a reduction in the
current market rate of interest or to the imposition of a tax on interest
income, means that a given holding of earning assets promises a smaller expected return for the same risk. This *may* induce the investor to decrease his
risk. [10] If so, we have the conclusion that the demand for money, for a given
value of wealth, is inversely related to the rate of interest after tax. Furthermore, value of wealth is itself inversely related to the rate of interest before
tax. Thus we have as before a liquidity preference curve that is downward
sloping. although we have no reason to expect it to approach perfect elasticity at any rate above zero. We have also, as before, an upward shift in the
curve as a result of an income tax. [11]

Investment Function

(5A) $\dfrac{I}{p} = I\left[\dfrac{Y}{p}, r\right]$ $\qquad\qquad$ $\dfrac{I}{p} = I\left[\dfrac{Y}{p}, r\right]$ (5F)

Orthodox theory states that the equilibrium level of the stock of capital is the level at which the marginal productivity of capital is equal to the rate of interest. [12] Keynes' relation between investment and the rate of interest evidently depends on the possibility of a discrepancy between the actual stock of capital, which he takes as given for the purpose of determining a short-run equilibrium, and the equilibrium stock. The rate of investment depends on the direction and amount of this discrepancy. [13] Both the equilibrium stock and its discrepancy from the actual stock of capital will be greater the lower the rate of interest; consequently investment is inversely related to the interest rate. At the same time, the schedule of marginal productivity of capital depends directly on the level of employment of the other factor of production, labor. The greater the employment of labor the higher will be the marginal productivity of our given capital stock. In the short run employment of labor is uniquely related to total output Y/p. Consequently at any given interest rate the discrepancy between actual and equilibrium capital stock is greater the larger the level of real income. These are the reasons that (5A) and (5F) make the rate of investment depend on both real income and the interest rate. This theory of investment does not allow in any essential way for uncertainty about the marginal productivity of capital.

Government expenditures for products which are complements or substitutes for private output would influence the marginal productivity of both capital and investment. This type of impact effect is eliminated by assumption. Interest transfers obviously have no direct influence on the productivity of investment. The implication of the orthodox theory for the effects of income taxation on investment is simply that there are no effects. A tax on net business income does not alter the maximum-profit position of any firm. Therefore, it does not alter the equilibrium stock of capital or rate of investment corresponding to given levels of real income and the interest rate. To view the problem from a different angle, the prospective return to an investor from adding to the stock of capital is indeed reduced by the tax. But the interest cost of such investment is reduced in the same proportion. If the funds are borrowed, the investor can deduct the interest charges from his returns in computing his taxable income. If the funds are his own, the opportunity cost of investment is reduced by the fact that earnings from alternative uses of funds are taxed at the same rate.

On theories of investment that allow for uncertainty regarding the marginal productivity of capital, the outcome is of course more doubtful and complicated. Consider first a tax with complete offsets for business losses. Given the probabilities that an investor attaches to various prospects of the return before taxes, a proportional tax reduces the expected value of the return after tax by an amount proportional to the tax rate. The tax also lowers the dispersion of possible after-tax returns. An individual neutral towards risk would not care about this reduction in dispersion. The expected value of a distribution of possible returns has the same significance for him as the single certain return expected by the investor in the paragraph above. For such an individual, the tax has no effect on investment decisions. The case is different for the risk-avoiding investor we encountered in discussing liquidity preference. He will regard the reduction in dispersion as increasing the attractiveness of real investment relative to other assets; he will therefore invest more at the same rate of interest after the tax. To the extent that provisions for offset of business losses are imperfect, the expected value of an after-tax return is reduced more than in proportion to the tax rate. This reduction would lead a risk-neutral investor to lower his investment; and it would offset, at least partially, the favorable effects of the reduction in dispersion on the investment of a risk-avoiding investor. [14]

Production Function

(6A) $$\frac{Y}{p} = f[N] \qquad\qquad\qquad \frac{Y}{p} = f[N] \qquad (6F)$$

Equation (6A) is the technological relationship between employment of labor and real income or output, given the stock of capital. This relationship is not altered with the introduction of the various government outlays and income tax. Government output is conceived to be produced with the same proportions of factors as in the private sector. This assumption is a device to avoid the troublesome index number problem: it has no important influence on the results of the analysis. Government transfers are not counted in real income, and cannot directly influence the production function.

Wage Rate-Productivity Relation

(7A) $$\frac{w}{p} = f'[N] \qquad\qquad\qquad \frac{w}{p} = f'[N] \qquad (7F)$$

This equation states the conditions governing the amount of labor employed in a purely competitive economy: the derivative of real income with respect to employment — the marginal physical product of labor — is equal to the real wage rate w/p. [15] This relationship is unchanged by the introduction of the several government transactions. Government expenditures have no direct impact on it. The wage rate w, the price level p, and the marginal physical product of labor are each the same in public and private employment. Government interest payments obviously do not influence directly the remuneration of labor. Income taxation has no impact on this equation. Firms pay no tax in hiring the marginal unit of labor since wages are a deductible expense.

Labor Supply Function

$$\text{(8A)} \qquad N = N\left[\frac{w}{p}, w\right] \qquad\qquad N = N\left[\frac{w}{p}, w, (1-t)\right] \qquad \text{(8F)}$$

Equation (8A) in its full generality makes the supply of labor N depend jointly on real and money wage rates. To simplify the subsequent analysis, we have restricted our attention to special cases where one or the other of the two variables can be omitted. We recognize only a few possibilities, subdivided between these two cases: (1) many sellers of labor, with real wages determining supply; (2) one or many sellers of labor, with a rigid money wage rate. The specific effects of government transactions on labor supply differ for these two cases, and equation (8F) only shows in a general way that the tax rate is a relevant variable.

In the first case, the impact of a proportional income tax is to change the determinant of supply to real wages after tax $w(1 - t)/p$. The tax reduces the net income from an hour of work, while leisure, the alternative to work, is untaxed. The effect of this reduction in real wages on labor supply depends upon the slope of the labor supply curve. Supply may vary with changes in real wages in the same direction, in the opposite direction, or not at all. At any given real wage rate the tax reduces supply in the first case, increases it in the second, and has no influence in the third. Government expenditures are assumed to be neutral with respect to labor supply. This assumption rules out as possible outlays government outputs which are substitutes or complements either for the goods and services in household budgets or for leisure. Interest transfers do not influence directly the supply of effort.

In the second case, here the money wage rate is fixed, the tax has an impact effect only if labor takes account of the tax in wage demands. The impact effect is to raise the money wage by the amount of the increase of the wage demand. If we assume that the pretax wage rate w_0 is increased to compensate entirely for the tax, the new money wage is $w_0/(1 - t)$.

Wealth-Income Identity

(9A) $\quad \dfrac{R}{p} = \dfrac{Y}{p} - \dfrac{w}{p} N$ $\qquad\qquad\qquad\qquad \dfrac{R}{p} = \dfrac{Y}{p} - \dfrac{w}{p} N$ $\qquad$ (9F)

Equation (9A) shows that real income Y/p less aggregate real wages wN/p is equal to real property income R/p. Since the government sector is assumed to produce its output with the same proportions of factors as the private sector, government expenditures do not directly affect the functional distribution of income. Interest transfers are excluded from real income and its components. Income taxation has no impact effects on this identity. The taxes payable on each of the functional shares and on real income as a whole are already included in the variables shown.

Tax Function

(10A)   . . . . $\qquad\qquad \dfrac{T}{p} = t\left(\dfrac{Y}{p} + \dfrac{B}{p} \right)$ $\qquad$ (10F)

This function serves to determine real tax collections T/p. As shown in equation (10F), collections are the product of the tax rate t and real disposable income before taxes (real income plus real interest transfers).

2. Total Effects

In the remaining parts of the essay, total effects of income taxation are examined for complete aggregative models. Throughout this discussion prices and real income are emphasized as key variables.[16] The total effects of government transactions are examined for three special cases of our general model. The characteristics distinguishing the three models are summarized in table 4.3. The models are called "classical," "neo-Keynesian" and "neoclassical"; but these labels are merely for descriptive convenience and are not meant to associate any particular authors with the assumptions of the models.

Values of the variables which satisfy simultaneously all the structural equations of a model constitute a solution of the system. For a static economic model of the type we are considering, a solution is an equilibrium. The total effects of a tax are given by comparing equilibrium or solution values of real income and prices in two situations, one with the tax and the other without the tax. It is instructive to examine this solution by classifying the variables and equations in two categories: (1) those which determine aggregate demand and (2) those which determine aggregate supply. Aggregate demand is the amount of real income (or real output) which the community demands

Table 4.3
Characteristics of selected models *

Structural Equation No. †	Classical	Neo-Keynesian	Neoclassical
(3F) Saving function	$S_2 > 0$ (interest effect) $S_3 = 0$ (no wealth effect)	$S_2 = 0$ (no interest effect) $S_3 = 0$ (no wealth effect)	$S_2 > \dot{0}$ (interest effect) $S_3 > 0$ (wealth effect)
(4F) Money demand-supply	$M = k(Y + B)$ (no interest effect)	$L_1 < 0$ (interest effect) $L_2 < 0$ (tax effect)	$L_1 < 0$ (interest effect) $L_2 < 0$ (tax effect)
(5F) Investment function	$I_2 < 0$ (interest effect)	$I_2 = 0$ (no interest effect)	$I_2 < 0$ (interest effect)
(8F) Labor supply	$N = N\left[\dfrac{w(1-t)}{p}\right]$ (no "money illusion")	$w = w_0$ (rigidity of money wage before tax) or $w = \dfrac{w_0}{1-t}$ (rigidity of money wage after tax)	$N = N\left[\dfrac{w(1-t)}{p}\right]$ (no "money illusion")

* The characteristics are mainly properties of the derivatives of the functions in the structural equations. The notation follows the following convention:

$$\text{given } F(X), F' = \frac{dF(X)}{dX} \text{ ; given } F(X_1, X_2, \ldots X_n), F_1 = \frac{\partial F(X_1, X_2, \ldots X_n)}{\partial X_1} \qquad \text{for } i = 1, 2, \ldots n \,.$$

† From Table 4.2.

through its decisions to spend; aggregate supply is the amount of real income (or output) which the community supplies through its decisions to produce.

In the models set forth in Tables 4.2 and 4.3, six structural relations (numbers 1-5 and 10) and the variables included in them determine aggregate demand. The remaining three structural relations (numbers 6-8) determine aggregate supply. In the neoclassical variant the ninth equation complicates the picture, since it bridges the demand and supply subsystems.

For either of the systems other than the neoclassical, the equilibrium solution may be described in terms of equality of aggregate demand and aggregate supply. Within the aggregate demand subsystem, the other variables may be expressed as functions of real income and the price level. Thus, solution of the subsystem yields a relation between real income and the price level. Similarly, an aggregate supply relationship between real income and price level may be derived from the supply equations. Together these two relationships determine the equilibrium solution levels of real income and price. In the neoclassical variant the demand relationship must express real income as a function of wealth as well as of the price level, and wealth is determined by the supply equations (numbers 6-9). Real income is also determined by these four equations; thus, the demand equations determine the price level.

2.1. Classical Model

According to the classical model of an anarchic economy, aggregate demand is larger the lower the price level. Since the level of money income is fixed by the quantity of money ($M = kY$), the relation between p and Y/p is a rectangular hyperbola. Spending is divided between consumption and investment in accordance with the saving and investment functions, and the rate of interest equates saving and investment. In contrast, aggregate supply is constant at all price levels. Labor demand and labor supply are both functions of only one variable, the real wage rate; their equality determines the level of employment and of the real wage. This solution is independent of the price level. The equilibrium aggregate supply of real income is uniquely determined by this level of employment. Figure 4.2 illustrates the combination of price level p_0 and real income $(Y/p)_0$ which satisfies both the demand (D) and supply (S) relations.

Government demand for goods and services and the consumer demand induced by government interest payments do not alter the demand relation. Extra final demand for output only increases the interest rate and reduces competing demands to a volume which is consistent with the real income level associated with a given price level. However, the extra transactions de-

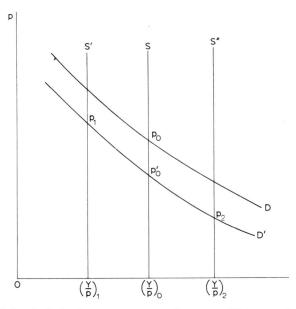

Fig. 4.2. Total effects of government transactions on equilibrium employment.

mand for money occasioned by government interest payments reduces the equilibrium level of real income at any price level, for the increased demand for money reduces the money income that can be supported with a given quantity of money. The net effect of this influence is to shift the demand relation to the left (to D' in Figure 4.2) and thus to reduce the price level (to p_0').

Introducing an income tax to finance part or all of a government deficit does not affect aggregate demand in the classical system. If the tax produces any impact effects that alter the spending equilibrium, the rate of interest adjusts so as to offset the disturbance and preserve the equilibrium of demand. Money income is determined in the money demand-supply equation, $M = k(Y + B)$, which is not affected by the tax (so long as there is no surplus in the new equilibrium). [17] However, the tax may produce a change in the equilibrium rate of interest. Since real consumption is the only one of the three components of aggregate demand directly affected by the tax, the existence and direction of a change in the interest rate depend upon the nature of the impact effect on consumption. Normally, this impact effect is to reduce consumption, and the interest rate must fall to offset it. It is conceivable, however, that the interest-reducing stimulus to consumption due to the tax could be greater than the income-reducing deterrent. In that case the interest rate would have to rise.

Aggregate supply, on the other hand, will be changed by an income tax if the supply of labor is responsive to changes in real wages. In this case, a tax alters the prior level of equilibrium employment and the equilibrium supply of real income. Figure 4.3 illustrates the effect of the tax on equilibrium employment for the two forms of labor supply functions in which real wages influence the supply of labor. If real wages and the supply of labor are positively related, the tax shifts the labor supply function (n) upward and to the left (n_t) and reduces equilibrium employment from N_1 to N_0; but if they are inversely related, it shifts the labor supply curve (g) upward and to the right (g_t) and increases equilibrium employment from N_1 to N_2. The tax would not change the equilibrium employment level if the supply function were vertical through N_1.

Any effects of the tax on the level of prices and real income are transmitted through the supply relation. As explained above, the tax does not affect aggregate demand. There are three possibilities, illustrated in Figure 4.2, corresponding to the three possible effects of the tax on aggregate supply. When the tax reduces aggregate supply, it increases the price level (p_1); when it increases aggregate supply, it depresses the price level (p_2); or it may produce no effect at all (p'_0). These effects constitute the total or

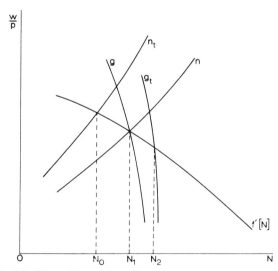

Fig. 4.3. Effect of income taxation on equilibrium employment.

economic effects of income taxation on prices and real income. Inasmuch as the economic effects of government spending were already taken into account in the pre-tax equilibrium of prices p'_0 and real income (Y/p_0), any alterations in the equilibrium values of these variables due to the tax are entirely attributable to its imposition.

2.2. Neo-Keynesian Model

Aggregate demand is inelastic with respect to the price level in the anarchic neo-Keynesian model. This characteristic is a consequence of the assumption that saving and investment are independent of the interest rate and are determined solely by real income. Variations in the price level do produce variations in the interest rate through the transactions demand for money. But these rate variations are of no significance in determining demand. [18]

Aggregate supply and the price level, however, are positively related. The higher the price level, the larger the amount of labor that can be profitably employed at the given money wage rate. Since the supply of labor varies as required, the larger the demand for labor, the greater is employment and real output.

Figure 4.4 illustrates these demand and supply relations (D and S) and the equilibrium values to which they lead (p_1 and $(Y/p)_1$).

Government expenditures and interest payments increase aggregate demand at any price level in this model, the amount of the increase being larger the lower the price level. At a given price level, the increased demand for final output, attributable to government expenditures and interest payments, exerts its full force on equilibrium demand for income. The enlarged transactions demand for money to finance the higher level of aggregate demand and interest payments raises the interest rate, but the components of aggregate demand are not affected. Multiplier analysis is applicable here, and the new equilibrium demand is higher by some multiple of the original stimuli, government expenditures and induced consumption from interest receipts. At a lower price level, the increase of aggregate demand due to given amounts of real government expenditures and money interest payments is larger, because the real value of the government interest payments is greater. Thus, the demand relation is shifted to the right and aggregate demand becomes sensitive to the price level. The aggregate supply function is not altered by government outlays. As illustrated in Figure 4.4 the shift in aggregate demand increases both real income (to $(Y/p)_2$) and the price level (to p_2).

Partial or complete financing of the government outlays with an income tax always reduces aggregate demand at any price level in this model. Since the saving-interest relation is absent, the tax always directly reduces consump-

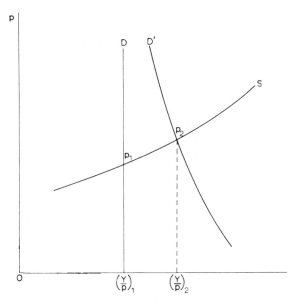

Fig. 4.4. Effect of government expenditure and interest payments on prices and real income.

tion; with the investment-interest relation also absent, saving and investment are equal only at a lower level of real income. The effects of the tax on the rate of interest are irrelevant in the determination of new equilibrium level of aggregate demand. The interest rate adjusts to produce equilibrium in the money market, but the commodities market, where the equality of saving and investment is attained, is effectively isolated from these adjustments.

Aggregate supply at any price level is either reduced or unaffected by the tax. The effect on aggregate supply depends on the labor supply function. In this model, the tax either increases or does not influence the money wage rate at which labor services are offered, depending on the characteristics of wage bargaining. When the tax does enter into wage negotiations, the labor supply curve shifts upward and equilibrium employment at any price level is re-duced, as shown in Figure 4.5. Two demand curves for labor, each relevant to a particular price level, are depicted. [19] The labor supply function (n) may be shifted by a tax to new position (n_t). At price level p_1, equilibrium employ-ment N_1 is reduced to N'_1, and the same occurs at any other price level, e.g., p_2. Aggregate supply of real income, which is determined by equilibrium employment, changes in the same direction. When the tax does not influence

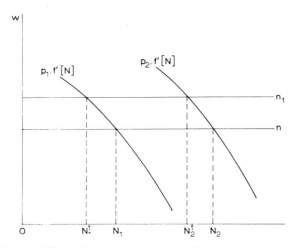

Fig. 4.5. Effect of income taxation on equilibrium employment.

wage demands, the equilibrium employment and aggregate supply corresponding to any given price level are not altered .

Figure 4.6 depicts shifts in the demand and supply relations and changes in equilibrium prices and real income resulting from the tax. If wage bargains are not influenced by the tax, both the price level and real income level are reduced from p_1, $(Y/p)_1$ to p_2 and the real income level corresponding to it. If wages are increased to compensate for the tax, the supply relation shifts upward to S', and the extent of this shift in relation to the movement of the D curve determines the new price level p_3.[20] When the marginal propensity to consume and the marginal propensity to invest are high, the reduction in aggregate demand – shift from D to D' – will be large and the new price level p_3 lower than the old. Whatever the price level change, real income will be lower in the new system equilibrium.

2.3. Neoclassical Model

The neoclassical model shares with the classical variant the characteristic that equilibrium real output Y/p is determined completely by the supply subsystem of equations. Since there is no "money illusion" in the labor supply function, real output is determined independently of the price level by the equilibrium of the labor market. So far as total output is concerned. therefore, the analysis of the effects of government transactions is the same as that presented above for the classical case. To summarize, government outlays have no effect; and the effect of income tax is positive, zero, or negative

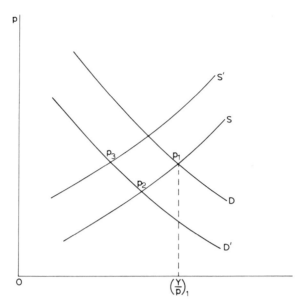

Fig. 4.6. Total effects of income taxation on prices and real income.

depending on whether the elasticity of labor supply with respect to the real wage is positive, zero, or negative.

Price level determination in the neoclassical case is, however, a more complex affair. The complexity arises principally from the wealth effect in the saving function. The real value of wealth is in the final model the sum of three components: R/pr the capitalized value of real private property income: B/pr the real value of the public debt; and M/p the real value of the money supply (which is assumed, it should be recalled, to consist entirely of currency and 100 per cent reserve bank deposits).

Given real private property income, the demand relationship between real income and the price level is negatively sloping. In this, the model again resembles the classical case. But here we have no quantity theory to insure that the curve is a rectangular hyperbola. And the neoclassical demand curve gets its negative slope from the wealth effect as well as from the monetary equation. The reasons for the negative slope are as follows: (a) A reduction in the price level lowers transactions requirements for money; since the liquidity preference curve is less than perfectly elastic, this release of cash lowers the interest rate. A lowering of the interest rate induces increases in both investment and consumption. The stimulus to consumption occurs not only from the direct effect of the reduced interest incentive to save but also through the wealth variable. Higher valuation is placed both on private property and on the public debt. (b) In addition, a reduction in the price level has a direct (Pigou) effect on consumption, which does not require any fall in the interest rate. The real value of the given stock of money rises, and so does the real value of the public debt.

The equilibrium price may be depicted as the intersection of a negatively sloped demand curve of this kind with the vertical supply curve. But the complexity arises because there are many such demand curves, and which of them is the relevant one depends on the supply-determined level of real output itself. Every demand curve assumes a given real property income; and real property income is determined by the same labor market equations that determine the level of employment and total output. These equations determine the real wage and the level of employment and thus the wage bill. The remainder of total output is the share of property owners.

So long as we do not consider autonomous changes in the labor market equation, this difficulty is easily met. The appropriate demand curve is the one which corresponds to the real property income associated with the unique supply-determined level of total output and employment.

Deficit financed government outlays do not alter the supply equations; hence we can analyze their effects without worrying about the dependence of demand on supply. As in the classical model, the transactions requirements incident to government interest transfers are depressing to demand. But in the neoclassical model, such transfers encourage consumption both by increasing disposable income and by increasing net private assets. The net effect may be to shift aggregate demand, at any given price level, in either direction. The shift varies directly with the marginal propensities to consume with respect to income and wealth, the income velocity of active money, and the numerical size of the elasticity of the liquidity preference curve.

Government expenditures on goods and services, on the other hand, always increase aggregate demand at a given price level. In this respect as in others, the neoclassical model stands between the classical and neo-Keynesian models. In the classical case, government expenditures do not affect total demand but only raise the interest rate enough to choke off an equal amount of private demand. In the neo-Keynesian case, they have a multiplier effect on aggregate demand, undiminished by any rise in the interest rate. In the present case, there is some rise in the interest rate but not enough to cancel the addition to total demand. Therefore in the ultimate equilibrium of the whole system, the job of keeping aggregate demand down to the given aggregate supply must be shared by rises in the interest rate and in the price level.

A similar analysis for the effects of the income tax is possible in the special circumstance of complete inelasticity of labor supply with respect to the real wage. In that circumstance the tax does not affect aggregate supply, and once again we need only look at the effect of the tax on the one demand curve associated with equilibrium aggregate supply. The investment function is not altered by the tax. The impact effects on the saving function we have already discussed above in connection with the classical model. The neoclassical saving function differs only in the addition of the wealth effect, and the value of wealth is not changed by the tax. Our conclusion above was that normally the tax would reduce consumption out of a given level of pretax income, although the opposite result, we found, was not inconceivable. At a given price level and interest rate, then, the tax will reduce consumption plus investment demand; the amount of this reduction will be the multiplied amount of the impact reduction in consumption, where the multiplier is the reciprocal of the marginal propensity to save plus the tax rate less the marginal propensity to invest. At the same time, the impact effect of the tax on the liquidity preference schedule is, we have seen, to raise the market interest rate required to make the community satisfied to hold a given amount of idle balances. This upward pressure on the interest rate reinforces the multiplier effect, and lowers the level of aggregate demand corresponding to any given price level. [21] Therefore the total effect of the tax, in the special case that now concerns us, is to shift the demand curve downwards and lower the price level.

We can no longer postpone the case where the tax affects labor supply and thus alters the equilibrium total output. Since it thereby alters real property income, it changes the demand curve relevant for the determination of the equilibrium price level. We can no longer confine ourselves to examining the shift in one demand curve, because we have at the same time a shift from one demand curve to another.

To prepare to examine this case, let us temporarily free our total system from the necessity of satisfying the labor supply equation and imagine that labor supply will adjust to any level of labor demand. Lacking this equation, the system will not determine unique values for any variable but it will determine a relation between any two variables. The two we are interested in are real income and the price level, and let us call this relation between them the supply-demand or *S-D* relation. In this relation, we embody not only movements along the demand curves discussed above but movements between them.

As production, thus freed from the shackles of labor supply, increases, what happens to the price level needed to equate aggregate demand to aggregate supply? On the one hand, we have the factors discussed above, which tend to lower the needed price level. These are the factors that make any one of our demand curves above negatively sloped. On the other hand, we have the increase in real property income associated with an increase in production. Via the wealth effect on consumption, this increase by itself would mean that a *higher* price level must be associated with a larger output. There is no a priori basis for saying that one effect outweighs the other. That it is conceivable for the wealth effect to be the stronger may be seen from the following numerical example. Assume an initial price level of unity, a marginal propensity to consume and marginal propensity to invest from income totalling 0.67, a marginal propensity to consume from wealth of 0.02, and an initial interest rate of 0.04. Assume that the elasticity of the demand for labor (the marginal productivity schedule) is unity; then an addition to total real income augments real property income by the same amount. An increase of $1 billion in real income adds $25 billion to the real value of wealth and induces $0.5 billion extra consumption. At the prevailing price level and interest rate, this direct increase in consumption means a total increase in aggregate demand of $1.5 billion, in accordance with the multiplier of 3. Thus the increment of demand exceeds the increment of supply. On the assumptions of the neoclassical model, the extra $0.5 billion of demand must be choked off both by a rise in the price level and by a rise in the interest rate. [22]

Given this S-D relation between real income and the price level, introduction of the level of real income as determined by the labor market equations determines both variables. We may now analyze the effects of a tax when the supply of labor and the level of output change. We have already argued (p. 67) that the effect of the tax is to lower the price level required to equate aggregate demand to a given aggregate supply. This means that the tax shifts the S-D curve downward. The net result is illustrated in Figure 4.7. In the figure, if the supply curve of labor is positively sloped the tax reduces labor supply and the level of real income, from S to S'. If the labor supply curve is negatively sloped, the tax increases real income to S''. The S-D curve is drawn positively sloped; the tax shifts it to $(S\text{-}D)'$. If real output is reduced to S', the price level falls from p_0 to p_1. In the other case, the new price p_2 is shown as lower than p_0, but it might be unchanged or even higher. Clearly a variety of results are possible, depending on the slopes and relative amounts of shifts of the labor supply and S-D relations. The figure illustrates two possible combinations, which of course are not necessarily empirically typical.

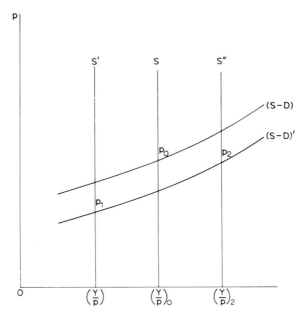

Fig. 4.7. Total effects of taxation on prices and real income.

2.4. *Conclusion*

The modifications of conventional conclusions that our analysis suggests may be illustrated by considering the celebrated balanced budget multiplier theorem. This theorem is that an increase of $1 billion in government expenditure on goods and services, financed by an increase of $1 billion in tax collections, will increase total real income by $1 billion. A corollary is that an increase of $1 billion in government transfer payments, financed by an equal increase in tax collections, will have no effect on total real income. Applied to the problem of inflation at a constant level of "full" employment, the theorem implies that an expansion of tax-financed expenditures is inflationary and that an expansion of tax-financed transfers is neutral. These conclusions follow from ignoring all equations and variables in a system except those used in simple multiplier analysis.

The neo-Keynesian model comes closest to embodying the assumptions implicit in the balanced budget multiplier theorem. Our conclusion for that model would agree that tax-financed transfer payments have no effect on real income. But, for tax-financed expenditure, our inclusion of total real income in the investment function, while disposable income appears in the saving function, means that the multiplier is greater than one. (For example, if the m.p. to save is 1/2 and to invest 1/4, $1 of expenditure leads to an increase of $4 of total income and $1 of taxes to a reduction of $2, so that the net effect is an increase of $2.)

In the classical and neoclassical models the effect on real income of tax-financed public outlays, whether expenditures or transfers, depends wholly on the effect of the tax on labor supply. This effect may of course be quite different from the effects of such transactions in a neo-Keynesian world. But it is instructive to compare the effects on prices, assuming that labor supply and real income are unchanged, with the expectations associated with the balanced budget theorem. In the classical case, neither expenditures nor taxes affect the price level. But transfers do; however they are financed, they add to transactions requirements and lower the price level supportable by a given quantity of money. In the neoclassical case, tax-financed expenditures have, on the one hand, a tendency to increase the price level, for the same reason that they augment aggregate demand in the neo-Keynesian model. This is reinforced under what we have considered normal circumstances, by the dis-incentive to saving due to the taxation of interest. But, on the other hand, the interest rate itself tends to rise because the tax shifts the liquidity-preference schedule upwards. The net effect may be either way. Nor is it clear that tax-financed transfers are neutral, although they are less inflationary, or more deflationary, than tax-financed expenditures. Transfers paid by taxes lack any direct expansionary multiplier effect; but, as in the case of expenditures, the tax may be a disincentive to saving. On the deflationary side, tax-financed transfers tend to increase the interest rate not only because of the impact of the tax on liquidity preference but also because of the extra transactions demand for money they entail.

Turning to the income tax as a weapon of short-run fiscal policy, our analysis suggests some qualifications of generally accepted views of the effects of changing the tax while outlays remain constant:

1. Increased income taxation is not necessarily anti-inflationary. There are situations in which the total effect is a wage and price rise. These situations are defined by certain kinds of behavior by consumers and producers. They do not depend on the ratio of tax collections to national income but can occur when tax rates are low as well as when they are high.

2. Reduction in the quantity of money by open-market operations may be a more effective way to reduce aggregate demand than a tax increase. Speaking broadly, the more "classical" the economy the more effective and neces-sary are monetary controls, and the more "neo-Keynesian" the economy the more reliance must be put on fiscal measures.

3. Under very special conditions neither income taxation nor changes in the monetary supply can be effective in reducing aggregate demand. This would be true if the market interest rate were at a Keynesian floor and if, as we have seen is conceivable, the interest elasticity of saving were so large that a tax actually increased consumption from a given pretax income. At the same time, a tax might have an inflationary effect from the supply side, through its effect on wage demands. In such an impasse, inflation must be fought by other measures, e.g., reduction of government expenditure, a spendings tax, direct controls.

The method of analysis followed here is of wide applicability to the theory of fiscal policy, although many questions of interest in the field cannot be approached by aggregative models. This paper has been concerned with a simple proportional income tax. But its methods and theoretical framework could be utilized in examining the economic effects of other taxes: a progressive income tax, a consumption tax, a savings tax, a payroll tax, and general import and export duties.

3. Stability Conditions for a General Neoclassical Model

The purpose of this part of the essay is to examine stability conditions for the general neoclassical model discussed above, specifically under circumstances where the total marginal propensity to spend of the economy at a given price level is greater than unity. We shall preface this discussion with three general methodological remarks on the relationship of dynamic stability analysis to static theory.

1. A static model provides by itself no clue as to the stability of the equilibrium represented by its solution. To determine whether this equilibrium is stable or not, it is necessary to make some explicit dynamic assumptions. To raise the question of stability is to admit the possibility that some or all of the variables of the system can assume at times nonequilibrium values and that therefore some or all of the equations of the system are not satisfied at every instant of time. How these departures can occur, and what will happen when they do occur, must be explicitly specified. In this specification the theorist has as much freedom of choice, among alternative assumptions regarding dynamic behavior, as he has in building a static model in the first place. On some assumptions, a given static equilibrium will be stable; on others, the same equilibrium will be unstable. It is never possible to prove that a given system is necessarily stable, in the sense that no dynamic assumptions could be found for which it would be unstable. One can at most show that on some plausible dynamic assumptions, a system is stable.

2. The reason for raising questions of stability about a static system is to determine whether the system is interesting or not. An equilibrium to which there is no dynamic force pushing a system is not an interesting one. Comparative statics traces the effects of exogenous changes on equilibrium solutions; the information it provides is quite irrelevant if the equilibria are unstable.

3. A finding that, for certain values of the parameters of the static functions and for certain dynamic assumptions, the solution of a static system will be an unstable equilibrium is by no means a finding that such parameter values cannot empirically exist. It is only a finding that, if those values do obtain, the economy cannot be represented by the static model. This point is worth emphasizing because of the frequent occurrence of such arguments as "The marginal propensity to spend cannot exceed one, because if it did the system would be unstable." It is a perversion of Samuelson's celebrated *correspondence principle* to imagine that stability conditions place limitations on empirical possibilities; they place limitations only on the relevance of static theories.

To return to our specific problem, the practice of using only a part of a complete aggregative system has been as frequent in analysis of the stability of aggregative equilibrium as in the comparative statics analysis of taxation. Concentration on the multiplier mechanism under the assumption of a constant price level has led to the accepted view that stability requires a marginal propensity to spend less than one. This ignores the possible stabilizing contribution of changes in the price level in systems where aggregate demand is inversely related to the price level. (If aggregate demand were positively associated with the price level − for example, for speculative reasons − price level changes would aggravate the problem of instability). As we shall see, this contribution can, on certain assumptions, overcome a marginal propensity to spend greater than one.

The contribution of price level changes to stability is important for the relevance of our static analysis because we allow for two effects which may well raise the marginal propensity to spend above unity. One is the positive relationship of investment to income; the dependence of the marginal productivity of capital on the level of employment of cooperating factors is one which, on the logic of the theoretical basis for aggregative models, can hardly be ignored. The second, in the neoclassical variant, is the effect of an increase in income on consumption demand via the indirect route of increasing real property income and hence the value of wealth.

In a dynamic analysis each of the variables must be viewed as a function of time t. Time may be imagined to move in discrete jumps, as in period analysis, or continuously. We shall adopt the latter view of time, but our results would not be different had we adopted the discrete convention. In what follows, therefore, Y means $Y(t)$, and similarly for other variables. The derivative of Y with respect to time, dY/dt, we shall represent simply by Y'.

We assume that the following equations of our model hold at all moments of time:

$$(1) \quad \frac{Y}{p} = \frac{C}{p} + \frac{I}{p} \qquad\qquad (6) \quad \frac{Y}{p} = f[N]$$

$$(2) \quad \frac{S}{p} = \frac{I}{p} \qquad\qquad\qquad (7) \quad \frac{w}{p} = f'[N] \qquad\qquad (A1)$$

$$(4) \quad M = kT + L(r) \qquad\qquad (9) \quad \frac{R}{p} = \frac{Y}{p} - \frac{Nw}{p}$$

But the other equations need not hold at every point in time. Thus, taking equation (3) for example, S/p can be different from $S[Y/p, r, R/pr + M/p]$, its schedule value, which we shall call $(S/p)^*$. Individuals are not necessarily saving at the rate, $(S/p)^*$, appropriate, according to the saving function, to the current values of the variables that determine saving. When individuals are not adjusted, in consumption and saving, to the current values of the determining variables, we assume that they are adjusting their consumption in a direction that would, if the determining variables remained constant, bring them on to the saving function. This adjustment they make by changing C, money consumption spending, a variable over which they have control. Formally:

$$C' = \Phi_C \left[\frac{S}{p} - \left(\frac{S}{p} \right)^* \right] \quad \text{where} \quad \Phi_C[x] \gtreqless 0 \text{ as } x \gtreqless 0. \qquad (A2)$$

In words, C will be increasing if real consumption is too low according to the saving function; C will be decreasing if it is too high; and C will be constant if saving and consumption are adjusted to the current values of their determining values.

Similarly, for investment:

$$I' = \Phi_I \left[\left(\frac{I}{p} \right)^* - \left(\frac{I}{p} \right) \right] \quad \text{where} \quad \Phi_I[x] \gtreqless 0 \text{ as } x \gtreqless 0. \qquad (A3)$$

Here $(I/p)^*$ is the schedule value of investment, $I[Y/p, r]$, according to equation (5) of the static model.

Now $Y(= C + I)$ is total money spending for goods and services. We shall assume that $\Phi_c \equiv \Phi_I$, so that (A2) and (A3) can be combined additively as follows: If the saving function and the investment function together call for a greater outlay on goods and services than is currently being made, then Y will increase. If, in combination, they call for a smaller outlay, then Y will decrease. If they call for the same outlay — whether consumption and investment are both adjusted to their schedule values or are out of adjustment by equal and opposite amounts — then total spending Y will be constant.

$$Y' = \Phi_Y\left[\left(\frac{I}{p}\right)^* - \left(\frac{S}{p}\right)^*\right] \quad \text{where} \quad \Phi_Y[x] \gtreqless 0 \text{ as } x \gtreqless 0. \quad \text{(A4)}$$

Thus spending will be increasing, constant, or decreasing according as schedule investment exceeds, equals, or falls short of schedule saving. This is our dynamic assumption concerning the behavior of demand.

Similarly, for the labor supply function, equation (8), we allow the possibility that labor supply will not be fully adjusted to the current real wage. Given the current real wage w/p the amount of employment N is determined by the marginal productivity of labor according to equation (7), which we have assumed to hold instantaneously. Let N^* be the employment appropriate to that same real wage according to the labor supply function (8). When N^* is greater than N, we assume that competition among wage earners lowers the money wage and increases employment; the opposite occurs when N^* is less than N.

$$N' = \Phi_N[N^* - N] \quad \text{where} \quad \Phi_N[x] \gtreqless 0 \text{ as } x \gtreqless 0. \quad \text{(A5)}$$

So long as the labor supply function (8) is above the labor demand function (7) to the right of their intersection, and below to the left, employment will always be moving towards its equilibrium value N_0 (This does not require the labor supply curve to be positively sloped.)

Real output Y/p and employment are positively related by (6), which we have assumed to hold at all moments of time. Consequently $(Y/p)'$ has the same sign as N'. It follows that, for a properly behaved labor supply curve, Y/p is always moving towards its equilibrium value $(Y/p)_0$.

$$\left(\frac{Y}{p}\right)' = \Phi_{Y/p}\left[\left(\frac{Y}{p}\right)_0 - \frac{Y}{p}\right] \quad \text{where} \quad \Phi_{Y/p}[x] \gtreqless 0 \text{ as } x \gtreqless 0. \quad \text{(A6)}$$

The condition for $(Y/p)' = 0$ is therefore simply that the system is somewhere on the vertical S curve shown above for the neoclassical model. (See, for example, Figure 4.7.)

Let us now consider the condition for $Y' = 0$, or for schedule saving to equal schedule investment. The locus of points $(Y/p, p)$ for which this is true is the S-D curve. Given the level of output Y/p, this curve shows the price level p necessary, according to the investment and saving functions, to equate saving and investment.

We are concerned with a rising S-D curve: since the total marginal propensity to spend exceeds unity, it takes a higher price level to keep investment from exceeding saving the larger the level of output. The S-D and S curves are shown in Figure 4.8. Their intersection E is the equilibrium solution of the static system, $((Y/p)_0, p_0)$. On our assumptions, if Y/p is to the right of S, Y/p will be decreasing; to the left, increasing. At any point above the S-D curve the price level is too high to bring investment-saving equality at the prevailing output level; saving exceeds investment, and spending Y will be falling. From any point below the S-D curve, Y will be rising. On these assumptions, E is a stable equilibrium. Imagine, for example, a displacement to point A.

At this point Y will be increasing, Y/p decreasing, therefore p will be increasing. From A, p and Y/p will follow a time path like the one indicated by the arrows; the path may be steeper or gentler in slope than the one shown, but its direction must in any case be somewhere between due north and due west. After the path crosses S-D, both Y and Y/p will be decreasing. The price level p may begin to decline, and eventually must decline. For when the path reaches S, Y/p will cease to fall while Y is still falling. The path leads inexorably to E, where both variables will be constant. The reader may verify that this is true regardless of the location of A and regardless of the relative strengths of the two dynamic effects.

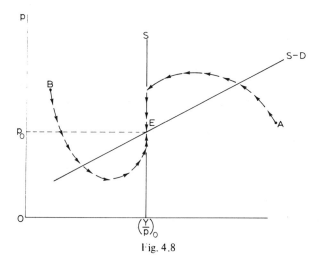

Fig. 4.8

It is possible to complicate this stability analysis in a number of directions without altering the basic conclusion. For example, we may drop the assumption that (7) holds instantaneously and allow divergence between the marginal productivity of labor and the real wage. (This causes complications on the demand side as well as the supply side, because there is no longer dynamically a unique relationship between property income and total income.) But so long as the labor demand-supply market is stable, the whole system will be stable.

The crucial dynamic assumption may be roughly expressed as follows: firms and wage earners determine the quantity of output, consumers and investors determine the volume of money outlay, and price adjusts to clear the market. An alternative approach would be to assume that spenders determine the quantity of output and producers the price level. It should be clear that this approach would give a high marginal propensity to spend a greater opportunity to create instability. We shall not give a formal analysis of such a dynamic model but only report that the equilibrium may be either stable or unstable, depending on the relative magnitudes of the two dynamic effects.

We believe that the first set of assumptions is more in accordance with the general premise of competition on which the aggregative model is based. But we need not argue the point. It is sufficient for our purposes that there are plausible dynamic assumptions on which the static analysis we have presented would be relevant and interesting because the static equilibrium is stable.

Notes

[1] The following articles are conspicuous exceptions: C. Clark, "Public Finance and Changes in the Value of Money," *Economic Journal*, 55 (Dec. 1945), 371-89; D.T. Smith, "Note on Inflationary Consequences of High Taxation," *Review of Economics and Statistics*, 34 (Aug. 1952), 243-47; O.H. Brownlee, "Taxation and the Price Level in the Short Run," *Journal of Political Economy*, 62, No. 1 (Feb. 1954), 26-33.

[2] In the second and third sections of this essay, Total Effects and Stability Conditions for a General Neoclassical Model, we examine the effects of taxation on the equilibrium solution of the complete system.

[3] Corporations are assumed to act in the interests of stockholders. Although this assumption recognizes only one aspect of corporate behavior — which is a useful approximation, considered by itself, only for closely held companies — there appears to be no consensus of opinion concerning the economic implications of the other aspects which might be taken into account. At the cost of increasing the complexity of the models, other hypotheses concerning corporate behavior could be introduced. For the purpose of this analysis, it does not seem worthwhile to increase its "realism."

Inasmuch as the treatment adopted here views the corporation-stockholder relation as similar to the partnership-partner relation, the personal income tax treatment of retained earnings is not important, so long as the latter are taxed only once, as is the case, for example, if they are included in the taxable incomes of owners only when earned.

[4] The money value of net private wealth is the aggregate of household net assets. Cf. J. Tobin, "Asset Holdings and Spending Decisions," *American Economic Review, Papers and Proceedings of the American Economic Association*, 42 (May 1952), 109-23, and the literature there cited. (Chapter 5 below.)

[5] Designating L as the demand for money, the two equations represented above in condensed form are: $L = k(Y) + L[r]$ and $M = L$.

[6] If the government is running a surplus, the same structural assumptions lead to a different expression for total transactions requirements, namely $k(Y + B + S')$ where S' is the surplus, or $k(Y + T - G)$. The additional requirement is due to the government's payment of the surplus to households to retire debt and to households' payment of this amount, in addition to their saving S, for private securities to finance business investment.

[7] Cf. Chapter 15 below.

[8] The argument is easily set forth algebraically in the case where the earning assets alternative to cash are perpetuities. Let r be the current market rate, r_e the individual's expected future rate, and t the tax rate. Then $r(1 - t)$ is the yield of an earning asset and $r/r_e - 1$ the expected capital gain or loss, assumed to be untaxed. The critical rate at any rate of tax, $r_c(t)$, is found as follows:

$$\frac{r_c(t)}{r_e} - 1 + r_c(t)(1 - t) = 0$$

$$r_c(t) = \frac{r_e}{1 + r_e(1 - t)}$$

Thus $r_c(t)$ is an increasing function of t. We may note, however, that the tax does not increase the critical rate by the amount necessary to offset the tax completely. That is $r_c(t)$ is less than $r_e 0/1 - t$. If the tax applied to capital gains and losses as well as to interest income, the critical rate would be unchanged by taxation.

[9] Inelasticity of interest rate expectations is an assumption of questionable propriety in a static model. It is an implicit way of introducing a dynamic relationship between current and past interest rates. In stationary equilibrium, then, liquidity preference would vanish. Cf. W. Leontief, "Postulates: Keynes' General Theory and the Classicists," Chapter 19 in S.E. Harris, *The New Economics* (New York: Knopf, 1947), 238-39. Moreover, whereas Keynes requires interest rate expectations to be inelastic, he requires price expectations to be of unitary elasticity. His overall conclusions would be very different if he were consistent. Cf. W.J. Fellner, *Monetary Policies and Full Employment*, rev. ed. (Berkeley: University of California Press, 1947), 150.

[10] It may induce the investor, even if he is averse to risk, to assume more risk in an effort to maintain his income. If so, his demand for cash, given the value of his wealth, would have a positive rather than a negative slope and would be shifted to the left rather than to the right by taxation. Analytically, this possibility is analogous to the possibility that a lowering of the interest rate will increase rather than reduce saving, or that a lowering of the wage rate will increase rather than reduce labor supply.

[11] Although the two approaches lead to similar conclusions regarding the effects of a tax on interest alone, they do not lead to similar conclusions when the tax is assumed to apply also to capital gains and losses. The first approach, we have seen, indicates no shift of the curve in that case. But the second approach suggests that the curve will shift down instead of up. Under this kind of tax, the government shares in risk to the same extent as in return. The terms on which the investor can "buy" return with risk are unchanged, and so therefore is his preferred combination of risk and return. But that combination requires a *greater* investment in earning assets the higher is the tax rate.

[12] The marginal product of capital is a rate of return of the same dimension as the interest rate. It shows the increment of product, measured in terms of real consumption, per unit of time, attributable to a unit of capital, measured in the same units of real consumption.

[13] Cf. A.P. Lerner, *The Economics of Control* (New York: Macmillan, 1946), Chapter 25.

[14] For a discussion of the effect of loss offsets cf. E. Domar and R.A. Musgrave, "Proportional Income Taxation and Risk Taking," *Quarterly Journal of Economics*, 58 (May 1944), 388-422; J.K. Butters and J. Lintner, *Effect of Federal Taxes on Growing Enterprises* (Boston: Harvard University, 1945), Chapter 3.

[15] Here, as in the case of other equations, we do not discuss the difficult aggregation problems involved.

[16] The direction of change in total real income and price level are not by themselves indicative of the "incidence" of taxation, or of any other government transaction. In its formal sense, tax incidence refers to the allocation to individuals of the difference between real income before taxes in the *posttax* equilibrium and real income after taxes in that same equilibrium. This difference, usually called the tax burden, is allocated among income recipients in accordance with the tax base. Thus, receipts from a proportional income are allocated in proportion to real incomes, classified according to size, functional source, or some other criterion. Tax-induced changes in total real income and the price level would not affect the incidence of an income tax in this formal sense. They would be relevant, however, if the comparison were between real income in the *pretax* equilibrium and real income after taxes in the *posttax* equilibrium. Here, the difference allocated includes changes in real income before taxes. Both changes in the price level and changes in real income affect the shares of wages, profits, and other property incomes, although in the formal sense of incidence a proportional income tax bears equally on all shares.

[17] A surplus raises the transactions demand for money (see p. 54 above) and, in this model, lowers aggregate demand. The effect is similar to that of government interest payments.

[18] For this reason it makes no difference whether the government budget shows a surplus, balance, or deficit. A surplus directly raises the transactions demand for money, but this impact has no influence on aggregate demand.

[19] These are the aggregative counterparts of the individual firm's money demand curve for labor, the marginal physical product of labor valued at its marginal revenue.

[20] The price level changes are qualitatively different in these two cases. When the money wage rate increases, any accompanying change in prices offsets both the higher wage rate and any variation in the marginal physical product of labor. When the wage rate is unchanged, any variation in prices compensates for alterations in the marginal physical product of labor only.

[21] In directly increasing the transactions demand for money, a surplus provides an extra deflationary influence.

[22] In this example, the total marginal propensity to spend of the economy exceeds unity, given the price level; and the reader may have some doubts of the stability of any equilibrium lying on an increasing S-D curve. This question is discussed in section 3 where it is shown that there are plausible dynamic assumptions for which such an equilibrium is stable.

CHAPTER 5

ASSET HOLDINGS AND SPENDING DECISIONS

A striking characteristic of recent discussion of monetary theory and policy has been the revival of interest in holdings of assets as determinants of the flow of spending. This revival followed a period during which the flow of spending was taken to depend almost exclusively on other flows – principally, of course, on income. One avenue of influence for asset stocks was even then kept open as a theoretical possibility, but its empirical importance was often considered small. This was the effect of the stock of money on spending via the interest rate. Since the war the fashion of dismissing interest rates as negligible factors in the spending decisions of households and business firms has waned, especially if the term "interest rates" is not interpreted literally but taken to cover the other dimensions of credit contracts. The faith of earlier monetary theorists, including Keynes, in the importance of interest rates has acquired renewed strength. Parallel to this development has been another one, logically quite distinct. This is the proposition that, whether or not spending is sensitive to interest rates, asset holdings have a direct influence on effective demand. It is with this proposition, in its several variants, that I shall be principally concerned in this paper.

In section 1 of the paper, alternative microeconomic and macroeconomic hypotheses concerning the dependence of spending on asset holdings will be stated. In section 2 the implications of these hypotheses for monetary theory and policy will be examined. In section 3 the plausibility of these hypotheses will be considered. In the concluding part, an attempt will be made to state, in brief and general terms, a hypothesis which is free from the objections which can be raised against the propositions under review but captures their essential meaning.

Reprinted from *American Economic Review* (*Papers and Proceedings*), 42 (May 1952), 109-23.

1. Alternative Hypotheses Relating Spending to Asset Holdings

Here, as elsewhere in economics, it is essential to distinguish micro-economic hypotheses, concerning the behavior of individual households or firms, from macroeconomic propositions, concerning the whole economy. Relationships postulated among aggregate variables, unless they are identities, depend on some assumptions regarding the behavior of basic economic units. These assumptions are not always made explicit by aggregative theorists, but it is nonetheless necessary to examine them in order to judge the plausibility of the corresponding macroeconomic hypotheses.

I shall list alternative microeconomic hypotheses first, and then consider their aggregate counterparts. I shall concentrate attention on hypotheses concerning the consumption spending behavior of households, but for the most part these hypotheses have analogues concerning the investment behavior of firms. The hypotheses differ from each other mainly in the stock variable to which the flow of current spending of a household is related.

1.1. *Hypotheses Concerning the Behavior of Individuals*

In each case, it should be remembered, the relationship of spending to asset holdings is a partial one, on the assumption that income, prices, interest rates, and other determinants of the household's spending decisions are constant. Each hypothesis, moreover, makes the basic assumption that there is no "money illusion" in household demand and that the functions determining that demand in physical units are homogeneous of order zero in all their variables of monetary dimension: money income, prices, and the value of the relevant stock of assets. It follows that a proportionate reduction of prices and money income with the money value of the appropriate stock of assets constant has, under each hypothesis, the same stimulating effect on real demand as an increase in the value of the asset holdings with money income and prices constant. It is the real value of the household's asset holdings – the volume of consumption goods which they could buy – which, with real income and interest rates given, is supposed to determine real spending.

1.1.1. Cash Balances

The first suggestion is to insert into the demand functions of a household its holdings of cash, on the hypothesis that, *ceteris paribus*, its total spending will be larger the larger its cash balances. Cash balances are taken to include holdings of currency, demand deposits, and possibly also time deposits.

This hypothesis must be carefully distinguished from what is virtually its opposite, which has long been generally accepted; namely, that the cash holdings of a spending unit depend, at least in part, on the amounts and the synchronization in time of its income and expenditures. This traditional explanation of the demand for cash treats cash balances as a dependent variable, subject to the decision of the spending unit. The hypothesis under review treats the same variable as an independent determinant of other decisions of the spending unit.

1.1.2. Liquid Assets

Since the war there has been widespread acceptance of the proposition that the spending of a household is directly dependent on its holdings of liquid assets. The strength of postwar demand has been widely attributed to the large accumulation of liquid assets during the war. A symptom of the popularity of this hypothesis is the interest of the Survey Research Center and the Federal Reserve Board in obtaining annual data on the liquid asset position of households and the widespread use of these data in assessing current economic prospects.

The category "liquid assets" is variously defined, and it is easier to list the types of assets selected for inclusion than to state the principle of selection. But for households, the category is essentially meant to include in addition to cash balances all obligations of banks (savings banks and savings and loan associations as well as commercial banks) and of the federal government which can be turned into cash on demand at an established price. The concept loses precision as soon as one asks such questions as whether an asset with an established redemption value in one month, but a price subject to the whims of the market meanwhile, qualifies as liquid. But such quibbling need not detain us. The meaning of the hypothesis is clear. It is the cash balances hypothesis 1.1.1 extended to recognize the existence of assets virtually indistinguishable from cash.

1.1.3. Net Worth

A third hypothesis relates the spending of a household to its net worth: the value of its assets of all kinds less its total indebtedness. The proposition is that the greater value of a household's accumulated savings, the greater will be its current consumption spending. The stimulating effects of asset holdings are not confined to any particular class of assets; and to debt is attributed a symmetrical depressing influence. The hypothesis implies that the composition of a household's wealth does not matter, that only its total value has significance for spending decisions.

The treatment of durable consumers' goods presents a problem for the net worth hypothesis. The value of these goods is surely a part of a household's wealth. But if outlay on these goods is, according to conventional practice, counted as consumption spending, this is one component of wealth which appears to have a negative instead of a positive effect on spending. This suggests that the categories "consumption" and "saving" appropriate to the net worth hypothesis are different from the conventional ones.

1.2. Aggregative Hypotheses

1.2.1. The Quantity of Money

The aggregative counterpart of 1.1.1 — the cash balances hypothesis for individuals — is simply the hypothesis that total spending will, other things being equal, vary directly with the quantity of money. This aggregative hypothesis cannot be derived from either of the other two microeconomic hypotheses.

The quantity of money hypothesis is often associated with the quantity theory, although it neither implies nor is implied by that theory. (A believer in the quantity theory need not assert that assets have anything to do with spending; he need only claim that the demand for cash balances is interest-inelastic. Similarly, a believer in the present hypothesis need not believe that the ultimate effects of an increase in the quantity of money are those described by the quantity theory; he needs only claim that one of the proximate effects will be to increase consumer spending.)

In his original exposition of what has come to be called "the Pigou effect," Pigou assigned a strategic role to the quantity of money. But, as he made clear later, this was not his real meaning. Evidently Pigou at first conceived the proposition that aggregate spending is positively related to the total quantity of money to be based on the proposition that the demand of that convenient Cambridge being, the "representative man," varies directly with the "value of his possessions." [1] That is, his hypothesis about individual behavior was evidently not 1.1.1. but 1.1.3. But Kalecki was quick to point out that the public is the debtor as well as the creditor of the banking system. [2] In his later article, Pigou amended his position to make the strategic variable not the total quantity of money but that part of it in excess of private indebtedness to the banks. This amended hypothesis does not follow from either 1.1.1. or 1.1.3., and doubtless what Pigou really intended is the variable defined by Patinkin, which will be discussed below under 1.2.3.

1.2.2. The Quantity of Liquid Assets

Similarly the aggregative counterpart of 1.1.2. is simply the hypothesis that total spending will, other things being equal, vary directly with the total value of private holdings of liquid assets. Significance in the determination of total spending may also be attached to the size distribution of liquid asset holdings among individuals and to their distribution among income classes.

1.2.3. Net Private Balances

This hypothesis, due to Patinkin, [3] relates private spending to the excess of private assets over private liabilities, excluding from private assets equities in physical goods. Net private balances correspond to the net indebtedness of the government, both interest-bearing and non-interest-bearing. Under American institutions, the variable is roughly equal to the monetary gold stock plus Treasury currency and interest-bearing federal debt held outside the federal government, whether by Federal Reserve banks, commercial banks, or others. The definition presents certain problems. What about state and local government debt? What about federal debt held by social security accounts? But there is no need here to enter into the refinements of the calculation of net private balances. [4]

This aggregative hypothesis follows from 1.1.3. – the net worth hypothesis for individuals – on the following assumptions: (1) that the stock of privately owned physical assets remains constant, and (2) that the marginal propensity to spend with respect to net worth is the same for individuals in different financial circumstances. The first assumption confines possible variation in the community's total real wealth to changes in the real value of net private balances. It is one of the assumptions of the static, short-run, Keynesian model and consequently is an appropriate one to make in exploring the implications of the net worth hypothesis for the workings of that model. The second assumption enables the distribution of wealth to be omitted from consideration.

1.2.4. Private Wealth

The natural macroeconomic counterpart of the net worth hypothesis, when the first assumption is not made, is that aggregate spending depends directly, other things equal, on total privately owned wealth. This amounts to the value of the community's stock of privately owned goods plus net private balances. As in the case of the previous hypothesis, focus of attention on the aggregate alone requires the second assumption.

This hypothesis applies not only to the conceivable alternative values of real wealth at a moment of time but also to capital accumulation over time. In this context it is traditional classical doctrine: the growth of wealth raises the representative man's rate of time preference and accordingly diminishes his saving at any given rate of interest. This was, indeed, restated by Pigou in the same two articles in which he set forth his hypotheses about the effects on spending of the money supply.

The wealth hypothesis applies only to consumption expenditure. Under unchanged technology, the accumulation of capital goods is unfavorable to further new investment; the net effect of accumulation on demand depends on the balance between this unfavorable effect and the stimulus to consumption. If consumers' durable goods are included in wealth, then their purchase must be considered investment and their use as consumption and income.

2. Implications of the Hypotheses for Theory and Policy

2.1. *The Absolute Price and Wage Level*

On any of the four hypotheses the real value of the appropriate stock of assets varies inversely with the absolute price level. Consequently, effective real demand will vary inversely with the price level. This — the Pigou effect — was a trump card in Pigou's long contest with the Keynesians over the theoretical possibility of underemployment equilibrium in the absence of wage rigidity. Pigou thought extremely unlikely the special cases of the Keynesian model in which wage and price flexibility are impotent to affect the level of real demand through the rate of interest, but he nevertheless provided an argument which is quite independent of the interest rate. Although the context of the controversy which inspired this argument was the analysis of deflation, the Pigou effect is no less applicable to the opposite problem, of more topical interest. It provides an automatic counterinflationary mechanism by which increases in the price level themselves tend to destroy the excess demand which generates them.

2.2. *The Efficacy of Monetary Policy*

One feature of Keynes' model was symmetry between changes in the quantity of money and changes in money wage and price levels. Whenever wage and price changes could affect employment and output, so also could changes in the quantity of money; and the same circumstances which might render wages and price flexibility impotent would also make monetary policy powerless. This symmetry follows from the fact that both must operate, if at all, through the interest rate. Deflation is the equivalent of an increase in the supply of money, because it releases money from transactions balances.

Hypothesis 1.2.1. — in which the quantity of money is the strategic variable — retains this symmetry. It gives to monetary policy, as well as to changes in money wage and price levels, direct power to influence employment and output, regardless of interest rate effects.

On hypothesis 1.2.2. — liquid assets — the effect of a change in the quantity of money depends on how it is accomplished. If assets which do not fall in the liquid category are monetized by the banking system, the hypothesis implies an increase in effective demand. But a mere exchange of money for other liquid assets would be of no consequence, aside from effects via the interest rate.

Hypothesis 1.2.3. − net private balances − gives to wage and price flexibility powers which it withholds from monetary measures. Open market operations by the banking system cannot change the quantity of net private balances. This quantity can change in money value only as a result of a change in the rate of interest or as a result of a fiscal deficit or surplus.

2.3. Secular Stagnation or Inflation

The hypotheses under discussion also have implications for a set of long-range problems connected with the effects of capital accumulation and fiscal policy on effective demand. The total private wealth hypothesis 1.2.4. leads to the conclusion that the growth of capital will automatically push up the propensity to consume. This tendency offsets, in part at least, whatever influence the accompanying increase in income may have in pushing down the propensity to consume. Growth of the federal debt, unaccompanied by increase in the economy's productive capacity, has even more pronounced effects on the side of long-run inflation. It stimulates consumption demand and does not offset this stimulus, as capital accumulation does, by enlarging full employment income (and thus possibly boosting the propensity to save) or by exhausting investment opportunities. [5] Similar effects are attributed to the public debt by hypothesis 1.2.3., and, to the extent that the debt is monetized or represented by liquid assets, by hypotheses 1.2.1. and 1.2.2.

3. Critique of the Hypotheses

3.1. The Control of Spending Units over the Independent Variables

A variable is not useful in explaining the behavior of an individual if its magnitude is just as much subject to his discretion as the behavior which it is supposed to explain. An explanation of spending decisions must relate the spending of a household to determinants outside its control. This is the fatal objection to the hypothesis 1.1.1. that the spending of an individual unit depends on the size of its cash balances, and to the macroeconomic hypothesis 1.2.1. derived from it. By exchanging cash for other assets, or vice versa, a household or firm can control the size of its cash balance extremely rapidly. One must beware of an optical illusion. A household which has decided to make an abnormal expenditure may in preparation build up its cash balance. It would be a mistake to conclude that the abnormally high cash balance caused the extraordinary expenditure. It is true that, in contrast to the cash balances of individuals, the total supply of money can be taken as an independent variable. But the effects of changing this supply on spending cannot occur in the naive direct manner depicted by these hypotheses. They must occur as a result of changes in other variables which are independent from the point of view of individual decisions — changes which induce individuals to adjust their cash balances to the altered total money supply.

The same criticism applies, with only slightly diminished force, to the liquid assets hypotheses. The category liquid assets excludes many other easily marketable assets; by purchasing or selling such assets an individual may change his liquid asset position at will. Like the total quantity of money, the total supply of liquid assets may be an independent variable. But changes in this supply must affect spending not directly but through interest rates and asset prices.

It would, however, be possible to hold the following view. There are lags in the adjustment both of spending and of cash (or liquid asset) holdings to the independent variables determining them. In consequence, both spending and cash (or liquid asset) holdings may be in disequilibrium with respect to the current values of those independent variables. It might be that these two disequilibria were uniquely related. In that case, it would not be necessary to look into the history of the household to explain its present spending behavior; that history would be summarized in the household's present holdings of cash balances or liquid assets; and with this knowledge and the present values of the variables determining spending, one could predict the household's current spending. This implies that any history of income, prices, interest rates, etc., which leads to the same current holding of cash (or liquid assets) leads also to the same current spending behavior. Even granting the possibility of such a remarkable coincidence, this modification of the hypotheses would rob them of most of their interesting implications.

In connection with the net worth hypothesis and its aggregative counterparts, the independence of the explanatory variables depends on whether the hypotheses are interpreted in a static or in a dynamic sense. At a moment of time, an individual is helpless to affect his present net worth. Over time, he can by his saving decisions control it within limits which become wider as the time horizon is extended. The problem of the present section is therefore inseparable from the plausibility of applying these hypotheses to changes over time, which will be discussed below.

3.2. Selected Assets Versus Total Wealth

It is difficult to justify restricting the effect of asset holdings on spending to any particular kind of asset, such as money or liquid assets. The criticism of the preceding section amounts to saying that any asset which can be turned into these forms either by sale or as security for debt has an equal right to be counted, at its market price, in the wealth relevant for spending decisions. Even assets which are not negotiable – for example, prospective social security benefits – can fulfill some of the purposes of holding wealth and consequently have some effect on spending. The quantity of money and the liquid assets hypotheses also neglect the indebtedness of the spending unit and imply that a given holding of cash or liquid assets has the same effect on spending, whatever this indebtedness.

The net worth hypothesis avoids all these difficulties and may indeed err in the other direction in its implication that only the value of wealth, not its composition, is relevant to spending decisions. Some assets which must be valued in reckoning total wealth are not marketable; and, because of market imperfections, an individual may be able to borrow, if at all, only at substantially higher interest rates than the rates at which he can lend. Consequently, an individual may get caught in a position in which, with the same net worth, he would spend more if his wealth were not tied up in nonmarketable assets.

3.3. The Public Debt as Private Wealth

The inclusion of the interest-bearing public debt in net private balances and in total private wealth raises an interesting question. How is it possible that society merely by the device of incurring a debt to itself can deceive itself into believing that it is wealthier? Do not the additional taxes which are necessary to carry the interest charges reduce the value of other components of private wealth? [6] There certainly must be effects in this direction. Additional taxes on the returns from income-producing property reduce, at a given rate of discount, the present value of that property. These doubts apply also to the role attributed to the interest-bearing public debt in the operation of the Pigou effect. The lower the price level, the greater must be the real outlays of the government for interest payments. The higher tax rates to meet these increased outlays mean that the stimulus to private demand from the increase in real value of the debt is offset, at least in part, by changes in private wealth which are unfavorable to spending.

Of course it may be that the fiscal policy of the government is and is expected to be to pay the interest on its debt, not by taxes, but by incurring further debt. In this case the debt does have a net expansionary effect, and the wealth-spending hypothesis points out that this effect may be greater than would be expected according to conventional income analysis. Still it would be more natural to attribute it to the influence of the debt on public spending rather than to its effect on private spending.

It is true that the creation of public debt, even if it does not alter the value of private wealth relevant for spending decisions, makes the composition of that wealth more liquid. In this respect it is similar to an increase in the money supply. On hypotheses which attribute to liquidity per se a stimulating effect on spending, the debt will be expansionary. The doubts expressed above apply to the inclusion of the debt at full value in connection with hypotheses which rely on the total value of private wealth rather than on its composition.

If public debt is incurred for government investment in assets which yield revenue to the government and reduce its tax requirements or in projects which contribute to the earning power of private property, it will have no depressing effects on spending to offset its stimulating effects. I suspect that, in reckoning the size of national wealth relevant to private spending decisions, just as in reckoning it for other purposes, it is nearer the truth to count the productive assets of the government than to include its debt.

3.4. *The Distribution of Wealth*

It was noted above that the Pigou effect, based on the net-worth hypothesis concerning individual behavior, requires an assumption eliminating the necessity for considering changes in the distribution of wealth among individuals. Such assumptions are common in aggregative economics; the conventional aggregate consumption function ignores in a similar way changes in the distribution of income. But the assumption is particularly vulnerable in the case of the Pigou effect. Only a small part of national wealth − net private balances −- changes in real value when the price level changes; the base on which the Pigou effect operates is even smaller if the criticism above of the inclusion of deadweight interest-bearing public debt is accepted. This leads to the possibility that changes in the distribution of wealth associated with changes in the price level may dwarf in significance the net change in total wealth. Moreover, these changes in distribution are systematic: creditors, debtors, shareholders, owners of goods − all fare differently. Without knowing both the income and wealth positions of these various groups and the differences in marginal propensity to spend with respect to net worth associated with differences in financial position, it is not possible to judge whether the redistribution of wealth due to a change in the price level would reinforce or oppose the Pigou effect.

3.5. *Effects of Wealth on the Supply of Labor*

If, as the hypotheses under review assert, an increase in wealth leads to an increased demand for consumption goods and services, it is logical to expect it to lead also to an increase in the demand for leisure; that is, to a decrease in the supply of labor. The Pigou effect has the unintended by-product of providing a rationale for the Keynesian labor supply function, although it is a different rationale from the one Keynes provided. The supply of labor will be larger, at the same real wage, the higher the money wage, not out of sheer "money illusion" but because households are poorer in wealth at the higher price level and can afford less leisure. Consequently the unemployment which, via the Pigou effect, is remedied by a decline in prices and money wages is remedied, not just by an increase in the demand for labor, but also by a decrease in the supply. The full employment which is achieved by deflation is not as large a full employment as would have been achieved by some other means. Indeed, Keynes himself was unwilling to consider an employment equilibrium full if a greater supply of labor would be forthcoming at the same or lower real wage at a higher price level.

This footnote to the long controversy which culminated in the Pigou effect is worth adding because of the modern tendency to insert wealth in some fashion into the Keynesian model and at the same time to dismiss Keynes' labor supply function as an excusable aberration of a great theorist. Following Klein, [7] Patinkin adopts the classical view that the supply of labor is a function solely of the real wage. This rules out unemployment as a possible equilibrium solution of a complete static Keynesian model and makes it necessary to attribute unemployment to the failure of the model to have a solution and the failure of the labor supply function to be satisfied. Pigou's amendment gives such a model a solution. But it also rehabilitates the original Keynesian view of the supply of labor.

3.6. The Dynamic Wealth-Spending Relationship

It was suggested above that the net worth hypothesis can have both a static and a dynamic interpretation. The static version relates the real spending of a consumer to the possible real values which his net worth may assume at a moment of time. His real wealth is variable because of possible variation in factors beyond his control; the prices of his assets and debts and the prices of consumption goods. It is this interpretation of the hypothesis which is used in the Pigou effect.

The dynamic interpretation applies the hypothesis also to changes in the individual's net worth which occur over time as a result of his saving decisions. This interpretation leads, as mentioned in section 2, to an optimistic or inflationary picture of the long-run prospects of effective demand. As the time horizon is lengthened, the control of the individual over his own net worth increases; once again the question arises whether a variable over which he has control can qualify as a determinant of his spending behavior. Does the fact that a household has saved and added to its wealth this year imply that it will save less from the same real income next year? This does not seem plausible unless this year's accumulation was for some reason unintentionally high. If a household is simply executing a saving plan previously decided upon, no special significance attaches to the year-to-year changes in its net worth. The plan may call for an even rate of saving over many years, or it may call for high saving in some years and low saving or dissaving in other years, in any sequence. Clearly there is variation over time in the saving behavior of a household due solely to its biology; and it would be a mistake to attribute such variations to the concurrent changes in other variables, either income or net worth.

What may be of significance, from an aggregative viewpoint, is the endowment of wealth with which a new generation of households commences economic life. It might be that the larger this endowment the lower will the generation scale its lifetime saving plans. Thus the growth of national wealth over time would gradually lift the propensity to consume, even though no meaningful relationship existed for a particular household between the time histories of its wealth and of its current saving. In this form, the hypothesis involves speculation about the propensity to bequeath. The secular lift to consumption would not occur if each generation scaled up in proportion to its own endowment its conception of the appropriate amount to leave to the next generation. The forces determining this propensity are surely very complex and difficult to discover either by speculation or by empirical investigation.

Aside from this possibility, there is one other sense in which wealth might plausibly be taken to influence spending over time. Unplanned increases or decreases in wealth may influence subsequent accumulation. If a household's wealth grows in one year more than had been anticipated, the household may in the following year spend somewhat more than if events had gone according to plan. Unplanned changes in real wealth can be the result of unexpected changes in the prices of the assets held by the household or in the prices of consumption goods. To be of significance in altering the saving behavior of the household, such changes must be viewed as relatively permanent. (Unexpected increases in real income may also lead to unplanned saving and accumulation of wealth, followed later by consumption greater than planned. But this sequence of events is better interpreted as a lagged response of spending to income than as a response of spending to wealth.)

3.7. Attempts to Measure the Strength of the Pigou Effect

In his articles stressing the theoretical importance of the Pigou effect, Patinkin disclaimed any belief in its practical significance. He reported experiments with interwar aggregate time series which showed that the real value of net private balances does not make a significant contribution to the explanation of observed variation in aggregate consumption. He also exhibited the weakness of the Pigou effect in the Great Depression by contrasting the 46 per cent rise he computes in the real value of net private balances from 1929 to 1932 with the 40 per cent fall in real national income in the same period.

Quite aside from the usual statistical difficulties, these tests are not appropriate for the hypotheses about individual and aggregate spending which are supposed to be tested.

The real value of net private balances becomes, in theory, a strategic aggregate variable only because, in the circumstances envisaged by the theory, it is the only variable determinant of the real value of total private wealth. During the span of a test based on time series, real private wealth changes for other reasons. Changes in the value, in terms of consumption goods, of the capital stock overshadow in importance changes in the real value of net private balances. The value of the capital stock changes over time, not only by physical investment or disinvestment, but by changes in the valuation, in terms of consumption goods, of existing capital. [8] Both of these sources of variation are excluded from the theoretical argument which leads to the focus of attention on the real value of net private balances.

Nor can the concentration of statistical attention on net private balances be justified as conforming to the dynamic interpretation of the wealth hypothesis discussed above. On this interpretation, it will be remembered, the only changes over time in private wealth which might be expected to affect the propensity to consume are changes which were unexpected departures from saving plans. There is no reason to expect these to coincide with changes over time in real net private balances, which may be either too narrow or too broad a category. Changes in the purchasing power of fixed-money-value assets and debts are not the only sources of surprises to holders of wealth. Over time. real net private balances change because the government runs a deficit or buys gold. Like saving which goes into private capital formation, saving which matches the increase in supply of net private balances may simply conform to consumers' plans and thus have no effect on their subsequent spending.

Whatever interpretation of the wealth hypothesis is adopted, the effects on consumption spending of changes in the distribution of wealth are likely to overshadow the effects of changes in the real value of net private balances.

4. Conclusion

It is difficult to state a plausible, simple hypothesis relating spending to wealth. Any hypothesis which makes spending depend on the holding of a particular kind of asset, such as cash or liquid assets, runs afoul of several objections: (1) other assets are good, often perfect, substitutes for the selected types; (2) the composition of an individual's wealth is, at any time, subject to his own decision; (3) indebtedness should be treated symmetrically with asset holdings. The hypothesis relating a consumer's spending to his net worth avoids these difficulties. But, since a consumer's wealth is, over time, determined in large part by his own saving plans, the dynamic interpretation of this hypothesis is questionable. Even in its static interpretation, there is no simple aggregative counterpart of the net worth hypothesis. It is doubtful that deadweight government debt should be included in net private balances. Without this component, the variable has little quantitative significance. In any case, the systematic redistribution of wealth accomplished by changes in the price level is likely to be of greater importance for real consumption demand than changes in the purchasing power of net private balances.

The main theoretical issues to which the hypotheses under discussion have been directed are the efficacy of monetary policy and the efficacy of flexibility in the absolute price and wage levels. The issues are whether, under circumstances when reactions through the rate of interest are negligible, a change in the level of employment and output can nevertheless be effected by changing the quantity of money and by changing the money wage rate. The discussion has contributed no basis for optimism concerning monetary policy. The hypothesis that spending will vary directly with the quantity of money is logically the weakest of the family of hypotheses relating spending to asset holdings. The Pigou effect argues for greater confidence in the efficacy of wage and price flexibility, but the issue is, for a number of reasons advanced above, both theoretically and empirically in doubt.

For monetary policy a stronger case can be made by questioning the skepticism of recent years about the significance of interest rates in spending decisions than by claiming that the quantity of money can influence spending directly, regardless of what happens to interest rates. In making this case, a wealth-spending hypothesis can be an ally rather than a replacement. Changes in the interest rate alter the real value of wealth and may affect spending by this route as well as by changing the terms on which future goods may be substituted for present goods.

A third theoretical issue to which the hypotheses under review are relevant is the behavior of saving in secular expansion. But there are special difficulties in a dynamic interpretation of these hypotheses. Even if one accepts the Pigou effect he should not jump to the conclusion that the same argument guarantees the passage of the rich-economy camel through the eye of the full-employment needle.

In spite of these negative comments, I do believe that there exist important relationships between wealth and current spending. Monetary theory is, I agree, taking the proper direction in seeking to end the artificial separation between decisions about stocks and decisions about flows to which Keynesian economics contributed. Doubtless the relationships between wealth and spending involve the composition of wealth as well as its total value. However, the effects of the composition of national wealth — the aggregate supplies of various kinds of assets — are felt by individuals mainly through the structure of interest rates and asset prices. It is to these interest rates and prices rather than to their holdings of different kinds of assets that the spending decisions of consumers — and business firms as well — must be related.

The formulation of plausible hypotheses is impeded by the custom of forcing theoretical concepts to conform to the categories used for reasons of statistical exigency, in national income accounting. If consumers' durable goods were counted as assets and the concepts of consumption and income revised accordingly, the following general hypotheses about consumer behavior might provide a framework for analysis:

1. An individual attempts to distribute his net worth among various kinds of assets and debts in a pattern which depends upon his net worth, his income, the prices of the various assets and debts, and the prices of nondurable consumption goods and services.

2. An individual divides his current income between consumption and saving in a manner which depends on the same four sets of factors.

On these hypotheses, the important thing about the supply of a particular kind of asset is not its absolute size but its amount relative to the supplies of other assets and to total wealth. As the stock of government bonds expanded in the last decade, the quantity of money had to rise to keep the interest rate from rising. The supply of liquid assets at the end of the war held inflationary dangers because it was, at prevailing interest rates and prices of durable and nondurable goods, a disproportionate share of total wealth. The same supply holds less inflationary danger when, both because of rises in the prices of goods and because of expansion of the physical stock of durable goods, it is a smaller share of total wealth. There is not space to show how other phenomena which the various hypotheses reviewed in this paper are designed to explain fall into place in the suggested framework. But of course the crucial questions about saving and spending behavior are empirical, and no general analytical framework can even begin to answer those.

Notes

[1] A.C. Pigou, "The Classical Stationary State," *Economic Journal* (1943), 343-51; "Economic Progress in a Stable Environment," *Economica* (1947), 180-90.

[2] M. Kalecki, "Professor Pigou on 'The Classical Stationary State' – A Comment," *Economic Journal* (1944), 131-32

[3] Don Patinkin, "Price Flexibility and Full Employment," *American Economic Review* (September 1948), 543-64.

[4] "Price Flexibility and Full Employment," comment by Herbert Stein and reply by Don Patinkin, *American Economic Review* (June 1949), 725-28.

[5] Cf. Gardner Ackley, "The Wealth-Saving Relationship," *Journal of Political Economy* (April 1951), 154-61.

[6] My doubts on this point were inspired by T.C. Schelling. See "The Dynamics of Price Flexibility," *American Economic Review* (September 1949), 911, foornote 2.

[7] L.R. Klein, *The Keynesian Revolution* (New York: Macmillan, 1947), pp. 80-90.

[8] This change in valuation incidentally, greatly limits the possibility of using the wealth hypothesis, as Ackley does in the article previously cited, to explain why consumption is a higher proportion of income in depression than it was at the same real income during an earlier prosperity. The decline in real income from full employment levels may not reduce the physical stock of capital but it certainly reduces its value.

CHAPTER 6

TAXES, SAVING AND INFLATION

During the postwar inflation in the United States, Professor Sumner Slichter proposed a reduction of personal income taxes on the portion of income saved. [1] The immediate objective of the proposal was to encourage individual saving as a means of fighting the inflation. In addition, Professor Slichter believes it to be social wisdom to devote a larger share of full employment national income to saving and investment. To this end he offered his plan as a permanent feature of the tax system. This suggestion was enthusiastically seconded by Professor David McCord Wright, [2] both because he favors more saving and investment and because he believes the long-run prospects of the economy are inflationary.

As an anti-inflationary weapon, the plan has the great advantage of being politically painless. [3] Conventional anti-inflationary measures are never popular. But this proposal offers taxpayers, instead of an increase in income tax rates, a reduction in their tax liability. Indeed, Professor Slichter claimed that cutting tax rates during the inflation in 1948 would be harmless if accompanied by his proposal. [4]

The plan is to permit the taxpayer to exclude his saving, or some fraction thereof, [5] from his taxable income. Saving would be a "deduction," like charitable contributions or medical expenses. From the individual taxpayer's viewpoint, the plan is equivalent to replacing part or all of the income tax by a tax on his consumption expenditures. [6] Thus the Slichter proposal is closely related to the expenditures tax advocated by Wallis and Friedman as a wartime measure. [7] But while Wallis and Friedman proposed to combat inflation by temporarily adding an expenditures tax to the existing income tax, Slichter proposes to replace permanently the existing income tax, or part of it, by a tax on consumption.

How effective would exemption of saving from taxation be in weakening inflationary pressure? The privilege would certainly raise the amount of

Reprinted from *American Economic Review*, 39 (December 1949), 1223-32.

saving forthcoming from any given level of income before taxes. But saving may be increased at the expense either of taxes or of consumption. Substitution of saving for tax payments is of no help in a fight against inflation; it may even be a step backwards. Giving consumers a larger cushion of accumulated savings may strengthen their propensity to consume in subsequent years. Moreover, substitution of saving for taxes means that more government obligations are outstanding; and these obligations are actually or potentially bank reserves under present monetary arrangements. [8] Professor Slichter argues that the availability of more current saving by individuals would facilitate the transfer of resources from consumption to investment without the necessity of bank credit expansion. [9] But if government expenditures are independent of tax receipts, any saving which merely replaces taxes will be matched by an increase in the government's demand for loanable funds. The needs of government and business to borrow from the banks will be undiminished, and the ability of the banks to meet these demands will be enhanced.

Therefore, if the plan is to realize its objectives, it must result in substitution of saving for consumption as well as for taxes. In evaluating the effects of the proposal on consumption, a temporary privilege of deducting saving must be distinguished from the permanent incorporation of this feature in the tax system. The plan has a better chance of reducing the propensity to consume out of income before taxes if it is regarded as temporary than if, as its proponents advocate, it is expected to be permanent. A principal motive for saving is provision for future consumption. The force of this motive is weakened if future consumption spending is expected to be taxed at the same rate as current consumption.

Even if the measure is understood to be temporary, its effectiveness is doubtful; consumer demand corresponding to a given level of personal income before taxes may even be increased. The deduction privilege is in effect a lowering of the price of saving in terms of income and consumption. Instead of costing one dollar of consumption, a dollar of saving costs one dollar less the tax deduction attributable to it. (If r is the applicable marginal income tax rate and b is the fraction of saving eligible for deduction from taxable income, the cost of a dollar of saving is $1 - br$ dollars of consumption.) Now lowering the price of saving has both substitution effects and income effects. The substitution effects are unfavorable to consumption. But any taxpayer who would save in the absence of the special incentive is given, under the proposal, an increase in disposable income equal to the tax on the deductible part of his normal saving. The increase in disposable income is favorable to consumption. There is no a priori way to decide whether the substitution effects or the income effects will predominate. But a measure which has income effects favorable to consumption is a weak method of fighting inflation.

Moreover, there are two features of the plan which limit its restrictive effects on consumption. First, the deduction privilege does not alter the price of dissaving. To qualify for tax relief, dissavers would have to cease dissaving and start saving. Short of a drastic revision of their budgets, the plan gives dissavers no incentive to reduce their consumption. Nor does it force them to consume less by imposing on them higher taxes. The plan could touch dissavers only by including a penalty for dissaving at the same rate as the bonus for saving. A penalty provision probably would not be acceptable on social and political grounds.

Second, due to the progressive structure of tax rates, the more a taxpayer saves the less he can gain by reducing his consumption further. His saving is excluded from the taxable income on which his marginal tax rate depends. Enough saving can move him to a bracket with a lower marginal tax rate. A taxpayer who would save in the absence of the plan gets a boost in his disposable income based on the marginal tax rate applicable to his taxable income before deduction of saving. His normal saving may be sufficient to move him to a lower tax bracket. When he considers whether to increase his saving at the expense of his consumption, his calculations are made at a lower marginal tax rate, i.e., a higher cost of saving. Consider, for example, a lowest-bracket taxpayer whose deduction for normal saving lowers his taxable income beyond the reach of the income tax. The deduction privilege gives him an increase in diposable income, some of which he may devote to increased consumption, but it offers him no incentive to substitute saving for consumption.

The difficulties due to varying marginal tax rates could be largely avoided by computing the tax deduction for saving in a different manner from the deductions now allowed. Instead of a deduction from taxable income, the privilege could take the form of a credit against tax liability computed by applying a uniform rate to the taxpayer's saving. Except for taxpayers with sufficient saving to reduce their tax liability to zero, the cost of saving to an individual would be independent of the amount of his saving.

The reduction in the price of saving in terms of income and consumption accomplished by the proposed tax revision is analogous to a general rise in interest rates. Both the deduction privilege and an increase in interest rates enable a saver to have larger funds at his disposal in the future for the same sacrifice of current consumption. Both increase the amount of future consumption which can be obtained with a given current income. Economic opinion has been uncertain and divided concerning the effects of interest rate changes on consumption and saving. Empirical evidence is inconclusive, and the current fashion is to attribute to interest rates little or no influence on the disposition of income. It is true that the tax proposal can accomplish much bigger changes in the price of saving than the usual range of variation of interest rates. On the other hand, a rise in interest rates does not suffer from the special features of the tax device which limit its effectiveness in inducing substitution of saving for consumption.

It is by no means certain, therefore, that the Slichter plan would restrict consumption spending even if it were regarded as temporary. The proposal has even less chance of achieving its anti-inflationary objective if it is expected to be permanent. This expectation will in no way weaken the income effects of the tax deduction privilege, which are favorable to consumption. But it will substantially weaken the substitution effects. Consider a taxpayer whose expectations of income and tax rates place him in the same marginal tax rate bracket in the future as today. Suppose that, in the absence of tax incentives, he plans to save in future years about the same amount he is currently saving, so that deduction of these savings from taxable income would not make his future tax brackets differ from his present bracket. A temporary exemption of saving from taxation might induce him to shift to the present some of the saving he had planned to do in the future and to postpone consumption. He would thereby avoid permanently tax payments on the increase in his current saving. But if the exemption of saving from taxation is permanent, the taxes are not avoided but only postponed. If the taxpayer shifts consumption from today until tomorrow, he adds to his future tax liability exactly what he deducts from his taxes today. Indeed, due to the progressive tax rate structure, he may add more to his future tax liability than he gains from tax exemption in the present. An increase in future consumption might carry the taxpayer into a higher tax bracket, because he would have less saving to deduct from future taxable income. Or a decrease in present consumption might take him into a bracket with a lower marginal tax rate.

For some taxpayers, whose income prospects and consumption and saving plans are not uniform over time, permanent exemption of saving from taxation could lead to a reshuffling of consumption and saving plans. But this reshuffling can work both ways; present consumption can be increased as easily as reduced. If a taxpayer expects to face different marginal tax rates in different years, the scheme gives him an incentive to shift his consumption to years when he expects to be in low tax brackets. Similarly the absence of a penalty for dissaving may lead to concentration of consumption spending in years when dissaving is planned anyway. For example, a taxpayer who anticipates dissaving when he retires will not increase his taxes in the years of retirement by planning to consume more at that time. He will receive current tax benefits by reducing his present consumption; consequently, for him the plan reduces the cost of future consumption in terms of present consumption. On the other hand, an individual who is currently dissaving in anticipation of higher future incomes which will permit him to save adds nothing to his current taxes and reduces his future taxes by dissaving more now and planning to save correspondingly more in the future.

A by-product of the scheme, whether adopted temporarily or permanently, would be to change regressively the size distibutions of disposable income, wealth, and possibly consumption. Big savers in the high-income groups would receive increases in disposable income, while low-income families with zero or negative saving would not. To the extent that the high-income groups save their gains, inequality of wealth is promoted. If the beneficiaries increase their consumption, even the distribution of consumers' goods is altered against the low-consumption groups who receive no advantage from the tax reduction. The regressive features of the plan would diminish its political appeal, one of the principal advantages claimed for the proposal, and might well increase inflationary pressure due to wage demands. Regressive effects could be lessened by placing a ceiling on the allowable deduction of saving or by varying the fraction of saving eligible for deduction inversely with the amount of saving claimed. But these provisions would also diminish, in the same manner as the progressive structure of tax rates, the incentive for substituting saving for consumption.

By a more fundamental revision, the Slichter proposal can be made both more effective against inflation and less regressive. Tax rebates would be allowed not for all saving but only for additions to the taxpayer's normal saving. This revision eliminates the perverse income effects; tax relief would be obtainable only by curtailing consumption. The economic meaning of "normal saving" is the amount the taxpayer would save given his income before taxes and given the tax law without the rebate provision. No legal formula can do more than approximate the economic meaning. A possible approximation would be a schedule of normal saving for tax purposes, determined by the government. Based on family budget data, the schedule would relate normal saving to income, number of dependents, and perhaps to other factors. The taxpayer could claim deduction only for saving in excess of the figure in the schedule applicable to him.

Such a schedule — or any other legal formula for normal saving, such as the taxpayer's saving in some previous year — is bound to overstate the normal saving of some and understate that of others. These inevitable errors reduce the anti-inflationary effectiveness of the plan. Taxpayers whose normal saving is understated will receive a windfall, with income effects favorable to consumption. Taxpayers whose normal saving is significantly overstated are unlikely to change the disposition of their incomes. Like the dissavers considered above in the analysis of the original proposal, they must take an unrewarded cut in consumption before they can begin to claim tax rebates for further cuts. The plan could be made certain to affect all taxpayers by including a penalty tax for undersaving as well as a tax deduction for oversaving.

To summarize, tax rebates for all saving are not a reliable method of restricting consumer demand and stopping inflation. They are especially ineffective if they are expected to be a permanent feature of the tax system. A temporary plan to exempt saving from taxation can be strengthened by confining the exemption to saving in excess of some normal amount. It can be further strengthened by penalizing taxpayers who save less than normal amounts as well as rewarding those who save more. Even with these amendments, the proposal requires for its success a high degree of substitutability between present and future consumption. And the amendments spoil the spectacular, if illusory, political appeal of a proposal which promises to stop inflation by reducing taxes.

The quest for anti-inflationary medicine which is both effective and palatable is, nevertheless, an important one. What means of restricting the consumption of a taxpayer to a given level will deprive him of the least satisfaction? This question is surely relevant to an appraisal of anti-inflationary tax measures, even though it is not to be expected that the constituents of political appeal can be discovered in the economic theory of consumer preference.

An answer to the question requires assumptions concerning the taxpayer's preferences. The following assumptions are made: (1) Given his level of current consumption, the taxpayer prefers more future purchasing power to less; (2) Given the terms of exchange of present consumption for future purchasing power, the taxpayer will both consume more and save more the higher his current disposable income; (3) To leave the taxpayer at a given level of satisfaction, it is necessary to provide him with increasing amounts of future purchasing power for every additional dollar of current consumption of which he is deprived.

We exclude from consideration measures which would involve a net gift by the Treasury to the taxpayer, either in cash or in government obligations.

Clearly the best way of restricting consumption to a given level, from the taxpayer's standpoint, is the one which leaves him the most saving to go along with that consumption. Also, the taxpayer will be better satisfied with this solution the greater the future value of the saving. Consequently, he will prefer a temporary measure, which will not restrict or tax his future disposition of the saving, to a permanent measure.

By this standard, a temporary expenditures tax — which amounts to the same thing as an income tax with saving exempted — is superior to an income tax. If each is levied at the rate necessary to induce the taxpayer to restrict his consumption to a given amount, the expenditures tax will leave him with more saving. This follows from the fact that the expenditures tax can take advantage of whatever substitutability there is between present and future consumption, while the income tax must rely wholly on income effects. In Figure 6.1 saving is measured on the vertical axis, and consumption on the horizontal axis. I_1, I_2, I_3 are indifference curves embodying the assumptions stated above concerning consumer preferences. Curve X is the locus of points of tangency of indifference curves with line of slope -1. Y on each axis represents the consumer's income before either of the taxes under consideration. Point A shows the consumption and saving chosen by the

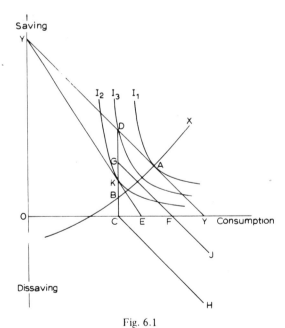

Fig. 6.1

consumer. C is the level of consumption to which he is to be restricted. An income tax would accomplish this restriction by moving him to point B, where a line parallel to $YDAY$ would be tangent to an indifference curve. An expenditures tax will be represented by a line which starts on the saving axis at Y and has a steeper slope than $YDAY$. The slope will be steeper the bigger the tax. (A progressive expenditures tax would be shown by a broken line convex upwards.) The expenditures tax which will induce the taxpayer to consume only C will be shown by a line tangent to some indifference curve at a point directly above C. Now the indifference curve through D has a slope at D steeper than -1, while the indifference curve through B has a slope at B equal to -1. The expenditures tax line through B has a slope steeper than -1, while the line through D has a slope equal to -1. Therefore there is a point K, between B and D, where an expenditures tax line YKE touches an indifference curve I_2. Thus an expenditures tax leaves the taxpayer better off than an equally effective income tax.

Neither of these measures, however, is as satisfactory to the taxpayer as a suitably designed compulsory savings levy. The major weakness of an ordinary compulsory savings plan is that the assets which consumers are forced to acquire are good substitutes for assets which they already own or would voluntarily acquire. Consequently, consumers damage their financial position very little by maintaining their consumption and reducing their voluntary saving or, if necessary, dissaving. This weakness can be avoided by a levy in return for which government obligations are issued only if the taxpayer's saving meets a specified standard. If the taxpayer cannot show the required amount of voluntary saving, the levy on him is simply an income tax.

A compulsory savings scheme with teeth can limit the taxpayer's consumption and give him the rest of his income in saving. This can be accomplished, for example, by levying a tax equal to CY in Figure 6.1 and by giving the taxpayer government bonds equal to the tax provided his dissaving during the year is zero. The line showing the alternatives open to the taxpayer is $YDCH$ and the best choice he can make is point D. Here he is better off than under an expenditures tax or income tax which holds him to the same consumption. On our assumptions, which imply some substitutability between present and future consumption, the same result can be achieved by a smaller levy (FY). In this case eligibility to receive government bonds would require positive saving equal to CF, the difference between income after the tax and the given consumption level. The alternatives open to the taxpayer lie along the line $YDGJ$. The tax must be large enough so that the line GF lies below I_3, the indifference curve through D, The important feature of compulsory savings schemes of this type is to give the taxpayer no intermediate choice; either he keeps his consumption down and commutes his tax payments into bond purchases or he fails to save the required amount and pays the tax in full without recompense.

In practice a compulsory savings levy of this kind would not supersede the existing income tax but would be added to it when an inflationary situation warranted. Complete conversion of the income tax into a compulsory savings scheme would change regressively the distribution of income after taxes and of wealth. It would also provide the public with an accumulation of assets which might prolong inflationary danger.

For the purposes of this plan the government would have to determine a schedule of the voluntary saving which taxpayers must perform in order to be eligible to receive government bonds in return for their tax payments. Together with the schedule of tax rates, this schedule would determine the levels of consumption to which the program would seek to hold taxpayers. The schedule should, therefore, be based not only on income but on number of dependents.

Administration and enforcement of a compulsory savings levy with teeth, or of an expenditures tax, or of rebates for saving would be complicated by the requirement that the taxpayer declare and be able to prove the amount of his saving. [10] The taxpayer would have to show such data as net purchases of sales of securities, changes in bank deposits, changes in indebtedness, changes in cash value of insurance policies. For the anti-inflationary purposes of these schemes, "saving" would have to exclude purchases of houses and other durable goods. Care would be required to prevent taxpayers from claiming capital gains, realized or unrealized, as saving. Administration of any of these plans would be difficult both for the tax collector and the taxpayer, but the information demanded and the problem of checking its accuracy are not basically different from the requirements of existing tax legislation.

Notes

[1] S. Slichter, "The Problem of Inflation," *Review of Economic Statistics*, 30, No. 1 (Feb. 1948), 5, and "Tax Formula: for Savers, Lower Levies," *The New York Times Magazine*, January 25, 1948. The argument that the income tax should not apply to saved income has a long history, which, together with a vigorous espousal of the thesis, may be found in Irving Fisher and H.W. Fisher, *Constructive Income Taxation* (New York, 1942).

[2] D. McC. Wright, "Inflation and Equality," *American Economic Review*, 38, No. 5 (Dec. 1948), 895.

[3] Cf. Slichter, "Tax Formula," *loc. cit.*

[4] *Ibid.*

[5] Professor Slichter suggests one-third.

[6] For a taxpayer with positive saving, the relationship between an income tax with saving exempted and a spending tax is as follows: Let Y be the taxpayer's income before taxes, C his consumption expenditure, S his saving, and R his tax liability. $C + S + R = Y$. Under conventional income taxation, R is a function of Y, $R(Y)$. Under the Slichter proposal, $R = R(Y - bS)$ where b is the fraction of saving permitted to be exempted from taxation. This implies $R = R(Y - bY + bC + bR)$. That is, R depends implicitly on income Y and consumption C. If $b = 1$ — all saving is freed from taxation — R depends only on C and the income tax is converted completely into an expenditures tax. The function $R(Y)$ is, under a progressive rate structure, a connected series of line segments of increasing slope. For taxable income in a range $Y_{n-1} < Y < Y_n$, the marginal tax rate $R'(Y)$ is a constant, r_n. Suppose that $R'(Y - bY + bC + bR) = r_n$. Then the marginal tax rate with respect to income is $(r_n - r_n b)/(1 - r_n b)$. The marginal tax rate with respect to consumption is $r_n b/(1 - r_n b)$.

The two plans differ in their treatment of dissaving. Under the Slichter proposal, dissavers would not be penalized; whatever their consumption, their tax would depend only on their income. Under a spending tax, dissavers, like everybody else, would pay taxes based on their consumption, regardless of their income.

[7] W.A. Wallis, "How to Ration Consumers' Goods and Control Their Prices," *American Economic Review*, 32, No. 3, Pt. 1 (Sept. 1942), 501-12. Milton Friedman, "The Spendings Tax as a Wartime Fiscal Measure," *American Economic Review*, 33, No. 1, Pt. 1 (Mar. 1943), 50-62.

[8] Before the Treasury-Federal Reserve Accord of 1951 the Federal Reserve was committed to purchase at par all government obligations offered to it. See Chapter 22.

[9] "Tax Formula," *loc. cit.*

[10] This subject can only be mentioned here. For an optimistic view of the administrative feasibility of such a requirement, see K.E. Poole, "Problems of Administration and Equity under a Spending Tax," *American Economic Review*, 33, No. 1, Pt. 1 (Mar. 1943), 63-73. For the opposite view, see H.H. Villard, "Monetary Theory," *A Survey of Contemporary Economics*, vol. 1 (Philadelphia: Irwin, 1948), 343.

CHAPTER 7

TOWARD A GENERAL KALDORIAN THEORY
OF DISTRIBUTION: A NOTE

If Mr. Kaldor is going to transform the Keynesian theory of employment into a Keynesian theory of distribution, [1] should he not aspire to a *General Theory of Distribution*? For all the flaws that Mr. Kaldor detects in it, neo-classical distribution theory is general; it will divide up the national product among 3 or 101 factors as well as or as badly as between 2. Mr. Kaldor's substitute should not do less. In limiting his contesting factors to Capital and Labor, he has been unduly modest. The purpose of the present note is to sketch the manner of generalization.

First, a brief review of Mr. Kaldor's two factor theory: Full employment national output is divided into two fractions, Investment y_1 and Consumption y_2 ($y_1 + y_2 = 1$), in proportions that are independent of the distribution of output between capitalists' share, s_1, and labor's share, s_2 ($s_1 + s_2 = 1$). Capitalists divide their income as follows: a fraction b_{11} for investment, a fraction b_{12} ($= 1 - b_{11}$) for consumption. For laborers the corresponding fractions are b_{21} and b_{22}. The following two equations can be solved for the shares s_1 and s_2:

	Capital	Labor	
Investment	$b_{11}s_1$	$+ b_{21}s_2$	$= y_1$
Consumption	$b_{12}s_1$	$+ b_{22}s_2$	$= y_2$

$$\text{The solution is: } s_1 = \frac{y_1 - b_{21}}{b_{11} - b_{21}} \qquad s_2 = \frac{b_{11} - y_1}{b_{11} - b_{21}}$$

Assuming, as Mr. Kaldor does, that in a state of nature $b_{11} > y_1 > b_{21}$, the solution gives positive shares for both factors. [2] If the economists for trade

Reprinted from *Review of Economic Studies*, Vol. 27, No. 73 (February 1960), 119-20.

union federations and capitalists' clubs are on the ball, the state of nature may not last. Assuming that the capitalists are asleep, Labor can raise its share by hoisting b_{21}, Labor's average and marginal propensity to save, towards y_1, difficult as it may be for union leaders hardened to bargaining tables and picket lines to shift their energies to thrift campaigns among their own members. But if the unions slumber while the capitalists are roused by the financial press, Capital will reduce its propensity to save b_{11}; investment in yachts and caviar will yield handsome returns.

Alas, if both sides take the theory seriously, their maneouvres will destroy it. There will be no longer any protection against singular matrices and other embarrassments, and the whole theory of distribution will have to be surrendered to the game theorists.

Meanwhile, however, let us proceed to the n-factor theory. Final output must be divided into n categories: e.g., Aspirin, Binoculars, Cadillacs, Dress suits, Electronic calculators, Football pools, Goose livers, Harrows, . . . Newspapers. Likewise, the population must be split into n mutually exclusive classes. Call them "factors" if you like, but the distinctive advantage of the theory is that the groups need have nothing at all to do with supplying productive services. Let the classes be, for example, Actors, Birdwatchers, Conservative peers, Dons, Executives, Farmers, Gourmets not elsewhere classified, Hoopers, . . . Nuclear physicists. Class i has income share s_i and divides it in proportions $b_{i1}, b_{i2}, . . . b_{in}$ ($\Sigma_{yj} = \Sigma_{si} = 1$). Kindly suppress any neoclassical atavisms that suggest that the output of Cadillacs might depend on Executives' share, the output of Goose livers on the income of Gourmets n.e.c., the production of Harrows on Farmers' fortunes, and so on. The assumption that they don't is just an extension of the two-factor assumption that the division of output between Investment and Consumption is independent of Profits and Wages. The equations that determine the shares s_i are as follows:

	Actors	Birdwatchers	Conserv. peers	....	Nuclear physicists
Aspirin	$b_{11}s_1$	$+ b_{21}s_2$	$+ b_{31}s_3$	$+ .... +$	$b_{n1}s_n = y_1$
Binoculars	$b_{12}s_1$	$+ b_{22}s_2$	$+ b_{32}s_3$	$+ .... +$	$b_{n2}s_n = y_2$
Cadillacs	$b_{13}s_1$	$+ b_{23}s_2$	$+ b_{33}s_3$	$+ .... +$	$n_{n3}s_n = y_3$
...	....				
...	....				
Newspapers	$b_{1n}s_1$	$+ b_{2n}s_2$	$+ b_{3n}s_n$	$+ .... +$	$b_{nn}s_n = y_n$

Now if the Dons will just hurry to make their marginal propensities conform to the fractions in which output is divided (the vector b_{41}, b_{42}, b_{43} . . . b_{4n} to equal y_1, y_2, y_3 . . . y_n), centuries of public neglect of education and educators will be avenged.

Notes

[1] N. Kaldor, "Alternative Theories of Distribution," *Review of Economic Studies*, 23 (1955-56), 94-100.

[2] In addition to imposing the restriction that both shares must be nonnegative, Mr. Kaldor warns us that there are narrower limits (classical or neoclassical?) set by means of subsistence for Labor and the minimum tolerable rate of profit for Capital.

ECONOMIC GROWTH

Five articles on the theory of economic growth are collected in Part II. The first three concern the interrelations of monetary phenomena and the growth process. Chapter 8, "A Dynamic Aggregative Model" was my first attempt at this problem, but it had some other objectives as well.

One was to provide a macroeconomic model of income determination differing from the usual Keynesian model in its treatment of capital stock and investment. I had long been troubled by the transiency of a Keynesian equilibrium which assumed a constant capital stock but yielded non-zero saving and investment. Moreover, I did not understand the logic of Keynes' investment function, which made the *rate of change* of the capital stock rather than the stock itself a function of the rate of interest. The Keynesian condition that the marginal efficiency of capital equal the rate of interest sounds more like a rule of stock or portfolio equilibrium than an investment rule. My model has no investment equation; the demand for capital is a demand for a stock, a matter of portfolio choice; and investment is simply the difference between output and consumption.

A second purpose of the article was to argue that capitalist economies are a good deal more robust with respect to capital deepening than the growth models popular at the time suggested. According to the models of Harrod, Domar, and Hicks, expansion at full employment was impossible if the saving-investment potential of the economy was so great that the stock of capital would grow faster than the effective supply of labor. Capital would become technologically redundant; its rate of return would collapse; investment would decline, taking income and employment with it. I sought to point out that this bleak picture could be considerably modified if a production function allowing variable proportions and a monetary sector were introduced.

In the nine years between Chapters 8 and 9, the neoclassical nonmonetary theory of growth was immensely clarified by Trevor Swan, Robert Solow, E.S. Phelps, and others. In the Fisher lecture, Chapter 9, I took advantage of these developments in returning to some of the themes of the earlier article and in trying to point out how monetary factors determine the capital intensity and interest rate of the system in long-run equilibrium.

The main argument of Chapter 9 is restated, with different diagrammatic apparatus, in the next essay. This paper, however, is also concerned with monetary welfare economics, specifically with the optimal quantities and rates of growth of government debt, means of payment, and financial intermediation. As the title of Chapter 10 indicates, much of it is more than usually tentative.

The welfare economics of growth policy is also the subject of my 1963 Ely lecture, Chapter 11. At that time economic growth, of which we had enjoyed very little for several years, was much more popular than it is today, after a decade of spectacular growth. Absence makes the heart grow fonder, and familiarity breeds contempt. Anyway, the essay was an attempt to sort out the reasons, good and bad, for the government to have a policy of promoting growth. I interpret growth policy to be simply a collective concern for future generations, on the ground that the free market by itself may shortchange them. I find it difficult to see why growth, so interpreted, should be anathema to contemporary conservationists and ecologists. They, too, are afraid that future generations will be shortchanged. The question then becomes what is the best way to provide for future generations — reproducible capital goods? unexploited mineral resources? education? scientific and technological research? Unfortunately I was not sufficiently foresighted to address this range of questions in 1963.

The last chapter of Part II is much more technical than the preceding one, although it is the least mathematical part of a long article written with three collaborators. The vintage fixed-proportion technology studied in this article is appealing in its simplicity and realism, and it is instructive to work out the standard lessons of growth and capital theory for an economy with this technology.

CHAPTER 8

A DYNAMIC AGGREGATIVE MODEL

Contemporary theoretical models of the business cycle and of economic growth typically possess two related characteristics: (1) they assume production functions that allow for no substitution between factors, and (2) the variables are all real magnitudes; monetary and price phenomena have no significance. Because of these characteristics, these models present a rigid and angular picture of the economic process: straight and narrow paths from which the slightest deviation spells disaster, abrupt and sharp reversals, intractable ceilings and floors. The models are highly suggestive, but their representation of the economy arouses the suspicion that they have left out some essential mechanisms of adjustment.

The purpose of this paper is to present a simple aggregative model that allows both for substitution possibilities and for monetary effects. The growth mechanism in the model is not radically different from the accelerator mechanism that plays the key role in other growth models. But it is unlike the accelerator mechanism in that there is not just one tenable rate of growth. As in accelator models, growth is limited by the availability of factors other than capital. But here these limitations do not operate so abruptly, and they can be tempered by monetary and price adjustments that the accelerator models ignore.

The cyclical behavior of the model is similar to the nonlinear cyclical processes of Kaldor, Goodwin, and Hicks. [1] But the cycle in the present

Reprinted from *Journal of Political Economy*, 63 (April 1955), 103-15. Figures and footnotes have been renumbered and section 6 has been rewritten. Copyright © 1955 by the University of Chicago Press.

I wish to acknowledge with gratitude helpful discussions of this subject with graduate students and colleagues at Yale University. In particular, Henry Bruton, Thomas F. Dernburg, William Fellner, Challis A. Hall, and Arthur Okun read the paper and made valuable comments. So did Robert M. Solow of M.I.T. But it is not their fault if I have failed to follow all their advice. The paper was written while I was holding a Social Science Research Council Faculty Fellowship.

model depends in an essential way on the inflexibility of prices, money wages, or the supply of monetary assets.

Furthermore, the model to be described here does not restrict the economic process to two possibilities, steady growth or cycles. An alternative line of development is continuing underemployment -- "stagnation" during which positive investment increases the capital stock and possibly the level of real income. This outcome, like the cycle, depends on some kind of price or monetary inflexibility.

In section 1 the structure of the model will be described, and in section 2 some of its implications will be examined.

1.

The building blocks from which this model is constructed are four in number: (1) the saving function; (2) the production function; (3) asset preferences; and (4) labor supply conditions.

1.1. The Saving Function

At any moment of time net output is being produced at a rate Y, consumption is occurring at a rate C, and the capital stock, K, is growing at the rate $\dot{K}$, equal to $Y - C$. The saving function tells how output is divided between consumption and net investment:

$$\dot{K} = S(Y). \tag{1}$$

This relationship is assumed to hold instantaneously. That is, consumption is adjusted without lag to the simultaneous level of output; any output not consumed is an addition to the capital stock. Whether or not it is a welcome addition is another matter, which depends on the asset preferences of the community, discussed below.

Of the saving function, it is assumed that $S'(Y)$ is positive and that $S(Y)$ is zero for some positive Y. Otherwise the shape of the saving function is not crucial to the argument. Variables other than Y -- for example, W, total real wealth -- could be assumed to affect the propensity to save without involving more than inessential complications.

1.2. The Production Function

The rate of output, Y, depends jointly on the stock of capital in existence, K, and the rate of input of labor services, N:

$$Y = P(K, N) \tag{2}$$

The production function is assumed to be linear homogeneous. It follows that the marginal products are homogeneous functions of degree zero of the two factors; in other words, the marginal products depend only on the proportions in which the two inputs are being used. The real wage of labor, w, is equated by competition to the marginal product of labor; and the rent, r, per unit of time earned by ownership of any unit of capital is equated to the marginal product of capital:

$$w = P_N(K,N) , \tag{3}$$

$$r = P_K(K,N) . \tag{4}$$

If labor and capital expand over time in proportion, then output will expand in the same proportion, and both the real wage and the rent of capital will remain constant. If capital expands at a faster rate than labor, its rent must fall, and the real wage must rise.

A production function with constant returns to scale, both at any moment of time and over time, is a convenient beginning assumption. In judging the appropriateness of this kind of production function to the model, it should be remembered that, if it ignores technical improvement, on the one hand, it ignores limitations of other factors of production, "land," on the other. In the course of the argument the consequences of technological progress will be briefly discussed.

1.3. Asset Preferences

Only two stores of value, physical capital and currency, are available to owners of wealth in this economy. The own rate of return on capital is its rent, r, equal to its marginal product. Currency is wholly the issue of the state and bears an own rate of interest legally and permanently established. This rate will be assumed to be zero. The stock of currency, M, is exogenously determined and can be varied only by budget deficits or surpluses. The counterpart of this "currency" in the more complex asset structure of an actual economy is not money by the usual definition, which includes bank deposits corresponding to private debts. It is, for the United States, currency in circulation plus government debt plus the gold stock. [2]

If p is the price of goods in terms of currency, the community's total real wealth at any moment of time is

$$W = K + \frac{M}{p} . \tag{5}$$

Given K, M, and p, the community may be satisfied to split its wealth so that it holds as capital an amount equal to the available stock, K, and as currency an amount equal to the existing real supply, M/p. Such a situation will be referred to as "portfolio balance."

Portfolio balance is assumed to be the necessary and sufficient condition for price stability ($\dot{p} = 0$). If, instead, owners of wealth desire to hold more goods and less currency, they attempt to buy goods with currency. Prices are bid up ($\dot{p} > 0$). If they desire to shift in the other direction, they attempt to sell goods for currency ($\dot{p} < 0$). These price changes may, in turn, be associated with changes in output and employment; but that depends on other parts of the model, in particular on the conditions of labor supply.

What, then, determines whether an existing combination of K and M/p represents a situation of portfolio balance or imbalance? Portfolio balance is assumed in this model to be defined by the following functional relationship:

$$\frac{M}{p} = L(K, r, Y), \quad L_K \geqslant 0, \quad L_r < 0, \quad L_Y > 0. \tag{6}$$

Requirements for transactions balances of currency are assumed, as is customary, to depend on income; this is the reason for the appearance of Y in the function. Given their real wealth, W, owners of wealth will wish to hold a larger amount of capital, and a smaller amount of currency, the higher the rent on capital, r. Given the rent on capital, owners of wealth will desire to put some part of any increment of their wealth into capital and some part into currency. It is possible that there are levels of r (e.g., negative rates) so low that portfolio balance requires all wealth to be in the form of currency and that there is some level of r above which wealth owners would wish to hold no currency. But the main argument to follow in section 2 concerns ranges of r between those extremes.

The assumption about portfolio balance has now been stated, and the reader who is more interested in learning its consequences than its derivation can proceed to the next section. But since this is the one of the four building blocks of the model that introduces possibly unconventional and unfamiliar material into the structure, it requires some discussion and defense.

The theory of portfolio balance implicit in most conventional aggregative economic theories of investment implies that rates of return on all assets must be equal. Applied to the two assets of the mythical economy of this paper, this theory would go as follows: Owners of wealth have a firm, certain, and unanimous expectation of the rate of price change, $\dot{p}_e$. This may or may not be the same as the actual rate of price change $\dot{p}$ at the same moment of time.[3] The rate at which a unit of wealth is expected to grow if it is held in the form of currency is, therefore $-\dot{p}_e/p$. Similarly, owners of wealth have a firm and unanimous view of the rate at which wealth will grow if it is held as physical capital. This rate is r_e, the expected market rent, which may or may not be the same as r. Owners of wealth will choose that portfolio which makes their wealth grow at the fastest rate. If $-\dot{p}_e/p$ were to exceed r_e, they would desire to hold all currency and no capital; if r_e were greater than $-\dot{p}_e/p$, they would desire to hold all capital and no currency. Only if the two rates are equal will they be satisfied to hold positive amounts of both assets; and, indeed, in that case, they will not care what the mix of assets is in their portfolios. On this theory of asset preferences the relative supplies of the assets do not matter. Whatever the supplies, portfolio balance requires that the real expected rates of return on the assets be equal. In particular, if $r_e = r$ and $\dot{p}_e = 0$, equilibrium requires that $r = 0$.

Keynes departed from this theory in his liquidity preference explanation of the choice between cash balances and interest-bearing monetary assets. He was able to show that, given uncertainty or lack of unanimity in the expectations of wealth owners, the rate of interest that preserves portfolio balance between cash and "bonds" is not independent of the supplies of the two kinds of assets. But he did not apply the same reasoning to the much more important choice between physical goods or capital, on the one hand, and monetary assets, on the other. His theory of investment was orthodox in requiring equality between the marginal efficiency of capital and the rate of interest.

The assumptions behind the portfolio balance equation in the present model, equation (6), may be briefly stated. Each owner of wealth entertains as possibilities numerous values of both r_e and $\dot{p}_e/p$, and to each possible pair of values he attaches a probability. The expected value of r_e, that is, the mean of its marginal probability distribution, is assumed to be r. The expected value of $-\dot{p}_e/p$ is assumed to be zero. In other and less precise words, the owner of wealth expects *on balance* neither the rent of capital nor the price level to change. But he is not sure. The dispersions of possible rents and price changes above and below their expected values constitute the risks of the two assets.

Owners of wealth, it is further assumed, dislike risk. Of two portfolios with the same expected value of rate of return, an investor will prefer the one with the lower dispersion of rate of return. [4] The principle of "not putting all your eggs in one basket" explains why a risk-avoiding investor may well hold a diversified portfolio even when the expected returns of all the assets in it are not identical. For the present purpose it explains why an owner of wealth will hold currency in excess of transactions requirements, even when its expected return is zero and the expected return on capital is positive. It also explains why, given the risks associated with the two assets, an investor may desire to have more of his wealth in capital the larger is r. The higher the prospective yield of a portfolio, the greater is the inducement to accept the additional risks of heavier concentration on the more remunerative asset. [5]

1.4. Labor Supply

The behavior of the model depends in a crucial way on assumptions regarding the relations of the supply of labor to the real wage, to the money wage, and to time. It will be convenient, therefore, to introduce alternative assumptions in the course of the argument of section 2.

2.

2.1. Stationary Equilibrium

The model would be of little interest if its position of stationary equilibrium were inevitably and rapidly attained, but, for the sake of completeness, this position will be described first. There are any number of combinations of labor and capital that can produce the zero-saving level of output. To each combination corresponds a marginal productivity of labor, to which the real wage must be equal; this marginal productivity is higher the more capital-intensive the combination. Suppose there is a unique relation between the supply of labor and the real wage. An equilibrium labor-capital combination is one that demands labor in an amount equal to the supply forthcoming at the real wage corresponding to that combination. The equilibrium absolute price level is then determined by the portfolio balance equation. Given the rent and amount of capital in the equilibrium combination and the supply of currency, portfolio balance must be obtained by a price level that provides the appropriate amount of real wealth in liquid form.

2.2. Balanced Growth

Proportional growth of capital, income, and employment implies, according to the assumed production function, constancy of capital rent, r, and the real wage, w. Maintenance of portfolio balance requires, therefore, an increase in M/p. Given the supply of currency, the price level must fall continuously over time. Balanced growth requires an expanding labor supply, available at the same real wage and at an ever decreasing money wage.

2.3. Growth with Capital Deepening

In this model, unlike those of Harrod, Hicks, and others, failure of the labor supply to grow at the rate necessary for balanced growth does not mean that growth at a slower rate is impossible. If the real wage must rise in order to induce additional labor supply, the rent of capital must, it is true, fall as capital grows. Portfolio balance requires, therefore, that a given increment of capital be accompanied by a greater price decline than in the case of balanced growth. But there is some rate of price decline that will preserve portfolio balance, even in the extreme case of completely inelastic labor supply. Although the rate of price decline per increment of capital is greater the less elastic the supply of labor with respect to the real wage and with respect to time, the time rate of price decline is not necessarily faster. The growth of income, saving, and capital is slower when labor is less elastic, and it takes longer to achieve the same increment of capital.

2.4. Technological Progress and Price Deflation

The preceding argument has assumed an unchanging production function with constant returns to scale. In comparison with that case, technological progress is deflationary to the extent that a more rapid growth of income augments transactions requirements for currency. But technological progress has offsetting inflationary effects to the extent that it raises the marginal productivity of capital corresponding to given inputs of capital and labor. Conceivably technical improvement can keep the rent on capital rising even though its amount relative to the supply of labor is increasing. This rise might even be sufficient to keep the demand for real currency balances from rising, in spite of the growth of the capital stock and of transactions requirements. At the other extreme, it is possible to imagine technological progress that fails to raise or even lowers the marginal productivity of capital corresponding to given inputs of the two factors. Progress of this kind contains nothing to counteract the deflationary pressures of a growing capital stock, declining capital rent, and increasing transactions needs.

2.5. Monetary Expansion as an Alternative to Price Deflation [6]

Price deflation is one way to expand the real supply of currency. Increase of the nominal supply is another. As noted above, monetary expansion cannot, in this model, be accomplished by monetary policy in the conventional sense but must be the result of deficit financing. [7] The simplest assumption, which will be followed here, is that the government deficit $\dot{M}$ takes the form of transfer payments.

The real value of transfer payments is $(\dot{M}/M)(M/p)$. The real gains (or losses) in monetary wealth due to price change are $(-\dot{p}/p)(M/p)$. Both represent accumulations of wealth, and both should be included in the disposable income to which the saving function applies. Thus equation (1) must be changed to read:

$$\dot{K} + \left(\frac{\dot{M}}{M} - \frac{\dot{p}}{p}\right)\frac{M}{p} = S\left(Y + \left(\frac{\dot{M}}{M} - \frac{\dot{p}}{p}\right)\frac{M}{p}\right). \tag{7}$$

With a marginal propensity to save less than one, monetary accumulation displaces capital accumulation. The greater the increment of monetary wealth, the smaller the part of a given real income Y which goes into investment $\dot{K}$ instead of consumption C.

When $\dot{M}/M$ is zero, we have seen that there is a deflationary price path that provides the growing real stock of currency necessary to balance the accumulation of capital. The same monetary growth can also be provided via $\dot{M}/M$ with prices stable, or by other combinations of $\dot{M}/M$ and $\dot{p}/p$.

However, monetary expansion and price deflation are not entirely symmetrical. Growth with continuous price deflation strains the assumption that wealth owners expect, on balance, the price level to remain constant. The process itself would teach them that the expected value of the real return on currency is positive, and it would perhaps also reduce estimates of the dispersion of possible returns on currency. The more attractive currency is as an asset, the larger will be its share in wealth and in new saving. Given the saving function, price deflation slows down capital accumulation more than the same monetary expansion accomplished via deficit finance.

2.6. Wage Inflexibility as an Obstacle to Growth

If the currency supply grows too slowly, the necessity that price deflation – possibly an ever faster price deflation – accompany growth casts considerable doubt on the viability of the growth processes described above. This doubt arises from the institutional limits on downward flexibility of prices, in particular money wage rates, characteristic of actual economies. The purpose of this and the two following sections is to analyze the behavior of the system when money wage rates are inflexible.

For this analysis it is convenient to work with two relationships between the price level, p, and employment of labor, N. Both relationships assume a constant capital stock, K. The first, called the "labor market balance" (*LMB*) relation, gives for any level of employment, N, the price level, p, that equates the marginal productivity of labor to the real wage. Given the money wage, this p is higher for larger values of N, because the marginal product of labor declines with employment with a given capital stock. This relation is shown in Figures 8.1 and 8.2 as curve *LMB*. The level of employment N_f is the maximum labor supply that can be induced at the given money wage. At that level of employment the money wage becomes flexible upward. If the money wage

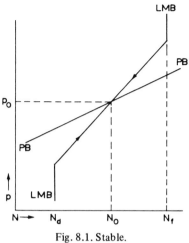

Fig. 8.1. Stable.

is raised or lowered, the *LMB* curve will shift up or down proportionately. If the capital stock is expanded, the *LMB* curve will shift downward, because an addition to capital will raise the marginal product of labor at any level of employment.

The second relation between the same two variables, p and N, is the

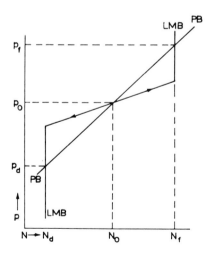

Fig. 8.2. Unstable.

"portfolio balance" relation *PB*, also shown in Figures 8.1 and 8.2. As the name indicates, it shows for any level of employment the price level required for portfolio balance between the given stock of capital K and the given supply of currency M. Its slope may be either positive or negative. The marginal productivity of the given stock of capital, and hence the rent of capital, is greater the higher the volume of employment. Currency is thus a relatively less attractive asset at higher levels of employment; so far as this effect is concerned, the price level must be higher at higher levels of employment in order to reduce the real supply of currency. The transactions relation of demand for currency to the level of real income works, however, in the opposite direction. Whatever its slope, the *PB* curve will, for obvious reasons, shift upward if currency supply M is expanded, and downward if capital expands.

It is not possible to establish a priori which curve, *LMB* or *PB*, has the greater slope. The two possibilities are shown in Figures 8.1 and 8.2. In Figure 8.1 the *LMB* curve has the greater slope; both curves are drawn with positive slopes, but the *PB* curve could equally well have a negative slope. In Figure 8.2 the *PB* curve has the greater slope. As indicated by the arrows, the intersection (p_0, N_0) is a stable short-run equilibrium in Figure 8.1 but an unstable one in Figure 8.2. This follows from the assumption that $\dot{p}$ will be positive, zero, or negative, depending on whether wealth owners regard their currency holdings as too large, just right, or too small. [8] In Figure 8.2 (p_f, N_f) is a stable short-run equilibrium. And there may be another stable intersection (p_d, N_d). Here N_d would be a level of employment so low and, correspondingly, a real wage so high that the rigidity of the money wage breaks down.

Capital expansion shifts both the *LMB* and the *PB* curve downward. How does capital expansion affect the point (p_0, N_0)? The following results are proved in the Appendix: When the intersection (p_0, N_0) is an unstable point (Figure 8.2) capital expansion increases both N_0 and p_0. The *PB* curve shifts more than the *LMB* curve, and their intersection moves northeast. The qualitative effect of capital expansion may be depicted graphically by imagining the *PB* curve to shift downward while the *LMB* curve stays put. The same argument shows that capital accumulation moves a point like (p_f, N_f) or (p_d, N_d) in Figure 8.2 downward, while capital decumulation moves it upward. When the intersection (p_0, N_0) is a stable point (Figure 8.1), the argument of the Appendix indicates that capital expansion necessarily lowers p_0 but may either increase or decrease N_0; the intersection may move either southeast or southwest. It is, in other words, not possible to say which curve shifts more as a consequence of a given change in the capital stock.

These results permit consideration of the question whether growth with full employment of labor is compatible with a floor on the money wage rate. Except in the case where labor supply grows as rapidly as capital or more rapidly, the growth' process brings about an increase of the real wage. A certain amount of price deflation is therefore compatible with rigidity of the money wage. But, according to the results reported in the previous paragraph, certainly in the unstable case and possibly in the stable case, too, the amount of price deflation needed to maintain portfolio balance is too much to enable employment to be maintained at a rigid money wage. Capital growth shifts the *PB* curve down more than the *LMB* curve. However, it is also possible in the stable case that the *LMB* curve shifts more than the *PB* curve, so that employment could be maintained and even increased while the money wage remains rigid and prices fall. But even this possibility depends on the assumption that wealth owners balance their portfolios on the expectation that the price level will remain the same. As noted above, it is only realistic to expect that a process of deflation would itself teach owners of wealth to expect price deflation rather than price stability. Such expectations would inevitably so enhance the relative attractiveness of currency as an asset that the process could not continue without a reduction of the money-wage rate.

2.7. Wage Inflexibility and Cyclical Fluctuations

It is the situation depicted in Figure 8.2 that gives rise to the possibility of a cycle formally similar to those of Kaldor, Goodwin, and Hicks. Suppose the economy is at point (p_f, N_f). Capital expansion will·sooner or later cause this point to coincide with (p_0, N_0) at a point like R in Figure 8.3. This day will be hastened by any inflation in the money-wage floor fostered by full employment; it may be that, once having enjoyed the money wage corresponding to (p_f, N_f) in Figure 8.2, labor will not accept any lower money wage. Once R is reached, any further capital expansion will require a price decline that will push the real wage of labor, given that the money wage cannot fall, above its marginal productivity. Employers will therefore contract employment. But this does not obviate the necessity of price deflation. Indeed, it aggravates it, because the reduction of employment lowers the marginal productivity of capital. Balance cannot be restored both in the labor market and in wealth holdings until a level of employment is reached at which the wage rate becomes flexible downward (N_d in Figure 8.3).

The permanence of this "floor" equilibrium depends upon the saving function. If positive saving occurs at the levels of income produced by labor supply N_d, capital expansion will continue; and so also will price and wage deflation. Increase of employment then depends on the willingness of labor

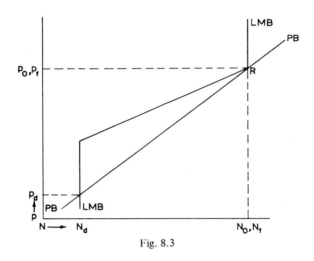

Fig. 8.3

to accept additional employment at the low level to which severe unemployment has driven the money wage. Willingness to accept additional employment at this money wage may be encouraged by the increase in the real wage due to continued capital accumulation. A sufficient lowering of the money-wage rate demanded for increased employment would result in a situation like that represented by point S in Figure 8.4, and full employment could be restored.

Alternatively, the "floor" may correspond to a level of income at which there is negative saving. The gradual attrition of the capital stock will then move the PB curve up relative to the LMB curve. As capital becomes scarcer, its marginal product rises; and for both reasons its attractiveness relative to that of currency increases. Whatever happens to the money wage terms on which labor will accept additional employment, the decumulation of capital will eventually lead to a position like S in Figure 8.4.

Once S is reached, any further reduction in the money wage, or any further decumulation of capital, will lead to an expansion of employment. But increasing employment only enhances the relative attractiveness of the existing stock of capital, causing the price level to rise and employment to be still further increased. As Figure 8.4 shows, the only stopping point is (p_f, N_f). Once N_f is reached, the money wage becomes flexible upward and follows the price level upward until portfolio balance is restored at the price level p_f. The cycle then repeats itself.

The floor in this model is provided by a level of employment so low, and a real wage correspondingly so high, that money-wage rates become flexible

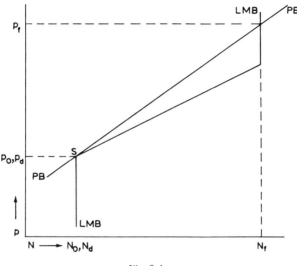

Fig. 8.4

downward. The breakdown of money-wage rigidity may be interpreted as a function of time; as Leontief has suggested, money-wage rigidity may not reflect any persistent "money illusion" on the part of workers and their organizations but only a lag in their perception of the price level to use in reckoning their real wage. [9] Trouble occurs at full employment, even when real wages are increasing, because the time rate of price deflation becomes too fast in relation to this lag. Likewise, contraction of employment can be stopped and even reversed when money wage demands have had time to catch up with what has been happening to the price level.

In this discussion of the floor it has been assumed that the rate of capital decumulation is controlled by the saving function. An interesting question arises when the saving function indicates dissaving at a rate higher than that at which the capital stock can physically decumulate. In the models of Goodwin and Hicks, in fact, the floor is the level of income at which dissaving equals the maximum possible rate of capital decumulation.

A physical limit on the rate of capital decumulation cannot really be handled within the framework of an aggregative model that takes account of only one industry, one commodity, and one price level. Such a model assumes that the output of the economy is essentially homogeneous and can equally well be consumed or accumulated in productive stocks, from which it can be withdrawn at will. If capital goods and consumers' goods are regarded as less than perfect substitutes, it is necessary to imagine that they have different price levels. Encountering a Goodwin-Hicks floor would then mean that the two price levels diverge. At any lower level of income the community would be unable to consume capital at the rate at which it wished to dissave. Consequently, the community would dissave from its holdings of currency. This would stop the fall in the price level of consumption goods and make the Goodwin-Hicks floor an equilibrium level of employment and income. The price of capital goods would continue to fall as owners of wealth attempted to convert capital into either currency or consumption. This fall in the value of capital goods would restore portfolio balance – even though consumers' goods prices ceased to fall and money-wage rates remained rigid -- by making capital a smaller proportion of the community's wealth.

With the model thus amended, the physical limit on capital decumulation provides a floor that will stop and eventually reverse a contraction even if the money-wage rate is intractable. But the contraction need not proceed to this extreme if the wage flexibility floor described above occurs at a higher level of employment and output.

2.8. *Wage Inflexibility and Stagnation*

The cycle just described arises from the situation depicted in Figure 8.2. But the situation of Figure 8.1, where the *LMB* curve has an algebraically greater slope than the *PB* curve and the intersection (p_0, N_0) is a stable equilibrium, also is a possibility. In this case the intersection may move to the left as the capital stock increases. Growth of capital is accompanied by reduction of employment, so long as the money-wage rate is maintained. This process may end in a stationary equilibrium position if it entails such a reduction in output (or, if wealth is relevant to the saving function, such an increase in wealth) as to reduce saving to zero. But it is also possible that a process with positive saving, growth of capital, and increasing unemployment will continue indefinitely.

2.9. *Summary*

The simple aggregative model that has been presented here differs from others used in discussions of growth and cycles in two main respects. The production function allows for substitution between capital and labor. The willingness of the community to hold physical capital depends on its rate of return and on the value of the liquid wealth held by the community. These two assumptions provide a link, generally absent in other models, between the world of real magnitudes and the world of money and prices. This link provides the model with some adjustment mechanisms ignored in other growth and cycle models. The following conclusions result:

1. Growth is possible at a great variety of rates and is not necessarily precluded when the labor supply grows slowly or remains constant.

2. The course of the price level as capital grows depends on (a) the accompanying rate of expansion of the labor force, (b) the rate at which the supply of currency is augmented by government deficits, and (c) the rate of technological progress. The first two factors are both inflationary. Technological progress has mixed effects. In the absence of monetary expansion and technological progress, price deflation is a necessary concomitant of growth even when the labor supply is increasing just as rapidly as capital. In these circumstances, therefore, growth with stable or increasing employment cannot continue if the money-range rate is inflexible downward.

3. Given wage inflexibility, the system may alternate between high and low levels of employment and, concurrently, between periods of price inflation and deflation. The ceiling to this cyclical process is provided by inelasticity of the labor supply. The floor may be provided either by the breakdown of the rigid money wage or by physical limits on the rate of consumption of capital. Alternatively, the system may "stagnate" at less than full employment, quite conceivably with capital growth and reduction of employment occurring at the same time. Whether the system behaves in this manner or with cyclical fluctuations depends on the relation between the conditions of portfolio balance and the rate of return on capital. The greater the shift in portfolios that owners of wealth wish to make when the rate of return on capital changes, the more likely it is that the system will have a cyclical solution.

Appendix

The equation of the labor-market-balance curve, for given K, is

$$pP_N(K, N) = w_0 , \tag{1}$$

where w_0 is the rigid money-wage rate. The slope of this curve is

$$\left(\frac{dp}{dN} \right)_{LMB} = \frac{-p^2 P_{NN}}{w_0} . \tag{2}$$

Since $P_{NN} < 0$, this slope is positive.

The equation of the portfolio balance curve, for given K and M, is

$$M = pL(K, r, Y) = pL(K, P_K[K, N], P[K, N]) . \tag{3}$$

The slope of this curve is

$$\left(\frac{dp}{dN}\right)_{PB} = \frac{-p^2}{M}(L_r P_{KN} + L_Y P_N) . \tag{4}$$

Since $L_r < 0$, $P_{KN} > 0$, and $L_Y > 0$, this slope may be either positive or negative.

The point (p_0, N_0) is determined by the intersection of (1) and (3). The problem is to find the changes in p_0 and N_0 associated with an increase in K. Differentiating (1) and (3) with respect to K gives

$$\frac{\partial p_0}{\partial K}\left(\frac{w_0}{p_0}\right) + \frac{\partial N_0}{\partial K}(p_0 P_{NN}) = -p_0 P_{NK} , \tag{5}$$

$$\frac{\partial p_0}{\partial K}\left(\frac{M}{p_0}\right) + \frac{\partial N_0}{\partial K}(p_0 L_r P_{KN} + p_0 L_Y P_N)$$

$$= -p_0 L_K - p_0 L_r P_{KK} - p_0 L_Y P_K . \tag{6}$$

Equations (5) and (6) give the following solutions:

$$\frac{\partial p_0}{\partial K} = -\frac{p^2}{D}(P_{NK}^2 L_r - P_{NN} P_{KK} L_r$$

$$- L_K P_{NN} + P_{NK} P_N L_Y - P_{NN} P_K L_Y) , \tag{7}$$

$$\frac{\partial N_0}{\partial K} = -\frac{1}{D}(w_0 L_K + w_0 L_r P_{KK} - M P_{NK} + w_0 L_Y P_K) , \tag{8}$$

where

$$D = w_0 L_r P_{KN} - M P_{NN} + w_0 L_Y P_N . \tag{9}$$

From (2), (4), and (9), it can be concluded that D will be positive, zero, or negative according as the slope of the LMB curve is greater than, equal to, or less than the slope of the PB curve. In the stable case (Figure 8.1), D is positive. In the unstable case (Figure 8.2), D is negative.

The production function is assumed to be homogeneous of degree one. Consequently,

$$P_N N + P_K K = P .$$

Differentiating this with respect to N and K gives

$$P_{NN} N + P_{KN} K = 0 , \tag{10}$$

$$P_{NK}N + P_{KK}K = 0 .$$ (11)

Using (10) and (11) in (7) gives

$$\frac{\partial p_0}{\partial K} = \frac{-p_0^2}{D} - (P_{NN}L_K + P_{NK}P_N L_Y - P_{NN}P_K L_Y) .$$ (12)

Since P_{NN} is negative, this derivative has the opposite sign of D. Consequently, in the stable case it is negative, and in the unstable case it is positive.

Using (9), (10), (11) in (8) gives

$$\frac{\partial N_0}{\partial K} = \frac{1}{D} \left(\frac{N}{K} D - w_0 L_K - w_0 L_Y \frac{Y}{K} \right) ,$$ (13)

where L_K and L_Y are positive. Consequently, if D is negative – the unstable case – $\partial N_0 / \partial K$ must be positive. But if D is positive – the stable case – the derivative may have either sign.

A point like (p_f, N_f) represents the intersection of the portfolio balance curve (3) with a vertical labor-market-balance curve. To find out whether employment can be maintained at N_f when K is increased, it is necessary only to find $\partial w_0 / \partial K$ for fixed N_f from (1) and (3). If this $\partial w_0 / \partial K$ is negative, then maintenance of employment is not consistent with maintenance of portfolio balance unless the money wage floor w_0 is lowered. If the derivative is zero or positive, then employment can be maintained or indeed increased even though the money-wage rate remains fixed or rises. Differentiating (1) and (3) with respect to K, for fixed N, gives:

$$\frac{\partial w_0}{\partial K} - \frac{\partial p_f}{\partial K} \left(\frac{w_0}{p_f} \right) = p_f P_{NK} ,$$ (14)

$$\frac{\partial p_f}{\partial K} \left(\frac{M}{p_f} \right) = -p_f L_K - p_f L_r P_{KK} - p_f L_Y P_K .$$ (15)

Therefore:

$$\frac{\partial w_0}{\partial K} = \frac{-w_0 L_K - w_0 L_r P_{KK} - w_0 L_Y P_K + M P_{NK}}{M/p_f} .$$ (16)

Comparing (8) and (16),

$$\left(\frac{\partial w_0}{\partial K} \right)_{N_{const.}} = \frac{D}{M/p_f} \left(\frac{\partial N_0}{\partial K} \right)_{w_{0_{const.}}}$$ (17)

From the conclusions previously reached with the aid of (13), it follows that, when D is negative (unstable case), $\partial w_0/\partial K$ is negative. But when D is positive (stable case), $\partial w_0/\partial K$ may have either sign.

Notes

[1] N. Kaldor, "A Model of the Trade Cycle," *Economic Journal,* 50 (March 1940), 78-92; R. Goodwin, "The Nonlinear Accelerator and the Persistence of Business Cycles," *Econometrica,* 19 (January 1951), 1-17, and "Econometrics in Business Cycle Analysis," in A.H. Hansen, *Business Cycles and National Income* (New York: W.W. Norton, 1951), chap. 22; J.R. Hicks, *A Contribution to the Theory of the Trade Cycle* (Oxford: Oxford University Press, 1950).

[2] This is the same concept developed in connection with discussions of the *Pigou effect*; see Herbert Stein, "Price Flexibility and Full Employment: Comment," *American Economic Review,* 39 (June 1949), 725-26, and Don Patinkin, "Price Flexibility and Full Employment: Reply," *American Economic Review,* 39 (June 1949), 726-28.

[3] An individual may be assumed to know the historical course of prices $p(t)$ up to the present (for $t \leqslant t_0$) and to expect a future course of prices $p_e(t)$ (for $\geqslant t_0$). Presumably the expected course starts at the same price at which the historical course ends ($p[t_0] = p_e[t_0]$). But there is no reason that one should start with the same slope with which the other ends: $p'(t_0)$, referred to in the text as $\dot{p}$, is not necessarily the same as $p_e'(t_0)$, referred to in the text as $\dot{p}_e$

[4] Risk aversion in this sense may be deduced from the assumption of generally declining marginal utility of income. Here, however, it is not necessary to go into the question of the usefulness of the concept of cardinal utility in explaining behavior under uncertainty.

[5] There is an "income effect" working in the opposite direction. The portfolio balance function, equation (6), assumes the substitution effect to be dominant.

[6] This section has been rewritten to eliminate errors and confusions in the original version. The subject is, I hope, clarified in Chapters 9 and 10.

[7] The implications of the approach of this paper concerning the effects of conventional monetary policy are left for discussion elsewhere. Clearly such a discussion requires the introduction of additional types of assets, including bank deposits and private debts.

[8] Employment has been assumed always to be at the point where the marginal product of labor equals the real wage. But the conclusions on the stability of (p_0, N_0) in Figures 8.1 and 8.2 would not be altered if it were assumed instead that $\dot{N}$ is positive, zero, or negative depending on whether the marginal product of labor exceeds, equals, or is less than the real wage.

[9] W. Leontief, "Postulates: Keynes' *General Theory* and the Classicists," in S.E. Harris (ed.), *The New Economics* (New York: A.A. Knopf, 1947), chap. 19.

CHAPTER 9

MONEY AND ECONOMIC GROWTH

Summary. In non-monetary neo-classical growth models, the equilibrium degree of capital intensity and correspondingly the equilibrium marginal productivity of capital and rate of interest are determined by "productivity and thrift," i.e., by technology and saving behavior. Keynesian difficulties, associated with divergence between warranted and natural rates of growth, arise when capital intensity is limited by the unwillingness of investors to acquire capital at unattractively low rates of return. But why should the community wish to save when rates of return are too unattractive too invest? This can be rationalized only if there are stores of value other than capital, with whose rates of return the marginal productivity of capital must compete. The paper considers monetary debt of the government as one alternative store of value and shows how enough saving may be channeled into this form to bring the warranted rate of growth of capital down to the natural rate. Equilibrium capital intensity and interest rates are then determined by portfolio behavior and monetary factors as well as by saving behavior and technology. In such an equilibrium, the real monetary debt grows at the natural rate also, either by deficit spending or by deflation.

1. The purpose of this paper is to discuss the role of monetary factors in determining the degree of capital intensity of an economy. The models I shall use in discussing this question are both aggregative and primitive. But I believe they serve to illuminate the basic points I wish to make. At any rate, I have taken the designation of this talk as a "lecture" as a license to emphasize exposition rather than novelty and sophistication. And my subject falls naturally and appropriately in the tradition of Irving Fisher of my own university.

Fisher and Keynes, among others, have drawn the useful and fruitful analytical distinction between choices affecting the disposition of income and choices affecting the disposition of wealth. The first set of choices determines

Reprinted from *Econometrica*, 33, No. 4 (October 1965), 671–84, with some revisions and corrections. This paper was presented as the Irving Fisher Lecture at the Joint European Conference of the Econometric Society and the Institute of Management Sciences in Zurich, on September 11, 1964.

how much is saved rather than consumed and how much wealth is accumulated. The second set determines in what forms savers hold their savings, old as well as new. Considerable economic discussion and controversy have concerned the respective roles of these two kinds of behavior, and their interactions, in determining the rate of interest.

2. Most models of economic growth are nonmonetary They offer no place for significant choices of the second kind – portfolio choices. They admit only one type of asset that can serve wealth owners as a store of value, namely reproducible capital. It is true that some of these models, particularly disaggregated variants, may allow savers and owners of wealth to choose between different kinds or vintages of capital. But this is the only scope for portfolio choice they are permitted. Different questions arise when monetary assets are available to compete with ownership of real goods. I shall proceed by reviewing how the intensity and yield of capital are determined in a typical aggregative nonmonetary model of economic growth, and then indicating how their determination is modified by introducing monetary assets into the model.

3. In a nonmonetary model of growth and capital accumulation, so long as saving continues it necessarily takes the form of real investment. And so long as saving and investment augment the capital stock faster than the effective supplies of other factors are growing, nothing prevents the yields on capital investment from being driven to zero or below. Of course, low or negative yields may cause people to reduce or discontinue their saving or even to consume capital. This classical reaction of saving to the interest rate may help to set an upper limit to capital deepening and a lower bound to the rate of return on capital. But clearly this kind of brake on investment causes no problems of underemployment and insufficiency of aggregate demand. Increased consumption automatically replaces investment.

4. I can illustrate in Figure 9.1 the manner in which saving behavior determines capital intensity and the rate of interest in a nonmonetary growth model. (For the basic construction of the diagram I am indebted to my Yale colleague, John Fei, but he is not responsible for my present use of it.)

In Figure 9.1 the horizontal axis measures capital intensity k, the quantity of capital (measured in physical units of output) per effective manhour of labor. The significance of the term "effective" is to allow for improvements in the quality of labor inputs due to "labor-augmenting" technological progress. Thus, if a 1964 manhour is equivalent as input in the production function to two manhours in the base period, say 1930, then k measures the amount of capital per man half-hour 1964 or per manhour 1930.

The vertical axis measures various annual rates. Curve AA' represents v, the average annual product of capital. Since output and capital are measured in

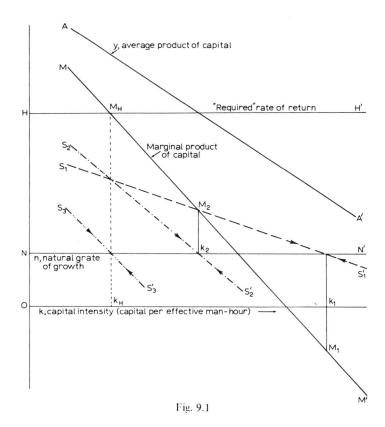

Fig. 9.1

the same physical units, this variable has the dimension, pure number per year. It is the reciprocal of the famous capital-output ratio. In accordance with usual assumptions about the production function, y is shown to decline as capital intensity k becomes deeper. Curve MM' represents the corresponding marginal product of capital. For present purposes it will be convenient to regard the average product y, shown by AA', and the corresponding marginal product of capital MM', as referring to output net of depreciation. If depreciation is a constant proportion δ of the capital stock, the average gross product of capital would simply be $y + \delta$, and the marginal gross product would likewise be uniformly higher than MM' by the constant δ. In Figure 9.1 MM' becomes zero or negative for sufficiently intense use of capital. There are, of course, some technologies — Cobb-Douglas, for example — in which the marginal gross product is always positive. But depreciation can nevertheless make the marginal net product negative.

Even after allowance for depreciation, the yield on durable capital relevant to an investment-saving decision is not always identical with the marginal product of capital at the time of the decision. The two will be identical if the marginal product is expected to remain constant over the lifetime of the new capital. But if it is expected to change because of future innovations or because of future capital deepening or capital "shallowing" in the economy, the relevant marginal efficiency of current new investment is a weighted average of future marginal products. I shall, however, ignore this distinction in what follows and use the marginal product in Figure 9.1 as at least an indicator of the true rate of return on capital. For the most part I shall be concerned with equilibrium situations where the two are stationary and therefore identical.

A curve like S_1S_1' reflects saving behavior. It tells the amount of net saving and investment per year, per unit of the existing capital stock. Therefore it tells how fast the capital stock is growing. In Harrod's terminology, this is the "warranted rate of growth" of the capital stock. The particular curve S_1S_1' is drawn so that its height is always the same proportion of the height of A_1A_1'. This represents the common assumption that net saving is proportional to net output.

The effective labor force, in manhours, is assumed to grow at a constant rate n, independent of the degree of capital intensity. The "natural rate of growth" n depends on the natural increase in the labor force and on the advance of labor-augmenting technology. This conventional growth model assumption is indicated in Figure 9.1 by the horizontal line NN'.

5. So much for the mechanics of Figure 9.1. Now what determines the development and ultimate equilibrium value, if any, of capital intensity? A rate of growth of capital equal to n will just keep capital intensity constant. If the "warranted" rate of growth of capital exceeds the "natural" rate of growth of labor n, then capital deepening will occur. If capital grows more slowly than labor, k will decline. These facts are indicated in the diagram by the arrows in curve S_1S_1'. With the saving behavior assumed in S_1S_1', the equilibrium capital intensity is k_1. The corresponding stationary marginal product is M_1. To emphasize the point suggested above, M_1 in the diagram is negative.

A different kind of saving behavior is depicted by S_2S_2'. Here the ratio of net investment to output declines with k. The reason would be that capital deepening lowers the yield on saving and therefore increases the propensity to consume. With saving behavior S_2S_2', the ultimate equilibrium has a capital intensity k_2 and a marginal product M_2.

6. The theory of interest sketched in section 5 is classical. The rate of return on capital, in long-run equilibrium, is the result of the interaction of

"productivity" and "thrift," or of technology and time preference. To dramatize the conflict of this theory and monetary theories of interest, I shall begin with an extreme case — so extreme that the crucial monetary factor is not even specified explicitly.

Some growth models assume a lower limit on the marginal product of capital of quite a different kind from the limit that thrift imposed in section 5. Harrod, for example, argues that investors will simply not undertake new investment unless they expect to receive a certain minimum rate of return. Savers, on the other hand, are not discouraged from trying to save when yields fall to or below this minimum. The result is an impasse which leads to Keynesian difficulties of deficient demand and unemployment. In Harrod's model these difficulties arise when the warranted rate of growth at the minimum required rate of profit exceeds the natural rate. The rate of saving from full employment output would cause capital to accumulate faster than the labor force is growing. Consequently, the marginal product of capital would fall and push the rate of return on investment below the required minimum.

In Figure 9.1, suppose HH to be the required minimum. Then, correspondingly, k_H is the maximum capital intensity investors will tolerate. Yet the saving behavior depicted in the diagram would, if it were actually realized, push marginal product toward M_1 and capital intensity toward k_1, given saving behavior $S_1 S_1'$ (or M_2 and k_2, given saving behavior $S_2 S_2'$). It is this excess of *ex ante S* over I which gives rise to the Keynesian difficulties.

The opposite problem would arise if there were a *maximum* return on investment *below* the equilibrium return (M_1 or M_2) to which saving behavior by itself would lead. At this maximum, the warranted rate of growth would fall short of the natural rate. So long as actual yields on investment exceeded the critical maximum, investment demand would be indefinitely large. In any event it would exceed saving.

The consequences of this impasse in Harrod's model are less clear than the events that follow the deflationary or Keynesian impasse. At this stage the two cases lose their symmetry. Though it is possible for output to fall short of the technologically feasible, when *ex ante* investment is less than *ex ante* saving, it is not possible for output to surpass its technological limits in the opposite case. Presumably an excess of *ex ante* investment is an "inflationary gap," and its main consequence is a price inflation which somehow — for example, through forced saving — eliminates the discrepancy. But this only makes the point that monetary assets had better be introduced explicitly. For it is scarcely possible to talk about inflation in a nonmonetary model where there is no price level to inflate.

7. I have spoken of Harrod's model, but I have the impression that the

concept of a required rate of profit plays a key role in other theories of growth, notably those of Mrs. Robinson and Mr. Kaldor. Indeed I understand one of the key characteristics of their models – one of the reasons their authors consider them "Keynesian" growth models in distinction to classical models of the type sketched in section 5 above – is that they separate the investment decision from saving behavior.

A minimal rate of return on capital (a required rate of profit) cannot exist in a vacuum, however. It must reflect the competition of other channels for the placement of saving. For a small open economy, a controlling competitive rate might be set by the yield available on investment abroad. This would, however, leave unexplained the existence of such a limit for a closed economy, whether a national economy or the world as a whole. In any case the growth models under discussion are closed economy models.

In a closed economy clearly the important alternative stores of value are monetary assets. It is their yields which set limits on the acceptable rates of return on real capital and on the acceptable degree of capital intensity. To understand these limits, both how they are determined and how they may be altered, it is necessary to introduce monetary assets into the model explicitly. It is necessary to examine the choices of savers and wealth owners between these assets and real capital. I continue, I remind you, to make the useful distinction between saving-consumption choices, on the one hand, and portfolio choices on the other. The choices I am about to discuss are portfolio choices; that is, they concern the forms of saving and wealth rather than their total amounts.

8. The simplest way to introduce monetary factors is to imagine that there is a single monetary asset with the following properties:

(a) It is supplied only by the central government. This means that it represents neither a commodity produced by the economy nor the debts of private individuals or institutions.

(b) It is the means of payment, the medium of exchange, of the economy. And it is a store of value by reason of its general acceptability in the discharge of public and private transactions.

(c) Its own-yield (i.e., the amount of the asset that is earned by holding a unit of the asset a given period of time) is arbitrarily fixed by the government. This may, of course, be zero but is not necessarily so.

Furthermore, it will be convenient for expository reasons to introduce money in two stages, avoiding in the first stage the complications of a variable value of money, a variable price level. Suppose, to begin with, that the value of money in terms of goods is fixed. The community's wealth now has two components: the real goods accumulated through past real investment and fiduciary or paper "goods" manufactured by the government from thin air.

Of course the nonhuman wealth of such a nation "really" consists only of its tangible capital. But, as viewed by the inhabitants of the nation individually, wealth exceeds the tangible capital stock by the size of what we might term the fiduciary issue. This is an illusion, but only one of the many fallacies of composition which are basic to any economy or any society. The illusion can be maintained unimpaired so long as the society does not actually try to convert all of its paper wealth into goods.

9. The simplest kind of two-asset portfolio behavior is the following: If the yields of the two assets differ, wealth owners will wish to place all of their wealth in the asset with the higher yield. If they are the same, wealth owners do not care in what proportions they divide their wealth between the two assets. Evidently, if there are positive supplies of both assets, they can be willingly held in portfolios only if the two yields are equal. On this assumption about portfolio behavior, it is easy to see how the institutionally determined rate of interest on money controls the yield of capital. In particular, it is this rate of interest which is the minimal rate of profit that leads to the deflationary impasse discussed in section 6 above.

At the same time, we can see two ways in which government policy can avoid this impasse. Returning to Figure 9.1, suppose that HH is the yield on money and therefore the minimal yield acceptable to owners of capital. The corresponding capital intensity is k_H. One measure the government could take is to reduce the yield on money, say to M_1. Such a reduction might – and in Figure 9.1 it does – entail a negative rate of interest on money, reminiscent of the "stamped money" proposals of Silvio Gesell. Manipulation of interest rates on monetary assets within more normal limits is, in more realistically complex models, accomplished by the usual instruments of central banking.

Alternatively, the government could channel part of the community's excessive thrift into increased holdings of money. Thus, let us now interpret $S_1 S_1'$ to measure the amount by which the public wishes to increase its total wealth relative to its existing holdings of capital. This leads to the Harrod impasse if all the saving must take the form of capital. But if only part of it goes into capital accumulation, if in particular the rate of increase of the capital stock can be lowered to $S_3 S_3'$, then all will be well. Equilibrium capital intensity will be k_H, consistent with maintaining the marginal product of capital at the required level HH. This can be done if the government provides new money to absorb the saving represented by the difference between $S_1 S_1'$ and $S_3 S_3'$.

The only way for the government to achieve this is continuously to run a deficit financed by issue of new money. The deficit must be of the proper size, as can be illustrated by Figure 9.2. Here saving is measured vertically,

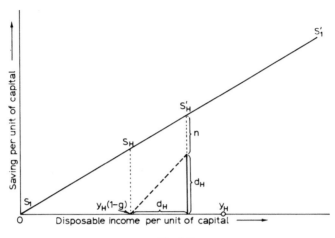

Fig. 9.2

and output and income horizontally. Both are measured in proportion to the capital stock, as in Figure 9.1. y_H is the output per unit of capital corresponding to the required equilibrium capital intensity k_H. Government purchases of goods and services are assumed to be a fraction g of output; Consequently, $y_H (1 - g)$ is output available for private use, and if the budget is balanced it is also the disposable income of the population. Taking $S_1 S_1'$ as the function relating saving to disposable income, S_H is the amount of private saving. (relative to the capital stock) when the budget is balanced. By assumption, however, this is too much investment — it causes the warranted rate to exceed the natural rate. Now n is the natural rate of growth; it is therefore the "right" amount of investment relative to the capital stock. A deficit of d_H (per unit of capital) will do the trick. It increases disposable income to $y_H (1 - g) + d_H$, and this raises total saving to S'_H. But of this, d_H is acquisition of government debt, leaving only n for new tangible investment.

The arithmetic is simple enough: Since

$$S = s[y(1-g)+d] = d + n , \tag{1}$$

$$\frac{d}{y} = \frac{s(1-g) - n/y}{1-s} \tag{2}$$

gives the required deficit as a fraction of income.

On these assumptions about portfolio choice, the size of the government debt, here identical to the stock of money, does not matter. The deficit must absorb .a certain proportion of income, as given in (2). But since wealth owners will hold money and capital in any proportions, provided their yields are in line, the size of the cumulated deficit is immaterial.

The opposite case would correspond to Harrod's inflationary impasse. Just as there is a deficit policy that will resolve the deflationary impasse, so there is a surplus policy that will remedy the opposite difficulty. In this case a balanced budget policy would leave the yield on capital so high that no one wants to hold money. To get the public to hold money it is necessary to increase capital intensity and lower the marginal product of capital. But a higher capital intensity takes more investment relative to output. To achieve a higher investment ratio, the resources that savers make available for capital formation must be supplemented by a government budget surplus. The mechanics of this can be seen by operating Figure 9.2 in reverse.

10. The portfolio behavior assumed in section 9 is too simple. A more realistic assumption is that the community will hold the two assets in proportions that depend on their respective yields. There is a whole range of rate differentials at which positive supplies of both assets will be willingly held. But the greater the supply of money relative to that of capital, the higher the yield of money must be relative to that on capital. I shall not review the explanations that have been offered for this kind of rate-sensitive portfolio diversification. One explanation runs in terms of risk-avoiding strategy where one or both yields are imperfectly predictable. Other explanations are associated with the specific functions of money as means of payment. Yield differentials must compensate for the costs of going back and forth between money and other assets. They must also offset the value of hedging against possible losses in case of unforeseen and exigent needs for cash.

The demand for money, presumably, depends also on income. Other things equal (i.e., asset yields and total wealth), more money will be required and less capital demanded the higher the level of output.

11. One implication of the assumption about portfolio behavior made in section 10 can be stated very simply. Capital deepening in production requires monetary deepening in portfolios. If saving is so great that capital intensity is increasing, the yield on capital will fall. Given the yield on money, the stock of money per unit of capital must rise. Provided the government can engineer such an increase, capital deepening can proceed. There is a limit to this process, however. As in the previous cases discussed, there is an equilibrium capital intensity. Monetary deepening cannot push capital intensity beyond this equilibrium because the deficit spending required would leave too little saving available for capital formation.

In such an equilibrium, the shares of money and capital in total wealth must be constant so that their yields can remain constant. To maintain the fixed relation between the stocks, money and capital must grow at the same rate. That is, new saving must be divided between them in the same ratio as old saving.

Let $m(k, r)$ be the required amount of money per unit of capital when the capital intensity is k and the yield of money is r. We know that m is an increasing function of r: more money is demanded when its yield is higher. At the moment, we are taking r as fixed. I take m to be also an increasing function of k because an increase in k lowers the yield of capital. It is true that an increase in k also lowers y and therefore reduces the strict transactions demand for means of payment. But I assume the yield effects of variations in capital intensity to be the more powerful.

Let w (for "warranted") be the rate of growth of the capital stock, and let d represent, as before, the deficit per unit of existing capital. Then, constancy of amount of money per unit of capital at $m(k, r)$ requires that $d = m(k, r)w$. Assuming as before that saving is a constant proportion of disposable income, the basic identity is essentially the same as (1) above:

$$S = s(y(1-g)+d) = d + w \ .$$

Using the fact that $d = m(k, r)w$, we have

$$w(k, r) = \frac{sy(k)(1-g)}{1 + (1-s)m(k, r)} \ . \tag{3}$$

In equilibrium $w = n$: the warranted and natural rates must be equal. The equilibrium degree of capital intensity is the value of k that equates $w(k, r)$ in (3) to n. I have written w and y in (3) as functions of k as a reminder that these variables, as well as m, depend directly or indirectly on capital intensity. Since y is a decreasing and m an increasing function of k, it is clear that w declines with k. Moreover, the amount by which w in (3) falls short of the hypothetical w for $m = 0$ ($sy(1-g)$) increases with k.

This analysis may be presented diagrammatically, following the format of Figure 9.1. In Figure 9.3, $S_1 S_1'$ reflects, as before, the balanced budget ($d = 0$) saving function, with saving a constant fraction of disposable income. This would be the warranted rate of growth of capital if m were zero. $W_1 W_1'$ represents for every capital intensity the warranted rate of growth of capital, assuming that the stock of money is adjusted to that capital intensity and maintained in that adjustment by deficit spending. The intersection of $W_1 W_1'$ with NN', the natural rate of growth, gives the equilibrium capital intensity k_1. As before, the equilibrium yield on capital is M', its marginal product at k_1. This yield, however, is not necessarily equal to the yield on money r.

The curve $W_1 W_1'$ is drawn for a particular yield on money r_1. Lowering the yield on money, say to r_2, would shift the curve to the right, to $W_2 W_2'$

increasing equilibrium capital intensity and lowering the equilibrium rate of return on capital.

12. I turn now to the more interesting and realistic case where value of money in terms of goods is variable. Its variability has two important consequences. The real value of the monetary component of wealth is not under the direct control of the government but also depends on the price level. And the real return on a unit of money – a favorite concept of Fisher – consists not only of its own-yield but also of the change in its real value.

Once again, we may ask whether there is an equilibrium capital intensity and, if so, how it is determined. The analysis of section 11 tells us that there is an equilibrium capital intensity associated with a stable price level. But this requires a particular fiscal policy that maintains through deficit spending of the right magnitude just the right balance between stocks of money and capital. Now what happens when fiscal policy is determined independently so that a stable price level cannot necessarily be maintained?

In particular, suppose that a balanced budget policy is followed and the nominal stock of money remains constant. Real capital gains due to deflation

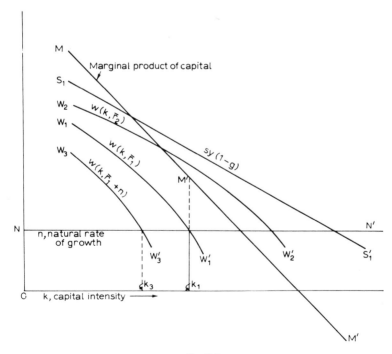

Fig. 9.3

play the same role as deficits did in section 11. That is, they augment real disposable income and they absorb part of the propensity to save. Therefore, we can use the same apparatus as before, illustrated in Figure 9.3, to find the equilibrium capital intensity.

There is, however, one important difference. In the equilibrium the real stock of money must be increasing as fast as the capital stock, namely at the natural rate n. In the present instance this can happen only if the price level falls at rate n. If so, the real return on money r is not simply the nominal yield r but $r + n$. Consequently the demand for money will be larger than if prices were expected to remain stable. Equilibrium will require a greater stock of money per unit of capital and a lower capital intensity if deflation is substituted for money creation. This is indicated in Figure 9.3 where $W_3 W_3'$ is the curve corresponding to a yield on money n points higher than the yield behind $W_1 W_1'$.

13. It is natural to ask whether there are symmetrical *equilibrium* situations in which a budget surplus or inflation is called for. The most obvious symmetrical case occurs when the natural rate of growth of the effective labor force is negative. But this is not a very interesting case of "growth."

The Harrod inflationary impasse, discussed above, would mean that at the hypothetical equilibrium capital intensity and rate of profit achievable when 100 per cent of saving goes into capital formation there is zero demand for money. Any money in existence, therefore, would have to be wiped out by surpluses or price increases; but these would be temporary rather than permanent.

One might, I suppose, imagine the public to desire a negative monetary position, i.e., to be net debtors to the government. Then there would be an equilibrium in which the public's net debt to the government grows in real value at the natural rate, thanks either to budget surpluses (with which the government acquires IOU's from its citizens) or to price inflation. In either case capital formation exceeds normal saving because the public saves extra either through taxes and the government budget or through the necessity to provide for the increased real burden of its debt to the government.

A negative monetary position is not as farfetched as it sounds, if "money" is interpreted in a broad sense to connote the whole range of actual fixed-money-value assets, not just means of payment. It is quite possible, then, for the government to be a net creditor over this entire category of assets, while still providing a circulating medium of exchange.

14. So far only the existence of an equilibrium path of the kind described in section 12 has been discussed. Its stability is something else again. I can only sketch the considerations involved.

What happens when the community is thrown out of portfolio balance either by some irregularity in technological progress, labor force growth, saving behavior, change in yield expectations, or portfolio preferences? If the result of the shock is that the public has too much capital and too little money for its tastes, goods prices will fall faster or rise more slowly than before. In the opposite case, the public will try to buy capital with money and will push prices up faster or retard their decline.

Evidently there are two effects, at war with each other. One we might call the Pigou effect, the other the Wicksell effect. The Pigou effect is stabilizing. Consider the case of a deflationary shock. The accelerated decline in prices, by augmenting the real value of existing money balances, helps to restore portfolio balance. Moreover, by increasing total real wealth it retards the flow of saving into capital formation. The Wicksell effect is destabilizing. An accelerated decline in prices means a more attractive yield on money and encourages a further shift in portfolio demand in the same direction as the original shock. The issue depends on the speed with which actual price movements are translated into expectations. If this process is sluggish – expectations are inelastic – then the stabilizing Pigou effect will win out. But if current experience has a heavy weight in formation of expectations, the system can be unstable. [1]

15. In classical theory, the interest rate and the capital intensity of the economy are determined by "productivity and thrift," that is, by the interaction of technology and saving propensities. This is true both in the short run, when capital is being accumulated at a rate different from the growth of the labor force, and in the long-run stationary or "moving stationary" equilibrium, when capital intensity is constant. Keynes gave reasons why in the short-run monetary factors and portfolio decisions modify, and in some circumstances dominate, the determination of the interest rate and the process of capital accumulation. I have tried to show here that a similar proposition is true for the long run. The equilibrium interest rate and degree of capital intensity are in general affected by monetary supplies and portfolio behavior, as well as by technology and thrift.

Note

[1] The last three sentences have been added to the original version, and the remainder of the stability discussion of section 14 deleted.

CHAPTER 10

NOTES ON OPTIMAL MONETARY GROWTH

The question of the optimal size and rate of growth of the money supply has at least as many meanings as there are definitions of *money*. Three possible interpretations of the question are: (1) What are the optimal size and the optimal rate of growth of the central government's deadweight debt to its citizens? (2) What are the optimal size and the optimal rate of growth of the supplies of currency and other means of payment? (3) What is the optimal degree of financial intermediation in an economy, and what is its optimal rate of expansion?

In some models one or two of these interpretations vanish, or merge. An important example is the simplest monetary extension of the standard aggregative neoclassical growth model. In this extension money as government debt and money as means of payment are identical. It is assumed, in other words, that all government debt takes the form of means of payment – either directly as currency or indirectly as demand deposits backed 100 per cent by currency or other government obligations – and that all means of payment are directly or indirectly obligations of the central government. Under these restrictive assumptions, interpretations (1) and (2) merge. At the same time these models ignore private financial markets and intermediaries, so that question (3) does not arise.

1. "Money" as Government Debt

I shall begin with the first interpretation of the question. The crucial property of "money" in this role is being a store of value, an alternative to repro-

Reprinted from *Journal of Political Economy*, 76 (July–August 1968), 833-59. Footnotes and figures have been renumbered. Copyright © 1968 by The University of Chicago Press. Paper presented at the 1967 Conference of University Professors, September 5–8.

The research described in this paper was carried out under a grant from the National Science Foundation. I have benefited from discussions with William Brainard, Harry Johnson, Alvin Marty, and E.S. Phelps. Roger Grawe helped with the diagrams.

ducible productive capital in satisfying the desires of the community to accumulate wealth. If the supply of government debt in real terms is increased, its acquisition may absorb private saving that would go into investment in productive capital. Thus the degree to which saving is absorbed in government debt helps to determine the equilibrium capital-labor ratio and the net marginal productivity of capital. The welfare question is whether this diversion of saving steers the economy toward or away from the optimal capital-labor ratio.

1.1. Properties of Neoclassical Growth Equilibrium

Let me review the well-known essential properties of a model capable of balanced growth paths of "moving stationary states" (for a good expository review, see Johnson, 1967, chap. 4). Output depends on two inputs, capital and labor, with constant returns to scale and diminishing positive marginal productivity of each factor; the production function remains constant over time except for technical progress that augments the effective labor input represented by a natural unit of labor; the "natural" rate of growth of the supply of effective labor is an exogenous constant, determined by population growth and technical progress. Under these conditions, there is a family of paths along which output, capital, and effective labor all grow steadily at the natural rate. Each path is characterized by its constant capital/output ratio and, related to that, its constant ratio of capital to effective labor. With a high capital/output path is associated a high efficiency wage and a low marginal productivity of capital. A path with low capital/labor and capital/output ratios will have a low wage and a high marginal productivity of capital.

Let g be the natural rate of growth, μ the capital/output ratio, and s the share of output that is invested in new capital. Along an equilibrium path the rate of growth of the capital stock, s/μ, must be equal to the natural rate, g. Therefore, a balanced growth path will be an equilibrium path if and only if it induces savers to hold capital in the technologically required ratio to output, μ, and accordingly to provide continuously the required addition to capital, namely a constant fraction of output equal to μg.

Figure 10.1 relates the capital/output ratio to the net marginal productivity of capital, R_K, for alternative balanced growth paths. Curve T represents the technological relationship between these variables implicit in the economy's production function. Paths with higher capital/output ratios will have lower marginal productivities of capital. A curve like S represents the amount of wealth savers desire, relative to national income, in a situation of balanced growth. As curve S illustrates, they may desire a higher wealth/income ratio along a path with a high real rate of interest than along one where the reward

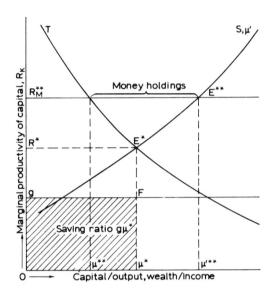

Fig. 10.1.

for saving is low. In an economy where the only store of value is capital, the wealth/income ratio must be the same as the capital/output ratio, and the rate of interest on saving is the net marginal productivity of capital. The equilibrium capital/output ratio is therefore μ^*; the corresponding amount of saving or investment relative to income is $g\mu^*$, graphically illustrated by the area of the rectangle $O\mu^*Fg$. A curve like S, and therefore an equilibrium like E^*, will exist if the properties of a balanced growth path suffice to determine a constant desired wealth/income ratio. This means that desired wealth and saving, relative to income, must not depend on the absolute level of population or of per capita income.

A special assumption about saving behavior, which has received the most attention in the literature, is that the saving ratio is a constant $\bar{s}$. This means, of course, that the wealth/income ratio desired along a balanced growth path is the same for every path, namely $\bar{\mu} = \bar{s}/g$. In other words, the S curve is vertical. Of the technologically possible paths, the one that has a capital/output ratio $\bar{\mu}$ is the equilibrium. This is illustrated in Figure 10.2.

Another conceivable special case is that consumer-savers have a fixed marginal rate of substitution of present for future consumption, will accumulate wealth indefinitely at a rate of interest greater than R^* or equal to that rate, and dissave indefinitely at any lower rate. If so, the S curve is horizontal, as

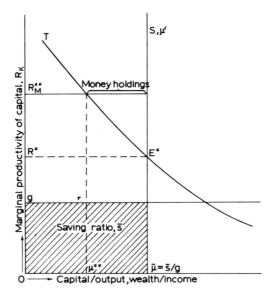

Fig. 10.2.

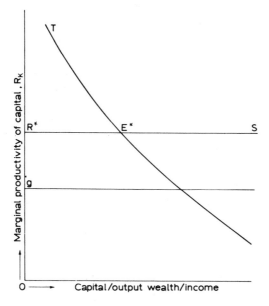

Fig. 10.3.

in Figure 10.3. The equilibrium capital/output ratio is the one that provides a marginal productivity of capital equal to this rate.

1.2. Growth with a Monetary Asset Perfectly Substitutable for Capital [1]

What happens when a second asset, a competing store of value, is introduced? Suppose that money — still in the sense of government debt — has a value $1/p$ in terms of goods; that the price level p is perfectly flexible; and that the government pays an own rate of interest, or nominal rate, of r on money.

One thing we know right away, of course, is that in a growth equilibrium the *real* quantity of government debt, like every other real magnitude, must be expanding at the natural rate of growth of the economy. That is, if M is the nominal quantity,

$$\frac{\dot{M}}{M} - \frac{\dot{p}}{p} = g .$$ (1)

We can also calculate the real rate of interest on money as

$$R_M = r - \frac{\dot{p}}{p} = r - \frac{\dot{M}}{M} + g .$$ (2)

Thus the question of the optimal value of $\dot{M}/M$ can be translated into the question of the optimal value of R_M, the real rate of return on money.

This question is easiest to answer in the most uninteresting case, that is, where it is assumed that money and capital are perfect substitutes in the portfolios of savers. This means that owners of wealth are indifferent about the proportions in which they hold the two assets so long as their real yields are equal (or differ by an exogenously determined constant) and otherwise will hold none of the lower-yielding asset. In this case, clearly, coexistence of the two assets requires:

$$R_K = R_M = r - \frac{\dot{M}}{M} + g .$$ (3)

Evidently the government can, by determining r and $\dot{M}/M$, determine R_K and, therefore, determine the equilibrium capital/labor ratio. In Figure 10.1, for example, by selecting R_M^{**}, the government steers the economy to a capital/output ratio μ^{**}. (An exception to this rule arises in the case exemplified by Figure 10.3. Here R_K is determined by the perfectly elastic supply of saving at the rate R^*. The government has no choice but to set R_M at the same level; otherwise there will be either no demand for capital or no demand for money.)

However, the capital/output ratio is no longer the same as the wealth/ income ratio. Wealth is now $K + (M/p)$. And "disposable" income exceeds output by the growth of the real stock of money, $g(M/p)$. Let $m = M/pK$, the ratio of money to capital holdings; this will be constant in equilibrium. Let μ' be the ratio of wealth to disposable income. Then

$$\mu' = \frac{K(1 + m)}{Y + gmK} = \frac{\mu(1 + m)}{1 + gm\mu}, \tag{4}$$

$$\mu = \frac{\mu'}{1 + m(1 - g\mu')}. \tag{5}$$

Here $g\mu'$ will be recognized as the ratio of total saving, including accumulation of money in real terms as well as of capital, to disposable income. Since this is smaller than one, the capital/output ratio μ is smaller than, equal to, or larger than μ' according as m is positive, zero, or negative. Now to interpret Figure 10.1 remember that in the case under consideration money and capital are perfect substitutes. Therefore, the curve S can still represent the desired wealth/income ratio μ'. When, for example, the real rate of interest, whether R_K or R_M, is set at R_M^{**} in Figure 10.1, the desired wealth/income ratio is given by curve S as μ'^{**}. This exceeds the capital/output ratio μ^{**}, and the two must be reconciled by a positive value of m necessary to satisfy equation (5). Since any value of m is acceptable to wealth owners, this situation is an equilibrium.

In Figure 10.1, R^* is the lowest real rate of interest compatible with positive quantities of money. Should the authorities establish a real rate lower than R^*, μ' would be less than μ and m would have to be negative. That is, the government would have to be a net creditor of the private economy, its net credit position rising at the natural rate of growth.

In the special case of Figure 10.2, the saving ratio is fixed at s. With the introduction of money, this ratio should now be applied to disposable income, so that the vertical S curve applies to $\mu' = s/g$. From equation (5) we have:

$$\mu = \frac{\bar{s}}{g} \cdot \frac{1}{1 + m(1 - \bar{s})}. \tag{6}$$

It is still true that, as in the case of Figure 10.1, m can adjust to any horizontal difference between the curves T and S that exists at the established real interest rate.

If the authorities can in effect set any real rate of interest they want, which should they set? First of all, they should not set one below g. A balanced growth path with a marginal productivity of capital below the growth rate is inefficient: All generations could have higher consumption by saving less and having a lower capital/output ratio. Conceivably the economy could, in the absence of money, be stuck on an inefficient equilibrium path of this kind. If so, the government could improve matters by issuing money with a real rate of interest equal to g, absorbing some of the excessive thrift of the population in this paper form and raising the marginal productivity of capital to g.

Note that a rate of g means that $\dot{M}/M = r$ and that $\dot{p}/p = r-g$. The debt increases solely by the government's incurring new debt to pay the interest. The considerations so far developed give us no criterion for choosing further a common value of $\dot{M}/M$ and r, for example, choosing between (a) $\dot{M}/M = = r = g$ and price stability, and (b) $\dot{M}/M = r = 0$ and price deflation at the natural rate g. In equilibrium the steady rate of price change is wholly anticipated, and one rate is as good as another.

If, in the absence of government debt, the equilibrium marginal productivity of capital would exceed g, it is not optimal to absorb any saving in government debt. In other words, if outside money is not competitive at a real rate g, the government should not try to make it competitive by offering a higher rate. The reasoning is as follows: a steadily growing economy with an indefinite life can always use claims against the government to trade present consumption for future consumption at the rate of interest g. In a moving stationary state, savers acquiring such claims can be assured of this return simply because the savers of the future will be more numerous and/or richer. By the time savers wish to cash in their paper assets, the market for them will have grown at the natural rate of increase g. But this is the maximum sustainable rate at which such trades can be made via government paper. If accumulation of physical capital offers a higher payoff in future consumption for current saving, then it dominates government paper as a vehicle for making such trades.

The question then arises whether the government should push the economy to the "golden rule" degree of capital intensity by augmenting the private saving of the economy with public saving from tax revenues. In equilibrium the government would lend at the interest rate g, which would also be the rate of increase of the private economy's debt to the government. There is a considerable literature discussing the sense, if any, in which the golden rule solution is optimal, and I will not review it here. The important conclusion of this discussion is that the situation is not symmetrical with the case in which government debt could rescue the economy from overcapitalization. If the society is originally endowed with a less-than-golden-rule capital stock, then the additional capital cannot be acquired without reducing the consumption and utility of consumers during the transition. These will be taxpayers who are, in effect, forced to save involuntarily in order to build up the government's stock of claims against the private economy.

1.3. Growth with a Monetary Asset Imperfectly Substitutable for Capital

The more interesting case is that in which capital and money are not perfect substitutes but can coexist in wealth/owners' portfolios even when they do not bear the same real rate of interest. The money/capital ratio is, by the same token, not a matter of indifference; it depends on the two rates R_K and R_M.

Let us provisionally suppose, although this assumption now has less logic, that the curves S still describe the relationship of the desired wealth/income ratio μ' to R_K and, what is more, do so independently of R_M. Given R_K and R_M, a portfolio-balancing value of m is determined. Equation (5) or (6) then shows how μ' and m together determine the value of μ, which satisfies both the saving and the asset preferences of the public. For positive m, μ will be smaller than μ'; for negative m, larger. Given R_M, increasing R_K will lower m and raise μ relative to μ'.

This is illustrated in Figures 10.4 and 10.5, where it is seen that the introduction of money, with a real rate that induces wealthowners to substitute

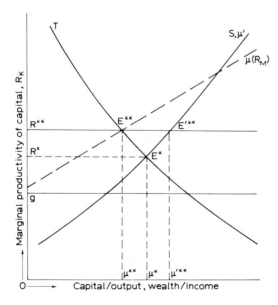

Fig. 10.4.

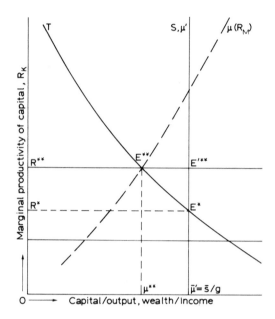

Fig. 10.5.

it for capital, lowers the equilibrium capital intensity and raises the equilibrium marginal productivity of capital. The curve $\mu(R_M)$ will be shifted upward by a rise in R_M. Thus the diversion of saving will be greater with a high R_M than with a low R_M. Once again, any substitution of money for capital – any positive m – will move the capital/output ratio in the wrong direction unless the marginal productivity would otherwise be below g.

If there were danger of an inefficient, "overcapitalized" equilibrium, then there is an optimal combination of r and $\dot{M}/M$ that will raise the marginal productivity of capital to the golden-rule rate g. This is illustrated in Figure 10.6. In this equilibrium the real rate on money will not necessarily be equal to $R_K = g$, but probably lower by an amount that reflects those imputed advantages of money that lead people to hold it even when its explicit rate is not competitive with the return on capital. Therefore, the optimal $\dot{M}/M$ is larger than the nominal interest rate r.

The general conclusion is that there is an optimal rate of growth of the supply of outside money, equal to or greater than the nominal interest rate r, only to the extent that diversion of saving into this vehicle is necessary to keep the marginal productivity of capital from falling below g. In the absence

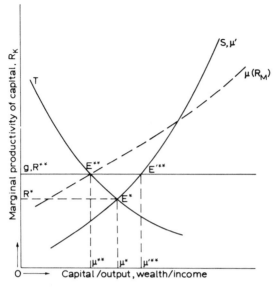

Fig. 10.6.

of such a tendency for oversaving, it is not optimal to absorb any saving in outside money or deadweight debt.

This does not mean that the government should not issue any liabilities for private savers to acquire. There may be good reason to do so, evidenced by the willingness of the public to hold such liabilities at a sacrifice of return. It does mean that the government should in turn invest the savings entrusted to it, either directly on its own account or indirectly by relending them to private investors, in capital bearing the prevailing real rate of return. The question which then arises, that is, how far such financial intermediation should be carried, will be discussed, though not answered, below.

1.4. Inflation and Unemployment

The preceding discussion has assumed that prices, and correspondingly money wages, are completely flexible, so that any rate of inflation or deflation can occur consistently with full employment of the exogenously given labor force. One implication is that the government cannot directly control the stock of outside money in real terms; whatever nominal stock is supplied will be instantaneously adjusted to the public's demand by movement of the price level. Thus the government controls the real supply, in the models so far discussed, only indirectly, by influencing the demand. As explained, the rate of change of the nominal supply helps to determine the size of the stock demanded.

A Phillips-curve model of wage and price determination has somewhat different implications. The rate of price inflation is an increasing function of the degree of utilization of the labor force. Steady growth at the natural rate can occur at any fixed degree of utilization; once this is chosen, a particular steady rate of inflation has also been chosen. Given the nominal rate r, the government's choice of $\dot{M}/M$ determines in equilibrium not only the rate of inflation $\dot{p}/p$ [equal to $(\dot{M}/M)-g$] but the degree of utilization associated with it. It also determines R_M [equal to $r-(\dot{p}/p)$] and, therefore, in the manner explained above, the equilibrium capital/output ratio.

Thus a deflationary policy – low $\dot{M}/M$ – not only diminishes the amount of capital per employed worker but also diminishes the number of workers employed. Even the use of a relatively deflationary policy to discourage over-investment in physical capital has an offsetting disadvantage in reducing utilization. But the possibility of manipulating r is another degree of freedom. An obvious way to have a rate of inflation compatible with high employment without having an excessively low real rate of return on money is to compensate for the inflation by a higher nominal interest rate.

The application of the Phillips-curve model to long-run growth equilibrium is questionable, but I will not enter that debate here. It is also questionable that the government's choice of a $\dot{M}/M$ policy can proceed as if all values of $\dot{p}/p$, negative and positive, were equally feasible.

2. "Money" as Means of Payment

The previous discussion has been concerned with the effects of the availability of monetary and financial assets on capital formation. In this context the important property of these assets is that they are stores of value with smaller yield uncertainties than physical capital. The optimal size and rate of growth of the supply of means of payment is quite another question. Means of payment can be supplied either as outside money or as inside money, without affecting in one way or another the optimal supply of saving for capital formation. What part of public or private debt should be monetized to provide a circulating medium is a narrower question.

2.1. Growth and the Demand for Means of Payment

In a balanced growth equilibrium, or golden age, of the type discussed above, our natural first presumption would be that the stock of means of payment, in real terms, must grow with every other real aggregate, at the pervasive growth rate of the economy. The nominal stock will then grow at this rate plus the rate of price inflation.

However, this initial presumption deserves closer examination. I shall consider it from the viewpoint of the inventory theory of the demand for cash, which focuses attention on the management of the temporary and fluctuating balances that people.hold to bridge gaps between their receipts and their outlays (Tobin, 1956, Chapter 14 below).

According to this theory, there are economies of scale in the management of these balances. These economies arise from the fact that at least a portion of the costs of transactions between cash and higher-yielding assets is independent of the size of the transactions and depends only on the number of transactions. Some individuals have temporary balances too small and short-lived to justify the costs of investing them; they simply hold the balances in cash. For others, the average amount of cash held depends inversely on the interest premium available and directly on the volume of receipts or outlays to the costs of making financial transactions. When the dollar volume of an individual's receipts and outlays increases, while his transaction costs remain unchanged, his average cash holdings rise less than in proportion.

It is an error of composition, however, to attribute to the theory the prediction that in a growing economy the demand for means of payment expands at a rate slower than total income and wealth. In the absence of technical progress, growth in neoclassical theory is simply an increase in the population of individuals, households, firms. But none of these units increases in average size – income, wealth, volume of receipts, and outlays. Nothing happens to transaction costs either; the opportunity costs of making transactions, measured either in human labor or in consumer goods, remain the same. Interest rates are constant. Consequently, the theoretical prediction is that the demand for means of payment increases like everything else at the natural rate of growth of the population and economy.

If there is labor-augmenting (Harrod-neutral) technical progress, the situation is more complicated. Now the scale of an economic unit – its income, wealth, and volume of transactions – increases at the rate of technical progress. What happens to transaction costs? If the making of transactions is purely a labor-using activity – either the labor of the transactor or of his agents – which does not benefit from labor-augmenting technical progress, then the costs are essentially wages. Wages rise at the rate of technical progress the same as the volume of transactions per economic unit. Once again, then, the conclusion is that the demand for means of payment rises at the natural growth rate – that is, the sum of the rates of population increase and technical progress. The nonlinearity of the inventory/theory approach does not carry over to the economy as a whole.

However, it might be more natural and more realistic to assume that the making of transactions benefits from labor-augmenting technical progress at the same rate as productive activity in the economy. In this event the scale of a typical transactor increases at the rate of technical progress, while transactions costs do not rise; the average cash holding of a transactor rises less than in proportion to the increase in the volume of his transactions. [2] Hence the aggregate demand for means of payment increases at a rate larger than n, the rate of population increase, but less than $n + \gamma$, the rate of growth of income and wealth — indeed, approximately at the rate $n + (\sqrt{1 + \gamma} - 1)$.

The conclusion that the velocity of means of payment should rise secularly in a growing economy would be even stronger if it were thought that technical progress in the making of transactions were faster than elsewhere in the economy. This is not farfetched. The innovations in business machines — calculating, automatic data processing, copying — are perhaps the most dramatic example of labor-augmenting technological progress. Among other things, these innovations have surely cut the costs of economizing cash balances. They have been accompanied by other cash-economizing innovations. Credit cards are a device by which small transactors are pooled into large units than can exploit the economies of scale in cash management.

It is possible that the growth of per capita income due to technical progress leads to a shift from work to leisure. If so, the supply of labor does not grow as fast as population. The natural rate of growth of the economy, both income and capital, is less than $n + \gamma$. Income and transactions volumes per unit grow less rapidly than the rate of technical progress, but the wage rate grows at the rate of technical progress. In this case it is possible that average cash holding requirements rise — provided little or no progress occurs in financial technology. [3]

On balance the inventory/theory model gives little support to the idea that the demand for means of payment should, at constant interest rates, rise secularly relative to national income. The model does not suggest that money behaves like a luxury durable consumer's good, generating services for which the income elasticity of demand exceeds one. This would work against the model if the empirical evidence advanced in support of the assertion that the long-run trend in velocity is downward were more convincing. But for the United States the "money" whose holdings have grown relative to income includes more than means of payment, specifically commercial bank time deposits. Before the first world war, these were the major monetary store of value available to savers. Since the second world war, the demand for time deposits has been increased by the dramatic rise in their yields relative to other vehicles of saving. There is no evidence that the services of means of payment per se are a luxury good.

2.2. The Optimal Supply of Means of Payment

The preceding discussion concerns the rate of growth in means of payment, in real terms, needed in a steadily growing economy. What is the optimal size of the growing stock of means of payment?

Scarcity of means of payment forces individuals, firms, and other economic units to economize their cash holdings. In order to gain the earnings possible from keeping their working balances heavily invested in assets which are not means of payment but yield higher real returns, they must make frequent transactions in and out of cash. These transactions have real costs, for example, the labor of the transactors themselves or their agents. Diversion of productive resources into the handling of in-and-out transactions is socially wasteful, because there is no cost to society in creating means of payment.

The way to avoid this waste is to supply a large enough stock of means of payment to absorb all working balances. This requires that means of payment bear a high enough real rate of return to remove the incentive to economize them. No resources should be devoted to the making of transactions to invest working balances temporarily in higher-yielding assets, either physical capital or public and private debt instruments. Since optimality will generally require positive real rates of interest on these alternative assets, means of payment will also have to bear a positive real rate.

If the nominal rate on means of payment is stuck at zero by law or by convention, the incentive to economize means of payment cannot be removed without persistent and anticipated deflation. When there are rigidities of money wages and prices that prevent such deflation and convert deflationary impulses into unemployment of labor and other resources, the social waste of economizing means of payment becomes one of the costs of avoiding the larger social wastes of underutilization. Deflation, of course, will also contribute to the real returns on other assets denominated in the monetary unit of account. Their nominal yields will have to be close enough to zero to prevent them from, on the one hand, diverting saving from capital formation and, on the other hand, diverting working balances away from means of payment.

A better way would be to allow means of payment to bear a nominal interest rate. Or, to put the same thing another way, interest-bearing assets defined in the monetary unit of account could be allowed to serve as means of payment. There seems no reason, for example, why checking should not be permitted .against savings accounts in commercial banks and thrift institutions, transforming these assets into interest-bearing means of payment. Freeing means of payment from the legal limitation of zero interest would make it theoretically possible to have an efficient growth equilibrium without deflation – efficient both in the sense that the real rate of interest is high enough to avoid overcapitalization and in the sense that real resources are not diverted into economizing means of payment.

3. Uncertainty, Saving, and Liquidity

I return now to the question dodged earlier by the assumption that the desired wealth/income ratio is independent of the menu of assets available to savers and the structure of their rates of return. The comparisons that this assumption tempts one to make between economies with and without outside money, illustrated in Figures 10.1 and 10.2, are likely to be misleading. [4] When money or other financial assets and real capital bear different real rates of return, clearly they are not perfect substitutes. If financial assets are not perfect substitutes for real capital in the portfolios of wealth owners, it is unlikely that they replace them dollar for dollar in saving decisions. The old Keynesian dichotomy – analyze separately decisions about total wealth and decisions about its composition – is useful for many purposes. I have generally found it convenient myself. But for our present problem it is not really appropriate, because the central question is precisely the bearing of alternative financial policies and institutional arrangements on the supply of saving available for capital formation.

Unfortunately, I have not found this to be a simple problem, and at the moment I cannot do more than indicate some directions for future analysis.

One of the principal reasons that savers hold financial assets with expected yields smaller than those on real capital is to diminish uncertainty about the amounts of their future consumption. We must begin, therefore, by considering the bearing of uncertainty on saving decisions – first without and then with financial assets available in addition to real assets.

3.1. General Remarks on Uncertainties and Saving Decisions
There are two ways in which uncertainty and risk aversion affect the quantity of saving for the future. One kind of uncertainty, *yield uncertainty*, relates to the return on saving, positive or negative – the individual does not know how much future consumption a dollar saved today will actually provide. The other kind of uncertainty, *need uncertainty*, relates to the size of the consumer's future needs and the degree to which resources other than

saving will be available for meeting them — he does not know what his wage income will be or whether he will confront extraordinary consumption needs, for example, for medical reasons.

As far as yield uncertainty is concerned, aversion to risk may either deter saving or increase it. It deters it by diminishing the attractiveness of the reward for saving — a kind of substitution effect. Some risk-averse consumers may save nothing for the future, even though they would save if the expected return on saving were sure. Uncertain of the return on saving, they prefer the certain utility of present consumption. On the other hand, yield uncertainty combined with risk aversion may increase saving via a calculation that, since the payoff may not be large, it is best to save enough to make sure of adequate future consumption, a kind of income effect.

Given this familiar ambiguity, it is not surprising that availability of less risky lower-yielding assets may work in either direction. Some savers, in particular those who previously saved nothing, will respond to the possibility of accumulating less risky portfolios by saving more. Conceivably they will even acquire more risky assets than when the opportunity to mix them with safer assets was not available. On the other hand, the possibility of saving in forms that give greater assurance of future return may diminish the need for saving felt by consumers dominated by the income effect.

Need uncertainty is the source of what might be termed precautionary saving — saving more than is actually required to meet future contingencies. Because of declining marginal utility of consumption, need uncertainty leads risk-averse savers to impute a higher value to a dollar provision for the future, relative to a dollar of current consumption, than they would if they anticipated with certainty the same average level of future consumption. Nevertheless, the uncertainties surrounding yield on risky assets may be so great that saving in this form will not improve the individual's position. The availability of safe assets will then increase precautionary saving. However, from an economywide standpoint, such saving may be excessive, providing *ex post* too generously for future consumption at the expense of current consumption. Insurance against unemployment, accident, illness, and longevity may be better social devices for accommodating individuals' reluctance to carry these risks.

3.2. *Yield Uncertainty and Saving: A Two-Period Example*

To reduce the problem to its most elementary terms, let us consider that old friend of the classroom and textbook, the consumer with a two-period life and horizon. Let his lifetime utility be the sum of two utilities, one depending on real consumption in period one, the other on real consumption in period two. That is, $U = u(c_1) + v(c_2)$. As is well known, this assumption of independence already gives us cardinal utility. When deciding how much to save in period one for use in period two, the individual knows for sure the consequences of his decision for c_1, but he does not know for sure what c_2 will result. He is assumed to maximize expected utility: $E(U) = u(c_1) + E[v(c_2)]$. Further simplifying the problem, I assume that the expected value of second-period utility is a function of two parameters of the probability distribution of second-period consumption, the mean $\bar{c}_2$ and the standard deviation σ_{c_2}. Thus

$$E(U) = u(c_1) + \varphi(\bar{c}_2, \sigma_{c_2}).$$

A simple and pure case of yield uncertainty is constructed by endowing the consumer with known incomes y_1 and y_2 in the two periods, with the possibility of saving in a single asset with uncertain prospects. Let x be the value in consumption of·period two of a unit saved from consumption of period one, $\bar{x}$ its expected value, σ_x its standard deviation. If $y_1 - c_1$ is saved, then $\bar{c}_2 = y_2 + (y_1 - c_1)\bar{x}$ and $\sigma_{c_2} = (y_1 - c_1)\sigma_x$. The expected value of period-two utility is then $\varphi(\bar{c}_2, \sigma_{c_2})$, and we define a certainty-equivalent level of second-period consumption as c_2^* such that $\varphi(c_2^*, 0)$ – the same as $v(c_2^*)$ – is equal to $\varphi(\bar{c}_2, \sigma_{c_2})$.

In Figure 10.7 the effect of yield uncertainty on the saving decision is illustrated. In the left panel, c_1 is measured right to left on the horizontal axis. and $\bar{c}_2$ and c_2^* are measured vertically. Indifference curves in the left quadrant, like U_A and U_B, represent constant levels of utility for consumption combinations actually achieved: $U = u(c_1) + v(c_2^*)$. For convenience y_2 is taken to be zero. The frontier of possible combinations of c_1 and $\bar{c}_2$ is the line from y_1 to $y_1\bar{x}$. If x were known in advance with certainty, or if the individual were risk-neutral, he would equate $\bar{c}_2$ and c_2^* and divide his income y_1 between current consumption and saving in the manner indicated by point A on the frontier.

Suppose, however, that x is not known with certainty and that our consumer is risk-averse. On the right hand panel σ_{c_2} is measured horizontally. The line from the origin OZ shows for each value of expected consumption $\bar{c}_2$ on the vertical axis the corresponding dispersion σ_{c_2} of future consumption. The indifference curves in the right quadrant represent constant values of $\varphi(\bar{c}_2, \sigma_{c_2})$. Their upward slope indicates risk aversion. Their intercepts with the vertical axis, where $\sigma_{c_2} = 0$, are their certainty equivalents c_2^*. Thus it is possible to convert any expected consumption $\bar{c}_2$ into its certainty equivalent c_2^* by following back to the axis the indifference curve that cuts OZ at the level $\bar{c}_2$. Consider, for example, the future consumption made possible by saving y_1 in full. Expected future consumption is $y_1\bar{x}$; risk is $y_1\sigma_x$; the indif-

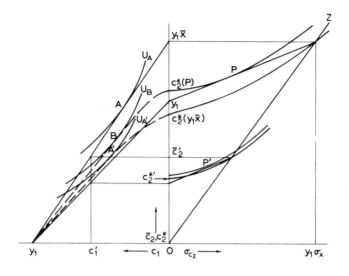

Fig. 10.7.

ference curve through this point hits the axis at $c_2^*(y_1\bar{x})$. Similarly, an amount of current consumption c_1' leads to expected future consumption $\bar{c}_2'$ with a certainty equivalent $c_2^{*'}$. Joining all the points like $(c_1', c_2^{*'})$ results in a pseudo-opportunity locus. The individual determines his consumption and saving so as to arrive at A' on this locus rather than at A. In the diagram this is shown to involve less saving, although this result is not inevitable. [5]

It is conceivable that indifference curves in the right panel cut the line OZ from below, not from above. In this case, c_2^* diminishes as additional saving increases $\bar{c}_2$, and the effective pseudo-opportunity locus vanishes almost to the point y. This situation is illustrated in Figure 10.8. With such pronounced risk aversion, yield uncertainty is a great obstacle to saving and capital formation.

Now suppose that a riskless asset is provided by which a dollar of current consumption c_1 can be turned into a dollar of future consumption with perfect safety. This possibility is depicted in Figures 10.7 and 10.8 by the 45-degree line from y_1 on the c_1 axis to y_1 on the c_2 axis. Since $\bar{x}$ is assumed greater than 1, the 45-degree line lies inside the original frontier. Now, a given amount of saving can result in a variety of combinations $(\bar{c}_2, \sigma_{c_2})$ depending on how the saving is split between the two assets. For example, saving all of y_1 can provide expected consumption c_2 of y_1 with no risk, or as before $\bar{c}_2 = y_1\bar{x}$ with risk of $y_1\sigma_x$, or any linear combination of these as indicated by

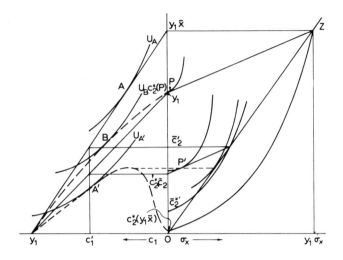

Fig. 10.8.

the line connecting the two points. The actual combination that would be chosen for highest expected utility is indicated by point P, and this has a certainty equivalent $c_2^*(P)$. Note that this certainty equivalent is higher than the equivalent of the same amount of saving in the absence of the safe asset. By repeating this procedure for other levels of saving, a new pseudo-opportunity locus can be constructed and a new equilibrium consumption-saving decision, point B, determined. The diagram shows more saving at B than at A', but less than at A. Figure 10.8 indicates a dramatic increase in saving, because the pseudo-opportunity locus scarcely existed in the absence of the safe asset. [6]

Thus the availability of a safe asset may very well increase saving and make the "as if" terms on which saving decisions are reached accord more closely with the opportunities actuarially available for transforming present consumption into future. But the safe asset itself absorbs saving, and it is unlikely, except in the case illustrated in Figure 10.8, that its availability actually increases the direct flow of risk-averse saving into capital formation. Increasing the total amount of capital formation will generally require that the savings placed in the safe asset flow indirectly, via the government or private financial intermediaries, into real investment. In the extreme it is possible to lead risk-averse investors to point A by offering them a safe asset with a guaranteed rate of return equal to the expected marginal efficiency of capital.

The same apparatus may be used to analyze need uncertainty and precau-

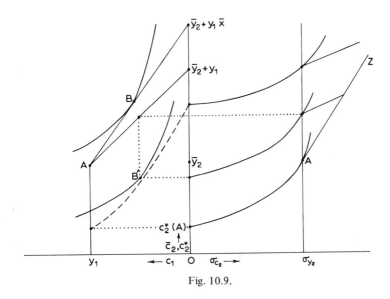

Fig. 10.9.

tionary saving. Figure 10.9 has the same general format as the previous diagrams. But now the zero saving position is indicated by points A in both diagrams. In period two expected income $\bar{y}_2$ is at the vertical level of these points; but the dispersion of this prospect is σ_{y_2}. The corresponding $c_2^*(A)$ is shown on the vertical axis. If saving can be done by acquiring an asset which will realize on average $\bar{x}$ per dollar at a risk of σ_x, further possibilities are opened. Expected consumption $\bar{c}_2$ becomes

$$\bar{y}_2 + (y_1 - c_1)\bar{x} ,$$

as indicated by the frontier line from A in the left panel. Risk σ_{c_2} becomes

$$[\sigma_{y_2}^2 + (y_1 - c_1)^2 \sigma_x^2 + 2\rho(y_1 - c_1)\sigma_{y_2}\sigma_x]^{1/2},$$

where ρ is the coefficient of correlation between second-period income and yield on saving. Conceivably, saving can reduce or even eliminate risk – provided the correlation is negative. But, in general, saving will increase expected period-two consumption only by increasing its dispersion also, as illustrated by curve AZ in Figure 10.9. Once again the points on AZ can be converted into certainty equivalents c_2^* and the resulting pseudo-opportunity locus plotted. It is easily possible that none of these c_2^* is higher than $c_2^*(A)$, so that positive saving cannot improve on zero saving. This is the case illustrated in Figure 10.9.

The manner in which the availability of a safe asset modifies the pseudo-opportunity locus is the same as in Figures 10.7 and 10.8. In the case illustrated by Figure 10.9, introduction of a safe asset leads to a large increase in saving, all in the safe asset. Not only does this saving exceed what would be forthcoming without any safe asset available; it also exceeds the amount that would be saved if there were no uncertainty about either need or yield (point B). At the actual equilibrium point B', the individual is behaving as if the marginal reward for saving exceeded that actuarially available. Thus the departure from risk-neutral behavior may be in the opposite direction from the pure case of yield uncertainty.

3.3. Borrowing and Intermediation

It takes two kinds of people, at least, to make a market. The consumer savers of the previous section are one kind. They have a positive demand for accumulation of the less risky monetary asset. In the market as a whole this can be satisfied only by governmental or private borrowers who create such assets. Potential private borrowers are individuals with little or no risk aversion. In the primitive diagrammatic framework introduced in the previous section, they prefer to stay on the locus OZ, placing all their saving in risky real investment rather than to move to the left and accumulate a diversified portfolio. The opportunity to borrow means that they can assume more risk than OZ. If the expected real rate of interest on their debt is smaller than that on real investment, assuming more risk also raises their expected amounts of future consumption.

The adjustment of such a borrower is illustrated in Figure 10.10, which follows the same format as the previous diagrams. As before, the lower dashed curve in the left panel is the pseudo-opportunity locus when only the risky asset is available. The opportunity to borrow — where $\bar{b}$, assumed greater than one but less than $\bar{x}$, is the amount to be repaid for each dollar borrowed — extends risk return opportunities to the right of OZ along lines like those drawn through P and P'. The points P and P' are the preferred risk return combinations. For example, if the individual consumes c_1', saves $y_1 - c_1'$, his real investment will be greater than his saving in the proportion $\overline{S'P'}$ to $\overline{S'Q'}$, and he will make up the difference by borrowing. This opportunity raises the pseudo-opportunity locus in the left panel, as illustrated.

The borrower of Figure 10.10 is risk-averse; his risk return indifference curves are almost flat, but still upward sloping. Risk-neutral or risk-seeking borrowers would in similar circumstances have an unlimited demand for loans. They would have to be rationed by some credit line or margin requirement. After all, the borrower, under bankruptcy law, cannot lose more than his own stake; the lender is really taking the remaining risk. A credit line proportional

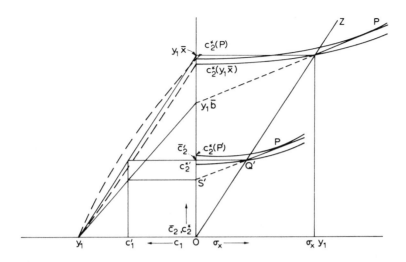

Fig. 10.10.

to the borrower's commitment of his own equity would be depicted by a ray to the right of OZ and the corresponding pseudo-opportunity locus would be a straight line from y_1 steeper than the line to $y_1\bar{x}$.

The borrower then has, from a welfare standpoint, an excessive incentive to save, because the more he saves himself the more he is permitted to borrow on what he regards as profitable terms. Somehow the market must ration borrowers, and it is not clear how it can simultaneously make an efficient allocation of risk among lenders and borrowers and an efficient social choice between present and future consumption. Loan markets and financial intermediaries transfer the risks of capital ownership from conservative savers, who find such risks distasteful, to adventurous investors, who like the risks but are short of wealth. But the pattern of expected yields, interest rates, and credit lines that accomplishes this allocation does not mean the same thing for the saving/consumption choices of all the participants in the market. Whereas lenders discount the prospects of capital ownership for its risks and the prospects of lending for risks of default, borrowers limited by credit lines add to the returns on new saving the value of enlarging their capacity to borrow.

4. Questions about Optimality

The two-period consumer can be the nucleus of a growth model with over-lapping generations. Each generation works and saves one period, retires and dissaves the second period, and does no net saving over its lifetime. Alternative steady growth paths imply different sequences of first-period consumption and second-period consumption. In the absence of technical change, each path involves the same consumption sequence for every generation (Samuelson, 1958; Diamond, 1965, esp. pp. 1126–35; Cass and Yaari, 1966). The set of sustainable sequences is limited by an opportunity locus of the type *ABC* in Figure 10.11. Curve *ABD* is the frontier of possibilities when all saving takes the form of acquiring productive capital. Its convexity to the origin reflects the diminishing marginal productivity of capital. At point *B*, the golden-rule point, this marginal productivity becomes equal to the rate of growth of population *g*. As observed above, it is inefficient to invest in capital beyond this point. Any further saving should take the form of paper earning a real rate of interest, *g*, with which each retired generation purchases some of the

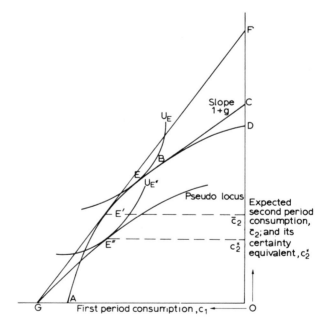

Fig. 10.11.

output of its younger contemporaries. This opportunity is represented in the diagram by the line BC with slope $1 + g$, tangent to ABD at point B.

In the absence of uncertainty, an equilibrium would be reached at a point like E, where the opportunity locus is tangent to an indifference curve of a representative consumer. The common slope would be the rate of return on saving sustained by a competitive market. This equilibrium growth path would also be the optimum. In the case illustrated, all saving is and should be acquisition of capital.

An equilibrium in which saving is influenced by uncertainty and risk aversion is exemplified by E'. Now the opportunity locus ABC refers to expected values of consumption. Each generation, when it saves, is unsure of the return its savings will earn. Although the actuarial opportunity presented by the market is described by a line $GE'F$ tangent to ABC at E', the representative individual determines his consumption and saving by reference to a pseudo-opportunity locus interior to the tangent $GE'F$. This leads him to point E'', where his first-period consumption is the same as at E'. The ordinate of E'', c_2^*, is the certainty equivalent of an expected value of second-period consumption, $\bar{c}_2$, indicated by E'.

As explained above, the availability of a safe asset bearing a lower return than physical capital brings the pseudo-opportunity locus closer to the actuarial price line. Therefore, it moves the equilibrium along ABC toward E – provided that all the saving goes into capital formation, that is, that the safe asset is "inside money" representing indirect investment in capital. Indeed, the equilibrium could be pushed all the way back to E by offering the safe asset at an interest rate equal to the expected rate of return on capital and investing in capital all saving placed in the safe asset. But it would not be possible for financial intermediation to do this if the risks that deter direct investment in capital are social as well as private risks. Not even the government can offer savers an asset that frees private saving of the risks intrinsic to the production processes of the economy as a whole.

The analysis is different for the case when the safe asset is outside money. Suppose that this bears a return of g, lower than the expected return of capital, and each generation of savers acquires both assets. This means – the golden rule case aside – that the society is not operating on the frontier ABC but inside it, along a frontier like AB^*C^* in Figure 10.12 where B^*C^* has the slope $1 + g$ and is parallel to BC. Suppose the chosen sequence of first-period consumption and expected second-period consumption is E^*. The return on physical investment is given by the slope of the locus ABC at B^* and shown by the slope of GB^*. Saving that goes into capital formation is represented by the projection of GB^* on the horizontal axis, and saving that goes into outside

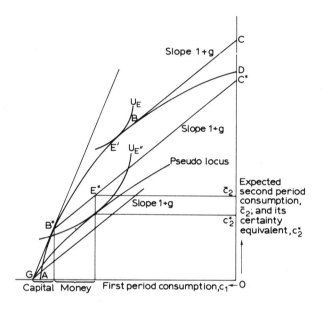

Fig. 10.12.

money by the projection of B^*E^*. For E^* to be an equilibrium, the typical individual must wish to save the total amount indicated in the proportions indicated. In other words, E^* must lie directly above the preferred position on a pseudo-opportunity locus from point G, a locus reflecting the opportunities for combining capital bearing the return indicated by line GB^* and money bearing the interest rate g. Although the availability of the safe asset might well increase total saving, as compared with a nonmonetary equilibrium with uncertainty E', it might also diminish the capitalization of the economy and even lower the expected value of future consumption.

What risks should be reflected in society's choices between present and future? There are technological and environmental uncertainties surrounding the efforts of a society to earn its livelihood from nature and from the rest of the world. If members of the society are risk averse with respect to consumption prospects, their caution should be reflected in social investment decisions. There are also private risks that are not social risks, and these should not influence one way or another the basic social choice between consumption now and consumption later. Personal hazards – for example, death, disability – should be, and frequently are, handled by insurance rather than by saving. Competition makes the risks of investment in any individual firm greater than the social risks of investment in the industry or in the economy at large. In principle, diversification should be able to cut the risks to any individual saver down to the irreducible social minimum. If so, competitive risks would not distort intertemporal choices.

However, competitive financial markets may not be able to do the whole job. Markets are not perfect; transactions costs, indivisibilities, and lack of information limit the possibilities of diversification for many savers. Private enterprise cannot guarantee the liquidity of means of payment or other financial assets against "runs" or against pervasive cyclical fluctuations in business activity or against changes in the purchasing power of currency. Only government can do these things, by making available its own obligations (possibly including purchasing-power-guaranteed obligations), by acting as a financial intermediary itself, and by guaranteeing certain private obligations like bank deposits.

The question is how the government can intervene in these essential ways while leaving to private financial markets the appraisal and accommodation of individual borrowers and the tailoring of assets to the preferences of individual lenders.

These issues are much more complicated, and also much more important, than specifying a rate at which the quantity of some narrow category of financial assets, arbitrarily designated as *money*, should grow.

Notes

[1] This and the next section draw on and elaborate my article, "Money and Economic Growth" (1965), Chapter 9 above.

[2] According to inventory theory, average holdings per unit are proportional to the square root of the size of the unit.

[3] If growth is not balanced but is accompanied by a general increase in capital per unit of output and per augmented unit of labor, this too leads to an increase both in income per capita and in the wage rate. But even so there is no need for an increase in cash holdings per capita unless the wage rate increases faster than per capita income. Whether it does or not depends on technology in ways that can be somewhat tediously described by the value of the elasticity of substitution. A higher wealth/income ratio may increase the demand for cash for transactions on capital account – a requirement somewhat similar to Keynes' finance motive. And the decline in interest rates due to higher capital intensity may also lower velocity. The price of transaction-making services will not change if labor productivity gains as much from higher capital intensity there as elsewhere. But it may rise if financial services are more labor intensive than productive activities.

[4] An economic historian would be puzzled by the implication of section 1 that the development of monetary and financial institutions is in some sense bad for real invest-

ment. Without the safe assets made available by these institutions, how would the thrift of the cautious saver have been mobilized? The conflict is largely superficial. Financing of capital accumulation is the story of inside money, not of outside money.

[5] The optimal choice of c_1 is found by setting equal to zero the derivative of

$$\psi(c_1) = u(c_1) + \varphi\{(y_1-c_1)\bar{x}, (y_1-c_1)\sigma_x\}: \psi'(c_1^*) = u'(c_1^*)-\varphi_1\bar{x}-\varphi_2\sigma_x = 0 ,$$

provided this has a solution between 0 and y_1. The second derivative must be negative:

$$\psi''(c_1^*) = u''(c_1^*) + (\varphi_{11}\bar{x}^2 + 2\varphi_{12}\bar{x}\sigma_x + \varphi_{22}\sigma_x^2) < 0.$$

Consider the relationship of c_1^* to σ_x:

$$\frac{\partial c_1^*}{\partial \sigma_x} \cdot \psi''(c_1^*) = \varphi_{12}\bar{x}(y_1-c_1^*) + \varphi_{22}\sigma_x(y_1-c_1^*) + \varphi_2 .$$

Given that ψ'', φ_{22}, and φ_2 are negative, $\partial c_1^*/\partial\sigma_x$ can be negative only if φ_{12} is positive. We know that if φ is the expected value of a quadratic utility function of c_2 then $\varphi = \bar{c}_2-b(\bar{c}_2^2 + \sigma_{c_2}^2)$, (where $b > 0$), and $\varphi_{12} = 0$. Alternatively for a more general $v(c_2)$

$$\varphi = \int_{-\infty}^{\infty} v(\bar{c}_2 + \sigma_{c_2}z)N(z)dz ,$$

where $N(z)$ is the normal probability density function with zero mean and unit standard deviation. In this case,

$$\varphi_{12} = \int_{-\infty}^{\infty} v''(\bar{c}_2 + \sigma_{c_2}z)N(z)dz$$

and may have either sign.

[6] The optimal choice of c_1 is found by setting equal to zero the derivatives with respect to c_1 and m of

$$u(c_1) + \varphi\{y_1-c_1\} [m + (1-m)x], (y_1-c_1)m\sigma_x\} ,$$

where m is the proportion of saving placed in the safe asset:

$$u'(c_1^*)-\varphi_1[\bar{x} + m(1-\bar{x})] -\varphi_2 m\sigma_x = 0 ;$$

$$\varphi_1(y_1-c_1^*) (1-\bar{x}) + \varphi_2(y_1-c_1^*)\sigma_x = 0 .$$

These may be reduced to the following pair of equations:

$$u'(c_1^*)-\varphi_1\bar{x} = 0 ;$$

$$\varphi_1(1-x) + \varphi_2\sigma_x = 0 .$$

Clearly c_1^* will be smaller, saving larger, than if m is constrained to be zero. Suppose that $\tilde{c}_1$ satisfies the equation of the previous footnote, so that

$$u'(\tilde{c}_1) = \bar{x}\varphi_1\{(y_1-\tilde{c}_1)\bar{x}, (y_1-\tilde{c}_1)\sigma_x\} + \sigma_x\varphi_2\{(y_1-\tilde{c}_1)\bar{x}, (y_1-\tilde{c}_1)\sigma_x\} .$$

Now consider the marginal utility of saving $(y_1-\tilde{c}_1)$ in the second regime:

$$\bar{x}\varphi_1\{(y_1-\tilde{c}_1) [\bar{x} + m(1-\bar{x})], (y_1-\tilde{c}_1)m\sigma_x\} .$$

The second φ_1 has smaller arguments than the first and — provided again that φ_{12} is non-positive — is larger. We know also that φ_2 is negative. Therefore, the marginal utility of saving $y_1 - \tilde{c}_1$ in the second regime exceeds the marginal utility of $\tilde{c}_1$. Thus, c_1 will have to be lower than $\tilde{c}_1$ to bring the marginal utilities of consumption and saving back into equality.

Similarly, consider $\hat{c}_1$ such that $u'(\hat{c}_1) = \bar{x}\varphi_1[(y_1 - \hat{c}_1)\bar{x}, 0]$, that is, the value of c_1 that would be chosen if $\bar{x}$ were regarded as a certain outcome. Reducing the first argument of φ_1 raises its value, but increasing the second argument may work in either direction. In the "quadratic" case where φ_{12} is zero,

$$\bar{x}\varphi_1\{(y_1 - \hat{c}_1)[\bar{x} + m(1 - \bar{x})], (y_1 - \hat{c}_1)m\sigma_x\}$$

will definitely be greater than $u'(\hat{c}_1)$. Thus, with both uncertainty and money present, c_1 will have to be smaller than $\hat{c}_1$ in order to equate the marginal utilities of consumption and saving.

References

Cass, D., and Yaari, M.E. "A Re-examination of the Pure Consumption Loans Model," *Journal of Political Economy*, 74 (August 1966), 353-67.

Diamond, P.A. "National Debt in a Neoclassical Growth Model," *American Economic Review*, 55 (December 1965), 1126-50.

Johnson, H.G. *Essays in Monetary Economics* (London: Allen & Unwin, 1967).

Samuelson, P.A. "An Exact Consumption-Loan Model of Interest with or Without the Social Contrivance of Money," *Journal of Political Economy*, 66 (December 1958), 467-82.

Tobin, J. "The Interest-Elasticity of Transactions Demand for Cash," *Review of Economics and Statistics*, 38 (August 1956), 241-47.

———. "Money and Economic Growth," *Econometrica*, 33 (October 1965), 671-84; Chapter 9 above.

CHAPTER 11

ECONOMIC GROWTH AS AN OBJECTIVE
OF GOVERNMENT POLICY

In recent years economic growth has come to occupy an exalted position
in the hierarchy of goals of government policy, both in the United States and
abroad, both in advanced and in less developed countries, both in centrally
controlled and decentralized economies. National governments proclaim
target growth rates for such diverse economies as the Soviet Union,
Yugoslavia, India, Sweden, France, Japan — and even for the United Kingdom
and the United States, where the targets indicate dissatisfaction with past
performance. Growth is an international goal, too. The Organization for
Economic Cooperation and Development aims at a 50 per cent increase in the
collective gross output of the Atlantic Community over the current decade.

Growth has become a good word. And the better a word becomes, the
more it is invoked to bless a variety of causes and the more it loses specific
meaning. At least in professional economic discussion, we need to give a
definite and distinctive meaning to growth as a policy objective. Let it be
neither a new synonym for good things in general nor a fashionable way to
describe other economic objectives. Let growth be something it is possible to
oppose as well as to favor, depending on judgments of social priorities and
opportunities.

1.

In essence the question of growth is nothing new, but a new disguise for an
age-old issue, one which has always intrigued and preoccupied economists:

Reprinted from *American Economic Review (Papers and Proceedings),* 54 (May
1964), 1-20.
I am greatly indebted to my colleagues at the Cowles Foundation, especially Tjalling
Koopmans, Arthur Okun, and E.S. Phelps, for clarifying many of the questions discussed
in this paper. But they do not necessarily share my opinions, and they certainly share no
responsibility for my mistakes.

the present versus the future. How should society divide its resources between current needs and pleasures and those of next year, next decade, next generation?

The choice can be formalized in a way that makes clear what is essentially at stake. A consumption path or program for an economy describes its rate of consumption at every time point beginning now and extending indefinitely into the future. Not all imaginable consumption paths are feasible. At any moment future possibilities are limited by our inherited stocks of productive resources and technological knowledge and by our prospects for autonomous future increase in these stocks. Of feasible paths, some dominate others; i.e., path *A* dominates *B* if consumption along path *A* exceeds consumption along path *B* at every point of time. I hope I will incur no one's wrath by asserting that in almost everyone's value scheme more is better than less (or certainly not worse), at least if we are careful to specify more or less of what. If this assertion is accepted, the interesting choices are between undominated or efficient feasible paths; e.g., between a pair *A* and *C* where *A* promises more consumption at some points in time but less at others. See Figure 11.1. In particular, I take *growthmanship* to be advocacy of paths that promise more consumption later in return for less earlier.

But *growthmanship* means more than that. Growthmen are usually willing to throw the weight of the government on to the scales in order to tip the balance in favor of the future. Here they fly in the face of a doctrinal

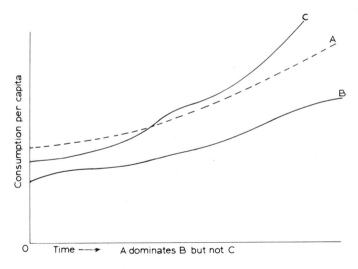

Fig. 11.1

tradition of considerable strength both in economics and in popular ideology. Does not the market so coordinate the free, decentralized decisions of individuals between present and future so as to reach an optimal social choice? Is not any government intervention in favor of growth, therefore, bound to tilt the scales toward the future to a degree that society does not "really" want?

The basic question raised by advocates of faster growth may be further formalized to emphasize this issue. Assuming that the economy is now on a feasible and undominated consumption path, the desirability of deviating from it can be expressed in the language of interest rates and present values. Any feasible and efficient path, including the prevailing path, implies two sets of interest rates. One, which we may call the *time preference set*, expresses the society's marginal rates of substitution as consumers between consumption at one date and consumption at another date. This set answers questions like the following: Given society's consumption prospect, how much increase in consumption five years or fifty years or *t* years from now is worth the loss of a dollar's worth of consumption today? The rates implied by the answers need not all be the same. The other set, which we may call the *technological set,* expresses the opportunities which present and prospective technology offers the society for marginal substitutions of consumption at one date for consumption at another. This set answers questions like the following: Given the consumption path, by how much could consumption be increased five years or fifty years or *t* years from now by the resources released from a dollar's worth of consumption today? Again, the rates can vary with time. A sacrifice in current consumption may yield, say, 10 per cent per year if its fruits are taken five years from now, but 20 per cent – or 2 per cent – if they are taken fifty years from now.

A small proposed feasible deviation from the existing path can in principle be tested as follows: Calculate the present values of the proposed deviations in consumption, negative and positive, discounting them by the time preference set of interest rates. If the sum is positive, the proposed deviation is worth while. If it is zero or negative, it is not worth while. We know that this sum will not be positive if it happens that the time preference and technological interest rates are identical.

Evidently growthmen believe that the two sets diverge in such a way that society would give a positive present value to feasible increases in future consumption purchased at the expense of current and near future consumption. Their opponents think the contrary. Many of them have faith in the capital markets and believe there is a presumption that these markets make the two sets of rates equal.

2.

This is the heart of the issue, I believe, and I shall return to it later in this lecture. First, however, I must discuss some questions raised by the formulation of the growth issue which I have just tried to sketch. What is the relationship between growth and other objectives of economic policy, in particular full employment of resources? Are there some noneconomic reasons for accelerating growth — reasons which this formulation excludes or evades? Exactly what is the "consumption" whose path is to be chosen? Finally, can government successfully influence the growth path?

2.1. *Growth Versus Full Employment*
To accelerate growth is not the same thing as to increase the utilization of existing resources, manpower, and capital capacity. In the formulation sketched above, a consumption path with underutilization is dominated or inefficient. By putting the idle resources to work, consumption can be increased both now and in future. The same is true of other measures to improve the efficiency of allocation of resources. We can all agree, I presume, on the desirability of growth measures free of any cost. If that is the meaning of growth policy, there is no issue.

For short periods of time, stepping up the utilization of capacity can increase the recorded rate of growth of output and consumption. But over the decades fluctuations in the utilization of capacity will have a minor influence compared to the growth of capacity itself. To express the same point somewhat differently, the subject of economic growth refers mainly to supply, or capacity to produce, rather than to demand. In the short run, accelerating the growth of demand for goods and services can, by increasing the rate of utilization of capacity, speed the growth of output. But in the long run, output and real demand cannot grow faster than capacity. If monetary demand is made to set a faster pace, it will be frustrated by a rate of inflation that cuts real demand down to size.

Public policy affecting aggregate demand should be aimed at maintaining a desired rate of utilization of capacity. Economists and other citizens will differ on how high this rate should be, because they differ in the weights they attach to additional employment and output, on the one hand, and to the risks of faster price inflation, on the other. But however this balance is struck, monetary and fiscal policies can in principle hit the target utilization rate just as well whether the economy's capacity is growing at 5 per cent or 3 per cent or zero per cent.

Full employment is, therefore, not a reason for faster economic growth;

each is an objective in its own right. In an economy suffering from low rates of utilization of manpower and capital resources, accelerating the growth of aggregate demand may well be the need of the hour. But this ought not be considered growth policy in the more fundamental sense. Tax reduction today has sufficient justification as a means of expanding demand and raising the rate of utilization. It is probably an unfortunate confusion to bill it as a growth measure too.

I do not mean, of course, that the rate of growth of the economy's capacity is in practice wholly independent of its rate of utilization. In principle they may be independent. Demand can be expanded in ways that do not accelerate, indeed may even retard, the growth in capacity itself. But as a rule some of the output resulting from an increase in utilization will be used in ways that expand future capacity. Thus the Great Depression deprived the nation and the world of investment as well as consumption; we, as well as our fathers, bear the cost. The proposed tax reduction, even though its major impact is to stimulate consumption, will nonetheless increase the share of national capacity devoted to capital accumulation. It is in this sense that it can be called a growth measure. But there may be ways to expand demand and utilization to the same degree while at the same time providing both more stimulus for and more economic room for capacity-building uses of resources now idle.

2.2. Noneconomic Reasons for Growth

Economic growth may be a national objective for noneconomic reasons, for national prestige or national strength or national purpose.

No doubt much of the recent dissatisfaction with U.S. growth is motivated by unfavorable comparisons with other countries, especially the Soviet Union. If current rates are mechanically extrapolated, it is easy to calculate that the U.S. will not be first in international statistical comparisons in our great grandchildren's textbooks. Presumably the American nation could somehow stand and even rationalize this blow to our national pride, even as we survive quadrennial defeats by Russian hordes in the Olympics. At any rate, it is not for professional economists to advise the country to act differently just to win a race in statistical yearbooks. The cold war will not be so easily won, or lost, or ended.

International competition in growth may, however, be of importance in the battle for prestige and allegiance among the "uncommitted" and less developed countries. These nations place a high premium on rapid economic progress. They will not -- so the argument runs -- choose the democratic way in preference to communism, or market economies in preference to centrally directed economies, unless our institutions show by example that they can outperform rival systems. A political psychologist rather than an economist should evaluate this claim. But it has several apparent weaknesses: (a) Rate of growth is not the only dimension of economic performance by which our society will be judged by outside observers. Equality of opportunity and of condition, humanity, understanding, and generosity in relation to less privileged people in our own society and abroad – these are perhaps more important dimensions. (b) The U.S. is not the only noncommunist economy. The examples of western Europe (in particular the contrast of West to East Germany) and Japan are more relevant to the rest of the world, and they give convincing evidence of the economic vitality of free societies. (c) What is much more important is a demonstration that an underdeveloped country can progress rapidly under democratic auspices. Without this kind of demonstration, faster growth of affluence in already affluent societies may cause more disaffection than admiration.

On the score of national strength, there is a case for growth. But it is more subtle than the facile association of military power with generalized civilian economic capacity. Nuclear technology has made this connection looser than ever. A country is not necessarily stronger than another just because it has a higher GNP. Great productive capacity may have been the decisive reserve of military strength in the last two world wars, but nowadays it is useless if it remains unmobilized until the cataclysmic buttons are pushed. A country with smaller GNP can be as strong or even stronger if it persistently allocates enough of its GNP to military purposes. And in the age of overkill, apparently there can be a point of saturation.

Should we grow faster to be better prepared to meet possible future needs for output for military purposes – or for other uses connected with national foreign policy? If we do not, we will have to meet such needs when they arise by depriving other claimants on national production, principally consumption, at the time. But in order to grow faster, we have to deprive these claimants now. Hence the national power argument seems to boil down to the economist's calculation after all; i.e., to the terms of trade between current and future consumption.

But there is an important exception. Some hazards are great enough to bias our choice to favor the future over the present, to accept less favorable payoffs than we otherwise would. We might conceivably be challenged one day to a duel of overriding priority, involving all-out commitment of resources to military uses, foreign aid, space adventures, or all of these together. A high GNP might be the difference between victory and defeat rather than the difference between more or less consumption. In other words, this contingency is one that could be met only by sacrifices of consumption in advance. not by sacrifices at the time.

As for national purpose, it is surely conceivable that a growth target could inspire. galvanize, and unite the nation. But it is not the only objective that could serve this purpose, nor is it necessarily the best candidate.

2.3. Growth in What?

The formulation of the growth issue sketched above presents it as a choice among available consumption paths. The concentration on consumption deserves some elaboration and explanation – especially because growth performance and aspiration are popularly expressed in terms of gross or net national product.

Some of the noneconomic reasons for favoring faster growth also suggest that GNP is the relevant measure, especially if it is the most usual and visible measure. But as economists we would make welfare or utility depend on consumption. We would require the investment part of GNP to derive its value from the future consumption it supports. After all, a future in which the rate of growth of GNP reaches fantastic heights has no appeal if the fruits of the achievement are never consumed. We must heed the "golden rule" of capital accumulation: there is a saving ratio and a corresponding capital intensity that maximize consumption. Persistent saving in excess of the rule makes GNP higher but consumption lower (see Phelps [5]).

Neither GNP nor consumption, as ordinarily measured, counts leisure. Yet I do not understand advocates of faster growth to be taking a stand in favor of goods and services priced in the market and against leisure. Should the trend toward shorter hours. longer vacations, and earlier retirements accelerate. the rate of growth of consumption as measured in the national accounts might decline. But a decline for this reason should not bother a growth-oriented economist. *The Affluent Society* to the contrary notwithstanding. the conventional wisdom of economics was long since liberated from the fallacy that only produced goods and services yield utility and welfare. Economists do have prejudices against biasing the price system in favor of leisure and against forcing the leisure of involuntary unemployment on anyone. But those are other matters. The consumption whose growth path concerns us should include leisure valued at the real wage. Needless to say, it should also allow for consumption goods and services provided by government.

Finally, is the relevant measure aggregate consumption or consumption per capita? Later I shall be concerned with social indifference curves between consumption at one date and at a later date. An example is pictured in Figure 11.2. What measure of consumption should the axes of such a diagram

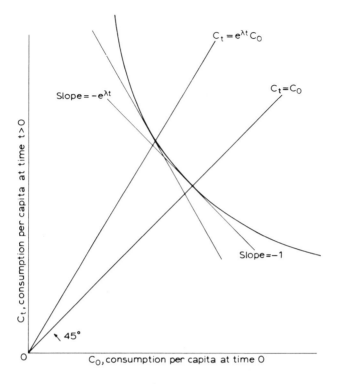

$C_t = e^{\lambda t} C_0$

$C_t = C_0$

Slope $= -e^{\lambda t}$

Slope $= -1$

C_t, consumption per capita at time $t > 0$

45°

O

C_0, consumption per capita at time O

Fig. 11.2

represent? The answer depends on questions like the following: Do we discharge our obligation to the next generation if we enable them to enjoy the same aggregate consumption even though there will be more of them to share it? Should we, on the other hand, sacrifice today in order to raise per capita consumption half a century from now just because there will then be more consumers? Or should generations count in some sense equally regardless of size?

These are not easy questions for the social philosopher, but revealed social preferences lean towards per capita consumption. Presumably we do not value increase in population for its own sake. We might if sheer numbers were important for national power. But in general we are content to leave population trends to free choice; indeed, we seek to enlarge parents' ability to limit births at their discretion. Neither immigration nor subsidies for childbearing are advanced as growth proposals. In the world at large, certainly, the commonly accepted aim is to retard the growth of population, not to accelerate it. (For discussion of some aspects of this problem, see Koopmans [3].)

2.4. *Government's Power to Influence Growth*

I come now to the question whether the government can influence growth, even if we wish it to. The growth objective is commonly framed in terms of an exponential growth rate. Those who advocate measures to promote growth frequently are expressing a preference for a higher per annum rate of growth, for 4 per cent instead of 3 per cent or 3½ per cent. But the thrust of much recent theorizing and model building is that in the really long run we have no choice about the growth rate. (See, for example, Phelps [6].) The long-run growth rates of GNP and aggregate consumption are exogenously determined by the growth of the labor force and the progress of technology. Or, to express the same conclusion somewhat differently, the rates of growth of productivity per man and of consumption per capita are in the long run controlled by the rate of advance of technology.

According to these models, there are various hypothetical paths which share the exogenously determined rate. These paths differ in level. On a higher path, consumption per capita is always larger than on a lower one. A higher path represents a higher capital intensity (so long as capital intensity does not exceed its golden-rule value), and a correspondingly higher propensity to save is required to maintain it.

An economy moving along one of these paths may "decide" to move to a higher one, by lowering its propensity to consume. For a while, its growth rate will be higher, as the effects of increasing capital intensity and modernization are added to those of the underlying progress of technology. Eventually, however, capital intensity will cease to increase and the growth rate will converge to its natural value. The process can be repeated by further increases in the saving ratio, but the golden rule argument cited above sets a limit long before the propensity to consume reaches zero – indeed, when the propensity to save is equal to the elasticity of output with respect to capital accumulation. This is the highest path for consumption per capita.

Asymptotically, then, it appears that we have no choice about our rate of growth, but can choose only between parallel paths of different levels. But asymptotically is a very long time. The period of transition from one path to another, short from the perspective of the model builder, may be measured in decades or generations. It is therefore not wholly misleading to regard society as choosing among growth rates.

Models of this kind take the rate of technological progress as exogenous. In fact, it is probably subject to improvement, like the degree of capital intensity, by expenditure of current resources. We still know very little about the technology that governs the production of applicable technological knowledge. What is required to keep the index of technology, which determines the productivity of labor and capital, growing at a constant exponential rate? Does it take simply a constant absolute amount of labor and capital? Does it take a constant fraction of the resources devoted to production? Does it take an input of resources growing at the same rate as the technology index itself? Only when we can answer such questions can we know whether and how the pace of economic growth is ultimately limited by the natural increase of the labor force.

A second reason for doubting that government measures can affect the intertemporal choices of society is the possibility that the private decisions of individuals can and will offset these measures. Suppose, for example, that the government levies new taxes and uses the proceeds for saving and investment, either through public expenditure or through public lending to private investors or through retirement of public debt. The government's purpose is to increase later consumption at the expense of earlier. But if this purpose is perfectly well understood, will not the public reduce its private saving in the knowledge that its collective saving is now doing part of the job?

I have two comments regarding this possibility. First, it may be that the government's saving corrects a situation of underinvestment, where public or private projects that would pay for themselves in social benefits (discounted at the time preference set of interest rates) were not being undertaken. In this case, the government's twist of the path will not be undone even if perfectly understood because the new path corresponds better to public preferences. Second, the assumption that the public correctly foresees all the consequences of government policy is farfetched. In the example above, economists would usually expect the new taxes to be paid in large part out of private consumption. Disposable income is reduced; and so, gradually, is the public's net financial claim on the government − a more tangible element in private balance sheets than the present value of future tax liabilities or of free services from government.

I conclude, therefore, that at least for the medium run, government can affect the growth of the economy; and I turn to the question whether it should.

3.

In this section I propose to argue: (1) that government might legitimately have a growth policy, and indeed could scarcely avoid having one, even if private markets were perfect; (2) that capital markets are far from perfect and that private saving decisions are therefore based on an overconservative estimate of the social return to saving; and (3) that the terms on which even so advanced an economy as our own can trade present for future consumption seem to be very attractive.

3.1. Government Neutrality in Intertemporal Choice

Many economists and many other citizens will argue that the government should be neutral as between present and future. In their view the capital markets produce an optimal result, balancing the time preferences of individuals, freely expressed through their consumption and saving behavior, against the technological opportunities for substituting consumption tomorrow for consumption today. Let us assume for the moment that government can be neutral in some meaningful sense and that the capital markets perform their assigned function. Even so, I believe government should have a growth policy, and only by accident a neutral one.

I fail to see why economists should advise the public that it is wrong for them collectively to supplement (or diminish) the provisions for the future they are making individually. I agree to the desirability of satisfying human preference – that is what our kind of society and economy is all about. But I have never been able to understand why the preferences of individuals are worthy of respect only when they are expressed in the market, why the preferences of the very same individuals expressed politically should be regarded as distortions. Sometimes economists come close to rationalizing all market results and private institutions by the argument that they would not occur and survive if they were not optimally satisfying individuals' preferences. But political results and public institutions are not granted the benefit of presumptive justification-through-existence.

In both arenas preferences certainly need to be guided by full and accurate information. In the arena of government policy, it is the business of economists to help the society know what it is doing, to understand the choices. benefits, costs, and risks it confronts, not simply to repeat *ad nauseum* that the best thing to do is nothing.

The case for explicit government policy in intertemporal social choice is especially strong. More than any other social institution, government represents the permanence and continuity of the society. And in a democracy one way in which each generation uses government is to protect the interest of unborn generations against its own shortsighted and selfish instincts.

We cannot be sure that lineal family ties will give individuals sufficient motivation to provide for society's future. Suppose the individuals of a whole generation, deciding that their children and grandchildren might better start from scratch, were to proceed to consume their capital. Good capital markets might reflect this epidemic of acute time preference in a perfectly Pareto-optimal way. But would we as a nation feel that we were collectively discharging our obligations to our successors?

Through many activities of government, including conservation and public education, we have recognized a generalized obligation to equip the next generation — an obligation wholly distinct from our individual provisions for our own children. This generalized obligation acquires special force if we take seriously our ideals of equality of opportunity. We like to think that our society gives the members of each generation an equal chance in the race, or at least that their chances are not predetermined by family backgrounds. Besides requiring investment in human beings on a basis other than ability to pay, this ideal suggests redistributive taxation of estates. And if estate taxation dulls incentives to save for specific heirs, the government needs to replenish saving collectively.

But what is growth-neutral government finance anyway? I have already dismissed as farfetched one answer; namely, that any government finance is growth-neutral when it is fully and accurately foreseen, and accordingly offset, by taxpayers and by the beneficiaries of government services. Often a balanced budget is considered a growth-neutral fiscal policy. The budget in this rule is not, of course, the conventional U.S. administrative budget. Rather the rule suggests that (a) net government investment should be covered by borrowing, with the Treasury competing in the capital markets with private investors for private saving, and that (b) other government expenditure, including allowance for consumption of public capital, should be covered by current taxes or fees.

The rule is clear cut and has intuitive appeal. But it seems to bias social choice against the future when there is simply a shift in public preference from private consumption, present and future, to collective consumption, present and future. The rule would levy only enough new taxes to cover the additional collective consumption. But the evidence is that taxpayers would pay some of these new taxes from saving (especially if the collective consumption the taxes finance were of regrettable necessities like national defense rather than of services that clearly yield utility now and in future). Interest rates would rise and investment would be curtailed, even though no shift in social time preference has occurred. Clearly the 10 per cent of GNP which the cold war has forced us to devote persistently to national defense has not come wholly from private or public consumption. True neutrality evidently would require a tighter fiscal policy the bigger the government's budget for current consumption.

But in any case, the quest for neutrality is probably a search for a will-of-the wisp. For it is not only the overall budget position of government but also the specifics of taxation and expenditure which affect intertemporal choices. We have not yet learned how to implement the welfare economist's lump-sum taxes. I have already given one example of a tax which is desirable in view of other social objectives but is bound to affect incentives for private accumulation of wealth. It will suffice to remind you also that our methods of taxation necessarily favor one kind of current consumption, leisure, both as against other current consumption and as against future consumption of products and leisure.

The major policy proposals of growthmen boil down to the suggestion that government should save – or save more – by making investments on its own account, subsidizing the investments of others, or by channeling tax money through the capital markets into private investment. This last item is the major purpose of the full employment budget surplus for which Councils of Economic Advisers longed under both Presidents Eisenhower and Kennedy.

It is now widely recognized that in principle the government can match aggregate demand to the economy's capacity in a variety of ways. Its various instruments for regulating or stabilizing demand affect consumption and investment differently. A strong progrowth policy would restrict consumption by taxation or by economy in government's current expenditure while stepping up public investment and encouraging private investment through tax incentives or low interest rates and high liquidity. The government cannot avoid choosing some combination of its demand-regulating instruments. Therefore government is bound to affect the composition of current output and society's provision for the future. Let us debate this choice of policy mixtures on its merits, weighing growth against its costs and against other objectives of policy, without encumbering the debate with a search for that combination which meets some elusive criterion of neutrality.

3.2. Imperfections in Private Capital Markets

I turn now to the second subject: the efficiency of the capital markets. Do private saving decisions reflect the real payoffs which nature and technology offer the economy? There are several reasons to believe that the answer is negative.

3.2.1. Monopoly and Restrictions of Entry

The evidence is that the rates of return required of real investment projects by U.S. business corporations are very high – typically more than 10 per cent after allowance for depreciation, obsolescence, and taxes. Rates of this magnitude are not only required *ex ante* but realized *ex post*. Why do these rates so greatly exceed the cost of borrowed funds, the earnings-to-price ratio of equity issues, and in general the rates of return available to savers?

One reason clearly is that the relevant markets are not purely competitive. A monopolistic or oligopolistic firm limits its expansion in product markets, its purchases in factor markets, and its calls on capital markets, because the firm takes into account that prices and rates in these markets will turn against it. The managers seek to maintain a market valuation of the firm in excess of the replacement cost of its assets, the difference representing the capitalized value of its monopoly power, often euphemistically called good will. Restrictions and costs of entry prevent other firms from competing this difference away. Foresighted and lucky investors receive the increases in the firm's market value in the form of capital gains. But the willingness of savers to value the assets of the firm above their cost, i.e., to supply capital at a lower rate of return than the firm earns internally, is not translated into investment either by this firm or others. One effect is to depress rates of return in more competitive sectors of the economy. But another result is to restrict total saving and investment.

3.2.2. Risks, Private and Social

Risks provide a second reason for the observed divergence between the rates of return satisfactory to savers and those typically required of real investment projects. Some of these are risks to the economy as well as to the owners of the business: technological hazards, uncertainties about consumer acceptance of new products, or uncertainties about the future availability and social opportunity cost of needed factors of production. Even though these are social as well as private risks, it is not clear that society should take a risk-averse position towards them and charge a risk premium against those projects entailing more uncertainties than others. Presumably society can pool such risks and realize with a very small margin of uncertainty the actuarial return on investments.

Moreover, some of the private risks are not social risks at all. Consider, for example, uncertainties about competition and market shares; if several rivals are introducing a new process or new product, the main uncertainties in the investment calculation of each are the future actions of the others. Consider, further, the high and sometimes prohibitive cost which many firms impute to external funds -- apparently as insurance against loss of control to new shareowners, or, with extremely bad luck, to bondholders. If savers were offered the rates of return asked of and earned by business investments, in the form of assets that impose no more risk on the holder than is commensurate to the social risks involved, presumably they would choose to save more.

It is true, on the other hand, that some net saving is now motivated by personal contingencies that are likewise social risks of a much smaller order. But our society has created insuring institutions, both private and public, to reduce the need for oversaving to meet such contingencies. Except in the field of residential construction, it has created few similar institutions to prevent private risk aversion from leading to underinvestment.

3.2.3. External Returns to Investment

Some investments yield benefits which cannot be captured by the individual or firm making the initial outlays. Research and development expenditures and outlays for training of personnel are obvious cases in point. Government policy has already recognized this fact both in tax law and in government expenditures, and it is difficult to judge whether this recognition is sufficient. Kenneth Arrow (1) has pointed out that not only research and development but all forms of investment activity share in some degree the property that B may learn from A's doing. The support which this observation gives to a general policy of encouraging investment is somewhat tempered by reflecting that the same social process of "learning by doing" can occur in production of goods and services for current consumption. However, experience is most important as a teacher in new situations, and innovations are likely to require investment.

In regard to investment in human capacities and talents, it is by no means clear that public outlays are yet sufficient to reap the external benefits involved, or even that the relevant capital markets are sufficiently developed to permit individuals to earn the private benefits. I recognize that calculations of the rate of return to educational outlays depend critically on how much of these outlays are charged to current consumption. As an educator and ex-student I am inclined to rate high the immediate utility-producing powers of education.

3.3. The Payoff to Social Saving

The burden of my remarks so far is that we cannot escape considering growth or, more precisely, intertemporal choice as an issue of public economic policy. We cannot assume, either, that the market settles the issue optimally or that government can be guided by some simple rules of neutrality. We must confront head-on the question whether the social payoff of faster growth in higher future consumption validates its cost in consumption foregone today. The issue that needs to be joined is typified by the contrast between Denison (2), who estimates a very high investment requirement for a one point increase in the medium-term growth rate (a ten point increase in the ratio of current gross investment to GNP) and Solow (8), who calculates a marginal investment requirement only about one-fifth as high.

Fortunately the profession has now begun the task of computing rates of return on various kinds of investment, tangible and intangible. Thanks to theoretical advances in growth models and in handling the knotty problems of technological progress, vintage capital, and obsolescence, we have a better conceptual foundation for these tasks than we did only a few years ago. Phelps (6) using the same conceptual approach as Solow (7), has estimated the overall rate of return on tangible investment in the United States to be about 14 per cent in 1954. And even this figure seems conservative in relation to some target rates of return of large industrial corporations reported by Lanzillotti (4).

But whatever the true rates are, they must be compared with appropriate social rates of time preference.

Consider a family of exponential balanced growth paths sharing a common growth rate; each member of the family has a constant saving ratio, and this ratio differs from path to path. It is also true that each path is characterized by a single technological interest rate, the same for all intervals of time. The theory of the golden rule tells us that the path of highest consumption per capita at every point in time is characterized by a gross saving ratio s equal to the elasticity of output with respect to capital α (this is also the share of nonlabor income in GNP if income distribution is governed by marginal productivity). Along the golden rule path the social rate of interest is constant and equal to the rate of increase of the "effective" labor force. This in turn is equal to the natural rate of increase in the labor force plus the annual rate of improvement in labor quality due to technical progress.

If there is no technical improvement, consumption per capita remains constant over time; and along the golden rule path a dollar of per capita consumption saved today will produce a dollar, no more and no less, in per capita consumption tomorrow. The return on aggregative saving is just enough to keep up with population growth.

This rate of return represents impartiality between generations in this sense. When consumption per capita is the same tomorrow as today, there is no time preference, a dollar of consumption per capita is valued the same whenever it occurs. (See Koopmans [3].)

When there is technical progress, both the real wage and consumption per capita will advance at the annual rate at which labor quality improves, say λ.

And along the golden rule path λ will also be the per annum rate of return, in future per capita consumption, on saving today. (A dollar of saving will yield in addition enough new capital to provide for the increment of population.) That is, an increase in per capita consumption of $1.00 at time t requires sacrifice of only $\$e^{-\lambda t}$ at time zero.

It is reasonable to regard this rate of discount, too, as intertemporally impartial. Absence of time preference means that at equal consumption levels society values equally a dollar of future consumption and a dollar of present consumption. But on a path of growing per capita consumption, it is natural that a dollar of future consumption should no longer trade for current consumption at par. To take the rate of improvement in labor quality and in the real wage λ, as the rate of time preference is to say in effect that saving is justified if and only if it earns more than future consumers will gain anyway through the inexorable progress of technology. Thus if the rate of technical progress is correctly foreseen, this principle meets a common criticism of growth; namely, that there is no reason to save for future generations when technological progress will make them better off anyway. Figure 11.2 illustrates a social indifference curve between present and future per capita consumption such that there is no time preference when the two are equal, but elsewhere a marginal rate of substitution that exceeds one in the same proportion that future consumption exceeds current consumption.

An economy saving at a constant rate s lower than α, the share of capital income in GNP, will be below its golden rule path. Its rate of return on saving will be accordingly higher than the golden rule rate. Indeed the present value of the stream of returns from a dollar of investment, computed at the golden rule rate on the theory that this is an appropriate impartial discount factor free of the taint of time preference, is equal to α/s. In the United States today the ratio α/s must exceed 1.5 and may be as high as 2.

For some models it is possible to compute the technological interest rate characteristic of a path with α/s greater than one; i.e., of a path below the golden rule path. This is, in effect, what Phelps did to arrive at his estimates of the return on investment in the United States, cited above. Consider a model based on a Cobb-Douglas production function with variable factor proportions both *ex ante* and *ex post*. Let capital elasticity be α and labor elasticity $1-\alpha$; the natural rate of increase in labor force n; constant technical progress expressed as improvement in the quality of labor at rate λ; a gross saving ratio s; depreciation of capital at a constant rate δ. The members of this family of growth paths share a rate of growth $n + \lambda$ in aggregate output investment, and consumption, and a rate of growth λ in the real wage and in per capita consumption. The rate of interest characteristic of a path is different depending whether technical progress is assumed to be (*a*) disembodied and affecting all capital old or new, or (*b*) embodied in new vintage capital only. The expressions for the rate of interest in the two cases are as follows (for their derivation see Appendix):

(a) disembodied technical progress

$$r = \frac{\alpha}{s}(n + \lambda + \delta) - \delta$$

(b) embodied technical progress

$$r = \frac{\alpha}{s}(n + \lambda + \delta) - \delta + \frac{\lambda(1-\alpha)}{s} - \frac{\lambda(1-\alpha)}{\alpha}$$

If, for example, $n = .015$, $\lambda = .03$, $\delta = .03$, $\alpha = .33$ and $s = .20$, then $r = .095$ in case (*a*) and $r = .135$ in case (*b*). The difference reflects the fact, originally emphasized by Solow (7), that additional saving moves the economy toward a higher path faster in the vintage-capital model and therefore is rewarded sooner with higher consumption.

The evidence is uncertain, and there is a clear need for more refined and reliable estimates of the parameters on which the issue turns. I believe the evidence suggests that policy to accelerate growth, to move the economy to a higher path, would pay. That is, the returns to a higher saving and investment ratio would be positive, if evaluated by a reasonable set of social time preference interest rates. This seems to me the strongest reason for advocating growth policy.

Appendix

1. Let $I(v)$ be gross investment at time (vintage) v, and let $\rho(v, t)$ be its marginal productivity at time t. Then the present value of the stream of returns from investment of one dollar at time v is

$$\int_{v}^{\infty} \exp(v^{-\int^{t} r(u)\, du}) \rho(v, t)\, dt \ .$$

Setting this present value equal to 1 for all v defines the series $r(u)$ of instantaneous technological interest rates.

In the models under discussion in the text calendar time does not affect $\rho(v, t)$, which can therefore be written as $\rho(t-v)$. It follows that $r(u)$ is a constant, and we may find it from:

$$\int_0^\infty \exp[-r(t-v)]\, \rho(t-v)\, d(t-v) = 1 \ . \tag{1}$$

The gross income to capital at time t, if capital of each vintage is paid its marginal product is,

$$\alpha Q(t) = \int_{-\infty}^t I(v)\, \rho(v, t)\, dv = \int_0^\infty I(t-v)\, \rho(t-v)\, d(t-v)$$

where $Q(t)$ is gross output summed over all vintages, and α is capital's share. Now if investment is growing exponentially at rate g — the rate of growth of output — then $I(t-v) = I(t) \exp[-g(t-v)]$. Therefore

$$\frac{\alpha Q(t)}{I(t)} = \frac{\alpha}{s} = \int_0^\infty \exp[-g(t-v)]\, \rho(t-v)\, d(t-v) \tag{2}$$

where s is the saving ratio, constant along the path. The right-hand side will be recognized at the present value of the stream of returns from investment when the discount factor is g rather than r. This present value exceeds 1 whenever α/s exceeds one.

2. The above argument shows that $r \gtrless g$ as $\alpha \gtrless s$. It remains to derive the explicit expressions for r given in the text.

(a) Disembodied progress:
Let $Q(v, t)$ be the output and $L(v, t)$ the labor input associated with capital made at time v.

$$Q(v, t) = A(I(v)\exp[-\delta(t-v)])^\alpha (L(v, t) \exp[\lambda t])^{1-\alpha} \tag{3}$$

The marginal product of capital:

$$\rho(v, t) = \alpha \frac{Q(v, t)}{I(v)} = A\alpha \exp[-\alpha\delta(t-v)] \exp[\lambda(1-\alpha)t] \left(\frac{L(v, t)}{I(v)}\right)^{1-\alpha} \tag{4}$$

The marginal product of labor:

$$w(t) = (1-\alpha) \frac{Q(v, t)}{L(v, t)} = A(1-\alpha) \exp[-\alpha\delta(t-v)] \exp[\lambda(1-\alpha)t] \left(\frac{L(v, t)}{I(v)}\right)^{-\alpha}$$

$$w(t)^{-(1-\alpha)/\alpha} = A^{-(1-\alpha)/\alpha}(1-\alpha)^{-(1-\alpha)/\alpha} \exp[(1-\alpha)\delta(t-v)] \tag{5}$$

$$\times \exp[-\lambda((1-\alpha)^2/\alpha)t] \left(\frac{L(v, t)}{I(v)}\right)^{1-\alpha}$$

$$\rho(v, t) = A^{1/\alpha}\alpha(1-\alpha)^{+(1-\alpha)/\alpha} \exp[-\delta(t-v)] \exp[((1-\alpha)/\alpha)\lambda t]\, w(t)^{-((1-\alpha)/\alpha)}$$

Since the real wage w grows at rate λ,

$$\rho(v, t) = A^{1/\alpha}\alpha(1-\alpha)^{(1-\alpha)/\alpha} \exp[-\delta(t-v)]\exp[((1-\alpha)/\alpha)\lambda t]$$
$$\times (w(0)\exp[\lambda t])^{-(1-\alpha/\alpha)}$$

$$\rho(v, t) = A^{1/\alpha}\alpha(1-\alpha)^{(1-\alpha)/\alpha} \exp[-\delta(t-v)]\, w(0)^{-((1-\alpha)/\alpha)}$$

Thus $\rho(v, t)$ can be written as $\rho(t-v)$ and indeed

$$\rho(v, t) = \rho(t-v) = \rho(v,v)\exp[-\delta(t-v)] = \rho(0)\exp[-\delta(t-v)] \quad (6)$$

To find r we set $\int_0^\infty \exp[-r(t-v)]\rho(t-v)d(t-v) = 1$.
Therefore

$$\rho(0)\int_0^\infty \exp[-r(t-v)]\exp[-\delta(t-v)]\,d(t-v) = 1 \quad (7)$$

and $r = \rho(0)-\delta$. From section 1 we know

$$\rho(0)\int_0^\infty \exp[-g(t-v)]\exp[-\delta(t-v)]\,d(t-v) = \frac{\alpha}{s}$$

Therefore

$$\rho(0) = \frac{\alpha}{s}(g+\delta) \quad (8)$$

Since $g = n + \lambda$ we have

$$r = \frac{\alpha}{s}(n+\lambda+\delta)-\delta \quad (9)$$

(b) Embodied progress:
In this case:

$$Q(v, t) = A(I(v)\exp[-\delta(t-v)])^\alpha(L(v, t)\exp[\lambda v])^{1-\alpha} \quad (10)$$

By reasoning similar to (a) we obtain

$$\rho(v, t) = A^{1/\alpha}\alpha(1-\alpha)^{(1-\alpha)/\alpha} \exp[-\delta(t-v)]\exp[((1-\alpha)/\alpha)\lambda v]$$
$$\times w(t)^{-((1-\alpha)/\alpha)}$$

$$\rho(v, t) = A^{1/\alpha}\alpha(1-\alpha)^{(1-\alpha)/\alpha}\exp[(-\delta-(1-\alpha)\lambda/\alpha)(t-v)]$$
$$\times w(0)^{-((1-\alpha)/\alpha)}$$

$$(11)$$

Once again $\rho(v, t)$ can be written as $\rho(t-v)$, and

$$\rho(t-v) = \rho(0) \exp[-(\delta +(1-\alpha)\lambda/\alpha)(t-v)]$$

The same procedure used in (a) gives:

$$r = \rho(0) - \delta - \frac{(1-\alpha)\lambda}{\alpha} \tag{12}$$

and

$$\rho(0) = \frac{\alpha}{s}\left(g + \delta + \frac{(1-\alpha)}{\alpha}\lambda \right)$$

$$= \frac{\alpha}{s}(n + \lambda + \delta) + \frac{(1-\alpha)}{s}\lambda \tag{13}$$

Therefore

$$r = \frac{\alpha}{s}(n + \lambda + \delta) - \delta + \left(\frac{1-\alpha}{s}\right)\lambda - \left(\frac{1-\alpha}{\alpha}\right)\lambda . \tag{14}$$

References

(1) Kenneth Arrow, "The Economic Implications of Learning by Doing," *Review of Economic Studies* (June 1962), 155-73.

(2) Edward F. Denison, *The Sources of Economic Growth in the United States and the Alternatives Before Us* (Washington, D.C.: Committee on Economic Development, 1962), Chapter 12.

(3) T.C. Koopmans, "On the Concept of Optimal Economic Growth," Cowles Foundation Discussion Paper No. 163, 1963, presented at a joint session of the American Economic Association and the Econometric Society, "Intertemporal Economic Theory," in the Boston Meetings, December, 1963.

(4) Robert F. Lanzillotti, "Pricing Objectives in Large Companies," *American Economic Review* **(December 1958), 921-40.**

(5) E.S. Phelps, "The Golden Rule of Accumulation," *American Economic Review* (September 1961), 638-42.

(6) E.S. Phelps, "The New View of Investment: A Neoclassical Analysis," *Quarterly Journal of Economics* (November 1962), 548-67.

(7) R.M. Solow, "Investment and Technical Progress," in K.J. Arrow, S. Karlin, and P. Suppes (eds.), *Mathematical Methods in the Social Sciences 1959* (Stanford, Calif.: Stanford University Press, 1960), 89-104.

(8) R.M. Solow, "Technical Progress, Capital Formation, and Economic Growth," *American Economic Review* (May 1962), 76-86.

CHAPTER 12

NEOCLASSICAL GROWTH WITH FIXED FACTOR PROPORTIONS

1. Introduction

We analyze in this paper a completely aggregated model of production in which output is produced by inputs of homogeneous labor and heterogeneous capital goods, and allocated either to consumption or to use as capital goods. Allocations are irreversible: capital goods can never be directly consumed. Fixed coefficients rule: any concrete unit of capital has a given output capacity and requires a given complement of labor. Technological progress continuously differentiates new capital goods from old. But we assume that the "latest model" in capital goods has no smaller capacity and no higher labor requirement than any older model capital goods with the same reproduction cost. Thus each instant's gross investment will take the form of the latest model capital. There is no problem of the optimal "depth" of capital. The main effect of an *increase* in gross investment is to modernize the capital stock in use.

One normal consequence of technological progress will be a rising trend of the real wage rate. Since existing capital operates under fixed coefficients, there will eventually come a time in the life of every vintage of investment when the wage costs of using it to produce a unit of output will exceed one unit of output. At that instant the investment may be said to have become obsolete as a result of the competition of more modern capital; it will be retired from production – permanently, unless the real wage should temporarily fall.

We have several motives for wishing to analyze so special a model.

1. Capital theory seems – perhaps inevitably – to consist of a catalog of special models, distinguished by the different ways time and durable com-

This is part of a paper prepared with R. Solow, C. von Weizsäcker, and M. Yaari, and is reprinted from *Review of Economic Studies*, 33 (April 1966), 79–89, and 98–103. Footnotes and figures have been renumbered.

modities enter the process of production. Since this simple, but not trivial, model has not been studied as a growth model before, we think it a worthwhile addition to the catalog. [1]

2. The model contributes something more than mere completeness to the catalog. It isolates the effects of what has been called "quickening" — hastening the practical introduction of newly discovered techniques into production — from those of "deepening" of capital. "Widening" can also be analytically excluded by considering the special case of a constant labor force.

3. The literature sometimes suggests, or seems to suggest, that what are called "neoclassical" *modes of analysis* — we emphasize that we do not refer to assumptions of Say's Law — require for their validity or utility that capital and labor be directly and smoothly substitutable for one another. This paper provides a counterexample. Although there is no scope for substitution *ex post* or *ex ante*, we show that the basic neoclassical methods do function and give the expectable results. No use is made of any "generalized stock of capital."

4. What is true is that the basic neoclassical methods apply when and only when output is limited by the availability of resources, not by effective demand. Most of our argument is conducted under the assumption that full employment of labor is the bottleneck to production. This assumption may be regarded as appropriate to a planned economy, or to a decentralized economy with an effective fiscal policy. An important task of economic theory is to find some way of unifying the theory of production and the theory of effective demand. The model of this paper is, we believe, particularly suited for this purpose, precisely because it gives effect to the common casual empirical belief that in the short run the scope for changing factor proportions is small. On the other hand, the model no doubt limits excessively the scope for changing factor proportions over long periods of time. Like all aggregate models, it must ignore the effects of intercommodity shifts.

5. Finally, it is sometimes asserted that in modern industrial economies *ex ante* choice of techniques is in fact unimportant; that at any instant of time one technique — the latest one — effectively dominates all others for all thinkable configurations of factor prices. We do not know how nearly true this assertion is (particularly in macroeconomic terms). But the model of production studied in this paper is presumably the appropriate vehicle for studying the implications of the assertion.

2. Physical Relations

2.1. Technological Assumptions

The model assumes fixed-coefficient technology with embodied technical progress. Once capital has been put into place, there is no possibility of substituting capital for labor or vice versa; the output-capital and output-labor coefficients are fixed for the life of the capital. Neither are there any effective possibilities of *ex ante* substitution between labor and capital. For a business investing in new capital, only one pair of these coefficients, the pair which will characterize this capital so long as it is operating, is available. (This is not strictly true, since an investing business could always use older technology characterized by different coefficients. But this is an empty qualification, because in the model an investor will never prefer older technology to new technology no matter what wage rate and interest rate he faces.) Technical progress consists of improvement in one or both of the output-input coefficients. But the improved coefficients apply only to new vintage capital, not to investments made in the past. Since the model has only one commodity, serving indifferently as capital good and consumer good, investment can be measured unambiguously in physical units equal to the opportunity cost of one unit of consumption.

Formally, let:

$Y(t, v)dv$ be the rate of gross output (physical units per year) at time t, produced on capital of vintage v, *i.e.* capital installed during a period $(v, v + dv)$, where necessarily $v \leqslant t$.

$I(v)$ the rate of gross investment (physical units per year) at time v.

$I(v)dv$ the amount of capital (physical units) installed in the period $(v, v + dv)$.

$N(t, v)dv$ the rate of employment of labor (men) at time t on capital of vintage v.

$\lambda(v)$ the technologically determined output per year per man producible on capital of vintage v.

$\mu(v)$ the technologically determined output per year producible with one unit of capital of vintage v.

$Y(t)$ total gross output per year, summed over all vintages of capital, at time t.

$N(t)$ total employment (men), summed over all vintages of capital, at time t.

$L(t)$ total labor supply at time t.

$w(t)$ the real wage rate (physical units per man-year).

$\rho(t, v)dv$ the quasi rent earned at time t on one unit of capital of vintage v (a pure number).

$m(t)$ the age of the oldest capital in use at time t (years).

The assumptions about production outlined verbally above can be summarized in the following production function for output from capital of vintage v ($\leqslant t$)

$$Y(t, v) = \text{Min}\{\lambda(v)N(t, v), \mu(v)I(v)\} . \tag{1}$$

This formulation ignores physical depreciation and assumes that capital is perfectly durable. This assumption has the advantage of simplicity, and it permits the model to bring out clearly the economics of obsolescence. Capital wears forever, but it is not in general used forever — better, more modern, capital displaces it. At the same time, physical depreciation of simple types can be allowed without essentially altering the behavior of the economy described by the model.

In general, we shall be interested in situations where, for vintages v in use:

$$Y(t, v) = \lambda(v)N(t, v) = \mu(v)I(v) . \tag{2}$$

Unless this condition is met, capital of vintage v is not being efficiently used. It makes no sense to overman capital, and in a continuous time model it will not be undermanned either. In a discrete time model, it would be conceivable that some but not all of the capital invested during period v might be in use at a later time t. This possibility does not arise here because there is not a finite mass of capital of any instantaneous vintage. If any vintage v capital is in use, all of it is. Note that there is no specifically "vintage v" labor. Any labor available at time t will do. One unit of vintage v capital employs $\mu(v)/\lambda(v)$ workers when it is in use.

2.2. Kinds of Technical Progress

The coefficients $\lambda(v)$ and $\mu(v)$ carry technical progress. We shall assume that each of these coefficients is a nondecreasing function of v. This guarantees that no earlier technology is ever preferred to the newest. The model does not explain the advance of technical knowledge; it is autonomous, requires no

productive resources, and cannot be accelerated or retarded. A more complete
model would relate progress not just to the passage of time but to production
experience (as is done, for instance, by Arrow, 1) and to the use of resources
in research and development (see, *e.g.*, Uzawa, 3).

Three special kinds of technical progress are depicted in Figures 12.1,
12.2, and 12.3. Capital-labor isoquants are shown for a fixed rate of output
under vintage v_0 technology, and under technology of a later vintage v_1. The
arrows show in each case the direction in which technical progress moves the
isoquant.

The three special cases are:

(a) $\lambda'(v) > 0, \mu'(v) = 0$ Purely labor-augmenting or "Harrod-neu-
                                             tral" progress

(b) $\dfrac{\lambda'(v)}{\lambda(v)} = \dfrac{\mu'(v)}{\mu(v)} > 0$ $\dfrac{\lambda(v)}{\mu(v)}$ constant. "Hicks-neutral" progress

(c) $\lambda'(v) = 0, \mu'(v) > 0$ Purely capital-augmenting progress

2.3. Aggregative Implications

At any time t, the total labor supply $L(t)$ is assumed to be given exogenously. This is not necessarily equal to aggregate employment $N(t)$. The past
history of gross investment $I(v)$ determines the capital available for use at
time t. The maximum possible employment which this investment history

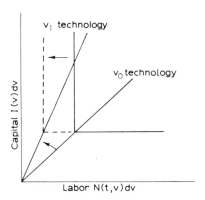

Fig. 12.1. Purely labor-augmenting technical progress, "Harrod-neutral." Capital-labor
ratio increases.

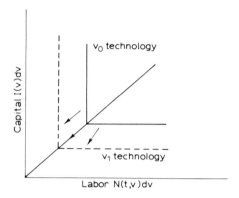

Fig. 12.2. "Hicks-neutral." Capital-labor ratio constant.

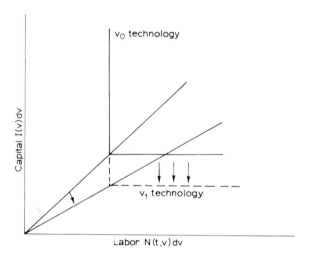

Fig. 12.3. Purely capital-augmenting technical progress. Capital-labor ratio falls.

permits is:

$$N^*(t) = \int_{-\infty}^{t} \frac{\mu(v)}{\lambda(v)} I(v)dv$$

and this requires all (surviving) capital to be in use. The integral may diverge, in which case labor can never be in surplus. For simplicity we assume $N^*(t)$

finite. There are three important possible regimes:

(I) $L(t) \geqslant N^*(t) = N(t)$.   Labor surplus

All capital is in use. Labor is unemployed because of a shortage of capital. Or, when $L(t) = N^*(t)$, labor is just adequate to man all the capital.

(II) $N(t) = L(t) < N^*(t)$.   Full employment

Some capital is left unused because the labor supply is insufficient.

(III) $N(t) < L(t) \leqslant N^*(t)$.   Keynesian unemployment

Some labor, and an associated amount of capital, is unemployed because demand is insufficient.

2.4. Allocation of Labor

What is the optimal allocation of labor over the available capital of various vintages? Or, to put the same question somewhat differently, which vintages should be used and which left unused? Let u be an unutilized vintage and v an utilized vintage. If an allocation is optimal, it should not be possible to increase total output by shifting a unit of labor from vintage v capital to vintage u capital. Such a shift would increase output by $\lambda(u)$ and diminish it by $\lambda(v)$. Hence an optimal allocation requires that:

$$\lambda(u) \leqslant \lambda(v) \text{ for any unutilized vintage } u \text{ and utilized vintage } v \text{ .} \qquad (3)$$

Provided $\lambda'(v) > 0$, optimal allocation is very simple and obvious: $\lambda(u) < < \lambda(v)$ if and only if $u < v$. No vintage should be left unutilized if an older vintage is in use. A rational planner allocating a given total employment $N(t)$ would first man the newest equipment, then the next newest, and so on until he runs out of labor (or out of equipment). This is also what the competitive market will do. As we shall see, except in the labor surplus regime, the competitive real wage rate makes it unprofitable to operate the oldest equipment. Quasi rents obtainable at time t vary inversely with the age of capital – highest for the most modern, zero for the "cutoff" age, and negative for economically obsolete vintages.

2.5. The Purely Capital-Augmenting Case

If technical progress is purely capital-augmenting – $\lambda'(v) = 0$, the third of the special cases listed above – the allocation of employment among competing vintages of capital is indeterminate. Technical progress lowers the real cost of a unit of productive capacity. But once the capacity is in being, the marginal and average variable cost of output is the same on every vintage.

Therefore, this case is not very interesting. It reduces to these possibilities:
(a) In regime I, there is always ample labor to man the whole capital stock.
When $\lambda(v) = \lambda$, this implies:

$$N(t) = N^*(t) = \frac{1}{\lambda} Y(t) = \frac{1}{\lambda} \int_{-\infty}^{t} \mu(v)I(v)dv . \tag{4}$$

Let $s(t)$ be the ratio of gross saving to gross output at time t. Correspondingly, $1/\mu(t)$ is the marginal or incremental capital requirement per unit of output. We have, therefore, the familiar Harrod-Domar equation for the rate of
growth of output and employment:

$$\frac{N'(t)}{N(t)} = \frac{Y'(t)}{Y(t)} = \mu(t)s(t) . \tag{5}$$

If labor is truly in excess supply, its marginal product is zero and so is its
competitive real wage, or its shadow price in a planned economy. Correspondingly, the rent on capital of vintage v is its average product: $\mu(v)$. If $L(t)$ is
just equal to $N(t)$, then the price of labor $w(t)$ is indeterminate between zero
and its average product λ. Correspondingly, the quasi rent $\rho(t, v)$ on vintage v
capital is indeterminate between $\mu(v)$ and zero:

$$\rho(t, v) = \mu(v) \left(1 - \frac{w(t)}{\lambda} \right) \geqslant 0 . \tag{6}$$

(b) In the other two regimes, labor supply is not large enough to permit
utilization of all vintages of capital. The marginal product of capital is zero,
whatever its vintage. New capital has no advantage over old. If labor is fully
employed, its real wage is λ, its average product. This situation may, of
course, lead to Keynesian difficulties: full employment incomes might generate saving but — since profits are zero — not corresponding investment. Then
the result would be underutilization of both capital and labor, with the efficiency prices of factors again indeterminate.

2.6. Obsolescence and Income Distribution

So much for purely capital-augmenting technical progress. In all other
cases new vintages will always be preferred to older vintages. We disregard the
labor surplus regime as atypical for advanced economies. In cases of interest,
then, the age of the oldest capital in use, $m(t)$, is related to total employment

by the equation

$$N(t) = \int_{t-m(t)}^{t} \frac{\mu(v)}{\lambda(v)} I(v)dv . \tag{7}$$

On the other hand, there is a relation between $m(t)$ and aggregate output:

$$Y(t) = \int_{t-m(t)}^{t} \mu(v) I(v) dv . \tag{8}$$

Employment of a unit of additional labor at time t would permit the use of capital just beyond the cutoff point $m(t)$, adding to total output the average product of labor on capital of this vintage. The marginal product of labor, therefore, is $\lambda(t-m(t))$. (This is the value of $\partial Y(t)/\partial N(t)$, as may be ascertained by differentiating (7) and (8) with respect to $N(t)$.) The marginal product of capital of any vintage may also be found. An additional unit of capital of an active vintage v (v greater than $t-m(t)$) would permit added output of $\mu(v)$. But it would require shifting $\mu(v)/\lambda(v)$ units of labor away from the oldest vintage capital, reducing output by $\mu(v)/\lambda(v) \lambda(t-m(t))$. An additional unit of capital of an idle vintage adds nothing to output.

Under competition, we can identify the marginal product of labor with the real wage and the marginal product of capital of any vintage with its quasi rent:

$$w(t) = \lambda(t-m(t)) , \tag{9}$$

$$\rho(t, v) = \begin{cases} 0 & \text{if } v \leqslant t-m(t) \\ \mu(v) \left(1 - \frac{\lambda(t-m(t))}{\lambda(v)}\right) & \text{if } v \geqslant t-m(t) . \end{cases} \tag{10}$$

Together wages and quasi rents exhaust the output of active capital.

The history of a particular investment is this: Its average product remains constant. At the beginning it earns a positive rent, because it is superior to earlier vintages. But as still better capital comes into existence, wages rise and the rents on the investment decline. Finally, wages are bid up so high by the owners of modern equipment that the rent on the investment vanishes. It is obsolete and ceases to operate.

2.7. The Growth of Income

The growth of income may be decomposed into a part attributable to the growth of the labor force and another part associated with new investment. Differentiating (7) and (8), we obtain:

$$N'(t) = \frac{\mu(t)I(t)}{\lambda(t)} - \frac{\mu(t-m(t))}{\lambda(t-m(t))} I(t-m(t)) (1-m'(t))$$

$$Y'(t) = \mu(t)I(t) - \mu(t-m(t))I(t-m(t)) (1-m'(t))$$

$$\lambda(t-m(t))N'(t) = \mu(t) \frac{\lambda(t-m(t))}{\lambda(t)} I(t) - \mu(t-m(t))I(t-m(t)) (1-m'(t))$$

$$Y'(t) = N'(t)\lambda(t-m(t)) + I(t)\mu(t) \left(1 - \frac{\lambda(t-m(t))}{\lambda(t)}\right)$$

$$= N'(t)w(t) + I(t)\rho(t, t) \tag{11}$$

$$\frac{Y'(t)}{Y(t)} = \left(\frac{w(t)N(t)}{Y(t)}\right) \frac{N'(t)}{N(t)} + \rho(t, t) \frac{I(t)}{Y(t)}. \tag{12}$$

This decomposition is analogous to the more conventional one for models with substitution.

In regime II, full employment, causation may be interpreted in this manner: $L(t) = N(t) \to m(t) \to Y(t)$ and $w(t)$. The first causal arrow stands for (7), the second for (8). In the Keynesian regime III, output is determined by effective demand. The causation then runs the other way: $Y(t) \to w(t)$ and $m(t) \to N(t) < L(t)$. Now the first arrow stands for (8), the second for (7). In this interpretation, one can easily allow for feedback effects of income distribution on effective demand. Equations (11) and (12) apply under either interpretation.

If aggregate demand falls, the model says that plants shut down in order of their age. Aside from the usual complications of aggregation, this is realistic enough. Its corollary, however, is that the average and marginal products of labor rise as labor is laid off from the oldest and least efficient plants. Cyclical statistics indicate the opposite, apparently because, in recessions believed to be temporary, employers continue to man, at least partially, facilities which they are not using (and/or because the right-hand side of (7) contains an "overhead" component independent of current output).

2.8. *Exponential Growth under Full Employment: Labor-augmenting Progress*

In what follows, both technical progress and labor force growth are assumed to be exponential:

$$\begin{cases} L(t) = L_0 e^{nt} \\ \mu(v) = \mu_0 e^{\mu v} \\ \lambda(v) = \lambda_0 e^{\lambda v} \end{cases} \tag{13}$$

The *full employment* regime is analyzed first: the labor supply is fully used but is insufficient to man all physically surviving capital. Moreover, the simplest kind of technical progress is assumed – the purely labor-augmenting, "Harrod-neutral" variety, *i.e.*, $\mu(v) = \mu_0$ for all v.

2.9. Balanced Growth Paths

Consider paths along which gross investment has been growing exponentially forever: $I(t) = I_0 e^{gt}$. From (7) and (13) we calculate:

$$L_0 e^{nt} = \frac{\mu_0 I_0}{\lambda_0(g-\lambda)} e^{(g-\lambda)t}(1 - e^{-(g-\lambda)m(t)}) \text{ for all } t .$$

If $g = n + \lambda$, this equation can be satisfied with $m(t)$ constant. If $g \neq n + \lambda$, the equation can not be satisfied even with variable $m(t)$; for $g < n + \lambda$, the left-hand side must eventually outstrip the right while $g > n + \lambda$ implies that $m(t) \to 0$ which in turn implies that gross investment eventually exceeds gross output (see 18). Therefore:

(i) $g = n + \lambda$, the usual formula for the "natural rate of growth" under Harrod-neutral technical progress; and

(ii) $m(t)$ is a constant, say m, satisfying

$$L_0 = \frac{\mu_0 I_0}{\lambda_0 n} (1 - e^{-nm}) .$$

$$m = -\frac{1}{n} \log \left(1 - \frac{\lambda_0 n L_0}{\mu_0 I_0}\right) . \tag{14}$$

For this formula to make sense, it is necessary that $\lambda_0 n L_0 < \mu_0 I_0$. The meaning of this restriction is easily seen after it is rewritten:

$$n L_0 e^{nt} < \frac{\mu_0 I_0 e^{gt}}{\lambda_0 e^{\lambda t}} .$$

In this form it says that the increment to the labor force must be smaller than the labor required to man the brand new capital: the gap is to be filled with the labor that had been operating the capital (of age m) now being retired. If the inequality is not satisfied, the length of life of capital will have to be extended indefinitely and, if N^* is finite, labor will eventually become surplus. This puts a lower limit on I_0 (cf. vi below).

(iii) $\rho(t, t)$ is constant;

$$\rho(t, t) = \mu_0(1 - e^{-\lambda m}) . \qquad (15)$$

(iv) $w(t)$ grows exponentially at rate λ;

$$w(t) = (\lambda_0 e^{-\lambda m}) e^{\lambda t} ; \qquad (16)$$

(v) $Y(t)$ grows exponentially at rate g; from (8)

$$Y(t) = \frac{\mu_0 I_0}{g} (1 - e^{-gm}) e^{gt} . \qquad (17)$$

(vi) From (17) it follows that the gross saving ratio, $s(t)$, defined as $I(t)/Y(t)$, is a constant depending on m:

$$s = \frac{g}{\mu_0(1 - e^{-gm})} = \frac{I_0}{Y_0} . \qquad (18)$$

If the saving rate thus calculated exceeds one, it means that even with consumption reduced to zero the economy is incapable of producing the minimal equipment required to employ the whole labor force, and eventually a labor surplus situation must emerge (cf. ii above).

2.10. Alternative Saving Rates

According to (18) the path corresponding to a high saving ratio is characterized by low m, quick obsolescence, modern capital. In the same sense, a low saving ratio means a long economic life for capital. Eliminating I_0 between (14) and (17) shows that a path with low m and high s has a high Y_0, as in Figure 12.4.

Not all values of s and m are consistent with balanced growth of this kind, at the "natural" rate $g = \lambda + n$. At one extreme, the lower limit on the saving ratio s is g/μ_0. This is the value of s for which m must be infinity in (18). It corresponds, therefore, to a situation in which, according to (14), the rate of investment is just sufficient to employ increments to the labor force without transferring any workers from obsolescent capital. $L(t)$ and $N(t)$ are equal to $N^*(t)$ and all are growing at rate n. But because full employment requires that infinitely old capital be left in use, the competitive equilibrium real wage, according to (16), must be zero!

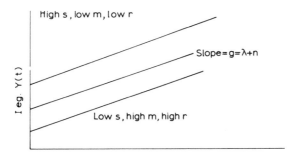

Fig. 12.4. Balanced Growth Rate.

Suppose the saving ratio is still smaller, so that $s\mu_0$ is less than g. If no capital ever becomes obsolete, the stock of capital will grow at the rate $s\mu_0$. But with the number of workers growing at rate n and the number of workers required per machine falling at rate λ, the stock of capital must grow at rate g to provide enough places. If $s\mu_0 < g$, therefore, new investment is insufficient to employ the natural increase in the labor force, much less to require release of any labor from older capital. So long as any capital is unused, previously submarginal vintages will be brought into use. As labor goes to work on older and older vintages, the real wage falls. The limit, of course, is the labor surplus regime.

The highest conceivable saving ratio (in a closed economy) is 1, and the correspondingly shortest capital lifetime m is given by

$$1 = \frac{g}{\mu_0(1 - e^{-gm})}.$$

(This has a positive solution for m provided $g < \mu_0$; otherwise, as remarked above, the need for new capital surpasses total output.) But this path, which yields the highest output path in Figure 12.4, is obviously not the path of highest consumption.

2.11. *The Golden Rule Path*

There is indeed a "golden rule" path — the balanced-growth path on which, given the development of the labor force $L(t)$, consumption is higher at every point in time than on any other balanced-growth path. Along this path, (1) the saving ratio is equal to the share of capital in gross product; and (2) the rate of interest or marginal efficiency of capital is equal to the growth rate.

These are familiar neoclassical or neo-neoclassical propositions, and it is of interest that they apply for the fixed-coefficient technology of the model under discussion here.

To prove the first proposition, it is necessary to show how the share of capital α depends on the obsolescence period m. The wage bill $N(t)w(t)$ is equal to $N(0)e^{nt}e^{\lambda(t-m)}$. Since $Y(t) = Y(0)e^{(n+\lambda)t}$, labor's share is constant over time along any path with exponential investment and, therefore, constant $\dot{m}$ and constant s:

$$1 - \alpha = \frac{N(t)w(t)}{Y(t)} = \frac{N(0)\lambda_0 e^{-\lambda m}}{Y(0)}. \tag{19}$$

From (14) and (17) this becomes:

$$1 - \alpha = \frac{g(e^{-\lambda m} - e^{-gm})}{n(1 - e^{-gm})}. \tag{20}$$

From (20) it follows that α is an increasing function of m — running from zero for $m = 0$, i.e., when all input is current labor input, to 1 for $m = \infty$, i.e., when labor is in surplus.

Similarly (18) shows that s, the saving ratio, is a decreasing function of m. Both these relationships are shown in Figure 12.5. At m^*, $s = \alpha$. That is:

$$\frac{g}{\mu(1 - e^{-gm^*})} = \frac{n(1 - e^{-gm^*}) - g(e^{-\lambda m^*} - e^{-gm^*})}{n(1 - e^{-gm^*})}. \tag{21}$$

We must show that this value of m^* also maximizes $C(0)$.

$$C(0) = (1-s)Y(0) = \frac{1-s}{s} \cdot \frac{\lambda_0 n N(0)}{\mu_0(1 - e^{-nm})}.$$

For given $N(0)$, $C(0)$ will be maximized if

$$\frac{1-s}{s(1 - e^{-nm})} \text{ is maximized},$$

i.e., if

$$\frac{\mu_0(1 - e^{-gm}) - g}{g(1 - e^{-nm})} \text{ is maximized with respect to } m.$$

The condition for the maximum,

$$g(1 - e^{-nm})\mu_0 g e^{-gm} = (\mu_0(1 - e^{-gm}) - g)gne^{-nm}, \tag{22}$$

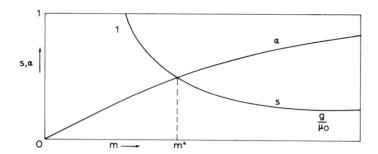

Fig. 12.5. Balanced growth paths. Relations of capital share α and saving ratio s to obsolescence period m.

reduces to (21), the condition for $\alpha = s$. Since this equation determines a unique local extremum, which is a maximum, the first formulation of the golden rule theorem is proved. The second version of the theorem states that along the balanced growth path with maximum consumption the rate of interest is equal to the growth rate. That statement is also true in this model, but the proof is postponed until the interest rate or marginal efficiency of capital has been introduced more formally.

3. Competitive Value Relations [2]

3.1. Wages, Quasi Rents, and Marginal Products

The impossibility of direct substitution between labor and capital goods in this model means that there is no "intensive margin." But there is an "extensive margin" at which, under competition, price relationships are determined. The elementary calculations have been made in section 2, (6 and 7), and we recapitulate them here.

Capital goods of age $m(t)$ are on the verge of obsolescence; they are "no-rent" capital. If they earned a positive rent their owners would not be about to withdraw them from production under tranquil competitive conditions. Since wages are the only prime cost in this model, the real wage must equal the average product of labor on no-rent capital. This yields, as before,

$$w(t) = \lambda(t-m(t)) . \tag{9}$$

Younger capital goods are intramarginal, and earn a differential quasi rent equal to the difference between output and labor costs; older ones could not cover prime costs if they were operated. Thus, with $\rho(t, v)$ representing the real quasi rent earned at time t by capital goods of vintage v,

$$\rho(t, v) = 0 \qquad\qquad\qquad v \leqslant t - m(t)$$

$$= \mu(v) \left(1 - \frac{\lambda(t-m(t))}{\lambda(v)}\right) \qquad v \geqslant t - m(t) . \qquad (10)$$

In 2, (6 and 7) it is shown that the competitive real wage and quasi rent play the role of social marginal product of labor and of capital goods of vintage v: $w(t)$ is the increase in aggregate output permitted by one extra unit of employment, and $\rho(t, v)$ is the increase in aggregate output permitted by the availability of one extra unit of vintage v capital.

3.2. Capital Values

Under conditions near to steady growth, the economic lifetime of capital will not change very much and, therefore, $\rho(t, v)$ will fall through time for each fixed v. (In the short run a sharp increase in output and employment may require a sudden increase in $m(t)$ and bring about a temporary rise in the quasi rents on existing capital. Even previously retired capital will be activated.) If $m(t)$ does not fluctuate much, it is reasonable to suppose that the market can foresee with fair accuracy the pattern of quasi rents a unit of capital can be expected to earn. The market value of any existing unit of capital will be the present value of the expected quasi rents, discounted at the market rate of interest. Let $P(t, v)$ be the price at time t of a unit of capital of vintage v, and let $r(t)$ be the rate of interest at time t. Then

$$P(t, v) = \int_t^\tau \rho(u, v) e^{-\int_t^u r(z)dz} \, du = \mu(v) \int_t^\tau \left[1 - \frac{\lambda(u-m(u))}{\lambda(v)}\right] e^{-\int_t^u r(z)dz} \, du . \qquad (23)$$

In this expression $\tau = \tau(v)$ is the root of the equation $\rho(\tau, v) = 0$; that is, it is the instant at which capital of vintage v will be retired. [3] If m is constant, then of course $\tau = v + m$, and in any case $\tau = v + m(\tau)$.

For existing capital (23) is all there is to be said. When $v = t$, (23) gives $P(t, t)$, the market price of a new machine at the moment of its construction. In tranquil competitive equilibrium, $P(t, t)$ must also equal the cost of production of a new machine of vintage t. ($P(t, t)$ can fall short of the cost of production if gross investment is zero, but we shall ignore that possibility.) Since this is a one-sector model we can, as mentioned in 2.1, measure capital goods in units identical with the unit of output. Thus $P(t, t) = 1$, and we have for every t

$$1 = \int_t^\tau \rho(u, t)e^{-\int_t^u r(z)dz} \, du \quad ^4 \tag{24}$$

or

$$1 = \int_0^{m(\tau)} \rho(x + t, t)e^{-\int_t^{t+x} r(z)dz} \, dx \, . \tag{24'}$$

From (23) we can extract the well-known equilibrium condition

$$\rho(t, v) + \frac{\partial P(t, v)}{\partial t} = r(t)P(t, v) \, . \tag{25}$$

The value of the stock of capital is

$$K(t) = \int_{t-m(t)}^t P(t, v)I(v)dv \, . \tag{26}$$

(Here we use again the assumption that the earnings of any particular investment fall eventually to zero and do not revive.) Now, by total differentiation with respect to t and use of (25) we find

$$I(t)-K'(t) = \int_{t-m(t)}^t \rho(t, v)I(v)dv - r(t)K(t) \, . \tag{27}$$

$K'(t)$ can be identified as net investment and $r(t)K(t)$ as net profits. Thus the difference between gross investment and net investment is the same as the difference between gross quasi rents and net profits. Both can be identified as "true depreciation"; since we have ignored physical depreciation, only "obsolescence" remains. We can let $Z(t)$ stand for net output and $C(t)$ for consumption and write the accounting identities

$$Y(t) = C(t) + I(t) = w(t)N(t) + \int_{t-m(t)}^t \rho(t, v)I(v)dv \, ,$$

$$Z(t) = C(t) + K'(t) = w(t)N(t) + r(t)K(t) \, .$$

Equipped with these definitions and relations we can experiment with hypotheses that make net saving depend in one way or another on net income or net profits. But not much can be accomplished at this level of generality, so we turn to our standard special case.

3.3. Harrod-Neutrality and Balanced Growth: The Interest Rate

Under the assumptions of section 2.9 technical progress is purely labor-augmenting and gross investment grows exponentially. Along such a path, as we saw, $m(t)$ is constant. From (10) and (13)

$$\rho(t, v) = 0 \qquad\qquad \text{if } v \leqslant t-m ,$$

$$= \mu_0(1 - e^{\lambda(t-v-m)}) ; \qquad \text{if } v \geqslant t-m . \qquad (28)$$

(24) becomes

$$1 = \mu_0 \int_t^{t+m} (1 - e^{\lambda(u-t-m)}) e^{- \int_t^u r(z)dz} \, du . \qquad (29)$$

Solution of this integral equation gives the equilibrium interest rate as a function of time on a balanced-growth path. Experience with Harrod-neutrality and balanced growth in other models suggests that the interest rate will be constant. Since the interest rate is required to discount to unity the stream of quasi rents expected from any newly built item of capital, and since (28) shows that the current quasi rent depends only on the age $(t-v)$ of a unit of capital, it is indeed hard to see how any nonconstant interest rate can do the trick. In fact, none can.

Substitution of $r(z) = r$ in (29) and integration yields

$$1 = \frac{\mu_0}{r} (1 - e^{-rm}) - \frac{\mu_0}{r-\lambda} (e^{-\lambda m} - e^{-rm})$$

$$= F(r) . \qquad (30)$$

It is easily seen that $F(-\infty) = \infty$ and $F(\infty) = 0$; since $F(r)$ is continuous, (30) has at least one root. Since $F'(r) < 0$ (best seen directly from (29)) there is exactly one root. (That root may be negative; but not if the undiscounted sum of quasi rents exceeds unity.) Thus if technical progress is Harrod-neutral there is one and only one constant interest rate compatible with competitive equilibrium along a path of steady growth. [5]

We have established that, with exponential, purely labor-augmenting technical progress, the only competitive equilibrium interest rate compatible with a permanent path of balanced growth is a constant interest rate, namely the unique real root of (30). Since the instantaneous interest rate is constant, the yield curve or term structure of interest rates is flat.

According to (30) r depends on μ_0, λ and m; through (18) r depends also on the other parameters, n and the gross saving ratio s. Holding μ_0 and λ constant, one can calculate that $\partial r/\partial m > 0$; if one compares two steady growth paths with the same μ_0 and λ but with different m, the path with longer lifetime for capital will be the one with higher interest rate. This sounds "un-Austrian"; indeed the mechanism is very different from the economics of roundaboutness. From (18), a higher m is associated with a lower s; with lower s, full employment requires the break-even margin to be pushed back to older machines. Thus a lower saving rate implies a higher m, which implies a higher rate of interest. This result is entirely conventional. Similarly (18) shows that, with given s $\partial m/\partial g > 0$. Since $g = n + \lambda$, a steady growth path with higher n will have higher m and higher r; other things equal, faster growth in the labor force favors a higher rate of profit. (Remember that full employment, or at least a constant unemployment rate, is simply assumed.)

The relation between r and λ for given s, is more complicated because λ appears directly in (29) or (30). Nevertheless, it can be shown from (29) and (18) that $\partial r/\partial \lambda > 0$. In this model faster Harrod-neutral technical progress with unchanged saving ratio always implies a higher rate of interest. The key to this result is that, from (18), $\partial m/\partial \lambda = 1/g(1/s\mu_0 - g) - m$; and, again from (18), $s\mu_0 - g = g/1 - e^{-gm} - g = g/e^{gm} - 1 < 1/m$. Thus $\partial m/\partial \lambda > 0$; with given s, a faster rate of technical progress actually lengthens the economic lifetime of capital. The greater initial productivity advantage of new capital must outweigh the more rapid rate of improvement of capital still to come.

By letting $r \to 0$ in (30), we find the m corresponding to a zero rate of interest. This m_1 satisfies

$$\lambda = \mu_0(\lambda m_1 - 1 - e^{-\lambda m_1}) .$$

Since the right-hand side increases monotonically from zero at $m = 0$ to $+\infty$ as $m \to \infty$, there is always a lifetime short enough to reduce the rate of interest to zero. From 2.11, however, the shortest m, say m_2, attainable by a closed economy in balanced growth is associated with $s = 1$, and satisfies $\mu_0(1 - e^{-gm_2}) = g$. Depending on the other parameters, m_1 may exceed, equal, or fall short of m_2. In the first case, $r = 0$ for some saving rate less than unity; in the second case $r = 0$ for $s = 1$; in the third case, the rate of interest remains positive even if all of output is saved and invested.

At the other end of the spectrum, as $m \to \infty$, $r \to \mu_0$ and this is the highest profit rate the technology can generate. For then the real wage is zero and investment of one unit of output earns a perpetuity of μ_0 units of output per unit time. The saving rate corresponding to infinite lifetime is $s = g/\mu_0$.

3.4. The Golden Rule Path Once More

In 2.12, it was shown that a steady growth path on which gross investment is, always equal to gross quasi rent generates the highest consumption path among all steady growth paths. We can now see that the other standard characterization of the "Golden Rule," that the rate of interest equals the rate of growth, also holds in this model. It is only necessary to put $r = g$ in (30) and observe that the resulting equation is the same as (21) or (22).

Notes

[1] The model was formulated and studied in detail by Salter (2), from a point of view which is somewhat different from ours.

[2] Section 3 of the original article has been omitted.

[3] We assume for simplicity that it is correctly foreseen that capital, once retired, will never be called back into production by a "cyclical" increase in output and employment.

[4] This can be regarded as an integral equation for the unknown interest rate as a function of time. The substitution

$$R(u) = \exp(-\int_0^u r(z)dz)$$ throws (24) into the more familar form

$$R(t) = \int^{\tau(t)} \rho(u, t)R(u)du.$$ Similarly for (24') .

[5] The more complicated proof that the interest rate *must* be constant is given in the original version, but omitted here.

References

[1] K.J. Arrow, "The Economic Implications of Learning by Doing," *Review of Economic Studies*, 29, 3, 1962.

[2] W.E.G. Salter, *Productivity and Technical Change,* Cambridge: 1960.

[3] H. Uzawa, "Optimum Technical Change in an Aggregative Model of Economic Growth," *International Economic Review*, 6, 1, 1965.

MONEY AND FINANCE

Chapter 13 can serve as a general introduction to Part III. It provides an overview of my approach to monetary theory and its relation to the important traditions in the field.

The significance of the question of the interest elasticity of the demand for money was mentioned above in connection with Chapter 3. The theoretical foundations for interest elasticity are discussed in Chapters 14 and 15, for transactions balances and "speculative" balances respectively.

The second article is also a contribution to the general theory of portfolio selection, developing and applying to economic analysis the mean-variance approach earlier introduced by Harry Markowitz. The article also states and proves what has come to be known as a separation theorem. The theorem concerns portfolios, in which one safe asset is mixed with n risky assets. The composition of the "mutual fund" of risky assets is independent of the degree of risk aversion of the investor. It depends only on the investor's estimates of the variances, covariances, and expected returns of the assets. Differences in risk aversion are reflected not in the composition of this fund but in the proportions in which the investor divides his wealth between the fixed-weight fund on the one hand and the safe asset on the other.

Considerable attention has been devoted to the theory of portfolio choice in general, and to the mean-variance simplification in particular, since 1958. For this reason I include as an Appendix to Chapter 15 a comment on two criticisms of the mean-variance approach, by Karl Borch and Martin Feldstein, published in the *Review of Economic Studies* in 1969.

While Chapters 14 and 15 concern the microeconomic behavioral foundations of monetary theory, the next six articles seek to place money in the economic and financial system as a whole. They present what I hope is a consistent and logical macroeconomic monetary theory. Chapter 22 complements the views on debt management presented in Chapter 21.

The theory presented in Part III assigns great power to monetary policy, but certainly not exclusive power. Fiscal policies and exogenous events in the private economy — even if they do not change monetary magnitudes — can and do affect the course of employment, production, and prices. The theory presented in Part III seeks, as one of its central purposes, to explain how various quantities of "money" are determined. But it does not regard changes in any of these quantities as necessary or sufficient measure of the impact of monetary policies and events on the economy. In these respects, the theory differs from the doctrines of "monetarism," whose leading exponent is Professor Milton Friedman. The final two chapters are articles in which I have commented on Professor Friedman's doctrines and findings.

CHAPTER 13

MONEY, CAPITAL, AND OTHER STORES OF VALUE

1. Monetary Economics and Rational Behavior

The intellectual gulf between economists' theory of the values of goods and services and their theories of the value of money is well known and periodically deplored. Twenty-five years after Hicks' eloquent call for a marginal revolution in monetary theory (4) our students still detect that their mastery of the presumed fundamental, theoretical apparatus of economics is put to very little test in their studies of monetary economics and aggregative models. As Hicks complained, anything seems to go in a subject where propositions do not have to be grounded in someone's optimizing behavior and where shrewd but casual empiricisms and analogies to mechanics or thermodynamics take the place of inferences from utility and profit maximization.

From the other side of the chasm, the student of monetary phenomena can complain that pure economic theory has never delivered the tools to build a structure of Hick's brilliant design. The utility maximizing individual and the profit maximizing firm know everything relevant about the present and future and about the consequences of their decisions. They buy and sell, borrow and lend, save and consume, work and play, live and let live, in a frictionless world; information, transactions, and decisions are costless. Money holdings have no place in that world, unless possession of green pieces of paper and yellow pieces of metal satisfies some ultimate miserly or numismatic taste. Wealth, of course, has the reflected utility of the future consumption it commands. But this utility cannot be imputed to money unless there are no higher yielding assets available. As Samuelson has pointed out (4, pp. 122-24), in a world of omniscient households and firms, dealing in strictly perfect markets, all vehicles of saving in use must bear the same rate of return. If "money" bears that yield, wealthholders will be indifferent

Reprinted from *American Economic Review (Papers and Proceedings)*, 51 (May 1961), 26-37.

between money and other stores of value – the demand for money will be indeterminate. If money fails to yield the going rate, no one will hold it. Even though money is required as a medium of exchange, transactors will suffer no cost or inconvenience by holding more lucrative assets at all times except the negligible microseconds before and after transactions.

The general sources of the "utility" of money have, of course, long been clear to monetary theorists. Lavington (9) and Pigou (13), for example, imputed to money a rate of return varying inversely with the size of money holdings relative to the transactions needs and total wealth of the holder. This return stands for the convenience and economy of having wealth readily available as means of payment, as well as the safety of money compared with other stores of value. The only alternative asset that these elders of the Cambridge school explicitly envisaged was capital investment. "This proportion [k] depends upon the convenience obtained and the risk avoided through the possession of [money], by the loss of real income involved through the diversion to this use of resources that might have been devoted to the production of future commodities. . . . k will be larger the less attractive is the production use and the more attractive is the rival money use of resources. The chief factor upon which the attractiveness of the production use depends is the expected fruitfulness of industrial activity" (13, pp. 166, 168). In short, an individual adjusts his money holding so that its marginal imputed return is equal to the rate available to him in capital investment. Paradoxically the Cambridge tradition did not build on these ideas of liquidity preference. Instead of being systematically related to the profitability of investment and to other variables affecting the rational calculations of wealth owners, the demand for money became a constant proportion of income. Marshall (11, p. 47) had explicitly mentioned wealth as well as income, but somehow wealth was dropped from the tradition. (k is not the only instance in English economics where a variable coefficient left unprotected by functional notation has quickly evolved into a constant in everyday use.) Hicks' prescription for monetary theory in 1935 was in much the same spirit as the approach of Lavington and Pigou. His strictures were nonetheless timely; the spirit of the original Cambridge theory had become obscured by the mechanical constant-velocity tradition.

Recent developments in economic theory have greatly improved the prospects of carrying out Hicks' "simplifying" suggestions and deriving rigorously the imputed return or marginal utility of money holdings in relation to their size. In the past decade theory has begun a systematic penetration of the murky jungle of frictions, market imperfections, and uncertainties. The theory of optimal inventory holdings, for example, shows how transactions and delivery costs must be balanced against interest and carrying costs. Applied to inventories of cash, the theory gives precision to the relation of cash holdings to the volume of nonfinancial transactions, the costs of asset exchanges, and the yields available on alternative assets (1) and (17). A parallel development has been the theory of choices involving risk. Applied to the general strategy of portfolio selection, the theory of risk aversion explains how money may find a place in a rationally diversified portfolio (10) and (18).

The new tools are constructing a bridge between general economic theory and monetary economics. More than that, they give promise at last of a general equilibrium theory of the capital account. Such a theory would explain both the balance-sheet choices of economic units as constrained by their net worths and the determination of yields in markets where asset supplies and demands are balanced. What characteristics of assets and of investors determine the substitutabilities or complementarities among a set of assets? Among the relevant properties with which the theory must deal are: costs of asset exchanges; predictability of real and money asset values at various future dates; correlations − positive, negative, or zero − among asset prospects; liquidity − the time it takes to realize full value of an asset reversibility − possibility and cost of simultaneously buying and selling an asset; the timing and predictability of investors' expected needs for wealth.

In a world of financial assets and well-developed capital markets, Keynes (7, pp. 166 and 168) was right in perceiving the tactical advantage to the theorist of treating separately decisions determining total wealth and its rate of growth and decisions regarding the composition of wealth. A theory of the income account concerns what goods and services are produced and consumed, and how fast nonhuman wealth is accumulated. The decision variables are flows. A theory of the capital account concerns the proportions in which various assets and debts appear in portfolios and balance sheets. The decision variables are stocks. Income and capital accounts are linked by accounting identities − e.g., increase in net worth equals saving plus capital appreciation − and by technological and financial stock-flow relations. Utilities and preference orderings attach to flows of goods and services; the values of stocks are entirely derivative from their ability to contribute to these flows. Some stock-flow relationships are so tight that this distinction is pedantic: the only way an art collector can obtain the flow of satisfactions of owning a particular *chef d'oeuvre* is to own it. But there is a vast menu of assets whose yields are generalized purchasing power, nothing less or more − investors do not have intrinsic preferences among engravings of security certificates.

2. The Capital Account in Aggregative Models

2.1. *Strictures on the Need for Explicit Assumptions*

Aggregative models of the income account reduce the dimensions of general equilibrium theory, purchasing definiteness in results at the risk of errors of aggregation. Commodities, prices, and factors of production are limited to one or two. For similar reasons, it is fruitful to limit the number of assets in aggregative theory of the capital account.

The first requisite of a theory of wealth composition is that decisions about assets and debts must, in the aggregate as for the individual, add up to the net worth of the moment, neither more nor less. Monetary theory needs to specify explicitly what forms the nonmonetary parts of wealth can take. Many confusions and disagreements can be traced to ambiguities and differences in assumptions about the nature of wealth. A theory should state the menu of assets assumed available, specifying which are components of net private wealth (capital stock plus government debt) and which are intermediate assets (private debts). Moreover, the independent interest rates in an aggregative system should be enumerated. An independent rate is one that is not tied to another yield by an invariant relationship determined outside the system; e.g., by a constant risk differential.

The basic means of payment of a country are generally demand "debts" of the central government. But there are also means of payment of private manufacture; indeed it is possible to imagine a pure credit economy without government debts of any variety, where all means of payment are private debts backed by private debts. Likewise it is possible to imagine a wholly nonmonetary public debt.

Monetary discussions suffer from confounding the effects of changing the supply of means of payment with the effects of changing the net value of private claims on the central government. The second kind of change takes time and requires private saving, absorbed in fiscal deficit, or dissaving equal to fiscal surplus. The first type of change can be accomplished instantaneously by exchanges of assets. When an author proposes to discuss the effects of changing the supply of money, is he imagining aggregate net worth to change simultaneously by the same amount? Effects that are due to increases of private wealth in the form of government debt should not be attributed to money per se. Sometimes we are asked to imagine that everyone wakes up to find his cash stock has doubled overnight and to trace subsequent adjustments. This mental experiment is harmless and instructive, provided its results are not considered indicative of changes in money supply engineered by normal central bank procedures. The overnight miracle increases equally money stocks and net worth; the gremlins who bring the money are not reported to take away bonds or IOU's. The repercussions are a mixture of effects: partly those of an unanticipated increase in net worth in the form of assets fixed in money value (as if the gremlins had brought bonds instead); partly those of an increase in the supply of means of payment relative to transactions needs and to other assets. The theory of real balance effect (12) is at the same time much more and much less than the theory of money.

Established procedure in aggregative model building is to specify the quantity of money, M, as an exogenous variable determined by the "monetary authorities." The practice is questionable when part of the money supply is manufactured by private enterprise. Banks are not arms of government. The true exogenous variables are the instruments of monetary control: the quantity of demand debt available to serve as primary bank reserves, the supplies of other kinds of government debt, required reserve ratios, the discount rate. Once these instrument variables are set, the interaction of bank and public preferences determines the quantity of money. No doubt a skillful central bank can generally manipulate its controls to keep M on target, but part of the job of monetary theory is to explain how. A theory which takes as data the instruments of control rather than M, will not break down if and when there are changes in the targets or the marksmanship of the authorities.

2.2. Two Models, Keynesian and Non-Keynesian

The assets of a formal model of Keynes' *General Theory* (7) appear to be four or possibly five in number: (1) government demand debt, serving either as means of payment or as bank reserves, (2) bank deposits, (3) long-term government bonds. (4) physical capital, i.e., stocks of *the* good produced on the income-account side of the model, and possibly (5) private debts, serving along with bonds (3) and demand debt (1) as assets held by the banking system against its monetary liabilities (2). Net private wealth is the sum of (1), (3), and (4).

Though there are four or five assets in this model, there are only two yields: the rate of return on money, whether demand debt or bank deposits, institutionally set at zero, and *the* rate of interest, common to the other two or three assets. For the nonmonetary assets of his systems, Keynes simply followed the classical theory of portfolio selection in perfect markets mentioned above; that is, he assumed that capital, bonds, and private debts are perfect substitutes in investors' portfolios. The marginal efficiency of capital must equal *the* rate of interest.

Keynes did not, of course, envisage literal equality of yields on consols, private debts, and equity capital. Indeed, he provides many perceptive observations on the sources and cyclical variations of the expectations and risk premiums that differentiate market yields. But in given circumstances these differentials are constants independent of the relative supplies of the assets and therefore inessential. Once one of the rates is set, the others must differ from it by appropriate allowances for risk and for expectations of price changes.

Thus Keynes had only one yield differential to explain within his theoretical model: the difference between the zero yield of money and *the* interest rate. This differential he explained in his theory of liquidity preference, which made the premium of bond yields above money depend on the stock of money relative to the volume of transactions and, presumably, aggregate wealth. Keynes departed from the classical model of portfolio choice and asset yields to explain money holdings, applying and developing an innovation borrowed from his own *Treatise* (8, pp. 140-44, 248-57), a rate differential that depends systematically on relative asset supplies.

Post-Keynesian aggregative theorists, whether disciples or opponents or just neutral fanciers of models, have stuck pretty close to the Keynesian picture of the capital account. For example, Patinkin (12) explicitly includes all the assets listed above, and no more, in his most comprehensive model. Like Keynes, he has only one interest rate to determine. His difference from Keynes is his real balance effect.

As Hicks (5), Kaldor (6), and others have pointed out, there are apparently no short-term obligations of fixed money value in the Keynesian scheme. Recognition of these near-moneys would add one asset category and a second interest rate to the Keynesian model of the capital account. Transactions costs become the major determinant of the money-short rate differential, and considerations of speculation and risk for investors of different types affect the size and sign of the short-long differential.

An entirely different monetary tradition begins with a two-asset world of money and capital and ignores to begin with all closer money substitutes of whatever maturity. Significantly, the authors of the Cambridge tradition, as mentioned above, regarded direct capital investment as *the* alternative to money holdings. Why did they fail to carry into their monetary theory the clear inference that the demand for money depends not only on the volume of transactions but also on the yield of capital? Perhaps the best guess is that for these economists the yield of capital was in the short run a constant. explained by productivity and thrift. Money balances were adjusting to a rate already determined, not to a rate their adjustment might help to determine.

On its own logic, therefore, the constant-velocity approximation is of little applicability in models where the rate of return on capital is variable. It is not applicable to cyclical fluctuations, where variations of employment affect the productivity of the given capital stock. It is not applicable to secular growth, if capital deepening or technological change alters the yield of capital.

Neither is the constant-velocity assumption applicable where money substitutes other than capital are available and have endogenously variable yields, for then the demand for money would depend on those yields. Paradoxically, the model of greatest popularity in everyday analysis of monetary policy really has no room for monetary policy per se. In the two-asset, money-capital economy there are no assets which the central bank and the banking system can buy or sell to change the quantity of money.

What is the mechanism by which a change in the quantity of money brings about the proportional change in money income that constant-velocity theory predicts? Sometimes the mechanism as described seems to assume a direct relationship between money holdings and spending on income account: When people have more money than they need, they spend it. It is as simple as that. Patinkin (12, Chapter 8) rightly objects that spending on income account should be related to excess wealth, not excess money. If the mechanism is a real balance effect, then it works only when new money is also new private wealth, accumulated by the public as a result of government spending financed at the printing press or the mint.

A mechanism more in the spirit of the arguments of Lavington, Pigou, and Hicks is that owners of wealth with excess money holdings seek to restore the balance of their capital accounts. Trying to shift from money to capital, they bid up the prices of the existing capital stock; and since new capital goods and old must bear comparable prices, prices also rise in commodity markets. The process ends when, and only when, money incomes have risen enough to absorb the new money into transactions balances. The real rate of return on the capital stock remains unchanged.

This mechanism can apply to increases in M due to expansion of bank lending – with private debts added to the menu of assets – as well as to increases associated with net saving. One aspect of the mechanism is then the process of which Wicksell (19) gave the classical description. Banks expand the money supply by offering to lend at a rate – the market rate – lower than the yield of capital -- the natural rate. Excess demand for capital by new borrowers bids up capital values, with the repercussions already described. Whether this process has an end or not depends on whether the banks' incentive to expand is extinguished by proportionate increases of money supply, money income, and prices. For a pure credit economy, where all means of payment are based on monetization of private debts, this model produces no equilibrium. The end to the Wicksellian process depends on banks' needs for reserves, whether enforced by legislation or by their own transactions and precautionary motives.

I have presented a modern version of a two-asset, money-capital economy in (16). Money and government debt are one and the same, and there are no private debts. The proportions in which owners of wealth desire to split their holdings between money and capital depend upon the volume of transactions and on the rate of return on capital. The yield of capital is not a constant, as it seems to be in the Cambridge model, but depends on the capital intensity of current production. The differential between the yield of capital and that of money depends on the relative supplies of the two basic assets; the liquidity preference mechanism is applied to a money-capital margin rather than a money-securities margin. The price level adjusts the relative supplies to the portfolio investors desire, given the ruling marginal productivity of capital. This portfolio adjustment is like the mechanism of response to increase in the quantity of money described above for the constant-velocity model; but here it does not necessarily maintain the same velocity or the same yield of capital. A real balance effect on consumption can be added if desired.

A trivial extension of the money-capital model is to include other kinds of government securities, on the assumption that given certain constant rate differentials they are perfect portfolio substitutes for money proper. Then "money" in the model stands for the entire government debt, whether it takes the form of media of exchange or money substitutes. The differential between the return on capital and the yield of any government debt instrument is determined by the relative supplies of total government debt and capital.

By a similar extension private debts could be added to the menu of assets. again with the proviso that they are perfect substitutes for government debt instruments but not for capital equity. This addition does not change the requirement of portfolio balance, that the net private position in assets of fixed money value stands in the appropriate relationship to the value of the capital stock.

Thus extended, the money-capital model winds up with the same asset menu as the Keynes-Patinkin model. Each has only one interest differential to be explained within the model. But there is a vast difference. The Keynes-Patinkin model assumes that all debt instruments are perfect substitutes for capital. The interest rate to be explained is the rate common, with the appropriate constant corrections, to all assets other than money itself. What explains this rate is the supply of money relative to transactions requirements and to total wealth. Monetary policy, altering the demand debt component of government debt, can affect the terms on which the community will hold the capital stock. Expansion of the real value of unmonetized debt cannot do so, although in Patinkin's version it can influence the level of activity via the real balance effect on current consumption. The money-capital model, in contrast, casts debt instruments on the side of money and focuses attention on the relationship between the total real value of government debt, monetized or unmonetized, and the rate of return the community requires of the capital stock. It contains no role for monetary policy; only the aggregate net position of the public as borrowers and lenders is relevant, not its composition.

The two models give different answers to important questions. Does retirement of government long-term debt through taxation have expansionary or deflationary consequences? The question refers not to the temporary multiplierlike effects of the surplus that reduces the debt – these are of course deflationary – but to the enduring effects, through the capital account, of having a smaller debt. The instinctive answer of economists schooled in the Keynesian tradition is "expansionary." The supply of bonds is smaller relative to the supply of money; *the* rate of interest goes down, and investment is stimulated until the marginal efficiency comes down correspondingly. The answer of the money-capital model is, as indicated above, "deflationary." The assumed substitutability of bonds and money will keep the bond rate up. The decline in the government debt component of net private wealth means that investors will require a higher rate of return, or marginal efficiency, in order to hold the existing capital stock.

Granted that both models are oversimplified, which is the better guide to instinct? Are long-term government debt instruments a better substitute for capital than they are for short-term debt and money? Reflection on the characteristic properties of these assets – in particular how they stand vis-a-vis risks of price level changes – surely suggests that if government securities must be assimilated to capital or money, one or the other, the better bet is money.

2.3. Towards a Synthesis

A synthesis of the two approaches must, of course, avoid the arbitrary choices of both, abandoning the convenience of assuming that all assets but one are perfect substitutes. The price of this advance in realism and relevance is the necessity to explain not just one market determined rate of return but a whole structure. The structure of rates may be pictured as strung between two poles, anchored at one end by the zero own-rate conventionally borne by currency (and by the central bank discount rate) and at the other end by the marginal productivity of the capital stock. Among assets that are not perfect substitutes, the structure of rates will depend upon relative supplies. In general, an increase in the supply of an asset – e.g., long-term government bonds – will cause its rate to rise relative to other rates, but less in relation to assets for which it is directly or indirectly a close substitute – in the example, short-term securities and money – than in relation to other assets – in the example, capital.

In such a synthesis, monetary policy falls in proper perspective. The quantity of money can affect the terms on which the community will hold capital, but it is not the only asset supply that can do so. The net monetary position of the public is important, but so is its composition.

One lesson of the simple money-capital model should be retained. The strategic variable – the ultimate gauge of expansion or deflation, of monetary tightness or ease – is the rate of return that the community of wealth-owners require in order to absorb the existing capital stock (valued at current prices), no more no less, into their portfolios and balance sheets. This rate may be termed the supply price of capital. If it is lower than the marginal productivity of capital, there will be excess demand for capital, stimulating increases in prices of capital goods and additions to the stock. If the supply price of capital is higher than its marginal productivity, demand for capital will be insufficient to absorb the existing stock; its valuation will tend to fall, discouraging production of new capital goods. The effects of deviation of supply price of capital from the marginal productivity of the existing stock are similar to those of discrepancies between Wicksell's market and natural rates.

In assessing policy actions and other autonomous changes, there is really no short-cut substitute for the supply price of capital. As the example of long-term debt retirement illustrates, *the* Keynesian interest rate, the long-term bond rate, can be a misleading indicator. Events that cause it to fall may cause the supply price of capital actually to rise. Another example of error due to concentration on the long-term bond rate is the following Keynesian argument: Expectation of a rise in *the* interest rate leads to liquidity preference and keeps the current interest rate high; a high interest rate discourages investment. However, what the marginal efficiency of capital must compete with is not the market quotation of the long-term rate, but that quotation less the expected capital losses. If the fact that the rate so corrected is close to zero causes substitution of money for bonds, should it not also cause substitution of capital for bonds?

If the long-term bond rate is an inadequate substitute for the supply price of capital, the same is true of another popular indicator: the quantity of money. The modern quantity-of-money theorist (2) (to be distinguished from the ancient quantity-theorist-of-money, who actually was a believer in the constancy of velocity), holds that virtually everything of strategic importance in the capital account can be studied by focusing on the supply and demand for money. This view, though seemingly endorsed by Shaw (15), has been persuasively opposed by Gurley and Shaw (3). As they point out, it is not hard to describe events and policies that raise the supply price of capital while leaving the quantity of money unchanged or even increasing it. Why concentrate on variables other than those of direct central interest?

How far to go in disaggregation is, as always, a matter of taste and purpose; it depends also on the possibilities of empirical application and testing. A minimal program for a theory of the capital account relevant to American institutions would involve: (1) four constituents of net private wealth: government demand debt, government short debt, government long debt, and capital stock; (2) two intermediate assets: bank deposits and private debts; (3) two institutionally or administratively fixed interest rates: zero on bank deposits and demand debt, and the central bank discount rate; (4) four market determined yields: the short-term interest rate, the long-term interest rate, the rate on private debts, and the supply price of equity capital.

In this model, the quantity of demand debt is divided between currency held outside banks and the net (unborrowed) reserves of banks. Required reserves depend on the volume of deposits. If required reserves exceed net reserves, banks must borrow from the central bank at the discount rate. The disposable funds of banks are their deposits less their required reserves. These are divided among net free reserves (net reserves less required reserves), short governments, long governments, and private debts in proportions that depend on the discount rate, the short rate, the long rate, and the private loan rate. The nonbank public apportions net private wealth among currency, bank deposits, the two kinds of interest-bearing government debt, private debt to banks (a negative item), and capital equity. All the yields except the discount rate are relevant to the public's portfolio choices. When the wealth constraints are allowed for, there are four independent equations in this system; e.g., a balance equation for each constituent of net private wealth. These equations can be used to find the four endogenous yields. The solution for the yield of capital is its supply price. There is equilibrium of the whole system, which would include also equations for the income account, only if the solution for the supply price of capital coincides with the marginal productivity of the existing stock.

References

(1) W.J. Baumol, "The Transactions Demand for Cash: An Inventory Theoretic Approach," *Quarterly Journal of Economics* (1952), 545-56.

(2) Milton Friedman, *Studies in the Quantity Theory of Money* (Chicago: University of Chicago Press, 1956), Chapter 1.

(3) J. Gurley and E.S. Shaw, *Money in a Theory of Finance* (Washington, D.C.: Brookings Institution, 1960).

(4) J.R. Hicks, "A Suggestion for Simplifying the Theory of Money," Chapter 2 of *Readings in Monetary Theory* (Homewood, Ill.: Irwin, 1951), reprinted from *Economica* NS II (1935), 1-19.

(5) ————. *Value and Capital* (Oxford, 1939), Chapter 13.

(6) N. Kaldor, "Speculation and Economic Stability," *Review of Economic Studies* (1939-40), 1-27.

(7) J.M. Keynes, *The General Theory of Employment, Interest and Money* (New York: Harcourt, Brace, 1936).

(8) ————. *A Treatise on Money,* I (New York: Harcourt, Brace, 1930).

(9) X. Lavington, *The English Capital Market*, 3d ed. (London: Methuen and Co., 1941), Chapter 6.

(10) H. Markowitz, *Portfolio Selection* (New York: Wiley, 1959).

(11) Alfred Marshall, *Money, Credit, and Commerce* (London: Macmillan, 1923), Chapter 4.

(12) Don Patinkin, *Money, Interest, and Prices* (Evanston, Ill.: Row Peterson, 1956).

(13) A.C. Pigou, "The Value of Money," Chapter 10 of *Readings in Monetary Theory* (Homewood, Ill.: Irwin, 1951), reprinted from *Quarterly Journal of Economics* (1917-18), 38-65.

(14) P.A. Samuelson, *Foundations of Economic Analysis* (Cambridge, Mass.: Harvard University Press, 1947).

(15) E.S. Shaw, "Money Supply and Stable Economic Growth," Chapter 2 of *United States Monetary Policy* (New York: American Assembly, 1958).

(16) J. Tobin, "A Dynamic Aggregative Model," *Journal of Political Economy* (1955), 103-15. Chapter 8 above.

(17) ————. "The Interest-Elasticity of Transactions Demand for Cash," *Review of Economics and Statistics* (1956), 241-47. Chapter 14 below.

(18) ————. "Liquidity Preference as Behavior Towards Risk," *Review of Economic Studies* (1958), 65-86. Chapter 15 below.

(19) K. Wicksell, *Lectures on Political Economy*, II (New York: Macmillan, 1935), pp. 190-208.

THE INTEREST ELASTICITY OF TRANSACTIONS DEMAND FOR CASH

One traditionally recognized source of demand for cash holdings is the need for transactions balances, to bridge the gaps in time between the receipts and the expenditures of economic units. By virtually common consent, this transactions demand for cash has been taken to be independent of the rate of interest. The relationship, if any, between the demand for cash holdings and the rate of interest has been sought elsewhere – in inelasticities or uncertainties of expectations of future interest rates. An exception is Professor Hansen, who has argued that even transactions balances will become interest-elastic at high enough interest rates. [1] Above some minimum, he conjectures, the higher the interest rate the more economical of cash balances transactors will be.

The purpose of this paper is to support and to elaborate Professor Hansen's argument. Even if there were unanimity and certainty that prevailing interest rates would continue unchanged indefinitely, so that no motive for holding cash other than transactions requirements existed, the demand for cash would depend inversely on the rate of interest. The reason is simply the cost of transactions between cash and interest-bearing assets. [2]

In traditional explanations of the velocity of active money, the amount of cash holdings needed for a given volume of transactions is taken as determined by the institutions and conventions governing the degree of synchronization of receipts and expenditures. To take a simple example, suppose that an individual receives $100 the first of each month, but distributes a monthly total outlay of $100 evenly through the month. His cash balance would vary between $100 on the first of each month and zero at the end of the month. On the average his cash holdings would equal $50, or 1/24 of his annual receipts and expenditures. If he were paid once a year this ratio would be ½ instead of 1/24; and if he were paid once a week it would be 1/104.

The failure of receipts and expenditures to be perfectly synchronized

Reprinted from *Review of Economics and Statistics*, 38 (August 1956), 241-47. Footnotes and figures have been renumbered. Footnote 2 is new.

certainly creates the need for transactions balances. But it is not obvious that these balances must be cash. By cash I mean generally acceptable media of payment, in which receipts are received and payments must be made. Why not hold transactions balances in assets with higher yields than cash, shifting into cash only at the time an outlay must be made? The individual in the preceding example could buy $100 of higher-yielding assets at the beginning of the month, and gradually sell these for cash as he needs to make disbursements. On the average his cash holdings would be zero, and his holdings of other assets $50. The advantage of this procedure is of course the yield. The disadvantage is the cost, pecuniary and nonpecuniary, of such frequent and small transactions between cash and other assets. There are intermediate possibilities, dividing the $50 average transactions balances between cash and other assets. The greater the individual sets his average cash holding, the lower will be both the yield of his transactions balances and the cost of his transactions. When the yield disadavantage of cash is slight, the costs of frequent transactions will deter the holding of other assets, and average cash holdings will be large. However, when the yield disadvantage of cash is great, it is worth while to incur large transactions costs and keep average cash holdings low. Thus, it seems plausible that the share of cash in transactions balances will be related inversely to the interest rate on other assets. The remainder of the paper is a more rigorous proof of this possibility.

Let *bonds* represent the alternative asset in which transactions balances might be held. Bonds and cash are the same except in two respects. One difference is that bonds are not a medium of payment. The other is that bonds bear an interest rate. [3] There is no risk of default on bonds, nor any risk of a change in the rate of interest. [4]

A transaction of $x, either way, between bonds and cash is assumed to cost $(a + bx), where a and b are both positive. Part of the cost of a transaction is independent of the size of the transaction, and part is proportional to that amount.

At the first of each time period ($t = 0$), the individual receives $Y. He disburses this at a uniform rate throughout the period, and at the end of the period ($t = 1$) he has disbursed it all. [5] Thus his total transactions balance, whatever its composition, $T(t)$ is:

$$T(t) = Y(1-t) . \qquad (0 \leqslant t \leqslant 1) . \qquad (1)$$

His average transactions balance:

$$\overline{T} = \int_0^1 Y(1-t)dt = Y/2 . \qquad (2)$$

$T(t)$ is divided between cash $C(t)$ and bonds $B(t)$:

$$T(t) = B(t) + C(t) \qquad 0 \leqslant B(t), C(t) .$$ (3)

Let $\bar{B}$ and $\bar{C}$ be average bond holding and cash holding respectively:

$$\bar{B} = \int_0^1 B(t)dt$$

$$\bar{C} = \int_0^1 C(t)dt \qquad \bar{B} + \bar{C} = \bar{T} = Y/2 .$$ (4)

The interest rate per time period is r. Bonds earn interest in proportion to the length of time they are held, no matter how short.

The problem is to find the relationship between $\bar{B}$ (and hence $\bar{C}$) and the interest rate r, on the assumption that the individual chooses $B(t)$ and $C(t)$ so as to maximize his interest earnings, net of transactions costs. The relationship may be found in three steps:

1. Suppose that the number of transactions during the period were fixed at n. Given r, what would be the optimal times $(t_1, t_2, \ldots t_n)$ and amounts of these n transactions? What would be the revenue R_n from this optimal plan? What are the corresponding values of $\bar{B}$ and $\bar{C}$?

2. Given r, but now considering n variable, what would be the value of n – call it n^* – for which R_n is a maximum?

3. How does n^*, the optimal number of transactions, depend on r? As n^* varies with r, so will $\bar{B}$ and $\bar{C}$. Also, incidentally, how do n^*, $\bar{B}$, and $\bar{C}$ depend on Y, the volume of transactions?

1. The first problem is the optimal timing and amounts of a given number of transactions. Consider this problem first for the case in which transaction costs are independent of the size of transactions ($b = 0$). In this case transactions costs are fixed by the number of transactions; and, for a given number, the optimal scheduling will be the one which gives the greatest interest earnings.

If there is one transaction, from cash into bonds, there must be at least a second transaction, from bonds back into cash. Bonds cannot be used for payments, and the entire initial transactions balance must be paid out by the end of the period.

In Figure 14.1, the total transactions balance T is plotted against time, as

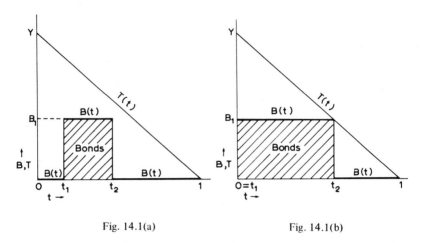

Fig. 14.1(a)   Fig. 14.1(b)

in equation (1). Figure 14.1 presents two possible ways of scheduling two transactions. The first way, shown in (a), is to hold all cash, no bonds, until time t_1; to buy B_1 bonds at that time; to hold these, and earn interest on them, until time t_2; and then to convert them into cash. Total interest earnings are proportional to the shaded area. The second way, shown in Figure 14.1(b) is to buy the same amount of bonds B_1 immediately on receipt of periodic income Y, and to hold them until they absolutely must be sold in order to get the cash necessary for subsequent payments. The revenue from this schedule is proportional to the shaded area in Figure 14.1(b), and is obviously greater than the revenue in Figure 14.1(a). The two general principles exemplified in the superiority of the second schedule to the first are as follows:

(a) All conversion from cash into bonds should occur at time 0. Whatever the size of a transaction in this direction, to postpone it is only to lose interest.

(b) A transaction from bonds into cash should not occur until the cash balance is zero. To make this transaction before it is necessary only loses interest that would be earned by holding bonds a longer time.

There are many schedules of two transactions that conform to these principles. Two possibilities are shown in Figure 14.2. In Figure 14.2(a) the initial transaction is obviously too great, and the second transaction must therefore be too early. The optimal schedule is to convert half of Y into bonds at time 0 and to sell them for cash at time ½. [6]

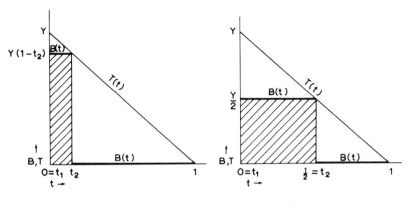

Fig. 14.2 (a)   Fig. 14.2 (b)

If three transactions are allowed, it is not necessary to sell all the bonds at one time. Some may be sold at time t_2 and the remainder at time t_3. This makes it possible to buy more bonds initially. Figure 14.3 shows the optimal schedule. In general, for n transactions, the optimal schedule is to buy at time zero $n-1/n$ Y bonds, and to sell them in equal installments of Y/n at times $t_2 = 1/n$, $t_3 = 2/n$, . . . $t_i = i-1/n$, . . . , $t_n = n-1/n$. The average bond holding, following this schedule, is half of the initial holding:

$$\bar{B}_n = \frac{n-1}{2n} Y . \qquad (n \geqslant 2) . \tag{5}$$

Revenue is $r\bar{B}_n$, or:

$$R_n = \frac{n-1}{2n} Yr . \qquad (n \geqslant 2) . \tag{6}$$

Transaction costs are equal to na, so that net revenue is:

$$\pi_n = \frac{n-1}{2n} Yr - na \qquad (n \geqslant 2) \tag{7}$$

where a is the cost of a transaction. These results are all proved in the Appendix.

Some modification in the argument is needed to take account of transaction costs proportional to the size of the transaction. If this cost is b per dollar, then every dollar of cash-bonds-cash round trip costs $2b$, no matter how quickly it is made. The interest revenue from such a circuit depends, on the other hand, on how long the dollar stays in bonds. This means that it is

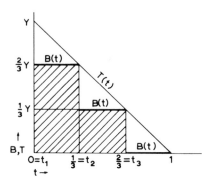

Fig. 14.3.

worth while to buy bonds only if they can be held long enough so that the interest earnings exceed $2b$. This will be possible at all only if r exceeds $2b$, since the maximum time available is 1. The minimum time for which all bonds purchased at time zero must be held, in order to break even, is $2b/r$. Holding bonds beyond that time, so far as transactions needs permit, will result in interest earnings which are clear gain. The problem is the same as in the simpler case without size-of-transaction costs, except that the effective beginning time is not $t_1 = 0$ but $t_1 = 2b/r$, and consequently the effective beginning total transactions balance is not Y but $Y[1-(2b/r)]$. With these modifications, the solution for the optimal scheduling of n transactions is the same: Put $(n-1)/n$ of the beginning balance into bonds, and sell these bonds for cash in equal installment at $n-1$ equally spaced dates. [7]

For $n = 3$, the solution is illustrated in Figure 14.4, which may be compared with Figure 14.3. In Figure 14.4 it is assumed that $2b/r = \frac{1}{2}$, i.e., that the size of transaction cost per dollar is ¼ of the interest rate. The effective beginning time is thus $t_1 = \frac{1}{2}$, and the effective beginning balance is $T(\frac{1}{2})$ or $Y/2$.

The initial purchase of bonds amounts to 2/3 of $Y/2$; half of this purchase is converted back into cash at $t_2 = 2/3$, and the remainder at $t_3 = 5/6$.

For the general case, the following results are proved in the Appendix.

$$\bar{B}_n = \frac{n-1}{2n} Y \left(1 - \frac{4b^2}{r^2}\right) \qquad (n \geqslant 2), \qquad (r \geqslant 2b) \qquad (8)$$

$$R_n = \frac{n-1}{2n} Yr \left(1 - \frac{2b}{r}\right)^2 \qquad (n \geqslant 2), \qquad (r \geqslant 2b) \qquad (9)$$

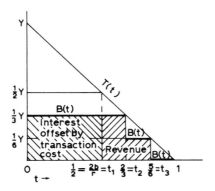

Fig. 14.4.

$$\pi_n = \frac{n-1}{2n} \, Yr \left(1 - \frac{2b}{r}\right)^2 - na. \qquad (n \geqslant 2), \qquad (r \geqslant 2b). \quad (10)$$

2. The next step is to determine the optimal number of transactions, *i.e.*, the value of n which maximizes π_n in (10). As shown in fig. 14.5, revenue R_n is a positive increasing function of n, which approaches $Yr/2 \, (1-2b/r)^2$ as n becomes indefinitely large. Marginal revenue, $R_{n+1}-R_n$, is a positive decreasing function of n, which approaches zero as n becomes infinite:

$$R_{n+1}-R_n = \frac{1}{2n(n+1)} \, Yr \left(1 - \frac{2b}{r}\right)^2 \qquad (n \geqslant 2), \qquad (r \geqslant 2b) \ (11)$$

Total cost, na, is simply proportional to a; and marginal cost is a constant.

There are four possible kinds of solution n^*, of which Figure 14.5 illustrates only one. These are defined by the relation of the interest rate to volume and costs of transactions, as follows:

(I) $a > 1/8 \, Yr(1-2b/r)^2$. π_2 is negative. In this case, π_n will also be negative for all values of n greater than 2. The optimal number of transactions is zero, because π_0 is equal to zero.

(II) $a = 1/8 \, Yr(1-2b/r)^2$. π_2 is zero. In this case, π_n will be negative for all values of n greater than 2; n^* is indeterminate between the two values 0 and 2.

(III) $1/8 \, Yr(1-2b/r)^2 > a > 1/12 \, Yr(1-2b/r)^2$; $n^* = 2$. Here π_n is positive for $n = 2$ but declines as n takes on greater values.

(IV) $1/12 \, Yr(1-2b/r)^2 \geqslant a$. The optimal number of transactions n^* is (or at least may be) greater than 2. This is the case illustrated in Figure 14.5.

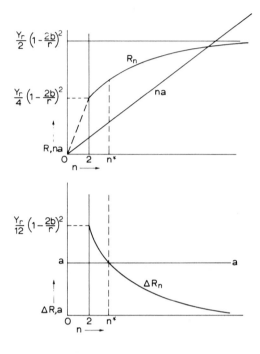

Fig. 14.5.

3. The third step in the argument concerns the relation of the optimal number of transactions, n^*, to the rate of interest r. From (9) and (11) it is apparent that both the total and the marginal revenue for a given n will be greater the larger is r. If an increase in r alters n^* at all, it increases n^*. Now $\bar{B}_{n^*}$, average bond holdings, is for two reasons an increasing function of n. As is clear from (8), B_n for given n depends directly on r. In addition, B_n increases with n; and n^* varies directly with r.

Thus it is proved that the optimal share of bonds in a transactions balance varies directly, and the share of cash inversely, with the rate of interest. This is true for rates high enough in relation to transaction costs of both kinds to fall in categories II, III, and IV above. Within category I, of course, r can vary without affecting cash and bond holdings.

Figure 14.6 gives an illustration of the relationship: r_{11} is the level of the rate of interest which meets the condition of category II, which is also the boundary between I and III.

The ratio of cash to total transactions balances is not independent of the

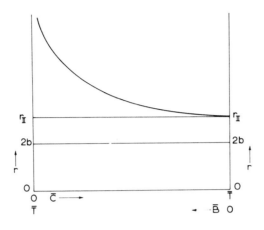

Fig. 14.6.

absolute volume of transactions. In equation (11), marginal revenue depends directly on Y, the amount of periodic receipts; but marginal cost a does not. Consequently n^* will be greater, for solutions in category IV, the greater the volume of transactions Y; and the ratio of cash holdings to Y will vary inversely with Y. Moreover, the range of values of r for which the demand for cash is sensitive to the interest rate (categories II,III,IV) is widened by increases in Y. Small transactors do not find it worth while even to consider holding transactions balances in assets other than cash; but large transactors may be quite sensitive to the interest rate. This conclusion suggests that the transactions velocity of money may be higher in prosperity than in depression, even if the rate of interest is constant. But it would not be correct to conclude that, for the economy as a whole, transactions velocity depends directly on the level of *money* income. It is the volume of transactions Y *relative to* transaction cost a that matters; and in a pure price inflation Y and a could be expected to rise in the same proportion.

Appendix

I. Suppose that $(1-t_2)Y$ bonds are bought at time $t = 0$ and held until $t = t_2$. From t_2 until t_3, $(1-t_3)Y$ bonds are held. In general, from t_{i-1} until t_i, $(1-t_i)Y$ bonds are held, and finally from t_{n-1} until t_n, $(1-t_n)Y$ bonds are held. After t_n, bond holdings are zero. Every dollar of bonds held from t_{i-1} until t_i earns interest in amount $(t_i-t_{i-1})r$. Since the total sales of bonds are the same as the initial pu chase, $(1-t_2)Y$, total transaction costs – ignoring those costs, na, which are fixed when the number of transactions is fixed – are $2b(1-t_2)Y$. Consequently, revenue R_n is given by the following expression:

$$R_n = (1-t_2)Y \cdot t_2r + (1-t_3)Y \cdot (t_3-t_2)r + \ldots$$
$$+ (1-t_n)Y(t_n-t_{n-1})r - 2b(1-t_2)Y. \qquad (A1)$$

It is convenient, for the purposes of this Appendix, to define t_1 as equal to $2b/r$. Then we may write R_n as follows:

$$R_n = Yr \sum_{i=2}^{n} (1-t_i)(t_i-t_{i-1}). \qquad (A2)$$

The t_i $(i = 2, \ldots n)$ are to be chosen so as to maximize R_n. Setting the partial derivatives equal to zero gives the following set of equations.

$$
\begin{aligned}
-2t_2 + t_3 &= -t_1 \\
t_2 - 2t_3 + t_4 &= 0 \\
t_3 - 2t_4 + t_5 &= 0 \\
\ldots\ldots \\
t_{n-2} - 2t_{n-1} + t_n &= 0 \\
t_{n-1} - 2t_n &= -1
\end{aligned}
\qquad (A3)
$$

The solution to (A3) is:

$$t_2 = t_1 + \frac{1-t_1}{n}$$

$$t_3 = t_1 + \frac{2}{n}(1-t_1)$$

$$\ldots\ldots \qquad (A4)$$

$$t_i = t_1 + \frac{i-1}{n}(1-t_1)$$

$$\ldots\ldots$$

$$t_n = t_1 + \frac{n-1}{n}(1-t_1).$$

From (A4) we have:

$$t_i - t_{i-1} = \frac{1}{n}(1-t_1). \qquad (i = 2, 3, \ldots n). \qquad \text{(A5)}$$

$$1-t_i = \frac{n-i+1}{n}(1-t_1). \qquad (i = 2, 3, \ldots n) \qquad \text{(A6)}$$

Substituting (A5) and (A6) in (A2) gives:

$$R_n = Yr \frac{(1-t_1)^2}{n^2} \sum_{i=2}^{n} (n-i+1) = Yr \frac{(1-t_1)^2}{n^2} \cdot \frac{n(n-1)}{2}. \qquad \text{(A7)}$$

From (A7), substituting $2b/r$ for t_1, expression (9) in the text is easily derived. Equation (6) in the text is a special case of (9).

$\bar{B}_n$, average bond holding, is obtained from the definition (4) as follows:

$$\bar{B}_n = Y \sum_{i=2}^{n} (1-t_i)(t_i - t_{i-1}) + Y(1-t_2)t_1$$

$$\bar{B}_n = \frac{Y(1-t_1)^2(n-1)}{2n} + \frac{2Yt_1(1-t_1)(n-1)}{2n}$$

$$\bar{B}_n = \frac{Y(n-1)(1-t_1^2)}{2n}. \qquad \text{(A8)}$$

Substituting $2b/r$ for t_1 in (A8) gives (8) in the text, of which (5) is a special case.

II. The model used in the present paper is much the same as that used by Baumol, and the maximization of my expression (10) gives essentially the same result as Baumol's equation (2), page 547, and his expression for R on page 549. There are, however, some differences:

1. I permit the number of transactions into cash, $n-1$, to take on only positive integral values, while Baumol treats the corresponding variable, I/C, as continuous. Consequently, it is possible to duplicate Baumol's equation (2) exactly only by ignoring differences between $n-1, n$, and $n+1$.

2. The present paper proves what Baumol assumes, namely that cash withdrawals should be equally spaced in time and equal in size.

3. Baumol does not consider the possibility that, in the general case where the individual has both receipts and expenditures, the optimal initial invest-

ment is zero. Of the four kinds of solution mentioned in the present paper, Baumol considers only case IV. In part this is because he treats the decision variable as continuous and looks only for the regular extremum. But it is also because of his definition of the problem. Baumol's individual, instead of maximizing his earnings of interest net of transaction costs, minimizes a cost which includes an interest charge on his average cash balance. This definition of the problem leads Baumol to overlook the question whether interest earnings are high enough to justify any investment at all. Baumol's calculation of interest cost is rather difficult to understand. By making it proportional to the average cash balance, he is evidently regarding as "cost" the sacrifice of earnings as compared with a situation in which the full transactions balance, which declines gradually from T to zero during the period, is invested and cash is held no longer than the split second preceding its expenditure. Since this situation would require infinitely many financial transactions and therefore infinitely large transactions costs, it hardly seems a logical zero from which to measure interest costs.

Notes

[1] Alvin H. Hansen, *Monetary Theory and Fiscal Policy* (New York: McGraw Hill, 1949), 66-67.

[2] The importance of these costs in explaining the demand for cash has been explicitly analyzed by W.J. Baumol, "The Transactions Demand for Cash: An Inventory Theoretic Approach," *Quarterly Journal of Economics*, 56 (November 1952), 545-56, a paper which I should have read before writing this one but did not. Baumol is mainly interested in the implications of his analysis for the theory of the transactions velocity of money at a given rate of interest, while the focus of this paper is on the interest elasticity of the demand for cash at a given volume of transactions. Other differences between Baumol's model and mine are discussed in the Appendix.

[3] I shall assume for convenience that the own-rate of interest on cash is zero; if cash bore interest, the argument would be essentially the same. By "the interest rate" is really meant the difference between the yield on bonds and the yield on cash.

[4] It is probably better to think of the alternative asset as time deposits or treasury bills rather than bonds.

[5] The argument would be changed only inessentially by considering instead an individual who receives cash at a uniform rate and must make a single periodic disbursement. It may not be too farfetched to claim that, at a given season, almost every transactor in the economy can be approximated by one of these two models. Either the transactor is accumulating a series of small receipts toward the day when large disbursements must be made, or he is gradually disbursing in small payments a prior large receipt. At different seasons of the year, or month, or week, the same transactor may sometimes be of one type and sometimes of the other. Of course actual transactions balances $T(t)$ need not decline, or grow, linearly, as assumed in this paper.

[6] For ½ is the value of t_2 which maximizes the expression representing interest revenue: $rY(1-t_2)t_2$.

[7] See Appendix for proof.

CHAPTER 15

LIQUIDITY PREFERENCE AS BEHAVIOR TOWARDS RISK

One of the basic functional relationships in the Keynesian model of the economy is the liquidity preference schedule, an inverse relationship between the demand for cash balances and the rate of interest. This aggregative function must be derived from some assumption regarding the behavior of the decision making units of the economy, and those assumptions are the concern of this chapter. Nearly two decades of drawing downward-sloping liquidity preference curves in textbooks and on classroom blackboards should not blind us to the basic implausibility of the behavior they describe. Why should anyone hold the non-interest bearing obligations of the government instead of its interest bearing obligations? The apparent irrationality of holding cash is the same, moreover, whether the interest rate is 6 per cent, 3 per cent or ½ of 1 per cent. What needs to be explained is not only the existence of a demand for cash when its yield is less than the yield on alternative assets but an inverse relationship between the aggregate demand for cash and the size of this differential in yields. [1]

1. Transactions Balances and Investment Balances

Two kinds of reasons for holding cash are usually distinguished: transactions reasons and investment reasons.

Reprinted from *Review of Economic Studies,* 25, No. 67 (February 1958), 65–86 and from *Risk Aversion and Portfolio Choice,* edited by J. Tobin and D. Hester (New York: Wiley, 1967), Cowles Foundation Monograph No. 19, Chapter 1. © 1967 by Cowles Foundation for Research in Economics at Yale University. Part 5 reprinted from *Review of Economic Studies,* 36, No. 1 (January 1969). Figures and footnotes have been renumbered. Footnote 6 is new.

I am grateful to Challis Hall, Arthur Okun, Walter Salant, and Leroy Wehrle for help-ful comments on earlier drafts of this paper.

1.1. Transaction Balances: Size and Composition

No economic unit — firm or household or government — enjoys perfect synchronization between the seasonal patterns of its flow of receipts and its flow of expenditures. The discrepancies give rise to balances which accumulate temporarily, and are used up later in the year when expenditures catch up. Or, to put the same phenomenon the other way, the discrepancies give rise to the need for balances to meet seasonal excesses of expenditures over receipts. These balances are transactions balances. The aggregate requirement of the economy for such balances depends on the institutional arrangements that determine the degree of synchronization between individual receipts and expenditures. Given these institutions, the need for transactions balances is roughly proportionate to the aggregate volume of transactions.

The obvious importance of these institutional determinants of the demand for transactions balances has led to the general opinion that other possible determinants, including interest rates, are negligible. [2] This may be true of the size of transactions balances, but the composition of transactions balances is another matter. Cash is by no means the only asset in which transactions balances may be held. Many transactors have large enough balances so that holding part of them in earning assets, rather than in cash, is a relevant possibility. Even though these holdings are always for short periods, the interest earnings may be worth the cost and inconvenience of the financial transactions involved. Elsewhere [3] I have shown that, for such transactors, the proportion of cash in transactions balances varies inversely with the rate of interest; consequently this source of interest elasticity in the demand for cash will not be further discussed here.

1.2. Investment Balances and Portfolio Decisions

In contrast to transactions balances, the investment balances of an economic unit are those that will survive all the expected seasonal excesses of cumulative expenditures over cumulative receipts during the year ahead. They are balances which will not have to be turned into cash within the year. Consequently the cost of financial transactions — converting other assets into cash and vice versa — does not operate to encourage the holding of investment balances in cash. [4] If cash is to have any part in the composition of investment balances, it must be because of expectations or fears of loss on other assets. It is here, in what Keynes called the speculative motives of investors, that the explanation of liquidity preference and of the interest elasticity of the demand for cash has been sought.

The alternatives to cash considered, both in this paper and in prior discussions of the subject, in examining the speculative motive for holding cash are assets that differ from cash only in having a variable market yield. They are obligations to pay stated cash amounts at future dates, with no risk of default. They are, like cash, subject to changes in real value due to fluctuations in the price level. In a broader perspective, all these assets, including cash, are merely minor variants of the same species, a species we may call monetary assets — marketable, fixed in money value, free of default risk. The differences of members of this species from each other are negligible compared to their differences from the vast variety of other assets in which wealth may be invested: corporate stocks, real estate, unincorporated business and professional practice, etc. The theory of liquidity preference does not concern the choices investors make between the whole species of monetary assets, on the one hand, and other broad classes of assets, on the other. [5] Those choices are the concern of other branches of economic theory, in particular theories of investment and of consumption. Liquidity preference theory takes as given the choices determining how much wealth is to be invested in monetary assets and concerns itself with the allocation of these amounts among cash and alternative monetary assets. [6]

Why should any investment balances be held in cash, in preference to other monetary assets? We shall distinguish two possible sources of liquidity preference, while recognizing that they are not mutually exclusive. The first is inelasticity of expectations of future interest rates. The second is uncertainty about the future of interest rates. These two sources of liquidity preference will be examined in turn.

2. Inelasticity of Interest Rate Expectations

2.1. *Some Simplifying Assumptions*

To simplify the problem, assume that there is only one monetary asset other than cash, namely consols. The current yield of consols is r per "year." $1 invested in consols today will purchase an income of r per "year" in perpetuity. The yield of cash is assumed to be zero; however, this is not essential, as it is the current and expected differentials of consols over cash that matter. An investor with a given total balance must decide what proportion of this balance to hold in cash, A_1, and what proportion in consols, A_2. This decision is assumed to fix the portfolio for a full "year." [7]

2.2. *Fixed Expectations of Future Rate*

At the end of the year, the investor expects the rate on consols to be r_e. This expectation is assumed, for the present, to be held with certainty and to be independent of the current rate r. The investor may therefore expect with certainty that every dollar invested in consols today will earn over the year ahead not only the interest $\$r$, but also a capital gain or loss g:

$$g = \frac{r}{r_e} - 1 . \tag{1}$$

For this investor, the division of his balance into proportions A_1 of cash and A_2 of consols is a simple all-or-nothing choice. If the current rate is such that $r + g$ is greater than zero, then he will put everything in consols. But if $r + g$ is less than zero, he will put everything in cash. These conditions can be expressed in terms of a critical level of the current rate r_e, where:

$$r_c = \frac{r_e}{1 + r_e}. \tag{2}$$

At current rates above r_c, everything goes into consols; but for r less than r_c, everything goes into cash.

2.3. Sticky and Certain Interest Rate Expectations

So far the investor's expected interest rate r_e has been assumed to be completely independent of the current rate r. This assumption can be modified so long as some independence of the expected rate from the current rate is maintained. In Figure 15.1 for example, r_e is shown as a function of r, namely $\varphi(r)$. Correspondingly $r_e/(1 + r_e)$ is a function of r. As shown in the figure, this function $\varphi/(1 + \varphi)$ has only one intersection with the 45° line, and at this intersection its slope $\varphi'/(1 + \varphi)^2$ is less than one. If these conditions are met,

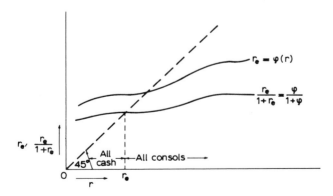

Fig. 15.1. Stickiness in the relation between expected and current interest rate.

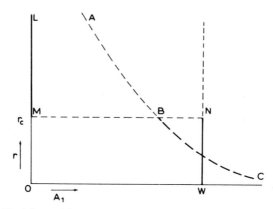

Fig. 15.2. Individual demand for cash assuming certain but inelastic interest rate expectation.

the intersection determines a critical rate r_c such that if r exceeds r_e the investor holds no cash, while if r is less than r_c he holds no consols.

2.4. Differences of Opinion and the Aggregate Demand for Cash

According to this model, the relationship of the individual's investment demand for cash to the current rate of interest would be the discontinuous step function shown by the heavy vertical lines *LMNW* in Figure 15.2. How then do we get the familiar Keynesian liquidity preference function, a smooth, continuous inverse relationship between the demand for cash and the rate of interest? For the economy as a whole, such a relationship can be derived from individual behavior of the sort depicted in Figure 15.2 assuming that individual investors differ in their critical rates r_c. Such an aggregate relationship is shown in Figure 15.3.

At actual rates above the maximum of individual critical rates the aggregate demand for cash is zero, while at rates below the minimum critical rate it is equal to the total investment balances for the whole economy. Between these two extremes the demand for cash varies inversely with the rate of interest r. Such a relationship is shown as $LMN \sum W$ in Figure 15.3. The demand for cash at r is the total of investment balances controlled by investors whose critical rates r_c exceed r. Strictly speaking, the curve is a step function; but, if the number of investors is large, it can be approximated by a smooth curve. Its shape depends on the distribution of dollars of investment balances by the critical rate of the investor controlling them; the shape of the curve in Figure 15.3 follows from a unimodal distribution.

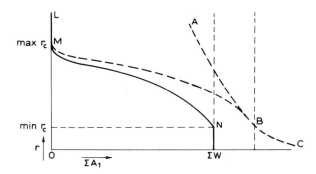

Fig. 15.3. Aggregate demand for cash assuming differences among individuals in interest rate expectations.

2.5. Capital Gains or Losses and Open Market Operations

In the foregoing analysis the size of investment balances has been taken as independent of the current rate on consols r. This is not the case if there are already consols outstanding. Their value will depend inversely on the current rate of interest. Depending on the relation of the current rate to the previously fixed coupon on consols, owners of consols will receive capital gains or losses. Thus the investment balances of an individual owner of consols would not be constant at W but would depend on r in a manner illustrated by the curve ABC in Figure 15.2. [8] Similarly, the investment balances for the whole economy would follow a curve like ABC in Figure 15.3, instead of being constant at $\sum W$. The demand for cash would then be described by $LMBC$ in both figures. Correspondingly the demand for consols at any interest rate would be described by the horizontal distance between $LMBC$ and ABC. The value of consols goes to infinity as the rate of interest approaches zero; for this reason, the curve BC may never reach the horizontal axis. The size of investment balances would be bounded if the monetary assets other than cash consisted of bonds with definite maturities rather than consols.

According to this theory, a curve like $LMBC$ depicts the terms on which a central bank can engage in open market operations, given the claims for future payments outstanding in the form of bonds or consols. The curve tells what the quantity of cash must be in order for the central bank to establish a particular interest rate. However, the curve will be shifted by open market operations themselves, since they will change the volume of outstanding bonds or consols. For example, to establish the rate at or below min r_c, the central bank would have to buy all outstanding bonds or consols. The size of the community's investment balances would then be independent of the rate of interest; it would be represented by a vertical line through, or to the right of, B, rather than the curve ABC. Thus the new relation between cash and interest would be a curve lying above LMB, of the same general contour as $LMN \sum W$.

2.6. Keynesian Theory and Its Critics

I believe the theory of liquidity preference I have just presented is essentially the original Keynesian explanation. The *General Theory* suggests a number of possible theoretical explanations, supported and enriched by the experience and insight of the author. But the explanation to which Keynes gave the greatest emphasis is the notion of a "normal" long-term rate, to which investors expect the rate of interest to return. When he refers to uncertainty in the market, he appears to mean disagreement among investors concerning the future of the rate rather than subjective doubt in the mind of an individual investor. [9] Thus Kaldor's correction of Keynes is more verbal than substantive when he says, "It is . . . not so much the uncertainty concerning future interest rates as the inelasticity of interest expectations which is responsible for Mr Keynes' 'liquidity preference function' . . . ." [10]

Keynes' use of this explanation of liquidity preference as a part of his theory of underemployment equilibrium was the target of important criticism by Leontief and Fellner. Leontief argued that liquidity preference must necessarily be zero in equilibrium, regardless of the rate of interest. Divergence between the current and expected interest rate is bound to vanish as investors learn from experience; no matter how low an interest rate may be, it can be accepted as "normal" if it persists long enough. This criticism was a part of Leontief's general methodological criticism of Keynes, that unemployment was not a feature of equilibrium, subject to analysis by tools of static theory, but a phenomenon of disequilibrium requiring analysis by dynamic theory. [11] Fellner makes a similar criticism of the logical appropriateness of Keynes' explanation of liquidity preference for the purposes of his theory of underemployment equilibrium. Why, he asks, are interest rates the only variables to which inelastic expectations attach? Why don't wealth owners and others regard predepression price levels as "normal" levels to which prices will return? If they did, consumption and investment demand would respond to reductions in money wages and prices, no matter how strong and how elastic the liquidity preference of investors. [12]

These criticisms raise the question whether it is possible to dispense with the assumption of stickiness in interest rate expectations without losing the implication that Keynesian theory drew from it. Can the inverse relationship of demand for cash to the rate of interest be based on a different set of assumptions about the behavior of individual investors? This question is the subject of the next section.

3. Uncertainty, Risk Aversion, and Liquidity Preference

3.1. *The Locus of Opportunity for Risk and Expected Return*

Suppose that an investor is not certain of the future rate of interest on consols; investment in consols then involves a risk of capital gain or loss. The higher the proportion of his investment balance that he holds in consols, the more risk the investor assumes. At the same time, increasing the proportion in consols also increases his expected return. In the upper half of Figure 15.4. the vertical axis represents expected return and the horizontal axis risk. A line such as OC_1 pictures the fact that the investor can expect more return if he assumes more risk. In the lower half of Figure 15.4, the left-hand vertical axis measures the proportion invested in consols. A line like OB shows risk as proportional to the share of the total balance held in consols.

The concepts of expected return and risk must be given more precision.

The individual investor of the previous section was assumed to have, for any current rate of interest, a definite expectation of the capital gain or loss g (defined in equation 1 above) he would obtain by investing one dollar in consols. Now he will be assumed instead to be uncertain about g but to base his actions on his estimate of its probability distribution. This probability distribution, it will be assumed, has an expected value of zero and is independent of the level of r, the current rate on consols. Thus the investor considers a doubling of the rate just as likely when the rate is 5 per cent as when it is 2 per cent, and a halving of the rate just as likely when it is 1 per cent as when it is 6 per cent.

A portfolio consists of a proportion A_1 of cash and A_2 of consols, where A_1 and A_2 add up to 1. We shall assume that A_1 and A_2 do not depend on the absolute size of the initial investment balance in dollars. Negative values A_1 and A_2 are excluded by definition; only the government and the banking system can issue cash and government consols. The return on a portfolio R is:

$$R = A_2(r + g), \qquad 0 \leqslant A_2 \leqslant 1 . \tag{3}$$

Since g is a random variable with expected value zero, the expected return on the portfolio is:

$$E(R) = \mu_R = A_2 r . \tag{4}$$

The risk attached to a portfolio is to be measured by the standard deviation of R, σ_R. The standard deviation is a measure of the dispersion of possible return around the mean value μ_R. A high standard deviation means, speaking roughly, high probability of large deviations from μ_R, both positive and negative. A low standard deviation means low probability of large deviations from μ_R; in the extreme case, a zero standard deviation would indicate certainty of receiving the return μ_R. Thus a high σ_R portfolio offers the investor the chance of large capital gains at the price of equivalent chances of large capital losses. A low σ_R portfolio protects the investor from capital loss,

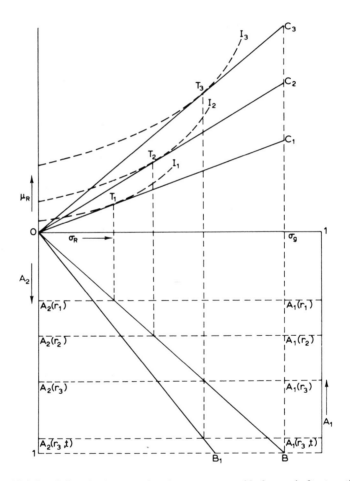

Fig. 15.4. Portfolio selection at various interest rates and before and after taxation.

and likewise gives him little prospect of unusual gains. Although it is intuitively clear that the risk of a portfolio is to be identified with the dispersion of possible returns, the standard deviation is neither the sole measure of dispersion nor the obviously most relevant measure. The case for the standard deviation will be further discussed in a following section.

The standard deviation of R depends on the standard deviation of g, σ_g, and on the amount invested in consols:

$$\sigma_R = A_2 \sigma_2 , \qquad 0 \leqslant A_2 \leqslant 1 . \tag{5}$$

Thus the proportion the investor holds in consols A_2 determines both his expected return μ_R and his risk σ_R. The terms on which the investor can obtain greater expected return at the expense of assuming more risk can be derived from equations (4) and (5):

$$\mu_R = \frac{r}{\sigma_g} \sigma_R , \qquad 0 \leqslant \sigma_R \leqslant \sigma_g . \tag{6}$$

Such an *opportunity locus* is shown as line OC_1 (for $r = r_1$) in Figure 15.4. The slope of the line is r_1 / σ_g. For a higher interest rate r_2, the opportunity locus would be OC_2; and for r_3, a still higher rate, it would be OC_3. The relationship (in equation 5) between risk and investment in consols is shown as line OB in the lower half of Figure 15.4. Cash holding $A_2(\mu 1 - A_2)$ can also be read off the diagram on the right-hand vertical axis.

3.2. Loci of Indifference between Combinations of Risk and Expected Return

The investor is assumed to have preferences between expected return μ_R and risk σ_R that can be represented by a field of indifference curves. The investor is indifferent between all parts (μ_R, σ_R) that lie on a curve such as I_1 in Figure 15.4. Points on I_2 are preferred to those in I_1; for given risk, an investor always prefers a greater to a smaller expectation of return. Conceivably, for some investors, *risk lovers*, these indifference curves have negative slopes. Such individuals are willing to accept lower expected return in order to have the chance of unusually high capital gains afforded by high values of σ_R. *Risk averters*, on the other hand, will not be satisfied to accept more risk unless they can also expect greater expected return. Their indifference curves will be positively sloped. Two kinds of risk averters need to be distinguished. The first type, who may be called *diversifiers* for reasons that will become clear below, have indifference curves that are concave upward, like those in Figure 15.4. The second type, who may be called *plungers*, have indifference curves that are upward sloping, but either linear or convex upward.

3.3. Indifference Curves as Loci of Constant Expected Utility of Wealth

The reader who is willing to accept the indifference fields that have just been introduced into the analysis may skip to section 3.4 without losing the main thread of the argument. But these indifference curves need some explanation and defense. Indifference curves between μ_R and σ_R do not necessarily exist. It is a simplification to assume that the investor chooses among the alternative probability distributions of R available to him on the basis of only two parameters of those distributions. Even if this simplification is accepted, the mean and standard deviation may not be the pair of parameters that concern the investor.

One justification for the use of indifference curves between μ_R and σ_R would be that the investor evaluates the future of consols only in terms of some two-parameter family of probability distributions of g. For example, the investor might think in terms of a range of equally likely gains or losses, centered on zero. Or he might think in terms that can be approximated by a normal distribution. Whatever two-parameter family is assumed – uniform, normal, or some other – the whole probability distribution is determined as soon as the mean and standard deviation are specified. Hence the investor's choice among probability distributions can be analyzed by μ_R-σ_R indifference curves; any other pair of independent parameters could serve equally well.

If the investor's probability distributions are assumed to belong to some two-parameter family, the shape of his indifference curves can be inferred from the general characteristics of his utility-of-return function. This function will be assumed to relate utility to R, the percentage growth in the investment balance by the end of the period. This way of formulating the utility function makes the investor's indifference map, and therefore his choices of proportions of cash and consols, independent of the absolute amount of his initial balance.

On certain postulates, it can be shown that an individual's choice among probability distributions can be described as the maximization of the expected value of a utility function. [13] The ranking or probability distributions with respect to the expected value of utility will not be changed if the scale on which utility is measured is altered either by the addition of a constant or by multiplication by a positive constant. Consequently we are free to choose arbitrarily the zero and unit of measurement of the utility function $U(R)$ as follows: $U(0) = 0$; $U(-1) = -1$.

Suppose that the probability distributions of R can be described by a two-parameter density function $f(R; \mu_R, \sigma_R)$. Then the expected value of utility is:

$$E[U(R)] = \int_{-\infty}^{\infty} U(R)f(R;\mu_R,\sigma_R)dR .$$ (7)

Let

$$z = \frac{R-\mu_R}{\sigma_R}.$$

$$E[U(R)] = E(\mu_R,\sigma_R) = \int_{-\infty}^{\infty} U(\mu_R + \sigma_R z)f(z;0,1)\, dz .$$ (8)

An indifference curve is a locus of points (μ_R, σ_R) along which expected utility is constant. We may find the slope of such a locus by differentiating equation 8 with respect to σ_R.

$$0 = \int_{-\infty}^{\infty} U'(\mu_R + \sigma_R z)\left[\frac{d\mu_R}{d\sigma_R} + z\right]f(z;0,1)\, dz .$$

$$\frac{d\mu_R}{d\sigma_R} = -\frac{\int_{-\infty}^{\infty} zU'(R)f(z;0,1)dz}{\int_{-\infty}^{\infty} U'(R)f(z;0,1)dz}.$$ (9)

$U'(R)$, the marginal utility of return, is assumed to be everywhere non-negative. If it is also a decreasing function of R, then the slope of the indifference locus must be positive; an investor with such a utility function is a risk averter. If it is an increasing function of R, the slope will be negative; this kind of utility function characterizes a risk lover.

Similarly, the curvature of the indifference loci is related to the shape of the utility function. Suppose that (μ_R, σ_R) and (μ_R', σ_R') are on the same indifference locus, so that $E(\mu_R, \sigma_R) = E(\mu_R', \sigma_R')$. Is

$$\left(\frac{\mu_R + \mu_R'}{2}, \frac{\sigma_R + \sigma_R'}{2}\right),$$

on the same locus, or on a higher or a lower one? In the case of declining marginal utility we know that for every z:

$$\tfrac{1}{2}U(\mu_R + \sigma_R z) + \tfrac{1}{2}U(\mu'_R + \sigma'_R z) < U\left(\frac{\mu_R + \mu'_R}{2} + \frac{\sigma_R + \sigma'_R}{2} z\right).$$

Consequently

$$E\left(\frac{\mu_R + \mu'_R}{2}, \frac{\sigma_R + \sigma'_R}{2}\right)$$

is greater than $E(\mu_R, \sigma_R)$ or $E(\mu'_R, \sigma'_R)$, and

$$\left(\frac{\mu_R + \mu'_R}{2}, \frac{\sigma_R + \sigma'_R}{2}\right),$$

which lies on a line between (μ_R, σ_R) and (μ'_R, σ'_R), is on a higher locus than those points. Thus it is shown that a risk averter's indifference curve is necessarily concave upwards, provided it is derived in this manner from a two-parameter family of probability distributions and declining marginal utility of return. All risk averters are diversifiers; plungers do not exist. The same kind of argument shows that a risk lover's indifference curve is concave downwards.

In the absence of restrictions on the subjective probability distributions of the investor, the parameters of the distribution relevant to his choice can be sought in parametric restrictions on his utility-of-return function. Two parameters of the utility function are determined by the choice of the utility scale. If specification of the utility function requires no additional parameters, one parameter of the probability distribution summarizes all the information relevant for the investor's choice. For example, if the utility function is linear $[U(R) = R]$, then the expected value of utility is simply the expected value of R, and maximizing expected utility leads to the same behavior as maximizing return in a world of certainty. If, however, one additional parameter is needed to specify the utility function, then two parameters of the probability distribution will be relevant to the choice; and so on. Which parameters of the distribution are relevant depends on the form of the utility function.

Focus on the mean and standard deviation of return can be justified on the assumption that the utility function is quadratic. Following our conventions as to the utility scale, the quadratic function would be:

$$U(R) = (1 + b)R + bR^2 . \tag{10}$$

Here $0 < b < 1$ for a risk lover, and $-1 < b < 0$ for a risk averter. However, equation (10) cannot describe the utility function for the whole range of R, because marginal utility cannot be negative. The function given in equation (10) can apply only for:

$(1 + b) + 2bR \geqslant 0$;

that is, for

$$R \geqslant -\left(\frac{1+b}{2b}\right)(b > 0) \qquad \text{(Risk lover)}$$

$$R \leqslant -\left(\frac{1+b}{2b}\right)(b < 0) . \qquad \text{(Risk averter)}$$

(11)

In order to use equation (10) therefore, we must exclude from the range of possibility values of R outside the limits of equation (11). At the maximum investment in consols $(A_2 = 1)$, $R = r + g$. A risk averter must be assumed therefore, to restrict the range of capital gains g to which he attaches non-zero probability so that, for the highest rate of interest r to be considered·

$$r + g \leqslant -\left(\frac{1+b}{2b}\right) . \tag{12}$$

The corresponding limitation for a risk lover is that, for the lowest interest rate r to be considered:

$$r + g \geqslant -\left(\frac{1+b}{2b}\right) . \tag{13}$$

Given the utility function of equation (10), we can investigate the slope and curvature of the indifference curves it implies: The probability density function for R, $f(R)$, is restricted by the limit of equation (12) or equation (13); but otherwise no restriction on its shape is assumed.

$$E[U(R)] = \int_{-\infty}^{\infty} U(R)f(R)dR = (1 + b)\mu_R + b(\sigma_R^2 + \mu_R^2) . \tag{14}$$

Holding $E[U(R)]$ constant and differentiating with respect to σ_R to obtain the slope of an indifference curve, we have:

$$\frac{d\mu_R}{d\sigma_R} = \frac{\sigma_R}{-\dfrac{1+b}{2b} - \mu_R} . \tag{15}$$

For a risk averter, $-[(1 + b)/2b]$ is positive and is the upper limit for R, according to equation (11); $-[(1 + b/2b]$ is necessarily larger than μ_R. Therefore the slope of an indifference locus is positive. For a risk lover, on the other hand, the corresponding argument shows that the slope is negative.

Differentiating equation (15) leads to the same conclusions regarding curvature as the previous alternative approach, namely that a risk averter is necessarily a diversifier.

$$\frac{d^2\mu_R}{d\sigma_R^2} = \frac{1 + \left(\dfrac{d\mu_R}{d\sigma_R}\right)^2}{-\dfrac{1+b}{2b} - \mu_R} . \tag{16}$$

For a risk averter, the second derivative is positive and the indifference locus is concave upwards; for a risk lover, it is concave downwards.

3.4. Effects of Changes in the Rate of interest

In section 3.3 two alternative rationalizations of the indifference curves introduced in section 3.2 have been presented. Both rationalizations assume that the investor (1) estimates subjective probability distributions of capital gain or loss in holding consols, (2) evaluates his prospective increase in wealth in terms of a cardinal utility function, (3) ranks alternative prospects according to the expected value of utility. The first rationalization derives the indifference curves by restricting the subjective probability distributions to a two-parameter family. The second rationalization derives the indifference curves by assuming the utility function to be quadratic within the relevant range. On either rationalization, a risk averter's indifference curves must be concave upwards, characteristic of the diversifiers, and those of a risk lover concave downwards. If the category defined as plungers exists at all, their indifference curves must be determined by some process other than those described in section 3.3.

The opportunity locus for the investor is described in section 3.1 and summarized in equation (6). The investor decides the amount to invest in consols so as to reach the highest indifference curve permitted by his opportunity locus. This maximization may be one of three kinds:

1. Tangency between an indifference curve and the opportunity locus, as illustrated by points T_1, T_2, and T_3 in Figure 15.4. A regular maximum of this kind can occur only for a risk averter, and will lead to diversification. Both A_1, cash holding, and A_2, consol holding, will be positive. They too are shown in Figure 15.4 in the bottom half of the diagram, where, for example, $A_1(r_1)$ and $A_2(r_1)$ depict the cash and consol holdings corresponding to point T_1.

2. A corner maximum at the point $\mu_R = r$, $\sigma_R = \sigma_g$, as illustrated in Figure 15.5. In Figure 15.5 the opportunity locus is the ray OC, and point C

represents the highest expected return and risk obtainable by the investor, *i.e.*, the expected return and risk from holding his entire balance in consols. A utility maximum at C can occur either for a risk averter or for a risk lover. I_1 and I_2 represent indifference curves of a diversifier; I_2 passes through C and has a lower slope, both at C and everywhere to the left of C, than the opportunity locus. I_1 and I_2 represent the indifference curves of a risk lover, for whom it is clear that C is always the optimum position. Similarly, a plunger may, if his indifference curves stand with respect to his opportunity locus as in Figure 15.6 (OC_2), plunge his entire balance in consols.

3. A corner maximum at the origin, where the entire balance is held in cash. For a plunger, this case is illustrated in Figure 15.6 (OC_1). Conceivably it could also occur for a diversifier, if the slope of his indifference curve at the origin exceeded the slope of the opportunity locus. However, case 3 is entirely excluded for investors whose indifference curves represent the constant-expected-utility loci of section 3.3. Such investors, we have already noted, cannot be plungers. Furthermore, the slope of all constant-expected-utility loci at $\sigma_R = 0$ must be zero, as can be seen from equations (9) and (15).

We can now examine the consequences of a change in the interest rate r, holding constant the investor's estimate of the risk of capital gain or loss. An increase in the interest rate will rotate the opportunity locus OC to the left. How will this affect the investor's holdings of cash and consols? We must consider separately the three cases.

Case 1. In Figure 15.7, OC_1, OC_2, and OC_3 represent opportunity loci for successively higher rates of interest. The indifference curves I_1, I_2, and I_3

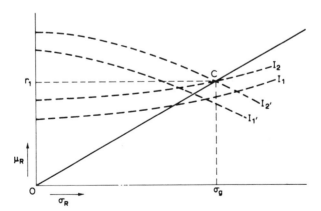

Fig. 15.5. "Risk-lovers" and "diversifiers": optimum portfolio at maximum risk and expected return.

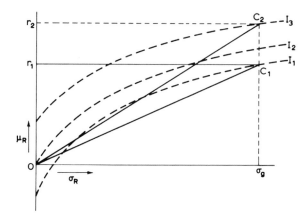

Fig. 15.6. "Plungers": optimum portfolio at minimum or maximum risk and expected return.

are drawn so that the points of tangency T_1, T_2, and T_3, correspond to successively higher holdings of consols A_2. In this diagram, the investor's demand for cash depends inversely on the interest rate.

This relationship is, of course, in the direction liquidity preference theory has taught us to expect, but it is not the only possible direction of relationship. It is quite possible to draw indifference curves so that the point of tangency moves left as the opportunity locus is rotated counterclockwise. The ambiguity is a familiar one in the theory of choice, and reflects the ubiquitous conflict between income and substitution effects. An increase in the rate of interest is an incentive to take more risk; so far as the substitution effect is concerned, it means a shift from security to yield. But an increase in the rate of interest also has an income effect, for it gives the opportunity to enjoy more security along with more yield. The ambiguity is analogous to the doubt concerning the effect of a change in the interest rate on saving; the substitution effect argues for a positive relationship, the income effect for an inverse relationship.

However, if the indifference curves are regarded as loci of constant expected utility, part of this ambiguity can be resolved. We have already observed that these loci all have zero slopes at $\sigma_R = 0$. As the interest rate r rises from zero, so also will consol holding A_2. At higher interest rates, however, the inverse relationship may occur.

This reversal of direction can, however, be virtually excluded in the case of the quadratic utility function. The conditions for a maximum is that the

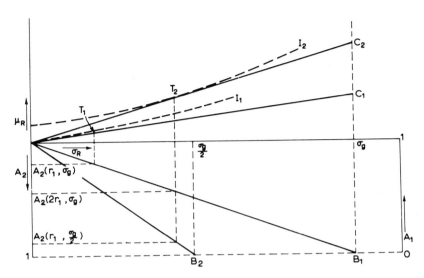

Fig. 15.7. Comparison of effects of change in interest rate (r) and in "risk" (σ_g) on holdings of consols.

slope of an indifference locus as given by equation (15) equals the slope of the opportunity locus of equation (6).

$$\frac{r}{\sigma_g} = \frac{A_2 \sigma_g}{-\dfrac{1+b}{2b} - A_2 r} \; ; \qquad A_2 = \frac{r}{r^2 + \sigma_g^2}\left(-\frac{1+b}{2b}\right) . \tag{17}$$

Equation (17) expresses A_2 as a function of r, and differentiating gives:

$$\frac{dA_2}{dr} = \frac{\sigma_g^2 - r^2}{(\sigma_g^2 + r^2)^2}\left(-\frac{1+b}{2b}\right) ; \qquad \frac{r}{A_2}\frac{dA_2}{dr} = \frac{\sigma_g^2 - r^2}{\sigma_g^2 + r^2} . \tag{18}$$

Thus the share of consols in the portfolio increases with the interest rate for r less than σ_g. Moreover, if r exceeds σ_g, a tangency maximum cannot occur unless r also exceeds g_{max}, the largest capital gain the investor conceives possible (see equation 12). [14] The demand for consols is less elastic at high interest rates than at low, but the elasticity is not likely to become negative.

Cases 2 and 3. A change in the interest rate cannot cause a risk lover to alter his position, which is already the point of maximum risk and expected yield. Conceivably a "diversifier" might move from a corner maximum to a regular interior maximum in response either to a rise in the interest rate or to a fall. A "plunger" might find his position altered by an increase in the interest rate, as from r_1 to r_2 in Figure 15.6; this would lead him to shift his entire balance from cash to consols.

3.5. Effects of Changes in Risk

Investors' estimates, σ_g, of the risk of holding monetary assets other than cash, "consols" are subjective. But they are undoubtedly affected by market experience, and they are also subject to influence by measures of monetary and fiscal policy. By actions and words, the central bank can influence investors' estimates of the variability of interest rates; its influence on these estimates of risk may be as important in accomplishing or preventing changes in the rate as open market operations and other direct interventions in the market. Tax rates, and differences in tax treatment of capital gains, losses, and interest earnings, affect in calculable ways the investor's risks and expected returns. For these reasons it is worthwhile to examine the effects of a change in an investor's estimate of risk on his allocation between cash and consols.

In Figure 15.7, T_1 and $A_2(r_1, \sigma_g)$ represent the initial position of an investor, at interest rate r_1 and risk σ_g. OC_1 is the opportunity locus (equation 6), and OB_1 is the risk-consols relationship (equation 5). If the investor now cuts his estimate of risk in half, to $\sigma_g/2$, the opportunity locus will double in slope, from OC_1 to OC_2, and the investor will shift to point T_2. The risk-consols relationship will have also doubled in slope, from OB_1 to OB_2. Consequently point T_2 corresponds to an investment in consols of $A_2(r_1, \sigma_g/2)$. This same point T_2 would have been reached if the interest rate had doubled while the investor's risk estimate σ_g remained unchanged. But in that case, since the risk-consols relationship would remain at OB_1, the corresponding investment in consols would have been only half as large, i.e., $A_2(2r_1, \sigma_g)$. In general, the following relationship exists between the elasticity of the demand for consols with respect to risk and its elasticity with respect to the interest rate:

$$\frac{\sigma_g}{A_2} \frac{dA_2}{d\sigma_g} = -\frac{r}{A_2} \frac{dA_2}{dr} - 1 . \tag{19}$$

The implications of this relationship for analysis of effects of taxation may be noted in passing, with the help of Figure 15.7. Suppose that the initial position of the investor is T_2 and $A_2(2r_1, \sigma_g)$. A tax of 50 per cent is now levied on interest income and capital gains alike, with complete loss offset provisions. The result of the tax is to reduce the expected net return

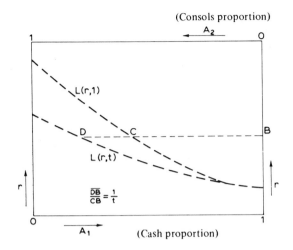

Fig. 15.8. Effect of tax (at rate $1-t$) on liquidity preference function.

per dollar of consols from $2r_1$ to r_1 and to reduce the risk to the investor per dollar of consols from σ_g to $\sigma_g/2$. The opportunity locus will remain at OC_2, and the investor will still wish to obtain the combination of risk and expected return depicted by T_2. To obtain this combination, however, he must now double his holding of consols, to $A_2(r_1, \sigma_g/2)$; the tax shifts the risk consols line from OB_1 to OB_2. A tax of this kind, therefore, would reduce the demand for cash at any market rate of interest, shifting the investor's liquidity preference schedule in the manner shown in Figure 15.8. A tax on interest income only, with no tax on capital gains and no offset privileges for capital losses, would have quite different effects. If the Treasury began to split the interest income of the investor in Figure 15.7 but not to share the risk, the investor would move from his initial position, T_2 and $A_2(2r_1, \sigma_g)$, to T_1 and $A_2(r_1, \sigma_g)$. His demand for cash at a given market rate of interest would be increased and his liquidity preference curve shifted to the right.

3.6. Multiple Alternatives to Cash

So far it has been assumed that there is only one alternative to cash, and A_2 has represented the share of the investor's balance held in that asset, "consols." The argument is not essentially changed, however, if A_2 is taken to be the aggregate share invested in a variety of noncash assets, e.g., bonds and other debt instruments differing in maturity, debtor, and other features. The return R and the risk σ_g on "consols" will then represent the average return and risk on a composite of these assets.

Suppose that there are m assets other than cash, and let x_i ($i = 1, 2, \ldots, m$) be the amount invested in the ith of these assets. All x_i are nonnegative, and

$$\sum_{i=1}^{m} x_i = A_2 \leqslant 1 \; .$$

Let r_i be the expected yield, and let g_i be the capital gain or loss, per dollar invested in the ith asset. We assume $E(g_i) = 0$ for all i. Let v_{ij} be the variance or covariance of g_j as estimated by the investor.

$$v_{ij} = E(g_i g_j) \qquad (i, j = 1, 2, \ldots, m) \; . \tag{20}$$

The overall expected return is:

$$\mu_R = A_2 r = \sum_{i=1}^{m} x_i r_i \; . \tag{21}$$

The overall variance of return is:

$$\sigma_R^2 = A_2^2 \sigma_g^2 = \sum_{i=1}^{m} \sum_{j=1}^{m} x_i x_j v_{ij} \; . \tag{22}$$

A set of points x_i for which $\sum_{i=1}^{m} x_i r_i$ is constant may be defined as a constant-return locus. A constant-return locus is linear in the x_j. For two assets x_1 and x_2, two loci are illustrated in Figure 15.9. One locus of combinations of x_1 and x_2 that gives the same expected return μ_R is the line from μ_R/r_2 to μ_R/r_1, through C; another locus, for a higher constant, μ_R', is the parallel line from μ_R'/r_2 to μ_R'/r_1, through C'.

A set of points x_i for which σ_R^2 is constant may be defined as a constant-risk-locus. These loci are ellipsoidal. For two assets x_1 and x_2, such a locus is illustrated by the quarter-ellipse from $\sigma_R/\sqrt{v_{22}}$ to $\sigma_R/\sqrt{v_{11}}$, through point C. The equation of such an ellipse is:

$$x_1^2 v_{11} + 2x_1 x_2 v_{12} + x_2^2 v_{22} = \sigma_R^2 = \text{constant}.$$

Another such locus, for a higher risk level, σ_R', is the quarter-ellipse from $\sigma_R'/\sqrt{v_{22}}$ to $\sigma_R'/\sqrt{v_{11}}$ through point C.

From Figure 15.9, it is clear that C and C' exemplify dominant combinations of x_1 and x_2. If the investor is incurring a risk of σ, somewhere on the ellipse through C, he will want to have the highest possible expectation of

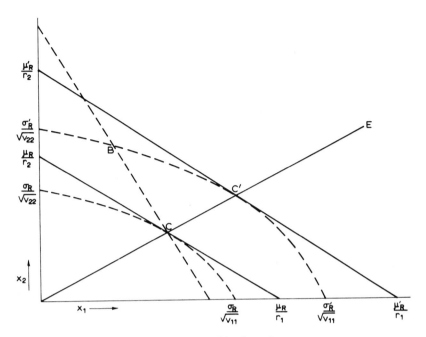

Fig. 15.9. Dominant combinations of two assets.

return available to him at that level of risk. The highest available expected
return is represented by the constant-expected-return line tangent to the
ellipse at C. Similarly C' is a dominant point: it would not be possible to
obtain a higher expected return than at C' without incurring additional risk,
or diminish risk without sacrificing expected return.

In general, a dominant combination of assets is defined as a set x_i which
minimizes σ_R for μ_R constant:

$$\sum_i \left(\sum_i v_{ij} x_i\right) x_i - \lambda\left(\sum_i r_i x_i - \mu_R\right) = \min , \qquad (23)$$

where λ is a Lagrange multiplier. The conditions for the minimum are that
the x_1 satisfy the constraint (equation 21) and the following set of m simultaneous linear equations, written in matrix notation:

$$[v_{ij}]\ [x_i] = [\lambda r_i] . \qquad (24)$$

All dominant sets lie on a ray from the origin. That is, if $[x_i^{(0)}]$ and $[x_i^{(1)}]$
are dominant sets, then there is some nonnegative scalar κ such that

$[x_i^{(1)}] = [\kappa x_i^{(0)}]$. By definition of a dominant set, there is some $\lambda^{(0)}$ such that:

$$[v_{ij}] \ [x_i^{(0)}] = [\lambda^{(0)} r_i] \ ,$$

and some $\lambda^{(1)}$ such that:

$$[v_{ij}] \ [x_i^{(1)}] = [\lambda^{(1)} r_i] \ .$$

Take $\kappa = \lambda^{(1)}/\lambda^{(0)}$. Then:

$$[v_{ij}] \ [\kappa x_i^{(0)}] = [\kappa \lambda^{(0)} r_i] = [\lambda^{(1)} r_i] = [v_{ij}] \ [x_i^{(1)}] \ .$$

At the same time.

$$\sum_i r_i x_i^{(0)} = \mu_R^{(0)}$$

and

$$\sum_i r_i x_i^{(1)} = \mu_R^{(1)} \ .$$

Hence, $\mu_R^{(1)} = \kappa \mu_R^{(0)}$. Conversely, every set on this ray is a dominant set. If $[x_i^{(0)}]$ is a dominant set, then so is $[\kappa x_i^{(0)}]$ for any nonnegative constant κ. This is easily proved. If $[x_i^{(0)}]$ satisfies equations (21) and (24) for $\mu_R^{(0)}$ and $\lambda^{(0)}$, then $[\kappa x_i^{(0)}]$ satisfies equations (21) and (24) for $\lambda^{(\kappa)} = \kappa \lambda^{(0)}$ and $\mu_R^{(\kappa)} = \kappa \mu_R^{(0)}$. In the two dimensional case pictured in Figure 15.9 the dominant pairs lie along the ray $OCC'E$.

There will be some point on the ray (say E in Figure 15.9) at which the investor's holdings of noncash assets will exhaust his investment balance ($\sum_i x_i = 1$) and leave nothing for cash holding. Short of that point the balance will be divided among cash and noncash assets in proportion to the distance along the ray; in Figure 15.9 at point C, for example, OC/OE of the balance would be noncash and CE/OE cash. But the convenient fact that has just been proved is that the proportionate composition of the noncash assets is independent of their aggregate share of the investment balance. This fact makes it possible to describe the investor's decisions as if there were a single noncash asset, a composite formed by combining the multitude of actual noncash assets in fixed proportions.

Corresponding to every point on the ray of dominant sets is an expected return μ_R and risk σ_R; these pairs (μ_R, σ_R) are the opportunity locus of section 3.1. By means of equation (24) the opportunity locus can be expressed in terms of the expected return and variances and covariances of the noncash assets. Let

$$[V_{ij}] = [v_{ij}]^{-1}.$$

Then:

$$\mu_R = \lambda \sum_i \sum_j r_i r_j V_{ij}, \tag{25}$$

$$\sigma_R^2 = \lambda^2 \sum_i \sum_j r_i r_j V_{ij}. \tag{26}$$

Thus the opportunity locus is the line:

$$\mu_R = \sigma_R \sqrt{\sum_i \sum_j r_i r_j V_{ij}} = \sigma_R \frac{r}{\sigma_g}. \tag{27}$$

This analysis is applicable only so long as cash is assumed to be a riskless asset. In the absence of a residual riskless asset, the investor has no reason to confine his choices to the ray of dominant sets. This may be easily verified in the two-asset case. Using Figure 15.9 for a different purpose now, suppose that the entire investment balance must be divided between x_1 and x_2. The point (x_1, x_2) must fall on the line $x_1 + x_2 = 1$, represented by the line through BC in the diagram. The investor will not necessarily choose point C. At point B, for example, he would obtain a higher expected yield as well as a higher risk; he may prefer B to C. His opportunity locus represents the pairs (μ_R, σ_R) along the line through BC $(x_i + x_2 = 1)$ rather than along the ray OC, and is a hyperbola rather than a line. It is still possible to analyze portfolio choices by the apparatus of (μ_R, σ_R) indifference and opportunity loci, but such analysis is beyond the scope of the present chapter. [15]

It is for this reason that the present analysis has been deliberately limited to choices among monetary assets. Among these assets cash is relatively riskless, even though in the wider context of portfolio selection, the risk of changes in purchasing power, which all monetary assets share, may be relevant to many investors. Breaking down the portfolio selection problem into stages at different levels of aggregation − allocation first among, and then within, asset categories − seems to be a permissible and perhaps even indispensable simplification both for the theorist and for the investor himself.

4. Implications of the Analysis for Liquidity Preference Theory

The theory of risk-avoiding behavior has been shown to provide a basis for liquidity preference and for an inverse relationship between the demand for cash and the rate of interest. This theory does not depend on inelasticity of expectations of future interest rates, but can proceed from the assumption that the expected value of capital gain or loss from holding interest-bearing assets is always zero. In this respect, it is a logically more satisfactory foundation for liquidity preference than the Keynesian theory previously described. Moreover, it has the empirical advantage of explaining diversification – the same individual holds both cash and "consols" – while the Keynesian theory implies that each investor will hold only one asset.

The risk aversion theory of liquidity preference mitigates the major logical objection to which, according to the argument on page 248, the Keynesian theory is vulnerable. But it cannot completely meet Leontief's position that in a strict stationary equilibrium liquidity preference must be zero unless cash and consols bear equal rates. By their very nature consols and, to a lesser degree, all time obligations contain a potential for capital gain or loss that cash and other demand obligations lack. Presumably, however, there is some length of experience of constancy in the interest rate that would teach the most stubbornly timid investor to ignore that potential. In a pure stationary state, it could be argued, the interest rate on consols would have been the same for so long that investors would unanimously estimate σ_g to be zero. So stationary a state is of very little interest. Fortunately the usefulness of comparative statics does not appear to be confined to comparisons of states each of which would take a generation or more to achieve. As compared to the Keynesian theory of liquidity preference, the risk aversion theory widens the applicability of comparative statics in aggregative analysis; this is all that need be claimed for it.

The theory, however, is somewhat ambiguous concerning the direction of relationship between the rate of interest and the demand for cash. For low interest rates, the theory implies a negative elasticity of demand for cash with respect to the interest rate, an elasticity that becomes larger and larger in absolute value as the rate approaches zero. This implication, of course, is in accord with the usual assumptions about liquidity preference. But for high interest rates, and especially for individuals whose estimates, σ_g, of the risk of capital gain or loss on "consols" are low, the demand for cash may be an increasing, rather than a decreasing, function of the interest rate. However, the force of this reversal of direction is diluted by recognition that the size of investment balances is not independent of the current rate of interest r. We have considered the proportionate allocation between cash and "consols" on the assumption that it is independent of the size of the balance. An increase in the rate of interest may lead an investor to desire to shift towards cash. But to the extent that the increase in interest also reduces the value of the investor's consol holdings, it automatically gratifies this desire, at least in part.

The assumption that investors expect on balance no change in the rate of interest has been adopted for the theoretical reasons explained rather than for reasons of realism. Clearly investors do form expectations of changes in interest rates and differ from each other in their expectations. For the purposes of dynamic theory and of analysis of specific market situations, the two theories discussed here are complementary rather than competitive. The formal apparatus considered previously will serve just as well for a non-zero expected capital gain or loss as for a zero expected value of g. Stickiness of interest rate expectations would mean that the expected value of g is a function of the rate of interest r, going down when r goes down and rising when r goes up. In addition to the rotation of the opportunity locus due to a change in r itself, there would be a further rotation in the same direction due to the accompanying change in the expected capital gain or loss. At low interest rates expectation of capital loss may push the opportunity locus into the negative quadrant, so that the optimal position is clearly no consols, all cash. At the other extreme, expectation of capital gain at high interest rates would increase sharply the slope of the opportunity locus and the frequency of no cash, all consols positions, like that of Figure 15.6. The stickier the investor's expectations, the more sensitive his demand for cash will be to changes in the rate of interest.

5. Comment on Borch and Feldstein [16]

Both Mr. Borch and Mr. Feldstein remind us that it is very difficult to derive propositions that are simultaneously interesting and general. In particular the Neumann-Morgenstern hypothesis of utility maximization will not, unaided, tell us much about portfolio choices. To get propositions with significantly more content than the prescription that the investor should maximize expected utility, it is necessary to place restrictions on his utility function or his subjective probability estimates or both. These propositions, naturally, will not hold if these restrictions are removed.

I do not believe that any of us who have found mean-variance analysis illuminating have been under any illusions on this basic point. We have known, and we have said, that "$\mu-\sigma$" indifference curves, as loci of constant expected utility, do not in general exist. I am not surprised that Mr. Borch can demonstrate their nonexistence by contriving probability distributions that the $\mu-\sigma$ criteria will rank incorrectly, given that the utility function meets everywhere his canons of good behaviour. We all know, to give another example, that no amount of risk aversion will cause an investor to prefer a portfolio with a certain return of zero to one with a wide dispersion of possible nonnegative returns.

We are considering an investor deciding how much, if any, of each of n assets to hold in his portfolio for a definite period of time: the portfolio is $(x_1, x_2, \ldots, x_n)$ where $\sum_i x_i = 1$. The portfolio return R will be $\sum_i x_i r_i$ where the r_i are random variables.

Strictly speaking, the portfolio choices of an expected-utility-maximizing investor can be analyzed in terms of the two parameters, mean and variance, of his subjective probability distributions of the returns from alternative possible portfolios only if one or both of the two following assumptions is met:

(a) the investor's utility function is quadratic;
(b) he regards the r_i as normally distributed.

In the absence of (a), the second assumption is required. Without it, the alternative possible portfolios $(x_1, x_2, \ldots, x_n)$ cannot be described and ranked in terms of mean and variance, even if the individual assets (pure portfolios with one $x_i = 1$ and all the rest equal to zero) can be so described and ranked.

As Mr. Feldstein points out, I tried erroneously to stretch the admittedly restricted generality of the approach. I should have recognized that the family of two-parameter distributions with the requisite property has only one member, the normal. In the "proof" which Mr. Feldstein critizes I used the property of replication under mixing mentioned in the preceding paragraph without realizing or stating that the normal is the only two-parameter distribution for which it holds. It is this same point – not, as Mr. Feldstein seems to assert in his third section, a different one – that is involved in the necessity to assume either quadratic utility or normal probability distributions in applying mean-variance analyses to choices involving more than one risky asset.

As for the convexity of the $\mu-\sigma$ indifference curves, my assertion was simply this: If they exist and are derived from expected utility maximization, then they must be convex. This is true whether (a) or (b) is the simplifying assumption made. Mr. Feldstein's indifference curve, with a concave range, is not a relevant example to counter this assertion. His logarithmic utility and log-normal probability distribution might be used to rank a designated list of basic portfolios all of which have by assumption log-normally distributed returns. But they could *not* be used to rank any portfolios that are linear blends of those portfolios, because the returns on the blends will not be log-normal. Now the fact that the market makes linear blends available to the investor is of the very essence of the portfolio choice problem. An analytical apparatus that does not handle this essential fact is as useless as a model of consumer choice that does not allow the consumer to move within his budget constraint to any market basket of goods he wants.

I do not believe it is an exaggeration to say that, until relatively recently, the basic model of portfolio choice in economic theory was a one-parameter model. Investors were assumed to rank portfolios by reference to one parameter only — the expected return, possibly corrected by an arbitrary "risk premium," constant and unexplained. This approach was rationalized, if at all, by assuming either subjective certainty or constant marginal utility. Is is now more than a decade ago that I participated in the modest endeavour of doubling the number of parameters of investors' probability estimates involved in economists' analyses of asset choice. This extension from one moment to two was never advertised as the complete job or the final word, and I think that its critics in 1969 owe us more than demonstrations that it rests on restrictive assumptions. They need to show us how a more general and less vulnerable approach will yield the kind of comparative-static results that economists are interested in. This need is satisfied neither by the elegant but nearly empty existence theorems of state preference theory nor by normative prescriptions to the individual that he should consult his utility and his subjective probabilities and then maximize.

Notes

[1] ". . . in a world involving no transaction friction and no uncertainty, there would be no reason for a spread between the yield on any two assets, and hence there would be no difference in the yield on money and on securities . . . in such a world securities themselves would circulate as money and be acceptable in transactions; demand bank deposits would bear interest, just as they often did in this country in the period of the twenties." Paul A. Samuelson, *Foundations of Economic Analysis* (Cambridge, Mass.: Harvard University Press, 1947), p. 123. The section, pp. 122-24, from which the passage is quoted makes it clear that liquidity preference must be regarded as an explanation of the existence and level not of the interest rate but of the differential between the yield on money and the yields on other assets.

[2] The traditional theory of the velocity of money has, however, probably exaggerated the invariance of the institutions determining the extent of lack of synchronization between individual receipts and expenditures. It is no doubt true that such institutions as the degree of vertical integration of production and the periodicity of wage, salary, dividend, and tax payments are slow to change. But other relevant arrangements can be adjusted in response to money rates. For example, there is a good deal of flexibility in the promptness and regularity with which bills are rendered and settled.

[3] "The Interest Elasticity of Transactions Demand for Cash," *Review of Economics and Statistics*, 38 (August 1956), 241-47, chapter 14 above.

[4] Costs of financial transactions have the effect of deterring changes from the existing portfolio, whatever its composition; they may thus operate against the holding of cash as easily as for it. Because of these costs, the status quo may be optimal even when a different composition of assets would be preferred if the investor were starting over again.

[5] For an attempt by the author to apply to this wider choice some of the same theoretical tools that are here used to analyze choices among the narrow class of monetary assets, see "A Dynamic Aggregative Model," *Journal of Political Economy*, 63 (April 1955), 103-15, chapter 8 above.

[6] For the purpose of this paper, "cash" should not necessarily be identified with means of payment, *i.e.*, currency and bank deposits. In most advanced economies these are dominated for investment balances by equally safe and lossproof assets which bear interest, notably time and saving deposits. This article really refers to the choice and interest differential between those assets and market instruments on which capital losses may occur as a result of interest rate movements. I must apologize that the "bonds" of the previous article, Chapter 14, are the "cash" of this article. Another way to put it is that Chapter 14 concerns the short-term rate, and this chapter the differential between long-term and short-term rates.

[7] As noted above, it is the costs of financial transactions that impart inertia to portfolio composition. Every reconsideration of the portfolio involves the investor in expenditure of time and effort as well as of money. The frequency with which it is worth while to review the portfolio will obviously vary with the investor and will depend on the size of his portfolio and on his situation with respect to costs of obtaining information and engaging in financial transactions. Thus the relevant "year" ahead for which portfolio decisions are made is not the same for all investors. Moreover, even if a decision is made with a view to fixing a portfolio for a given period of time, a portfolio is never so irrevocably frozen that there are no conceivable events during the period which would induce the investor to reconsider. The fact that this possibility is always open must influence the investor's decision. The fiction of a fixed investment period used here is, therefore, not a wholly satisfactory way of taking account of the inertia in portfolio composition due to the costs of transactions and of decision making.

[8] The size of their investment balances, held in cash and consols, may not vary by the full amount of these changes in wealth; some part of the changes may be reflected in holdings of assets other than monetary assets. But presumably the size of investment balances will reflect at least in part these capital gains and losses.

[9] J.M. Keynes, *The General Theory of Employment, Interest, and Money* (New York: Harcourt Brace, 1936), Chapters 13 and 15, especially pp. 168-172 and 201-203. One quotation from p. 172 will illustrate the point: "It is interesting that the stability of the system and its sensitiveness to changes in the quantity of money should be so dependent on the existence of a variety of opinion about what is uncertain. Best of all that we should know the future. But if not, then, if we are to control the activity of the economic system by changing the quantity of money, it is important that opinions should differ."

[10] N. Kaldor, "Speculation and Economic Stability," *Review of Economic Studies*, 7(1939), 15.

[11] W. Leontief, "Postulates: Keynes' General Theory and the Classicists," Chapter 19 in S. Harris, editor, *The New Economics* (New York: Knopf, 1947), pp. 232-42.

Section 6, pp. 238-239, contains the specific criticism of Keynes' liquidity preference theory.
[12] W. Fellner, *Monetary Policies and Full Employment* (Berkeley, Calif.: University of California Press, 1946), p. 149.
[13] See J. von Neumann and O. Morgenstern, *Theory of Games and Economic Behavior*, 3d edition (Princeton, N.J.: Princeton University Press, 1953), pp. 15-30, pp. 617-632; I. N. Herstein and J. Milnor, "An Axiomatic Approach to Measurable Utility," *Econometrica*, 23 (April 1953) 291-297; J. Marschak, "Rational Behavior, Uncertain Prospects, and Measurable Utility," *Econometrica*, 18 (April 1950), 111-141; M. Friedman and L. J. Savage, "The Utility Analysis of Choices Involving Risk," *Journal of Political Economy*, 56 (August 1948), 279-304, and "The Expected Utility Hypothesis and the Measurability of Utility," *Journal of Political Economy*, 60 (December 1952), 463-474. For a treatment which also provides an axiomatic basis for the subjective estimates here assumed, see Savage, *The Foundations of Statistics* (New York: Wiley, 1954).
[14] For this statement and its proof, I am greatly indebted to my colleague Arthur Okun. The proof is as follows: If $r^2 \geq \sigma_g^2$, then by equations (12) and (17):

$$1 \geq A_2 \geq \frac{r}{2r^2}\left(-\frac{1+b}{2b}\right) \geq \frac{1}{2r}(r + g_{max}) \, .$$

From the two extremes of this series of inequalities it follows that $2r \geq r + g_{max}$ or $r \geq g_{max}$. Professor Okun also points out that this condition is incompatible with a tangency maximum if the distribution of g is symmetrical. For then $r \geq g_{max}$ would imply $r + g_{min} \geq 0$. There would be no possibility of net loss on consols and thus no reason to hold any cash.
[15] Harry Markowitz, in *Portfolio Selection* (New York: Wiley, 1959), treats the general problem of finding dominant sets and computing the corresponding opportunity locus, for sets of securities all of which involve risk. Markowitz's main interest is prescription of rules of rational behavior for investors; the main concern of this paper is the implications for economic theory, mainly comparative statics, that can be derived from assuming that investors do in fact follow such rules. For the general nature of Markowitz's approach, see his article, "Portfolio Selection," *Journal of Finance*, 7 (March 1952) 77-91.
[16] Reprinted from *Review of Economic Studies*, 36, No. 1 (January 1969), 13-14, as a note replying to comments in the same issue by Karl Borch and Martin Feldstein.

CHAPTER 16

COMMERCIAL BANKS AS CREATORS OF "MONEY"

1. The Old View

Perhaps the greatest moment of triumph for the elementary economics teacher is his exposition of the multiple creation of bank credit and bank deposits. Before the admiring eyes of freshmen he puts to rout the practical banker who is so sure that he "lends only the money depositors entrust to him." The banker is shown to have a worm's-eye view, and his error stands as an introductory object lesson in the fallacy of composition. From the Olympian vantage of the teacher and the textbook it appears that the banker's dictum must be reversed: depositors entrust to bankers whatever amounts the bankers lend. To be sure, this is not true of a single bank; one bank's loan may wind up as another bank's deposit. But it is, as the arithmetic of successive rounds of deposit creation makes clear, true of the banking system as a whole. Whatever their other errors, a long line of financial heretics have been right in speaking of "fountain pen money" money created by the stroke of the bank president's pen when he approves a loan and credits the proceeds to the borrower's checking account.

In this time honored exposition two characteristics of commercial banks – both of which are alleged to differentiate them sharply from other financial intermediaries – are intertwined. One is that their liabilities – well, at least their demand deposit liabilities – serve as widely acceptable means of payment. Thus, they count, along with coin and currency in public circulation, as "money." The other is that the preferences of the public normally play no role in determining the total volume of deposits or the total quantity

Reprinted from *Banking and Monetary Studies*, edited by Deane Carson (Homewood, Ill.: Richard D. Irwin, 1963), pp. 408-19, and from *Financial Markets and Economic Activity*, edited by J. Tobin and D. Hester (New York: Wiley, 1967), Cowles Foundation Monograph No. 21, Chapter 1. © 1967 by Cowles Foundation for Research in Economics at Yale University. Footnotes have been renumbered.

of money. For it is the beginning of wisdom in monetary economics to observe that money is like the "hot potato" of a children's game: one individual may pass it to another, but the group as a whole cannot get rid of it. If the economy and the supply of money are out of adjustment, it is the economy that must do the adjusting. This is as true, evidently, of money created by bankers' fountain pens as of money created by public printing presses. On the other hand, financial intermediaries other than banks do not create money, and the scale of their assets is limited by their liabilities, i.e., by the savings the public entrusts to them. They cannot count on receiving "deposits" to match every extension of their lending.

The commercial banks and only the commercial banks, in other words possess the widow's cruse. And because they possess this key to unlimited expansion, they have to be restrained by reserve requirements. Once this is done, determination of the aggregate volume of bank deposits is just a matter of accounting and arithmetic: simply divide the available supply of bank reserves by the required reserve ratio.

The foregoing is admittedly a caricature, but I believe it is not a great exaggeration of the impressions conveyed by economics teaching concerning the roles of commercial banks and other financial institutions in the monetary system. In conveying this melange of propositions, economics has replaced the naive fallacy of composition of the banker with other half-truths perhaps equally misleading. These have their root in the mystique of "money" – the tradition of distinguishing sharply between those assets which are and those which are not "money," and accordingly between those institutions which emit "money" and those whose liabilities are not "money." The persistent strength of this tradition is remarkable given the uncertainty and controversy over where to draw the dividing line between money and other assets. Time was when only currency was regarded as money, and the use of bank deposits was regarded as a way of economizing currency and increasing the velocity of money. Today scholars and statisticians wonder and argue whether to count commercial bank time- and savings-deposits in the money supply. If so, why not similar accounts in other institutions? Nevertheless, once the arbitrary line is drawn, assets on the money side of the line are assumed to possess to the full properties which assets on the other side completely lack. For example, an eminent monetary economist, more candid than many of his colleagues, admits that we do not really know what money is, but proceeds to argue that, whatever it is, its supply should grow regularly at a rate of the order of 3 to 4 per cent per year. [1]

2. The "New View"

A more recent development in monetary economics tends to blur the sharp traditional distinctions between money and other assets and between commercial banks and other financial intermediaries; to focus on demands for and supplies of the whole spectrum of assets rather than on the quantity and velocity of "money"; and to regard the structure of interest rates, asset yields, and credit availabilities rather than the quantity of money as the linkage between monetary and financial institutions and policies on the one hand and the real economy on the other. [2] In this chapter I propose to look briefly at the implications of this "new view" for the theory of deposit creation of which I have above described or caricatured the traditional version. One of the incidental advantages of this theoretical development is to effect something of a reconciliation between the economics teacher and the practical banker.

According to the "new view," the essential function of financial intermediaries, including commercial banks, is to satisfy simultaneously the portfolio preferences of two types of individuals or firms. On one side are borrowers, who wish to expand their holdings of real assets — inventories, residential real estate, productive plant and equipment, etc. — beyond the limits of their own net worth. On the other side are lenders, who wish to hold part or all of their net worth in assets of stable money value with negligible risk of default. The assets of financial intermediaries are obligations of the borrowers — promissory notes, bonds, mortgages. The liabilities of financial intermediaries are the assets of the lenders — bank deposits, insurance policies, pension rights.

Financial intermediaries typically assume liabilities of smaller default risk and greater predictability of value than their assets. The principal kinds of institutions take on liabilities of greater liquidity too; thus, bank depositors can require payment on demand, while bank loans become due only on specified dates. The reasons that the intermediation of financial institutions can accomplish these transformations between the nature of the obligation of the borrower and the nature of the asset of the ultimate lender are these: (1) administrative economy and expertise in negotiating, accounting, appraising, and collecting; (2) reduction of risk per dollar of lending by the pooling of independent risks, with respect both to loan default and to deposit withdrawal; (3) governmental guarantees of the liabilities of the institutions and other provisions (bank examination, investment regulations, supervision of insurance companies, last-resort lending) designed to assure the solvency and liquidity of the institutions.

For these reasons, intermediation permits borrowers who wish to expand their investments in real assets to be accommodated at lower rates and easier terms than if they had to borrow directly from the lenders. If the creditors of financial intermediaries had to hold instead the kinds of obligations that private borrowers are capable of providing, they would certainly insist on higher rates and stricter terms. Therefore, any autonomous increase – for example, improvements in the efficiency of financial institutions or the creation of new types of intermediaries – in the amount of financial intermediation in the economy can be expected to be, *ceteris paribus*, an expansionary influence. This is true whether the growth occurs in intermediaries with monetary liabilities, i.e., commercial banks, or in other intermediaries.

Financial institutions fall fairly easily into distinct categories, each industry or "intermediary" offering a differentiated product to its customers, both lenders and borrowers. From the point of view of lenders, the obligations of the various intermediaries are more or less close, but not perfect, substitutes. For example, savings deposits share most of the attributes of demand deposits; but they are not means of payment, and the institution has the right, seldom exercised, to require notice of withdrawal. Similarly there is differentiation in the kinds of credit offered borrowers. Each intermediary has its specialty, e.g., the commercial loan for banks, the real estate mortgage for the savings and loan association. But the borrowers' market is not completely compartmentalized. The same credit instruments are handled by more than one intermediary and many borrowers have flexibility in the type of debt they incur. Thus there is some substitutability, in the demand for credit by borrowers, between the assets of the various intermediaries. [3]

The special attention given commercial banks in economic analysis is usually justified by the observation that, alone among intermediaries, banks "create" means of payment. This rationale is on its face far from convincing. The means-of-payment characteristic of demand deposits is indeed a feature differentiating bank liabilities from those of other intermediaries. Insurance against death is equally a feature differentiating life insurance policies from the obligations of other intermediaries, including banks. It is not obvious that one kind of differentiation should be singled out for special analytical treatment. Like other differentia, the means-of-payment attribute has its price. Savings deposits, for example, are perfect substitutes for demand deposits in every respect except as a medium of exchange. This advantage of checking accounts does not give banks absolute immunity from the competition of savings banks; it is a limited advantage that can be, at least in some part for many depositors, overcome by differences in yield. It follows that the community's demand for bank deposits is not indefinite, even though demand deposits do serve as means of payment.

3. The Widow's Cruse

Neither individually nor collectively do commercial banks possess a widow's cruse. Quite apart from legal reserve requirements, commercial banks are limited in scale by the same kinds of economic processes that determine the aggregate size of other intermediaries.

One often cited difference between commercial banks and other intermediaries must be quickly dismissed as superficial and irrelevant. This is the fact that a bank can make a loan by "writing up" its deposit liabilities. while a savings and loan association, for example, cannot satisfy a mortgage borrower by crediting him with a share account. The association must transfer means of payment to the borrower; its total liabilities do not rise along with its assets. True enough. but neither do the bank's, for more than a fleeting moment. Borrowers do not incur debt in order to hold idle deposits, any more than savings and loan shares. The borrower pays out the money, and there is of course no guarantee that any of it stays in the lending bank. Whether or not it stays in the banking system as a whole is another question. about to be discussed. But the answer clearly does not depend on the way the loan was initially made. It depends on whether somewhere in the chain of transactions initiated by the borrower's outlays are found depositors who wish to hold new deposits equal in amount to the new loan. Similarly, the outcome for the savings and loan industry depends on whether in the chain of transactions initiated by the mortgage are found individuals who wish to acquire additional savings and loan shares.

The banking system can expand its assets either (a) by purchasing. or lending against, existing assets; or (b) by lending to finance new private investment in inventories or capital goods, or buying government securities financing new public deficits. In case (a) no increase in private wealth occurs in conjunction with the banks' expansion. There is no new private saving and investment. In case (b), new private saving occurs, matching dollar for dollar the private investments or government deficits financed by the banking system. In neither case will there automatically be an increase in savers' demand for bank deposits equal to the expansion in bank assets.

In the second case, it is true. there is an increase in private wealth. But even if we assume a closed economy in order to abstract from leakages of capital abroad the community will not ordinarily wish to put 100 per cent of its new saving into bank deposits. Bank deposits are, after all, only about 15 per cent of total private wealth in the United States; other things equal, savers cannot be expected greatly to exceed this proportion in allocating new saving. So, if *all* new saving is to take the form of bank deposits, other things cannot stay equal. Specifically, the yields and other advantages of the competing assets into which new saving would otherwise flow will have to fall enough so that savers prefer bank deposits.

This is *a fortiori* true in case (*a*) where there is no new saving and the generation of bank liabilities to match the assumed expansion of bank assets entails a reshuffling of existing portfolios in favor of bank deposits. In effect the banking system has to induce the public to swap loans and securities for bank deposits. This can happen only if the price is right.

Clearly, then, there is at any moment a natural economic limit to the scale of the commercial banking industry. Given the wealth and the asset preferences of the community, the demand for bank deposits can increase only if the yields of other assets fall. The fall in these yields is bound to restrict the profitable lending and investment opportunities available to the banks themselves. Eventually the marginal returns on lending and investing, account taken of the risks and administrative costs involved, will not exceed the marginal cost to the banks of attracting and holding additional deposits. At this point the widow's cruse has run dry.

4. Banks and Other Intermediaries Compared

In this respect the commercial banking industry is not qualitatively different from any other financial intermediary system. The same process limits the collective expansion of savings and loan associations, or savings banks, or life insurance companies. At some point the returns from additional loans or security holdings are not worth the cost of obtaining the funds from the public.

There are of course some differences. First, it may well be true that commercial banks benefit from a larger share of additions to private savings than other intermediaries. Second, according to modern American legal practice, commercial banks are subject to ceilings on the rates payable to their depositors – zero in the case of demand deposits. Unlike competing financial industries, commercial banks cannot seek funds by raising rates. They can and do offer other inducements to depositors, but these substitutes for interest are imperfect and uneven in their incidence. In these circumstances the major readjustment of the interest rate structure necessary to increase the relative demand for bank deposits is a decline in other rates. Note that neither of these differences has to do with the quality of bank deposits as "money."

In a world without reserve requirements the preferences of depositors, as well as those of borrowers, would be very relevant in determining the volume of bank deposits. The volume of assets and liabilities of every intermediary, both nonbanks and banks, would be determined in a competitive equilibrium, where the rate of interest charged borrowers by each kind of institution just balances at the margin the rate of interest paid its creditors. Suppose that such an equilibrium is disturbed by a shift in savers' preferences. At prevailing rates they decide to hold more savings accounts and other nonbank liabilities and less demand deposits. They transfer demand deposits to the credit of nonbank financial institutions, providing these intermediaries with the means to seek additional earning assets. These institutions, finding themselves able to attract more funds from the public even with some reduction in the rates they pay, offer better terms to borrowers and bid up the prices of existing earning assets. Consequently commercial banks release some earning assets — they no longer yield enough to pay the going rate on the banks' deposit liabilities. Bank deposits decline with bank assets. In effect, the nonbank intermediaries favored by the shift in public preferences simply swap the deposits transferred to them for a corresponding quantity of bank assets.

5. Fountain Pens and Printing Presses

Evidently the fountain pens of commercial bankers are essentially different from the printing presses of governments. Confusion results from concluding that because bank deposits are like currency in one respect – both serve as media of exchange – they are like currency in every respect. Unlike governments, bankers cannot create means of payment to finance their own purchases of goods and services. Bank created "money" is a liability, which must be matched on the other side of the balance sheet. And banks, as businesses, must earn money from their middleman's role. Once created, printing press money cannot be extinguished, except by reversal of the budget policies which led to its birth. The community cannot get rid of its currency supply; the economy must adjust until it is willingly absorbed. The "hot potato" analogy truly applies. For bank created money, however. there is an economic mechanism of extinction as well as creation, contraction as well as expansion. If bank deposits are excessive relative to public preferences, they will tend to decline; otherwise banks will lose income. The burden of adaptation is not placed entirely on the rest of the economy.

6. The Role of Reserve Requirements

Without reserve requirements, expansion of credit and deposits by the commercial banking system would be limited by the availability of assets at yields sufficient to compensate banks for the costs of attracting and holding the corresponding deposits. In a regime of reserve requirements, the limit which they impose·normally cuts the expansion short of this competitive equilibrium. When reserve requirements and deposit interest rate ceilings are effective, the marginal yield of bank loans and investments exceeds the marginal cost of deposits to the banking system. In these circumstances additional reserves make it possible and profitable for banks to acquire additional earning assets. The expansion process lowers interest rates generally – enough to induce the public to hold additional deposits but ordinarily not enough to wipe out the banks' margin between the value and cost of additional deposits.

It is the existence of this margin – not the monetary nature of bank liabilities – which makes it possible for the economics teacher to say that additional loans permitted by new reserves will generate their own deposits. The same proposition would be true of any other system of financial institutions subject to similar reserve constraints and similar interest rate ceilings. In this sense it is more accurate to attribute the special place of banks among intermediaries to the legal restrictions to which banks alone are subjected than to attribute these restrictions to the special character of bank liabilities.

But the textbook description of multiple expansion of credit and deposits on a given reserve base is misleading even for a regime of reserve requirements. There is more to the determination of the volume of bank deposits than the arithmetic of reserve supplies and reserve ratios. The redundant reserves of the 1930's are a dramatic reminder that economic opportunities sometimes prevail óver reserve calculations. But the significance of that experience is not correctly appreciated if it is regarded simply as an aberration from a normal state of affairs in which banks are fully "loaned up" and total deposits are tightly linked to the volume of reserves. The 1930's exemplify in extreme form a phenomenon which is always in some degree present; the use to which commercial banks put the reserves made available to the system is an economic variable depending on lending opportunities and interest rates.

An individual bank is not constrained by any fixed quantum of reserves. It can obtain additional reserves to meet requirements by borrowing from the Federal Reserve, by buying "Federal Funds" from other banks, by selling or "running off" short-term securities. In short, reserves are available at the discount window and in the money market, at a price. This cost the bank must compare with available yields on loans and investments. If those yields are low relative to the cost of reserves, the bank will seek to avoid borrowing reserves and perhaps hold excess reserves instead. If those yields are high relative to the cost of borrowing reserves, the bank will shun excess reserves and borrow reserves occasionally or even regularly. For the banking system as a whole the Federal Reserve's quantitative controls determine the supply of unborrowed reserves. But the extent to which this supply is left unused, or supplemented by borrowing at the discount window, depends on the economic circumstances confronting the banks – on available lending opportunities and on the whole structure of interest rates from the Federal Reserve's discount rate through the rates on mortgages and long-term securities.

The range of variation in net free reserves in recent years has been from −5 per cent to +5 per cent of required reserves. This indicates a much looser linkage between reserves and deposits than is suggested by the textbook exposition of multiple expansion for a system which is always precisely and fully "loaned up." (It does not mean, however, that actual monetary authorities have any less control than textbook monetary authorities. Indeed the net free reserve position is one of their more useful instruments and barometers. Anyway, they are after bigger game than the quantity of "money"!)

Two consequences of this analysis deserve special notice because of their relation to the issues raised earlier in this chapter. First, an increase – of, say, a billion dollars – in the supply of unborrowed reserves will, in general, result in less than a billion-dollar increase in required reserves. Net free reserves will rise (algebraically) by some fraction of the billion dollars – a very large fraction in periods like the 1930's, a much smaller one in tight money periods like those of the fifties. Loans and deposits will expand by less than their textbook multiples. The reason is simple. The open market operations which bring about the increased supply of reserves tend to lower interest rates. So do the operations of the commercial banks in trying to invest their new reserves. The result is to diminish the incentives of banks to keep fully loaned up or to borrow reserves, and to make banks content to hold on the average higher excess reserves.

Second, depositor preferences do matter, even in a regime of fractional reserve banking. Suppose, for example, that the public decides to switch new or old savings from other assets and institutions into commercial banks. This switch makes earning assets available to banks at attractive yields – assets that otherwise would have been lodged either directly with the public or with the competing financial institutions previously favored with the public's savings. These improved opportunities for profitable lending and investing will make the banks content to hold smaller net free reserves. Both their deposits and their assets will rise as a result of this shift in public preferences, even though the base of unborrowed reserves remains unchanged. Something of this kind has occurred in recent years when commercial banks have been permitted to raise the interest rates they offer for time and savings deposits.

7. Concluding Remarks

The implications of the "new view" may be summarized as follows:

1. The distinction between commercial banks and other financial intermediaries has been too sharply drawn. The differences are of degree, not of kind.

2. In particular, the differences which do exist have little intrinsically to do with the monetary nature of bank liabilities.

3. The differences are more importantly related to the special reserve requirements and interest rate ceilings to which banks are subject. Any other financial industry subject to the same kind of regulations would behave in much the same way.

4. Commercial banks do not possess, either individually or collectively, a widow's cruse which guarantees that any expansion of assets will generate a corresponding expansion of deposit liabilities. Certainly this happy state of affairs would not exist in an unregulated competitive financial world. Marshall's scissors of supply and demand apply to the "output" of the banking industry, no less than to other financial and nonfinancial industries.

5. Reserve requirements and interest ceilings give the widow's cruse myth somewhat greater plausibility. But even in these circumstances, the scale of bank deposits and assets is affected by depositor preferences and by the lending and investing opportunities available to banks.

I draw no policy morals from these observations. That is quite another story, to which analysis of the type presented here is only the preface. The reader will misunderstand my purpose if he jumps to attribute to me the conclusion that existing differences in the regulatory treatment of banks and competing intermediaries should be diminished, either by relaxing constraints on the one or by tightening controls on the other.

Notes

[1] E.S. Shaw, "Money Supply and Stable Economic Growth," in *United States Monetary Policy* (New York: American Assembly, 1958), pp. 49-71.

[2] For a review of this development and for references to its protagonists, see Harry Johnson's survey article, "Monetary Theory and Policy," *American Economic Review* 52 (June 1962), 335-84. I will confine myself to mentioning the importance, in originating and contributing to the "new view," of John Gurley and E.S. Shaw (yes, the very same Shaw cited in the previous footnote, but presumably in a different incarnation). Their viewpoint is summarized in *Money in a Theory of Finance* (Washington, D.C.: Brookings Institution, 1960).

[3] These features of the market structure of intermediaries, and their implications for the supposed uniqueness of banks, have been emphasized by Gurley and Shaw, *op. cit.* An example of substitutability on the deposit side is analyzed by David and Charlotte Alhadeff, "The Struggle for Commercial Bank Savings," *Quarterly Journal of Economics,* 72 (February 1958), 1-22.

CHAPTER 17

FINANCIAL INTERMEDIARIES AND
THE EFFECTIVENESS OF MONETARY CONTROLS

Does the existence of uncontrolled financial intermediaries vitiate monetary control? What would be the consequences of subjecting these intermediaries to reserve requirements or to interest rate ceilings? This chapter is addressed to these questions, but it treats them theoretically and at a high level of abstraction. The method is to set up models of general equilibrium in financial and capital markets and to trace in these models the effects of monetary controls and of structural changes. Equilibrium in these models is an equilibrium of stocks and balance sheets – a situation in which both the public and the financial institutions are content with their portfolios of assets and debts, and the demand to hold each asset is just equal to the stock supply. This approach has obvious limitations, among which the most important is probably that it has nothing to say about speeds of adjustment and other dynamic effects of crucial practical importance. On the other hand, monetary economics has long suffered from trying to discuss these effects without solid foundation in any theory of general financial equilibrium. We feel that we can advance the discussion by outlining a systematic scheme for comparative static analysis of some of the questions at issue. [1]

The models discussed in the text are simple ones, designed to bring out the main points with few enough assets and interest rates so that graphical and verbal exposition can be used. The exposition in the text takes advantage of the fact that introducing nonbank financial intermediaries, uncontrolled or controlled, into a system in which banks are under effective monetary control

By James Tobin and William C. Brainard. Reprinted from *American Economic Review* (*Papers and Proceedings*), 53, No. 2 (May 1963), 383-400; and from *Financial Markets and Economic Activity*, edited by J. Tobin and D. Hester (New York: Wiley, 1967), Cowles Foundation Monograph No. 21, Chapter 3. Footnotes, tables, and figures have been renumbered, and parts repetitive of Chapter 16 have been omitted. © 1967 by Cowles Foundation for Research in Economics at Yale University.

presents essentially the same problems as introducing commercial banks as an intermediary, uncontrolled or controlled, into a system in which the government's essential control is the supply of its own currency. The analysis therefore centers on the more primitive question: the effects of financial intermediation by banks, the consequences of leaving their operation unregulated, and the effects of regulating them in various ways. The conclusions have some interest in themselves, in clarifying the functions of reserve and rate controls on commercial banks. By analogy they also bear on questions concerning the extension of such controls to other financial intermediaries.

The main conclusions can be briefly stated. The presence of banks, even if they are uncontrolled, does not mean that monetary control through the supply of currency has no effect on the economy. Nor does the presence of nonbank intermediaries mean that monetary control through commercial banks is an empty gesture. Even if increases in the assets and liabilities of uncontrolled intermediaries wholly offset enforced reductions in the supplies of controlled monetary assets, even if monetary expansion means equivalent contraction by uncontrolled intermediaries, monetary controls can still be effective. However, substitutions of this kind do diminish the effectiveness of these controls; for example, a billion-dollar change in the supply of currency and bank reserves would have more effect on the economy if such substitutions were prevented.

Whether it is important that monetary controls be more effective in this sense is another question, to which this chapter is not addressed. When a given remedial effect can be achieved either by a small dose of strong medicine or a large dose of weak medicine, it is not obvious that the small dose is preferable. Increasing the responsiveness of the system to instruments of control may also increase its sensitivity to random exogenous shocks. [2] Furthermore, extension of controls over financial intermediaries and markets involves considerations beyond those of economic stabilization; it raises also questions of equity, allocative efficiency, and the scope of governmental authority.

1. Substitution among Financial Intermediaries

The essential functions of banks and other financial intermediaries have been discussed in Chapter 16. In the interests of concise terminology, "banks" will refer to commercial banks and "nonbanks" to other financial institutions, including savings banks. Moreover, "intermediary" will refer to an entire species, or industry, of financial institutions. Thus all commercial banks constitute one intermediary, all life insurance companies another, and so on. An "institution" will mean an individual member of the species, an individual firm in the industry – a bank, or a life insurance company, or a retirement program.

Financial institutions fall fairly easily into distinct categories, each industry offering a differentiated product to its customers, both lenders and borrowers. There is also product differentiation within intermediaries, between institutions, arising from location, advertising, and the other sources of monopolistic competition. But this is of a smaller order of importance than the differentiation between intermediaries. For present purposes, the products offered by the institutions within a given intermediary can be regarded as homogeneous.

These observations about the nature of financial intermediaries and the imperfect competition among them lead to a basic assumption of the following analysis. The liabilities of each financial intermediary are considered homogeneous, and their appeal to owners of wealth is described by a single market rate of interest. The portfolios of wealthowners are made up of currency, real capital, and the liabilities of the various intermediaries. These assets are assumed to be imperfect substitutes for each other in wealthowners' portfolios. That is, an increase in the rate of return on any one asset will lead to an increase in the fraction of wealth held in that asset, and to a decrease or at most no change in the fraction held in every other asset. Similarly, borrowers are assumed to regard loans from various intermediaries as imperfect substitutes. That is – given the profitability of the real investment for which borrowing is undertaken – an increase in one intermediary lending rate will reduce borrowing from that intermediary and increase, or at least leave unchanged, borrowing from every other source.

2. The Criterion of Effectiveness of Monetary Control

A monetary control can be considered expansionary if it lowers the rate of return on ownership of real capital that the community requires to induce it to hold a given stock of capital, and deflationary if it raises that rate of return. (The words expansionary and deflationary are used merely to indicate the direction of influence; the manner in which the influence is divided between price change and output change depends on aspects of the economic situation that are not relevant here.) The value of the rate of return referred to is a hypothetical one: the level at which owners of wealth are content to absorb the given stock of capital into their portfolios or balance sheets along with other assets and debts. In full equilibrium, this critical rate of return must equal the expected marginal productivity of the capital stock, which depends technologically on the size of the stock relative to expected levels of output and employment. If a monetary action lowers the rate of return on capital owners of wealth will accept, it becomes easier for the economy to accumulate capital. If a monetary action increases the rate of return on equity investments demanded by owners of wealth, then it discourages capital accumulation.

This chapter concerns the financial sector alone, and we make no attempt here to describe the repercussions of a discrepancy between the rate of return on capital required for portfolio balance and the marginal productivity of capital. These repercussions occur in the market for goods and services and labor, and through them feed back to the financial sector itself. Let it suffice here to say that they are qualitatively of the same nature as the consequences of a discrepancy between Wicksell's natural and market rates of interest.

We assume the value of the stock of capital to be given by its replacement cost, which depends not on events in the financial sphere but on prices prevailing for newly produced goods. We make this assumption because the strength of new real investment in the economy depends on the terms on which the community will hold capital goods valued at the prices of current production. Any discrepancy between these terms and the actual marginal productivity of capital can be expressed alternatively as a discrepancy between market valuation of old capital and its replacement cost. But the discrepancy has the same implications for new investment whichever way it is expressed.

This required rate of return on capital is the basic criterion of the effectiveness of a monetary action. To alter the terms on which the community will accumulate real capital — that is what monetary policy is all about. The other criteria commonly discussed — this or that interest rate, this or that concept of the money supply, this or that volume of lending — are at best only instrumental and intermediate and at worst misleading goals.

3. Summary of Regimes

The argument proceeds by analysis of a sequence of regimes. A regime is characterized by listing the assets, debts, financial intermediaries, and interest rates which play a part in it. In all the regimes to be discussed, net private wealth is the sum of two components: the fixed capital stock, valued at current replacement cost; and the non-interest-bearing debt of the government, taking the form either of currency publicly held or of the reserves of banks and other intermediaries. In the models of this chapter, there is no government interest-bearing debt. [3] Consequently there are no open market operations proper. Instead the standard monetary action analyzed is a change in the supply of non-interest-bearing debt relative to the value of the stock of capital. (Only the proportions between the two components of wealth matter, because it is assumed that all asset and debt demands are, at given interest rates, homogeneous of degree one with respect to the scale of wealth.)

The public is divided, somewhat artificially, into two parts: wealthowners and borrowers. Wealthowners command the total private wealth of the economy and dispose it among the available assets, ranging from currency to direct ownership of capital. Borrowers use the loans they obtain from financial intermediaries to hold capital. This split should not be taken literally. A borrower may be, and usually is, a wealthowner – one who desires to hold more capital than his net worth permits.

A final simplification is to ignore the capital and nonfinancial accounts of intermediaries, on the ground that these are inessential to the purposes of the chapter. Table 17.1 provides a summary of the regimes to be discussed.

Table 17.1
Summary of financial regimes

| Regime | Structure of assets and debts | | Yields to be determined on |
	Holder	Assets (+), debts (−)	
I	Private wealth-owners	+ Currency, + capital	Capital
II	Private wealth-owners	+ Currency, + capital, + intermediary liabilities	Capital, intermediary liabilities and loans
	Private borrowers	− Loans, + capital	
	Intermediary	− Liabilities, + loans, (+ reserves)	
III	Private wealth-owners	+ Currency, + capital + deposits	(A) Capital, loans, deposits
	Private borrowers	− Loans, + capital	(B) Capital, loans (deposit rate fixed)
	Intermediary (banks)	− Deposits, + loans, + reserves (currency)	

4. Regime I: A Currency-Capital World

It is instructive to begin with a rudimentary financial world in which the only stores of value available are currency and real capital. There are no intermediaries, not even banks, and no credit markets. Private wealth is the sum of the stock of currency and the value of the stock of capital. The stock of currency is, in effect, the government debt, all in non-interest-bearing form. The required rate of return on capital R_0 is simply the rate at which wealthowners are content to hold the existing currency supply, neither more nor less, along with the existing capital stock, valued at replacement cost. The determination of R_0 is shown in Figure 17.1. In Figure 17.1, the return on capital R_0 is measured vertically. Total private wealth is measured by the horizontal length of the box OW, divided between the supply of currency OC and the replacement value of capital CW. Curve DD' is a portfolio choice curve, showing how wealthowners wish to divide their wealth between currency and capital at various rates R_0. It is a kind of "liquidity preference" curve. The rate which equates currency supply and demand – or, what amounts to the same thing, capital supply and demand – is $\bar{R}_0$.

In this rudimentary world, the sole monetary instrument is a change in the supply of currency relative to the supply of capital. An increase in currency supply relative to the capital stock can be shown in Figure 17.1 simply by moving the vertical line CC' to the right. Clearly this will lower the required rate of return R_0. Similarly, the monetary effect of a contraction of the currency supply can be represented by a leftward shift of the same vertical line.

5. Regime II: An Uncontrolled Intermediary

Now imagine that a financial intermediary arrives on the scene. The liabilities of the intermediary are a close but imperfect substitute for currency. Its assets are loans which enable private borrowers to hold capital in excess of their own net worth. How does the existence of this intermediary alter the effectiveness of monetary policy? That is, how does the intermediary affect the degree to which the government can change $\bar{R}_0$ by a given change in the supply of currency?

We will assume first that the intermediary is not required to hold reserves and does not hold any. Its sole assets are loans. To any institution the value of acquiring an additional dollar liability to the public is the interest at which it can be reloaned after allowance for administrative costs, default risk, and the like. Consequently, in unrestricted competition this rate will be paid to

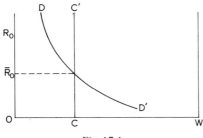

Fig. 17.1

the intermediary's creditors. In equilibrium, the borrower's demand for loans at the prevailing interest rate on loans will be the same as the public's supply of credits to the intermediary at the corresponding rate.

This regime is depicted in Figure 17.2. The axes represent the same variables as in Figure 17.1, and the supplies of currency and capital are shown in the same manner. But the demand for capital is now shown in two parts. The first, measured leftward from the right vertical axis to curve KK', is the direct demand of wealthowners. The second part, measured rightward from line CC' to curve LL', is the demand for capital by borrowers. This distance also measures the demand of borrowers for loan accommodation by the intermediary. Curve DD' represents, as in Figure 17.1, the demand of wealthowners for currency. The horizontal difference between DD' and KK' is their demand for the liabilities of the intermediary.

In this regime there is a second interest rate to be determined, the rate R_2 on intermediary liabilities. The rate on intermediary loans, r_2, is uniquely determined by R_2; competition among institutions keeps the margin between these rates equal to the cost of intermediation. The position of the three curves in Figure 17.2 and the demands which they depict depend on this rate as well as on R_0. The three dashed curves represent a higher intermediary rate R_2 than the solid curves. However, only the solid curves represent an

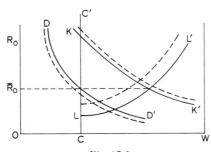

Fig. 17.2

equilibrium combination of the two rates, at which (1) the demands for capital absorb the entire capital stock, (2) the loan assets of the intermediary equal its liabilities, and (3) the demand for currency is equal to the supply.

We may presume, of course, that the introduction of the intermediary lowers the required rate of return on capital R_0. For wealthowners, the intermediary's liabilities satisfy some of the same needs which would be met in Regime I by an increase in the supply of currency. At the same time, some of the capital which wealthowners formerly held can now be lodged with borrowers, at a lower rate of return. These borrowers were unable to obtain finance to hold capital in Regime I.

An autonomous growth of the intermediary can be formally represented by a reduction in the margin between the intermediary's lending and borrowing rates. As the intermediary becomes more efficient in administration, risk pooling, and in tailoring its liabilities and assets to the preferences of its customers on both sides, this margin will decline under the force of competition. It can be shown that a reduction in the margin always lowers the required rate of return on capital and increases the intermediary's assets and liabilities.

A reduction in the supply of currency will, in this regime, as in the first regime, raise the required rate of return on capital. It will also raise the intermediary's rates. The existence of the intermediary does not, therefore, mean that monetary control is ineffective. However, it normally means that the control is less effective, in the sense that a dollar reduction in the supply of currency brings about a smaller increase in R_0 when it can be counteracted by expansion of the intermediary. The possibility of substituting the intermediary's liabilities for currency offers a partial escape from the monetary restriction. But as long as the intermediary's liabilities are an imperfect substitute for currency, the escape is only partial.

6. Regime II: A Controlled Intermediary

The proposition that the intermediary weakens monetary control can be demonstrated by imagining that we can impose some quantitative restriction on the expansion of the intermediary. We can then compare the strength of monetary restriction in Regime II, with and without this quantitative control.

Assume, therefore, that the government's non-interest-bearing debt is divided into two segregated parts: currency held by the public and reserves held by the intermediary pursuant to a legal fractional reserve requirement. Assume further that this requirement is effective, i.e., that the aggregate size of intermediary liabilities permitted by the reserve requirement is smaller than the size which would result from unrestricted competition. When the reserve requirement is effective, the margin between the intermediary's lending and borrowing rates is greater than is needed to compensate for risk and administrative costs. Let the supply of currency to the public be reduced. In an uncontrolled Regime II, this will in certain circumstances lead to an expansion of intermediary assets and liabilities. In those circumstances, preventing such expansion by a reserve requirement will increase the effectiveness of monetary control. That is, a dollar reduction in the currency supply will raise R_0 more if an expansionary response by the intermediary is prevented. There are also circumstances — probably less plausible — where monetary restriction would, in an uncontrolled regime, result in a contraction of the intermediary. In these cases, of course, control of the intermediary does not strengthen monetary control.

The example just discussed is a simple and artificial one. But the point it makes is of quite general applicability. In the more complex real world, currency and commercial bank liabilities are together subject to control via monetary policy, while the scales of operations of other financial intermediaries are not. The freedom of these intermediaries offers an escape from monetary controls over commercial banks, but only a partial escape. Likewise, the effectiveness of monetary controls would be enhanced if each nonbank intermediary was subject to a specific reserve requirement which would keep it from expanding counter to policies which contract commercial banks.

7. Regime III: Commercial Banking

The reserve requirement introduced in Regime II was expressed in terms of a specific government debt instrument, available only for this purpose and only in amounts determined by the government. The more familiar situation is that the reserve asset is, for all practical purposes, currency itself. Currency, that is, can serve either as a means of payment in the hands of the public, or as reserves for the intermediary. The government determines the total size of its non-interest-bearing debt, but its allocation between currency and reserves is a matter of public choice. It is, of course, this kind of reserve and reserve requirement that we associate with commercial banks — the most prominent intermediary. Indeed, the traditional business of banks is to accept deposit liabilities payable in currency on demand, and this obligation is the historical reason for banks' holding reserves in currency or its equivalent in "high-powered" money.

Let us consider, therefore, a third regime in which the one intermediary is a commercial banking system required to hold as reserves in currency a certain fraction of its deposit liabilities. Total private wealth is, as in the first two regimes, the sum of currency supply and the capital stock. Wealthowners divide their holdings among currency, bank deposits, and direct ownership of capital. Banks dispose their deposits between reserves in currency and loans to borrowers, in proportions dictated by the legal reserve requirement. Borrowers hold that part of the capital stock not directly held by wealthowners. So far as interest rates are concerned, there are two important variants:

A. Interest on bank deposits is competitively determined, and stands in competitive relation to the interest rate on bank loans. This relationship will depend on, among other things, the reserve requirement, which compels a bank to place a fraction' of any additional deposit in non-interest-bearing reserves.

B. Interest on deposits is subject to an effective legal ceiling, and at the same time the reserve requirement normally restricts the banking industry to a scale at which the loan rate exceeds this fixed deposit interest rate by more than the competitive margin.

In this regime, there are two sources of demand for currency. One is the direct demand of the public. The other is the banks' reserve requirement; in effect, the public demand for deposits creates a fractional indirect demand for currency. This creates an interesting complication, as follows: The basic assumption about the portfolio behavior of wealthowners is that assets are all substitutes for each other. Essentially the same assumption is applied to the behavior of borrowers, that is, a rise in the interest rate on any asset (A) induces, *ceteris paribus,* an increase in desired holdings of (A) and a decrease, or at most no change, in the desired holdings of every other asset. It is this assumption which enabled us to state unambiguously the direction of the effects of monetary actions in the regimes previously discussed. In the present regime the same substitution assumption still applies to the portfolio behavior of wealthowners and borrowers. This means, among other things, that the public's direct demand for currency is assumed to decline, or at most not to rise, in response to an increase in the rate offered on bank deposits. But, of course, an increase in this rate also increases the demand for bank deposits. Thus it indirectly increases the demand for currency to serve as bank reserves.

It is certainly conceivable, especially if the required reserve ratio is high, that the indirect effect of an increase in the deposit rate outweights the direct effect. In that event, currency and deposits are, taking account of public and banks together, complements rather than substitutes. The possibility is the simplest example of a very general phenomenon. Even though the substitution assumption applies to the portfolio choices of the public, and of every intermediary, taken separately, it is possible that assets will be complements in the system as a whole. This can happen whenever the public and intermediaries hold the same assets (currency, or government bonds, or other securities) or whenever one intermediary holds as assets the liabilities of another intermediary. Some of the implications of complementarity for both the stability of the system and its responses to various changes in parameters and in structure can be illustrated in the present regime.

Equilibrium in Regime III may be depicted by considering separately the conditions of equilibrium in the market for currency and in the market for loans. In Figure 17.3 the supply of currency is shown as the vertical line CC'. The demand for currency, in relation to the deposit rate R_2, is the curve AA'. This includes both the direct and the indirect demand for currency. As noted above, this relationship may be either downward-sloping as in (a) or upward-sloping, as in (b). The upward-sloping case is that of complementarity. In each case the position of the demand curve depends on the level of R_0; the dashed curve represents a higher R_0, which tends to reduce the demand for currency. From the relationships involved in Figure 17.3 can be derived a locus of pairs of rates R_0 and R_2 which equate demand and supply for currency. Such a relationship is shown in Figure 17.5 by the curve E_c. In the "substitutes case," corresponding to Figure 17.3(a), it is downward-sloping, as shown in Figure 17.5(a). In the "complements case," correspond-

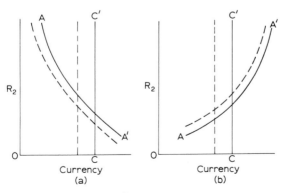

Fig. 17.3

ing to Figure 17.3(b), it is upward-sloping, as shown in Figures 17.5(b) and (c).

In Figure 17.4 the loan market is shown, the volume of loans on the horizontal axis and the deposit rate on the vertical axis. The supply of loans, BB', is essentially the public demand for deposits, after allowance for the fractional reserve requirement. The demand for loans, LL', is the amount of loan accommodation borrowers wish at various deposit rates, taking account of the fact that the loan rate systematically exceeds the deposit rate for the reasons already mentioned. The positions of the loan supply and demand curves depend on R_0, the rate of return on capital. A higher R_0 shifts both curves upward, as indicated by the dashed curves. From these relationships a second locus of the two rates R_0 and R_2 can be derived, the pairs of rates which equilibrate the loan market. This is the upward-sloping relationship E_l, also shown in Figure 17.5.

Three possible cases for the system as a whole are shown in the three parts of Figure 17.5: the first, or substitutes case, in Figure 17.5(a), a moderate complements case in Figure 17.5(b). Now if there is a reduction in the supply of currency, equilibrium in the currency market can be maintained only by an increase in the rate on capital R_0 associated with any given deposit rate R_2. This can be seen by a shift left in the currency supply in Figure 17.3. Consequently the effect of a reduction in the currency supply can be shown in Figure 17.5 by a rightward shift in the curve E_c. In the first two cases, Figures 17.5(a) and 17.5(b), this means an increase in both rates, as would be expected. However, in the extreme complements case, Figure 17.5(c), it indicates a decrease in both rates!

This implausible result arouses the suspicion that the solution indicated in Figure 17.5(c) is an unstable equilibrium. We have examined the question of stability under the assumption that excess demand for capital leads to a fall in

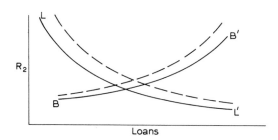

Fig. 17.4

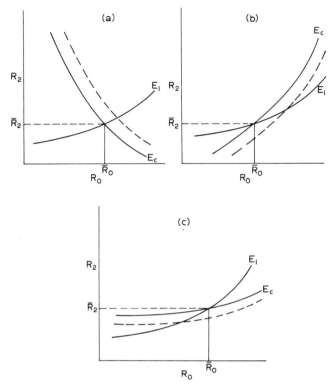

Fig. 17.5

the rate of return on capital R_0, while excess borrowers' demand for loans, relative to the supply permitted by reserve requirements and depositor preferences, leads to a rise in loan-deposit rate R_2. The case exhibited in Figure 17.5(c) is indeed unstable, while the other two cases are stable.

Consider now alternative (B), in which the interest rate on deposits is subject to an effective legal ceiling. The competitive link between the deposit and loan rates is broken by this regulation. In Figure 17.3, in other words, there is only one applicable level of the deposit rate. Consequently, there is only one rate on capital which is consistent with equilibrium in the "market" for currency. Figure 17.6 exhibits this situation. The currency equilibrium curve of Figure 17.6 is simply a vertical line; although the loan rate r_2 measured on the vertical axis of Figure 17.6 can vary, its variation does not affect either the deposit rate or equilibrium in the currency market.

The effect of an increase in the controlled deposit rate depends on

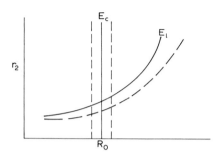

Fig. 17.6

whether currency and deposits are, when both indirect and direct demands are taken into account, substitutes or complements. If they are substitutes, an increase in the controlled deposit rate will reduce the net demand for currency. Therefore, the rate on capital R_0 which balances the supply and demand for currency will be lower. In Figure 17.6, this means a movement to the left in the vertical line. An increase in the deposit rate also increases the supply of loans, causing a downward shift in the E_l schedule. For any given rate on capital a lower loan rate will be required to clear the loan market. In the new equilibrium both the rate on capital and the loan rate will be lower. An increase in the deposit rate is an expansionary monetary action. [4] If, on the other hand, currency and deposits are complements, the result of an increase in the controlled deposit rate is the reverse. An increase in the rate on capital will be required to restore equilibrium in the currency market; the increase in deposit rate is a deflationary monetary action. However the loan rate r_2 may move either way. As in the substitutes case, a rise in the deposit rate increases the supply of loans, shifting E_l downward. But the rise in the rate of return on capital R_0 raises the demand for loans.

With a fixed deposit rate, a reduction in currency supply is always deflationary. This is true, of course, whether currency and deposits are substitutes or complements. But the question of real interest is whether monetary restriction is more deflationary — i.e., produces a bigger increase in the return on capital — when the deposit rate is flexible or when it is fixed. Monetary restriction will, in the flexible case, increase the deposit rate; in the other case the legal ceiling prevents this reaction. Now if currency and deposits are substitutes, an increase in the deposit rate is expansionary; it opposes and weakens the monetary contraction. But if they are complements, the reverse is true; flexibility in the deposit rate reinforces and strengthens quantitative monetary control.

Once there is a reserve requirement, variation in the required ratio is another instrument of monetary control. There are two questions to ask about such variation. The first concerns its effect upon the required rate of return on capital. The second concerns its effect on the strength of quantitative monetary control.

With a fixed deposit rate, an increase in the reserve requirement is always deflationary. With a given currency supply, the higher reserve requirement necessarily means that the public must curtail its holdings of currency or deposits or both. The only way they can be induced to do so is by an increase in R_0.

With a flexible deposit rate the same conclusion applies when currency and deposits are substitutes. However, it is conceivable, when they are complements, that an increase in the reserve requirement will be expansionary. [5]

We may now ask what is the effect of introducing, or in general of increasing, the reserve requirement on the strength of quantitative monetary control. The answer may depend on whether the deposit rate is fixed or flexible. With a fixed deposit rate an increase in the reserve requirement will decrease the response to changes in currency supply. This can be seen by imagining that uncontrolled Regime II is modified, first, by fixing the deposit rate and, second, by imposing a reserve requirement. With a fixed deposit rate and no reserve requirement, any reduction in the supply of currency is at the expense of the public's direct holdings of currency. The increase in the rate of return on capital necessary to reconcile the public to these reduced holdings of currency will also diminish their demand for bank deposits. But when banks hold no reserves, this cannot release any currency.

On the other hand, once banks are required to hold reserves, a contraction of bank deposits releases currency. Therefore, direct holdings of currency do not have to absorb the full reduction in the currency supply. Consequently, the necessary increase in the rate of return on capital is smaller.

When the deposit rate is free to rise, we would expect an increase in the rate in the wake of currency contraction to increase the volume of bank deposits. This expansion tends to offset the reduction in the public's currency holdings. Substitution of deposits for currency moderates the increase in R_0 necessary to reconcile the public to smaller holdings of currency. When banks hold no reserves, this substitution can proceed without any brake. But when banks are subject to a reserve requirement, it can proceed only to the extent that the public is induced to give up additional currency to serve as bank reserves. Therefore, a reserve requirement means that a larger increase in R_0, the rate of return on capital, is needed to make the public content with a larger reduction in its direct holdings of currency.

Table 17.2
Summary of Results for Regime III

Currency and deposits are	Substitutes	Complements	Extreme complements
System is	Stable	Stable	Unstable
Increase in deposit rate is	Expansionary	Deflationary	
Variation of currency supply more effective when deposit rate is	Fixed	Flexible	

This is the essential reason why regulations preventing or limiting expansion of the intermediary strengthen monetary control. It may be observed that such regulations are of two kinds: either a rate ceiling which prevents the intermediary from bidding for funds, or a reserve requirement, or both. Once there is an effective rate ceiling, however, increasing the required reserve ratio — though itself an effective instrument of control — reduces the effectiveness of a given change in the supply of currency. It is possible, even when the deposit rate is flexible, that bank deposits decline in response to a contraction of the currency supply. Then, just as in the case of a fixed deposit rate, increasing the reserve requirement diminishes the response of the system to such contraction. A reserve requirement is not necessary to prevent expansion of the intermediary from offering an escape from monetary control, because the intermediary would not expand anyway. [6]

The principal results for Regime III are summarized in Table 17.2.

These conclusions have been reached by adding one intermediary, banks, to a currency-capital model and then imposing rate and reserve regulations on banks. But they are illustrative of more general conclusions. In a many-intermediary world, similar propositions apply to the extension to nonbank intermediaries of the rate and reserve regulations to which banks are subject.

Appendix

1. Notation and Assumptions

Suppose there are n types of financial assets that owners of wealth can hold; the first currency, the remaining $(n-1)$ the liabilities of $(n-1)$ financial intermediaries. An $(n+1)$ asset, direct equity in capital, is designated by subscript 0. Let $D_i \geqslant 0$ be the proportion of the value of total wealth the public desires to hold in the ith asset $(i = 0, 1, 2, ..., n)$. Let R_i be the rate of return offered owners of the ith asset. Since the first financial asset is currency, R_1 is taken to be fixed at zero. Each D_i may be taken to be a function of all the R_i. We shall further assume that the demand for the various assets is homogeneous in wealth, i.e., the D_i do not depend on the level of wealth. There are n independent functions to distribute total wealth into $n+1$ categories. Thus we may represent wealth-owners' desired allocation by:

$$D_i = D_i(R_0, R_2, ..., R_n) \qquad (i = 1, 2, ..., n) . \tag{A1}$$

The assets are assumed to be imperfect substitutes, so that the effect of a reduction in the jth interest rate, other rates remaining constant, is to diminish D_j and to increase or at least to leave unchanged the demand for each of the other assets, including D_0. Similarly, it is assumed that the effect of a reduction in R_0 is to increase or leave unchanged every financial asset holding. Using the notation D_{ij} to represent the partial derivative of the function D_i with respect to the jth rate, these assumptions are as follows:

$$D_{ij} > 0 \ (i = j) \qquad (i, j = 1, 2, ..., n)$$

$$D_{ij} \leqslant 0 \ (i \neq j)$$

$$\sum_{i=1}^{n} D_{ij} > 0 \qquad (j = 2, ..., n) \tag{A2}$$

$$D_{i0} \leqslant 0$$

Each of the financial intermediaries offers its own variety of loan to individuals who would like to hold capital beyond their net worth. The demands of borrowers for loans of each type depend jointly on the rate of return on capital, R_0, and on the $(n-1)$ different borrowers' interest rates r_i:

$$L_i = L_i(R_0, r_2, ..., r_n) \qquad (i = 2, 3, ..., n) \tag{A3}$$

Debts of different types are assumed to be gross substitutes, so that the effect of a reduction in the jth borrower's rate, other rates remaining constant, is to increase both total borrowing $\Sigma_{i=2}^{n} L_i$ and L_j specifically and to diminish or leave unchanged all other debts. The effect of a reduction in R_0 is to diminish or leave unchanged borrowers' demands for each type of loan. These assumptions are as follows:

$$L_{ij} < 0 \; (i = j)$$

$$L_{ij} \geq 0 \; (i \neq j)$$

$$\sum_{i=1}^{n} L_{ij} < 0 \qquad (i, j = 2, ..., n) \qquad (A4)$$

$$L_{i0} \geq 0$$

In addition to loans, an intermediary may hold other assets. The regimes considered in section 2 (and their n-intermediary counterparts in section 3) make different assumptions about intermediaries' portfolios of loans, currency and other assets. The portfolio choices of intermediaries are constrained by the requirement that their assets equal their liabilities. (For the present purposes no harm is done by assuming shareholders' equity in intermediaries to be zero.) To simplify presentation, the balance sheet identity for each financial intermediary will be used to translate wealthowners demand for each intermediary's liability into indirect demand for loans, currency, etc. Equilibrium in the various asset markets may then be represented by a system of equations of the following form:

Capital $\quad A_0(R_0, R_2, ..., R_n, r_2, ..., r_n) = S_0$

Currency $\quad A_1(R_0, R_2, ..., R_n, r_2, ..., r_n) = S_1$

Loans $\quad \underline{A_i(R_0, R_2, ..., R_n, r_2, ..., r_n) = 0} \qquad (i = 2, ..., n) \qquad (A5)$

$$\sum_{0}^{n} A_i \qquad\qquad = \sum S_i = 1$$

The functions A_0, A_1, and A_i are derived from the demand functions D_i and L_i already discussed. A_0 and A_1 represent the total private demand for capital and currency respectively. The supply of these assets, which comprise private wealth, are S_0 and S_1. The A_i in the remaining $(n-1)$ equations represent the excess demand functions for the various types of intermediary loans. When there are additional forms of government debt, this system is correspondingly augmented with equations like that relating to currency. The last equation indicates that the demands for the various assets always sum up to private wealth; hence one of the preceding demand equations is redundant. We follow the convention of omitting the first equation.

The n independent equations of (A5) contain $(2n-1)$ rates: R_0 the yield of capital, $(n-1)$ intermediary lending rates, and $(n-1)$ intermediary borrowing rates. Consequently, $(n-1)$ additional equations are needed. For example, lending and borrowing rates may be assumed equal for all intermediaries in a competitive regime where intermediaries hold no assets but loans. Then

$$R_i = r_i \qquad (i = 2, ..., n) \ . \tag{A6}$$

This need not be literally interpreted to mean that competition among financial institutions within a given intermediary brings the rates into equality. The assumption could be relaxed to permit a premium to compensate for administrative costs and risks of default and illiquidity, without essential difference so long as the premium is a constant or increasing function of the total volume of assets and liabilities of the intermediary.

When the deposit rates are regulated, or competition is ineffective, a different set of $(n-1)$ conditions will apply to the rates.

Use of equations (A6) or their counterpart will enable us to eliminate all but n variables from the system of equations (A5). The effects of changes in parameters on the rates, and in particular on R_0, may then be found by differentiating this system. The results depend crucially upon the partial derivatives of the demand equations A_i, which differ from regime to regime.

2. Analysis of Regimes

2.1. Regime I

$$D_1(R_0) = S_1 \qquad \text{Currency}$$

$$\frac{\partial R_0}{\partial S_1} = \frac{1}{D_{10}} < 0 \tag{A7}$$

2.2. Regime II

2.2.1. Uncontrolled Intermediary

$$D_1(R_0, R_2) = S_1 \qquad \text{Currency}$$

$$D_2(R_0, R_2) - L_2(R_0, r_2) = 0 \qquad \text{Intermediary} \tag{A8}$$

$$r_2 - R_2 = a \qquad \text{Relation between rates}$$

(i) Effect of reduction in margin between rates

$$
\begin{bmatrix}
D_{10} & D_{12} \\
D_{20} - L_{20} & D_{20} - L_{22}
\end{bmatrix}
\begin{bmatrix}
\dfrac{\partial R_0}{\partial a} \\
\dfrac{\partial R_2}{\partial a}
\end{bmatrix}
=
\begin{bmatrix}
0 \\
L_{22}
\end{bmatrix}
\tag{A9}
$$

The restrictions on D_i and L_i assumed in section 1 assure that the determinant of the Jacobian is negative, that $\partial R_0/\partial a \geqslant 0$, that $\partial R_2/\partial a \leqslant 0$, and that $\partial D_2/\partial a = D_{20}(\partial R_0/\partial a) + D_{22}(\partial R_2/\partial a) \leqslant 0$. That is, an increase in the efficiency of intermediation lowers the required return on capital, raises the deposit rate, and expands the liabilities and assets of the intermediary.

(ii) Effect of change in currency supply.

$$
J'
\begin{bmatrix}
\dfrac{\partial R_0}{\partial S_1} \\
\dfrac{\partial R_2}{\partial S_1}
\end{bmatrix}
=
\begin{bmatrix}
1 \\
0
\end{bmatrix}
\tag{A10}
$$

where J' is the Jacobian of equation (A9). It follows that $\partial R_0/\partial S_1$, $\partial R_2/\partial S_1$, $\partial r_2/\partial S_1 \leqslant 0$. However $\partial D_2/\partial S_1 = D_{20}(\partial R_0/\partial S_1) + D_{22}(\partial R_2/\partial S_1)$ may have either sign.

2.2.2. Controlled Intermediary

$$D_1(R_0, R_2) = S_1 \qquad \text{Currency}$$
$$eD_2(R_0, R_2) = S_2 \qquad \text{Specific reserve} \quad \text{(A11)}$$
$$(1-e)D_2(R_0, R_2) - L_2(R_0, r_2) = 0 \qquad \text{Intermediary}$$

Here S_2 is the supply of government debt in the form of the reserve asset, expressed as a proportion of total wealth. The required ratio is $0 \leqslant e \leqslant 1$. There are three equations in the three rates R_0, R_2, r_2; the third equation of (A8) drops out. (However, the inequality $r_2 - R_2 \geqslant a$ must hold; otherwise equations (A11) are supplanted by equations (A8).)

(i) Effect of change in currency supply.

$$\begin{bmatrix} D_{10} & D_{12} & 0 \\ D_{20} & D_{22} & 0 \\ (1-e)D_{20}-L_{20} & (1-e)D_{22} & -L_{22} \end{bmatrix} \begin{bmatrix} \dfrac{\partial R_0}{\partial S_1} \\ \dfrac{\partial R_2}{\partial S_1} \\ \dfrac{\partial r_2}{\partial S_1} \end{bmatrix} = \begin{bmatrix} 1 \\ 0 \\ 0 \end{bmatrix} \quad (A12)$$

The first two equations can be solved separately, and it is easily seen that $\partial R_0/\partial S_1$, $\partial R_2/\partial S_1 \leqslant 0$. Since $D_{20}(\partial R_0/\partial S_1) = -D_{22}(\partial R_2/\partial S_1)$ from the second equation the third equation reduces to

$$-L_{20}\frac{\partial R_0}{\partial S_1} = L_{22}\frac{\partial r_2}{\partial S_1}.$$

Therefore $\partial r_2/\partial S_1$ is also nonpositive.

(ii) Comparison with uncontrolled regime.

The effect of restraining the expansion of the intermediary can be found by subtracting equation system (A10) from the first two equations of (A12).

$$\begin{bmatrix} D_{10} & D_{12} \\ D_{20} & D_{22} \end{bmatrix} \begin{bmatrix} \dfrac{\partial R_0}{\partial S_1} \\ \dfrac{\partial R_2}{\partial S_1} \end{bmatrix}_{(A12)} - \begin{bmatrix} D_{10} & D_{12} \\ D_{20}-L_{20} & D_{22}-L_{22} \end{bmatrix} \begin{bmatrix} \dfrac{\partial R_0}{\partial S_1} \\ \dfrac{\partial R_2}{\partial S_1} \end{bmatrix}_{(A10)} = \begin{bmatrix} 0 \\ 0 \end{bmatrix}$$

$$\begin{bmatrix} D_{10} & D_{12} \\ D_{20} & D_{22} \end{bmatrix} \begin{bmatrix} \left(\dfrac{\partial R_0}{\partial S_1}\right)_{(A12)} - \left(\dfrac{\partial R_0}{\partial S_1}\right) \\ \left(\dfrac{\partial R_2}{\partial S_1}\right)_{(A12)} - \left(\dfrac{\partial R_2}{\partial S_1}\right)_{(A10)} \end{bmatrix}$$

$$= \begin{bmatrix} 0 & 0 \\ -L_{20} & -L_{22} \end{bmatrix} \begin{bmatrix} \dfrac{\partial R_0}{\partial S_1} \\ \dfrac{\partial R_2}{\partial S_1} \end{bmatrix}_{(A10)} = \begin{bmatrix} 0 \\ -\left(\dfrac{\partial D_2}{\partial S_1}\right)_{(A10)} \end{bmatrix} \quad (A13)$$

It follows that

$$\text{sign}\left(\frac{\partial R_0}{\partial S_1}\right)_{(A12)} - \left(\frac{\partial R_0}{\partial S_1}\right)_{(A10)} = \text{sign}\left(\frac{\partial D_2}{\partial S_1}\right)_{(A10)}$$

$$\text{sign}\ \left(\frac{\partial R_2}{\partial S_1}\right)_{(A12)} - \left(\frac{\partial R_2}{\partial S_1}\right)_{(A10)} = \text{sign}\ -\left(\frac{\partial D_2}{\partial S_1}\right)_{(A10)}$$

If reduction of currency supply would lead to an expansion of the intermediary when it is uncontrolled, then preventing this expansion will enhance the effectiveness of the currency restriction.

2.3. Regime III

2.3.1. Deposit Rate Flexible

$$D_1(R_0, R_2) + cD_2(R_0, R_2) = S_1 \quad \text{Currency}$$
$$(1 - c)D_2(R_0, R_2) - L_2(R_0, r_2) = 0 \quad \text{Intermediary (banks)} \quad \text{(A14)}$$
$$\frac{R_2}{1 - c} - r_2 = 0 \quad \text{Relation between rates}$$

Here the required reserve is in currency, and the required ratio is $0 \leqslant c \leqslant 1$. The three equations determine R_0, R_2, r_2.

2.3.2. Deposit Rate Fixed

$$D_1(R_0, \bar{R}_2) + cD_2(R_0, \bar{R}_2) \quad = S_1 \quad \text{Currency}$$
$$(1 - c)D_2(R_0, \bar{R}_2) - L_2(R_0, r_2) = 0 \quad \text{Intermediary (banks)} \quad \text{(A15)}$$

Here the deposit rate is fixed at $\bar{R}_2$, and the two equations determine R_0, r_2. In order for this regime to apply, the following inequality must hold:

$$\frac{\bar{R}_2}{1 - c} \leqslant r_2\ .$$

(i) Change in fixed deposit rate in B.

$$\begin{bmatrix} D_{10} + cD_{20} & 0 \\ \\ (1 - c)D_{20} - L_{20} & -L_{22} \end{bmatrix} \begin{bmatrix} \dfrac{\partial R_0}{\partial \bar{R}_2} \\ \\ \dfrac{\partial r_2}{\partial \bar{R}_2} \end{bmatrix} = - \begin{bmatrix} D_{12} + cD_{22} \\ \\ (1 - c)D_{22} \end{bmatrix} \quad \text{(A16)}$$

The determinant of the Jacobian is negative. Therefore

$$\text{sign}\ \frac{\partial R_0}{\partial \bar{R}_2} = \text{sign}\ (D_{12} + cD_{22}) \quad \text{(A17)}$$

Currency and deposits are defined to be *substitutes* if $(D_{12} + cD_{22}) < 0$, and *complements* if $(D_{12} + cD_{22}) > 0$. Thus equation (A17) says that raising the fixed deposit rate is *expansionary* if currency and deposits are substitutes and *deflationary* if they are complements.

The sign of $\partial r_2/\partial R_2$ is also ambiguous:

$$\text{sign}\,\frac{\partial r_2}{\partial \bar{R}_2} = \text{sign}\,\begin{vmatrix} D_{10} + cD_{20} & D_{12} + cD_{22} \\ (1-c)D_{20} - L_{20} & (1-c)D_{22} \end{vmatrix}$$

In the substitutes case $\partial r_2/\partial \bar{R}_2 < 0$.

(ii) Complementarity and stability.

The sign of $D_{12} + cD_{22}$ is also important in determining the stability of the equilibrium represented by the solution of equations (A14). Let the Jacobian of equations (A14) be:

$$J' = \begin{bmatrix} D_{10} + cD_{20} & D_{12} + cD_{22} \\ (1-c)D_{20} - L_{20} & (1-c)D_{22} - L_{22} \cdot \dfrac{1}{1-c} \end{bmatrix}$$

The solution is stable if $|J'| < 0$ and unstable if $|J'| > 0$. If $D_{12} + cD_{22} < 0$, $|J'| < 0$. That is, a sufficient condition for stability is that currency and deposits be substitutes. This is not a necessary condition. But "extreme" complementarity is associated with instability. The proof that stability depends on the sign of $|J'|$ is as follows.

Assume that excess demand for capital leads to a fall in the rate of return on capital and that an excess of borrowers' demand for loans over banks' supply of loans leads to a rise in the deposit rate R_2 and accordingly in the loan rate r_2. [7]

$$\begin{aligned} \dot{R}_0 &= -K_0 A_0 (R_0, R_2) \\ \dot{R}_2 &= -K_2 A_2 (R_0, R_2) \end{aligned} \qquad (A18)$$

where $K_0, K_2 > 0$ are speeds of adjustment, which by choice of units may be taken as unity.

Here,

$$\begin{aligned} A_0 &= 1 - D_1 - D_2 + L_2 - S_0 \\ &= S_1 - D_1 - D_2 + L_2 \end{aligned}$$

and

$$A_2 = (1-c)D_2 - L_2$$

By Taylor's theorem we can approximate A_i in the neighborhood of equilibrium by the linear expression:

$$A_i = \sum_j a_{ij}(R_j - \bar{R}_j) \qquad i = 0, 2 \tag{A19}$$

where a_{ij} is the partial derivative of excess demand for the ith asset with respect to the jth rate and $\bar{R}_j$ is the equilibrium R_j.

Substituting equation (A19) in equation (A18) and using the relationships given in equation (A14) we obtain:

$$\begin{bmatrix} \dot{R}_0 \\ \\ \dot{R}_2 \end{bmatrix} = \begin{bmatrix} D_{10} + D_{20} - L_{20} & D_{12} + D_{22} - \dfrac{L_{22}}{1-c} \\ \\ -(1-c)D_{20} + L_{20} & -(1-c)D_{22} + \dfrac{L_{22}}{1-c} \end{bmatrix} \begin{bmatrix} R_0 - \bar{R}_0 \\ \\ R_2 - \bar{R}_2 \end{bmatrix}$$

$$= A[R_i - \bar{R}_i] \tag{A20}$$

This system is stable if and only if the real parts of the characteristic roots of the Jacobian A are all negative. A 2 by 2 matrix with negative diagonal elements (always the case in our system) has the real parts of its characteristic roots negative if and only if the determinant of the matrix is positive. That is, stability under our assumptions requires $|A| > 0$.

By adding the last row of the determinant of A to the first row it can be seen that:

$$|J'| = -|A|$$

hence $|J'| < 0$ is a necessary and sufficient condition for stability under our assumptions.

In the text we defined "extreme" complementarity as the case where the currency equilibrium curve E_c cuts the loan equilibrium curve E_l above from the left as in fig. 17.5(c). Let $E_l(R_0)$ be the value of R_2 which clears the loan market, and $E_c(R_0)$ the value of R_2 which clears the currency "market."

The for the "extreme" complements case

$$\frac{\partial E_l}{\partial R_0} > \frac{\partial E_c}{\partial R_0} > 0 \quad \text{for} \quad (D_{12} + cD_{22}) > 0$$

since

$$\frac{\partial E_l}{\partial R_0} = \frac{-[(1-c)D_{20} - L_{20}]}{[(1-c)D_{22} - L_{22}/(1-c)]}$$

and

$$\frac{\partial E_c}{\partial R_0} = \frac{-(D_{10} + cD_{20})}{(D_{12} + cD_{22})}$$

and

$$|J'| = (D_{10} + cD_{20})\left[(1-c)D_{22} - \frac{L_{22}}{1-c}\right] - [(1-c)D_{10} - L_{20}](D_{12} + cD_{22})$$

it is clear that in the complements case:

$$\frac{\partial E_l}{\partial R_0} \gtrless \frac{\partial E_c}{\partial R_0} \quad \text{implies } |J'| \gtrless 0$$

The "extreme" complements case is unstable; the "moderate" complements case is stable.

(iii) Effect of change in currency supply.

(a) Deposit rate flexible.

Differentiating equations (A14) gives:

$$J' \begin{bmatrix} \dfrac{\partial R_0}{\partial S_1} \\[2ex] \dfrac{\partial R_2}{\partial S_1} \end{bmatrix} = \begin{bmatrix} 1 \\[2ex] 0 \end{bmatrix} \tag{A21}$$

Assuming stability, $|J'| < 0$, and $\partial R_0/\partial S_1$, $\partial R_2/\partial S_1 \leqslant 0$.

(b) Deposit rate fixed:

Differentiating equations (A15) and letting J^2 be the Jacobian of this system, written out in (A16) we have:

$$J^2 \begin{bmatrix} \dfrac{\partial R_0}{\partial S_1} \\[2ex] \dfrac{\partial r_2}{\partial S_1} \end{bmatrix} = \begin{bmatrix} 1 \\[2ex] 0 \end{bmatrix} \tag{A22}$$

Again,

$$\frac{\partial R_0}{\partial S_1}, \frac{\partial r_2}{\partial S_1} \leqslant 0 .$$

We can compare the responses in the two cases by assuming a restriction of currency supply beginning at the same equilibrium. In one case, (b), the deposit rate is prevented from rising, but the loan rate may rise. In the other case, (a), the two rates remain in the equilibrium relationship given by the third equation of (A14). However, in order to make the comparison, we must use that equation to eliminate R_2, rather than r_2, from the first two equations of (A14). Denoting the solutions to (A14) and (A15) by 1 and 2 respectively we find:

$$
\begin{bmatrix} D_{10} + cD_{20} & (D_{12} + cD_{22})(1-c) \\ \\ (1-c)D_{20} - L_{20} & (1-c)^2 D_{22} - L_{22} \end{bmatrix} \begin{bmatrix} \dfrac{\partial R_0}{\partial S_1} \\ \\ \dfrac{\partial r_2}{\partial S_1} \end{bmatrix}_1
$$

$$
- \begin{bmatrix} D_{10} + cD_{20} & 0 \\ \\ (1-c)D_{20} - L_{20} & -L_{22} \end{bmatrix} \begin{bmatrix} \dfrac{\partial R_0}{\partial S_1} \\ \\ \dfrac{\partial r_2}{\partial S_1} \end{bmatrix}_2 = \begin{bmatrix} 0 \\ \\ 0 \end{bmatrix} \qquad \text{(A23)}
$$

Therefore

$$
\begin{bmatrix} D_{10} + cD_{20} & (D_{12} + cD_{22})(1-c) \\ \\ (1-c)D_{20} - L_{20} & (1-c)^2 D_{22} - L_{22} \end{bmatrix} \begin{bmatrix} \left(\dfrac{\partial R_0}{\partial S_1}\right)_1 - \left(\dfrac{\partial R_0}{\partial S_1}\right)_2 \\ \\ \left(\dfrac{\partial r_2}{\partial S_1}\right)_1 - \left(\dfrac{\partial r_2}{\partial S_1}\right)_2 \end{bmatrix}
$$

$$
= - \left(\dfrac{\partial r_2}{\partial S_1}\right)_2 \begin{bmatrix} (D_{12} + cD_{22})(1-c) \\ \\ (1-c)^2 D_{22} \end{bmatrix} \qquad \text{(A24)}
$$

The determinant of the Jacobian in equation (A24) is $(1-c)|J^2|$, and is therefore negative whenever the system is stable. We know also that $(\partial r_2/\partial S_1)_2$ is negative. Therefore:

$$
\left(\frac{\partial R_0}{\partial S_1}\right)_1 - \left(\frac{\partial R_0}{\partial S_1}\right)_2 = \frac{-(\partial r_2/\partial S_1)_2}{|J^2|} \cdot \begin{vmatrix} D_{12} + cD_{22} & 0 \\ (1-c)^2 D_{22} & -L_{22} \end{vmatrix}
$$

Therefore

$$
\text{sign} \left[\left(\frac{\partial R_0}{\partial S_1}\right)_1 - \left(\frac{\partial R_0}{\partial S_1}\right)_2 \right] = \text{sign} - (D_{12} + cD_{22}),
$$

or

$$\text{sign} \left[\left| \left(\frac{\partial R_0}{\partial S_1} \right) \right|_1 - \left| \left(\frac{\partial R_0}{\partial S_1} \right)_2 \right| \right] = \text{sign} (D_{12} + cD_{22})$$

That is, changes in currency supply are more (less) effective with a *fixed* deposit rate if currency and deposits are substitutes (complements).

(iv) Effect of change in reserve requirement.

(*a*) Deposit rate flexible.

Differentiating equation (A14) gives:

$$J' \begin{bmatrix} \dfrac{\partial R_0}{\partial c} \\[3mm] \dfrac{\partial R_2}{\partial c} \end{bmatrix} = \begin{bmatrix} -D_2 \\[3mm] D_2 + \dfrac{L_{22}R_2}{(1-c)^2} \end{bmatrix} \qquad\qquad \text{(A25)}$$

Since $|J'|$ is negative for stable solutions,

$$\text{sign} \frac{\partial R_0}{\partial c} = \text{sign} \begin{vmatrix} D_2 & D_{12} + cD_{22} \\[3mm] -D_2 - \dfrac{L_{22}R_2}{(1-c)^2} & (1-c)D_{22} - \dfrac{L_{22}}{1-c} \end{vmatrix}$$

$$= \text{sign} \begin{vmatrix} D_2 & D_{12} + cD_{22} \\[3mm] -\dfrac{L_{22}R_2}{(1-c)^2} & D_{12} + D_{22} - \dfrac{L_{22}}{1-c} \end{vmatrix}$$

Therefore, if $D_{12} + cD_{22} < 0$, then $\partial R_0/\partial c > 0$ (substitutes case). But if $D_{12} + cD_{22} > 0$ (complements case), $\partial R_0/\partial c$ may be negative. For example, let $D_2 = 0$.

(*b*) Deposit rate fixed.

Differentiating equation (A15) gives

$$J^2 \begin{bmatrix} \dfrac{\partial R_0}{\partial c} \\[3mm] \dfrac{\partial r_2}{\partial c} \end{bmatrix} = \begin{bmatrix} -D_2 \\[3mm] D_2 \end{bmatrix} \qquad\qquad \text{(A26)}$$

Therefore,

$$\frac{\partial R_0}{\partial c} = \frac{D_2 L_{22}}{|J^2|} > 0 .$$

(v) Effect of change in reserve requirement on response of system to change in currency supply.

(a) Deposit rate flexible.

Differentiating equation (A21) with respect to c gives:

$$
J' \begin{bmatrix} \dfrac{\partial}{\partial c}\left(\dfrac{\partial R_0}{\partial S_1}\right) \\[2ex] \dfrac{\partial}{\partial c}\left(\dfrac{\partial R_2}{\partial S_1}\right) \end{bmatrix} = - \begin{bmatrix} D_{20} & D_{22} \\[2ex] -D_{20} & -D_{22} - \dfrac{L_{22}}{(1-c)^2} \end{bmatrix} \begin{bmatrix} \dfrac{\partial R_0}{\partial S_1} \\[2ex] \dfrac{\partial R_2}{\partial S_1} \end{bmatrix}
$$

$$
= - \begin{bmatrix} \dfrac{\partial D_2}{\partial S_1} \\[2ex] -\dfrac{\partial D_2}{\partial S_1} - \dfrac{L_{22}}{(1-c)^2}\dfrac{\partial R_2}{\partial S_1} \end{bmatrix}
$$

$$
\text{sign}\,\frac{\partial}{\partial c}\left(\frac{\partial R_0}{\partial S_1}\right) = \text{sign} \begin{vmatrix} \dfrac{\partial D_2}{\partial S_1} & D_{12}+cD_{22} \\[2ex] -\dfrac{\partial D_2}{\partial S_1} - \dfrac{L_{22}}{(1-c)^2}\dfrac{\partial R_2}{\partial S_1} & (1-c)D_{22} - \dfrac{L_{22}}{1-c} \end{vmatrix}
$$

$$
= \text{sign} \begin{vmatrix} \dfrac{\partial D_2}{\partial S_1} & D_{12}+cD_{22} \\[2ex] -\dfrac{L_{22}}{(1-c)^2}\dfrac{\partial R_2}{\partial S_1} & D_{12}+D_{22} - \dfrac{L_{22}}{1-c} \end{vmatrix}
$$

If $D_{12}+cD_{22} < 0$ (substitutes case) and $\partial D_2/\partial S_1 < 0$, then $\partial(\partial R_0/\partial S_1)/\partial c < 0$, i.e., an increase in c increases the response. In particular $D_{12}+cD_{22} < 0$ when $c=0$. If $D_{12}+cD_{22} > 0$ (complements case) and $\partial D_2/\partial S_1 > 0$, then $\partial(\partial R_0/\partial S_1)/\partial c > 0$.

(b) Deposit rate fixed.

Differentiating equation (A22) with respect to c gives:

$$
J^2 \begin{bmatrix} \dfrac{\partial}{\partial c}\left(\dfrac{\partial R_0}{\partial S_1}\right) \\[2ex] \dfrac{\partial}{\partial c}\left(\dfrac{\partial r_2}{\partial S_1}\right) \end{bmatrix} = \begin{bmatrix} -D_{20}\,\dfrac{\partial R_0}{\partial S_1} \\[2ex] D_{20}\,\dfrac{\partial R_0}{\partial S_1} \end{bmatrix}
$$

Therefore

$$\frac{\partial}{\partial c}\left(\frac{\partial R_0}{\partial S_1}\right) = \frac{D_{20}L_{22}(\partial R_0/\partial S_1)}{|J^2|} > 0 .$$

That is, increasing the required reserve ratio always diminishes the response.

3. Extention to Many Intermediaries

The discussion of regimes below parallels section 2.

3.1. *Regime II*

3.1.1. Uncontrolled Intermediaries

$$D_1(R_0, R_2, ..., R_n) = S_1 \qquad \text{Currency}$$

$$D_i(R_0, R_2, ..., R_n) - L_i(R_0, r_2, ..., r_n) = 0 \qquad \text{Intermediaries} \qquad (A27)$$

$$r_i - R_i = a_i \qquad \text{Relation between the rates}$$

$$i = 2, ..., n$$

(i) Effect of change in currency supply.

Using the $(n-1)$ rate relations to eliminate the r_i and differentiating with respect to S_1:

$$
\begin{bmatrix}
D_{10} & D_{12} & \cdots & D_{1n} \\
D_{20} - L_{20} & D_{22} - L_{22} & \cdots & D_{2n} - L_{2n} \\
\cdot & \cdot & \cdots & \cdot \\
\cdot & \cdot & \cdots & \cdot \\
\cdot & \cdot & \cdots & \cdot \\
D_{n0} - L_{n0} & D_{n2} - L_{n2} & \cdots & D_{nn} - L_{nn}
\end{bmatrix}
\begin{bmatrix}
\dfrac{\partial R_0}{\partial S_1} \\
\dfrac{\partial R_2}{\partial S_1} \\
\cdot \\
\cdot \\
\cdot \\
\dfrac{\partial R_n}{\partial S_1}
\end{bmatrix}
=
\begin{bmatrix}
1 \\
0 \\
\cdot \\
\cdot \\
\cdot \\
0
\end{bmatrix}
\qquad (A28)
$$

By the assumptions of (A2) and (A4) in section 1 the first column of the n by n matrix in equation (A28) is composed entirely of nonpositive elements. In the remaining columns, the diagonal elements are positive and the rest non-positive. Moreover, the sum of the elements in every column but the first is positive. It is shown in section 4 that the determinant of such a matrix is negative and that all the cofactors of the first row are positive. Hence all the derivatives that solve equation (A28) are negative. An increase in the supply of currency will lower rates at all intermediaries and will lower the acceptable return on direct equity in capital.

The change in the volume of each intermediary $\partial D_i/\partial S_1 = \Sigma_j D_{ij}(\partial R_j/\partial S_1)$, $(i = 2, ..., n)$, and the corresponding derivative for aggregate intermediary liabilities $\Sigma_{i=2}^n(\partial D_i/\partial S_1) = \Sigma_i\Sigma_j D_{ij}(\partial R_j/\partial S_1)$ may have either sign.

3.2. Controlled Intermediaries

$$D_1(R_0, R_2, ..., R_n) = S_1 \qquad \text{Currency}$$

$$e_i D_i(R_0, R_2, ..., R_n) = S_i \qquad \text{Specific Reserves}$$

$$(1 - e_i)D_i(R_0, R_2, ..., R_n) - L_i(R_0, r_2, ..., r_n) = 0 \qquad \text{Intermediaries}$$

$$i = 2, ..., n \qquad \text{(A29)}$$

Here S_i is the supply of the reserve asset specific to the ith intermediary expressed as a proportion of total wealth. The required ratio for the ith intermediary is $0 \leqslant e_i \leqslant 1$. There are $(2n - 1)$ equations in the $(2n - 1)$ rates R_0, R_i, r_i; the last $(n - 1)$ equations in equations (A27) drop out. (However, the inequalities $r_i - R_i \geqslant a_i$ must hold.)

(i) Effect of change in currency supply

$$\text{(A30)}$$

The first n equations can be solved separately from the last $(n-1)$ equations for the n derivatives $\partial R_0/\partial S_1$, $\partial R_i/\partial S_1$. Since this subsystem has the same features as system (A28) it is easily seen that $\partial R_0/\partial S_1$, $\partial R_i/\partial S_1 \leqslant 0$ $(i = 2, ..., n)$.

The remaining $(n-1)$ equations may be solved for the $\partial r_i/\partial S_1$. Since the first n equations are satisfied, $\Sigma_j e_j D_{ij}(\partial R_j/\partial S_1) = 0$, this system reduces to:

$$
\begin{bmatrix}
-L_{22} & \cdots & -L_{2n} \\
\cdot & & \\
\cdot & & \\
\cdot & & \\
-L_{n2} & \cdots & -L_{nn}
\end{bmatrix}
\begin{bmatrix}
\dfrac{\partial r_2}{\partial S_1} \\
\cdot \\
\cdot \\
\cdot \\
\dfrac{\partial r_n}{\partial S_1}
\end{bmatrix}
=
\begin{bmatrix}
L_{20} \\
\cdot \\
\cdot \\
\cdot \\
L_{n0}
\end{bmatrix}
\dfrac{\partial R_0}{\partial S_1}
\qquad \text{(A31)}
$$

The diagonal elements of the matrix in equation (A31) are all positive, the off diagonal elements nonpositive, and the column sums positive. In section 4 it is shown that the determinant of such a matrix is positive and that the cofactors of each element are positive. Hence

$$
\frac{\partial r_i}{\partial S_1} \leqslant 0 , \qquad i = 2, ..., n .
$$

(ii) Comparison with uncontrolled regime.

The effect of restraining the expansion of each intermediary can be found by subtracting equation system (A28) from the first n equations of (A31).

$$
J_4
\begin{bmatrix}
\dfrac{\partial R_0}{\partial S_1} \\
\cdot \\
\cdot \\
\cdot \\
\dfrac{\partial R_n}{\partial S_1}
\end{bmatrix}_4
- J_2
\begin{bmatrix}
\dfrac{\partial R_0}{\partial S_1} \\
\cdot \\
\cdot \\
\cdot \\
\dfrac{\partial R_n}{\partial S_1}
\end{bmatrix}_2
= 0
\qquad \text{(A32)}
$$

where J_4 is the sub-Jacobian in equation (A30) and J_2 the Jacobian in equation (A28).

$$J_2 = J_4 + \begin{bmatrix} 0 & \cdots & 0 \\ -L_{20} & \cdots & -L_{2n} \\ & \cdot & \\ & \cdot & \\ & \cdot & \\ -L_{n0} & \cdots & -L_{nn} \end{bmatrix} = J_4 + \Delta$$

$$J_4 \left[\left[\frac{\partial R_i}{\partial S_1} \right]_4 - \left[\frac{\partial R_i}{\partial S_1} \right]_2 \right] = \Delta \left[\frac{\partial R_i}{\partial S_1} \right]_2 = - \begin{bmatrix} 0 \\ \frac{\partial D_2}{\partial S_1} \\ \cdot \\ \cdot \\ \cdot \\ \frac{\partial D_n}{\partial S_1} \end{bmatrix}_2 \qquad (A33)$$

Given $J_4 < 0$ it follows that

$$\text{sign} \left[\left(\frac{\partial R_0}{\partial S_1} \right)_4 - \left(\frac{\partial R_0}{\partial S_1} \right)_2 \right] = \text{sign} \begin{vmatrix} 0 & D_{12} & \cdots & D_{12} \\ \left(\frac{\partial D_2}{\partial S_1} \right)_2 & D_{22} & \cdots & D_{2n} \\ \cdot & \cdot & & \cdot \\ \cdot & \cdot & & \cdot \\ \cdot & \cdot & & \cdot \\ \left(\frac{\partial D_n}{\partial S_1} \right)_2 & D_{n2} & \cdots & D_{nn} \end{vmatrix} \qquad (A34)$$

If all the $(\partial D_2/\partial S_1)_2$ are negative the determinant at the right will be negative; this is a sufficient, not a necessary, condition.

If reduction of the currency supply would lead to an expansion of all the intermediaries when they are uncontrolled, then preventing this expansion will enhance the effectiveness of currency restriction.

3.3. Regime III

3.3.1. Deposit Rates Flexible

$$D_1(R_0, R_2, ..., R_n) + c \sum_2^n D_i(R_0, R_2, ..., R_n) = S_1 \qquad \text{Currency}$$

$$(1-c)D_i(R_0, R_2, ..., R_n) - L_i(R_0, r_2, ..., r_n) = 0 \qquad \text{Intermediaries}$$

$$\frac{R_i}{(1-c)} - r_i = 0 \qquad \begin{array}{l}\text{Relation between} \\ \text{rates}\end{array}$$

$$i = 2, ..., n \qquad (A35)$$

Here the required reserve for each intermediary is in currency, and the required ratio is $0 \leqslant c \leqslant 1$. For convenience we assume the required ratio for all intermediaries is equal. The $(2n-1)$ equations determine the $(2n-1)$ variables $R_0, R_i, r_i; (i = 2, ..., n)$.

3.3.2. Deposit Rates Fixed

$$D_1(R_0, \overline{R}_2, ..., \overline{R}_n) + c \sum_{2}^{n} D_i(R_0, \overline{R}_j) = S_1 \qquad \text{Currency}$$

$$(1-c)D_i(R_0, \overline{R}_2, ..., \overline{R}_n) - L_i(R_0, r_2, ..., r_n) = 0 \qquad \text{Intermediaries}$$

$$i = 2, ..., n \qquad (A36)$$

Here the deposit rate at the ith intermediary is fixed at $\overline{R}_i$, and the n equations determine the n variables $R_0, r_i (i = 2, ..., n)$. In order for the regime to apply, the following inequality must hold:

$$\frac{\overline{R}_i}{(1-c)} \leqslant r_i$$

(i) Effect of change in currency supply.
(a) Deposit rates flexible.
Differentiating equation (A35) gives:

$$
\begin{bmatrix}
D_{10} + c \sum D_{i0} & D_{12} + c \sum D_{i2} & \cdots & D_{1n} + c \sum D_{in} \\
(1-c)D_{20} - L_{20} & (1-c)D_{22} - \dfrac{L_{22}}{(1-c)} & \cdots & (1-c)D_{2n} - \dfrac{L_{2n}}{(1-c)} \\
\vdots & \vdots & & \vdots \\
(1-c)D_{n0} - L_{n0} & (1-c)D_{n2} - \dfrac{L_{n2}}{(1-c)} & \cdots & (1-c)D_{nn} - \dfrac{L_{nn}}{(1-c)}
\end{bmatrix}
\begin{bmatrix}
\dfrac{\partial R_0}{\partial S_1} \\
\dfrac{\partial R_2}{\partial S_1} \\
\vdots \\
\dfrac{\partial R_n}{\partial S_1}
\end{bmatrix}
=
\begin{bmatrix}
1 \\
0 \\
\vdots \\
0
\end{bmatrix}
$$

$$(A37)$$

Since the cofactors of the first row are all positive, the derivatives that solve equation (A37) are all of the same sign:

$$\text{sign} \begin{bmatrix} \dfrac{\partial R_0}{\partial S_1} \\[2mm] \dfrac{\partial R_2}{\partial S_1} \\[2mm] . \\ . \\ . \\ \dfrac{\partial R_n}{\partial S_1} \end{bmatrix} = \text{sign} \, |J^3|$$

where J^3 is the Jacobian in equation (A37).

A sufficient, but not necessary, condition that $|J^3| < 0$ is that all the deposits be "substitutes" with currency:

$$\left(D_{1j} + c \sum_{i=2}^{n} D_{ij} \right) \leqslant 0 \, , \qquad j = 2, ..., n \, .$$

This condition is analogous to the substitutes case discussed in the text and section 2 of the Appendix. In this case however an increase in the ith rate causes a decrease in the demand for currency reserves by the other intermediaries as well as an increase in the demand for reserves by the ith intermediary.

(b) Deposit rate fixed.

Differentiating equation (A36) gives:

$$\begin{bmatrix} D_{10} + c \sum D_{i0} & 0 & \cdots & 0 \\[2mm] (1-c)D_{20} - L_{20} & -L_{22} & \cdots & -L_{2n} \\ . & . & . \\ . & . & . \\ . & . & . \\ (1-c)D_{n0} - L_{n0} & -L_{n2} & \cdots & -L_{nn} \end{bmatrix} \begin{bmatrix} \dfrac{\partial R_0}{\partial S_1} \\[2mm] \dfrac{\partial r_2}{\partial S_1} \\[2mm] . \\ . \\ . \\ \dfrac{\partial r_n}{\partial S_1} \end{bmatrix} = \begin{bmatrix} 1 \\ 0 \\ . \\ . \\ . \\ 0 \end{bmatrix} \qquad (A38)$$

The Jacobian in this system of equations meets the same sign conditions as the Jacobian in system (A28), hence $\partial R_0/\partial S_1$, $\partial r_i/\partial S_1 \leqslant 0$; $(i = 2, ..., n)$.

Following the procedure discussed in section 2, Regime III (iii) we may compare the responses in the two cases by subtracting system (A37) (but using the rate relations to eliminate the deposit rather than loan rates) from system (A38):

$$
J^4 \begin{bmatrix} \dfrac{\partial R_0}{\partial S_1} \\[2mm] \dfrac{\partial r_2}{\partial S_1} \\[1mm] . \\ . \\ . \\[1mm] \dfrac{\partial r_n}{\partial S_1} \end{bmatrix}_4 - J^{3'} \begin{bmatrix} \dfrac{\partial R_0}{\partial S_1} \\[2mm] \dfrac{\partial r_2}{\partial S_1} \\[1mm] . \\ .. \\ . \\[1mm] \dfrac{\partial r_n}{\partial S_1} \end{bmatrix}_{3'} = \begin{bmatrix} 0 \\[2mm] 0 \\[1mm] . \\ . \\ . \\[1mm] 0 \end{bmatrix}
\tag{A39}
$$

where J^4 is the Jacobian in equation (A38) and $J^{3'}$ is the Jacobian of the system (A37) when the deposit rates rather than the loan rates are eliminated.

$$
J^4 \left\{ \begin{bmatrix} \dfrac{\partial R_0}{\partial S_1} \\[2mm] \dfrac{\partial r_2}{\partial S_1} \\[1mm] . \\ . \\ . \\[1mm] \dfrac{\partial r_n}{\partial S_1} \end{bmatrix}_4 - \begin{bmatrix} \dfrac{\partial R_0}{\partial S_1} \\[2mm] \dfrac{\partial r_2}{\partial S_1} \\[1mm] . \\ . \\ . \\[1mm] \dfrac{\partial r_n}{\partial S_1} \end{bmatrix}_{3'} \right\} = -[J^4 - J^{3'}] \begin{bmatrix} \dfrac{\partial R_0}{\partial S_1} \\[1mm] . \\ . \\ . \\[1mm] \dfrac{\partial r_n}{\partial S_1} \end{bmatrix}_{3'}
\tag{A40}
$$

$$
= (1-c) \begin{bmatrix} 0 & \left(D_{12} + c \displaystyle\sum_2^n D_{i2} \right) & ... & \left(D_{1n} + c \displaystyle\sum_2^n D_{in} \right) \\[4mm] & (1-c)D_{22} & ... & (1-c)D_{22} \\ . & . & & . \\ . & . & & . \\ . & . & & . \\ 0 & (1-c)D_{n2} & ... & (1-c)D_{n2} \end{bmatrix} \begin{bmatrix} \dfrac{\partial R_0}{\partial S_1} \\[2mm] \dfrac{\partial r_2}{\partial S_1} \\[1mm] . \\ . \\ . \\[1mm] \dfrac{\partial r_n}{\partial S_1} \end{bmatrix}_{3'}
$$

Since $|J^4| < 0$ and the cofactor of the first element in the first row of J^4 is positive:

$$\text{sign}\left[\left(\frac{\partial R_0}{\partial S_1}\right)_4 - \left(\frac{\partial R_0}{\partial S_1}\right)_{3'}\right] = \text{sign} - \sum_{j=2}^{n}\left(D_{1j} + c\sum_{i=2}^{n} D_{ij}\right)\left(\frac{\partial r_j}{\partial S_1}\right)_{3'}$$

when $|J^3| < 0$, $(\partial r_j/\partial S_1)_{3'} \leqslant 0$ for all j.

Changes in currency supply are more (less) effective with *fixed* deposit rates if currency and each variety of "deposits" are substitutes (complements).

(ii) Effect of change in reserve requirement on response of system to change in currency supply.

(*a*) Deposit rate flexible.

Differentiating equation (A37) with respect to c gives:

$$J^3\left[\frac{\partial\left(\frac{\partial R_i}{\partial S_1}\right)}{\partial c}\right] = -\begin{bmatrix} \sum_{2}^{n} D_{i0} & \sum_{2}^{n} D_{i2} & \cdots & \sum_{2}^{n} D_{in} \\ -D_{20} & -D_{22}-\dfrac{L_{22}}{(1-c)^2} & \cdots & -D_{2n}-\dfrac{L_{22}}{(1-c)^2} \\ \cdot & \cdot & \cdots & \cdot \\ \cdot & \cdot & & \cdot \\ \cdot & \cdot & & \cdot \\ -D_{n0} & -D_{n2}-\dfrac{L_{n2}}{(1-c)^2} & \cdots & -D_{nn}-\dfrac{L_{nn}}{(1-c)^2} \end{bmatrix}\begin{bmatrix} \dfrac{\partial R_i}{\partial S_1} \end{bmatrix}$$

$$(A41)$$

where J^3 is the Jacobian in equation (A37).

This reduces to:

$$J^3\left[\frac{\partial\left(\frac{\partial R_i}{\partial S_1}\right)}{.\ \partial c}\right] = -\begin{bmatrix} \dfrac{\partial \sum D_i}{\partial S_1} \\ -\dfrac{\partial D_2}{\partial S_1} - \sum_{2}^{n}\dfrac{L_{2i}}{(1-c)^2}\dfrac{\partial R_i}{\partial S_1} \\ \cdot \\ \cdot \\ \cdot \\ -\dfrac{\partial D_n}{\partial S_1} - \sum_{2}^{n}\dfrac{L_{ni}}{(1-c)^2}\dfrac{\partial R_i}{\partial S_1} \end{bmatrix}$$

$$(A42)$$

Assuming $|J^3| < 0$: if $\partial D_i/\partial S_1 < 0$ $(i = 2, ..., n)$, $(D_{ij} + c\Sigma_{i=2}^n D_{ij}) < 0$ $(j = 2, ..., n)$ (all substitutes case), and $\Sigma_{i=2}^n [L_{ji}/(1 - c)^2]$ $(\partial R_i/\partial S_1) > 0$ then $\partial(\partial R_0/\partial S_1)/\partial c < 0$, *i.e.*, an increase in c increases the response of the rate on capital.

(b) Deposit rates fixed.

Differentiating equation (A38) with respect to c gives:

$$
J^4 \left[\frac{\partial \left(\dfrac{\partial R_i}{\partial S_1} \right)}{\partial c} \right] = - \begin{bmatrix} \displaystyle\sum_{i=2}^n D_{i0} \\ -D_{20} \\ \cdot \\ \cdot \\ \cdot \\ -D_{n0} \end{bmatrix} \frac{\partial R_0}{\partial S_1}
$$

Therefore,

$$
\frac{\partial(\partial R_0/\partial S_1)}{\partial c} = \frac{-(\partial R_0/\partial S_1)}{|J^4|} \begin{vmatrix} \displaystyle\sum_{i=2}^n D_{i0} & 0 & \cdots & 0 \\ -D_{20} & -L_{22} & & -L_{2n} \\ \cdot & \cdot & & \cdot \\ \cdot & & \ddots & \cdot \\ \cdot & \cdot & & \cdot \\ -D_{n0} & -L_{n2} & \cdots & -L_{nn} \end{vmatrix} > 0
$$

That is, increasing the required reserve ratio always diminishes the response of the rate on capital to changes in the supply of currency.

4. Some Basic Propositions about Matrices

Let A be a nonsingular square matrix with nonpositive off-diagonal elements, positive diagonal elements, column sums $\Sigma_i a_{ij}$ positive. To prove that $\det(A)$ is positive.

Consider the matrix B where $b_{ij} = -a_{ij}/a_{jj}$ for $i \neq j$ and $b_{jj} = 0$. Then B is a matrix of nonnegative elements with column sums $\Sigma_i b_{ij} < 1$. $\det(A)$ will be positive if $\det(I - B)$ is positive, for $\det(I - B) = (1/\Pi_j a_{jj}) \det(A)$.

4.1. *Proof that* $\det (I - B) > 0$ [8]

Suppose $\det (I - B) \leqslant 0$. Since for sufficiently large λ, $\det (\lambda I - B) > 0$, there must exist a root $\lambda_0 \geqslant 1$ with $\det (\lambda_0 I - B) = 0$. The equation system $[\lambda_0 I - B]'x = 0$ has a solution vector $x \neq 0$. Let x_j be the element of largest absolute value $|x_j| > 0$. $|x_j| \leqslant |\lambda_0 x_j|$. By the jth equation of the system, $|\lambda_0 x_j| = |\Sigma_i b_{ij} x_i|$. $|\Sigma_i b_{ij} x_i| \leqslant \Sigma_i b_{ij}|x_i| \leqslant \Sigma_i b_{ij}|x_j| < |x_j|$. This contradicts $\lambda_0 \geqslant 1$. Hence $\det (I - B) > 0$.

Consider a nonsingular matrix A_1 formed by substituting for the first column of A a vector of nonpositive elements. The proposition is that $\det (A_1)$ is negative.

4.2. *Proof by induction*

If the proposition is true for n by n square matrices, then it is true for $(n + 1)$ by $(n + 1)$ square matrices. Add to $A(n)$ a new first row and first column so that the resulting matrix is $A_1(n + 1)$. Expand A_1 by the first row. The first cofactor is $\det [A(n)]$, which is positive according to the first note above. The cofactors of the remaining elements of the first row all involve n by n minors of which the first column consists entirely of nonpositive elements, while the remaining columns come from $A(n)$. The minor of the second element is $A_1(n)$ and by assumption negative; thus the second cofactor is positive. The minor of the third element can be made into an $A_1(n)$ by placing the third row at the top of the minor. This interchange alters the sign; hence the minor and cofactor are both positive. In general, the minor of the ith element can be made into an $A_1(n)$ by the $(i - 2)$ interchanges necessary to place the ith row at the top of the minor. The minors will be positive for i odd and negative for i even; therefore all the cofactors are positive. Since all the elements of the first row are nonpositive, $A_1(n + 1)$ is negative.

The proposition is true for $n = 2$. $A_1(2) = \begin{vmatrix} - & - \\ - & + \end{vmatrix}$.

If the first and last rows of the matrix of coefficients in equation (A28) are interchanged, the resulting matrix is $A_1(n + 1)$. Hence the matrix in equation (A28) has a positive determinant, with negative cofactors for the last row.

Notes

[1] This essay is based on work by both authors. Some of its topics were treated in a preliminary way in a Cowles Foundation Discussion Paper (No. 63, January 1958, mimeographed) of the same title, by James Tobin. The general approach of that paper was elaborated and extended in a systematic way by William Brainard in "Financial

Intermediaries and a Theory of Monetary Control," in the *Yale Economic Essays*, 4, No. 1 (Fall 1964), 431-82.

[2] The balancing of these considerations and the desirability of finding structural changes which increase the first kind of responsiveness without increasing the second are discussed in the Brainard paper cited above.

[3] This complication has been discussed in other works of the authors; in Brainard, *op. cit.*, and in Tobin, "An Essay on Principles of Debt Management," *Fiscal and Debt Management Policies*, prepared for the Commission on Money and Credit (Englewood Cliffs, N.J.: Prentice-Hall, 1963), pp. 143-218, Chapter 21 below.

[4] It is perhaps not too fanciful to refer, as an example of this kind of effect, to the consequences of the increases in Regulation Q ceiling rates on time and savings deposits in commercial banks permitted in 1961. Contrary to many predictions, these increases led to lower, rather than higher, mortgage lending rates; they were expansionary. Given the low reserve requirement against these deposits, especially when compared to demand deposits, it is to be expected that time and savings deposits are strong substitutes for currency and reserves.

[5] This may be seen in the following way: The initial effect of an increase in the reserve requirement may be divided into two parts: (a) the increase in the demand for currency and decrease in the supply for loans which result from banks' attempts to meet the higher reserve requirement; and (b) the increased margin banks will require between their deposit and loan rates when they have to place a higher proportion of deposits in non-interest-bearing reserves. The first of these effects is always contractionary. The second effect will also be contractionary in the substitutes case. In the complements case, however, the effect of increasing the margin between the rates is expansionary, and may even outweigh the first effect. At the same loan rate the deposit rate will be lower; as we have already noticed, lowering the deposit rate is expansionary in the complements case.

[6] This statement needs to be somewhat qualified to allow for the fact that a higher reserve ratio enlarges the competitively required margin between deposit and loan rates. This strengthens the contribution of a higher reserve requirement to the effectiveness of a reduction in the currency supply, and makes it possible for this contribution to be positive even when deposits do not expand.

[7] We assume that the relation $R_2/(1 - c) - r_2 = 0$ always holds. Our results would not be altered if we allowed a "profit" margin in disequilibrium and assumed that it tends toward zero.

[8] For this proof, we are much indebted to Martin Beckmann.

CHAPTER 18

A GENERAL EQUILIBRIUM APPROACH TO
MONETARY THEORY

I will take the opportunity provided by the first issue of a journal devoted to monetary economics to set forth and illustrate a general framework for monetary analysis. It is not a new approach, but one shared at least in spirit by many monetary economists. My purpose here is exposition and recapitulation.

1. The Capital Account

The approach focuses on the capital accounts of economic units, of sectors of the economy, and of the economy as a whole. A model of the capital account of the economy specifies a menu of the assets (and debts) that appear in portfolios and balance sheets, the factors that determine the demands and supplies of the various assets, and the manner in which asset prices and interest rates clear these interrelated markets. In this approach, monetary assets fall into place as a part, but not the whole, of the menu of assets; and the commercial banking system in one sector, but not the only one, whose balance sheet behavior must be specified.

Treatment of the capital account separately from the production and

Reprinted from *Journal of Money, Credit, and Banking*, 1 (February 1969), 15-29. Footnotes, figures, and tables have been renumbered. Copyright © 1969 by the Ohio State University Press, Columbus, Ohio.

Among many debts, I will acknowledge here a special one to my colleague and, on occasion, collaborator, William C. Brainard, who has helped to develop and clarify the approach here expounded. He is not responsible, however, for errors and confusions that may remain in this particular exposition. See also Tobin and Brainard, "Financial Intermediaries and the Effectiveness of Monetary Controls," *American Economic Review*, 53 (May 1963) 383-400 (Chapter 17 above); and Brainard, "Financial Intermediaries and a Theory of Monetary Control," *Yale Economic Essays*, 4 (Fall 1964), 431-82. These papers are reprinted as Chapters 3 and 4 in *Financial Markets and Economic Activity*, ed. Hester and Tobin. Cowles Foundation Monograph 21, (New York: Wiley, 1967).

income account of the economy is only a first step, a simplification to be justified by convenience rather thán realism. The strategy is to regard income account variables as tentatively exogenous data for balance sheet behavior, and to find equilibrium in the markets for stocks of assets conditional upon assumed values of outputs, incomes, and other flows. Of course the linkages run both ways. Some of the variables determined in asset markets affect the flows of spending and income. In a complete equilibrium the two sides of the economy — one is tempted to call them "financial" and "real" — must be mutually consistent. That is, the financial inputs to the real side must reproduce the assumed values of the real inputs to the financial side.

A familiar and simple example of this strategy is the "*LM* curve." Macroeconomics texts and lectures have immortalized Hicks's decomposition of the Keynesian system into submodels. One of these tells what asset stock equilibrium corresponds to any tentative assumption about aggregate real income and the commodity price level. In this conditional equilibrium "the" interest rate equates the demand and supply of money and clears the markets for other assets. Of the many *LM* equilibria, only one is in general consistent with the other relationships in the complete system.

The key behavioral assumption of this procedure is that spending decisions and portfolio decisions are independent — specifically that decisions about the accumulation of wealth are separable from decisions about its allocation. As savers, people decide how much to add to their wealth; as portfolio managers, they decide how to distribute among available assets and debts the net worth they already have. The propensity to consume may depend upon interest rates, but it does not depend *directly* on the existing mix of asset supplies or on the rates at which these supplies are growing.

Figure 18.1 (p. 328) illustrates schematically the approach just sketched.

2. Accounting Framework

The general accounting framework for a theory of the capital account is indicated in Table 18.1. Rows represent assets or debts. A row might be labeled "money" or "physical capital," or in a finer classification "demand deposits" or "producers' durable equipment." Columns represent sectors of the economy: for example, commercial banks, central government, nonbank financial institutions, public. Entries in cells, in general, can be positive, negative, or zero. A negative entry means that the sector in question is a debtor in the kind of asset indicated by the row. All holdings must be valued in the same numéraire, *e.g.*, either in the monetary unit of account or in terms of purchasing power over consumer goods. The sum across a row is the net exogenous supply of the asset to the economy as a whole. For stocks of goods, this exogenous supply is the economy's inheritance from the past. For internally generated financial assets the net exogenous supply is, of course, zero. If from the sums in the final column the central government's holdings of an asset are subtracted (or its debt added), the net holdings of the private economy result. The sum of a column represents the net worth of a sector. The sum of the final column is national wealth. As indicated, private wealth differs from this total by the amount of the government's net worth. If the government is a net debtor, as will typically be the case, at least if its stocks of goods are ignored, then private wealth exceeds national wealth. The framework illustrated by Table 18.1 is intended for a closed economy, although it could be extended to include capital account relations with the rest of the world.

3. The Analytical Framework

The accounting framework of Table 18.1 can be brought to life as a framework for monetary analysis by (a) assigning to each asset a rate of return r_i, $(i = 1, 2, \ldots n)$ and (b) imagining each sector $j (j = 1, 2, \ldots m)$ to have a net demand for each asset, f_{ij}, which is a function of the vector r_i and possibly of other variables as well. Of course in practice many of the cells are

Table 18.1
General Accounting Framework

Assets	Sectors of the Economy							Central government	Net total holdings = Exogenous supply
	1	2	3	.	.	.	m		
1									
2									
3									
.									
.									
.									
n									
Net worth	Total private wealth (= National wealth less government net worth)							Government net worth	National wealth

empty; certain sectors are just not involved with certain assets, either as holders or as debtors.

Each sector is, at any moment of time, constrained by its own net worth. Its members are free to choose their balance sheets — the entries in the columns of Table 18.1 — but not to choose their net worth — the sum of the column entries. This is determined by their past accumulations of assets and by current asset prices. The individual economic unit can neither change the legacy of the past nor, it is assumed, affect by his own portfolio choices the current market valuations of his assets. Of course, as time passes the individual may save and may make capital gains or losses. A year later his net worth will be different, but it will be once again a constraint on his portfolio behavior.

This adding-up requirement has certain obvious and simple implications. For any sector, the sum over all assets of responses to a change in any rate of return r_k is zero:

$$\sum_{i=1}^{n} \frac{\partial f_{ij}}{\partial r_k} = 0 .$$

This is also true for any other variable that enters the sector's asset demand functions. The exception is the sector's net worth itself; clearly the sum of asset changes due to a change in wealth is equal to one:

$$\sum_{i=1}^{n} \frac{\partial f_{ij}}{\partial W_j} = 1 .$$

These same properties will hold for demand functions aggregated over sectors, that is for

$$f_i = \sum_{j=1}^{m} f_{ij} .$$

Each row in Table 18.1 corresponds to one market-clearing equation, by which the net demands of the m private sectors add up to the available supplies, whether issued by the government or otherwise exogenous. But these n equations are not independent. Whatever the values of the determining variables, the left-hand sides (net private demands) of these n asset equations sum to the same value as the right-hand sides (supplies), namely to aggregate private wealth. Therefore, contrary to superficial first impression, the n equations will not determine n rates of return but only $n-1$ at most.

The value of aggregate or sectoral wealth may depend on asset prices, which are themselves related to the r_i, the market rates of return, determined by the system of equations. This will be true of all assets whose life exceeds the length of the assumed period of portfolio choice. For example, the outstanding supplies of durable physical capital and of long-term government bonds change in value as their market rates of return change. Consequently, the $n-1$ market-clearing equations actually include rates of return in two roles, as arguments in the asset demand functions and as determinants of the values of existing asset supplies and total wealth.

In some applications of the analysis there are fewer than $n-1$ rates of return free to be determined. There are fewer endogenous rates of return than there are independent market-clearing equations. Some rates are institutionally or legally fixed — consider the conventional zero own-rate of interest on currency, the prohibition of interest on demand deposits, effective ceilings on interest paid on time and savings accounts. Some are constrained, at least in the long run, by real factors — for example, by the technological marginal productivity of physical capital assets. In these cases the capital account equations cannot be satisfied unless some asset supplies are not exogenous but adjust to clear the markets, or unless some relevant variables from the real side of the economy — income, price level, price expectations — assume appropriate values. I will return to these problems in the illustrations that follow.

4. A Money-Capital Economy

I turn now to some simple applications of the approach just described. First, consider an economy with only one private sector and only two assets: money issued by the government to finance its budget deficits, and homogeneous physical capital. Let p be the price of currently produced goods, both consumer goods and capital goods. I shall, however, allow the value of existing capital goods, or of titles to them, to diverge from their current reproduction cost — let qp be the market price of existing capital goods. Let r_M and r_K be the real rates of return available from holding money and capital respectively. Let p_p^e be the expected rate of change in commodity prices, let r_M' be the nominal rate of interest on money (generally, zero), and let R be the marginal efficiency of capital relative to reproduction cost. Let W be wealth and Y income, both measured in goods.

Model I is as follows:

Wealth definition:

$$W = qK + M/p .$$ (I.0)

Balance equations:

$$f_1(r_K, r_M, Y/W)W = qK \qquad \text{capital } (r_K) \tag{I.1}$$

$$f_2(r_K, r_M, Y/W)W = M/p \qquad \text{money } (r_M) \tag{I.2}$$

Rate-of-return equations:

$$r_K q = R \qquad \text{capital} \tag{I.3}$$

$$r_M = r'_M - \rho_p^e \qquad \text{money} \tag{I.4}$$

The two portfolio behavior functions have been written in a special form. They are homogeneous in wealth; the proportions held in the two assets are independent of the absolute scale of wealth. The "adding-up" requirement tells us that $f_1 = 1 - f_2$; therefore, one of the two balance equations, let it be I.1, can be omitted. It is natural to assume that the own-rate derivatives $\partial f_1/\partial r_K$ and $\partial f_2/\partial r_M$ to be positive and the cross-derivatives therefore to be negative.

The ratio of income to wealth appears in both asset demand functions; if it appears in one, it must be in the other one too. The conventional assumption is that more money will be "needed for transactions purposes" at higher income levels. The implication is that the demand for capital will, other things equal, be reduced by a rise in income. However, "other things" will not be equal if on the real side of the economy there is a positive connection between Y and R, and therefore between Y and r_K.

Whether income falls with wealth constant or wealth rises with income constant, a smaller fraction of wealth is needed to meet transactions requirements. The demand for money will fall relative to the demand for capital. I shall make the usual Keynesian assumption that the partial elasticity of demand for money with respect to income is positive but does not exceed one. The reasoning is that transactions demand is, at most, proportional to income (elasticity equal to one), but transactions balances are only part of money holdings. The assumption is, then, that

$$0 < \frac{\partial (f_2 W)}{\partial Y} \bigg/ \frac{f_2 W}{Y} = \frac{\partial f_2}{\partial (Y/W)} \bigg/ \frac{f_2}{Y/W} \leqq 1 .$$

Equation I.3 expresses an inverse relation between the market valuation of capital equity and the market rate of return upon it. Suppose that the perpetual real return obtainable by purchasing a unit of capital as its cost of production p is R. If an investor must pay qp instead of p, then his rate of return is R/q. The consol formula of I.3 applies strictly only for perfectly durable capital. For depreciating capital, or physical assets of finite life, the relation of r_K and q will not be so simple or so pronounced. But there will still be an inverse relation.

Note that the commodity price level p does not affect the real rate of return on capital, calculated either on reproduction cost or on market value. However, the expected rate of inflation of commodity prices does enter portfolio behavior, as one of the constituents of the real rate of return on money in I.4.

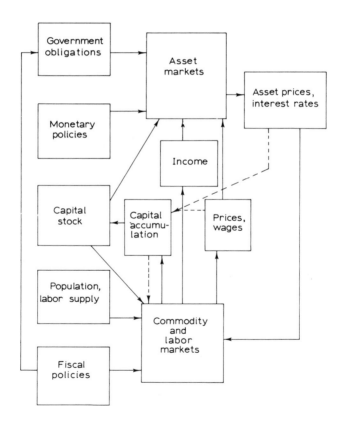

Fig. 18.1. Capital Account Approach (Schematic).

With I.1 omitted as redundant, Model I consists of four equations. The interpretation of the model depends on which four variables are taken as endogenous.

5. Short-run Interpretation of the Money-Capital Model

One interpretation (IA) is the following:

Endogenous variables: r_K, r_M, W, q;
Exogenous variables: $K, M, Y, p, R, \rho_p^e, r_M'$.

Then, by (I.4) r_M is, in effect, exogenous. By various substitutions the model can then be expressed as a single equation in q:

$$f_2\left(R/q, r_M, \frac{Y}{qK + M/p}\right)(qK + M/p) = \frac{M}{p}.$$ (I.5)

The assumptions made in the previous section are sufficient, not necessary, to assure that $\partial q/\partial M > 0$, in words that an increase in the quantity of money is expansionary, causing a rise in the valuation of existing capital and stimulating investment. The same conditions assure that $\partial q/\partial R > 0$, i.e., that an increase in the marginal efficiency of capital pulls up its price; that $\partial q/\partial r_M < 0$, i.e., that an increase in the real rate of interest on money diminishes the

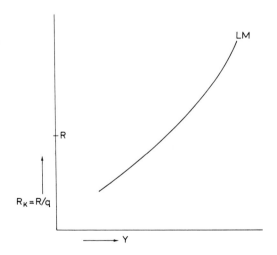

Fig. 18.2. *LM* Curve Drawn from Equation (I.5).

valuation of capital; and that $\partial q/\partial Y < 0$, *i.e.*, that asset equilibrium requires a lower valuation of capital the higher the level of income relative to asset stocks.

This last result leads to the observation that, as part of a short-run model of income determination, equation (I.5) can be interpreted as a species of the standard Keynesian *LM* curve. That is, it tells what combinations of real income Y and the rate of return on capital equity, r_K or R/q, are compatible with equilibrium in asset markets (Figure 18.2). Like the textbook *LM* curve, this relationship shifts to the right when M increases or p diminishes. The difference is that the interest rate on the vertical axis here is the return on capital equity rather than Keynes's long-term bond rate. However, Keynes was assuming the two rates to be equal, or to differ only by a constant risk premium. If this assumption is dropped, R/q is the appropriate variable for the diagram, which needs to be completed by an *IS* curve. The *rate* of invest-ment — the speed at which investors wish to increase the capital stock — should be related, if to anything, to q, the value of capital relative to its replacement cost.

The *LM* curve of Figure 18.2 was drawn on the assumption of a fixed marginal efficiency of capital, R. If R rises with Y, $\partial q/\partial Y$ will be smaller than with R constant, and may even be negative. In Keynesian theory there has always been ambivalence on this point, between the apparent view of Keynes

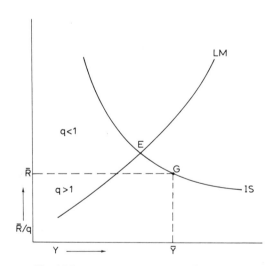

Fig. 18.3. *LM* Curve Plotted with *IS* Curve.

himself that investors' estimate of the marginal efficiency of capital is related to a future largely independent of the current level of income and the view that investors simply expect the current rate of profit on capital to continue. If, in line with the second view, some dependence of R on Y is built into the LM curve, there is no one-to-one relation between r_K and q.

Consequently, Figure 18.3 plots the LM curve against $\bar{R}/q$, where $\bar{R}$ is the marginal efficiency of the existing capital stock K at a standard real income $\bar{Y}$. This standard income $\bar{Y}$ is the level at which saving would just suffice to increase the capital stock at the natural rate of growth of the economy. For example, let this growth be g and the saving ratio s; then $gK = s\bar{Y}$. Investment at this rate will, under the usual assumptions of neoclassical growth theory, keep $\bar{R}$ unchanged. Consequently, investment at this rate is compatible with $q = 1$, $r_K = \bar{R}$. In other words, the IS curve goes through the point $(\bar{R}, \bar{Y})$. [1] At an income lower than $\bar{Y}$, this normal rate of investment will exceed saving; therefore, investment-saving equality requires a q less than one. The short-run equilibrium – for a given real money supply M/p – is shown as E in Figure 18.3; in this illustration it occurs at a lower income level and equity valuation than the steady growth position G.

6. Long-run Equilibrium in the Money-Capital Model

An alternative interpretation of Model I (IB) requires that capital be valued at its reproduction cost, $i.e.$, that $q = 1$. This may be regarded as a condition of equilibrium in the long run. In a long-run growth equilibrium, E and G in Figure 18.3 must coincide; moreover this income $\bar{Y}$ must also represent equilibrium of labor supply and demand. Then if M/p, R, Y, and K are given, they determine r_K and W. Equation I.2 must then determine r_M, the real rate of interest on money. That is, either expectations of price change ρ_p^e or the own-rate on money r_M' must be market determined rather than institutionally or legally fixed. Otherwise, there is no way of reconciling wealthowners to the supplies of capital and real balances that history and policy have determined.

Alternatively, if r_M is fixed, the supplies of capital and money, measured in real terms, must be free to adjust to public portfolio preferences. Models of the role of outside money in long-run growth show how this adjustment can occur. [2] One mechanism is flexibility in the price level p, which assures that any nominal supply of money M can be turned into the real supply that the public wants at the prevailing set of real interest rates. Another possible mechanism is fiscal policy itself, adjusting the size and rate of expansion of the government debt so as to achieve equilibrium.

7. A Money-Securities-Capital Model

In model I there is no monetary policy as this term is generally understood. The supply of money is identical with the government debt. It is not possible to increase money by a dollar without simultaneously increasing private wealth by a dollar. They rise together in money value when the government runs a budget deficit and prints money to cover it, or in real value when the price level falls. An increase in the nominal money stock is a monetary consequence of fiscal policy rather than monetary policy in the usual sense. The closest conceivable thing to monetary policy in model IA is variation of r'_M, the institutionally determined rate of interest on money.

Monetary policy can be introduced by allowing some government debt to take nonmonetary form. Then, even though total government debt is fixed at any moment of time, at least in terms of its original money value, its composition can be altered by open market operations – or by debt management operations, which are really the same thing. In Model II let $\hat{r}$ stand for the vector of real rates of return (r_K, r_M, r_S):

Wealth definition:

$$W = qK + \frac{M + S}{p}.$$

(II.0)

Balance equations:

$$f_1(\hat{r}, Y/W)W = qK \qquad \text{capital } (r_K) \tag{II.1}$$

$$f_2(\hat{r}, Y/W)W = M/p \qquad \text{money } (r_M) \tag{II.2}$$

$$f_2(\hat{r}, Y/W)W = S/p \qquad \text{gov't. securities } (r_S) \tag{II.3}$$

Rate-of-return equations:

$$r_K q = R \qquad \text{capital} \tag{II.4}$$

$$r_M = r'_M - \rho_p^e \qquad \text{money} \tag{II.5}$$

$$r_S = r'_S - \rho_p^e \qquad \text{gov't. securities} \tag{II.6}$$

Here it is assumed for simplicity that securities are short-term, so that their market value is independent of their interest rate r'_S. Otherwise a relationship between the two could be introduced, like (II.4) for capital, and allowed for in the calculation of wealth.

An interpretation analogous to IA takes as exogenous Y, M, S, K, R, r'_M, ρ^e_p, and p, leaving $q, W, r_K, r_S, r_M, r'_S$ to be determined by the six independent equations. Consolidation gives the following two equations, along with the definition of W, to determine q and r_S:

$$f_2(R/q, r_M, r_S, Y/W)W = M/p \tag{II.7}$$

$$f_2(R/q, r_M, r_S, Y/W)W = S/p. \tag{II.8}$$

It is assumed, as before, that the own derivatives of the f_i

$$\left(\frac{\partial f_1}{\partial r_K}, \frac{\partial f_2}{\partial r_M}, \frac{\partial f_3}{\partial r_S} \right)$$

are positive, and that all the cross-derivatives are nonpositive. (It will be remembered also that $\Sigma_i \partial f_i / \partial x = 0$ for any x that appears as an argument in the functions f_i.) In other words, the assets are gross substitutes: the demand for each asset varies directly with its own rate and inversely with other rates.

It is also assumed, as before, that the partial elasticity of demand for money with respect to income is positive but does not exceed one. Moreover, now that government securities are available, it is assumed that they, rather than capital, absorb changes in transactions requirements for money. That is,

$$\frac{\partial f_2}{\partial(Y/W)} = -\frac{\partial f_2}{\partial(Y/W)} \quad \text{and} \quad \frac{\partial f_1}{\partial(Y/W)} = 0.$$

These assumptions lead to the conclusions presented in Table 18.2.

The first two columns represent increases in government debt taking one form or the other. The third column represents monetary policy in the shape

Table 18.2
Effects on Endogenous Variables of Increase in Specified Exogenous Variables, with All Others Held Constant

Endo-genous variables	Exogenous variables							
	M	S	M at expense of S	r'_M	Y	R	p	ρ^e_p
q	+	?	+	−	−	+	−	+
r_S	−	+	−	+	+	?	?	−
r_K	−	?	−	+	+	+	+	−

of open market purchases. Here, unlike Model IA, it is possible to shift the *LM* curve of Figures 18.2 and 18.3 to the right by monetary policy in the usual sense. The fourth column represents monetary policy in the guise of an increase in the legally determined interest rate on money.

What is the feature of money that leads to the results tabulated in the first three columns? That is, why does an increase in government debt in monetary form have a more expansionary effect than increase in government debt in the form of securities? And why is substitution of money for securities via open market purchases expansionary?

It is not because asset No. 1 has been called "money" and asset No. 2 "securities." It is not because asset No. 1 is a means of payment or has any other intrinsic properties asset No. 2 lacks. It is not that asset No. 1 bears no interest — it may or may not. These properties have nowhere entered the analysis, except in the general sense that they explain why the assets are not perfect substitutes for each other. The essential characteristic — the only distinction of money from securities that matters for the results given above — is that the interest rate on money is exogenously fixed by law or convention, while the rate of return on securities is endogenous, market determined.

When the supply of any asset is increased, the structure of rates of return, on this and other assets, must change in a way that induces the public to hold the new supply. When the asset's own rate can rise, a large part of the necessary adjustment can occur in this way. But if the rate is fixed, the whole adjustment must take place through reductions in other rates or increases in prices of other assets. This is the secret of the special role of money; it is a secret that would be shared by any other asset with a fixed interest rate.

As observed above, an n-asset economy will provide no more than $n-1$ independent market-clearing equations. The system will determine, therefore, no more than $n-1$ real rates of return. If the rate on one asset, "money," is fixed, then the market rate of return on capital can, indeed must, be among the $n-1$ rates to be determined. This enables the monetary authority to force the market return on physical capital to diverge from its technological marginal efficiency — or, what is the same thing, to force the market valuation of existing capital to diverge from its reproduction cost. By creating these divergences, the monetary authority can affect the current rate of production and accumulation of capital assets. This is the manner in which the monetary authority can affect aggregate demand in the short run — diagrammatically, by moving the *LM* curve of Figure 18.3 to the left or right and changing its intersection with the *IS* curve.

If the interest rate on money, as well as the rates on all other financial assets, were flexible and endogenous, then they would all simply adjust to the marginal efficiency of capital. There would be no room for discrepancies between market and natural rates of return on capital, between market valuation and reproduction cost. There would be no room for monetary policy to affect aggregate demand. The real economy would call the tune for the financial sector, with no feedback in the other direction. As previously observed, something like this occurs in the long run, where the influence of monetary policy is not on aggregate demand but on the relative supplies of monetary and real assets, to which all rates of return must adjust.

8. A Model with Bank Deposits and Loans

As a third and final illustration of the approach, consider an economy with two sectors rather than one. Model III has a banking system as well as a general public sector and adds two new assets — deposits and private loans — to the economy's menu of assets. There are also two new real rates of interest to be determined, r_D on deposits and r_L on loans, and two new nominal rates, r'_D on deposits and r'_L on loans, to be established either exogenously or endogenously. A new interest rate relevant to the banks, the central bank discount rate d', (d in real terms) can also be introduced; this is another instrument of monetary control.

Let $\hat{r}$ be the vector of real interest rates $(r_K, r_M, r_S, r_D, r_L, d)$. For convenience, both bank and public portfolio choices will be written as functions of $\hat{r}$. But it will be understood that the discount rate d is irrelevant to the public, and that the market rate on capital r_K is irrelevant to the banks, which are assumed not to hold such equity. For the same reason, the banks' asset demands could be expressed equally well in money values and related to money interest rates rather than real. The legal reserve requirement enters as k.

Asset No. 2 is still the demand debt of the government, inclusive of the central bank. The size of this debt, net of the banks' borrowings from the central bank at the discount window, is the supply of currency and unborrowed reserves to the banks and the public. But of course M no longer corresponds to the quantity of money as conventionally defined. Rather it represents "high-powered" money. The money stock would include the public's share of M plus bank deposits (or perhaps only demand deposits if, as is not done here, time deposits were distinguished). Thus the money stock would be an endogenous quantity.

Wealth definition:

$$W = qK + \frac{M+S}{p} \tag{III.0}$$

Balance equations:

Banks   *Public*

$$f_{1P}(\hat{r}, Y/W)W = qK \text{ (capital } (r_K)) \tag{III.1}$$

$$kD + f_{2B}(\hat{r})D(1-k) + f_{2P}(\hat{r}, Y/W)W = M/p \text{ (currency and} \atop \text{reserves) } (r_M, d) \tag{III.2}$$

$$f_{3B}(\hat{r})D(1-k) + f_{3P}(\hat{r}, Y/W)W = S/p \text{ (government} \atop \text{securities } (r_S)) \tag{III.3}$$

$$f_{4B}(\hat{r}) + f_{4P}(\hat{r}, Y/W)W = 0 \text{ (deposits } (r_D)) \tag{III.4}$$

$$D = f_{4P}(\hat{r}, Y/W)W \text{ (definition of } D) \tag{III.4a}$$

$$f_{5B}(\hat{r})D(1-k) + f_{5P}(\hat{r}, Y/W)W = 0 \text{ (loans } (r_L)) \tag{III.5}$$

Rate-of-return equations:

$$r_K q = R \text{ (capital)} \tag{III.6}$$

$$r_M = r'_M - \rho_p^e \text{ (currency and reserves)} \tag{III.7}$$

$$r_s = r'_S - \rho_p^e \text{ (government securities)} \tag{III.8}$$

$$r_D = r'_0 - \rho_p^e \text{ (deposits)} \tag{III.9}$$

$$r_L = r'_L - \rho_p^e \text{ (loans)} \tag{III.10}$$

$$d = d' - \rho_p^e \text{ (discount rate)}. \tag{III.11}$$

The equity of bank shareholders is ignored, so that the items in the bank column sum to zero, just as the items in the public column sum to private net worth W.

There are eleven independent equations. As before, $Y, M, S, K, R, r'_M, \rho_p^e$, p, d', and K may be taken as exogenous and the system solved for the eleven variables q, W, r_K, r_M, r_S, r'_S, r_0, r'_D, r_L, r'_L, and d. In this interpretation of model III, the interest rate paid on deposits is endogenous, market determined. The banks' deposit supply function f_{4B} tells, for given values of other interest rates, the quantity of deposits banks wish to accept at any given deposit rate. In equilibrium this must be equal to the quantity of deposits the public wishes to hold at this same set of rates.

As before, the effects of various instruments of monetary policy and of other exogenous variables on the key variable q represents their impact on aggregate demand. With the same assumptions about asset substitution, and about income elasticity of demand for high-powered money, the results will be qualitatively the same as in the other models. They will be quantitatively very different, of course. Fractional reserve banking means that a bigger re-shuffling of portfolios and larger changes in rates of return are needed to absorb a given increase in the supply of high-powered money. To the extent the banks are not induced to add the new supply to their excess reserves, the public must be induced to hold some multiple of it as deposits. The change in rates of return necessary to accomplish either of these results, or any combination of them, may be very large in comparison with the 100 per cent money regime depicted in models I and II.

An alternative interpretation is to take the deposit rate r'_D as institution-ally or legally fixed. Adding it to the list of exogenous variables means that one equation must be deleted. The one to delete, of course, is (III.4). With an effective ceiling on the interest banks are allowed to pay, banks fall short of their supply curve $(-f_{4B})$. They accept all the deposits the public is willing to leave with them at the prevailing set of interest rates, and they would gladly accept more. Thus (III.4) becomes an inequality: $f_{4B} + f_{4P} < 0$. The remaining equations in the model, including (III.4a), still apply.

This interpretation is the one customarily made. It accords with United States institutions — prohibition of interest on demand deposits and a ceiling on time deposit interest. Once again the effects on q of policy measures and other exogenous changes can be analyzed. Here, however, there is a new possi-ble source of abnormal results. The "gross substitutes" assumption may be violated in the market as a whole even though it is satisfied by each sector — banks and public — separately. For example, an increase in the deposit rate or a reduction in the securities rate might increase rather than diminish the net demand for currency or government securities. While the public's direct de-mands fall as they shift into deposits, the banks' demands may increase simply because they have more deposits [3]

This formulation adds the deposit rate ceiling to the list of monetary policy instruments and permits analysis of the question whether an increase in the ceiling is expansionary or contractionary.

9. Concluding Remarks

The models discussed here were meant to be illustrative only, and to give meaning to some general observations about monetary analysis. The basic framework is very flexible. It can be extended to encompass more sectors and more assets, depending on the topic under study. Other financial intermediaries can be introduced. More distinctions can be made among categories of government debts and types of private debts. Equally important, the assumption that physical capital is homogeneous can be dropped, and a number of markets, prices, and rates of return for stocks of goods introduced – distinguishing among houses, plant, equipment, consumers' durables, etc.

According to this approach, the principal way in which financial policies and events affect aggregate demand is by changing the valuations of physical assets relative to their replacement costs. Monetary policies can accomplish such changes, but other exogenous events can too. In addition to the exogenous variables explicitly listed in the illustrative models, changes can occur, and undoubtedly do, in the portfolio preferences – asset demand functions – of the public, the banks, and other sectors. These preferences are based on expectations, estimates of risk, attitudes towards risk, and a host of other factors. In this complex situation, it is not to be expected that the essential impact of monetary policies and other financial events will be easy to measure in the absence of direct observation of the relevant variables (q in the models). There is no reason to think that the impact will be captured in any single exogenous or intermediate variables, whether it is a monetary stock or a market interest rate. [4]

Notes

[1] Jerome Stein has insisted on this property of the short-run investment schedule. See his paper, "Money and Capacity Growth," *Journal of Political Economy*, 74 (October 1966), 451-65.

[2] See Tobin, "Money and Economic Growth," *Econometrica*, 33, No. 4 (October 1965), 671-84 (Chapter 9 above).

[3] These problems are analyzed in the Tobin-Brainard and Brainard papers cited above.

[4] This point has been illustrated in simulation of a numerical model on the order of Model III above. See Brainard and Tobin, "Pitfalls in Financial Model Building," *American Economic Review*, 58 (May 1968), 99-122.

CHAPTER 19

DEPOSIT INTEREST CEILINGS AS A MONETARY CONTROL

The most important weapons of the Federal Reserve System in its battles
with inflation during the past three years have been its traditional tools: open
market operations, the discount rate and the administration of discount
"windows," and required reserve ratios. But ceilings on the rates which member banks, and insured nonmember commercial and mutual savings banks,
may pay on savings and time deposits have played a more important and
controversial role than ever before. During this period, moreover, similar
ceilings were imposed on federally insured savings and loan associations.

The history of Regulation Q since 1962 is given in table 19.1. The general
policy since 1965 has been to keep the lid on these rates while market interest rates have risen dramatically. Indeed one important action, taken in September 1966 in the aftermath of the "crunch," was to lower the rates banks
could pay on small time deposits. The objective was to help the savings and
loan associations. Since March 1965 their regulatory authority, the Federal
Home Loan Bank Board (FHLBB), had been trying to prevent competitive
increases in savings and loan dividends by threatening to deny credit to associations that exceeded its informal ceilings, which had reached 4.75 per cent
on regular accounts for most associations. In September 1966 the Board was
empowered to impose formal ceilings, to be coordinated with the regulations
issued by the Federal Reserve and the Federal Deposit Insurance Corporation
for commercial banks and mutual savings banks. Since that date savings and
loan dividends on regular accounts have been limited to 4.75 per cent or 5 per
cent, depending on region and on rates paid locally by competing institutions;
somewhat higher rates are allowed on special accounts. [1]

I propose to comment in turn on the macroeconomic, allocative, and distributive implications of the policy. I conclude that the overall monetary

Reprinted from *Journal of Money, Credit, and Banking,* 2 (February 1970), 4-14.
Copyright © 1970 by the Ohio State University Press, Columbus, Ohio.
The research described in this paper was carried out under grants from the National
Science Foundation and the Ford Foundation.

Table 19.1
Maximum Interest Rates Payable on Time and Savings Deposits (Per Cent Per Annum)*

Rates Jan. 1, 1962 – July 19, 1966

Type of deposit	Jan. 1, 1962	July 17, 1963	Nov. 24, 1964	Dec. 6, 1965
		Effective date		
Savings deposits: †				
12 months or more	4	4	4	4
Less than 12 months	3.5	3.5	4	4
Other time deposits: ‡				
12 months or more	4	4	4	5.5
6 months to 12 months	3.5	4	4.5	5.5
90 days to 6 months	2.5	4	4.5	5.5
Less than 90 days (30–89 days)	1	1	4	5.5

Rates beginning July 20, 1966

Type of deposit	July 20, 1966	Sept. 26, 1966	Apr. 19, 1968
		Effective date	
Savings deposits	4	4	4
Other time deposits: ‡			
Multiple maturity: #			
90 days or more	5	5	5
Less than 90 days (30–89 days)	4	4	4
Single-maturity:			
Less than $100,000	5.5	5	5
$100,000 or more:	5.5	5.5	
30–59 days			5.5
60–89 days			5.75
90–179 days			6
180 days and over			6.25

* *Federal Reserve Bulletin* (Nov. 1969). Note: rates given are maximum rates that may be paid by member banks as established by the Board of Governors under provisions of Regulation Q; however, a member bank may not pay a rate in excess of the maximum rate payable by state banks or trust companies on like deposits under the laws of the state in which the member bank is located. Beginning Feb. 1, 1936, maximum rates that may be paid by nonmember insured commercial banks as established by the FDIC, have been the same as those in effect for member banks.

† Closing date for the Postal Savings System was March 28, 1966. Maximum rates on postal savings accounts coincided with those on savings deposits.

‡ For exceptions with respect to certain foreign time deposits, see *Federal Reserve Bulletin* (Oct. 1962), 1279; (Aug. 1965), 1084; and (Feb. 1968), 167.

Multiple-maturity time deposits include deposits that are automatically renewable at maturity without action by the depositor and deposits that are payable after written notice of withdrawal.

effects of ceiling regulations are small and easy to neutralize by traditional monetary controls. The allocative and distributive effects are, however, unfortunate. The root of the policy was an exaggerated and largely unnecessary concern for the technical solvency of savings and loan associations. These institutions should be reformed so that monetary policy is not again constrained by solicitude for the appearance of their balance sheets.

1. Ceiling Rates as Anti-Inflationary Policy

Is an increase in rate ceilings an easing or a tightening of monetary policy? Superficial arguments point in both directions. Raising the ceilings is after all an increase in interest rates, and is that not deflationary? But it also brings in deposits and promotes intermediation by banks and thrift institutions — is that not expansionary? The Federal Reserve, if one may judge from the tenacity with which it sticks to the present policy, adheres to the latter view.

Suppose that the Federal Reserve does not change the settings of its other policy instruments, the supply of unborrowed reserves, the discount rate, and reserve requirements. What does a rise in deposit rates do to the excess demand for bank reserves? The sign of this impact is not an infallible indicator of the direction of ultimate effect. But it gives a strong presumption, and it is the same first-order effect that underlies our confidence that we know the directions in which the conventional instruments move the economy.

For every dollar drawn into time deposits, banks' required reserves rise by k_T cents, their disposable funds by $1-k_T$ cents, and their demand for net free reserves rises by $e_T(1-k_T)$ cents, where e_T is the fraction, positive or negative, of disposable funds placed in net free reserves. Where do the funds come from? Suppose that d cents of every new dollar of time deposits come from demand deposits, while $1-d$ cents come from assets outside banks. The reduction of demand deposits lowers banks' demands for reserves by $d[k_D + e_D(1-k_D)]$. Given that the Fed holds the supply of unborrowed reserves constant, the net increment in excess demand for reserves is:

$$k_T - dk_D + e_T(1-k_T) - e_D(1-k_D)d \qquad (1)$$

(We shall ignore the possibility that some of the new time deposits are dishoardings of currency, not only because it is unlikely but because by assumption the Fed maintains unborrowed reserves constant in the face of changes in public currency holdings.)

In the case of certificates of deposit, k_T is currently .06 for the large banks in the CD market; k_D is .175; take e_T and e_D both to be --.005. Therefore expression (1) will be positive, the impact effect deflationary, if d is less than .32; the impact effect will be inflationary if d is greater than .32. Gramlich and Kalchbrenner, [2] who have carefully estimated own- and cross-effects of interest rates on demands for liquid assets, find d to be about .37. This is probably too high an estimate for our current purpose. It does not allow for substitutions into time deposits from other than liquid assets (currency, treasury bills, demand deposits, deposits in mutual savings banks and savings and loan associations). Also, demand deposits are probably a less important marginal source of time deposits now, when the interest differential is already so large, than on average during the period of estimation. I guess that d is smaller than the crucial value, that the impact effect of a rise in rates on excess demand for reserves would therefore be restrictive, but that there is not much in it one way or the other. Even if ceilings were raised enough so that banks could recapture the $10 billion in certificates of deposit they have lost in the past year their required reserves would rise by at most $600 million, and by $175 million less for every billion that came out of demand deposits.

The situation is somewhat different for savings deposits and small time deposits. The critical value of d is lowered by as much as 50 per cent; thanks to reductions made in 1967, reserve requirements on savings deposits and the first $5 million of time deposits are only 3 per cent. This increases the chance that the reserve impact of a ceiling increase is expansionary. If, as in the period prior to September 1966, commercial bank ceilings are raised and other thrift institutions are not able to meet the competition, banks will gain deposits at the expense of those institutions. Gramlich and Kalchbrenner find a high degree of substitutability. One third of the funds going into commercial bank time and savings deposits due to a rise in their interest rates come from other savings accounts and this estimate would be higher if CD's were distinguished from other deposits. Almost 90 per cent of the own-effect of a rise in interest rates in savings institutions is, these authors find, due to substitution out of commercial bank time deposits. In these circumstances a rise in commercial bank ceilings alone might have a restrictive impact. However, under current circumstances ceilings in all these institutions would undoubtedly be raised together or not at all. The shift into commercial banks would be small per interest rate point, but a substantial fraction would have to come from demand deposits. One way in which the Fed could soak up the reserves thus released would be to raise the reserve requirements on savings and time deposits. Under present legislation they can be set as high as 10 per cent.

Reserve calculations are not, of course, the whole story. A rise in deposit rates will also induce some swaps of assets between banks and the public.

These may dominate, and conceivably even reverse, the reserve effects just discussed. Assuming that the reserve effects wash out, the public sells to the banks $1-d$ of assets for every dollar of new time and savings deposits. At prevailing interest rates the public will not necessarily want to sell the same package of assets that banks want to buy with their new funds. In the case of CD's there could be initially an excess supply of Treasury bills and marketable commercial paper, and excess demand for less liquid commercial loans, longer term securities, and mortgages. The macroeconomic upshot of this increase in intermediation is probably not large, but is seems definitely expansionary. As for savings deposits, the nature of the asset shifts depends, once again, on whether the ceiling increase applies only to commercial banks or to all institutions. If it is confined to commercial banks, the main result is a shift from mortgages to business loans. If it is general, the main result will be excess demands for mortgages and business loans matched by excess supplies in securities markets.

The prevalent view that an increase in ceilings is expansionary seems to be based on these asset shifts. Reserve effects are ignored on the ground that the Fed's normal operating procedures stabilize money market interest rates, not the supply of unborrowed reserves. Indeed, in 1962–64, when the Fed was following a "bill rate only" policy, the greatest triumphs of Operation Twist were due to increases in Regulation Q ceilings, which eased the markets for mortgages and long-term securities while short-term rates were kept at internationally safe levels.

A rise in ceilings may, *ceteris paribus*, be expansionary, but this is no reason for maintaining low ceilings even in inflationary times. The Fed does not have to supply reserves to support any induced inflow of deposits, certainly not for any period longer than the three weeks between Federal Open Market Committee meetings. In principle, the same degree of effective monetary restraint can be maintained with low ceilings, with high ceilings, or, for that matter, with no ceilings. Higher deposit interest rates would mean more time deposits, less demand deposits, probably more total deposits, higher money market rates, and more intermediation. But these differences in simple monetary indicators are all consistent with zero macroeconomic impact. The common fallacy is to identify an expansion of bank deposits which is bought from the public by making deposits more attractive with a forced expansion to which the public can be reconciled only if competing assets become less attractive. [3]

2. Allocative and Distributive Implications

Although the macroeconomic effects are small and easily neutralized, the maintenance of effective low ceilings during a tight money period has important allocative and distributive consequences. Here again it is necessary to distinguish the interest ceilings on large denomination CD's from those on small time deposits and savings accounts. The latter are much more important.

Funds priced out of CD's have become available to the banks' borrowing customers in ingenious indirect ways that bypass the ceiling. Funds shifted to Eurodollar deposits have been borrowed by U.S. banks. Through their parent holding companies banks have borrowed in the open market. Prime corporate borrowers have sold their own short-term obligations in the market. The Fed finds itself in a perpetual and probably losing race to block these detours.

Presumably there is some deadweight loss in these arrangements for connecting lender and borrower, in comparison with the CD-bank loan nexus. But some of the inefficiency may be transient, and some of the new arrangements may be here to stay. The reluctance of big name corporations to use the commercial paper market has always been something of a mystery. If there has been an irreversible improvement of short-term loan markets outside banks, the Fed's policy of forcing disintermediation will have weakened its future control.

How do CD rate ceilings affect the allocation of funds among potential borrowers, as compared with an equally restrictive monetary policy with higher CD rates? Large metropolitan banks are hit the hardest when CD's become uncompetitive, but it is precisely they and their customers who can most easily use the alternative channels. Perhaps the main victims are the smaller, riskier, less well-known customers or potential customers of these banks.

The ceilings on small accounts favor commercial and business borrowers at the expense of mortgage borrowers. This was, of course, dramatically evident in 1966 before the September regulations. In 1969 the mortgage lending thrift institutions have not had to suffer rate competition from commercial banks, but the competition of rising open market yields slowed their growth to a halt at midyear and led to net withdrawals thereafter. As in 1966, the main burden of monetary restriction has fallen on mortgage borrowing and on residential construction.

Does the heavy impact of tight money on homebuilding reveal that it is an especially dispensable and postponable investment activity? Or does it reflect a financial structure that distorts the true priorities of the society? The truth is somewhere in between. Regardless of the structure of financial institutions and markets, long-lived durable goods of which a large stock already exists are especially vulnerable to increases in interest rates. If the capital shortage is transient and the rate increase is only short-term, there is good reason to postpone new construction. A permanent rate increase, on the other hand, depresses the present value of a house much more than that of a machine or truck. But the intrinsic sensitivity of residential construction to monetary restriction is exaggerated by the specialization of mortgage lending in institutions that are not allowed to complete for funds in periods of high interest rates. Home buyers are not able to shift to other forms of borrowing, and alternate lenders are slow to move in. Of course, if the burdens of monetary restriction were spread more evenly and more equitably, it would take higher interest rates to accomplish the same degree of overall restraint.

One of the least attractive features of recent policy has been discrimination against the small saver. He cannot earn market interest (although the small borrower must pay it). The ceiling rate differentials detailed in table 19.1 are by no means the full measure of the discrimination. The small saver cannot easily go into the open market in search of higher yields. He is impeded by the significant minimum denominations and lot sizes of market instruments, by brokerage fees, by his own unfamiliarity and ignorance. Of course, the policy makers were counting on precisely this segmentation of the market; without it the ceiling rate policy could not work at all. But from a larger perspective, the reason that financial intermediaries exist and receive government support is to overcome just this kind of segmentation, to make markets more perfect rather than to exploit their imperfections. One important reason for the rise in nominal interest rates in the last three years is the increased speed of inflation, but the government as a matter of policy denies the small saver this compensation. A government that fails to provide purchasing power bonds is in a poor moral position to deny savers competitive interest rates during an inflationary period.

This discriminatory policy will gradually be eroded by the arbitrage which it makes possible. The gaps between market lending rates and the ceiling rates on small savings will encourage new ways of bringing together small lenders and large borrowers. What mutual funds have done in equities can be done in other markets; the growing popularity of mortgage trusts is indicative. Here again the authorities, by stimulating some irreversible creation of institutions outside their control, may have bought future trouble in return for present expediency.

3. Tight Money and Savings and Loan Associations

At the root of the policy was the predicament of the savings and loan associations. The official line of the FHLBB has been that the associations could
not pay higher rates for savings as long as their portfolios were full of mortgages made at low market interest rates in the past. Like anyone else who
borrows short and lends long, the associations suffered capital losses when
there was a general rise in interest rates. The objective of the FHLBB has been
to make sure that these losses do not show up either in their balance sheets or
in their income statements. The Board's hope, successfully realized so far, has
been that the ceiling regulations would (a) hold dividends below net interest
income so that the associations would not have to draw on their accumulated
reserves and surplus, but (b) not result in net withdrawals of savings from the
associations beyond the Board's capacity to offset with advances of its own
funds. The Board's concern for the cosmetics of the savings and loan associations took priority, not only in its own policies but in those of the entire
government, over equitable treatment of the housing industry and of small
savers.

Some figures will place the Board's concerns in perspective. At the end of
1965 the reserves and surplus of savings and loan associations totalled $8.7
billion. Over the years this sum had been withheld from the owners of the
institutions (mostly mutual associations) to protect them against just such
contingencies as occurred in 1966-69. And was it so used? No, during the
period of crisis the aggregate reserves and surplus of the associations rose
every year and now stand at $10.7 billion. There can be no justification for
holding dividend rates down, and interest rates in competing institutions too,
so that the undistributed nonprofits of savings and loan associations can grow
at their normal pace. With the passage of time, low-rate mortgages are
replaced by high-rate mortgages, and the original rationalization for the
Board's policy becomes weaker and weaker. [4]

Suppose that beginning in 1966 the associations had paid one percentage
point higher dividends. The average annual cost would have been $1.2 billion
on the savings capital the associations actually had during the period. Instead
of growing, the reserves and surplus of the associations would have declined
to about their 1962 level. But the associations would now have more assets.
On the conservative assumption that a more flexible rate policy would have
enabled the associations to continue to attract net inflows of $10 billion per
year, as in the early 1960's, they would at the end of this year have $150
billion in savings capital instead of $133 billion. The additional $17 billion
new savings would have been invested in mortgages at current high market

rates, which would be particularly valuable to the associations if interest rates fall. If, under this alternative policy, the FHLBB had needed to buttress the reserves of the weaker associations, it could have done so by acquiring long-term claims upon them, junior to the claims of shareowners and depositors.

Whether or not is was avoidable this time, we certainly should not again let the whole financial policy of the country be constrained by the need to paper over the capital losses of these financial institutions. Any of a number of structural reforms would help. The associations could offer borrowers the optional alternative of mortgage contracts with variable interest charges geared to current market conditions, the variation to be absorbed in the number rather than the size of monthly payments. In any event, the associations should moderate the extreme spread between their assets and their liabilities. This could be done by diversifying assets, for example, going into the finance of consumer credit. But diversification on the liability side, which has already begun on a modest scale, seems more consistent with the purposes of the institutions. With some imagination the associations could offer savers an attractive variety of maturities, terms, and rates.

4. Appendix

The basic points of the text regarding overall monetary impact can be made with the following simple model. [5] The assets are reserves, bills. loans, and capital. The vector of interest rates $\hat{r}$ includes r_D the discount rate, r_B on bills, r_L on loans, r_K on capital, and r_T on time deposits. Government debt is given in total, R in the form of unborrowed reserves and $G-R$ in interest-bearing bills. A monetary policy is expansionary if it lowers r_K, deflationary if it raises r_K, neutral if it leaves it unchanged. The four balance equations are as follows:

Reserves:

$$[k_D + e_D(\hat{r})\,(1-k_D)]\ D(\hat{r}) + [k_T + e_T(\hat{r})\,(1-k_T)]\ T(\hat{r}) = R\ . \qquad (1)$$

$D(\hat{r})$ and $T(\hat{r})$ are the public's demands for demand deposits and time deposits; k_D and k_T are the legal reserve requirements per dollar of these deposits. After these are met, banks are free to dispose of $(1-k_D)\,D$ and $(1-k_T)\,T$; $e_D(\hat{r})$ and $C_T(\hat{r})$ are the fractions, positive or negative, of these disposable funds they choose to hold in net free reserves.

Bills:

$$b_D(\hat{r})\,(1-k_D)\,D(\hat{r}) + b_T(\hat{r})\,(1-k_T)\,T(\hat{r}) + B(\hat{r}) = G-R\ . \qquad (2)$$

Here $b_D(\hat{r})$ and $b_T(\hat{r})$ are the fractions of disposable funds banks choose to hold in bills, and $B(\hat{r})$ is the public's demand for bills.

Loans:

$$l_D(\hat{r})\,(1-k_D)\,D(\hat{r}) + l_T(\hat{r})\,(1-k_T)\,T(\hat{r}) + L(\hat{r}) = 0 \; . \tag{3}$$

Since banks' liabilities and assets must balance for any interest vector, $e_D + b_D + l_D = 1 = e_T + b_T + l_T$.

Capital:

$$C(\hat{r}) = K \tag{4}$$

(Sum of 1–4)

$$D(\hat{r}) + T(\hat{r}) + B(\hat{r}) + L(\hat{r}) + C(\hat{r}) = G + K \; . \tag{5}$$

The last equation is an identity saying that, whatever the vector of interest rates, the public allocates all its wealth and no more. Accordingly, any one of the four balance equations can be derived from the wealth identity and the other three.

The first case discussed in the text takes r_D, R and r_T as given. The equations determine r_B, r_L, r_K. The question at issue is the sign of $\partial r_K / \partial r_T$. It is convenient to omit (2) and to differentiate (1), (3), and (4) with respect to r_T:

$$\begin{bmatrix} ER_{r_B} & ER_{r_L} & ER_{r_K} \\ EL_{r_B} & EL_{r_L} & EL_{r_K} \\ C_{r_B} & C_{r_L} & C_{r_K} \end{bmatrix} \begin{bmatrix} \partial r_B / \partial r_T \\ \partial r_L / \partial r_T \\ \partial r_K / \partial r_T \end{bmatrix} = - \begin{bmatrix} ER_{r_T} \\ EL_{r_T} \\ C_{r_T} \end{bmatrix} \tag{6}$$

Here ER_{r_x} is the partial derivative of demand for reserves with respect to r_x, equal to:

$$[k_D + e_D(1-k_D)]\,D_{r_x} + e_{D_{r_x}}(1-k_D)\,D$$
$$+ [k_T + e_T(1-k_T)]\,T_{r_x} + e_{T_{r_x}}(1-k_T)\,T$$

where D_{r_x}, T_{r_x}, $e_{D_{r_x}}$, and $e_{T_{r_x}}$ are the partial derivatives of these functions with respect to r_x. Note that ER_{r_T} is the expression examined in the text for reserve impact, taking $d = D_{r_T} / T_{r_T}$ and assuming $e_{D_{r_T}} = e_{T_{r_T}} = 0$.

Similarly, EL_{r_x} is

$$l_D(1-k_D)\,D_{r_x} + l_{D_{r_x}}(1-k_D)\,D + l_T(1-k_T)\,T_{r_x} + l_{D_{r_x}}(1-k_T)\,T + L_{r_x} \; .$$

We assume that, both for the public and for the banks, all own-rate derivatives are positive and all cross-rate derivatives nonpositive. The matrix of coefficients in (6) therefore has the sign pattern

$$
\begin{matrix}
- & - & - \\
- & + & - \\
- & - & +
\end{matrix}
$$

Its determinant is necessarily negative if the minor

$$
\begin{vmatrix}
EL_{r_L} & EL_{r_K} \\
C_{r_L} & C_{r_K}
\end{vmatrix}
$$

is positive. Each diagonal element is greater in absolute value than the other element of the same column. This must be so because an own-rate derivative is equal in absolute value to the sum of *all* the cross-rate derivatives in the same column, and here we do not have them all. Therefore the minor in question is positive, and the determinant is negative.

It follows that the sign of $\partial r_K / \partial r_T$ is the sign of the determinant

$$
\begin{vmatrix}
ER_{r_B} & ER_{r_L} & ER_{r_T} \\
EL_{r_B} & EL_{r_L} & EL_{r_T} \\
C_{r_B} & C_{r_L} & C_{r_T}
\end{vmatrix}
$$

which is equal to

$$
\alpha ER_{r_T} - \beta EL_{r_T} + \gamma C_{r_T}
$$

where α and γC_{r_T} are necessarily positive, and β is positive on the empirically plausible assumption that the bill rate has more direct effect on the demand for reserves than on the demand for capital, while the reverse is true of the loan rate. Now ER_{r_T} is what was discussed in the text as the "reserve effect" – when it is positive (low d) a rise in the time deposit rate increases excess demand for reserves. EL_{r_T} is what was discussed in the text as the "asset swap" effect – when it is negative, a rise in the time deposit rate decreases the excess demand (of lenders) for loans. These signs guarantee a deflationary result, *i.e.*, a positive $\partial r_K / \partial r_T$. The opposite signs – a negative impact on reserve demand and a positive impact on loan demand – do not assure an expansionary result unless the third term, involving direct substitution of time deposits for capital (C_{r_T}), can be ignored.

The second case discussed in the text differs from the first in making r_B policy determined and exogenous, and R an endogenous variable. The equations are then:

$$
\begin{bmatrix} -1 & ER_{r_L} & ER_{r_K} \\ 0 & EL_{r_L} & EL_{r_K} \\ 0 & C_{r_L} & C_{r_K} \end{bmatrix}
\begin{bmatrix} \partial rR/\partial r_T \\ \partial r_L/\partial r_T \\ \partial r_K/\partial r_T \end{bmatrix}
= -
\begin{bmatrix} ER_{r_T} \\ EL_{r_T} \\ C_{r_T} \end{bmatrix}
\tag{8}
$$

The determinant of the matrix of coefficients is again negative. The sign of $\partial r_K/\partial r_T$ is the sign of

$$
\begin{vmatrix} -1 & ER_{r_L} & ER_{r_T} \\ 0 & EL_{r_L} & EL_{r_T} \\ 0 & C_{r_L} & C_{r_T} \end{vmatrix}
= C_{r_L} ER_{r_L} - EL_{r_L} C_{r_T}
$$

Since C_{r_L} is negative and $-EL_{r_L} C_{r_T}$ is positive, $\partial r_K/\partial r_T$ is definitely positive if the "asset swap" impact is negative, but may be negative (expansionary) if that impact is positive.

The third case discussed in the text is neutrality: $\partial r_K/\partial r_T$ equal to zero. The endogenous variables will be r_B, r_L, and R, and the equations are:

$$
\begin{bmatrix} ER_{r_B} & ER_{r_L} & -1 \\ EL_{r_B} & EL_{r_L} & 0 \\ C_{r_B} & C_{r_L} & 0 \end{bmatrix}
\begin{bmatrix} \partial r_B/\partial r_T \\ \partial r_L/\partial r_T \\ \partial R/\partial r_T \end{bmatrix}
= -
\begin{bmatrix} ER_{r_T} \\ EL_{r_T} \\ C_{r_T} \end{bmatrix}
\tag{9}
$$

The determinant is again negative, and it is clear that $\partial R/\partial r_T$ here has, naturally enough, the same sign as $\partial r_K/\partial r_T$ in the first case, (7).

Notes

[1] The FHLBB Annual Report for 1968 summarizes the regulations as follows:

(a) Associations with home offices in Alaska, California, Hawaii, and Nevada (and branches in these states of associations with home offices in other states) could offer 5 per cent on regular accounts; 5.25 per cent on bonus accounts requiring a 3-year holding period to obtain the bonus; and 5.50 per cent on accounts representing funds that were in 3-year bonus accounts before the effective date of rate control.

(b) Associations with home offices in Standard Metropolitan Statistical Areas, or in counties outside an SMSA, where a mutual savings bank was offering more than 4.75 per cent on regular accounts, could offer 5 per cent on all types of accounts. (This also applied to associations with home offices in SMSA's or counties where there were branches of associations that were offering more than 4.75 per cent on regular accounts because of mutual savings bank practice in their home area.)

(c) All associations with home offices in other areas (and at their option, associations in areas cited above) could offer 4.75 per cent on regular accounts and 5.25 per cent on minimum term-minimum balance accounts requiring a 6-month holding period.

[2] Edward M. Gramlich and John K. Kalchbrenner, "A Constrained Estimation Approach to the Demand for Liquid Assets," unpublished paper, Board of Governors of the Federal Reserve System, April 1969.

[3] The Appendix gives some of the arguments of this section in mathematical form.

[4] See remarks of Donald D. Hester, "Financial Disintermediation and Policy." *Journal of Money, Credit, and Banking*, 1 (1969), 615. In January 1969, while this paper was in press, some small increases in ceiling rates were finally – and grudgingly – made, but they were too late and too little.

[5] For description and explanation of this type of model see J. Tobin, "A General Equilibrium Approach to Monetary Theory," *Journal of Money, Credit, and Banking*, 1 (1969), 15-29 (Chapter 18 above).

CHAPTER 20

PITFALLS IN FINANCIAL MODEL BUILDING

Most monetary economists agree that the financial system is a complex of interrelated markets for assets and debts. The prices and interest rates determined in these markets and the quantities to which they refer both influence and are influenced by the "real economy," the complex of markets for currently produced goods and services. These interdependences are easy to acknowledge in principle but difficult to honor in practice, either in theoretical analysis or in empirical investigation. All of us seek and use simplifications to overcome the frustrating sterility of the cliché that everything depends on everything else. But we all know that we do so at some peril.

In this paper we argue for the importance of explicit recognition of the essential interdependences of markets in theoretical and empirical specifications of financial models. Failure to respect some elementary interrelationships — for example, those enforced by balance sheet identities — can result in inadvertent but serious errors of econometric inference and of policy. This is true equally of equilibrium relationships and of dynamic models of the behavior of the system in disequilibrium.

We will try to illustrate the basic point with the help of computer simulations of a fictitious economy of our own construction. This procedure guarantees us an Olympian knowledge of the true structure that is generating the observations. Therefore, it can exhibit some implications of specifications and misspecifications that are inaccessible both to analytical inspection and to econometric treatment of actual data.

We fully realize, of course, that this procedure cannot tell us anything

By William C. Brainard and James Tobin. Reprinted from *American Economic Review* (*Papers and Proceedings*), 58 (May 1968), 99–122. Tables have been renumbered.

The research described in this paper was carried out under a grant from the National Science Foundation. We are grateful to Sanford Berg and Jon Peck for skillful and loyal help with the computations and to Donald Hester for use of his macrosimulation program. We have benefited from the comments of Carl Christ on the original version of the paper.

about the real world. You can't get something for nothing. We realize further that lessons derived or illustrated by simulations of our particular structure will not be very convincing or even interesting to people who believe that the model bears no resemblance to the processes which generate actual statistical data. We have tried to formulate a model we believe in qualitatively, though of course the numerical values of the parameters are arbitrary.

1. An Equilibrium System

We begin by setting forth the equations of a static equilibrium of a simple financial system. The model contains the following six assets: currency and bank reserves, Treasury securities, private loans, demand deposits, time deposits, equities. With each asset is associated an interest rate; some rates are market determined, some are policy variables, some are institutional constants. There are three sectors: government, commercial banks, public. The constituents of their balance sheets and the symbols used for them in the paper are given in table 20.1.

The interest rates involved in the model are:

r_F central bank discount rate
r_S Treasury security rate
r_L loan rate
$\bar{r}_D$ demand deposit rate, legal ceiling (generally zero)
$\bar{r}_T$ time deposit rate, legal ceiling
r marginal efficiency of real investment
r_K market yield on equity
$\hat{r}^P$ the vector of interest rates relevant to public portfolio decisions, $(r_S, r_L, \bar{r}_D, \bar{r}_T, r_K)$.
$\hat{r}^B$ the vector of interest rates relevant to banks' asset choices, (r_F, r_S, r_L).

In addition to the interest rates and the accounting variables of table 20.1, the following symbols are used:

q the market valuation of equities; the replacement value of the physical assets to which the equities give title is taken to be 1 and serves as the numeraire of the system;
K the stock of capital at replacement cost;
Y national income;
k_D and k_T required reserve ratios for demand and time deposits, respectively.

Table 20.1.

Debts of	Assets of			
	Government	Banks	Public	Total Debts
Government		S^B Treasury Bills	S^P Treasury Bills	$G-R$ Treasury Bills
		E Required Reserves Net Free Reserves	C Currency	R Reserves of Currency
Banks			D Demand Deposits T Time Deposits	D Demand Deposits T Time Deposits
Public		$-L$ Loans		$-L$ Loans
Equities in physical capital			V Equities	V Equities
Net worth assets–debts	$-G$ Government Debt	0	W^P Equities + Government Debt	

$I = \Delta K$ net investment at replacement cost
$\underline{H}$ private saving
$\overline{GP}$ government purchases
$\overline{tx}$ the marginal tax rate.

The equations are:

Public asset holdings and debts

$$C = C^P(\hat{r}^P, Y) W^P$$ Currency (assumed zero in simulation model)

$$D = D^P(\hat{r}^P, Y) W^P$$ Demand deposits   (1)

$$T = T^P(\hat{r}^P, Y) W^P$$ Time deposits   (2)

$$S^P = S^P(\hat{r}^P, Y) W^P$$ Treasury securities   (3)

$$-L = -L^P(\hat{r}^P, Y)\, W^P \qquad \text{Borrowing} \qquad (4)$$

$$[V = V^P(\hat{r}^P, Y)\, W^P \qquad \text{Equities}$$

$$= (1-L^P-S^P-T^P-D^P-C^P)\, W^P] \qquad \text{[implied by other equations]}$$

Bank asset holdings

$$E = E_D^B(\hat{r}^B)(1-k_D)\, D + E_T^B(\hat{r}^B)(1-k_T)\, T \qquad \text{Net free reserves} \qquad (5)$$

$$S^B = S_D^B(\hat{r}^B)(1-k_D)\, D + S_T^B(\hat{r}^B)(1-k_T)\, T \qquad \text{Treasury securities} \qquad (6)$$

$$L = L_D^B(\hat{r}^B)(1-k_D)\, D + L_T^B(\hat{r}^B)(1-k_T)\, T \qquad \text{Loans}$$

$$= (1-E_D^B-S_D^B)(1-k_D)\, D + (1-E_T^B-S_T^B)(1-k_T)\, T \qquad (7)$$

Balance equations

$$k_D D + k_T T + E + C = R \qquad \text{Currency and bank reserves} \qquad (8)$$

$$S^P + S^B = G-R \qquad \text{Treasury securities} \qquad (9)$$

$$[L^P + L^B = 0 \text{ implied by (4) and (7)]} \qquad \text{Loans}$$

$$V = qK \qquad \text{Market value of equity} \qquad (10)$$

$$W^P = G + V \qquad \text{Public wealth} \qquad (11)$$

$$q r_K = r \qquad \text{Yield and value of equity} \qquad (12)$$

$$r = \alpha_0 + \alpha_1 \frac{Y}{K} \qquad \text{Relation of marginal to average product of capital.} \qquad (13)$$

In addition, two inequalities must be satisfied in order for the ceiling rates on deposits to be effective. Banks must be willing to accept demand and time deposits at prevailing interest rates in at least as large volume as the public wishes to hold.

The thirteen equations (leaving aside public currency holdings) determine seven quantities $(D, T, S^P, S^B, L, E, V)$, four rates (r_S, r_L, r, r_K), the market value of equity q, and of wealth W^P. Exogenous variables are of two kinds: policy variables $r_F, \bar{r}_T, R, k_D, k_T$ and other variables G, K, α_0, Y. Alternative interpretations are possible, depending on the *modus operandi* or objectives of the central bank. Although the supply of reserves R is one of the quantities the central bank directly controls, it may nevertheless be an endogenous variable and r_S an exogenous one if the central bank supplies whatever reserves are needed to peg the market interest rate at some target level.

A number of the features of this model need explanation:

1. The structure of the balance sheet desired by the public is taken to depend on the vector of relevant interest rates and on its net worth W^P in a special way. Desired holdings of the various assets and debts are homogeneous in wealth; a change in W^P with given interest rates changes all items in the balance sheet in the same proportion. With respect to interest rate effects, the assets are assumed to be gross substitutes. An increase in the rate on a particular asset increases the public's demand for the asset but diminishes or leaves unchanged its demand for any other.

2. Similar behavior is assumed of banks with regard to the allocation of their "disposable assets" – deposits less required reserves – among net free reserves, [1] government securities, and loans. However, allowance is made for possible differences between the allocations of disposable demand deposits and disposable time deposits. Since time deposits are, from the individual banker's viewpoint, less volatile than demand deposits, they may be more adventurously invested.

The vector of interest rates relevant to the banks is somewhat different from the one relevant to the public. It includes the central bank discount rate, which is irrelevant to the public, but excludes the rate on equities, which the banks do not hold. It is also assumed, though this is not essential, that asset allocations of deposits are independent of the rates that are paid to depositors.

3. In each case, banks and public, the entire list of relevant interest rates occurs in each equation. The reason for this is as follows: The total effect of an interest rate change, summed over the whole portfolio or balance sheet, must be zero. Thus if a particular rate is entered only as a positive factor in the demand for its own asset and not included in any other equation, the offsetting negative effect is being implicitly assigned to the missing equation. (In the above model, bank demand for loans and public demand for capital play this residual role.)

It is always important to check the specification of the unwritten equation that is implied by the explicit specification of the others. For example, one might be tempted, either because it is theoretically convenient or because of econometric results and significance tests, to regard the time deposit interest rate as important for time deposits but of negligible importance in public demand for any other particular asset – demand deposits, currency, securities, loans. But to drop it out of those equations is to assume that all the funds attracted into time deposits come from equities. If this is an assumption one would not make deliberately, neither should he make it inadvertently. It is quite possible that cross-effects are so diffused that none of them appears significant in empirical regressions. Yet it is a mistake to drop them out, because their sum is not zero but equal in absolute value to the own-effect.

4. The same observation applies to other variables affecting balance sheet or portfolio choice. In the model, income Y is entered to represent the standard influence of transactions volume on desired holdings for demand deposits and for currency. By the same token, Y belongs in the other asset demand functions of the public. If an increase in income induces the public to add to their money holdings, it induces them to diminish their holdings of something else. If this something else is not specified, the implicit assumption is that all the movement into cash is at the expense of the residual asset, the one whose equation is not written down.

5. The influence of Y on asset choice is one causal link from the real economy to financial markets. An additional link is the influence of r, the marginal efficiency of capital, another variable exogenous to the financial sector. An increase in r, for example, will raise either the market value of equities, and with it the public's wealth, or the market yield of equities, or both. In any event it will lead to a general reshuffling of portfolios, and a new structure of rates. The marginal efficiency of capital itself is linearly related to its average product Y/K; both Y and K are exogenous to the financial sector.

6. One of the basic theoretical propositions motivating the model is that the market valuation of equities, relative to the replacement cost of the physical assets they represent, is the major determinant of new investment. Investment is stimulated when capital is valued more highly in the market than it costs to produce it, and discouraged when its valuation is less than its replacement cost. Another way to state the same point is to say that investment is encouraged when the market yield on equity r_K is low relative to the real returns to physical investment.

An increase in q, the market valuation, can occur as a result of an increase in the marginal efficiency of capital r; i.e., as a result of events exogenous to the financial sector. But an increase in q may also occur as a consequence of financial events that reduce r_K, the yield that investors require in order to hold equity capital. Indeed, this is the sole linkage in the model through which financial events, including monetary policies, affect the real economy. In other words, the valuation of investment goods relative to their cost is the prime indicator and proper target of monetary policy. Nothing else, whether it is the quantity of "money" or some financial interest rate, can be more than an imperfect and derivative indicator of the effective thrust of monetary events and policies. As some of our examples below will show, such indicators can be quite misleading.

In the actual economy, of course, the single linkage just described is a multiple one. There are many kinds of physical capital and many markets where existing stocks are valued — not just markets for equities, but other markets for operating businesses and for houses, other kinds of real estate, cars and other durable goods, etc. The value of these stocks then helps to determine the profitability of new production of the same kind of capital or of close substitutes. Here this variety is ignored by aggregating all capital and attributing to it a single market price and a single replacement cost.

7. The effects of changes in Regulation Q ceiling rates on time deposits have been much debated in recent years, among both monetary theorists and men of affairs. In our view this discussion has not paid enough attention to the general equilibrium effects of such regulatory measures and has been too preoccupied with the effects on commercial bank loans or deposits. A reduction in the ceiling may in some circumstances be deflationary, but the fact that it drives funds out of banks and forces them to contract their loans is no proof at all of this assertion. Erstwhile depositors will be looking for places to invest their funds, and they may be glad to acquire, either directly or through other intermediaries, the assets the banks have to sell and to accommodate the borrowers the banks turn away. Whether the ultimate result is to bid interest rates and equity yields down or up is a complicated question: the answer depends, among other things, on whether time deposits are in wealth-owners' portfolios predominantly substitutes for demand deposits and currency or for loans and equities. The former substitution pattern tends to make a reduction in time deposit rates deflationary, the latter pattern, expansionary. The answer depends also, of course, on what is assumed about the supply of unborrowed reserves and other instruments of monetary control.

For some purposes it will be useful to make explicit the connections between the financial system and the real economy, extending the model to encompass endogenous determination of income, investment, and the marginal productivity of capital. Our extensions are of the most primitive sort; our purpose is not to build a complete model but to include the linkages necessary to illuminate the problems of constructing a model of the financial sector. The explicit equations, (14), (15), and (16), are given below in section 3.7. Net investment depends, for the reasons already stated, on the market value of capital, q. The model is a stationary one — alternatively, it could be interpreted to describe deviations from trend. In an equilibrium with $q = 1$, net investment will be zero. Government expenditures are exogenous; tax revenues and saving are linear functions of income; the level of income is determined by the usual multiplier process. The marginal productivity of capital has an exogenous component but also varies directly with income. Both income and the marginal productivity of capital feed back into the equations of the financial sector in the manners already described. The model does not determine a commodity price level; everything is expressed in terms of newly produced capital goods, the numeraire.

2. Dynamics of Adjustment

No one seriously believes that either the economy as a whole or its financial subsector is continuously in an equilibrium. Equations like those of the model described above do not hold every moment of time. Consequently analysts and policy makers can hope to receive no more than limited guidance from comparative static analysis of the full effects of "changing" exogenous variables, including the instruments of policy. They need to know also the laws governing the system in disequilibrium. Since there are many dynamic specifications that have the same static equilibrium, the model builder has great freedom. Moreover, economic theory, although it imposes some a priori constraints on specification of equilibrium models, has almost nothing to say on mechanisms of adjustment. The burden on empirical testing and estimation is very heavy, but it is precisely in the estimation of lag structures and autoregressive effects that statistical and econometric techniques encounter greatest difficulties.

There are, of course, some identities – e.g., balance sheet or income identities – that apply out of equilibrium as well as in. Our strictures in section 1 on the need for model builders to pay explicit attention to these identities apply with equal force to dynamic specifications. A common and useful dynamic equation is that the deviation of a variable from its "desired level" – i.e., its value according to one of the equations of the equilibrium model – is diminished by a certain proportion each unit of time. This specification is incomplete when the model includes a number of such variables constrained to add up to a given total, the same total for actual values and desired values. Deviations of actual from desired values must always add up to zero. If, for example, the public is raising its holdings of demand deposits to bring them closer to the quantity desired at current levels of income and interest rates, the public must also be reducing its holdings of some other assets, taking those holdings either toward or away from equilibrium.

In general, the adjustment of any one asset holding depends not only on its own deviation but also on the deviations of other assets. The public might have exactly the right amount of demand deposits and yet change this holding in the course of adjusting other holdings to their desired levels. Failure to specify explicitly these dynamic cross-adjustment effects has the unintended consequence that they are all thrown into the omitted equation. In the model of section 1, for example, the equity equation happens to be the one which is arbitrarily omitted, since by Walras' law its specification is implicit in the other equations. If no cross-effects were allowed in the explicit equations of adjustment of the other asset demands, then the counterparts of all the own-adjustments specified would be loaded into the implicit adjustment equation for equities. The assumption would be, for example, that when people increase their demand deposits to bring them up to desired levels they get all the funds by selling equities. It is doubtful that a model builder would want to make an assumption of this sort, but he might do so inadvertently.

The necessity for the effects of a change in a variable to sum to zero across an exhaustive list of asset holdings applies separately to every lagged value introduced as an explanatory variable. Model builders are tempted, of course, to choose for each equation, one at a time, the lag structure that seems best to fit their commonsense judgements and the data. They should remember that they are implicitly building the reflection of this lag structure into other equations. For example, it would be hard to make sense of a model that relates one asset holding to interest rates lagged two and three quarters and relates a close substitute to the same interest rate lagged one and four quarters.

We are pleading, in short, for a "general disequilibrium" framework for the dynamics of adjustment to a "general equilibrium" system. This is the spirit in which the simulation model, described in the next section, has been constructed.

3. Description of the Structure of the Model

The model which has been simulated is as follows:

3.1. Public's Desired Balance Sheet

Each desired asset holding is of the form $X^P = (a_0 + a_1 r_T + a_2 r_S + a_3 r_L + a_4 r_K + a_5 Y) W^P$. The assumed coefficients of the linear forms are given in table 20.2; we do not attempt to defend the realism of these numbers or the ones in later tables. We shall designate by $X^{**}(t)$ the value of X^P which this function yields for contemporaneous r's, Y, and W^P. The sum of X^{**}/W^P

Table 20.2.
Desired Balance Sheet of Public

Coefficients of:	Const.	r_T (Time Deposits)	r_S (Securities)	r_L (Loans)	r_K (Equities)	Y (Income)	
C^{**}/w^P	0	0	0	0	0	0	Currency*
(1) D^{**}/w^P	+ 0.55	−0.20	−0.10	0	0	+ 0.10	Demand Deposits
(2) T^{**}/w^P	−0.55	+ 0.40	−0.20	0	0	−0.03	Time Deposits
(3) S^{P**}/w^P	+ 0.20	−0.15	+ 0.40	0	−0.025	−0.05	Treasury Securities
(4) L^{**}/w^P	0	0	0	+ 0.20	−0.125	−0.05	Loans (in negative sense)
V^{**}/w^P	+ 0.30	−0.05	−0.10	−0.20	+ 0.15	+ 0.03	Capital
Totals	1.00	0	0	0	0	0	

* Public is assumed not to hold currency.

must be identically equal to 1; therefore, the constant terms must add up to 1 and the other coefficients to 0.

3.2. Public's Adjustment Behavior

This is assumed to take the following form

$$\Delta X_i(t) = X_i(t) - X_i(t-1) = \sum_j \alpha_{ij}(X_j^{**}(t) - X(t-1)) + \beta_i H(t) + \gamma_i K(t-1) \, \Delta q(t) \, .$$

The first terms simply represent the stock adjustment terms previously discussed, including "cross" as well as "own" terms. The last two terms represent initial allocations of new saving $H(t)$ and of capital gains on equities $K(t-1)\Delta q(t)$. Together these two variables account for the change in public wealth $\Delta W^P(t)$. As the column sums of table 20.3 indicate, the sum of the reactions to a particular deviation, with wealth constant, must be 0, and the sum of the reactions to change in wealth must be 1.

There are five deviations $X^{**}(t) - X(t-1)$ and two wealth increments $H(t)$ and $K(t-1)\Delta q(t)$. But they are linearly dependent: the sum of the five deviations must equal the sum of the two wealth increments. Therefore, there are

Table 20.3.
Adjustment Behavior of Public

Coefficient of:	Deviation from Desired Stocks				Changes in Wealth	
	Demand Deposit $D^{**}(t)-D(t-1)$	Time Deposit $T^{**}(t)-T(t-1)$	Securities $SP^{**}(t)-SP(t-1)$	Loans $L^{**}(t)-L(t-1)$	Saving $H(t)$	Capital Gains $K_{t-1}(q_t-q_{t-1})$
(1') $\Delta D(t)$	+0.30	-0.08	-0.08	-0.30	1.00	0
(2') $\Delta T(t)$	-0.10	0.20	-0.10	0	0	0
(3') $\Delta SP(t)$	-0.15	-0.10	0.20	0	0	0
(4') $\Delta L(t)$	0	0	0	0.40	0	0
$\Delta V(t)$	-0.05	-0.02	-0.02	-0.10	0	1.00
Totals	0	0	0	0	1.00	1.00

only six identifiable coefficients, not seven, in each ΔX adjustment equation. We have chosen to leave out $V^{**}(t)-V(t-1)$, which can be derived as the sum of the last two variables – column headings in table 20.3 – less the sum of the first four. Therefore, each of the first four columns of table 20.3 describes the pattern of reactions to a unit deviation in the designated variable offset by a unit deviation of opposite sign in equity holdings. Likewise, each of the last two columns describes the pattern of reactions to a unit increment of wealth matched by a unit deviation of the same sign in equity holdings.

The numerical values in the table embody some preconceptions of the authors. One is that new saving is initially accumulated as demand deposits, later to be distributed among other assets if holdings of demand deposits are too large. Another is that capital gains are initially held in the assets that gave rise to them; later they may be at least partially realized and distributed across the whole portfolio. The fourth column has the following interpretation: If people are in debt more than they like (and have equivalently more equity capital than they would like), they repay 40 per cent of the excess, selling equities for one quarter of the repayment and using demand deposits for the other three quarters. Conversely, if their debt is less than desired, they borrow 40 per cent and divide the newly borrowed funds in the same one-to-three ratio between equities and cash. Subsequently the borrowed money finds its way into equities, which the equilibrium equations tell us is the purpose of incurring debt.

3.3. Banks' Desired Allocation of Deposited Funds

As explained in section 1, banks accept as given and beyond their control the quantities of time and demand deposits forthcoming at the ceiling rates. They allocate these deposits, after meeting the reserve requirements upon them, among excess reserves, securities, and loans. These allocations are not the same for the two kinds of deposits; banks are more willing to lend out their time deposits, which are regarded as less likely to be withdrawn. The form of the equation for banks' desired holding of an asset is $X^B = (1-k_D) D\{a_D + a_1(r_S - r_F) + a_2(r_L - r_F)\} + (1-k_T) T\{a_T + a_1(r_S - r_F) + a_2(r_L - r_F)\}$. We shall call the value of X^B for contemporaneous values of interest rates and deposits $X^*(t)$.

3.4. Banks' Adjustment Behavior

The dynamics of bank behavior are similar in structure to the dynamics of public portfolio adjustment. Changes in bank portfolio allocations depend, on the one hand, on deviations from desired allocations and, on the other hand, on changes in disposable deposits. The assumed structure of the former res-

Table 20.4.
Desired Portfolio of Banks

	Constants		Coefficients of Differentials Above Discount Rate		
	a_D Demand Deposits	a_T Time Deposits	a_1 Securities Rate r_S-r_F	a_2 Loan Rate r_L-r_F	
(5) E^*	0.01	0.0	−0.04	−0.01	Net free reserves
(6) S^{B*}	0.67	0.34	+ 0.06	−0.09	Treasury securities
(7) $-L^*$	0.32	0.66	−0.02	+ 0.10	Loans
Totals	1.00	1.00	0	0	

Table 20.5.
Adjustment Behavior of Banks

	Coefficients of:				
	Deviation from Desired Stocks		Changes in Disposable Assets		Changes in Loan Demand
	Net free Reserves	Treasury Securities	Demand Deposits	Time Deposits	
	$E^*(t)-E(t-1)$ $+\Delta k_D D(t-1)$ $+\Delta k_T T(t-1)$	$S^{B*}(t)-S^B(t-1)$	$(1-k_D)\Delta D$ $-\Delta k_D D(t-1)$	$(1-k_T)\Delta T$ $-\Delta k_T T(t-1)$	$-\Delta L$
(5') ΔE	0.5	−0.5	1	1	−1
(6') ΔS^B	−0.5	0.5	0	0	0
$-\Delta L$	0	0	0	0	1
Totals	0	0	1	1	0

ponses is given in the first two columns of table 20.5, for net free reserves and securities. A unit deviation in either of these has as its counterpart a unit deviation of opposite sign in loans.

The structure of responses to changes in disposable assets is given in columns 3 and 4; very simply, all changes are initially absorbed in net free reserves. As indicated in those columns, disposable assets may change either because deposits change or because reserve requirements are altered. Reserve requirement changes also figure in column 1: banks are assumed to realize, for example, that net free reserves of last period are already less excessive if reserve requirements have meanwhile been increased.

Finally, the last row and column of table 20.5 recognize that in the short run banks meet from excess reserves whatever loan demand comes their way at the established interest rate. However, banks adjust the loan rate up or down, depending on whether $L^*(t)-L(t-1)$ is greater or smaller than zero:

$$\Delta r_L = 10 \left\{ \frac{L^*(t)-L(t-1)}{(1-k_D)\,D(t-1) + (1-k_T)\,T(t-1)} \right\} \qquad (7')$$

This is the *modus operandi* of the loan market and determines the loan rate. There are two other balance equations, one for bank reserves (currency) and one for interest-bearing government debt. These equations determine the two remaining interest rates, on securities and equities. These must adjust contemporaneously as necessary to clear these markets.

$$E(t) + k_D D(t) + k_T T(t) = R(t) \qquad \text{Reserves} \qquad (8)$$

$$S^P(t) + S^B(t) = G(t)-R(t) \qquad \text{Securities} \qquad (9)$$

As in the static model, we have equations for the market value of the capital stock and for total public wealth:

$$V(t) = q(t)\,K(t) \qquad (10)$$

$$W^P(t) = G(t) + V(t) \qquad (11)$$

3.5. Market Value of Equity

As explained in section 1, there is an inverse relation (12) between the market value of equity and the return it bears. Their product is equal to the marginal productivity of capital, r. This in turn was assumed to be positively and linearly related to the average product of capital; in the dynamic version this relation is lagged.

$$r_K(t)\,q(t) = r(t) \qquad (12)$$

$$r(t) = \alpha_0 + \alpha_1 \frac{Y(t-1)}{K(t-1)} \qquad (13')$$

In some simulation runs α_0 is varied in a cyclical pattern in order to "drive" the economy. Two pairs of normal values of (α_0, α_1) are used — one is $(9,2.5)$ and the other $(8,5)$. The second gives a more powerful endogenous determination of r. Since the equilibrium value of the average product of capital is taken to be 0.4, the equilibrium value of marginal productivity is in both cases 10 (per cent).

3.6. Changes in Wealth

Equation (11) implies that $\Delta W^P(t) = \Delta V(t) + \Delta G(t)$. Likewise, equation (10) says that $\Delta V(t)$ may be the result either of real investment $I(t) = \Delta K(t)$ or of capital gains or losses on existing capital. The allocation of changes in wealth between saving ($H(t) = \Delta G(t) + q(t) I(t)$) and capital gains makes a difference in the adjustment process – see table 20.3.

The 13-equation static model has now been augmented by the seven adjustment equations (1') through (7'). Correspondingly, actual values of the seven quantities are augmented by seven desired levels D^{**}, T^{**}, S^{P**}, L^{**}, E^*, S^{B*}, L^*.

The model so far described tells how the financial system operates in response to monetary policy changes or to other shocks arising either inside the financial sector or in the real economy. This model can trace the effects of these shocks on time paths of interest rates, financial quantities, and the market valuation of capital. Among the variables whose time paths are treated as exogenous to the financial system are income Y, the exogenous component of marginal efficiency of capital α_0, the real capital stock K, the government debt G.

In a rough sense, this model is analogous to the LM sector of the textbook Keynes-Hicks macroeconomic model. That is, it tells what interest rates will be associated – via monetary and financial institutions, markets, and behavior – with different states and paths of income and other "real economy" variables.

3.7. The Model Extended to Endogenous Determination of Income

As noted in section 1, we have also constructed a primitive extension of the model to allow for endogenous determination of income. The dynamic version of this extension consists of the following equations:

$$Y(t)(1-c(1-\overline{tx})) = c_0 + \Delta K(t) + \overline{GP}(t) \tag{14}$$

This is the conventional multiplier relation. Here c is the marginal propensity to consume from disposable income, c_0 is the consumption intercept, $\overline{tx}$ is the marginal tax rate, and $\overline{GP}$ is government purchases. No lags are introduced; (14) holds for contemporaneous values of the variables.

$$\Delta G(t) = \overline{GP}(t) - \overline{tx}Y(t) - \overline{tx}_0 \tag{15}$$

The increase in government debt is identical to the budget deficit, which is the excess of government purchases over tax revenue. Tax revenue is a linear function of income.

$$\Delta K(t) = \gamma_0(q(t)-1) + \gamma_1(q(t-1)-1) \tag{16}$$

As explained in section 1, the valuation of equity is the channel through which financial policies and events are transmitted to the real economy. Equation (16) expresses this linkage. In one numerical version (γ_0, γ_1) is $(1.5,0)$; in an alternative version (γ_0, γ_1) is $(1.5,1.5)$. These three equations convert Y, G, and K into endogenous variables and introduce $\overline{GP}$, $\overline{tx}_0$ and $\overline{tx}$ as new policy parameters.

The extended model can be driven by three kinds of shocks (a) exogenous changes in r — i.e., changes in the α_0 part of r, (b) monetary instruments, in particular changes in R, the supply of bank reserves, and (c) fiscal policy, represented by variation of government purchases GP while tax rates remained constant.

4. Description of Simulations

The dynamic systems described in section 3 are systems of simultaneous nonlinear first-order difference equations in 20 or 23 variables. There are three such systems: one for the financial sector alone, and two variants of the extended model, with "weak investment" and "strong investment" responses to changes in income Y. Simulations of the following types have been run:

4.1. Unit Impulses
The system is displaced from equilibrium by a once-for-all increase of 10 per cent in a single exogenous variable, holding all others at their initial equilibrium values, and the paths of the endogenous variables to the new equilibrium are traced.

4.2. Exogenous Cycles
The system is displaced from equilibrium by a sinusoidal fluctuation in a single exogenous variable, with a period of 24 units of time. At its peaks the variable is 5 per cent above, at its troughs 5 per cent below, its initial value.

There are both monetary cycles, in which the driving force is R, the supply of unborrowed reserves, and nonmonetary cycles. In the several nonmonetary cycles, the driving forces are $\overline{GP}$, government purchases, and r, the marginal efficiency of capital or its exogenous component α_0. There are two kinds of nonmonetary cycles, corresponding to alternative assumptions about the behavior of the central bank. In one set of simulations, the monetary authority holds R constant and lets interest rates fluctuate. In another set, the monetary authority desires to peg the Treasury security rate, and therefore engages heavily in open market operations designed to keep the rate on target.

The results of these simulations are summarized in tables 20.6-20.11. They form the basis for some observations in the subsequent sections of this paper.

5. Equilibrium Responses, Financial Sector

The comparative static properties of the model, a number of which were discussed qualitatively in section 1, are illustrated in table 20.6. How to read it may be explained by reference to the first column, which concerns the ultimate effects of a 10 per cent or 0.17 change in unborrowed bank reserves R, accomplished by open market operations. Note that the public eventually sold not only 0.17 securities to the central bank but another 0.34 to the banks. With the reserve requirements in force, the increase in reserves could legally have supported an expansion of 1.13 in demand deposits or 3.40 in time deposits, or any linear combination. However, this does not happen. Both demand and time deposits have elasticities less than one (0.43 and 0.69) with respect to reserve changes, and their total increase is only 0.84. Banks keep 0.10 of the new reserves idle. Even so, the public has considerably reshuffled its wealth, selling securities and borrowing as the counterpart of its increased deposits. These portfolio shifts, and their counterparts in the banks' portfolios, are induced by a general reduction in interest rates, with which goes an increase in the valuation of equity capital, q. Thus the column says that open market purchases have an effect in the expected expansionary direction.

The other columns are to be interpreted similarly. A number of properties of the model worth noting are illustrated in table 20.6:

1. In several instances D and q move in opposite directions, and increases in D accompany increases rather than reductions in interest rates. Thus column 3 concerns an increase in wealth which takes the form entirely of equity capital; no government debt in monetary or other form is provided to balance it. As might be expected, this is highly deflationary. But the public does acquire more bank deposits, and the banks are induced by higher interest rates to cut their excess reserves drastically.

Columns 4 to 7 concern 10 per cent increases in demand deposits as a result of autonomous changes in asset preferences, the shift in each case com-

Table 20.6.
Financial Sector Model
Equilibrium responses to once-for-all 10 per cent increases in single variables (units in upper left of cell; elasticity in lower right)

Shock, and Amount / Variable	Reserves R 0.17	Government Debt G 0.75	Real Capital K 1.25	Preferences for Demand Deposits				Marg. Prod. r 1.10	Income Y 0.5	Reserve Requirements		Ceiling Rate R_T 0.25
				from T^{**} 0.70	from S^{**} 0.70	from K^{**} 0.70	from L^{**} 0.70			Demand Deposits k_D 1.5%	Time Deposits k_T 0.5%	
Demand deposits D	0.30 / 0.43	0.15 / 0.21	0.57 / 0.82	0.53 / 0.76	0.45 / 0.65	0.41 / 0.59	0.46 / 0.66	0.19 / 0.27	0.73 / 1.05	-0.18 / -0.26	-0.07 / -0.10	-0.94 / -1.35
Time deposits T	0.54 / 0.69	0.10 / 0.13	0.52 / 0.66	-0.88 / 1.12	-0.38 / -0.48	-0.36 / -0.46	-0.31 / -0.40	0.20 / 0.25	-0.71 / -0.90	-0.30 / -0.38	-0.12 / -0.15	2.04 / 2.54
Security holdings S^P	-0.51 / -1.92	0.67 / 2.52	0.47 / 1.76	0.08 / 0.30	-0.09 / -0.34	0.08 / 0.30	0.16 / 0.60	0.18 / 0.68	0.05 / 0.19	0.26 / 0.97	0.09 / 0.34	-0.31 / -1.18
Loans $-L$	0.33 / 0.33	0.18 / 0.18	1.58 / 1.58	-0.26 / -0.26	-0.01 / -0.01	0.14 / 0.14	0.32 / 0.32	0.57 / 0.57	0.08 / 0.08	-0.22 / -0.22	-0.10 / -0.10	0.79 / 0.79
Excess reserves E	0.10 / (n.a.)	-0.02 / (n.a.)	-0.11 / (n.a.)	-0.04 / (n.a.)	-0.05 / (n.a.)	-0.04 / (n.a.)	-0.05 / (n.a.)	-0.04 / (n.a.)	-0.07 / (n.a.)	-0.06 / (n.a.)	-0.02 / (n.a.)	0.04 / (n.a.)
Bank securities S^B	0.34 / 1.09	0.08 / 0.26	-0.47 / -1.50	-0.09 / -0.29	0.09 / 0.29	-0.09 / -0.29	0.16 / 0.51	-0.18 / -0.58	-0.05 / -0.16	-0.26 / -0.83	-0.09 / -0.29	0.31 / 0.99
Security rate r_S	-0.09 / -0.46	0.06 / 0.30	0.09 / 0.44	0.02 / 0.10	0.08 / 0.39	0.04 / 0.20	0.04 / 0.20	0.03 / 0.15	0.09 / 0.44	0.05 / 0.24	0.02 / 0.10	0.04 / 0.20
Yield on capital r_K	-0.25 / -0.24	-0.03 / -0.03	1.16 / 1.13	0.27 / 0.26	0.18 / 0.18	0.49 / 0.48	0.38 / 0.37	0.46 / 0.45	0.32 / 0.31	0.20 / 0.20	0.08 / 0.08	-0.31 / -0.30
Loan interest r_L	-0.20 / -0.38	0.04 / 0.08	0.63 / 1.22	0.20 / 0.38	0.10 / 0.19	0.20 / 0.39	0.28 / 0.54	0.24 / 0.47	0.28 / 0.54	0.14 / 0.27	0.05 / 0.10	-0.34 / -0.66
Equity value* q	0.02 / 0.20	+0.00 / +0.00	-0.13 / -1.30	-0.03 / -0.30	-0.02 / -0.20	-0.05 / -0.50	-0.04 / -0.40	0.05 / 0.50	-0.03 / -0.30	-0.02 / -0.20	-0.01 / -0.10	0.03 / 0.30

* Numbers are inexact because changes in q were reported only to one significant figure.

ing from the asset indicated. All such shifts are of course deflationary, even though demand deposits increase and satisfy partially the public's desire to hold more of them. Banks are again induced to economize reserves by increases in interest rates.

2. Changes in excess reserves are also an unreliable guide to the thrust of the financial system, as measured by q. When monetary policy is expansionary, excess reserves go up along with q. When, as in column 8, nonmonetary events are raising both q and the demands on the banking system, net free reserves fall.

3. Although interest rates move together in all the cases in table 20.6, they too can be misleading indicators. Consider, for example, an autonomous shift from securities into capital, whose effects could be calculated by subtracting

Table 20.7.
Financial Sector Model: Amplitude (peak less trough) relative to amplitude of driving force. Equilibrium elasticities (absolute values) from Table 20.6 in parentheses

Variable	Exogenous cycles in:			
	Income Y	Income Y Investment ΔK^*	Government Debt G	Reserves R
Demand deposits D	1.07 (1.05)	3.20	0.40 (0.21)	0.46 (0.43)
Time deposits T	0.60 (0.90)	0.34	0.34 (0.13)	0.39 (0.69)
Security holding S^P	0.53 (0.19)	3.24	2.34 (2.52)	1.73 (1.92)
Loans $-L$	0.25 (0.08)	2.31	0.06 (0.18)	0.17 (0.33)
Excess reserves E†	0.09 (0.07)	0.33	0.03 (0.02)	0.13 (0.10)
Banks' reserves S^B	0.45 (0.16)	2.78	0.48 (0.26)	1.03 (1.09)
Security rates r_S	0.39 (0.44)	0.49	0.44 (0.30)	0.39 (0.46)
Yield on capital r_K	0.32 (0.31)	2.92	0.17 (0.03)	0.37 (0.24)
Loan interest r_L	0.45 (0.54)	2.04	0.08 (0.08)	0.41 (0.38)
Equity value q	0.20 (0.30)	2.70	0.20(+ 0.00)	0.40 (0.20)

* In this simulation ΔK was always $1/2$ (actual Y –equilibrium Y), corresponding to a multiplier of 2; the capital stock varied accordingly, whereas in column 1 the capital stock is held constant.

† Amplitudes given in units.

column 6 from column 5. Then r_S would rise by $0.04, r_K$ would fall by 0.21 and q would rise.

In table 20.7 the equilibrium responses of the endogenous variables to three exogenous variables, Y, G, and R are compared to the relative amplitudes of the same endogenous variables in cycles driven by the same three exogenous variables. Thus demand deposits had a relative amplitude 1.07 times as large as income in an income driven cycle; this compares with a comparative-statics elasticity of 1.03. The table shows that for some variables such elasticities are a misleading indicator of cyclical sensitivities. The magnitude of the cyclical fluctuations in T, for example, is on the order of two-thirds its equilibrium response for both the Y and R cycles. On the other hand, in the Y cycle, the security holdings of both the banks and the public fluctuate more than two-and-a-half times their equilibrium response. Similarly, fluctuations in bank reserves cause bigger fluctuations in r_K and q than would be expected from the corresponding once-for-all elasticity. This suggests that it may be difficult to obtain accurate estimates of the demand relationships from cyclical data.

6. Adjustment Speeds

The speed with which a simultaneous difference equation model returns to equilibrium when subjected to a change in an exogenous variable cannot be inferred by inspection of individual behavioral equations. Systems with slow adjustment in individual behavioral equations may move quickly to a new equilibrium, and systems incorporating rapid adjustment in individual equations may be slow to reach a new equilibrium. This reflects two features of a "general disequilibrium" system.

First, some variables can be taken as given by individual decision makers or in particular markets but are endogenous to the system as a whole. Slow response of individuals in one dimension may merely result in a compensating large and rapid adjustment of other endogenous variables. This process may get the system to equilibrium in a short time. [2]

Second, adjustments made in one market, while moving it towards equilibrium, may move other markets away from equilibrium. Even for the relatively simple model of the financial sector we have constructed, the dynamics of adjustment would be extremely difficult to obtain analytically. Although the system is nonlinear, one might expect the endogenous variables to exhibit behavior similar to that generated by a high order linear difference equation. Hence we should not be surprised to find that the speed with which particular

Table 20.8.

Extended Model Cycles. Amplitudes (peak less trough) relative to amplitude of driving force (10 per cent of equilibrium value)

	Strong Investment Variant						Weak Investment Variant			
	Exogenous cycle in:									
	$\bar{GP}$, Govt. Purchases		r, Marg. Product		Reserves R	Reserves R	$\bar{GP}$, Govt. Purchases		r, Marg. Product	
	r_S pegged	R fixed	r_S pegged	R fixed	R	R	r_S pegged	R fixed	r_S pegged	R fixed
Demand deposits D	1.42	0.83	1.31	1.16	0.66	0.63	1.32	0.79	1.08	1.03
Time deposits T	0.33	0.52	0.41	0.25	0.42	0.41	0.34	0.54	0.40	0.23
Security holdings S^P	1.24	0.94	0.56	0.79	1.73	1.73	1.20	0.90	0.53	0.75
Loans L	0.38	0.20	1.02	0.95	0.37	0.34	0.28	0.17	0.91	0.85
Excess reserves* E	0.10	0.07	0.09	0.12	0.09	0.11	0.04	0.06	0.07	0.11
Banks' securities S^B	0.83	0.22	0.61	1.09	0.87	0.90	0.90	0.16	0.61	0.94
Security rate r_S	0.05	0.39	0.00	0.20	0.39	0.39	0.05	0.39	0.00	0.20
Yield on capital r_K	0.10	0.16	0.91	0.93	0.06	0.12	0.03	0.13	0.76	0.81
Loan interest r_L	0.14	0.33	0.70	0.80	0.21	0.27	0.10	0.29	0.58	0.70
Equity value q	0.00	0.00	0.20	0.20	0.00	0.20	0.00	0.00	0.40	0.40
Reserves R	1.00	0.00	0.41	0.00	1.00	1.00	0.93	0.00	0.41	0.00
Income Y	0.80	0.68	0.34	0.30	0.12	0.10	0.76	0.26	0.68	0.24

* Amplitude given in units.

Table 20.9.
Financial Sector Model. Speeds of adjustment to once-for-all 10 per cent increases in single variables. (Smallest number of periods after which variable's distance from new equilibrium is 25 per cent or less of full equilibrium response. Starred entries (*) designate adjustment paths that overshoot and oscillate.)

Shock / Variable	Reserves R	Govt. Debt G	Real Cap. K	Preferences for Demand Deposits				Marg. Prod. r	Income Y	Reserve Req.	
				from T**	from S**	from K**	from L**			kD	kT
Demand deposits D	5	5*	10*	2	3	2	2	9	2	4	5
Time deposits T	7	14*	10*	6	7	6	5	7	6	8	8
Security holdings S^P	4	1	12*	5	1*	8	8	10	8	4	4
Loans −L	4	11	7*	13*	20*	11*	3	5	18*	10	9
Excess reserves E	4*	5*	5*	5	2	4	5	7	5	4*	1
Banks' securities S^B	5	4*	12*	6	6*	9	8	10	8*	5	4
Security rate r_S	1	2*	2*	5	1	2	3	6	3	2	3
Yield on capital r_K	3*	15*	10*	15*	2	5*	7	8	4	2	2
Loan interest r_L	4	4*	9*	4*	4	5	5	7	5	4	3
Equity value q	3*	15*	9*	15*	2	5*	7	6*	6	2	2

variables adjust to their new equilibrium depends on the particular exogenous variable which is changed. Moreover, there is no simple way to infer from the speeds of adjustment to each of two or more individual shocks how fast the system would adjust to a combination of shocks, either simultaneous or sequential.

In our simulations (see table 20.9) it appears that most variables are relatively slow to reach a new equilibrium following an increase in the supply of real capital or an increase in the marginal product of capital, and adjust relatively fast to an injection of reserves. Similarly, on the basis of the analogy with linear difference equations, we would expect to find some variables responding relatively fast to some shocks and relatively slow to others. Demand deposits, for example, complete 75 per cent of their adjustment to a change in income within two periods, whereas loans require 18 periods for a similar adjustment. In response to a change in the marginal product of capital, however, loans adjust 75 per cent of the way in 5 periods whereas the similar adjustment requires 9 periods in the case of demand deposits.

In spite of the fact that relative speeds of adjustment depend on which exogenous variable is changing, some endogenous variables seem to adjust relatively slowly for almost all of the shocks we have considered. Even though individuals always hold the desired quantity of loans, L is frequently among the last of the variables to come within 25 per cent of its new equilibrium value. In two-thirds of the cases, the loan rate, which banks adjust "slowly," achieves 75 per cent adjustment before the quantity of loans. With the exception of the adjustment to a change in the marginal product of capital, demand deposits adjust more rapidly than time deposits.

7. Cyclical Timing Patterns

In a highly interdependent dynamic system, the chronological order in which variables reach cyclical peaks and troughs proves nothing whatever about directions of causation. Although few people would seriously claim that cyclical lead-lag patterns are a reliable guide to direction of causal influence, believers in the causal primacy of monetary variables have offered the timing order of variables in business cycles as partial evidence for their position. Simulation of cycles of known exogenous or causal source is a good way to show that observed timing order can be very misleading.

The dangers involved in relying on the timing of peaks and troughs as an indication of causality are illustrated in tables 20.10 and 20.11. In every case considered, some endogenous variable leads the exogenous variable driving

Table 20.10.
Lag (+) or Lead (−), Compared with Exogenous Cycles (24 Periods) Financial Sector.

Endogenous Variables	Exogenous Variables			
	Y	R	G	$Y, \Delta K$
D	½	2½	−2½	0
T	(2½)	3	(−2½)	(4)
S^P	(2)	(2)	½	(−5½)
$-L$	−1	5½	(−4½)	2
E	(0)	−1	(−2)	(0)
S^B	−4	3½	−1	−5½
r_S	1	(½)	−2½	3½
r_K	3	(2½)	(1)	2½
r_L	2½	(3)	−4½	4
q	(4)	2½	1	(2½)
R	−	0	−	−
Y	0	−	−	0
ΔK	−	−	−	0

Note: Comparison is with second cyclical peak of cyclically fluctuating exogenous variable in simulation run. Numbers in parentheses refer to timing of a trough in comparison with this reference cycle's peak; this comparison is made for variables that move countercyclically.

the system. In each of the reserve cycles, for example, free reserves lead the total supply of reserves. Similarly, an exogenous cycle in the marginal product of capital generates a cycle in income which leads it in both variants of the extended model.

Even though leads and lags do not provide information about causation, if they could be depended on they would be extremely useful in forecasting the future course of the economy. Unfortunately, the tables provide numerous examples of variables which lead another endogenous variable when the economy is driven by one exogenous variable and lag it when the economy is driven by another exogenous variable.

For example, in the extended model with reserves fixed, loans lead income when government purchases are the driving force, but lag income in cycles driven by fluctuations in the marginal product of capital.

Similarly, in the financial sector simulations, the rate on securities leads the rate on equities by two periods when income alone varies exogenously, but lags it by one period when fluctuations in investment accompany the variations in income.

Not surprisingly, the leads and lags are also sensitive to the policy actions

Table 20.11.
Lag (+) or Lead (−), Compared with Exogenous Cycles (24 Periods)

	Extended Model–Strong Investment					Extended Model–Weak Investment				
	r_S pegged R endogenous		R-cycle	r_S endogenous R fixed		r_S pegged R endogenous		R-cycle	r_S endogenous R fixed	
	$\overline{GP}$-cycle	r-cycle		$\overline{GP}$-cycle	r-cycle	$\overline{GP}$-cycle	r-cycle		$\overline{GP}$-cycle	r-cycle
D	2	−1	1	1	$-\frac{1}{2}$	2	$-\frac{1}{3}$	$1\frac{1}{2}$	1	−2
T	(−1)	$4\frac{1}{2}$	$3\frac{1}{2}$	(2)	$5\frac{1}{2}$	$(-\frac{1}{2})$	5	$3\frac{1}{2}$	$(2\frac{1}{2})$	4
S^P	(+ 1)	$(-1\frac{1}{2})$	$(1\frac{1}{2})$	$(-5\frac{1}{2})$	$(-5\frac{1}{2})$	(1)	−1	$(1\frac{1}{2})$	$(-5\frac{1}{2})$	6 or (−6)
$-L$	2	$1\frac{1}{2}$	$3\frac{1}{2}$	−2	2	$2\frac{1}{2}$	2	4	$-2\frac{1}{2}$	$\frac{1}{2}$
E	0	$(-2\frac{1}{2})$	−1	(0)	(0)	0	$(-1\frac{1}{2})$	$-1\frac{1}{2}$	$(\frac{1}{2})$	(−2)
S^B	3	$(5\frac{1}{2})$	2	−3	−6 or (6)	$3\frac{1}{2}$	−6 or (6)	2	$-1\frac{1}{2}$	$(4\frac{1}{2})$
r_S	–	–	(1)	$1\frac{1}{2}$	3	−4	–	(1)	$1\frac{1}{2}$	1
r_K	$\frac{1}{2}$	2	$(-\frac{1}{2})$	1	$2\frac{1}{2}$	$-3\frac{1}{2}$	2	$(\frac{1}{2})$	1	1
r_L	$\frac{1}{2}$	2	$(1\frac{1}{2})$	2	$3\frac{1}{2}$	−1	3	(1)	2	2
q	–	−2	0	–		–	−2	$\frac{1}{2}$	–	−3
R	$1\frac{1}{2}$	$1\frac{1}{2}$	0	–	–	$1\frac{1}{2}$	$1\frac{1}{2}$	0	–	–
Y	$\frac{1}{2}$	−2	0	0	$-1\frac{1}{2}$	$\frac{1}{2}$	$-1\frac{1}{2}$	$\frac{1}{2}$	0	−3
ΔK	1	−2	0	0	$-1\frac{1}{2}$	3	$-1\frac{1}{2}$	$\frac{1}{2}$	–	−3

Note: Comparison is with second cyclical peak of cyclically fluctuating exogenous variable in simulation run. Numbers in parentheses refer to timing of a trough in comparison with this cycle's peak; this comparison is made for variables that move countercyclically.

of the monetary authority. If the supply of reserves is fixed and government purchases cause fluctuations, free reserves trough when income peaks. When the monetary authority pegs the rate on securities, however, free reserves actually peak with income. Similarly, in the "strong investment" variant, loans lead government purchases by two periods when the rate on securities is endogenous and lag government purchases when it is pegged.

Notes

[1] Banks' net free reserves are equal to excess reserves less debt to the central bank; the model does not attempt to explain the two items separately.

[2] For example, consider the following trivial model:

$$X_D^*(t) = B_0 - B_1 P(t)$$

$$\Delta X_D(t) = \alpha(X_D^*(t) - X_D(t-1))$$

$$\overline{X}_S(t) = X_D(t)$$

where X_D^* is the desired quantity of a commodity, P its price, ΔX_D the change in actual demand, $\alpha \neq 0$ the speed of adjustment, and $\overline{X}_S$ the exogenously determined supply. Irrespective of the speed of adjustment α, the system will be in long-run equilibrium two periods after a change in the supply.

CHAPTER 21

AN ESSAY ON THE PRINCIPLES OF DEBT MANAGEMENT

1. The Federal Debt and Its Composition

1.1. *The Relevant Concept of Federal Debt*

Claims against the federal government held by individuals and institutions outside the federal government are of several kinds: (a) transferable demand obligations, (b) marketable short-term securities, (c) marketable long-term securities, (d) nonmarketable securities, and (e) other commitments. The first category (a) includes currency issued by the Treasury and Federal Reserve, and deposit obligations of the Federal Reserve. Between categories (b) and (c) there is, of course, no sharp line. Maturities at issue vary from three months to forty years. In Table 21.1, the dividing line between short-term and long-term is taken to be one year. Savings bonds are the principal example of category (d), securities obtainable only from the Treasury and disposable only by redemption at the Treasury. These securities are redeemable at specified values on demand, though often with some delay and inconvenience of collection. Although they are demand obligations, they cannot be traded among private holders, and in this important respect they differ from category (a).

The last category, (e), comprises a vast array of statutory commitments difficult to calculate in amount and timing, expressed in ways other than unconditional obligations to pay fixed sums of money at specified future dates. Examples are social security benefits, veterans' pensions, grants-in-aid to state and local governments. Quite possibly these obligations are a more weighty burden on future budgets than the conventional national debt, which receives so much attention because it can be precisely calculated. The extent of these obligations is the result of congressional decisions of social policy. It cannot be altered by administrative decisions of the Treasury or the Federal

Reprinted from *Fiscal and Debt Management Policies* (Englewood Cliffs, N.J.: Prentice-Hall, 1963), pp. 143-218. Prepared for the Commission on Money and Credit. Footnotes, figures, and tables have been renumbered.

Table 21.1
Composition and Distribution of Federal Debt, December 31, 1955 and 1969 *
(billions of dollars)

Category of debt	Total outside Treasury and Federal Reserve		Held by commercial banks		Held by others	
	1955	1969	1955	1969	1955	1969
Demand obligations (currency and Federal Reserve deposits)	$ 51	73	22	28	29	45
Short-term marketable securities (maturity under one year)	43	80	10	15	33	65
Long-term marketable securities (maturity more than one year)	113	82	52	30	61	52
Nonmarketable securities	59	57	–	–	59	57
Total	$ 266	292	84	73	182	219

* Original article gave data for 1955 and 1959.

Reserve. These agencies have administrative discretion to increase one of the first four categories at the expense of another. But they cannot substitute obligations of the first four types for obligations of type (e), or vice versa.

The *federal debt* for the purposes of this paper is the total of the first four kinds of obligations outstanding at any moment, the net cumulation of past federal *deficits* and *surpluses*. Total debt grows over time when federal *outlays* exceed *receipts* and declines as *receipts* exceed *outlays*. The course of the total over time depends, therefore, on budgetary policies that determine the balance of receipts and outlays. The distribution of the total, at any moment of time, among the various categories of debt can be altered by the Treasury and Federal Reserve. The size of the debt results from fiscal policies; its composition is the province of debt management and monetary policies.

The concepts of *debt, surplus, deficit, receipts*, and *outlays,* must be mutually consistent, and the definitions chosen should be relevant to the choices available to the makers of government stabilization policy. The set of concepts used in this paper differs in several important respects from the conventions of federal government accounting.

1. Since obligations of the fifth type are excluded from the *debt*, as defined here, payments by the public which give rise to such obligations can be counted as *receipts* which, other things equal, reduce federal debt. Social security taxes are the principal example. Receipt of these taxes enables the Treasury to reduce its obligation, in the first four categories, to the public. Likewise, expenditures to discharge obligations in the fifth category must be counted as *outlays*, which, other things equal, increase federal debt. To pay social security benefits, the Treasury must increase its financial *debt* to the public. In reckoning the relevant *surplus* or *deficit*, receipts and outlays of this kind must be included, although they are not included in the conventional budget. Correspondingly, the relevant concept of debt does not include the intragovernmental debts of the Treasury to social security and other trust funds.

2. Unlike the usual concept, *debt* here includes non-interest-bearing demand obligations, category (a). Accordingly in reckoning the current surplus or deficit, *outlays* must include purchases which, like those of gold and silver, are financed by printing or coining money. *Receipts* include proceeds of the sale of gold. This is not the practice in conventional federal budget accounting. When the Treasury acquires precious metals, it is permitted to pay for its purchases by printing money. These purchases are not counted as expenditures in the conventional federal budget, evidently on the theory that the government has acquired an asset of equal value. Other outlays of the federal government must be financed by taxes or by selling interest-bearing debt, and must be counted as current expenditures in federal budgeting.

3. In reckoning the composition of the federal debt, the artificial distinction between the Treasury and Federal Reserve in the conventions of federal accounting should be ignored. A debt of the Treasury to the Federal Reserve is a debt of the left hand to the right. It does not enlarge the public's claims. The holder of a claim of a given category does not care whether it is a Treasury or Federal Reserve obligation. Treasury currency and Federal Reserve notes circulate interchangeably. The monetary impact of the debt depends on the composition of the public's holdings, not on the composition of what the Treasury originally issued. The Treasury's debt by conventional reckoning might consist substantially of long-term bonds at high interest rates. But if those bonds are held by the Federal Reserve banks, which have in turn incurred demand obligations to the banks and the public, the debt that counts is a non-interest-bearing demand debt. What counts in assaying monetary impact also counts in calculating the net interest costs to the taxpayer. Interest payments from the Treasury to the Federal Reserve are not a net cost. The profits of the Federal Reserve banks, above a fixed payment

on the stock member banks are compelled to subscribe, belong to the Treasury. In Table 21.1 the Treasury and Federal Reserve are consolidated, and the composition of claims against them on two sample dates is shown.

1.2. Fiscal Versus Monetary Effects

Government debt has two kinds of impact on aggregate demand for goods and services. The first occurs when the debt is acquired, and only then. This is the direct fiscal effect of the budget, of government expenditures in excess of receipts from the public. As is well understood from multiplier theory, the higher expenditures are in relation to receipts, the greater is aggregate demand. (It is not true, however, that the budget's impact on aggregate demand can be gauged simply by knowing its balance, the net deficit or surplus. Increase in government expenditures is generally expansionary even if offset dollar for dollar by increase in revenues.) The fiscal effect depends much more on the rate at which the debt is changing than on the size of the debt itself. To gauge the fiscal effect it is much more important to know, along with the size of the budget, whether the budget shows a deficit of 14 billion or a surplus of 3 billion than to know whether the debt at the beginning of the year is 30 billion, 150 billion, or 300 billion. No doubt the initial size of the debt affects somewhat the size of the multipliers that determine how much a budget deficit is magnified by its repercussions on private income and spending. But this is a second-order effect compared to the magnitude of the deficit itself and of the income it generates.

The second type of impact with which this paper is concerned, is the monetary effect of the debt. This is the effect on aggregate demand of private ownership of claims against the central government. It depends on the total magnitude of those claims, and on their nature. The monetary effect of debt outlasts the deficits that produced it and their temporary fiscal effects. It endures as long as the debt itself. Aggregate demand for goods and services throughout the postwar period would have been different without the 250-300 billion dollar federal debt inherited from the war, even if postwar federal budgets had been the same. The fiscal effect works through the influence of budget expenditures and receipts on private income. The monetary effect works through the impact of the debt on the size and composition of private wealth.

1.3. Fiscal Versus Monetary Policy Decisions

Within the second type of impact, a distinction must be made between the monetary effect of a change in the size of the debt and the monetary effect of a change in the composition of a debt of given total size. The distinction is important because only the latter kind of change is within the powers of those government authorities, whether at the Federal Reserve or the Treasury, charged with responsibility for monetary policy and debt management. These authorities can make swaps with the public, one kind of government debt for another. If they wish, they can alter the composition of the outstanding federal debt drastically within a very short time – a day or a week or a month. They cannot, however, change the size of the debt. (Here *size of the debt* means the total amount the government received from the public for its outstanding obligations, i.e., the net cumulative total of past budget deficits less surpluses. The monetary and debt management authorities can to a limited degree affect the market value of the debt, which may at any moment be greater or smaller than *the size of the debt.*)

Changes in the size of the debt require budget deficits or surpluses. They are a by-product of fiscal policy rather than of monetary policy. They result from decisions of Congress and the Executive regarding government expenditures and taxes. Changes in the size of the debt also require time. A budget running a deficit at a rate of 12 billion a year will add only 1 billion to the debt in a month. Indeed it will take between two and three years to increase the outstanding debt by 10 per cent. A change in the size of the debt will have a different monetary effect depending on what form it takes. If an addition to debt takes the form of long-term obligations, for example, its monetary effect will be less expansionary than if it takes the form of demand or even short-term obligations. The monetary and debt management authorities can decide that. Given the change in the debt willed by the fiscal powers-that-be, the monetary authorities can and must choose the composition of the change. That decision is of the same nature as their choice of the composition of a debt of given size, and does not require separate analysis.

To summarize, changes in the size of the debt are the province of fiscal policy. They have two effects on demand. One, the fiscal effect, is temporary. The other, the monetary effect, is permanent. The strength of the monetary effect depends on the composition of the change in debt. This is the province of the authorities in charge of monetary policy and debt management. Indeed their province is wider. They are not confined to deciding the form of marginal changes of the debt. They can alter the composition of the whole debt whether it is changing in size or not.

1.4. Monetary Control and Debt Management

How can the Treasury and Federal Reserve affect the composition of the total debt? The Treasury can replace security issues when they come due – at which time they are virtually demand obligations – with time obligations. By *advance refunding* offers or conceivably by repurchasing its own debt, the Treasury can convert short-term debt before it matures into long-term debt, or vice versa. The Treasury can increase nonmarketable debt at the expense of other categories by offering more attractive terms on savings bonds. The Treasury can increase the public's holdings of federal demand obligations by drawing down its deposit balance in the Federal Reserve banks. Within limits the Treasury can issue new currency, i.e., literally print new money, to replace interest-bearing debt. Since 1933 the Treasury has generally owned a margin of unmonetized gold, against which it could issue gold certificates.

The Federal Reserve also can change the composition of the debt, principally by its open market operations. By purchasing short-term secur- ities, for example, the Federal Reserve at the same time increases the quantity of demand obligations outstanding and decreases by an equal amount the quantity of outstanding debt in the short-term marketable category. Federal Reserve sales of long-term securities diminish the outstanding demand debt and increase the outstanding long debt by an equal amount. By purchasing shorts and at the same time selling an equivalent quantity of longs the Federal Reserve could lengthen the marketable debt, leaving the demand debt unchanged. The Federal Reserve does not set the terms of nonmarketable securities kept on tap by the Treasury. But it may influence the demand for such securities indirectly by altering yields of marketable debt instruments.

There is no neat way to distinguish monetary policy from debt manage- ment, the province of the Federal Reserve from that of the Treasury. Both agencies are engaged in debt management in the broadest sense, and both have powers to influence the whole spectrum of debt. But monetary policy refers particularly to determination of the supply of demand debt, and debt management to determination of the amounts in the long and nonmarketable categories. In between, the quantity of short debt is determined as a residuum. From 1953 to 1961 this specialization was institutionalized in the United States. The Federal Reserve controlled the size of the demand debt, independently of the Treasury. The Treasury decided the amount of long- term and nonmarketable debt; under its "bills only" policy, the Federal Reserve normally refrained from buying or selling long-term securities. Since February 1961, however, the Federal Reserve has operated in all maturities.

Although variation of the quantity of demand debt outstanding through open market operations is perhaps the principal instrument of monetary policy, it is not the only one. The Federal Reserve sets the discount rate at which the banks can borrow reserves. Within limits set by Congress, the Federal Reserve sets required reserve-to-deposit ratios for commercial banks. Although these are purely monetary tools, how they are used has a great deal to do with both the economic impact and the net interest cost of a given federal debt structure.

Semantic distinctions and institutional specializations should not be permitted to obscure the essential indivisibility of the problem. The need for coordination in policy-making, commensurate with the economic unity of the task of debt management, will be argued at length below. The monetary authorities at the Federal Reserve cannot make sensible decisions about demand debt, or about the other instruments they control, without taking into account the Treasury's actions regarding the supply of long debt. Neither can the Treasury, whatever its debt management objectives, pursue them intelligently without considering how much interest-bearing debt the Federal Reserve will leave outstanding.

2. Monetary Effects of Changes in Size and Structure of Debt

2.1 Net Private Wealth and its Composition

Suppose that at a given moment of time the net worth of every economic unit in the United States other than the federal government is calculated. Net private [1] wealth is the aggregate of these net worths. In the aggregation private debts wash out. They appear as assets on the balance sheets of some units, but in equal amount on the liability side of other balance sheets. What remains? There are three basic components of net private wealth: (1) claims against the federal government, i.e., the federal debt defined in section 1; (2) the value of the United States physical capital stock, other than capital owned by the federal government, and (3) net claims of United States economic units, again excepting the federal government, against the rest of the world. The first component grows with federal deficits or declines with federal surpluses, as explained in section 1. The second component grows with net investment in plant and equipment, residential construction, and stock of goods. It changes also with market valuations of existing capital goods and real estate. The third component grows when United States residents acquire claims against foreigners or invest in property and capital abroad; it declines when foreigners acquire claims against us or equity in property here. [2] In what follows, the third category will be ignored, or consolidated with the second. The net capital position of the United States vis-a-vis the rest of the world is an important topic in its own right, but it is not the subject here. It will not distort the analysis of debt management to assume a closed economy in order to focus attention on the relative magnitudes of the first two components of net private wealth.

2.2. Stabilization Policy and the Supply Price of Capital

Control of the course of aggregate economic activity — economic stabilization — is the principal purpose of monetary and debt management. What is the route by which management of money and public debt may affect economic activity? Ultimately its effectiveness depends on its ability to influence the terms on which investors will hold the existing stock of real capital and absorb new capital. If investors demand a higher rate of return on capital than the existing stock can yield, given the state of technology and the supplies of labor and other factors of production, investment will decline and the economic climate will be deflationary. If investors are willing and anxious to expand their holdings of capital at a rate of return lower than the marginal productivity of the capital stock, investment will tend to outrun saving and the outlook will be inflationary.

The same point may be expressed in another way. If investors are content with a low rate of return on equity in real capital, relative to its marginal productivity, their bids for existing capital will cause its valuation to exceed its replacement cost; the difference will be an incentive to expand production of capital goods. But if investors require a relatively high rate of return on equity in real capital, the valuation of capital in place will be low relative to its replacement cost and will deter further production of investment goods. The course of economic activity, then, depends on the difference between two rates of return on ownership of capital. One is the anticipated marginal productivity of capital, determined by technology, factor supplies, and expectations about the economy. This cannot be controlled by the managers of money and public debt, except in the indirect sense that if they somehow successfully control the economy they control all economic magnitudes. The second rate of return on capital equity is that rate at which the public would be willing to hold the existing stock of capital, valued at current prices. It is this rate of return, the *supply price of capital,* which the monetary and debt authorities may hope to influence through changing the supplies and yields of assets and debts that compete with real capital for place in the portfolios and balance sheets of economic units

Broadly speaking, the authorities can lower the supply price of capital by lowering the yields of competing assets. But it is important to remember that these yields — interest rates on national debt instruments, bank loan rates, mortgage rates, etc. — are means rather than ends. The target is the supply price of capital. This rate, although influenced by the yields of other assets, is not identical with any of them. It is a mistake to use the rate on long-term government or corporate bonds, for example, as an unerring gauge of the tightness of monetary control of the economy. The differential between a long-term bond interest rate and the rate of return investors require of equity is surely as variable as any differential in the whole gamut of the structure of interest rates. Lowering the long-term government bond rate is not expansionary if the premium above it required for investment in real capital is at the same time commensurately increased. Increasing the long-term bond rate is not deflationary if the means that increase it at the same time lower in equal degree the equity bond differential.

What is the monetary effect of an increase in the public debt? Other things equal, what difference does the size of the debt make to the supply price of capital? Will a larger debt change the rate of return that the community of private investors require in order to hold a given stock of capital? The answer of this section is that the monetary effect of an increase in the debt is to lower the required rate of return on capital, to make it easier to absorb a growing capital stock into portfolios and balance sheets. The magnitude of the effect depends on the form that the increase in debt takes. The expansionary effect is strongest, of course, if the increment of debt is "monetized," i.e., if it takes the form of demand debt. The effect is weaker for short debt and still weaker for long debt. But, it is argued here, the direction of the effect is unambiguous. Given the present assortment of debt instruments, the enduring monetary effect of increase in government debt is expansionary. To have a neutral or restrictive effect on the demand for capital, an increase in debt would have to take unconventional form. This is a principal motivation for the proposal set forth in section 4 below for new debt instruments geared to the purchasing power of the dollar.

A $1 billion increase in public debt, while the value of the capital stock is given, means a $1 billion increase in net private wealth. At given rates of return on debt instruments and on equity in capital, owners of wealth would be unlikely to choose to concentrate the whole of a billion dollar increase in wealth on public debt. Rather they would choose a balanced expansion of their holdings. Their new acquisitions would be divided between public debt and capital. Consequently to induce the community to absorb the whole of an increase in wealth in the form of public debt, yields of public debt instruments must rise relative to the rate of return on capital. The differential of capital equity over public debt must fall. If the public debt were homogeneous and the yield on the uniform debt instrument were fixed, the result of debt expansion would be perfectly clear. The differential in favor of capital would have to fall; otherwise the public would not be content with portfolios in which capital forms a smaller proportion and government debt a larger proportion. Given a fixed yield on government debt, the differential could fall only if the supply price of capital were to fall.

In practice, the public debt is not homogeneous, and the yields on debt instruments are not absolutely fixed. However, there are certain fixed anchors to the structure of yields on public debt. First, the rate on the transferable demand debt of the government – currency for nonbank holders, reserve balances in Federal Reserve banks for banks – is zero. The rate on demand deposits is likewise legally set at zero; every dollar of public holding of deposits is indirectly a holding of a fraction of a dollar, the required reserve ratio, for government demand debt. Second, banks can obtain additional holdings of demand debt at the Federal Reserve discount rate. So long as it is maintained constant, the discount rate provides another fixed pivot for the structure of rates.

About a quarter of the marketable U.S. federal debt is demand debt, subject to legally or administratively fixed yield. The rest takes the form of instruments whose yields are determined in the market. Although they are market determined, these yields cannot stray too far from the fixed yields of the demand debt. The time obligations of the government – the Treasury or the Federal Reserve – are more or less substitutable for its demand obligations, and an effective chain of substitution keeps the yields even of long maturities in line. Therefore, if yields on public debt must rise relative to the rate of return on capital, the main brunt of the adjustment falls on the latter. The inducement to increase the proportion of wealth held as public debt, decreasing the share held as capital equity, must be in substantial part a fall in the yield of equity.

To say that an increase in debt is expansionary, and likewise that debt retirement has a deflationary monetary effect, is not to say that neutralization of these effects is beyond the powers of the monetary and debt authorities. The assertion is merely that effects in the indicated direction will occur, in the absence of deliberate action to offset them. The Federal Reserve may be able to neutralize the expansionary influence of an increase in debt by raising the discount rate. Or the effect of a change in the size of the debt may be counteracted by a change in the composition of the initial debt. For example. expansion of long-term debt might be neutralized by a tighter monetary policy, open market sales substituting short debt for demand debt. The effects of changes in the composition of debt of a given total size are discussed in section 2.7.

2.3. Effects of Change in the Supply of Demand Debt

The expansionary effect of an increase in debt is clearest and strongest when it takes the form of demand debt. Suppose that federal demand debt is increased by $1 billion, while the quantities of short and long government debt outside the Treasury and the Federal Reserve are unchanged. Assume that the Federal Reserve discount rate remains unchanged. Take the money value of the stock of capital, and the prices of goods, as given also. (Of course, in fact the stock of capital is always changing both in real amount and in money value at the same time as the federal debt. The assumption of a fixed amount and value of capital is made for analytical purposes, because the gauge of the impact of change in debt is what it does to the rate of return investors require of a *given* quantity of capital. As is usual in comparative static analysis, the purpose is to describe the difference it makes whether a parameter – in this case demand debt – is smaller or larger. The analysis is timeless, even though it would be impossibly puristic to try to explain it without chronological language.)

Private wealth increases by $1 billion, and interest rates must adjust so that owners of wealth are content to put the whole increment into demand debt, either directly or. through banks and other intermediaries. Public currency holdings are quite inelastic; it will not strain fact too much to assume them constant. Then the whole of the billion dollars must find its home with the banks, either as required reserves or as free reserves. Initially the deposits of the public in the banks will increase by the same amount as the increment in private wealth, and the free reserves of the banks will increase by a large fraction – five-sixths if the required reserve ratio is one-sixth – of that amount. As banks try to convert these excessive holdings of free reserves into earning assets, they bid government and private debt away from the public. The nonbank holders of these assets are induced to sell them, and to hold bank deposits instead, by a fall in their yields. Banks are willing to acquire them in spite of their reduced yields because they are, within limits, more profitable than free reserves. How far this process of expansion of banks' deposits and assets goes depends on the banks' preferences for cash and for freedom from debt to the Federal Reserve, relative to the yields of less liquid assets. If the banks' equilibrium demand for free reserves is constant, deposits and earning assets will expand by the textbook multiples of the original accretion of reserves. For example, if the average required reserve ratio is one to six, deposits will expand by 6 billions and earning assets by 5 billions, from an increase in demand debt of 1 billion. However, these classic multiples probably overstate the expansion. The expansion is inevitably accompanied by a fall in the yields of government and private debts. With the Federal Reserve discount rate unchanged, this fall diminishes the inducement to borrow from the Federal Reserve. It increases the attractiveness of excess reserve balances. As a result, banks' equilibrium demand for free reserves will be higher. A part of the increment in demand debt will serve to satisfy an enhanced appetite for free reserves; not all of the billion will go into higher required reserves.

What is the adjustment of the public outside the banks? Suppose, provisionally, that in the end the banks keep free reserves unchanged. In order to absorb as required bank reserves a billion dollar increase in demand debt, the public must absorb a multi-billion dollar increase in bank deposits. At the assumed required reserve ratio, the public must increase deposits by six times the increase in its wealth. Here is the significance of fractional-reserve banking. A substantial change in yields is required to effect a drastic shift in portfolio composition. A part of the increase in public willingness to hold bank deposits will be induced by reduction in yields of interest-bearing government debt. Short debt, in particular, is regarded by many corporations and institutions as a close substitute for cash. But it is hardly likely that these yields can fall enough to make the public *reduce* its holdings of federal debt by anything like five or six times the increase in net private wealth. In the balance sheet of the public, most of the room for the multiple expansion of deposits must come from an increase in the debt of the public to the banks, in response to a reduction in interest rates on private loans. This adjustment is a shift by private lenders from direct lending or from lending through nonbank intermediaries, which become less profitable, to bank deposits; the banks acquire the loan business given up. But unless the rate of return on capital falls too, the reduction in loan rates will stimulate new borrowing to finance new capital investment. But in the hypothetical example the stock of capital is assumed constant. To prevent the demand for capital from exceeding the existing stock, the yield of capital must fall. Its fall is the measure of the expansionary effect of the increase in debt.

Even if banks increase their equilibrium free reserve holdings, deposits will in all probability expand by a multiple — though smaller than the reciprocal of the required reserve ratio — of the increment of demand debt. Substantial reduction in the yields of alternative assets, including capital equity, would be necessary to induce the public to make this shift in the composition of their balance sheets.

Is it conceivable that banks' demand for free reserves would be so elastic with respect to yields on earning assets that they would absorb as free reserves five-sixths of the increment of demand debt? If so, the expansion of deposits would be limited to the growth of private wealth. Even an expansion of deposits thus limited would require, in general, some reductions in yields on other assets. Without the inducement provided by lower yields elsewhere, the public would not wish to keep even as little as 100 per cent of an increase in its net worth in deposits. Conceivably the reduction in yields that would

Table 21.2
Hypothetical Illustration: Assets (+) and Liabilities (−) of Banks and Public Before and After an Increment of Demand Debt and Private Wealth Equal to 1 Per Cent of Wealth

	Banks			Public			Total		
	Before	After	Change	Before	After	Change	Before	After	Change
Currency	0	0	0	+30	+30	0			
Required reserves	+20	+27	+7						
Free reserves	0	+3	+3						
Demand debt total	+20	+30	+10	+30	+30	0	+50	+60	+10
Short debt	+20	+30	+10	+60	+50	−10	+80	+80	0
Long debt	+10	+15	+5	+60	+55	−5	+70	+70	0
Private debt	+80	+97	+17	+320 −400	+303 −400	−17	0	0	0
Deposits	−120	−162	−42	+120	+162	+42	0	0	0
Capital	−10	−10	0	+810	+810	0	+800	+800	0
Total	0	0	0	+1000	+1010	+10	+1000	+1010	+10

accomplish this reallocation of assets by the public might be sufficient to persuade the banks to hold their initial gain idle in free reserves. Something like this happened in the thirties when yields on earning assets were low and the banks were saturated with reserve funds. In normal times, and in the usual range of interest rates, the banks' demand for free reserves is much more easily satisfied.

Table 21.2 is a hypothetical illustration of the change in bank and public balance sheets necessary to absorb an increment of demand debt and private wealth equal to 1 per cent of initial wealth. The table is meant to be indicative of behavior and circumstances between the extremes discussed above. That is, a multiple expansion of deposits occurs, but not the full textbook multiple. Free reserves also increase.

2.4. Change in the Supply of Short Debt

Suppose that private wealth is increased by government deficit financed by short debt. Demand debt, long debt, and the capital stock remain constant in supply, and the Federal Reserve maintains a fixed discount rate.

An extreme assumption will provide a useful point of departure for analysis of this case. The assumption is that the banks do, and the public does not, regard bills and free reserves as perfect substitutes at the prevailing bill rate. (Not all short debt is in the form of Treasury bills, but since the differences among short debt instruments are not of great moment, it is not misleading to use "bills" as a convenient synonym for short debt.) In this case an increase in bank holdings of short debt would have the same consequences as an equal increase in bank holdings of demand debt. In the "after" column of the example of Table 21.3 banks have absorbed an extra 9 of short debt. Net free reserves have become –6; banks have to borrow to meet reserve requirements. But banks act the same as if their free reserves had been increased by 3 (9–6). They expand loans and deposits. The public makes room for part of the expansion of deposits, which exceeds the increment in private wealth, by selling long debt to the banks, but for most of it by relinquishing private loan business to the banks. Reductions in the long rate, loan rate, and return on capital equity are necessary to achieve this reconstitution of bank and public balance sheets. Because of the assumed perfect substitutability of short debt for cash in bank portfolios, the short

Table 21.3

Hypothetical Illustration: Assets (+) and Liabilities (−) of Banks and Public Before and After an Increment of Short Debt and Private Wealth Equal to 1 Per Cent of Wealth Assuming Short Debt a Perfect Substitute for Free Reserves

	Banks			Public			Total		
	Before	After	Change	Before	After	Change	Before	After	Change
Currency	0	0	0	+30	+30	0			
Required reserves	+20	+26	+6						
Free reserves	0	−6	−6						
Demand debt	+20	+20	0	+30	+30	0	+50	+50	0
Short debt	+20	+29	+9	+60	+61	+1	+80	+90	+10
Long debt	+10	+16	+6	+60	+54	−6	+70	+70	0
Private debt	+80	+101	+21	+320 −400	+299 −400	−21	0	0	0
Deposits	−120	−156	−36	+120	+136	+36	0	0	0
Capital	−10	−10	0	+810	+810	0	+800	+800	0
Total	0	0	0	+1000	+1010	+10	+1000	+1010	+10

rate remains unchanged. For this reason, the public increases its holdings of shorts (+1) as well as of bank deposits.

The assumption behind Table 21.3 is farfetched but it is instructive. Short debt is not a perfect substitute for demand debt in bank portfolios, but it is within limits a good substitute. A bank needs a defensive buffer between its commercial loans and its required reserves. The purpose of the buffer is to enable it to withstand a loss of deposits and reserves, on the one hand, or compelling demands for loan accommodation, on the other hand. In neither case does the bank wish the necessity of meeting the reserve requirement to force it to disappoint customers, many of whom have earned the right to loan accommodation by faithfulness as depositors. Excess reserve balances are the most obvious defensive asset. Overnight loans of such balances — federal funds — to other banks are another. Treasury bills fill the defensive function almost as well. They can be sold quickly in a well-organized market. Since they are of short maturity, they subject the bank to very little risk of capital loss. Indeed by staggering maturities the bank can contrive to meet most reserve stringencies by letting bills "run off" and need worry very little about the chance that it would have to sell bills in a declining market. In any case bills can be used, like other government securities, as collateral for advances from the Federal Reserve. This further reduces the chance of capital loss involved in using them as secondary reserves; if the bill market is down when the bank needs reserves, the bank may find it advantageous not to sell bills but to borrow the needed reserves, repaying the loan when its bills mature or its reserve position is replenished.

These considerations suggest that for the banking system as a whole, short Treasury debt is a good though imperfect substitute for net free reserves. When the bill rate is very low, banks will prefer excess reserves in order to avoid the slight risks and transactions costs involved in using bills as secondary reserves. This preference will be very little affected by the discount rate. Even at a very low discount rate, banks would not find it profitable to borrow in order to acquire or to retain bills. But at higher rates, banks' demand for bills relative to net free reserves will be sensitive to the differential between the discount rate and the bill rate. When the bill rate is high relative to the discount rate, banks short of reserves will borrow rather than sell bills, and banks with free funds will buy bills rather than repaying debt or adding to excess reserves. When the bill rate is low relative to the discount rate, banks short of reserves will sell bills rather than incur debt to the Federal Reserve and banks with free funds will repay debt or hold cash rather than buy bills.

Table 21.4 is a hypothetical illustration of the absorption of an increase in

Table 21.4

Hypothetical Illustration: Assets (+) and Liabilities (−) of Banks and Public Before and After an Increment of Short Debt and Private Wealth Equal to 1 Per Cent of Wealth

	Banks			Public			Total		
	Before	After	Change	Before	After	Change	Before	After	Change
Currency	0	0	0	+30	+30	0			
Required reserves	+20	+23	+3						
Free reserves	0	−3	−3						
Demand debt	+20	+20	0	+30	+30	0	+50	+50	0
Short debt	+20	+27	+7	+60	+63	+3	+80	+90	+10
Long debt	+10	+10	0	+60	+60	0	+70	+70	0
Private debt	+80	+91	+11	+320 −400	+309 −400	−11	0	0	0
Deposits	−120	−138	−18	+120	+138	+18	0	0	0
Capital	−10	−10	0	+810	+810	0	+800	+800	0
Total	0	0	0	+1000	+1010	+10	+1000	+1010	+10

the supply of short debt, on the assumption that bills are a good but imperfect substitute for free reserves in bank portfolios. Here the short rate must rise slightly to provide banks the incentive to reduce net free reserves. Banks add to their holdings of short debt by more than they lower their free reserves. With their overall defensive position thus strengthened, they expand private loans and deposits, lowering the loan rate. The rate on long government debt also falls; there may be some reallocation of long debt between banks and public, but none is assumed in Table 21.4. The fall in the rate on private debt induces the public to switch to deposits, surrendering loan business to the banks. As before, the rate of return on equity capital − the supply price of capital − must fall to prevent an increase in demand for capital, as against the fixed supply, resulting from the reduction in long and private loan rates and from the increment of wealth.

How great the expansionary effect of short debt is depends crucially on whether the banks regard short debt as a better substitute for cash than the public does, or vice versa. The reason is that substitution of short debt for bank reserves economizes "high-powered money," demand debt, while public substitution of short debt for deposits economizes "low-powered money." In one case a dollar of bills takes the place of a dollar of demand debt. In the other case a dollar of bills takes the place of one-sixth of a dollar of demand debt. To take an example that is in a sense the opposite of Table 21.3, suppose that the public will substitute bills for cash without a change in the bill rate but that the banks will not. Banks will have no incentive to reduce their net free reserve position, since public demand will keep the bill rate from rising. Deposits will not increase. The only reductions in other interest rates, including the supply price of capital, will be those that suffice to induce the public to concentrate the increase in their wealth on holdings of short debt.

2.5. Change in the Supply of Long Debt

On the direction of the effects discussed in sections 2.3 and 2.4 there is general agreement, although on their magnitudes there is of course great uncertainty and disagreement. In respect to the monetary effect of a change in the supply of *long* debt, other things equal, there is not even general agreement as to direction. It is sometimes argued that the monetary effect of an increase in the supply of long-term debt is deflationary, the effect of retirement of long-term debt expansionary. After all, an increase in long debt will raise the long-term rate of interest, and retirement of long debt will lower it; many economists are accustomed to judge the direction of impact on aggregate demand of any monetary event by what happens to "the" rate of interest, approximated by the yield of long-term government bonds. However, the differential of the yield of equity over the long rate may not be constant but systematically variable. If an increase in long debt lowers this differential more than it raises the long rate, it lowers the supply price of capital and is expansionary.

The effects of an increase in the supply of long-term government securities, keeping the supplies of other components of public debt constant, depend on whether these securities are directly and indirectly a better substitute for demand and short debt, on the one hand, or for ownership of capital, on the other hand. The concept of *better substitute* can be given precision, and this is done below. The meaning can be conveyed by considering two extreme models: (A) in which long-term securities are a perfect substitute for demand debt, and not for capital, and (B) in which long-term securities are a perfect substitute for capital, and not for demand debt. In the case of either pair, the term *perfect substitute* means that the two yields are held in a certain relation to each other — not necessarily equal — by the fact that investors will make wholesale substitutions of one asset for the other in their portfolios if the yield differential deviates in the slightest degree from normal.

Model (A) amounts to the case discussed above (section 2.2), where the public debt is homogeneous, at a fixed rate. For even though there are a variety of debt instruments, the structure of yields is not affected by the relative supplies of the various kinds of debt. Long securities are such a good substitute for cash, either directly or through the substitution chain of intermediate and short-term securities, that the rate on long securities cannot be changed by altering their supply. In a given state of market expectations. with a given Federal Reserve discount rate, the long rate is as good as pegged. On the other hand, the expansion of debt means that the equity-bond differential must change in favor of debt; capital and long-term debt are not perfect substitutes, and debt has become relatively more abundant. In Model (A), therefore, the supply price of capital must fall.

In Model (B) it is the differential between capital and long-term government bond yields which substitution maintains unchanged. Issue of long-term bonds is essentially an increase in the combined supply of capital and capital substitutes. Meanwhile the supply of assets, government short and demand debt, which are imperfect substitutes for capital and long-term bonds is maintained. Accordingly the yield differential of capital over demand debt must rise. The rates on demand debt being fixed, the supply price of capital must rise. Likewise the rate on long-term securities must rise.

Is the world better approximated by (A) or by (B)? There are good reasons for believing that (A) is the better approximation, that debt instruments of varying maturities are better substitutes for each other than for equity in physical capital. The argument will be presented below. Economics has, however, been dominated by the tradition of Model (B), and the trained intuition of economists faced with a problem such as analyzing the monetary effects of deficit financing by long-term debt is to apply that model. The tradition of Model (B) is involved in the proposition, common to Keynesians and anti-Keynesians, that investment in capital will be carried to the point where the marginal efficiency (or productivity) of capital equals "the rate of interest." *The rate of interest* is identified with the rate on long-term government bonds. The equality need not be taken strictly; some premium for risk may be subtracted from the expected return on capital to obtain the rate that is to be equated to the bond yield. Nevertheless implicitly or explicitly capital investment and bond holding are regarded as perfect substitutes for each other at the proper rate differential. The risk premium, whatever else it depends on, does not vary systematically with the relative supplies of capital and long securities. Just as it conforms to Model (B) in regarding capital and long securities as perfect substitutes. so the prevailing theoretical tradition regards cash and long securities as quite imperfect substitutes. The theory of liquidity preference, and of the maturity structure of interest rates, explains the differential of long rates over the yields of short securities and demand debt. In this explanation the relative supplies of the various imperfect substitutes play a crucial role. In the simple Keynesian model "*the* rate of interest" − the very same one to which the marginal efficiency of capital must be equated − is wholly determined by the supply of cash relative to the supply of bonds. It is quite remarkable that Keynes devoted so much attention to the cash-bond yield differential and so little to the capital-bond differential, and that he failed to apply to the second the principle, that yield differentials depend on relative supplies, he developed for the first. It is perhaps even more surprising that the general theoretical tradition of economics has followed him in these regards so closely so long.

If Model (A) is the better approximation, though an imperfect one, the consequences of issue of long-term government debt may be described as follows: The public and· the banks together have greater overall net worth, with the same holdings of capital equity, short debt, and demand debt as before but larger holdings of long-term government debt. It is of course highly unlikely that the public will wish to absorb the increase in net worth entirely in an increase of holdings of long-term government securities unless there is some change in the structure of yields and asset prices. The saving corresponding to the government deficit would not automatically take the permanent form of investment in long-term government bonds. As the public attempts to maintain portfolio balance, with their larger net worth, they will try to sell long-term governments in order to buy equity, private debt, short-term government debt, and deposits. Yields of long-term securities will rise relative to those of competing assets: this process will continue until the change in structure of yields reconciles investors to the new structure of relative asset supplies. Since long securities are good substitutes for short debt, the short rate may be pulled up too. The improvement in yields of interest-bearing debt will induce the banks to diminish net free reserves and the public to hold more debt relative to deposits and currency. Banks, with an overall increase in their holdings of defensive assets, may expand loans and reduce the loan rate even though the yields on these assets are higher. In any case it takes a decrease in the rate of return on equity to induce the public to increase their holdings of liquid assets, deposits plus government debt, by more even than the increase in their wealth. What might happen to bank and public balance sheets is illustrated in Table 21.5.

In the end the long-term rate is higher absolutely, and higher relative to the yield on capital equity and to the rates on shorter-term government securities. However, the rise in the long rate is limited by the readiness with

Table 21.5

Hypothetical Illustration: Assets (+) and Liabilities (−) of Banks and Public Before and After an Increment of Long Debt and Private Wealth Equal to 1 Per Cent of Wealth

	Banks			Public			Total		
	Before	After	Change	Before	After	Change	Before	After	Change
Currency				+30	+30	0			
Required reserves	+20	+21	+1						
Free reserves	0	−1	−1						
Demand debt	+20	+20	0	+30	+30	0	+50	+50	0
Short debt	+20	+22	+2	+60	+58	−2	+80	+80	0
Long debt	+10	+12	+2	+60	+68	+8	+70	+80	+10
Private debt	+80	+82	+2	+320 −400	+318 −400	−2	0	0	0
Deposits	−120	−126	−6	+120	+126	+6	0	0	0
Capital	−10	−10	0	+810	+810	0	+800	+800	0
Total	0	0	0	+1000	+1010	+10	+1000	+1010	+10

which many holders will substitute long debt for shorter securities or cash. The short–long differential will not have to change much to induce banks and other institutional investors to shorten the average maturity of their holdings. Short securities are in turn a close substitute for cash; for banks, government bills are a close substitute for excess reserves or for reduction of debt to the Federal Reserve. Consequently short rates are fairly firmly anchored to the Federal Reserve discount rate and to the zero rate on demand debt and on deposits. Given these basic rates, the yields of short-term government securities can be changed substantially only by considerable shift in the relative supplies of demand and short debt. Here these supplies are taken to be constant. The rise in the long rate is, for these reasons, limited. But the differential of equity yield − the supply price of capital − over the long rate must fall. Indeed this differential must fall more than the differential, positive or negative, of short rates over long. That is a consequence of the assumption of Model (A) that long debt is a better substitute for other government debt than for capital. Accordingly the supply price of capital must fall.

Debt issue is on balance expansionary, in spite of the fact that the long-term rate rises. Instead of being an indication that the operation has deflationary results, the rise in the long-term rate is in large part a symptom of the expansionary impact of the transaction. It results mainly from the effort to restore portfolio balance between capital equity and government debt. Another result of the same effort is a decrease in the supply price of capital.

The argument applies in reverse, of course, for retirement of government debt. Other things equal, a decrease in government debt due to budget surplus has an enduring deflationary monetary effect, superimposed on its transient deflationary fiscal effect. This is true even if debt retirement is concentrated entirely on long-term bonds. Given the supplies outstanding of short debt and demand debt, and given the discount rate, retiremant of long-term securities from budget surplus will raise the supply price of capital.

2.6. Correlations of Risks among Debt Instruments and Capital Equity

What are the reasons for believing that government debt instruments are better substitutes for each other than any of them, even those of long maturity, are for equity in physical capital?

In general, an asset which is a candidate for an investor's portfolio may be characterized by two attributes of his estimate of the probability distribution of gains and losses from holding the asset for a given period ahead. One is the expectation of return, the means of the distribution. The other is a measure of dispersion or risk, the standard deviation of returns. Considering a number of assets together, the investor may be imagined to estimate a joint probability distribution, with possible positive or negative correlations in the returns on any pair of assets.

In general two assets are good substitutes for each other to the extent that they share the same risks, i.e., to the extent that their future rates of return are positively correlated with each other. If the same future contingencies that would make asset X turn out more profitably than expected on average would also make asset Y exceptionally remunerative, then X and Y are good substitutes. If the correlation is perfect, holding both X and Y in a portfolio does not accomplish any spreading of risk or hedging, in comparison with concentrating the same total investment on either asset alone. Considering two assets with high positive correlation of returns, which asset the investor chooses to concentrate on, or the proportions in which he holds the two assets, will be very sensitive to the difference between his expectations of return on the two assets.

When two assets have uncorrelated rates of return, the investor can reduce his risk by dividing his investment between them. The worst may happen to one but it will be very unlikely to happen to both at the same time. This is, of course, the basic reason for portfolio diversification. To reduce overall risk, a portfolio manager balances his holdings of assets by seeking independent risks. Some assets he holds have less expected return than others; the justification for their inclusion in the portfolio is reduction of risk. To maintain balance and diversification as wealth grows, an investor will expand the risk-independent components of his portfolio together in rough proportion. He will sacrifice risk-spreading and diversification only under the inducement of a higher expected rate of return on the riskier assets. A larger expected return differential is required for two reasons. There is an increase in overall risk due to the simple fact that one asset is riskier than the other. Added to this, in the case where the risks are independent, is an increase in risk due to loss of risk pooling.

When two assets have returns with negative correlation – i.e., events that would make X a big loser would more or less surely make Y a big winner – then real hedging is possible to reduce risk.

What are the risks of holding government obligations? All categories of government debt are free of risk of default. All categories of government debt, including demand debt, share their principal risk, namely uncertainty about the purchasing power of the dollar. Presumably each investor assigns to cash and to other obligations fixed in units of currency a real rate of return based on his expectation of the change in the price level. If his mean expectation is inflation at a rate of 3 per cent per annum, his expected real rate of return on cash is −3 per cent per annum. Likewise he will subtract 3 per cent from the expected money return on any other obligation of fixed money value, in order to arrive at its expected real rate of return. But no one is sure about the price level. It may rise more than the expected 3 per cent, or it may rise less, even fall. This is a risk in holding any asset of this kind. It is shared equally by all government debt instruments. If inflation takes away 50 per cent of the value of cash during the next decade, it will also take away 50 per cent of the value of a 10-year bond. If deflation adds 20 per cent to the value of cash, it will also add 20 per cent to the value of a bond. An investor cannot defend himself against risks of this kind by spreading investments among different kinds of maturities of government obligations.

The second risk of government obligations is due to uncertainty about future interest rates. This risk affects differently obligations of different maturities. An investor interested in the money value of his asset three months from now can be perfectly sure of it by holding cash or an obligation with maturity of three months or less. If he holds a debt of longer maturity, the value of his investment in three months will depend on the vagaries of the market. If the interest rate rises, he will suffer a capital loss; if it falls, he will gain. The degree of this uncertainty depends on the length of maturity. A one-point change in interest rate cannot alter very much the capital value of an obligation due in another three months or a year. It can alter considerably the capital value of a distant maturity. If interest rates for various maturities are expected most probably to move together, the prospects of short-period return on obligations of different maturities are positively correlated, with greater risks on greater maturities. For investors of short horizon, therefore, the risk associated with interest rate changes works in the same direction as the risk associated with price level changes. It makes government obligations of different maturities good substitutes for each other.

Some investors have long horizons; they are interested in their aggregate return over ten or twenty or thirty years, or more. They anticipate little or no probability that they will need to consume their capital at an earlier date. Accordingly they attach little importance to the value of their investments at intervening dates but concentrate on their ultimate value. For long horizon investors, so far as risks of interest rate change are concerned, the ranking of maturities with respect to risk is reversed. One can be more certain of the amount of money he will have in twenty years by buying a twenty-year bond than by buying a ten-year bond and planning to reinvest in a second ten-year bond when the first one matures. Uncertainty about the level of interest rates ten years from now affects the second strategy but not the first. Uncertainty about the future of interest rates adds even more to the risk of a shorter initial investment, a five-year or one-year maturity instead of a ten-year bond. If interest rates fall next month and stay down, the long-horizon investor with a twenty-year bond will nevertheless earn the original higher rate over the twenty-year period. If he has a ten-year bond, he will at least enjoy the higher interest over a ten-year period. With a one-year obligation, he will be stuck with a low rate of return over the nineteen subsequent years. Similarly the long-horizon investor will gain more from a rise in interest rates the shorter his initial investment.

Although the ranking of maturities with respect to risk is reversed for a long-horizon investor, the risks of the various maturities are positively correlated. As in the case of short-horizon investment, this positive correlation makes obligations of different maturities good substitutes for each other. Investors will be sensitive to the structure of yields in choosing among alternative ways of accumulating a sum of money for a target date twenty years in the future. If the current rate on ten-year bonds is enough higher than that on twenty-year bonds, they will buy ten-year bonds and take their chances on the interest rate ten years from now. After all the absolute worst that can happen is that they will hold cash at zero interest for the last ten years.

There is a third situation, in which the target date is neither at the beginning nor at the end of the maturity spectrum. Maturities both longer and shorter than the horizon entail risk, the more risk the more they diverge from the target date. But longer and shorter maturities can be combined as an imperfect hedge; and in this situation they are complements, rather than substitutes. Suppose an investor is holding both, and a rise in interest rates occurs before the target date. He suffers a capital loss on the longer maturities, but makes this up by increased earnings of interest as he reinvests the proceeds of his shorter maturities. Similarly, if interest rates fall, he loses as he reinvests the proceeds of the short maturities but makes a capital gain on the longer maturities. *Hedging combinations* of short and long securities are of course, a substitute for the simple matching of maturity with timing of obligation or need. Likewise there are various possible hedging combinations – very short and very long, moderately short with moderately long, etc. Which procedure is followed depends on which promises the highest yield. In this sense various maturities are again substitutes for each other.

Gains or losses from ownership of capital depend on quite a different set of events and contingencies. To begin with, capital ownership is specific. It requires betting on particular kinds of capital goods, particular industries, particular managements. The risks of a poor specific choice are of the same nature as the risks of default of private obligations of fixed money value. Government obligations are free of such risk. It is true that the specific risks of capital ownership can be reduced, though not wholly eliminated, by diversification. The rise of mutual funds and of conglomerate corporations tends to make diversified portfolios generally available, even to small investors. What diversification cannot begin to do, of course, is to eliminate the risks common to capital ownership of all kinds. Though there are tremendous variations in the fortunes of specific equities, they are variations on a common theme. To judge the prospects, either short-run or long-run, of a particular equity investment, one must guess not only its specific merits relative to other equities but also the course of "the market" in general.

The long-run prospects of capital ownership in general depend upon what happens to the relative prices of capital and consumption goods, rather than what happens to the absolute consumers' price level. In the short run there can, of course, be considerable discrepancy between the market's valuation of capital in place and the replacement cost of capital, even of the most up-to-date technological vintage. Market valuations fluctuate violently and erratically as investors speculate regarding the prospects of the economy and regarding each others' speculations. Whether in the stock market or in the markets for real capital goods, the terms of trade between capital ownership and consumption-goods may turn in favor of owners of capital or against them. But what happens to these terms of trade is quite independent of what happens to the terms of trade between consumption goods and money. The main sources of inflation or deflation cause both capital goods and consumption goods prices to rise. Ownership of capital is therefore a good though incomplete hedge against the risks of changes in the consumer price index. Ownership of government debt or its equivalent avoids the risks due to changes in the relative prices of investment goods, either as measured day to day in the stock market valuations of capital in place or as measured by the real cost of new capital equipment.

Another risk of capital ownership is due to uncertainty about the rate of technological obsolescence. All capital may be expected to decline in value in relation to its replacement cost as time and technological advance bring better ways of doing the same things. The anticipated rate of return on replacement cost that initially induces investors to acquire a capital item contains some allowance for the expected decline in value of the item due to obsolescence. If obsolescence is slower than anticipated, the net return on the item will be better than anticipated. But if obsolescence occurs faster than this guess, the return on the investment will be disappointing. Diversification of capital investments is a way of avoiding the consequences of miscalculation of obsolescence prospects in a particular line. But uncertainty about the rate of technological progress in the economy as a whole remains. Again, this is a risk that is not shared by government debt instruments nor correlated with their characteristic risks.

The conclusion is that there is substantial independence of risk between ownership of capital and ownership of government obligations. In contrast, there is considerable positive correlation of real rates of return within each of the two categories, among different kinds of government debt, on the one hand, and among different capital equities, on the other. The public will use government debt and capital equity to balance each other in diversified portfolios. They will shift the proportions of this balance only in response to changes in the differential real rates of return expected on the two categories. If, for example, the public must absorb a greater proportion of capital equity, the expected rate of return on capital equity must rise relatively to the expected rate on government debt. The rise must be sufficient to induce investors not only to assume more of the intrinsic risks of capital ownership but also to forego some of the defense against these risks afforded by a balanced holding of claims fixed in money value.

2.7. Changes in the Composition of a Given Debt

Previous sections have discussed the monetary effects of increasing the debt in each of the three forms: demand, short, and long. If those sections are shifted into reverse gear, they describe the effects of reducing the debt outstanding in each of these forms. Most of the operations of the monetary and debt management authorities involve changes in the composition of a given debt, i.e., increasing the supply of one kind of debt and reducing the supply of another. The effects of such operations are already implicitly described in the previous sections. For example, the effects of open market purchases of bills can be inferred from section 2.3 with the hypothetical example of Table 21.2, which describes an increase in the supply of demand debt, and from a reverse reading of section 2.4 and the hypothetical example of Table 21.4, which would describe an equal decrease in short debt. The assumptions about substitutabilities among assets made in the preceding sections already imply: (1) substitution of demand debt for short debt is expansionary, (2) substitution of demand debt for long debt is even more expansionary, and (3) substitution of short debt for long debt is expansionary, but probably less so, dollar for dollar, than either of the other two operations. These conclusions all assume that no category of debt is a perfect substitute for another, either in bank portfolios or public balance sheets. If, contrary to this view, banks regarded bills as perfect substitutes for free reserves, open market purchases and sales of bills would have little effect. Or, if the public, say, regarded short and long debt as perfect substitutes, it would not matter whether open market operations were conducted in the one kind of security or the other [operations (1) and (2) would have the same effect] and lengthening or shortening the interest-bearing debt [operation (3)] would make no difference to the state of aggregate demand.

Tables 21.6, 21.7, and 21.8 provide hypothetical examples of each of the three shifts in debt composition mentioned. These examples are consistent with those of Tables 21.2, 21.4, and 21.5.

2.8. Gross Versus Net Federal Debt

The activities of the federal government as a financial intermediary and the activities of quasi-governmental agencies and institutions serving as financial intermediaries with obligations bearing government guarantee, have not been discussed so far. These activities do not add to the net debt of the government or to the net private wealth of the community. Nonetheless they may have very significant monetary effects. Even when no government subsidy is involved, they reduce the supply price of capital by accommodating private borrowers at lower rates than they could otherwise obtain. This is

Table 21.6
Hypothetical Illustration: Open Market Purchases of Bills (Assets (+) and Liabilities (−) of Banks and Public Before and After Increase in Demand Debt Offset by Equal Decrease in Short Debt)

	Banks			Public			Total		
	Before	After	Change	Before	After	Change	Before	After	Change
Currency	0	0	0	+30	+30	0			
Required reserves	+20	+24	+4						
Free reserves	0	+6	+6						
Demand debt	+20	+30	+10	+30	+30	0	+50	+60	+10
Short debt	+20	+23	+3	+60	+47	−13	+80	+70	−10
Long debt	+10	+15	+5	+60	+55	−5	+70	+70	0
Private debt	+80	+86	+6	+320 −400	+314 −400	−6	0	0	0
Deposits	−120	−144	−24	+120	+144	+24	0	0	0
Capital	−10	−10	0	+810	+81(	0	+800	+800	0
Total	0	0	0	+1000	+1000	0	+1000	+1000	0

Table 21.7
Hypothetical Illustration: Open Market Purchases of Long Securities (Assets (+) and Liabilities (−) of Banks and Public Before and After Increase in Demand Debt Offset by Equal Decrease in Long Debt)

	Banks			Public			Total		
	Before	After	Change	Before	After	Change	Before	After	Change
Currency	0	0	0	+30	+30	0			
Required reserves	+20	+26	+6						
Free reserves	0	+4	+4						
Demand debt	+20	+30	+10	+30	+30	0	+50	+60	+10
Short debt	+20	+28	+8	+60	+52	−8	+80	+80	0
Long debt	+10	+13	+3	+60	+47	−13	+70	+60	−10
Private debt	+80	+95	+15	+320 −400	+305 −400	−15	0	0	0
Deposits	−120	−156	−36	+120	+156	+36	0	0	0
Capital	−10	−10	0	+810	+810	0	+800	+800	0
Total	0	0	0	+1000	+1000	0	+1000	+1000	0

Table 21.8
Hypothetical Illustration: Shortening of Interest-Bearing Debt (Assets (+) and Liabilities (–) of Banks and Public Before and After Increase in Short Debt Offset by Equal Decrease in Long Debt)

	Banks			Public			Total		
	Before	After	Change	Before	After	Change	Before	After	Change
Currency	0	0	0	+30	+30	0			
Required reserves	+20	+22	+2						
Free reserves	0	−2	−2						
Demand debt	+20	+20	• 0	+30	+30	0	+50	+50	0
Short debt	+20	+25	+5	+60	+65	+5	+80	+90	+10
Long debt	+10	+8	−2	+60	+52	−8	+70	+60	−10
Private debt	+80	+89	+9	+320 −400	+311 −400	−9	0	0	0
Deposits	−120	−132	−12	+120	+132	+12	0	0	0
Capital	−10	−10	0	+810	+810	0	+800	+800	0
Total	0	0	0	+1000	+1000	0	+1000	+1000	0

accomplished by the substitution of the government's credit for the private borrowers' credit. The agency either obtains the funds by issuing Treasury obligations or the equivalent, or by guaranteeing the private obligation. In either event, the lenders will supply the funds at lower yield than if they were supplying them directly to the borrowers. Nor is the reduction of private loan rates confined to borrowers served by the government. Competition will reduce loan rates to borrowers served by private lenders as well. The availability of a larger gross supply of government obligations, which can serve as secondary reserves and as hedges in portfolios, will lower private loan rates and the supply price of capital. This will be true even though these intermediary activities tend to raise somewhat government rates themselves. The earlier analysis of section 2.2 applies. Here again there is an increase in government debt relative to the other component of private wealth, the capital stock. Indeed here it is virtually as if the capital stock that must be placed in private portfolios is decreased concurrently with the increase in government debt. Though capital is not actually bought by the government, it is acquired by borrowers served by the government. So much less, then, needs to be lodged in private hands through the normal channels and incentives of capital markets and private financial institutions.

The intermediary activities of the federal government have monetary effects but they are not under the control of the monetary authorities. On occasion these activities have expanded when monetary policy was restrictive, and vice versa. Conceivably government intermediaries could thwart monetary policy more than private financial intermediaries. Private institutions are held in rein by interest rates which are within reach of the Federal Reserve. The scope of governmental intermediary operations is determined not by profit opportunities but by legislative and executive decision.

Greater coordination of activities that give rise to federal debt, under the control of the monetary and debt management authorities, is desirable. This does not mean, of course, abandonment of the aims for which Congress has authorized selective interventions in the credit market, though some economists may regard these interventions as unwise. Government credit and intermediation can still be used to channel funds to categories of borrowers or kinds of capital formation that Congress desires to foster. Selectivity of this kind cannot be practiced by the Federal Reserve itself. So long as open market operations are confined to government securities, the monetary authorities have no way to exert direct influence over the structure of private interest rates, e.g., to lower mortgage rates relative to corporate bond yields, or to lower rates on loans to finance farm crops while raising rates for commercial construction.

Government financial intermediation is one way of practicing selective monetary control. Selective regulations applicable to private lenders are another way. The Federal Reserve administers regulations concerning stock market credit and at times has regulated consumer and residential mortgage lending. If security reserve requirements of some kind were imposed on private financial intermediaries other than banks, variation of these requirements would be a third type of selective control, perhaps more powerful than either of the other two. Whatever administrative discretion exists in selective credit control, through government financial intermediaries and by other means, should be coordinated and to some degree centralized. Otherwise it may be used counter to the prevailing overall objectives of monetary and debt management policy. And it may not even add up to a consistent policy with respect to the structure of private interest rates and credit availabilities. For example, it would not make sense to expand the federal government's open market operations in mortgages, via "Fanny May," at the same time the Federal Reserve is stiffening regulations about mortgage down payments and maturities.

Federal debt instruments serve so many purposes in the contemporary monetary and financial system that observers sometimes wonder what the system would do if the debt were eliminated by a miraculous series of budget surpluses. What would we do for a currency supply, for bank reserves, for the money market, for secondary reserves of all kinds, etc? One answer is that private obligations would adapt to fill the vacuum. Private obligations of the quality, design, and maturity appropriate for money market transactions and for secondary reserves would increase in supply. Banks would take advantage of Federal Reserve willingness to make advances on private collateral or to rediscount. Relieved of the competition of government bills for the attention of dealers and of the money market, bankers' acceptances might flourish, fulfilling an ancient Federal Reserve dream. Banks might operate to a much greater degree than at present on borrowed reserves; this was the practice in the 1920's in the United States and is the practice today in France and other countries. But even these adaptations would not be necessary. The net debt could vanish – the government might even acquire net claims against the private economy – while a gross debt still remains. Government debt instruments to serve the useful purposes they serve today could be issued to finance the lending activities of government financial intermediaries. If more demand debt were needed, for example, the Federal Reserve could monetize the obligations of government lending agencies. This would keep the Federal Reserve itself free of the difficulties that would attend direct open market dealings in private securities on any scale.

2.9. The Central Bank Discount Rate

In addition to its powers over the composition of the debt, the Federal Reserve has at its command certain control instruments that do not alter the structure of the debt. The most important are the power to set the discount rate at which member banks can borrow reserves and the power to set required reserve ratios. Within broad limits, either or both of these tools may be substituted for open market operations in government securities. Whatever degree of monetary restraint the authorities desire, there are a variety of combinations of controls that can achieve it. Since these purely monetary instruments are close substitutes for debt management operations, they cannot be omitted from a consideration of debt management policy.

What are the monetary effects of lowering the discount rate, while the supplies of all categories of government debt and of capital remain unchanged? A word of caution is in order regarding interpretation of the phrase *lowering the discount rate*. What is really to be analyzed is the difference it makes to equilibrium bank and public balance sheets and to the structure of interest rates whether the discount rate stands at one level rather than another, *ceteris paribus*. Among the other things to be taken as equal are the expectations of the market, its estimates of the future of the economy and of interest rates. The exercise is one of comparative statics. No attempt is made to trace the process of change from one level of discount rate to another, in particular the alterations in expectation generated by the central bank's announcement of a new discount rate. For many students of central bank policy the psychology of the announcement is the most important and perhaps the only important aspect of the discount rate. Unfortunately there is little of a systematic character that can be said about it. Will the public conclude from the announcement of a fall in the discount rate that predictions of recession are now confirmed by the expert economic intelligence of the central bank, and therefore regard the announcement as a deflationary portent? Or will the market judge that the authorities have thus indicated their resolute intention of preventing deflation, arresting and reversing the recession, and accordingly interpret the announcement as an inflationary sign? What do the authorities themselves regard as the likely psychological effects of their announcements? Clearly it is easy to become enmeshed in a game of infinite regress between the central bank and the market. A conclusive justification for separating the analysis of discount policy from expectational effects is that the central bank can, if it chooses, separate them in practice. The authorities can and do make announcements, with calculated psychological impact, *without* changing the discount rate. The distinctive thing about lowering the discount rate is that it reduces the cost of advances to the banks.

Reduction of the discount rate gives banks incentive to reduce their net free reserves by increasing their debt to the Federal Reserve, substituting secondary reserve assets, in particular short government debt, for free reserves. As bank demand for bills increases, in response to the improved differential of the bill rate over the discount rate, the bill rate falls. The fall in the bill rate leads the public to supply bills to the banks, substituting deposits. The lower bill rate also stimulates banks to bid long debt and private debt away from the public; lower yields on these assets induce the public to shift to deposits. All rates, including the supply price of capital, fall, although not in proportion to the initial fall in the discount rate. The new structure of rates provides banks incentive to decrease their net free reserves (increase their borrowing at the Federal Reserve) and at the same time provides the public inducement to expand their deposits by six times the reduction in banks' free reserves.

A rise in the discount rate has the opposite effects. Other rates rise, though not in proportion to the discount rate. Banks increase their free reserves, and the public diminishes its deposits by a multiple of the increase in banks' free reserves. The change in the rate structure must accomplish both of these portfolio shifts at the same time.

There are limits to discount policy at both ends. Banks may be so heavily indebted to the Federal Reserve that they will not respond to further incentive to borrow. Or the bill rate may be so low that it would not compensate banks for the trouble and risk of borrowing to hold bills, even at a zero discount rate. At the other extreme, the discount rate may be so high as to be "out of touch" with the money market. That is, banks are already free of debt to the Federal Reserve, or substantially so, and increasing the bill rate cannot make them reduce indebtedness further. The relevant basic money rate is then the conventional zero rate paid on excess reserves and currency rather than the discount rate charged on borrowed reserves.

2.10. *Changes in Required Reserve Ratios*

The second "purely monetary" instrument is prescription of required reserve ratios. Within specified limits, Congress has delegated this power to the Federal Reserve. Changes outside those limits would require congressional action.

Changing required reserve ratios is an extremely powerful tool. Compare it, for example, with open market operations in bills. The Federal Reserve can effect a given initial increase in free reserves, calculated against an unchanged volume of deposits, either by open market purchases of bills from the banks or by a reduction in required reserve ratios. The first method does not alter the banks' overall defensive position; their holdings of free reserves plus bills amount to the same fraction of their disposable assets (total assets less required reserves) as before. The second method, reduction of required reserve ratios, improves the banks' overall defensive position at the same time that it augments their free reserves. Banks' free reserves plus bill holdings become a larger share of their disposable assets. The second method, therefore, gives the banks the greater incentive to expand loans. In the case of open market operations, reduction of free reserves to desired levels entails a multiple deposit expansion based on established reserve ratios. In the case of a lowering of required reserve ratios, reduction of free reserves to desired levels entails deposit expansion by a higher multiple, based on the new reserve ratios.

In the example of Table 21.4 the increase of demand debt was 10. This could be regarded as the initial increase in free reserves, calculating reserve requirements against the original deposit volume, 120. A similar increase in free reserves could be provided by halving required reserve ratios, so that required reserves against deposits of 120 would be only 10 instead of 20. But this 10 in free reserves is more high-powered than the 10 in free reserves provided by open market operations. It could support a deposit expansion of 120 instead of 60. In neither case will the full potential deposit expansion eventuate. As banks expand loans and deposits, interest rates will fall; and this fall in rates will restrain banks from converting all their new free reserves into required reserves. Banks will push the expansion of deposits farther in the second case than in the first; they will be willing to do so, even though they encounter lower yields on earning assets, because they are better supplied with free reserves and other defensive assets. At the same time they will probably not push the expansion of deposits twice as far in the second case; yields on earning assets would be too low to induce banks to accept an expansion of that magnitude in less liquid assets relative to free and secondary reserves. Clearly the lowering of required reserve ratios will accomplish a bigger reduction in yields of long debt, private debt, and capital than open market purchases of equivalent initial magnitude. Table 21.9 provides a hypothetical illustration which may be compared with 21.6.

An implication of the foregoing comparison is that the Federal Reserve can have a net expansionary impact by simultaneously (a) reducing required

Table 21.9

Hypothetical Illustration: Assets (+) and Liabilities (−) of Banks and Public Before and After a Reduction in Reserve Requirements Providing Initial Free Reserves Equal to 1 Per Cent of Wealth

	Banks			Public			Total		
	Before	After	Change	Before	After	Change	Before	After	Change
Currency	0	0	0	+30	+30	0			
Required reserves	+20	+16	−4						
Free reserves	0	+4	+4						
Demand debt	+20	+20	0	+30	+30	0	+50	+50	0
Short debt	+20	+35	+15	+60	+45	−15	+80	+80	0
Long debt	+10	+17	+7	+60	+53	−7	+70	+70	0
Private debt	+80	+130	+50	+320 −400	+270 −400	−50	0	0	0
Deposits	−120	−192	−72	+120	+192	+72	0	0	0
Capital	−10	−10	0	+810	+810	0	+800	+800	0
Total	0	0	0	+1000	+1000	0	+1000	+1000	0

reserve ratios so as to free 10 of reserves and (b) mopping up those freed reserves by open market sales of bills. The immediate consequence of these two moves is that banks have the same free reserves as before, but a larger supply of bills. As banks seek to swap bills with the public for long and private debt, the bill rate will rise and the yields on less liquid assets will fall. The rise in the bill rate will induce some reduction in banks' net free reserves, and each dollar reduction means a deposit expansion at the new higher multiple. This expansion is a further reason for reduction in the yields of private loans, and in the supply price of capital. The net result of the two operations is definitely expansionary. Likewise the Federal Reserve can have a net restrictive effect by raising reserve requirements and supplying the newly needed reserves by open market purchases.

3. Debt Management Policy

3.1. *Criterion for Optimal Policy: Minimum Cost for Required Economic Impact*

The objective of government policies for economic stabilization is to maintain balance between aggregate supply and demand at a desired degree of full employment. Whether the target should be 2 per cent unemployment, or 3 per cent, or 5 per cent is a matter of judgment, in which the advantages of greater production and employment must be weighed against their costs, in particular the hazards of faster secular increase in the price level. Whatever target is chosen, there are a variety of ways to pursue it. If aggregate demand threatens to become excessive, it can be restricted by fiscal means or by monetary means. Taxes can be increased to curtail private spending; which taxes are increased will determine whose spending and what kinds of spending are curtailed. Alternatively, demand may be restricted by higher interest rates and lower availability of credit. On what criteria shall these choices of stabilization tools be made? If a number of alternatives will have the same consequences so far as stabilization is concerned, the choice among them must depend on their other consequences.

The composition of national output is an important criterion. Depending on the choice of tools, the national output will be divided in different proportions between investment and consumption. If the government seeks a higher rate of growth, it may prefer a selection of stabilization tools that favors investment demand at the expense of consumption demand. For example, investment may be stimulated by low interest, "easy" monetary and debt management policies, while consumption is restrained by taxes reducing the spendable incomes of households. Other criteria include equity in the distribution of income and wealth and efficiency in the allocation of resources to accord with the needs and preferences of the society. A stabilization policy which encourages saving by shifting income to higher-income groups might be regarded by some as inequitable, by others as equitable. A stabilization policy which works through curtailing the school construction programs of local governments might raise some objections on the score of efficiency.

One implication of the goal of efficiency is the desirability, other things equal, of minimizing taxes. Taxation by any known feasible method imposes some burden or "deadweight" loss, even if the proceeds are returned to the community of taxpayers rather than used to commandeer productive resources for governmental purposes. This burden is not simply the cost of administration and enforcement. Beyond that, the tax causes taxpayers to adjust their decisions between leisure and work, one job and another job, saving and consuming, risk-taking and security, consumption of this and consumption of that, in directions that reduce their tax liability. These adjustments may alter the allocation of national resources and the consumption of national output in socially undesirable directions. Taxation does not always cause misallocation. A certain amount of taxation, skillfully designed, may improve resource allocation, correcting distortions that would otherwise occur. But the size of modern government gives ample scope for corrective taxation. The marginal amounts of taxation involved in decisions to rely more heavily on fiscal measures to restrict demand, and less heavily on other measures, will almost surely cause distorting rather than correcting adjustments in taxpayers' economic decisions. Against this consideration must be placed, of course, the objectives that can be served by relatively heavy reliance on fiscal measures, in particular the stimulation of saving, investment and growth.

Here it may be assumed that the target of stabilization policy has been decided, and the broad choice between fiscal and monetary instruments has been made. These decisions have the effect of assigning to the monetary and debt management authorities a certain stabilization task. They must aim at a certain degree of monetary restraint, or stimulus, upon the economy. The required degree of monetary restraint will be smaller the more restrictive is fiscal policy; and it will be smaller, for given fiscal policy, the lower the chosen unemployment target.

In achieving their assigned stabilization task, in maintaining the desired degree of monetary restraint or stimulus, the central bank and the managers of the debt have, in their turn, alternative instruments and combinations of instruments. Which should be used? What are the criteria of choice? In the absence of more important criteria, preference could be given to methods of monetary control that minimize the long-run costs of the federal debt to the Treasury. For the reasons given above, taxation to pay interest on the debt has disadvantages on grounds of allocative efficiency. It is logical, therefore, to ask that the monetary and debt management authorities achieve their stabilization task with as little burden on the federal taxpayer as possible. It is worth while pursuing the implications of this mandate, even though the course of the pursuit will encounter some constraining criteria – equity, avoidance of controls and regulations.

The problem of debt management, then, can be put in these terms: How are long-run interest costs on a given volume of federal debt to be minimized, given the contribution that debt management and monetary policy jointly make to economic stabilization? The proviso is, of course, crucial. It is easy to think of ways to minimize interest costs that do not meet it. Interest costs could be reduced to zero by monetizing the entire debt, but that would clearly not maintain intact the restraint that monetary policy and debt management now impose on aggregate demand. The trick is to reduce interest costs without impairing that restraint.

To state the criterion of debt management policy in this way is not to assign minimization of interest transfers a high priority among the goals of national economic policy. These transfers are in the main internal transfers from taxpayers to the Treasury's creditors. They are not a draft on the productive capacity of the country; unlike government purchases of goods and services, they do not require labor or capital equipment or natural resources that might be used for other purposes. This elementary fact was rightly stressed by advocates of "functional finance" who were urging deficit financing to combat unemployment and depression. Those who were ready to welcome increases in interest charged due to expansion of debt have in logic little license now to oppose increases in interest payments due to higher rates on the same total debt. In either case, we are still paying it to ourselves. Similarly the equanimity with which advocates of orthodox finance view increase in total interest burden today, when they result from higher rates, is scarcely consistent with the alarm they expressed over increases in the interest burden yesterday, when they resulted from expansion of debt.

How much taxation is necessary to cover a dollar expansion of interest payments? Enough to neutralize its effect on the demand for national output: if the recipients of a marginal dollar of interest transfer will spend 50 cents of this dollar increase in income, while taxpayers will reduce their spending by 75 per cent of any increase in their tax payments, tax revenues need be increased only 66.7 cents (50/.75) for every dollar increase in interest transfers. It is probable that the marginal propensity to spend from interest transfers is in fact smaller than the marginal propensity to spend from reduction of federal taxes. Indeed the fact that interest recipients are in general individuals of higher wealth and income than taxpayers is one of the stock objections to interest transfers. It is a valid objection, but its validity to some extent weakens the force of the efficiency objection, because the very regressivity of interest transfers makes less taxation necessary to neutralize them. The concept of fiscal neutrality is the relevant criterion. Balancing marginal revenues and outlays dollar for dollar has no economic logic, except as a rough approximation to fiscal neutrality. Usually it is a poor approximation. In the particular case at hand it overstates the need for additional taxation. For expenditures on goods and services and transfer payments other than interest, it generally understates the need for additional taxation.

Maximum production, full employment, economic growth, equity in distribution of income and wealth, efficient allocation of resources, balance of payments equilibrium, stabilization of prices -- these are prime goals of economic policy. We should not sacrifice much in our pursuit of them just to lower the interest burden on the debt. But we probably do not have to. The tools available for monetary control and debt management are sufficient in number and in power to permit us to minimize interest costs, within limits, without impairing the contribution that monetary control and debt management can make to the achievement and reconciliation of the prime goals. Unfortunately this does not mean that the government possesses sufficient tools of economic policy in general to pursue simultaneously all the prime goals. There are some irreconcilable conflicts among them, and hard choices have to be made. The relative abundance of monetary and debt management tools cannot, unhappily, be used to eliminate these conflicts. It is because they can contribute little in that arena that these tools are free to be used for the secondary purpose of minimizing interest transfers. An exception to this statement is that outflows of funds abroad may be more sensitive to short-term interest rates than to long-term rates, at least in the short run. When interest-oriented outflows are a danger, it may be possible to prevent them or diminish them by monetary and debt management techniques which keep short rates relatively high without tightening the overall domestic impact of monetary policy. This objective may well take priority over minimization of interest cost to taxpayers.

A noneconomic reason for concern over the size of government interest payments may be found in the symbolic status that the government's conventional budget has achieved. The size of conventional budget expenditures in a fiscal year is the number that enters political debate, newspaper editorials, and popular discussion. The state of balance of the conventional budget, judged by the eternal knife-edge precepts of Mr. Micawber, is the badge of fiscal success or failure. From the economist's point of view, the focus of attention on the size and state of balance of the conventional budget is quite misplaced. Its size does not measure the government's draft on the productive resources of the economy. Its balance does not measure the effect of the government's transactions with the public on the overall economic balance between supply and demand. But given its symbolic status, the conventional budget is difficult to increase even when the increase is of no economic significance. And given the magical significance vested in the concept of balance of the conventional budget, it is difficult to substitute the criterion of fiscal neutrality. As a matter of political fact, therefore, an increase in interest payments on the national debt may well come at the expense of government outlays on programs of national importance — defense, or school construction, or urban renewal. For it will be argued that the nation cannot afford higher outlays, which would have to be covered dollar for dollar by higher taxes to preserve budget balance. So long as government uses of resources for national purposes are rationed by this set of attitudes — and not merely by collective judgment concerning the marginal utility of the alternative private uses — it makes sense to try to keep interest transfers from impinging on the conventional budget.

The interest entry in the conventional budget is already an exaggerated one. including interest payments from the Treasury to other agencies of the government, principally the social security funds and the Federal Reserve banks, as well as to the general public. It would be desirable to reduce the apparent size of these nominal transfers by creating a special instrument for intragovernmental debt, — a simple memorandum of indebtedness without specific maturity, bearing no interest or a nominal interest rate of, say, 1 per cent. A substantial part of the Federal Reserve's current holdings of government securities will almost certainly never be sold to the public. These could be converted into interagency debt, leaving the Federal Reserve with an ample working stock of marketable securities for possible open market sale. If the working stock later became depleted, contrary to initial expectation, the Federal Reserve would have the right to ask the Treasury for marketable securities of any specification desired, in exchange for nonmarketable interagency memoranda of debt.

3.2. Reserve Requirements on Banks and Other Institutions
The debt management problem, as defined in section 3.1, may be exam-

ined either (a) assuming unchanged the existing institutional framework: existing legislation, financial institutions; markets, debt instruments, or (b) considering certain institutional changes that would contribute to the objective. The discussion is usually carried on solely in the first context, in which the problem reduces to the question how the total debt outstanding should be divided among the various maturities of conventional debt instruments. This question is discussed below, in section 3.3. Quite possibly, however, the potential contributions of optimal management of the maturity structure in the existing institutional framework are small compared to the savings of interest costs that institutional changes could accomplish. It is remarkable how sacrosanct prevailing institutions become even when they have emerged and survived by quite accidental and arbitrary processes.

One institutional change that would reduce interest costs is the introduction of bonds with purchasing power escalation, discussed in section 4 below. These bonds have other important advantages, and interest reduction is only a by-product. The introduction of such bonds might be economical to the Treasury because the general public would be willing to accept lower yields in order to avoid the risks of changes in the price level. The authorities could permit these lower yields to take effect, because they would not signify any reduction in the supply price of capital, any relaxation in the degree of monetary restraint. This is because the low yields on purchasing power bonds would reflect in part a shift out of capital equity, by investors who would prefer a safe hedge against inflation to the risky hedge of capital ownership. Indeed this initial process of substitution of purchasing power bonds for capital equity would tend to raise the supply price of capital. In order to avoid this tightening of the degree of monetary restriction, the Federal Reserve would have to take expansionary measures, further reducing interest charges on the government debt.

The second major category of possible institutional change is to impose on financial institutions new requirements to hold government securities. These requirements would increase the captive market for government securities. That would leave a smaller quantity of government debt to be placed in the voluntary market, consequently it could be placed on better terms. The authorities could acquiesce in the resulting reduction of yields on government obligations, because the new reserve requirements would accomplish some of the restriction of private demand that now must be achieved by high interest rates. The more the job of restricting private borrowing from financial institutions is done by compelling the institutions to hold larger reserves of government debt, the less the job must be done by higher interest rates.

The principal captive market for government debt at present is, of course,

the reserve requirement imposed on member commercial banks. This requirement makes it possible to place about $20 billion of federal debt, 7 per cent
of the total, as non-interest-bearing demand debt. [3] Within limits set by
Congress, the Federal Reserve can raise or lower required reserve/deposit
ratios. This is one of its instruments of monetary control, but of course the
Federal Reserve has others. The Board always has a choice among several
combinations of instruments all of which would achieve the same impact on
the economy via the banking system. The Federal Reserve could increase
reserve requirements, offsetting the restrictive effects of this action by open
market purchases of government securities. (See section 2.7 above.) Even if
the net result was that market interest rates were maintained, the government
would save interest by converting interest-bearing debt into non-interest-
bearing demand debt. But the Federal Reserve would have to go even farther,
and reduce interest rates, either by additional open market purchases or by
lowering its discount rate, in order to neutralize the increase in reserve
requirements. Unless interest rates on government securities fall, banks will
absorb part of the increase of required reserves by restricting their lending to
private borrowers and making the terms of such loans more severe. The fall in
government debt interest rates not only encourages banks to maintain private
lending relative to defensive holdings of government securities: it also induces
the public to switch from government securities to bank deposits, providing
securities for the Federal Reserve and the banks to buy. The necessary
reduction in yields of government obligations adds to the saving of Treasury
interest costs that can be accomplished by an increase in reserve requirements
neutralized by expansionary manipulation of other monetary controls.

There is an economic limit to this process, probably well beyond the upper
limits on required reserve ratios currently set by Congress. If reserve
requirements of banks are increased enough, banks will be able to maintain
their lending only by dispensing entirely with defensive holdings of government securities. This they would be unwilling to do even if short-term rates
were pushed to zero. After the Federal Reserve has pushed short-term rates to
their lower limit, it no longer has the power to neutralize increases in reserve
requirements. Clearly the banking system is very far from this limit today.

The same argument can show that neutralized reductions of reserve
requirements increase Treasury interest costs on two counts: they replace
zero-interest debt with interest-bearing debt, and they involve an increase in
interest rates on government securities. This has, in fact, been Federal Reserve
policy over the last eight years: reserve requirements have been relaxed when
monetary ease was desired, but subsequent tightening has been accomplished
by open market sales or increases of the discount rate.

Contrary to widely held assumptions of the strategic importance of fractional reserve requirements for monetary control, it would be possible to exercise monetary controls much as at present with zero reserve requirements. It would be possible, but expensive. It would be necessary merely to impose the same periodic reserve tests as at present, with the same penalties for deficiencies, (overdrafts of the Federal Reserve), and the same facilities for borrowing. The government would lose a substantial captive market for its debt, and the Federal Reserve would have to make up for the absence of reserve requirement by a high discount rate and substantial open market sales of government securities. The extreme example will suffice to drive home the point that the Congress and the Federal Reserve, in deciding by what combination of reserve requirements and other instruments to exercise a given degree of monetary restraint, are helping to decide how much the debt costs the Treasury.

In the short run, what the taxpayers lose by such decisions the shareholders of existing commercial banks gain, and vice versa. How true this is in the long run depends on how well competitive mechanisms work in the banking industry. When reserve requirements are lower and interest rates on safe government securities are higher, the marginal dollar of deposits is worth more to the individual bank. Although banks are prevented from competing for deposits by offering interest, imperfect competition for deposits does occur, with ancillary services, promotional expenses, and preferential loan treatment for good depositor-customers taking the place of outright interest rate competition. Thus bank depositor-customers share with bank shareholders the gains of a policy of low reserve requirements neutralized by high interest rates. In the still longer run, higher bank profits may encourage entry into the industry, so that the Treasury's losses are spread among a wider group of shareholders, not concentrated on those of existing banks. Although some observers may find this less objectionable on grounds of equity, encouragement of new enterprises is not to be welcomed on grounds of efficiency in an industry which already seems to exhibit the wastes of monopolistic competition.

One obvious way to save the Treasury money, then, is to increase the required ratios of reserves, as presently defined, to commercial bank deposits. Under present legislation, the Federal Reserve has discretion to increase required reserves on the present volume of demand and time deposits by $5.7 billion, 2 per cent of the outstanding federal debt. [4] Further increases would depend on new legislation.

Additional reserve requirements on commercial banks do not have to take the same form as present requirements. Congress could authorize the Federal

Reserve to impose a secondary requirement, for which not only primary reserve assets but also holdings of specified interest-bearing Treasury obligations would be eligible. The form of the requirement might be, for example, that total holdings of eligible assets must average 30 per cent of average deposits of all kinds over the reserve test period, while at the same time holdings of reserve balances and currency must meet the usual primary reserve requirements on demand and time deposits. This kind of required "liquid asset" ratio occurs in banking systems abroad, including England and Canada. If additional reserve requirements on banks take this form, the Treasury sacrifices the first of the two sources of economy of interest payments discussed above. The secondary requirement does not enlarge the captive market for interest-free demand debt. But the other source of interest saving remains. The supplementary requirement permits the Federal Reserve to let interest rates on government obligations fall, without diluting the restrictive impact of monetary policy. These interest rates would tend to fall of their own accord, as banks sought securities to meet the new requirement.

One of the greatest fallacies in discussions of proposals of this kind is the assertion that they will expand the banks' demand for the eligible assets only to the extent, if any, that the imposed requirement exceeds the voluntary practice of the banks. It is alleged, therefore, that if banks now find it prudent to carry 30 per cent of their deposits as liquid assets, a compulsory 30 per cent requirement would not affect bank portfolios but would merely formalize prevailing secondary reserve practices. This position is based on a misunderstanding of the role of voluntary secondary reserves. Banks hold certain quantities of excess reserves or of other assets which – from the point of view of a single bank – can be quickly and safely converted into primary reserves, in order to be able to pass the *present* primary reserve tests. In case of unusual losses of deposits or demands of good customers for loans, they wish to be able to meet their reserve requirements without cost or loss or embarrassment. It is true that assets held to meet a compulsory secondary reserve requirement will still be available, as at present, to meet the primary cash requirement. But banks will also have to worry about meeting the overall 30 per cent liquid asset requirement. The same contingencies – loss of deposits or extraordinary loan demands – would put them in danger of failing this test. To guard against this danger, they will have to hold additional voluntary secondary reserves, on top of the compulsory secondary reserves.

A simple numerical example will illustrate the point. Consider a bank subject to a 10 per cent primary reserve requirement which, in the absence of any secondary requirement, finds it prudent to hold secondary reserves of 15 per cent. The bank is protected against a 20 per cent (15/75) increase in demands upon it for illiquid loans at its present volume of deposits, or against a 16.7 per cent loss of deposits without the necessity for curtailing its lending (of the 16 2/3, 15 is covered by liquidation of secondary reserve and 1 2/3 by reduction of required reserves.) Suppose that the bank is now subjected to a 25 per cent overall liquid asset requirement. To retain the same protection as before, the bank would need an additional 12.5 per cent voluntary holding of secondary reserves. This would take care of a 20 per cent (12.5/62.5) increase in lending requirements or a 16.7 per cent decline in deposits (of the 16 2/3, 12 1/2 is covered by liquidation of the voluntary secondary reserve and 4 1/6 by reduction of overall required reserves). However, banks would in all likelihood be content with a somewhat weaker defensive position than before. Defensive assets would fall in yield relative to bank loans; as a result, banks would be content with somewhat less protection. To continue the simple numerical example, the loan/deposit ratio might fall only to 67.5 per cent instead of to 62.5 per cent; the bank has a defensive position of 7.5 per cent of deposits instead of 15 per cent. It would be protected against an 11 per cent (7.5/67.5) increase in loans or a 10 per cent loss of deposits (by 7.5 excess reserves and 2.5 reduction of reserve requirements).

A by-product of the reduction on government security yields that would result from imposition of additional reserve requirements on banks would be substitution by the public of bank deposits for government securities. Indeed only by inducing such substitution could the banking system as a whole obtain the assets necessary to meet the new requirements, with the same margin of safety as before. The resulting expansion of bank deposits and the money supply would be an innocuous one, for which the central bank could safely provide the cash reserves. It would not signify an expansion of bank lending or an easing of terms to private borrowers. Without an increase in bank deposits, in fact, bank credit would contract and tighten. (In the numerical example above, the representative bank changes from a 75 per cent loan/deposit ratio to a 67.5 per cent loan/deposit ratio. If this change in ratio is to leave the absolute volume of bank lending unchanged, deposits must increase by 11 per cent. If banks started out with liquid assets equal to 25 per cent of initial deposits, public substitution of deposits for direct holdings of government securities enough to increase deposits 11 per cent would give the banks reserve asset holdings of 32.5 per cent of their new volume of deposits [36/111]. To enable banks to meet the cash requirement against the new deposits, the Federal Reserve would absorb 1/10 of the securities surrendered by the public.)

This expansion of bank deposits should not be forgotten in calculating the impact of additional required reserves on bank profits. As a first approximation to neutralizing a new requirement, the Federal Reserve can permit the volume of bank lending and the terms of bank credit to private borrowers to remain unchanged. This means that the only change in the portfolio earnings of the banking system would be on account of bank holdings of government debt. These, in turn, can be divided into two categories; required reserves, and voluntary secondary reserves. Voluntary secondary reserve earnings will be smaller; for reasons given above, the yields of these assets will be lower and banks' holdings of excess secondary reserves smaller.

If the increase of reserve requirements takes the form of a simple increase in the required ratio of primary zero-interest reserves to deposits, earnings on required reserves are zero both before and after the change. Bank earnings as a whole unambiguously fall. The Treasury saves money partly on this account, and partly at the expense of the nonbank public. The public is induced by lower yields on government securities to substitute indirect holdings, via bank deposits at zero interest, for direct holdings; and the public receives lower yields on the direct holdings it retains.

If, however, the additional reserve requirements can be met by marketable interest-bearing government securities, the upshot for bank earnings is not so clear. Here there is an increase in earnings on the required reserve portion of banks' portfolios, which now consist of a primary reserve earning no interest and a secondary reserve earning interest. Conceivably this might do more than offset the decline in earnings on voluntary secondary reserves. In the numerical example above, reserve assets on which interest is earned (required and voluntary secondary reserves) increase from 15 to 25 (in per cent of initial deposit level). If the yields of such assets fall less than 40 per cent, the banks gain from the new requirement. The loss to the nonbank public is the same no matter what form the new requirement on the banks takes. To the extent that the government permits the banks to earn interest on reserves, the Treasury shares with the banks what can be gained from the public.

Reference to "losses" by the nonbank public does not mean, of course, that holders of unmatured government securities at the time the new reserve requirement is imposed will lose. They will in fact enjoy capital gains. The loss of the nonbank public, and the corresponding saving to the Treasury, is that as issues mature their holders will be able to replace them only at lower yields.

Commercial banks are not the only possible captive market for government securities. Congress might authorize the Federal Reserve to impose new reserve requirements, or increase existing ones, on the other financial intermediaries — life insurance companies, pension funds, savings and loan associations, mutual savings banks. Analysis of the consequences of such requirements is much the same as in the case of commercial banks, and gives much the same results. Yields on government securities eligible for the requirements, and others closely substitutable for them, will tend to fall. The monetary authorities can permit them to fall without loosening the bite of monetary control. The Treasury will save interest payments, certainly at the expense of its ultimate creditors, and possibly also at the expense of the intermediary institutions.

There is one important difference, however, between banks and other intermediaries. Banks do not, except in indirect and imperfect ways, compete for deposits by offering interest. The other intermediaries compete for their creditors' funds via the interest or dividends they offer. The equilibrium of an intermediary industry or category other than banks is one in which the interest or dividend offered to creditors is adjusted to the additional earnings an enterprise in the industry can obtain by investing an extra dollar of funds. The word "adjusted" is used deliberately in place of "equated," for these are not perfectly competitive industries, but ones in which each of the competing firms has distinctive appeal to certain savers and special opportunities for lending to a particular market of borrowers. This equilibrium condition does not apply in the case of banks. In that industry the total volume of assets and liabilities is controlled by adjusting the earnings from an additional dollar of loans not to the cost of an additional dollar of deposits, but to the cost and risk of holding a dollar less of net reserves.

If a reserve requirement, to be met by holdings of government securities. is imposed on a nonbank financial intermediary, the investment value of the marginal dollar of its liabilities is reduced. Consequently these institutions will seek to meet the requirement partly by selling their private investments and curtailing their private loans, substituting government securities, and partly by lowering the inducements they offer their creditors, thereby contracting their liabilities. The public shifts out of government securities and out of the liabilities of intermediaries. Into what? Partly into the private securities and loans the intermediaries get rid of, or into the capital equities those debts were financing. Partly, perhaps principally, into bank deposits. The authorities can – and indeed must, if they are going to neutralize the effects of the new controls and on balance keep private loan rates and the supply price of capital from rising – countenance this expansion of bank deposits and permit banks to fill the gap created by contraction of the lending of intermediaries. The banks and the Treasury gain, and the newly regulated intermediaries and their creditors lose. Borrowers specifically adjusted to the intermediaries lose, and borrowers in a position to profit from cheaper bank credit gain.

Clearly there is a ticklish question of equity involved in the present special treatment of banks, and no judgment on it will be essayed here. Competing financial intermediaries are not subject to the reserve requirements now imposed on banks. On the other hand, neither do they have the advantage of a government enforced covenant to avoid price competition for funds. When banks chafe under the bit of the interest-barren reserves they are compelled to hold, they are inclined to forget the advantages of having industry equilibrium maintained where marginal asset earnings considerably exceed the interest paid on deposits. Banks would have a better case for asking that the burden of reserve requirements be spread more widely if they were willing at the same time to restore competitive determination of interest on demand and time deposits.

Economy to the Treasury and equity to banks are not the only possible reasons for advocating reserve requirements for other financial intermediaries. Another reason is to strengthen the effectiveness of monetary control and to make its impact more immediately felt. The unregulated activities of other financial intermediaries provide the economy a partial escape from central bank control measures. When the availability of bank credit is restricted, borrowers denied credit or discouraged by stiffer terms can turn to other intermediaries for accommodation. At the same time the intermediaries can attract additional funds – which in the absence of restrictive measures would take the form of bank deposits – without more than a slight sweetening of the terms offered their creditors. Private loan rates and the supply price of capital rise less, in response to a given restrictive action by the monetary authority, than if nonbank intermediaries were prevented from expanding. This does not mean that the existence of these intermediaries makes monetary policy impotent. But it does mean that central bank action must be more drastic – e.g., a larger volume of open market sales – in order to achieve a given effect, and that the lag between action and effect is longer. If nonbank intermediaries were subject to a security reserve requirement, any central bank action raising government security yields would tend to make them contract like banks. For one thing, the increase in yields might induce the intermediaries themselves to hold more excess reserves. More important, the increase in yields may cause the public to substitute direct ownership of government securities for holdings of intermediary liabilities. A dollar of such substitution means a multiple contraction in intermediary private lending. Unlike commercial banks, other intermediaries can counter this threat to their reserves by offering higher yields on their own liabilities. [5] But this increase in the cost of funds will be reflected in harsher terms to private borrowers, and thus in a rise in the supply price of capital. Credit would be tighter, and the volume of lending smaller, at both banks and other intermediaries. The actions of the nonbank intermediaries would support rather than oppose the objectives of the central bank.

Is enlargement of the captive market for government securities to be abhorred as a violation of the principles of a free economy? Much official and private opposition to proposals for supplementary reserve requirements, either on banks or on other financial intermediaries, is expressly based on high ideological grounds. Interest rates, it is said, including those at which the government borrows, should be set in the free market, not by government fiat. The government should not rig the capital market in its own favor, discriminating against other claimants on the people's savings.

These expressions of ideological principle will not withstand careful analysis. Interest rates are already under government control. The market that determines them does so under the watchful eyes of the monetary authorities, and in an environment of their making. If the Federal Reserve and Treasury do not like the market's results they can and do intervene to change them. Without such interventions, the prospects of monetary stabilization would be very dim. There already exists a substantial captive market for government debt, indeed for zero-interest demand debt. Ideological consistency would require abolition of commercial bank reserve requirements. Matters of degree are poor material for invocation of "the basic principles of a free economy." There is no escape from the necessity to judge proposals for extension of reserve requirements on the more pragmatic grounds of the efficiency of stabilization policy, administrative possibility and inconvenience. and equity to various institutions, savers, borrowers, and taxpayers.

The kernel of truth in the ideological objections is that Congress and the President should to some extent be guided, in their decisions as to the scope of government investment programs and other public uses of resources, by the productivity of capital and other resources in the private sector of the economy. If a high interest rate on government securities is a signal that saving is in heavy demand for highly productive private investment projects, it is right that Congress and the President should be deterred from further borrowing and indeed encouraged to run a surplus. Similarly, a low interest rate on government securities, indicative that saving is not in great demand for private expansion of capital, should encourage the federal government to borrow for public investment. The signal, and the deterrent or incentive, provided by fluctuating interest rates on government securities should not be destroyed. Nor would they be. Extension of reserve requirements would mean a general lowering of the average over time of, interest rates on government debt, but not a stabilization of rates. The rates would fluctuate as now, but around a lower mean. The timing signal that these fluctuations send to the government would not be lost. It is *not* proposed to vary reserve requirements in a countercyclical way so that monetary control could be exercised without variation of interest rates on government debt. The signal given by *changes* in rates would be retained, and more than that cannot be expected. The absolute level of interest rate on government debt is very far from measuring the opportunity cost of capital. The social productivity of private investment is not the same as its private productivity, and the latter is related to a government bond yield only through a complicated and variable system of risk premiums. The social productivity of public expenditure is even more difficult to quantify. The accounting procedures of the government are irrational; they probably work to restrict public investment unduly, since they force the Treasury to count the complete cost of highly durable assets as current expense. The fiscal balance of the government is necessarily the result of a complex of policy considerations and objectives. In its decisions on fiscal policy the central government should be above the economic deterrents and incentives that operate on other economic units. For all these reasons, the importance to the allocative efficiency of government investment decisions of the level of interest rates on government securities is quite small. It is, in any case, not a significant objection to new reserve requirements.

3.3. Management of the Maturity Structure of Debt

3.3.1. The Criterion

The narrower problem of debt management is to arrange the maturity composition of the debt so as to obtain a given economic impact at minimal cost to the Treasury, without any change in reserve requirements, or in types of debt instruments.

A useful simplification, which still retains the essentials of the problem, is to consider only three categories of debt: Demand Debt, bearing zero interest rate; Short Debt, yielding r_s; and Long Debt, yielding r_l. Denote the Federal Reserve Discount rate by r_d. The following are important identities:

(1) Total Debt, a Constant = Demand Debt + Short Debt + Long Debt

(2) Net Cost = $(0 \times$ Demand Debt$) - (r_d \times$ Borrowed Reserves$) + (r_s \times$ Short Debt$) + (r_l \times$ Long Debt$)$

(3) Demand Debt = Currency Outside Banks + Required Reserves + Excess Reserves − Borrowed Reserves

(There is a certain asymmetry here, in that the discount rate is charged on Borrowed Reserves but not paid to banks on Excess Reserves.) The authorities have three instruments of control: fixing the magnitudes of any two of the three categories of debt, and setting the discount rate.

Which authorities? It is evident from the statement of the problem that debt management is not a task that is divisible into two provinces, monetary control on the one hand and management of the interest-bearing debt on the other. The problem is a unit, and it is anomalous to attempt, as we do in the United States, to split it into two administrative packages. The current division of labor and responsibility appears to assign to the Federal Reserve the fixing of the quantity of demand debt and of the discount rate, and to the Treasury determination of the amount of long debt. [6] Unless there is coordination and agreement between the two agencies, this division of the task cannot produce optimal, or even satisfactory results. Even if the two agencies concur in their diagnoses of current money and capital markets and business trends, and in their objectives, neither can make an intelligent use of the control instruments at its disposal without knowing what the other is doing. In analyzing the problem of debt management, we should not be imprisoned by current administrative arrangements or by conventional and artificial distinctions between monetary policy and debt management. It is best to attack the problem as a whole, as if there were a unified or coordinated authority to make and execute the three decisions. Some administrative recommendations consistent with the economics of the problem will be offered below.

Imagine the three decisions to be made for a certain planning period, the next quarter or the next year. What is the cost which the authorities should seek to minimize over that period, subject to the fulfillment of their responsibility for economic stabilization? The relevant cost — the cost to the government of owing its debt over the planning period — may be expressed as

(4) Net Cost = Net Interest Outlays + Increase in Market Value of the Debt.

In other words, the cost to the government of owing the debt over the period is simply the negative of the gains to the public of owning the debt. Under this concept, what the creditors gain, the debtors lose, and vice versa.

Now why should the government concern itself with changes in the market value of its obligations, when they involve no actual outlays of cash? Suppose that market interest rates on long-term bonds are expected to fall over the period ahead from 4 per cent to 3 per cent. This expectation should, other things equal, deter the Treasury from new long-term borrowing — better to wait for the lower interest rate. In effect, the rate on new long-term borrowing over the period is more than 4 per cent. It is 4 per cent plus the capital gain associated with a fall in the rate to 3 per cent; this gain depends on the exact maturity and coupon of the bonds — say the effective rate is 4 1/2 per cent. If the authorities can borrow the funds short for less than 4 1/2 per cent, even for 4 1/4 per cent, without compromising their stabilization responsibilities, they should do so. But if the attention of the authorities were confined to interest outlays, they would regard 4 per cent on the new long-term borrowing as quite satisfactory. Including changes in market value of the debt in the criterion is the way to make the authorities pay proper attention to the timing of long-term borrowing.

But that is not all. If the expectation of a fall in long-term market yield from 4 per cent to 3 per cent were sufficient to deter the Treasury from issuing new long-term debt, it should also be a signal to the government to purchase outstanding long-term bonds from the public, selling the appropriate neutral quantity of shorts to replace them. From the taxpayer's point of view, it is better for the Federal Reserve to enjoy the capital gains on longs than for the public to receive them.

The definition of *Net Cost* in (4) is the same as in (2), provided that the yields r_s and r_l are correctly defined. The yield r_l on a long bond during a period is the interest accrual to which ownership of the bond entitles the holder plus the appreciation of the value of the bond over the period, expressed as per cent of the initial market value of the bond, and converted to a *per annum* basis. This is the 4 1/2 per cent rate in the example above. This — rather than coupon yield on face value or coupon yield on market value — is the relevant rate an investor considers. It is also the relevant rate for the borrower, even the government. A similar definition applies for short rates. However, here the simplification has been made that there is only one short security, and its maturity will be assumed not to exceed the planning period. Thus the government does not have to worry about capital gains and losses on its short obligations. In practice, of course, the distinction of long and short, in this as in other regards, is not so sharp. If the authorities minimize (2), with the rates thus defined, they will also minimize (4).

Another illustration will make clear the importance of attention to market yields rather than simply to coupons. Suppose 20-year 2 1/2's with ten years to run are available at prices below par in the market, yielding their holders 4 1/2 per cent. Suppose that, as in the previous example, 4 1/2 per cent is too high a rate, considering prevailing short-term rates, at which to issue a new 10-year bond. Then by the same token it is to the government's advantage to buy back the old bonds now at 84 rather than ten years from now at 100. This saving overshadows the economy of the 2 1/2 per cent coupon.

The government does not, of course, borrow in a perfect market. As the government makes security transactions, it turns the market against itself. Government purchases of longs and sale of shorts to replace them will cause the long rate to fall and the short rate to rise. The rate differential that made the switch advantageous to the government will tend to vanish as the authorities exploit it. This does not mean that it is fruitless to take advantage of favorable opportunities. They should be exploited until they are exhausted, and no farther. It does mean that pursuit of the suggested criterion (4) involves less drastic and frequent reshuffling of the debt structure than might at first appear.

Even so, the minimization objective is not to be regarded as something to be precisely and continuously achieved. It indicates the direction in which adjustments of the debt structure should be sought. The authorities may well wish to sacrifice some apparent economy of interest cost in order to avoid too frequent and drastic interventions in the market. Nevertheless, present administrative arrangements probably keep the debt structure too rigid and too unresponsive to the requirements of debt management.

One component of the relevant long-term yield is observable in the market, the other, the capital gain or loss, will be known for certain only after the event. The authorities are in a somewhat better position than the public to guess at it, but their best guess is subject to considerable uncertainty. So also is the response of the yield to the government's own operations. What effect should this uncertainty have on the government's behavior? The answer is, None. The government should act on the basis of the statistical expectations of the values of the uncertain variables, ignoring the degree of uncertainty. If anyone is in the position to be his own insurer, clearly it is the Secretary of the Treasury. It would be inappropriate for him to pay the public in order to avoid risks. Indeed, the contrary should be the case. The government should gain for the taxpayer the amounts that owners of the debt will pay, through sacrifices of yields, in order to reduce private risks.

When the appropriate yields are considered, and when the maturity structure of the debt is sufficiently flexible, the authorities can make their decisions for the period immediately ahead without considering more distant periods. Suppose, for example, that the long-term rate is now 3 per cent, is expected to rise to 4 per cent next period, and then after several more periods to fall to 2 per cent. Assume an alternative short-term financing cost of 4 per cent. Should the government wait until the long-term rate reaches 2 per cent before borrowing long? In the period immediately ahead, the government should borrow long provided a rate in the neighborhood of 2 1/2 per cent (3 per cent less the expected capital loss) is highly satisfactory in the light of the prevailing short rate. At the time when the fall from 4 per cent to 2 per cent is expected, the long-term yield will be higher than 4 per cent, and the authorities should seek to replace longs with shorts temporarily, borrowing long again to take advantage of the 2 per cent rate. Applying the criterion successively in each period leads to the correct long-run strategy. It fails to do so only when the authorities attribute some cost to going in and out of the market. In that case, they may prefer to reduce the number of transactions by waiting until the rate reaches 2 per cent, even though waiting adds to the government's interest costs.

Are the interest rates that determine how expensive the debt is to the government the same interest rates that determine the monetary impact of the debt on the economy? This is the assumption of the argument concerning optimal debt management. The yields relevant to the government, it was argued above, are market yields corrected for expectation of capital gain or loss. Thus if the long-term interest rate is expected to rise, the relevant long yield is smaller than the prevailing market yield. This is as true for the managers of private portfolios and balance sheets as it is for the Treasury's debt managers. The attractiveness of long bonds, relative to other investments, is clearly lessened by expectation of capital loss and enhanced by anticipation of capital gain. The market yield must be thus corrected, whether bonds are being compared in investment worth with cash and short-term securities or with physical capital.

Discussions of monetary theory and policy contain some confusion on this point. Although it is generally assumed, following Keynes, that expectations of capital gain or loss on bonds influences the demand for bonds relative to more liquid alternatives, it seems also to be generally assumed, again following Keynes, that the market yield of bonds *un*corrected for such expectations is the "interest rate" against which "the marginal efficiency of capital" must be tested. But if capital losses are expected on bonds, is this not as good reason to prefer equities as to prefer cash? Is not a private borrower encouraged to borrow long for investment purposes when long-term interest rates are temporarily low? If this principle is symmetrically and consistently applied. it appears that long-term rates are by no means as sticky over the trade cycle as they appear to be. Relevant long rates fluctuate a good deal more than observed market rates. At the bottom of recession, long-term rates are lower than they seem, because market yields are expected to rise. In high prosperity long-term rates are higher than they seem because market yields are expected to fall. On the other hand, in incipient recession apparent reductions in the long-term rate may be nullified by expectations of further declines in market yields. The effective rate contains allowance for capital gains and is still high. Similarly if a rise in rates generates expectations of a further rise, the relevant interest rate may not have increased at all. The authorities will do better, for this reason, to move with decisively large steps rather than to feel their way in gradual and small moves that lead the public to expect further steps in the same direction.

Generally speaking, then, the same concept of the interest rate is relevant both for governmental decision and for private decision. But of course expectations are not concrete and observable, like market yields. The government may not agree with the "market." Indeed the participants in the market do not agree with each other, and most of them are uncertain of their own best guesses. Moreover, private investors and borrowers may differ widely from each other, and from the government, in the length and timing of investment planning periods. It is these uncertainties and differences of opinion and circumstance that prevent widely held expectations from realizing themselves immediately.

The government must take into account its disagreements with the market. Cost depends on the government's view, provided of course it is the government experts who are right. Monetary restraint depends on the market's view. Suppose, for example, the market decides that long-term interest rates are going to rise, while the government does not think so. This means that the government can no longer purchase the same degree of monetary restraint at the same expected cost. To offset the expansionary effect of the market's anticipations, the authorities will have to take restrictive measures. In other instances divergence of public expectations from government predictions may enable the government to purchase the required degree of restraint more cheaply. To some degree market expectations are self-fulfilling, because the actions the authorities have to take to offset their monetary effects tend to move interest rates in the direction the market expects.

3.3.2. Administration

If the expected long rate r_l is too high, the amount of long debt should be reduced. How can this be done? The mere passage of time is constantly transferring some debt from the long category to the short. But this reduction of the long portion of the debt may at times be much too small for optimal debt management. Refundings at maturity, of course, can never reduce the quantity of long debt. At the time of refunding, maturing issues are by definition short. The only way to effect a significant reduction in long debt in the short run is for the government to buy back its own long securities, or refund them in advance with short debt. The obvious instrument for such purchases is the Federal Reserve Open Market Committee. It would have to undertake open market operations in the interests of Treasury costs as well as in the interests of stabilization. In the present example, open market purchases of longs would be compensated, for stabilization purposes, by open market sales of shorts, very likely in an amount exceeding the purchases. At other times, the appropriate long rate may signal that the amount of long debt should be increased. This is easier for the Treasury to do, simply by issuing longs in place of maturing shorts. The Federal Reserve can move easily in either direction.

The cleanest administrative solution, if the problem of debt management is to be taken seriously, is to concentrate all security dealings with the public in a single agency, responsible for issue of new securities to the public, redemption of maturing issues, and purchases and sales of old securities. Refundings and new issues would be integrated with open market operations. The agency would be in complete command of the maturity distribution of the debt at all times. Its mandate would be to minimize long-run interest costs to the government, i.e., to minimize Net Cost as defined above, subject to the achievement of the stabilization (and balance of payments) objectives that are the task of monetary control. With its mandate thus broadened, the Federal Reserve would be the logical repository of this responsibility. The arrangement would have many incidental advantages, among them providing the government with an underwriting service that, alone among major borrowers, it now lacks through a perverse sense of self-denial.

Under the proposed arrangement, increases in debt to meet fiscal deficit would be accomplished in the first instance by replenishing the Treasury's cash balance in Federal Reserve Banks. The Federal Reserve would receive in return Treasury securities, with maturities and other terms designed to Federal Reserve specifications. The Federal Reserve would sell these or other securities from its portfolio to the public in amounts and at times of its own discretion, in pursuit of its joint mission of debt management and stabilization. Similarly, when budget surplus augments the Treasury balance, the Treasury may use the excess over its working balance to reclaim some securities from the Federal Reserve stock.

3.3.3. Discount Policy

Federal Reserve discount rate policy is a purely monetary matter, if anything is. But since the discount rate affects both the net costs of government debt and the degree of monetary restraint upon the economy, its level is a part of the problem of debt management. To considerable degree, moreover, it can be considered separately from the problem of optimal proportions of shorts and longs.

The Federal Reserve generally has a choice between maintaining a given degree of monetary restraint by (a) a low discount rate, a low volume of demand debt, negative net free reserves, with bank borrowing at the discount window encouraged by a favorable differential between yields on government securities and the discount rate, or (b) a high discount rate, a high volume of demand debt, positive net free reserves, with bank borrowing discouraged by an unprofitable differential between market yields on bills and other securities and the discount rate. Of course there are many more than two alternatives. The two contrasting possibilities are stated in order to dramatize the decision problem involved. In other words, it is generally possible to preserve the existing levels of deposits and bank loans either by lowering the discount rate and simultaneously making open market sales, or by raising the discount rate and simultaneously making open market purchases. There are limits to these possibilities, at both ends, as described in section 2.9.

What is the optimal combination of discount policy and open market operations? It is evidently of type (b), close to the second of the two extremes just outlined. The reasoning is as follows: Starting from some arbitrary combination of discount rate and demand debt, consider the change in net cost due to a dollar of open market purchases neutralized by an increase in the discount rate. The dollar of open market purchases will save the government r_s, the rate on short-term securities, which is to remain unchanged. On the other hand borrowed reserves will be reduced, but by less than a dollar. Net free reserves will be increased by a dollar, but a part of this increase will be in excess reserves, and only a fraction, say k, in reduction of debt. When the discount rate is higher, some banks, even some which rarely if ever borrow, will hold more excess reserves in order to diminish the probability that they will need to borrow in case of loss of deposits or heavy demand for customer loans. Let δr_d be the increase in discount rate necessary to bring about a reduction of k in borrowed reserves accompanied by an increase in $1 - k$ excess reserves. The increase in revenue of the Federal Reserve is $\delta r_d (B - k) - r_d k$ where B is the original volume of borrowing. In order for the change to be worthwhile, the total saving must be positive:

$$r_s + \delta r_d B - (r_d + \delta r_d) k > 0$$

Clearly changes in this direction are profitable so long as the discount rate is lower than r_s/k, and even longer if allowance is made for some residual bank borrowing (B), inelastic to interest differential, on which the Federal Reserve can profit.

As in the case of reserve requirement policy, the optimal policy for the government is to convert as much debt into non-interest-bearing demand debt as the Federal Reserve can neutralize. Here the instrument of neutralization is a high discount rate, which has the incidental advantage of bringing in more revenue from insensitive borrowers. If this kind of policy is followed, the Federal Reserve will keep the discount rate *above* market short-term rates, and keep the banking system operating with positive net free reserves. The more the banks can be induced to carry as defensive assets non-interest-bearing government debt rather than interest-bearing debt, the cheaper it is for the government.

3.3.4. Optimal Debt Composition

The strategy for determining the optimal proportions of shorts and longs can be described in general and formal terms. But it is not so easy to derive concrete conclusions concerning the optimal structure of maturities or of interest rates. Concrete conclusions depend on empirical estimates of the behavior relationships involved.

Suppose that a given degree of monetary restraint is to be maintained. Starting from an arbitrary composition of debt that accomplishes this task, consider an addition of $1 billion to Short Debt. Between them, Demand Debt and Long Debt must be diminished by $1 billion. How must this reduction be divided between these two categories? To concentrate the entire reduction on Demand Debt would certainly be deflationary, and to concentrate it all on Long Debt would generally be inflationary. To neutralize the addition to Short Debt, a fraction of it must replace Demand Debt and the remainder Long Debt. The fraction is a variable one, dependent on many circumstances. Among other things, it depends on the initial proportions of Short and Long Debt. Suppose Short Debt is already abundant relative to Demand Debt and Long Debt. To increase Short Debt further will not be giving the public a very good substitute for cash, and substitution of Short Debt for Long will not be very expansionary. Therefore the fraction of Demand Debt replaced by Short Debt must be small if deflation is to be avoided. But if Short Debt is relatively scarce to begin with, its expansion will have to be offset mainly by reduction of Demand Debt, and only to a small extent by reduction of Long Debt.

Chart Figure 21.1 shows combinations of Short Debt (horizontal axis) and Long Debt (vertical axis) that produce a given degree of monetary tightness. i.e., a given supply price of capital. The combinations lie along the curve L_1S_1. The curve applies, of course, only for a given total debt T_1, shown on both axes. The sum $L + S$, implied by the curve L_1S_1 is shown as the vertical

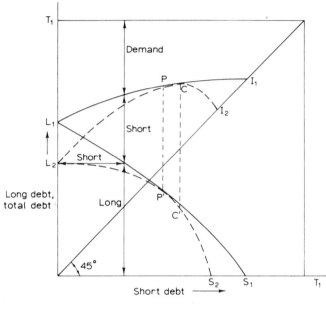

Fig. 21.1

distance below the curve $L_1 I_1$. This is the total interest-bearing debt, and the vertical difference between it and T_1 is the amount of Demand Debt. As the chart shows, Demand Debt and Long Debt increase together, as the amount of Short Debt is reduced. A greater degree of monetary restraint, i.e., a higher supply price of capital, would be indicated by a curve of the same general shape as $L_1 S_1$ but above and to the right. Corresponding to each point on $L_1 S_1$ are the interest rates, short and long, required to induce the public, including the banks, to hold the indicated quantities of Short and Long Debt. At L_1 the long rate is high relative to the short rate; this differential declines as the quantity of Short Debt is increased, towards S_1. As the differential between the two rates declines, their general level increases, reflecting the fall in the quantity of Demand Debt.

In similar manner, loci of constant cost to the government can be constructed, without regard for the degree of monetary restraint. $L_2 S_2$ is an example of such a locus. All combinations of Short and Long Debt on this curve represent the same cost to the government; they do not all, of course, represent the same degree of monetary restraint. The total interest-bearing debt corresponding to $L_2 S_2$ is shown as $L_2 I_2$. The assumption made in the chart is that more interest-bearing debt can be placed in the hands of the banks and the public at given cost when it is a mixture of Short and Long Debt than when it is concentrated heavily in either category. Some investors and institutions have special needs for longs, and other have special needs for shorts. It is economical for the government to cater to these special needs. Otherwise the government will have to pay the holders of its debt to take securities less well-tailored to their needs and preferences, or attract other holders by higher yields. The maximum interest-bearing debt that can be placed at the cost represented by L_2S_2 is at point C, with a distribution between Short and Long as indicated by point C'. But C and C' do not accomplish the degree of monetary restriction represented by L_1S_1. As the chart is drawn, that is the maximum degree of monetary restraint that can be purchased at the cost corresponding to L_1S_1. It can be purchased by a total interest-bearing debt of P, somewhat smaller than C, divided between Short and Long as indicated by P', with less Short and more Long than at C'.

The two kinds of loci — constant monetary restraint, and constant interest cost — are not independent of each other. The same asset preferences and interest rate sensitivities that determine the shape of one determine the shape of the other. This may be illustrated by some examples of extreme assumptions about asset preferences, some of which are the foundation, implicit or explicit, for current views about monetary policy and debt management.

a. One extreme view is that only the quantity of demand debt matters, whatever may be the distribution of interest-bearing debt as between Short and Long. The locus of constant restraint L_1S_1 is then a line with unit slope, and the corresponding curve of total interest-bearing debt L_1I_1 is horizontal. The rate changes necessary to induce substitution of a dollar of Short Debt for a dollar of Long would, on this view, have no net effect on the willingness of the community to hold capital at a given yield. To put the same point another way, it is the quantity of cash provided or absorbed in open market operations that matters, not what is bought or sold. This will be recognized as the core of "bills only" doctrine: Bank reserves can be controlled as well by buying and selling bills as by dealing in other securities. and there are various technical advantages to confining operations to bills. Buying a dollar of Shorts and selling a dollar of Longs will affect to some degree the Short-Long rate differential, but that is all it will affect. On this view, once the requisite amount of Demand Debt is provided, the task is simply to find the cheapest way to place the remainder of the Debt at interest. Point C coincides with P, in the chart, and point C' with P'. See Figure 21.2(a).

This is a consistent point of view, although its assumptions about the behavior of banks and other investors seem implausible. What is not

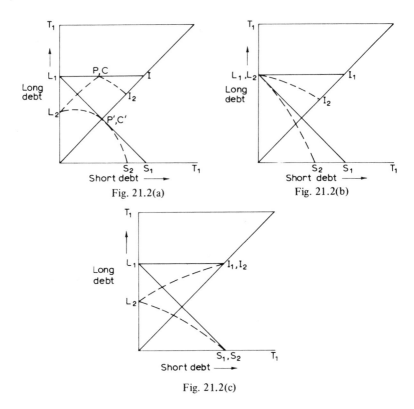

Fig. 21.2(a)

Fig. 21.2(b)

Fig. 21.2(c)

consistent is to couple "bills only" with stress on the urgency of lengthening the interest-bearing debt. If "bills only" is correct then the Treasury can safely turn its attention to minimizing the cost of placing at interest the quantity of debt which the Federal Reserve does not monetize. If this requires substitution of $100 million of "more liquid" Shorts for $100 million of "less liquid" Longs, the authorities can rest secure in the knowledge that the increase in the short rate necessary to induce the substitution will automatically render the Shorts as inocuous and as firmly held as the Longs they replace. Neither is it consistent to berate at the same time the Treasury for wishing to lengthen the debt and the Federal Reserve for its adherence to "bills only." If the Treasury should stick to the job of minimizing the cost of the interest-bearing debt, if it is indeed safe to ignore stabilization consequences of changing the maturity structure of the debt, it must be because the Federal Reserve can do what is needed for stabilization just by fixing the amount of demand debt.

A variant of this view has it that Short and Long securities are perfect substitutes for each other. Again, the degree of monetary restraint depends on the total quantity of a given debt represented by Short Debt and Long Debt combined, not on the split between them. But in addition, the interest rates on the two kinds of securities do not depend on their relative supplies. Whether the differential of longs over shorts is positive, zero, or negative may depend on the economic circumstances at the time. But it is not to be affected by changing the relative amounts of the two categories of debt. This may be referred to as the "arbitrage" variant of "bills only" doctrine. Although open market operations take place in shorts and affect the short rate in the first instance, arbitrage quickly spreads the effect throughout the range in maturities, restoring the appropriate structure of rates. In diagrammatic terms, the isocost curve is a straight line. In Figure 21.2(b) the long rate is lower, and optimal debt management would place the entire interest-bearing debt in longs. In Figure 21.2(c), the opposite is the case. If the appropriate structure of rates happens to be equality, then the maturity distribution of the debt does not matter.

b. Another common extreme view is associated with the tradition of aggregative economic theory, strongly reinforced by Keynes, that long-term government debt and private capital ownership are perfect substitutes for each other. "The marginal efficiency of capital must equal the rate of interest." (Some misleading implications of this tradition have been discussed elsewhere in this chapter.) Here this means that along a locus of constant monetary restraint the long rate is constant, in the appropriate relation to the constant supply price of capital. At these constant rates, the more Long Debt the community is asked to absorb, the lower must be the yield on Short Debt, and the greater the volume of Demand Debt. An interesting implication of this view is that optimal debt management requires a short rate below the long rate. This may be shown as follows: The cost of adding a dollar of Long Debt, while maintaining the degree of monetary restraint, is

$$r_l + S \frac{\delta r_s}{\delta L} + r_s \frac{\delta S}{\delta L}$$

where S is the quantity of Short Debt, L the quantity of Long Debt, r_l the constant long rate, and r_s the short rate. Long Debt should not be increased, but decreased if this cost is positive, i.e., if

$$r_l > r_s \left(-\frac{\delta S}{\delta L} \right) + S \left(-\frac{\delta r_s}{\delta L} \right)$$

Long Debt should be increased if the inequality is the other way. Now both derivatives are negative, and $\delta S/\delta L$ exceeds one in absolute value. Thus if the short rate is as high as the long rate, or higher, the quantity of Long Debt is insufficient. In interpreting this result, it is important to remember the definitions of yields relevant to the debt management problem. They include a correction of market yields for expected capital gains or losses due to interest rate changes.

    c. A third possible simple and extreme view is, in a sense, the opposite of the first. It is that Short Debt and Demand Debt are perfect substitutes for each other, at a given rate differential between them. The degree of monetary restraint then depends wholly on the *quantity* of Long Debt — not as in (b), on the long *rate*. As shown in Figure 21.3, the constant-restraint locus is a horizontal line. Clearly the cheapest way to achieve such restraint is to have no Short Debt whatever, but to convert it all into Demand Debt. Given the current division of labor between the Treasury and Federal Reserve, this view would assign the whole responsibility of monetary restraint to the Treasury, which decides the outstanding quantity of Long Debt, and leave the Federal Reserve with the task of cost minimization. Extreme emphasis on the importance of lengthening the federal debt sometimes approximates this view.

    The beliefs about bank and public behavior underlying this essay, as

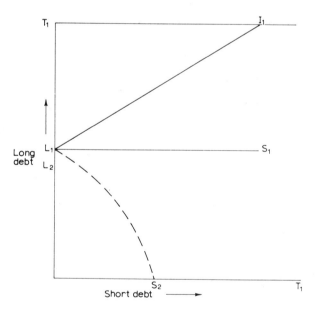

Fig. 21.3

expounded and illustrated in section 2, lead to none of these special views, but to the general picture described in Figure 21.1.

4. Bonds with Purchasing Power Escalation

4.1. *Improving the Effectiveness of Monetary Control*

The power of the monetary and debt authorities to control the economy would be enhanced if they could deal in equities themselves or at least in debt instruments that are closer substitutes for equities than conventional government obligations. At present the authorities try to affect the supply price of capital by exchanging with the public one kind of government debt for another – demand debt for short debt, demand debt for long debt, short debt for long debt. These exchanges do not, of course, affect the overall size of the debt relative to the stock of capital. They do affect the composition of the debt and its rate structure. But the effects upon the rate structure are limited to the degree necessary to induce the public to make the exchanges. If investors regard one kind of debt as a good substitute for another, they will require little movement in rates. Accordingly they will require little change in the rate of return they receive on capital ownership. In contrast, imagine that the authorities could exchange government debt for equities. Then open market and debt management operations would alter the relative supplies of government debt and capital outstanding, and the supply price of capital would change. Open market and debt management operations would be a tremendously powerful tool of economic stabilization. Clearly Federal Reserve and Treasury dealings in equities are out of the question. The choice of specific issues to buy or sell, with private fortunes riding on every arbitrary choice would be political dynamite. From a strictly economic point of view, it would involve unintended and arbitrary distortion of the allocative mechanism of the capital markets. What the authorities need is a way to intervene in the market in a general way, affecting the overall rate of return investors require of capital equity without distorting the relative positions of specific equities. No private security can fill this role. What is required is a new government debt instrument, which is a better substitute for capital equity than conventional instruments and a worse substitute for other species of government debt. Exchanges with the public involving the new instrument would effect substantial changes in its rate of return; and the supply price of capital would tend to move with the rate of return on an instrument closely substitutable for equity.

This is where a marketable bond expressed in terms of purchasing power comes in. A substantial part of the independence of risk between current debt instruments and capital equity arises from their difference in status with respect to uncertainties of the future purchasing power of money. A purchasing power bond would share the role of capital equity as a hedge against changes in the price level. It would therefore be a much better substitute than existing debt instruments for ownership of capital. There would remain, of course, the additional risks of capital ownership, for which capital would command a premium over the rate of return on purchasing power bonds. This premium would vary with, among other things, the relative supplies of purchasing power bonds and real capital. For its part, the marketable purchasing power bond would involve risks of interest rate change, in the same manner as conventional bonds. But there would be less reason to expect its interest rate to move together with other government debt interest rates. The purchasing power bond would be substantially independent of other debt instruments in risk. It would be a much poorer substitute for other government obligations than long-term bonds are at present for short-term obligations and cash.

The most appropriate index for escalation of bond principal and interest is, all things considered, the Consumer Price Index. In principle, escalation to a capital goods price index, or even to an index of equity share prices, would provide a more effective medium of control. But such an index is too slippery conceptually and too difficult practically to provide a basis of escalation in which everyone would have confidence. The CPI is solidly entrenched in public confidence, and there are precedents for its use as an escalator. Moreover, there are compelling reasons, quite apart from improvement of techniques of economic control, for adding to the menu of financial assets available to the public government bonds with purchasing power guarantees.

4.2. *Improving the Financial Menu*

The menu is seriously deficient. It does not provide the variety of asset choices necessary to match the variety of needs, tastes, financial knowledge, and circumstance of American households.

We take pride in the subtlety and articulation of our financial institutions and markets, which tailor instruments and contracts to meet an enormous variety of needs, tastes, expectations, and circumstances, both on the borrowing side and on the lending side. But these institutions and markets do not provide, at any price, a riskless way of accumulating purchasing power for the future, whether for old age or for college educations or for heirs. They cannot do so without government help. Meanwhile we force savers to take risk, even if they would gladly pay for the privilege of avoiding it. What is worse, the government lends its own prestige to perpetuating via advertising and other public appeal the falsehood, or at best half-truth, that its own obligations are free of risk.

If the price level were certain to remain stable, various riskless investments would be available. These would include demand obligations of the government, both currency and savings bonds, and the obligations of banks and other savings institutions guaranteed by government insurance programs. The marketable time obligations of the Treasury would be riskless if held to maturity, though subject to the risks of interest rate fluctuation in the intervening period. Many private contractual obligations would be virtually riskless, carrying only negligible possibility of default. These would include many corporate bonds, for example, and most life insurance contracts. At the same time there would be ample opportunity for taking risk, even without the possibility of making bets on the course of the price level. An investor would be able to mix riskless and risky investments in proportions suitable to his need, taste, and temperament. In a world dominated by risk averters, no doubt willingness to assume risk would be rewarded by a higher average expectation of return.

This is presumably the theory of our financial system, if indeed a congeries of institutions that have emerged without conscious comprehensive plan can be said to have a theory. But in practice we do not have a system like this, and we never have had. No government, whatever may be its intentions and financial scruples, is able to guarantee the constancy of the price level even for its own tenure of office, much less for all time. No government has ever been able to do so, and none ever will be. It is just beyond the power of government in a free and decentralized economy with a democratic political order. It is sufficient to recall that war and its aftermath are the main generators of changes in the price level. No one, alas, can guarantee perpetual peace.

In the present circumstances the only way to avoid the risk of price level change is to accept another set of risks, those inherent in ownership of capital. In spite of the growth of mutual funds, it is still costly – in terms of brokerage and management costs and other transactions charges – for a small and intermittent saver to obtain the protection of diversification in equity investment. Even this protection leaves the irreducible *general* risks of equity investment. The stock market may happen to be low relative to consumer prices just when the investor needs his money.

Present institutions virtually compel the participant in a contributory retirement program and the life insurance policyholder to accept the risk of change in the purchasing power of the dollar. In both these cases saving is combined with actuarial provision; there is ample reason supported by experience why joint packages of this kind are economical both for buyer and seller. But it is most unfortunate that the saving part of this package should be confined to acquisition of claims fixed in money amounts. In recent history. of course, yields of such claims did not contain adequate allowance for the increase in the price level; the war and postwar inflations were not anticipated. Even now it is surprising how large a part of the population fail to realize the vulnerability to inflation of investment fixed in money value. Many who do realize it still make such investments, precisely because they come as an inseparable part of the joint packages of retirement and life insurance. In this way the inadequacies of our financial institutions help to perpetuate their own injustices -- a principal reason that yields on bonds and other fixed-money-value investments fail to reflect adequately the expected rate of inflation is that these assets command a captive investment demand so long as retirement programs and life insurance companies are limited to the conventional contract. But even if the yields were high enough to offset the average expected rate of decline of purchasing power of money, present retirement and insurance contracts would still be deficient. There is a difference between providing sufficient yield on the average and providing it in every concrete case. Yields may be adjusted to the rate of inflation anticipated in advance by the market. There is a difference between the rate of inflation as now anticipated, and the rate of inflation that is actually realized over the lifetimes of a policyholder and his beneficiaries. With conventional contracts the saver necessarily takes a risk; the yield of his savings through retirement and insurance programs may overcompensate him for the actual change in the cost of living, or it may undercompensate him.

The variable annuity is a long overdue reform. One effect of it will be to help to correct the systematic bias of conventional contracts by liberating some of the captive demands for contracts with benefits fixed in money value and the corresponding captive demand of the insurance companies and retirement programs for bonds, mortgages, and other investments of fixed money value. The saving component of retirement and insurance packages can instead be equity investment. This option will benefit, through higher average returns, not only those who choose it but also those who stick with contracts of conventional type. The diversion of customers will cause the yields of conventional contracts to rise. But the variable annuity will not make it possible to choose a riskless retirement or insurance program. The beneficiaries cannot escape the irreducible risks of diversified equity investment.

No private institution can fill this gap. No insurance company or pension fund could assume the risk of offering purchasing power escalation to its creditors, without similarly escalated securities in which to invest at least part of their funds. Only the federal government is in a position to issue such securities. Once they are available, private financial institutions could offer the corresponding insurance and retirement policies. These should be available alongside conventional contracts, and contracts involving equity investment. In time, presumably, contracts with purchasing power guarantee would yield less than the other two, since they would involve less risk.

Nonmarketable savings bonds are also an important vehicle of long-run saving by small savers. To meet their preferences for a risk-free asset, the government should offer savings bonds with purchasing power escalation.

If purchasing power escalation were available in these forms of saving, what would happen to other saving institutions, the savings departments of commercial banks, mutual savings banks, and savings and loan associations? One possibility would be to leave them unchanged. The important thing is to enable small savers to eliminate the risk from long-run saving, where changes in the purchasing power of money can make a substantial difference. A savings deposit or savings and loan association share can be used to accumulate money for next summer's vacation or next April's taxes, without great risk of loss of purchasing power. To keep the longer-run savings of informed conservative households, these institutions would have to offer higher interest and dividends to their depositors and shareowners. To some extent they would be enabled to do so by the rise in yields of fixed-money-value bonds and mortgages, which would accompany the introduction of purchasing power bonds and variable annuities. But this rise would not be sufficient to avoid some loss of business to these institutions, relative to the channels of saving that offer purchasing power escalation.

A second possibility would be to permit these institutions to offer to the public escalated deposits or shares. These liabilities would be backed by holdings of marketable purchasing power bonds, the same issues that would be used by insurance companies and retirement funds. The institutions would serve as middlemen, overcoming for the small savers the obstacles to direct ownership of bonds: indivisibilities, transaction costs, and interest rate risks. In this regard the institutions would serve many of the same functions that the Treasury's own savings bonds serve. But this would be no change from the current situation; these channels of saving are already competitors. Some savers prefer the divisibility and reversibility of savings deposits and saving and loan shares, and some prefer the long-run assurance of interest earnings given by a savings bond. At the savings institution one can add or subtract any amount at any time. One can withdraw a sum today, and redeposit it tomorrow, with no penalty except loss of interest from the previous crediting date; and even that loss can be avoided by a passbook loan. In contrast, if one cashes in a nine-year old government savings bond today, he cannot buy it back tomorrow. He can buy only a brand-new bond, with ten years to maturity instead of one. But savings bonds have the advantage of guaranteeing a schedule of interest accumulation over a long period in advance. The savings institutions cannot give a forward guarantee. These differentia would continue to exist under the proposal, even if the savings institutions would be serving only as middlemen between the government and the saver in the field of escalated savings.

The third possibility would be to introduce escalated private mortgage contracts with FHA insurance, and to let them serve along with government purchasing power bonds as the basis for escalated savings deposits and shares. This innovation would permit these savings institutions to compete in the field of escalated savings without abandoning their traditional role in housing finance. An escalated mortgage does not appear to be any less appropriate obligation for an average homeowner to assume than a conventional mortgage. Both house values and wages are probably more stable in terms of the Consumer Price Index than in terms of the dollar. In any event, both options would be available. It would even be possible to arrange mixtures to suit the circumstances and tastes of the mortgager.

As it works out, our present financial system is an anachronism, appropriate perhaps to a small country dependent on external trade and finance but not to a great nation with a vast internal market, financing economic growth with its own savings. Our present arrangements can assure a saver, if he so desires, of a claim to a certain weight of gold. The claim is a highly theoretical one, and the gold is of no use anyway. If the United States were a small and undeveloped country, and if the gold represented a stable claim on the amenities of civilization elsewhere, a risk-free method of accumulating gold might be of some importance. In the United States today, provision of a risk-free method of accumulating claims to domestically produced consumer goods is much more pertinent.

4.3. Objections Considered

The principal argument against providing saving media with purchasing power escalation is that they would promote inflation.

Inflation is not an intrinsic evil, like famine or unemployment or juvenile deliquency. If it is an evil, that is because its consequences are evil. What are the evil consequences? Serious lists are rare. Economists, editorial writers, financiers, and politicians are better at denouncing inflation then in providing a rational account of its damage to the body economic, politic, and social. However, the principal damage almost always boils down to this: inflation causes erratic, unanticipated, and inequitable changes in the distribution of income and wealth. Those who have saved in fixed-money-value media lose. Those whose incomes directly or indirectly depend on investments in fixed-money-value assets lose. Those who borrow money from these unfortunate investors and acquire equity in goods gain. The purpose of purchasing power bonds and related opportunities for escalated saving is precisely to avoid the redistributions of wealth and income that are the principal objection to inflation in a closed economy.

A single country in a world economy linked by fixed exchange rates can of course incur balance-of-payments difficulties if its price level rises relative to the price levels of other countries. This consideration applies with force to the United States today. Avoidance of relative inflation is necessarily a prime objective of United States economic policy.

Nevertheless, it is far from clear that a regime with purchasing power bonds would actually be more susceptible to inflation than the present financial regime. In the first place, purchasing power bonds would strengthen the controls over the economy possessed by the monetary and debt management authorities. In the second place, the availability of a more satisfactory menu of assets might well increase noninflationary saving, encouraging the saving appetites of individuals and households of modest incomes. The experience of the last twenty years might discourage saving in the liquid media now available; better to consume a dollar's worth now than fifty cents worth twenty years from now. Or at any rate, better to save in the form of durable goods and houses rather than in liquid form. The opponents of purchasing power bonds always point out that they weaken the natural or built-in defense the economy now puts up against inflation. These defenses are the reductions in consumption spending by individuals and households who suffer capital losses, in real terms, when a rise in the price level impairs the purchasing power of their fixed-money-value assets. The ethical logic of this argument is rather strange. The main evil of inflation turns out to be a principal built-in brake upon it. Don't remove the evil or you will destroy the brake. What this observation neglects is the possibility that prospective savers may anticipate the contingency that they will have to serve involuntarily as a brake upon inflation, and save less – at least in liquid form – in the first place. If inflation is more likely because of the absence of suitable saving media, it is small consolation to know that the inequities that constitute the built-in brakes upon inflation are intact.

The political argument is more difficult to assess. The allegation is that escalation will vitiate the strength of political forces opposed to inflation. Presumably these forces now consist of people who stand to lose from inflation. If no one stands to lose, who will oppose it? The advent of purchasing power bonds will not mean that no one stands to lose from inflation. As at present, it will still be possible to bet that the accumulation of interest on fixed-money-value assets will outrun the price level. Those who take that side of the bet will favor anti-inflationary governmental policies. But in any case economists are probably inclined to exaggerate the degree to which positions on government economic policy reflect calculated self-interest with respect to inflation or deflation. To a large degree they seem to reflect ideological and moral attitudes, primitive economic reasoning, and entrenched political positions.

A frequent objection to purchasing power bonds is that they saddle upon the government an incalculable and possibly enormous future burden in terms of dollars. But the burden of the present debt is incalculable in terms of purchasing power and in terms of tax base of the federal government. These are much more relevant bench-marks for measuring the debt than the nominal dollar, and in terms of these bench-marks a purchasing power debt would be more calculable rather than less. Moreover, at the present time the federal government has undertaken many incalculable future obligations, outside the tidy little package formed by the conventional debt. Who can say what is the present value of the federal government's commitments under the Old Age and Survivor's Insurance program, for example? As for the possible size of the burden of a purchasing power debt, if it grows in dollars the tax base will grow with it. It is true that the federal government will, to the extent that it uses purchasing power obligations, forego the possibility of attrition of the real burden of its debt via inflation. (Should not the removal of this temptation strengthen rather than weaken political defenses against inflation?) But there will be countervailing gains. The Treasury should be able to borrow more cheaply with purchasing power bonds, since the public will pay the Treasury for assuming a risk which the government, and the government alone thanks to its taxing power, can assume without cost. Indeed in the long run exclusion of purchasing power bonds from the repertoire of debt instruments will cause greater debt costs to the Treasury, unless the public remains deceived concerning the possibilities of inflation. Should we follow a policy of debt management by which the Treasury gains only to the extent that the public is deceived?

Evidently for many people the clinching argument against purchasing power bonds is that their introduction would be a signal that the government had given up its battle to control the price level. Similarly unemployment insurance might be interpreted as a signal that the government had given up the battle to prevent unemployment. Civil defense might be regarded as an indication that the government no longer believed it possible to keep the peace or to defend the country from hydrogen bombing. To take precautions to protect people from unfortunate events does not mean that the government regards the events as inevitable, or even that the government intends to slacken its own efforts to prevent them. The public can understand that. The situation would be different were it easy or even possible to guarantee the price level. This is a guarantee a democratic government cannot give in our kind of economy and in the present state of the world. Debt policy should not be based on the myth that the government can guarantee the price level if it only musters the political will to do so.

5. Summary and Concluding Remarks

Monetary control and debt management are jointly concerned with the composition of the net claims of the economy against the federal government. The total of these claims is the province of congressional and presidential fiscal policy; net federal debt grows with budget deficit and declines with budget surplus. The composition of the total, and of changes in the total, is for the Federal Reserve and the Treasury's debt managers to decide.

The *monetary effect* of changes in federal debt must be distinguished from the *fiscal effect*. The monetary effect is permanent and depends upon the size of the debt. The fiscal effect is temporary and depends upon the rate at which deficit or surplus is changing the size of the debt. The monetary effect may be measured by the supply price of capital, the rate of return at which the community is willing to hold in its portfolios and balance sheets the existing stock of privately owned productive physical capital. Events and policy measures that lower the supply price of capital are expansionary; events and measures that raise it are deflationary.

On this criterion, increases in federal debt — whether as demand debt or as interest-bearing debt of short or long maturity — are expansionary. Likewise, substitution of demand debt for short or long debt, and substitution of shorter debt for longer debt, are expansionary. Altering the composition of the debt in one of these ways, or in reverse if contraction of aggregate demand is desired, is the principal tool of monetary control. In addition, the monetary authorities have the power to vary the discount rate and required reserve ratios.

The extent of the task of economic stabilization that falls on monetary control and debt management depends on how much of the job is assigned to taxation and other fiscal measures. The balance among instruments of stabilization must be decided with a view to the composition of output, economic growth, the distribution of wealth and income, and economic efficiency. Once the share of monetary measures in the control of aggregate demand is defined, the authorities have a wide choice of means. What criterion of choice should guide them? In the absence of more compelling criteria, minimization of net long-run interest cost to the Treasury is a sensible goal.

Optimal debt management, then, consists in accomplishing the task of monetary stabilization at the least cost to the Treasury. Some of the implications of this criterion are:

1. In achieving a given monetary effect, the Federal Reserve should give preference to measures that require or induce banks to increase their holdings of non-interest-bearing debt. The government saves money when monetary restriction is achieved by raising reserve requirements, or by raising the discount rate, rather than by open market sales of bills.

2. Costs could be lowered, without sacrifice of monetary effect, by enlarging the captive market for government debt through a secondary reserve requirement on banks, and through reserve requirements on other financial intermediaries. These requirements would also improve the efficiency of monetary control. Against them must be weighed considerations of equity to the owners and customers of banks and other financial intermediaries.

3. The government – comprising both the Federal Reserve and the Treasury – should continuously adjust the maturity structure of the debt, seeking to minimize its net cost while achieving the required restriction of aggregate demand. For this purpose, net cost to the government includes not only interest outlays but also increases in the market value of the outstanding debt. If this concept is used as the guide, the relevant interest rate on each maturity is the quoted market rate plus the capital gain (or minus the expected loss) due to interest rate changes anticipated in the immediate future. The Treasury should not borrow long if long rates are about to fall. On the contrary, at such times the government should repurchase or refund in advance its long obligations, replacing them with short maturities. To maintain monetary restriction intact, it is generally necessary to contract demand debt whenever the interest-bearing debt is shortened, and to expand demand debt whenever the interest-bearing debt is lengthened. That is, a dollar change either way in long debt must be accompanied by more than a dollar change in the opposite direction in short debt. Allowance must be

made for this necessity in calculating the advantage to the government of lengthening or shortening the debt.

4. The present administrative division of debt management responsibilities is inadequate to the economic unity of the problem. The Federal Reserve cannot make rational decisions of monetary policy without knowing what kind of debt the Treasury intends to issue. The Treasury cannot rationally determine the maturity structure of the interest-bearing debt without knowing how much debt the Federal Reserve intends to monetize. Serious pursuit of the optimum in debt management would require more centralization of government security purchases and sales than now exists. The suggestion is to assign the entire task of debt management to the Federal Reserve, with the mandate to minimize cost to the extent consistent with stabilization objectives. There would no longer be any distinction between Federal Reserve open market operations and security issues or redemptions. The Federal Reserve would be provided with a varied inventory of securities and would sell them or buy them back from the public, as their mandate required. The Treasury would provide the Federal Reserve with new securities when its working balance needs to be augmented because of budget deficit or "redeem" securities held by the Federal Reserve from budget surplus. (A base core of securities now held by the Federal Reserve represents a permanent monetization of federal debt, and it may be convenient to convert these into an intragovernmental memorandum of debt at zero or nominal interest.) Under this arrangement the Federal Reserve would be, like the Bank of England, the government's underwriter.

5. The government should issue marketable and nonmarketable bonds with purchasing power escalation, principal and interest geared to the Consumer Price Index. Marketable bonds of this type would greatly improve the effectiveness of monetary control. The Federal Reserve, by buying or selling these securities, would be dealing in assets much closer to equity capital than conventional public debt instruments. The monetary authorities would thereby gain a much greater leverage over the supply price of capital. At the same time, purchasing power bonds would fill, either directly or through the intermediation of insurance companies and other institutions, a shameful gap in the available menu of financial assets. Savers of limited means and knowledge should not be forced to gamble either on the price level or on the stock market. Since investors will pay the government to avoid such risks, purchasing power bonds would save the taxpayer interest outlays. Various objections to purchasing power bonds are considered and refuted in section 4.3.

Except under the stress of obvious and serious malfunction, society seldom takes the trouble to examine with real detachment the logic and utility of institutions ordinarily taken for granted. The fresh look at the nation's monetary and financial system undertaken by the Commission on Money and Credit is an exception, offering both an opportunity for constructive social engineering and a temptation to ratify the status quo. Existing arrangements are not necessarily inevitable or optimal or unique, but they are likely to seem so to people deeply involved in operating or observing them. Traditions and customs and commitments arise in remarkably short time. What seems natural and obvious procedure today was novel and revolutionary fifty or twenty or ten years ago. By the same token, changes that appear radical today will be defended by vested champions of the status quo tomorrow. The Commission should not be too tender of existing institutions. They are expendable if they fail to accomplish their functions — the functions they ought to perform today, which are generally quite different from the functions they were designed to perform. There are many respects in which our present arrangements for monetary control and debt management are irrational and anachronistic. They were not designed for a public debt that is so large a part of aggregate private wealth, so strategic a factor in monetary control, and so important a burden on the federal budget. They were not designed for a world in which economic stabilization has such a high priority on the agenda of government, and in which monetary control bears so large a responsibility for stabilization. They were not even designed for a system in which general economic stabilization — rather than prevention of panic and responsiveness to "needs of trade" — is the principal goal of the central bank. They were not designed for an era in which inevitable uncertainty about the price level makes gambles of fixed money value assets, traditionally regarded as perfectly safe. Sooner or later, slowly or rapidly, our institutions will evolve so that they more adequately meet the needs of the day. The Commission on Money and Credit has the opportunity to speed, to smooth, and to guide that evolution.

Notes

[1] The word *private* is not altogether appropriate, since among the economic units in the aggregate would be state and local governments. *Private* should be interpreted, in this context, as nonfederal.

[2] One implication of the concept of federal debt adopted in section 1 should be noted. When the United States finances a balance of trade deficit by selling gold or by foreign acquisition of U.S. government securities, it is the federal debt component of private wealth that declines. When the same deficit is financed by U.S. banks' incurring

deposit obligations to foreigners, it is the third component of private wealth that declines.

[3] As of 1970, the figures were $28 billion, nearly 10 per cent of the total.

[4] As of 1970, the figures were $12 billion, 4 per cent of the total.

[5] This is no longer true. See Chapter 19 for discussion of ceiling rates now imposed on savings institutions.

[6] This division still exists, though it was somewhat blurred by the Federal Reserve's decision in February 1961 to operate in all sectors of the government securities market.

Appendix

The analysis in the text is based on a model that can be explicitly stated in formal terms.

1. Definitions of Variables and Parameters

M_1 Amount of demand debt outside the Federal Reserve and Treasury.

M_2 Amount of short debt outside the Federal Reserve and Treasury.

M_3 Amount of long debt outside the Federal Reserve and Treasury.

C Value of the privately owned capital stock, at current prices.

L Net indebtedness of private borrowers to banks.

D Bank deposits.

k Required ratio of bank reserve to deposits.

E Shareowner's equity in banks.

M_{ib} Amount of debt of category i held by banks ($i = 1, 2, 3$).

M_{ip} Amount of debt of category i held by nonbank public ($i = 1, 2, 3$).

M_{1b}' Banks' net free reserves.

W Net private wealth.

r_1 Federal Reserve Discount rate.

r_2 Rate on short-term government securities.

r_3 Rate on long-term government securities.

r_4 Rate on private loans.

r_5 Supply price of capital.

2. Accounting Identities and Definitions

$$M_1 + M_2 + M_3 + C = W \tag{A1}$$

Net private wealth is equal to claims against the government plus the value of the privately owned capital stock.

$$M_{1p} + M_{2p} + M_{3p} + D - L + C + E = W \tag{A2}$$

The sum of assets held by the nonbank public, less its indebtedness, is equal
to net private wealth.

$$M_{ib} + M_{ip} = M_i \qquad (i = 1, 2, 3) \tag{A3}$$

Outstanding debt, in each form, is divided between bank holdings and nonbank public holdings.

$$M_{1b} + M_{2b} + M_{3b} + L - D - E = 0 \tag{A4}$$

Bank liabilities plus shareowner's equity equal bank assets. This can be
derived, from (1), (2), and (3).

$$M_{1b} = kD + M'_{1b} \tag{A5}$$

Bank holding of demand debt is equal to required reserves plus net free
reserves.

3. Behavioral relations

3.1. Banks

$$M'_{1b} = m_{1b}(r_1, r_2, r_3, r_4)(1-k)D \tag{B1}$$

The proportion (positive, zero, or negative) of bank disposable assets held as
net free reserves depends directly on the discount rate and inversely on the
interest rate on the three types of earning assets in banks' portfolios. The
most important determinants are r_1 and r_2. Banks have incentive to borrow
reserves when the differential between r_2 and r_1 is favorable. At the same
time, with a given differential, the demand for net free reserves will diminish
when these two rates are higher.

$$M_{2b} = m_{2b}(r_1, r_2, r_3, r_4)(1-k)D \tag{B2}$$

$$M_{3b} = m_{3b}(r_1, r_2, r_3, r_4)(1-k)D \tag{B3}$$

$$L = l_b(r_1, r_2, r_3, r_4)(1-k)D + E \tag{B4}$$

These three equations, together with the first, say that the proportions in
which banks divide their disposable assets among the four categories depend
on the four interest rates. Shareowners' equity is assumed to take entirely the
form of private loans. In each case demand for an asset is assumed positively
related to its own rate, negatively to the other rates. The discount rate might
be omitted from the last three equations, following the same logic that would
omit r_3 and r_4 from (B1). In any case, only three of these equations are
independent. The fourth may be derived from the other three with the help
of the identities (A4), (A5), (A6).

3.2. Nonbank public

$$M_{1p} = m_{1p}W \tag{P1}$$

Public currency holdings may be taken to be a constant proportion of wealth – given the volume of transactions and other determinants.

$$M_{2p} = m_{2p}(r_2, r_3, r_4, r_5)W \tag{P2}$$

$$M_{3p} = m_{3p}(r_2, r_3, r_4, r_5)W \tag{P3}$$

Direct holdings of short government debt, as a proportion of private wealth, depend directly on the short rate and inversely on the rates that compete for place in public portfolios. A similar relationship holds for long debt.

$$L = l_p(r_2, r_3, r_4, r_5)W \tag{P4}$$

L, net public borrowing from banks, is a negative number and becomes smaller algebraically, larger absolutely, when r_4, the loan rate declines and when the other rates rise. These reactions are due both to the direct lending behavior of the public and to its borrowing behavior. When the loan rate declines and other rates rise, the lending sector of the public will prefer other assets to private loans. When the loan rate declines and other rates rise, particularly r_5, the borrowing sector of the public will wish to increase its debt. On both counts, there will be more demand for bank loans.

$$D = d_p(r_2, r_3, r_4, r_5)W \tag{P5}$$

Public demand for deposits is negatively related to all the rates and is probably especially sensitive to the short rate r_2.

$$C = c_p(r_2, r_3, r_4, r_5)W \tag{P6}$$

Public demand for capital is higher the greater is r_5, and the lower are the other rates. Since much capital holding is financed by borrowing, the private loan rate r_4 is especially important.

Public equity in bank enterprises, E, may be taken as a constant. The six equations for the public balance sheet are not all independent. Using (A2) one of them can be derived from the other five.

4. Balance equations

Demand debt, from (A5), (B1), (P1), and (P5).

$$kd_p(\quad)W + m_{1b}(\quad)(1-k)d_p(\quad)W + m_{1p}W = M_1 \tag{1}$$

Short debt, from (B2) and (P2):

$$m_{2b}(\ )(1-k)d_p(\ )W + m_{2p}(\ )W = M_2 \qquad (2)$$

Long debt, from (B3) and (P3):

$$m_{3b}(\ )(1-k)d_p(\ )W + m_{3p}(\ )W = M_3 \qquad (3)$$

Loans, from (B4) and (P4)

$$l_b(\ )(1-k)d_p(\ )W + E - l_p(\ )W = 0 \qquad (4)$$

Capital, from (P6)

$$c_p(\ )W = C \qquad (5)$$

Where parentheses follow a symbol, e.g., $c_p(\ )$, a function is indicated, with the arguments, interest rates, as previously noted.

Since one of the bank portfolio equations can be derived from the other bank equations, and one of the public asset demand equations from the other public equations, the five balance equations are not independent. One can be eliminated, for example (4). Then equations (1), (2), (3), (5) determine simultaneously the four market interest rates r_2, r_3, r_4, r_5, given M_1, M_2, M_3, K, and therefore given W, their sum; given the discount rate r_1; and given the required reserve ratio k. The monetary effect of an increase in debt of a given category, say M_1, can be found by differentiating the system of equations partially with respect to M_1, remembering that $\partial W/\partial M_1 = 1$, and solving for $\partial r_5/\partial M_1$. The monetary effect of open market purchases of short debt would be $\partial r_5/\partial M_1 - \partial r_5/\partial M_2$; of open market purchases of long debt, $\partial r_5/\partial M_1 - \partial r_5/\partial M_3$; of substitution of short debt for long debt $\partial r_5/\partial M_2 - \partial r_5/\partial M_3$. In a similar manner, $\partial r_5/\partial r_1$ and $\partial r_5/\partial k$ can be found (remembering that $\partial W/\partial r_1$ and $\partial W/\partial k$ are zero). The effects of a parameter change on any item in a bank or public balance sheet may be found by using the solutions of the four differentiated equations and behavior equations of section 3. For example, the effects of a change in reserve requirements on bank deposits would be, using (P5),

$$\frac{\partial D}{\partial k} = W\left(\frac{\partial d_p}{\partial r_2}\frac{\partial r_2}{\partial k} + \frac{\partial d_p}{\partial r_3}\frac{\partial r_3}{\partial k} + \frac{\partial d_p}{\partial r_4}\frac{\partial r_3}{\partial k} + \frac{\partial d_p}{\partial r_5}\frac{\partial r_5}{\partial k}\right).$$

To find debt combinations that give equivalent restraint on demand, r_5 can be held constant in the four equation system (1), (2), (3), (5). Holding W and K constant also, the four equations can then be regarded as giving r_2, r_3, r_4, and M_3 as functions of M_2. In particular $\partial M_3/\partial M_2$ gives the quantity by which long debt must be changed to offset the effect on r_5 of a dollar change in outstanding short debt. Since total debt is fixed, M_1 can be found as a residual.

In similar manner debt combinations of equal cost (where cost is $r_2 M_2 + r_3 M_3$) can be determined from the same system of equations.

CHAPTER 22

MONETARY POLICY AND THE MANAGEMENT OF THE PUBLIC DEBT: THE PATMAN INQUIRY

The documents produced by the Patman inquiry [1] are a remarkable contribution to monetary literature. The first title, *Compendium* for short, consists of replies to questions propounded by the committee. [2] The first volume of the *Compendium* contains the careful answers of the Treasury and the Board of Governors of the Federal Reserve System to the lengthy questionnaires submitted to them. The second volume includes replies from the Presidents of Federal Reserve Banks, the Council of Economic Advisers, federal and state bank-examining authorities, the Reconstruction Finance Corporation, economists, bankers, life insurance executives, and dealers in United States government securities. The questionnaires varied with the respondent and were designed to obtain both factual information and expressions of opinion. The answers provide a wealth of legal, institutional, statistical, and historical information. Whether you wish, for example, a complete chronology of Federal Reserve policy actions since 1914, a summary of the reserve requirements of nonmember banks, a world survey of Treasury-central-bank relationships, or a study of the density of banking offices relative to population in the several states, the Patman *Compendium* is your source. The replies also provide a variety of opinion, comment, and theory concerning the role of monetary policy in the postwar United States economy.

The second title, *Hearings* for short, reports oral testimony on these same subjects and includes also numerous documents [3] and written statements submitted to the committee. The committee heard testimony from the principal contributors to the *Compendium* and from many others; the witnesses represented a wide variety of experience, interest, and viewpoint. The *Hearings* include four panel discussions on aspects of monetary policy.

Reprinted from *The Review of Economics and Statistics*, 35 (May 1953), 118-27. Footnotes have been renumbered.

Two of these, "How should our monetary and debt management policy be determined?" (pp. 747 ff.) and "What should our monetary and debt management policy be?" (pp. 685 ff.), are especially deserving of the attention of the reader who can only hit the high spots of these volumes.

The third title, *Report* for short, gives the findings and recommendations of the committee majority, with dissenting observations by Senator Douglas. [4] The *Report* is an admirable review of the events investigated by the committee; and its findings on the issues discussed in the *Compendium* and *Hearings* are, in my opinion, well balanced and moderate. For this *Report*, and indeed for the skillful design of the whole inquiry, there can be no doubt that Henry C. Murphy, the committee's economist, deserves tremendous credit.

It is patently impossible for a review to do justice to the masses of material in these three documents. I hope I have given some idea of their scope. For the rest, I shall confine myself to three major topics of the committee's inquiry; (1) the Treasury-Federal Reserve conflict, (2) the theory of the operation of monetary controls, (3) the place of monetary restriction in an anti-inflationary program.

1. Drama: The Treasury-Federal Reserve Conflict

The struggle between the Treasury and the Federal Reserve gave to monetary theory and policy a dramatic interest which economic issues seldom achieve. The drama is now over. The accord of March 1951 and the Patman inquiry were its concluding acts. The advent of new leadership in the Treasury makes it unlikely that the struggle will be resumed.

As the last act of the drama, the Patman inquiry was anticlimactic. The Douglas committee, which investigated the same subject in 1949, had strongly criticized the Treasury and had recommended Federal Reserve independence in the formation of credit policy. This token of congressional sentiment, even though the mandate to the two agencies favored by Senator Douglas was never passed, may well have stiffened the Federal Reserve in the subsequent conflict. (See *Hearings*, p. 535.) The Patman investigation, it was widely predicted and feared, was to be the Treasury's day of revenge and a challenge to the independence of the Federal Reserve. Nothing of the sort happened. The inquiry only consolidated the victory the Federal Reserve had already won in March 1951. Representative Patman conducted the inquiry, so far as a reader can discern, with the utmost fairness and impartiality. Although he was widely regarded beforehand as an "easy money" man, he gave no sign of dissatisfaction with the accord. He proved to be less interested in issues of monetary policy — except for selective credit controls, of which he strongly disapproved — than in emphasizing that the Federal Reserve System is a public agency responsible to Congress, not a chain of bankers' banks. Some of the organizational recommendations in the *Report* reflect this concern, but none would significantly weaken the autonomy of the Federal Reserve.

The extent of the Federal Reserve victory is indicated by changes in Federal Reserve attitudes on two proposals: one for an advisory council on monetary policy and one for granting the Board of Governors discretion to impose supplementary reserve requirements. In the days of its weakness the Federal Reserve had supported similar proposals. Now its spokesmen opposed them.

In 1949 Chairman McCabe of the Board of Governors and the Presidents of the Reserve Banks indorsed the Hoover Commission recommendation for a national monetary and credit council to facilitate consultation among the Treasury, The Federal Reserve, and the major federal credit agencies. [5] Such a council was one of the recommendations of the Douglas committee. In the Patman investigation, Secretary Snyder, who had given the plan only lukewarm support in 1949, revived the proposal. The Federal Reserve was now cool to the proposal, and Senator Douglas even colder. Formerly the council was considered an opportunity for increasing Federal Reserve influence with executive agencies; now it was viewed as a threat to Federal Reserve independence. The Patman committee majority nevertheless recommended the establishment of a council by executive order as an experiment.

The shift of attitude on supplementary reserves is of greater importance. In 1947 the Board of Governors sought powers to require supplementary bank reserves in government securities, as a step toward insulating the public debt from the interest rate fluctuations incident to a flexible monetary policy. As late as May 1951, two months after the accord, the report of the President's Four-Member Committee on this problem (Defense Mobilizer Wilson, Secretary Snyder, Chairman Martin of the Board of Governors, and Chairman Keyserling of the Council of Economic Advisers) stated, "Within a few days the Board of Governors will ask the Congress to consider definitive legislation providing for supplementary [reserve] requirements." (*Hearings*, p. 132.) The request was never made. By the time of the Patman inquiry, the Board of Governors had apparently been won over to the view of President Sproul of the New York Bank, who had always opposed the scheme. Federal Reserve spokesmen were extremely cool to any innovations in reserve requirements. Practical difficulties which had not seemed insurmountable before seemed so now. Having waged and won a fight on the moral principle that you cannot have your cake and eat it too, the Federal Reserve was in no mood to look with favor on devices for reconciling flexibility of monetary policy and stability of government securities prices. The committee majority did not agree. Representative Bolling repeatedly inquired why the Board should not have supplementary powers over reserves as a standby even if they were not immediately needed, and he never got a good answer. The *Report* favored granting such powers and pointed out that the time to provide them is precisely when they are not needed. But in the absence of a specific proposal by the Federal Reserve, this recommendation is certain to remain an expression of sentiment rather than a basis for legislation. Since the Federal Reserve was riding as high in the sympathy and esteem of Congress and the public as it is ever likely to be, its unreceptiveness to additional power may in future prove to be unfortunate. It is all very well to say there is no need for insulation when, under the Board's monetary policy, long-term governments fall no lower than 95. But if it becomes necessary to let them fall to, say, 80, the old dilemma will recur and the Board might again wish for a way out. [6] For there is no evidence that the Federal Reserve has either the disposition or the political strength to heed the extremists who would have it hew to the monetary line, letting bonds fall where they may.

The Patman inquiry was not only the last act of the Treasury-Federal Reserve drama. It was a revival of the whole play for the benefit of a wider audience, and it provided most of us with a much better view of the preceding acts than we had originally. Both the Treasury (*Compendium*, pp. 50-74) and the Board of Governors (*Compendium*, pp. 346-63) provided narratives of the events from the end of the war to the accord. The Treasury's account is both more informative and more combative, although their newfound friendship put both agencies under restraint in discussing their past differences. [7] The Federal Reserve reply is really given by President Sproul's testimony (*Hearings*, pp. 519-23, 541-43) on the period from August 1950 on, a narrative to which two other key Federal Reserve figures, Mr. Eccles and Mr. McCabe, signified their concurrence. Further light on the history of the struggle is shed by the confidential correspondence between the two agencies from June 1950 to March 1951 (*Hearings*, pp. 942-66), published by the committee over the cogent objection of Mr. Martin concerning the effects of this practice on the public service. Finally, the historically minded reader should not omit the account by Aubrey Lanston (*Compendium*, pp. 1253-65) of the market's day-by-day reactions to the pulling and hauling between the agencies.

The *Report* itself (pp. 25-28) provides an excellent and judicious summary of these events. On the evidence, there is no reason to doubt the committee's conclusion that "the record shows principally the actions of men of good will trying to work out the solution for an exceedingly complex problem." Nor is the record a history of Treasury domination of an unwilling Federal Reserve, suddenly ended in 1950-51 by an abrupt turn of the worm. Ever since the war, beginning with the question of termination of the preferential discount rate, the Federal Reserve has been pecking away at the structure of interest rates inherited from the war. The Treasury has resisted and delayed each step, but eventually the Treasury has always yielded. (Almost invariably the initial Treasury view is that any change in the status quo is risky – depression or war may be coming – or unnecessary or both.) Throughout the period the Federal Reserve has influenced not only the structure of rates but the types and maturities of Treasury issues. Only once, in the refunding operation in the fall of 1950, did the struggle explode into openly conflicting actions by the two agencies. The Treasury learned its lesson, and its next refunding followed Federal Reserve recommendations. Ultimately, in early 1951, the Federal Reserve had nothing left to peck at except the 2½ per cent long-term rate itself. Once again, in spite of some public verbal combat and the enlistment of the President on the Treasury side, the Federal Reserve prevailed. The accord came only one month after it was proposed to the Treasury by the Open Market Committee and only two months after the first intimation that the Federal Reserve had its eyes on the long-term rate. As in previous instances, the Treasury followed Federal Reserve advice regarding types and maturities of securities to issue.

Naturally the spheres of decision of the two agencies and their relationships with each other were problems of great concern to the committee. Both agencies took the attitude that the status quo, vague and informal though it may be, was satisfactory. Leave us alone, they said in effect, and we can work things out in cooperation and harmony. Skeptical outsiders were more worried about defining formally the spheres and powers of the two agencies. Most respondents were for asserting and safeguarding the independence of the Federal Reserve from the executive, and there was considerable support for a mandate of the kind advocated by Senator Douglas. Others held that "independence" is an unrealistic slogan, because monetary policy neither can nor should be made in a compartment separate from the other economic policies of the government. In the panel discussion on this subject. (*Hearings*, pp. 747 ff.) G.L. Bach and Harold Stein were persuasive advocates of this viewpoint, arguing that it is more important to enhance the influence of the Federal Reserve in the administration than to attempt to increase its independence. Some of the recommendations of the committee majority were directed to this end: in particular, the proposal that the Chairman of the Board of Governors have cabinet rank and be designated, from the membership of the Board, [8] for a four-year term concurrent with that of the President; and the proposal for a consultative and advisory council on monetary problems.

2. Theory: Operation of Monetary Controls

The Patman inquiry inspired, both in written replies and in oral testimony, numerous expositions of the theory of monetary control. A large majority of the respondents assigned to general monetary controls considerable influence on the level of economic activity. Only a few voiced the skepticism of their effectiveness so common five or ten years ago. These volumes are impressive evidence of the "rediscovery of money," as Howard Ellis has called this reversal in economic fashion.

The fluctuation of economic thought on the importance of the money supply is an interesting phenomenon in itself. Like the rise and fall of other fashions in the social sciences, it does little credit to our "science." Neither the initial skepticism about money nor its recent rediscovery has been solidly grounded on empirical evidence. Skepticism arose from the apparent impotence of monetary measures from 1929 on, received intellectual support from the Keynesian revolution, [9] and acquired reinforcement from an uncritical exaggeration of the importance and relevance of empirical findings that businessmen assign interest rates a low rank among factors influencing investment decisions. To some extent, skepticism grounded in the inadequacy of monetary measures to stimulate recovery from depression was applied to the opposite problem of preventing inflation. The reversal of fashion has had perhaps an even thinner empirical foundation. No new evidence has been adduced to prove the importance of monetary factors, [10] or to reverse previous impressions of the insensitivity of businessmen and other spenders to interest rates. The new confidence in the power of monetary weapons has been acquired just by giving the matter further thought — often one suspects, wishful thought. Absence is said to make the heart grow fonder, and to monetary policy has been attributed power to avoid the evils which flourished during its suspension in the interests of debt management. If the performance of the economy in response to monetary controls between the wars was an inadequate basis for pessimism about their efficacy, the performance of the economy since the war in the absence of monetary controls is surely an inadequate basis for optimism.

The important varieties of monetary theory espoused to the committee may be, with some violence to the individualities of some respondents, classified into three schools. One group, whose intellectual headquarters is Chicago, believes that aggregate spending is sensitive enough to the rate of interest, and hoarding insensitive enough, to make the quantity theory a good approximation. A second group agrees that the issue hinges on the sensitivity of spenders and hoarders to interest rates. But this group is skeptical about the interest elasticity of spending and is impressed more with the variability than with the constancy of monetary velocity. These two schools fit easily into the traditional framework of monetary discussion. Their disagreement, although it contributes to a marked difference in policy recommendations, is less a difference of theory than of empirical judgment. In the panel discussion (*Hearings,* pp. 685 ff.) Milton Friedman and Paul Samuelson represented ably these two points of view.

The third school, however, sets forth a new theory of monetary control which claims that both of the old schools are asking the wrong questions. Under the leadership of Robert V. Roosa [11] and others, the new theory has developed and spread rapidly in recent years. It has been inspired by postwar Federal Reserve policy, before and after the accord; the theory, in turn, inspires the policy. The Federal Reserve replies in the *Compendium* indicate that it is the official rationale of current policy. Because of its intellectual interest and its evident practical importance, the new theory deserves careful examination. In the Patman inquiry only Professors Samuelson and Whittlesey (*Hearings,* pp. 691-710, 736-43) gave it the critical attention which it merits.

According to this theory, monetary controls work much more through restricting the availability of credit than through increasing its cost, much more through restraints on lenders than through reactions of borrowers. It is possible, according to the theory, to curtail spending significantly by limiting the availability of bank reserves, without raising significantly market rates of interest. Some upward pressure on rates there is bound to be. But this is largely incidental, and one cannot judge the impact of a monetary restriction by the height to which it pushes interest rates. There are evidently two related parts to this proposition. The first is that it is possible to restrict reserves without raising interest rates appreciably. The second is that such restriction will curtail aggregate demand. Thus the new theory provides an answer to those of the other two schools who question the importance of fractional increases in interest rates. The significance of the new doctrine may be most clearly appreciated from the fact that it implies that monetary restriction will curtail aggregate demand even if the most extreme skepticism about the interest elasticity of borrowing and spending were justified.

To put the theory in an overformal but nonetheless perhaps an illuminating way, the substance of it is that an *increasing* yield on government bonds is an extremely good substitute for a *high* yield. At a given interest rate, the demand to hold government bonds, relative to other assets, will be higher if the interest rate is increasing or has recently increased than if it is stable. This is due to a combination of factors neglected in the older theories: first and most important, imperfections in the money markets which prevent the yields on other assets from adjusting to compensate for the increased attractiveness of government bonds; second, irrational and conventional behavior by financial institutions, so that portfolio decisions are not based wholly on yield comparisons but partly on considerations such as a reluctance to realize capital losses; third, uncertainties and expectations associated with increases in bond yields, which may make both borrowers and lenders appraise the economic future with more caution. Against these factors works the more familiar speculative effect: expectations and fears that interest rates will continue to rise tend to reduce the demand for bonds. But the new theory contends that if the favorable factors are skillfully exploited by the central bank, they will more than offset the speculative effect.

The consequences of a restriction of bank reserves are, according to the theory, as follows: The central bank restricts reserves by selling government securities or by lowering the price at which it will buy them. In either case there is some increase in their yield. This increase in yield deters banks and other lending institutions from selling government securities to make alternative loans and investments. It deters them for two principal reasons. First, they do not like to take a capital loss on government securities, even if an alternative asset offers a higher yield. [12] Second, and more important, the increase in yield makes government securities more attractive relative to alternative investments because the rates on other assets are kept from rising by institutional rigidities in the market. Lenders will, therefore, ration credit to private borrowers, and some willing borrowers will simply not be accommodated. For example, convention will keep the rate charged by banks to their commercial customers from rising; loan applications which previously would have been accepted will be refused. Again, the rate on mortgages will be sticky, in part because of government regulations; fewer mortgages will be bought. Similarly, corporations and state and local governments will find it impossible to float bond issues to finance investment projects. In all of these cases, it is argued, the disappointed borrower and spender does not have open to him in the market the alternative of offering a higher rate and obtaining the funds. Hence, even if borrowers are not likely to be deterred by higher interest charges, even if it is true that spending is insensitive to interest rate levels, monetary restriction is effective in curtailing spending.

This argument relies, as Professor Samuelson pointed out, on an increase in the imperfection of the market as a consequence of the initial rise in bond yields. There must be more rationing of credit than there was before. The importance of the argument depends on the persistence of the increase in imperfection. If the rates available to private borrowers are fixed for a long period, the theory uncovers important new potentialities for monetary control. If these rates are within a short time free to adjust upward to compensate for the increased yield and attractiveness of government securities, the contribution of the new theory is more modest. It points out some dynamic effects, neglected by the older theories, which temporarily enhance the influence of a monetary restriction. But as these effects wear off, the lasting influence of the restriction depends on the answer to the question the older theories ask: how interest-elastic are the demands for the alternatives to bonds, goods and cash? As the transient effects die, lenders will satisfy the needs of borrowers who are willing to pay higher rates. In order to do so, they will shift out of government securities; and given the volume of bank reserves, security yields will rise. To the extent that the increase in bond yields induces corporations and individuals to hold securities rather than cash reserves, lenders are provided with funds to satisfy the needs of borrowers who were previously rationed out of the market. In the ultimate equilibrium, rates on different assets will stand in a normal relationship to each other; the former degree of market imperfection will be restored; and the effect on spending will depend on what the monetary restriction has done to the level of interest rates and how borrowers and spenders react to that. Even so, the transient effects may be exceedingly useful to a central bank which wishes to dampen spending without raising interest rates much, or fears that demand is in any case not very responsive to the level of rates. If the inflationary pressure which the central bank wishes to oppose is itself temporary, the transient effects may be enough to do the job. Otherwise it would be necessary to administer successive doses of the medicine until the level of interest rates is pushed high enough to handle the situation.

The strength and persistence of these "availability effects" are empirical questions crucial to the new monetary theory. Inferences on the subject are drawn from events following the accord. But this should be done with great caution. Certainly the general economic stability of 1951 and 1952, compared with 1950, cannot be considered proof of the effectiveness of monetary policy, any more than it can be considered proof of the effectiveness of the direct controls introduced in 1951. Many other explanations of this phenomenon are at hand. But even if more specific evidence indicated that monetary policy should receive substantial credit for halting the inflation, the accord had unique characteristics which limit its usefulness as a basis for generalization. It was a departure from a policy and a rate to which the market had long been accustomed. It was natural for the market to react with confusion and imperfection and to transmit the change only slowly to the rates on private credit. Once the market is again accustomed to flexibility of basic rates, it may adjust with more speed. The first dose of the new medicine is likely to be the most effective, and it can only be administered once.

The evidence that the accord produced substantial effects of the kind envisaged by the new theory is not, in any case, impressive. (See testimony of Professor Whittlesey, *Hearings*, pp. 698-710.) Bank loans continued to grow. Insurance companies continued to dispose of government securities in favor of other assets, even though by 1951 they had reduced governments to something like a normal proportion of their portfolios. Although some new bond issues may have been postponed following the accord, the statistics of new issues suggest that it was not long before it was possible to place issues at rates acceptable to the market. (Professor Whittlesey argued also that anticipation of the accord greatly increased security offerings in the first quarter of 1951.)

In assessing the inflexibility of lending rates in the face of monetary restriction, it is essential to remember that lenders have at their disposal a number of devices for raising the effective rate of interest to the borrower while the nominal quoted rate remains the same. Bankers, for example, can be more insistent that borrowers keep certain amounts on deposit. Their replies to the committee (*Compendium*, pp. 1133-46) indicate that in many cases this was in fact their reaction to monetary tightness in 1950 and 1951.

It is easy to understand why the new theory of monetary control should be eagerly seized as the rationale of Federal Reserve policy. For it offers the hope that monetary policy can be effective without the large fluctuations of interest rates which used to be considered essential. And even now, for better or for worse, the Federal Reserve is not realistically free to pursue a policy which disregards the prices of government bonds. A great deal of Federal Reserve and Treasury effort must still, as ever since the war, be devoted to increasing private investors' willingness to hold government securities by measures other than increasing their yields. [13] The new theory reaches the cheerful conclusion that these measures will also be an effective curb on private spending, because they reduce the availability of credit to private borrowers.

Such a policy does not imply that rates must never rise; indeed occasional small changes in rates are, according to the theory, necessary to bring into play the effects on which the policy relies. It does require that, at any given level of rates, private willingness to hold government securities be as large as possible and, consequently, the supply of bank reserves and of money as small as possible. To this end the Treasury and Federal Reserve have available many devices, for example: judicious adjustment both of the types and maturities of public debt instruments and of the composition, in distinction to the size, of the Federal Reserve's government portfolio; "moral suasion" to prevent holders of government securities from selling – this went to extremes in 1950, and the Open Market Committee has now penitently forsworn its use (see *Compendium*, pp. 630-32, 1253-56, and *Hearings*, pp. 398-400.); setting the rediscount rate in such relation to the short-term government rate as to induce banks in need of reserves to borrow them, so that both the traditional distaste of bankers for indebtedness and the Federal Reserve's discretionary powers in respect to the privilege of rediscounting may be exploited; "pinning in" private bond holdings by penalizing sales, redemptions, or conversions before maturity with capital losses; manipulation of market uncertainties and expectations about future rates. Experience with this kind of policy has led to increased awareness of lags, imperfections, and institutional conventions in the money markets. These the policy seeks to exploit to make monetary measures effective, at least temporarily. As the market adapts itself to one measure, the ingenuity of the monetary authorities may be taxed to find another.

Only the future will tell whether this kind of monetary policy will do the job to the satisfaction of the monetary authorities themselves, or whether in the end they will conclude that monetary control can only be successful through the more pronounced changes in interest rates on which central banks traditionally relied in the past.

3. Policy: Monetary Restriction in an Anti-inflationary Program

Concerning the wisdom of the accord, the Patman inquiry disclosed virtually no dissent. Many thought that par support should have been abandoned earlier; almost no one, except an occasional banker, thought it should have been perpetuated. Concerning the importance of the accord, there was considerable disagreement. Senator Douglas and Professor Friedman were inclined to blame the 1950 inflation on the failure of the Federal Reserve to cease support at that time, and to attribute the stability of 1951 and 1952 to the new policy. Most others, including Federal Reserve spokesmen, were more modest in their claims for monetary measures. At the opposite extreme, Mr. Keyserling thought monetary policy a relatively insignificant factor both before and after the accord. But even he did not suggest that the accord was bad policy.

There was, however, substantial division of opinion on how far monetary policy should be pushed. At one extreme is Professor Friedman's position that it should be pushed as far as necessary to remove any inflationary pressure which fiscal policy does not remove, regardless of the consequences in the government securities markets. At the other – if we leave aside the bizarre views of Mr. John D. Clark (*Compendium*, p. 892) – Mr. Keyserling found so many disadvantages in higher interest rates that he would rely on direct controls instead of monetary restriction to supplement fiscal policy and would indeed prefer moderate inflation to the consequences of higher interest rates. In between, most respondents found some reasons for placing limits on monetary restriction, though their limits would be less confining than Mr. Keyserling's.

Reasons for limiting reliance on monetary restriction fall into two classes: those connected with the public debt, and those which would have force even if the public debt did not exist or were "insulated." For the most part, the reasons offered of the first class will not survive rational examination. Long ago Paul Samuelson demonstrated that the solvency of banks and other financial institutions is not threatened by a decline in government bond prices. [14] As for the higher interest charges to the Treasury, the issue is essentially the same as in the old controversy on the burden of the debt. It may seem strange to hear "after all, we owe it to ourselves" from financiers pleading for higher interest rates rather than from Harvard professors dispelling alarm over the size of the debt. But the substantial truth of the argument holds in either context. The only objection to a rise in debt charges is the friction and possible injury to incentives involved in taxing to pay the interest without unwelcome distributional consequences. [15]

More weight must be assigned the second class of reasons for limiting monetary policy. Prevention of inflation is not the only national economic objective. There are several instruments available for preventing inflation, and they can be combined in varying proportions. Among the several combinations which can do the anti-inflationary job, the optimum mix of policy instruments is the one most favorable to other social objectives. The Patman inquiry inspired surprisingly little discussion of this problem. The prevalent assumption seemed to be that, since an adequate anti-inflationary program is unlikely to be adopted, the best tactic is to urge stronger measures all around. This may be a realistic view, but is it the proper attitude to take in advising a committee of Congress? Congress, after all, has the authority to decide how much use shall be made of all anti-inflationary weapons. Should one say to Congress, in effect: We know you fellows haven't the guts to raise taxes, so you'd better go all out for monetary restriction? Or should one offer some guidance on the relative degrees to which Congress should rely on tax policy, monetary restriction, and direct controls?

One formula which often seems implicit [16] in discussions of the problem is that the budget should be balanced and any remaining inflationary pressure removed by monetary means. Although this prescription has the practical appeal that a balanced budget may be the best one can expect from Congress, it is not consistent with the countercyclical fiscal policy, including surpluses in boom times, which economists have been educating the public to accept. Moreover, should the formula apply regardless of the size of the budget? A large balanced budget would put more of a burden on monetary measures than a small one.

The choice between monetary restriction and tax increases is largely a choice between consumption and investment. (It is not entirely so, both because taxes may deter investment as well as consumption, and because monetary restriction, even excluding selective credit controls, may curtail consumption as well as investment.) Mr. Keyserling's objection to heavy reliance on general credit control was that he preferred to obtain resources for defense from consumption rather than from investment. Furthermore, given a decision that investment must bear a certain share of the burden, what lines of investment should be curtailed? General monetary restriction will result in one pattern; direct controls in another. Mr. Keyserling was not sure he would like the pattern of private investment produced by general monetary restriction. Professor Friedman and other exponents of the free market were sure they would not like a pattern produced by direct controls. Incidentally, if the description of the money market given by the new monetary theory is correct, the choice is less between a pattern produced by the price system and one produced by direct controls than between a pattern produced by decentralized rationing of credit and one produced by governmental controls of materials allocations and prices. These issues are, much more than the charges on the national debt, the ones to consider in judging the extent to which inflation should be fought by monetary weapons.

Another relevant consideration is the expected duration of the inflationary pressure and the economic forecast after it subsides. Experience with high and variable rates of interest during a period of inflationary pressure may well decrease the demand for bonds in the future and make it more difficult to achieve the lower rates suitable to a deflationary economic climate. Therefore, it can reasonably be argued (see *Report*, p. 35, and statement of Roy

Blough, *Hearings*, p. 253), a temporary inflationary storm should be fought by measures which can be more easily put into reverse. But the importance of this consideration should not be exaggerated, even if the assumption that normal economic weather is deflationary is accepted. Just as there are other ways of dealing with inflation, so there are other ways of coping with deflation; indeed it is widely agreed that monetary measures are less effective against deflation than against inflation. The economy will not be doomed to depression just because the monetary authorities find it takes time to undo the uncertainties and expectations about interest rates created by their previous anti-inflationary moves. If the long-run economic outlook is really deflationary, the central bank will be able in time to bring rates back down to their pre-inflation levels both by monetary expansion and by gradually reducing investors's rate expectations and uncertainties.

In recent years the subject of monetary policy has excited emotion as well as analysis. The end of the Treasury-Federal Reserve conflict has made the subject one of less absorbing interest, but also one which can be approached with less passion and more perspective. The volumes produced by the Patman inquiry will contribute to the serious study of monetary problems for a long time to come.

Notes

[1] *Monetary Policy and the Management of the Public Debt: Their Role in Achieving Price Stability and High-level Employment.*

[2] *Replies to Questions and Other Material for the Use of the Subcommittee on General Credit Control and Debt Management*, Joint Committee on the Economic Report, 82nd Congress, 2nd session (Washington: U.S. Government Printing Office, 1952). 2 Parts. Part 1 pp. xvii + 632. Part 2 pp. vii + 633-1302.

[3] *Hearings before the Subcommittee on General Credit Control and Debt Management*, Joint Committee on the Economic Report, 82nd Congress, 2nd session. March 10-31, 1952 (Washington: U.S. Government Printing Office, 1952), pp. v + 993.

[4] *Report of the Subcommittee on General Credit Control and Debt Management*, Joint Committee on the Economic Report, 82nd Congress, 2nd session (Washington: U.S. Government Printing Office, 1952), pp. vi + 80.

[5] Joint Committee on the Economic Report, *A Compendium of Materials on Monetary, Credit and Fiscal Policies* (81st Congress, 2nd session; Senate document 132), pp. 77-79, 180-86.

[6] A supplementary reserve requirement such as the Board proposed in 1947 would not eliminate the possibility of declines in long-term bond prices. But it would, even if indirectly, remove some of the pressure on the long-term market. To the extent that short-term debt was locked in the banks, the supply of short-terms to other investors would be diminished. The resulting rate structure would increase the willingness of these

investors to hold long-terms. Or the Treasury and Federal Reserve could, without expanding bank reserves, reduce the outstanding supply of long-terms and satisfy the needs of nonbank investors for short-term obligations.

[7] Compare the pre-accord letter of the Treasury General Counsel to the Joint Committee on the Economic Report, *General Credit Control, Debt Management, and Economic Stabilization*, pp. 38-40.

[8] Board members, according to the majority *Report*, should have terms of six instead of fourteen years, be eligible for reappointment, be reduced in number from seven to five, be chosen without geographical restraints, and receive increased salaries.

[9] Formally Keynes's theory justifies skepticism about monetary policy only in special circumstances. But Keynes himself and many Keynesians believed these circumstances to be typical of modern economics.

[10] Milton Friedman has presented figures showing a fairly close correspondence between the monetary expansions and the price inflations associated with three wars. "Price, Income, and Monetary Changes in Three Wartime Periods," *American Economic Review*, 42 (Proceedings, 1952), 612-25. Even accepting an interpretation of these data favorable to the quantity theory, it remains quite possible that over shorter spans of time the relationship between money and prices is loose.

[11] See his essay, "Interest Rates and the Central Bank," *Money, Trade, and Economic Growth*, pp. 270-95. For the development of the doctrine, beginning with prewar writings, see pp. 275-76 of that essay and the works there cited.

[12] The replies of insurance executives (*Compendium*, pp. 1234-44) do not provide unequivocal support to the view that they are irrationally "pinned in" to government securities by capital losses. (Neither do the figures on changes in insurance company portfolios since the accord.) Several executives explicitly denied that such losses were of any concern if higher-yielding investments were available. Others considered losses a deterrent, but it is not clear that they meant anything more than that higher yields on governments make them more competitive with other assets.

[13] And evidently by means other than compulsion. As noted above, the Federal Reserve is now not interested in supplementary reserve proposals designed to "insulate" part of the debt.

[14] "The Effect of Interest Rate Increases on the Banking System," *American Economic Review*, 35 (1945), 16-27.

[15] On the other hand, objections to "insulation" devices designed to save interest charges on the Treasury without hamstringing the Federal Reserve seem equally insubstantial. A rise in the interest rates the Treasury pays may do little harm, but neither is it a good thing in itself. The argument, frequently encountered in these volumes, that the government should be as subject to the discipline of the capital market as any other borrower is inconsistent with the argument that higher interest charges do not matter. If the transfer of interest from taxpayer to bondholder is properly of little concern to the government, why should a high market rate deter the government from spending? It is true, of course, that resources should be diverted from private investment to public investment only if they have as high a marginal social productivity in public use as in private. But the connection between this principle of rational allocation and the interest rate the Treasury has to pay to borrow is surely extremely tenuous.

[16] For fairly explicit statements of this formula, see the reply of Milton Friedman (*Compendium*, p. 1069), and the statement of Lester V. Chandler in *General Credit Control, Debt Management, and Economic Mobilization* (Joint Committee on the Economic Report, 82nd Congress, 1st session), p. 65.

CHAPTER 23

THE MONETARY INTERPRETATION OF HISTORY
(A REVIEW ARTICLE)

This monumental "monetary history of the United States" [1] since the Civil War is at the same time a critical history of monetary events, institutions, and policies and a monetary interpretation of the general economic — and even political – history of the century. I shall discuss these two aspects of the work in turn, although it is impossible to keep them entirely separate. In a sense the first aspect is the determination of the stock of money, M, while the second concerns the stability of the velocity of money, V. In the third and final section I shall review some of the judgments of the authors concerning particular episodes in the history of monetary policy.

1. The Stock of Money

Milton Friedman and Anna Schwartz provide a statistical account of the stock of money in the United States since 1867. Much of this is new, the product of long and painstaking statistical research. The profession is greatly indebted to them for constructing monetary series homogeneous in concept and definition over so long a span of time. The numerical account is dexterously and gracefully interwoven with a history of monetary institutions, legislation, policies, personalities, and politics. The resulting narrative is fascinating and absorbing, and it is written in a consistently lucid and lively style.

"The Monetary Interpretation of History" is a review of *A Monetary History of the United States 1867-1960* by M. Friedman and A. Schwartz. Reprinted from *American Economic Review* 55, No. 3 (June 1965), 464-85.

A version of this review article was given at the American Bankers Association Conference of University Professors, Princeton, N.J., September 1, 1964. In revising the paper, the author has benefited from the discussion at the conference, which included comments by James Duesenberry, Allan Meltzer, Milton Friedman, and Anna Schwartz. He is especially grateful to Friedman for providing a written version of his remarks. L.Charles Miller and Marshall Pomer carried out the calculations.

1.1. What is Money?

The "money" whose stock the authors trace and explain consists of currency and commercial bank deposits held outside the federal government and the banks. The main questions raised by this definition are these: Why are time and savings deposits in commercial banks, which are not means of payment, included? If they are included, why are similar claims on other financial institutions – notably deposits in mutual savings banks and shares in savings and loan associations – excluded?

On the first question, a decisive practical answer is that it is evidently impossible to distinguish time from demand deposits in commercial banks prior to 1914. But Friedman and Schwartz do not stand on this answer. They do not think that their inability to exclude deposits not subject to check impairs the utility or relevance of their series for the stock of money. They cannot contend, of course, that their M measures the stock of means of payment, but they do not regard this as a defect.

More basic, in their view, is a concept of money as "a temporary abode of purchasing power enabling the act of purchase to be separated from the act of sale" (p. 650). I am not sure what this means; on its face the concept seems to allow all forms of wealth, all stores of value, to qualify as money. Clearly purchasing power can find temporary abodes other than currency and commercial bank deposits, for example in other savings institutions.

The authors recognize that, once the means-of-payment criterion is dropped, drawing the lines that define *money* is a matter of expediency. What statistical quantity works best? That is, what measure bears the closest and most predictable relationship to measures of economic activity? This is fair enough scientific procedure. But such open-minded pragmatism in the concept and definition of money is an unconvincing prelude to policy conclusions which stress the overriding importance of providing money in precisely the right quantity. Sometimes Friedman and his followers seem to be saying: "We don't know what money is, but whatever it is, its stock should grow steadily at 3 to 4 per cent per year."

Friedman and Schwartz are entitled to use words the way they please, and their "money" is a very worthwhile magnitude to measure. Being an aggregative economist by nature myself, I am not as disposed as many critics might be to point out how much information any particular aggregate conceals. All global measures do conceal information. That is their virtue as well as their vice, and the task of science, in economics as elsewhere, is to find and devise aggregates which retain mostly essential information and discard mainly irrelevant information.

Nevertheless the central place which Friedman and Schwartz give their money stock in theoretical analysis, historical interpretation, and policy recommendation invites critical scrutiny. Imagine a balance sheet expressing on one side the financial claims of the rest of the economy on the federal government (including the Federal Reserve) and the commercial banking system and on the other side the debts of the public to the government and the banks. (The balancing item is that amount of private net worth represented by the net debt of the central government to the public.) Both the government and the commercial banks have demand liabilities to the public, currency and demand deposits. Both have time liabilities to the public, securities and deposits. The total on which the authors focus is the sum of the government's demand liabilities to the public and all of the commercial banking system's deposit liabilities, time as well as demand. In their view, this seems to be the only feature of the consolidated balance sheet which matters.

Do Friedman and Schwartz really think that the composition of this magnitude is of no consequence? Do they, for example, expect the velocity of a given M to be the same after a shift from demand to time deposits? And is their answer to this question the same whether such a shift is the autonomous result of a change in preferences or the induced effect of an increase in time-deposit interest rates? In special cases they recognize that compositional shifts are not neutral. They argue, for example, that shift to currency induced by bank failures will raise velocity – that is, it will reduce the demand for money because currency is an imperfect substitute for the safe deposits it replaces. But this attention to special cases suggests that there may be general and systematic compositional effects which the authors have ignored. I shall return to this question in section 2 in discussing the stability of velocity.

What about the liabilities omitted from M, the interest-bearing government debt held by the public? Are its size and composition of no monetary consequence? Friedman and Schwartz tend to take an extreme either/or black-or-white view. Generally they do not regard this debt as money or as affecting the significance for economic activity of the liabilities that are money. But there is an important exception. In 1942-51, Federal Reserve support of government security prices made them the equivalent of money, indeed of high-powered money. The true money stock should include these securities, valued at their support prices. By the same logic the 1951 Accord would abruptly shrink money to its usual constituents. [2]

I think most readers will agree with me that this is farfetched. There is uncertainty about government security prices in normal times, but it does not prevent them from being good substitutes for bank deposits. This is especially true of short maturities, but it is true of any maturities the holders can match with their own future-payments schedules. Uncertainty was doubtless reduced, but it was not eliminated, by the Fed's wartime support commitment. There was considerable doubt, justified in the event, that the policy would be permanently continued. There is no evidence – either in interest rates on government obligations or in velocity figures – of such radical and abrupt revisions of public attitude towards government securities.

Moreover, I cannot see the logic which makes the authors so anxious to assimilate completely to money marketable government securities temporarily supported at par, and so reluctant to assimilate to money the liabilities of thrift institutions which are always "supported at par."

Finally, are they justified in neglecting the asset side of the consolidated balance sheet of the government and the commercial banking system? The authors are strongly opposed to giving attention to "credit" as against "money." The word "credit" in this dichotomy has a host of meanings, whose only common bond is concern for features of bank operations and financial markets other than the quantity of money. In Federal Reserve history, credit policy was long associated with the real-bills fallacy written into its very charter. According to this doctrine, the Federal Reserve could and should enable the banking system to meet the legitimate needs of trade and industry to finance productive activity, so long as its credit was not used for speculation or for unsound accumulation of inventories. This hardy tradition survives to this day insofar as the state of confidence or anxiety over the quality and direction of credit influences general monetary policy. The authors are properly critical of this tradition and of the surprisingly complete neglect of the quantity of money in prewar Federal Reserve theory.

The real-bills "credit" tradition also neglects interest rates. For example, the credit situation is judged satisfactory if all borrowers of good credit standing are being accommodated, regardless of the rates and other terms prevailing in the market. All that matters is equality of supply and demand, the absence of queues, regardless of the price and quantity at which the market is cleared.

I stress this point because Friedman and Schwartz lump under the same heading – that of excessive attention to "credit" – all concerns with the interest rate effects of monetary measures. Indeed they blame Keynes for elevating "credit" above "money" because of the role of the long-term interest rate in the *General Theory* – even though the only way to get at the interest rate in the Keynesian model is to manipulate *M*.

Personally I think that interest rates rank high among the gauges that measure the impact of monetary policies and conditions on economic activity, and that central bankers surely ought to consider the interest rate effects of their policies. But whether this view is right or wrong, it is certainly not cut from the same cloth as the real-bills and credit quality fallacies.

Interest rates aside, does the composition of bank assets make no difference? Will the effect on economic activity be the same whether a given increase in the money stock reflects (a) commercial loans by banks to private business borrowers, or (b) exchange of bank certificates of deposit for Treasury bills previously held by the public? The monetization of commercial loans (or really indirectly of the inventories of goods which they finance) seems to me to be alchemy of much deeper significance than semimonetization of Treasury bills. By this I mean simply that I would expect (a) to stimulate more spending on GNP than does (b). If so, the same M packs a bigger wallop if it is the counterpart of operations like (a) than if it is the result of asset swaps like (b). You will never detect the difference if you confine your attention to the liabilities of the banking system.

1.2. The Proximate Determinant of the Stock of Money

Friedman and Schwartz explain the irregular growth of the stock of money, M, in terms of three "proximate determinants": (1) the stock of high-powered money, H, i.e., currency and Federal Reserve deposit liabilities held outside the federal government; (2) the ratio D/C of the public's commercial bank deposits, D, to the public's holdings of currency, C; and (3) the ratio D/R of deposits owned by the public, D, to the total high-powered money reserves, R, of the commercial banking system. It is purely arithmetic tautology to express the stock of money in terms of these three factors and to explain its development over time by variations in these "proximate determinants." Since $M = D + C$ and $H = R + C$,

$$M = H \left(\frac{\dfrac{D}{R}\left(1 + \dfrac{D}{C}\right)}{\dfrac{D}{R} + \dfrac{D}{C}} \right)$$

The authors breathe life into this tautology as they trace the three factors over the century.

The concept of "high-powered money" is indispensable to understanding a monetary and banking system like that of the United States. The essential feature of the system is the commitment of the banks, with only fractional reserves of currency, to maintain convertibility at par and on demand between their deposit liabilities and currency. Since 1914 the major portion of bank reserves has not been literally in the form of currency but rather in deposits in Federal Reserve Banks. But this difference of form is inconsequential, because the Federal Reserve maintains for banks two-way convertibility between these deposits and currency.

In the United States today the government – i.e., the Treasury and the Federal Reserve together – determines the quantity of high-powered money. The behavior of the public and the banks determines how much of this stock is in circulation as currency and how much serves as reserves for multiple creation of deposits by the banking system. The authors do not say so explicitly, but the logic of the three "proximate determinants" evidently is this: the stock of high-powered money is determined by the government, the deposit currency ratio by the public, and the deposit/reserve ratio by the banks. Of course this is an oversimplification, because each of the three sectors can, at least indirectly, affect all of the determinants. For example, the government, by determining reserve requirements, strongly influences the deposit/reserve ratio which the banks seek and achieve. Nevertheless I agree that this is an illuminating way to discuss the determination of the stock of money.

For the Federal Reserve era, I would find it more illuminating, and more in keeping with the spirit of the scheme, to exclude from high-powered money reserves borrowed by member banks from the Federal Reserve Banks. Then member bank decisions to use the discount window would affect the deposit/reserve ratio rather than the stock of high-powered money. The amount of borrowing is of course influenced by Federal Reserve policy in setting the discount rate and administering the discount window. But the initiative is the banks', and it seems to be more natural to regard decisions to borrow reserves in the same light as decisions to hold smaller excess reserves. This, however, is a matter of taste and analytical convenience rather than of principle.

1.3. The Stock of High-powered Money

The federal government's control – even its proximate control – over the stock of high-powered money was considerably tightened by the establishment of the Federal Reserve System in 1914. In earlier times national banks could expand the supply of high-powered money on their own initiative by issuing national bank notes; they never exploited their note-issue privilege to the legal maximum permitted. (Since note issue appears to have been profitable, the authors frankly say that this is a puzzle they cannot explain [p. 23].) Private gold transactions provided another gap in government control of high-powered money. Banks needing reserves, for example, could buy gold in London. For the system as a whole this expedient was limited by the "gold points" in periods when the United States was on the gold standard. But in the greenback period, before 1879, the banks could in effect increase their high-powered money reserves by depreciating the dollar relative to gold and sterling. I am indebted to Friedman and Schwartz for these points, but I do not think they stress sufficiently their implications – i.e., the government's control over the stock of high-powered money was relatively loose over much of the period which they cover.

Governmental actions to increase the stock of high-powered money have been of three kinds: (1) purchase and monetization of gold, (2) printing or coining of currency to meet other government expenditure, including the purchase of silver, and (3) the extension of Federal Reserve credit through open market purchases of securities, purchases of acceptances from banks, or discounting of paper for member banks. The reverse actions, of course, diminish the stock. Although these various sources of high-powered money are arithmetically equivalent, given the values of the two ratios, in their effects on the stock of money, I think it is misleading to regard them as economically equivalent.

In some cases high-powered money is created as a by-product of income-generating expenditures by the government or by foreign purchases of U.S. exports. In others, high-powered money arises simply from exchanges of assets between the government or central bank and private banks or individuals. In the former cases, the new high-powered money also reflects additions to private net worth; in the latter cases, it does not. Some of the expansionary economic consequences of growth in high-powered money may be due to income and wealth directly generated. These cannot be duplicated by purely monetary policy, which is confined to the third of the three ways of engineering increases in high-powered money. You cannot repeat the consequences for employment, income, and spending of purchasing a million dollars of newly mined gold by purchasing a million dollars of old government securities – even though both operations increase high-powered money by a million dollars.

1.4. The Deposit/Currency Ratio

Over the long run this ratio reflects the habits, institutions, and preferences of the community with respect to the use of currency and bank deposits. Over most of the short runs in this history, variations in the ratio reflect the fluctuating confidence of the public in banks' ability to maintain convertibility of their deposits into currency.

Secularly, banks gained steadily and dramatically at the expense of currency until 1929, although most of the gains after 1915 were in time deposits rather than in the ratio of demand deposits to currency in public use. But the banks have never restored the position they lost in the Great Depression and World War II. Although heavier income taxation has presumably promoted the use of currency, the success of deposit insurance and the general growth of income and wealth should have favored the use of banks. Bankers might well ask themselves why their liabilities are not as preferred a medium of exchange as they were thirty-five or forty years ago. Could service charges be a factor?

Much monetary history concerns the maintenance of convertibility between deposits and currency, and it is a dismal record of panics, crises, failures, and lessons never learned. The worst episode was of course that of 1930-33. The Federal Reserve System, established precisely to defend the monetary and banking structure against an "internal drain," failed utterly to do so. The authors make a convincing case that a better job would have been done without the Fed. Following earlier precedent, the banks would have stayed open while the conversion of deposits into currency was temporarily restricted. This would have been done, the authors think, as early as 1930; and this timely therapy would have prevented the subsequent disastrous scrambles for liquidity.

However this may be, the authors are surely right to regard federal deposit insurance as the real remedy, and therefore as the most important banking reform since the National Banking Act nationalized the issue of currency. Ironically enough, deposit insurance was stubbornly opposed as unsound by the banking fraternity it has so greatly benefited.

The deposit/currency ratio is broadly descriptive of the community's balance of preference between currency and deposits and of the state of confidence in banks. It is often used in another sense, as a parameter in calculation of the increase in money stock to be expected from a dollar's increase in high-powered money. I have doubts about this use of the ratio. It implies behavior that does not seem plausible, namely that currency and deposits are rigidly complementary – for every X dollars the community adds to its deposits, it will acquire also one dollar of currency. It is more likely that the demand for stocks of currency varies in the short run with money income, or more precisely with the volume of retail and wage transactions in which currency is used. If so, an increase in deposits will bring in its wake an increase in demand for currency only to the extent that it increases economic activity. Likewise increases in activity against an unchanged volume of deposits will tend to increase the demand for currency and to pull down the deposit/currency ratio. This hypothesis is borne out by the cyclical behavior of the ratio, so far as this can be divorced from fluctuations of confidence in banks. The ratio tends to fall prior to cyclical peaks, and thanks to the "return flow" of currency to banks to rise prior to troughs.

1.5. The Deposit/Reserve Ratio

This ratio reflects both legal reserve requirements and voluntary precautions against deposit withdrawal. I should perhaps repeat the authors' warning that both the numerator and denominator of the ratio exclude interbank deposits. Hence the use of correspondent balances as required or voluntary reserves tends to raise the ratio, and their replacement by high-powered money (as for reserves required of all Federal Reserve member banks) to lower it. In a sense the ratio measures the degree of protection the banking system as a whole has against withdrawals of currency. But this is so only on the assumption, contrary to fact, that in an emergency reserves would not be immobilized by legal requirements. It would have been better if the authors could have provided statistical series distinguishing between required and excess reserves, but evidently this was not technically possible.

Much of the short-run variation in this ratio, as in the previous one, is connected with the state of public confidence in banks. When confidence weakened, banks sought to protect themselves by increasing their reserves. Here was another element in the inherent instability of the system prior to deposit insurance. In classic banking crises banks and public joined in a mad scramble for high-powered money. There was never enough to go round.

Banks' demand for excess reserves — and banks' willingness to borrow reserves — depend on their assessments of the risks of deposit withdrawals, their appraisals of the possibilities and costs of obtaining reserves in emergency, and the earning opportunities on nonreserve uses of funds. Friedman and Schwartz are not inclined to stress the importance of interest rates in the liquidity preferences of banks — or, as we shall see later, in the liquidity preferences of the public.

The issue is clearly posed by the excess reserves of the banks after 1933. These reached $2.5 billion, 42 per cent of total reserves, in 1936. Even after the doubling of reserve requirements in 1936-37, excess reserves were $1.2 billion, 18 per cent of total reserves. And they grew again to $6.3 billion, 48 per cent of total reserves, in 1940. On one common interpretation, this accumulation meant that the banks were "loose," in the sense that gains or losses of reserves, over a considerable range, would affect very little or not at all their holdings of nonreserve assets. Friedman and Schwartz on the other hand, believe that the banks were about as "tight" as ever. True, their demand for excess reserves had greatly increased as a result of the 1930-33 experience; but it was just as important to satisfy this demand as it had been to satisfy the more modest reserve demands of the previous decade. Banks would respond to losses of reserves by reducing their other assets and their deposits, and to gains in reserves by significant increases in loans and investments and deposits.

Another way to put this difference of opinion is as follows: According to the first, or Keynesian, interpretation, banks were by the mid-'thirties moving along a fairly flat liquidity preference curve. Having invested in short-term Treasury and commercial paper until the rates were virtually zero, they would hold in cash any further accretions of reserves. The more high-powered money, the lower the deposit/reserve ratio — and these two proximate determinants certainly do show strong negative correlation in this period. (It is, of course, not at all inconsistent with this interpretation to agree with Friedman and Schwartz that the unhappy events of the early 1930's had also moved the banks' liquidity preference curves bodily to the right [Chart 44, p. 537].)

According to the authors' interpretation, this correlation is a coincidence. The decline in the deposit/reserve ratio is due much more to shifts of the banks' cash preference schedule than to movements along it. While shifting, the schedule remained steep. One shift was a result of the 1930-33 experience, the bank runs and the demonstration that the Federal Reserve was no help. A second shift in the same direction was the result of the 1936-37 increases in reserve requirements, reinforced by the 1937 economic contraction. This shift reflected not just the increase in required reserves but, more important and more permanent, an increase in demand for excess reserves to hold against the possibility that the Fed might again raise requirements. The authors believe that these shifts proceeded at their own pace, largely independent of the growth of the stock of high-powered money. The banks and the money supply were never out of the control of the Fed. By changing the supply of reserves, or reserve requirements, the Fed could at any time alter the deposits and earning assets of the banks by the usual multiple expansion process.

For these reasons the authors regard gold sterilization, failure to engage in open market operations, and the raising of reserve requirements as disastrous errors of policy. On the other interpretation, they were mistakes all right, but relatively harmless ones.

I find the interpretation of the authors unconvincing. I do not see why shifts in preference resulting from discrete events should proceed so smoothly, and in particular with such striking negative correlation with the growth of high-powered money. Did bankers never take heart again, even when the deposit/currency ratio was rising and bank runs seemed to be a thing of the past? It may be that the introduction of variation of reserve requirements into the Federal Reserve's tool kit occasioned an increase in the demand for excess reserves. If so, it would be more reasonable to expect this to occur in 1935 when the legislation was passed but the powers were yet to be used, rather than after 1937 when requirements were already at, or very near, the maximum permitted by Congress.

No doubt the depression led to an increase in banks' demand for safe short-term assets, whether excess cash reserves or Treasury bills. As banks' excess cash spilled into short-term securities, short-term rates were driven almost to zero. In these circumstances Federal Reserve open market purchases of bills were useless — almost like trading cash for cash. Surely there is this much truth, at least, in the Keynesian interpretation. Long-term rates and commercial loan rates were sticky, and it might have been hoped that banks' accumulation of excess reserves and low-yielding short-term securities would eventually put pressure on these other rates. But their differentials above short-term rates stubbornly reflected the lessons of the depression regarding risks of illiquidity and default. In spite of the substantial liquidity of the banks and the public they did not give way until war altered the whole economic climate. Open market purchases of long-term securities might have helped to depress their rates and to push banks and other financial institutions into more private lending. As it was, the gold sterilization policy kept these institutions supplied with safe income from government bonds during much of this period. The Federal Reserve Board does not deserve the scorn with which the authors treat their statement that in the circumstances of 1939 open market purchases were more important for their direct effects on the capital market than for their influence on member bank reserves (p. 534). [3]

2. The Velocity of Money

2.1. The Trend in Income Velocity of Money

Before World War II, the income velocity of Friedman and Schwartz money showed a sharp downward trend. Actually velocity did not begin its decline until after 1880, when it reached a record high of 4.97. It had fallen to 1.91 by 1914. No trend is apparent from 1914 to 1929. Velocity generally declined from 1929 to 1946. There were wartime bulges in 1918-19 and 1942-44. Since 1946 the trend has been upward, but V remains lower than in the 1920's or in 1914.

The authors believe that the normal trend of velocity is down. The reason is that the services of money stocks are a luxury, with income elasticity greater than one. As its per capita income rises, society devotes an increasing fraction of its income to purchase of the services of stocks of money. That is, society increases its holdings of money relative to money income.

Irving Fisher would be surprised to read this theory and history of velocity. He would have expected an account of the demand for money to be closely tied to its function as means of payment. He would have wished to hear about the frequency and timing of wage payments and bill settlements, the speed and cost of communications, the trend of industrial integration, the scope of the barter and subsistence economy relative to the money economy, the volume of total transactions relative to income-generating transactions, and so on.

Friedman and Schwartz provide no such discussion, and not even an excuse for omitting it. Partly, I suppose, this is because their money includes time deposits, which are not means of payment. Mainly, I think, it is because **they don't regard the properties of money as particularly relevant to an explanation of the demand for money. Here is a consumer good much like any other. Empirically, it turns out — but for reasons that have almost nothing to do with the distinctive properties of money — that this commodity is a luxury**, i.e., has an income elasticity greater than one. Like butter, or automobile mileage, or cameras. The big difference is that the supply of money does not respond to changes in income in accordance with its income elasticity, but instead makes income dance to its tune.

The treatment of money as a luxury consumer durable good seems to me a strained analogy. For one thing, it does not apply very easily to business firms, which hold most of the money stock. In any case, there are no identifiable services yielded by ownership of a stock of money: I don't believe the authors are referring to the joys of numismatics or to the satisfactions of a miser. The services of a stock of money are indirect. They can be measured only by comparing the implications of holding on average large stocks of money and small stocks of other assets with the alternative policy of holding on average smaller stocks of money and larger stocks of other assets. Possible advantages of the first policy over the second are smaller costs in effort or in fees and smaller risks of loss when it is necessary or expedient to make payments. The disadvantages of the first policy are the sacrifice of earnings when alternative assets yield more than monetary assets. Individuals and business firms presumably adjust their money holdings until these advantages and disadvantages balance at the margin.

It is certainly not obvious why this process should lead to a secular decline in velocity. If this is the model the authors have in mind, then they should tell us how time and the growth of incomes have altered the relevant costs, risks, and yields. But then they would have to assign much greater importance to interest rate differentials as a determinant of velocity than they are prepared to do. They prefer to leave the alleged downward trend in velocity unexplained — for saying that money is a luxury is just another way of saying that its velocity declines with income.

This inadequacy of theory would not be so damaging if the empirical evidence for the downward trend were more convincing. On the authors' interpretation of the series, there is a downward trend from 1869 to 1946. This leaves the period since 1946 as the principal aberration to be explained; but it also leaves the 1920's as a disconcertingly long period during which the trend was interrupted. For the most recent period, the authors' hypothesis is that the demand for money has been reduced by the favorable postwar experience of economic stability. [4] Another *ad hoc* shift in preferences! Since adaptation to this experience will sooner or later be complete, the authors expect a resumption of the normal downward trend.

To me it seems strange to rely on a trend which regards the 1930's and 1940's as normal and the 1920's and 1950's as abnormal. The only convincing trend evident in the velocity series is 1880-1915. Since 1915 the series is dominated by fluctuations associated with wars and depression. Latané has shown that the velocity of money excluding time deposits since 1909 can be explained by interest rates, independent of the trend of real income. [5] Friedman and Schwartz state that the two velocity series differ since 1915 only in periods when identifiable special circumstances affected the demand for time deposits. So it is not the difference in the denominators of the two velocity ratios which is at issue. The authors object that interest rates cannot explain low velocity in 1932-33 and in 1946. But given the wealth of particular explanations their own book provides for abnormally high demands for money in those years, this criticism of Latané's results does not seem very damaging. Friedman and Schwartz are left, therefore, with the assertion that Latané and other "Keynesians" cannot explain, via interest rates, the downward trend in velocity before 1915.

Actually, the long-term rate "explains" 60 per cent of the variation of velocity from 1869-1914 (Table 23.1, regression 1.7). It is true that simple trend explains much more (92 per cent, regression 1.5). After 1914, trend explains only 51 per cent; short-term interest rate 56 per cent; long-term interest rate 45 per cent (regressions 1.8, 1.9, 1.10). The introduction of either interest rate into a multiple regression (regressions 1.12 and 1.13) lowers the absolute size of the trend coefficient.

The interest rate explanation, although it succeeds well enough so that the authors have no right to dismiss it, is at a disadvantage in respect to the velocity of Friedman and Schwartz money. For their money includes deposits, which bear an interest rate that can be expected to be correlated with market rates. The proper variable would be the differential of the market rate from the rate on time deposits. It is not surprising that interest rates are more closely related to the velocity of money exclusive of time deposits (regressions 2.9, 2.10, 2.12, 2.13).

Table 23.1
Regression of Velocity.
Dependent variables: V_1 velocity of Friedman and Schwartz money, which includes time deposits, V_2 velocity of Friedman and Schwartz money less time deposits

Regression number	Period	Dependent variable	Constant term	Coefficients (and their ratio to their standard errors) of					Proportion of variance of V explained	Standard error of residual
				Year 1914	Rate of change of money income	Short-term interest rate	Long-term interest rate			
			1	t	$\Delta Y/Y$	R_1	R_2		R^2	
1.1	1869-1959	V_1	2.43	-0.035 (-20.5)					0.82	0.42
1.2	1869-1959	V_1	2.38	-0.034 (-20.2)	-0.220 (-0.5)				0.82	0.42
1.3	1869-1959	V_1	2.44	-0.034 (-14.6)	-0.221 (-0.5)	-0.000 (-0.0)			0.82	0.43
1.4	1869-1959	V_1	1.74	-0.030 (-14.0)	-0.005 (-0.0)		+0.175 (3.0)		0.84	0.41
1.5	1869-1914	V_1	1.70	-0.064 (-22.3)					0.92	0.26
1.6	1869-1914	V_1	2.18			+0.192 (2.1)			0.10	0.87
1.7	1869-1914	V_1	0.13				+0.707 (8.0)		0.60	0.58
1.8	1915-1959	V_1	2.06	-0.016 (-6.7)					0.51	0.21
1.9	1915-1959	V_1	1.35			+0.121 (+7.4)			0.56	0.20
1.10	1915-1959	V_1	0.83				+0.235 (+5.9)		0.45	0.22

Table 23.1 (continued)

Regression number	Period	Dependent variable	Constant term (1)	Coefficients (and their ratio to their standard errors) of				Proportion of variance of V explained R^2	Standard error of residual
				Year 1914 t	Rate of change of money income $\Delta Y/Y$	Short-term interest rate R_1	Long-term interest rate R_2		
1.11	1915-1959	V_1	2.06	−0.016 (−6.6)	−0.009 (−0.0)			0.51	0.21
1.12	1915-1959	V_1	1.59	−0.009 (−3.7)	+0.438 (+2.0)	+0.096 (+5.5)		0.72	0.16
1.13	1915-1959	V_1	1.43	−0.010 (−2.7)	+0.224 (0.8)		+0.130 (+2.2)	0.56	0.20
2.8	1915-1959	V_2	3.26	−0.034 (−11.3)				0.64	0.33
2.9	1915-1959	V_2	1.81			+0.241 (+8.9)	+0.541 (+10.1)	0.65	0.33
2.10	1915-1959	V_2	0.49					0.70	0.31
2.11	1915-1959	V_2	3.32	−0.034 (−9.9)	−0.932 (−2.5)			0.70	0.30
2.12	1915-1959	V_2	2.59	−0.022 (−6.5)	−0.207 (−0.6)	+0.150 (6.0)		0.83	0.24
2.13	1915-1959	V_2	1.70	−0.018 (−3.8)	−0.293 (−0.8)		+0.335 (+4.3)	0.78	0.27

Sources: V_1 and V_2, Friedman and Schwartz Table A-5, p. 774. $\Delta Y/Y$ derived from Friedman and Schwartz money income series, described on p. 775. R_1 (commercial paper rate) and R_2 (basic yield on long-term corporate bonds) are series charted and described in Friedman and Schwartz, pp. 640-641. I am grateful to the authors for providing me with the series Y, R_1, and R_2.

You have your choice. The authors' income-luxury theory seems to work up to World War II but has to rely on considerable *ad hoc* explanation since. The Keynes-Latané interest rate theory of velocity seems to work since 1909 or so, but needs help for the preceding period.

This help is not hard to find. The downward trend in velocity coincided with a strong upward trend in the public's holdings of deposits relative to currency, the deposit/currency ratio already discussed. Neither trend started until about 1880. The correlation between these two variables before 1915 is 90. [6] The trend toward deposits, after interruption during World War I, seems to have continued until 1930, thanks to growth of time deposits. During the same period 1880–1915, commercial bank deposits grew relative to mutual savings banks. Mutual savings banks were almost as important as commercial banks around 1880, when the decline in velocity began. Their deposits were 80 per cent as large as those in commercial banks in 1877, 60 per cent as large in 1880, only 25 per cent as large as their rivals in 1915. During these years, of course, the territory covered by mutual savings banks became a smaller part of the continental economy.

I suspect, therefore, that over this period there was a considerable thrift element in the accumulation of commercial bank deposits. The character of Friedman and Schwartz money changed radically as currency became less important. Some deposits replaced currency as stocks of means of payment. Other deposits replaced mutual savings deposits; commercial banks became the principal available savings institutions.

Perhaps 1880-1915 was the great day for commercial banking, and the decline in velocity reflects its successful spread. Similarly savings and loan associations have been the spectacular success of the period since World War II. Their spread has helped to increase the velocity of money, just as the spread of commercial banks increased the velocity of currency. To the extent, however, that the spread of SLA's has also taken business from the security markets, the velocity of money-plus-SLA shares has declined, just as the velocity of currency-plus-bank-deposits did before 1915.

The regressions of Table 23.1 include both a cyclical variable $\Delta Y/Y$ and interest rates. They indicate that the association of velocity with interest rates is not due simply to the fact that both are procyclical. Inclusion of interest rates invariably reduces or eliminates the apparent significance of the cyclical variable. In the case of V_2, the velocity of money without time deposits, the cyclical variable $\Delta Y/Y$ has a negative coefficient. This suggests that the procyclical behavior of V_1, the velocity of Friedman and Schwartz money, is wholly due to time deposits. Most of it is in any case explained by one or the other interest rate. More generally, in boom times deposits lose out to other thrift accounts, to securities, including equities, and to real investments, while in recessions these alternatives become relatively less attractive. When a phenomenon is so simply explained, is it necessary to construct an elaborate theory, in which estimates of unobserved variables like permanent income and permanent prices are invested with an altogether spurious reality?

2.2. Cyclical Fluctuations in Velocity

Whatever its secular trend, velocity increases in cyclical expansions and declines in contractions. Several interpretations are consistent with this observation. One is that the cycle is nonmonetary: Money income is driven along its cyclical course by exogenous factors, the money supply is sluggish, and the cyclical behavior of velocity is the arithmetic result. The authors present convincing narrative evidence that at least on some crucial occasions this has not been true.

A second interpretation (not necessarily at odds with the first) is that velocity follows the procyclical movement of interest rates. This has the scientific virtue of providing a unified theoretical and statistical (see, for example, the findings of Latané previously discussed) explanation of both trend and cycle in velocity.

A third explanation is Friedman's. The demand for real balances in the form of money grows with *permanent* real income – indeed, as we have already seen, more than proportionately. Measured incomes run ahead of permanent incomes in cyclical upswings, making the velocity statistic high, and behind in downswings, making it low. Some day perhaps Friedman will tell us what transient income is used for. We know from his work on the consumption function that none of it is consumed. We now know that none of it is saved in monetary form. Does it all go into the stock market? A priori I should have thought that money balances were a likely repository of windfalls. After all, Friedman and Schwartz define money as a "temporary abode of purchasing power . . . "?

The trend-cycle explanation of velocity leaves many episodes unexplained, and the authors provide a fascinating account of the special forces operating on the demand for money from time to time. A recurrent favorite is price expectations. When the public expects prices to fall, their demand for money will be increased.

This is the authors' explanation of one of the most puzzling phenomena in their narrative, the extraordinarily high demand for money, and for other liquid assets, between 1946 and the Korean conflict. (The low velocity of money in those years is the more surprising to Friedman and Schwartz because they believe that their figures *over*state the true velocity. They overstate it for a reason I have already commented upon, namely that in their view "money" ought to include marketable government obligations during the period the Fed was committed to support their prices.) It is easy to forget that before Korea the economy had apparently reached a noninflationary equilibrium with a high degree of liquidity and interest rates on government securities not exceeding 2½ per cent.

I am inclined to agree with the authors' interpretation of the 1946-50 period, the more so because there is survey evidence, thanks to George Katona, that the public actually held the expectations attributed to it. There are other instances as well in which the imputation of price expectations up or down seems a reasonable way to make sense of otherwise puzzling movements of velocity. But the authors bring in these expectations only when they are obviously needed, leaving the reader with the uneasy feeling that their introduction at other times might be embarrassing. More important, I find it hard to reconcile their attention to price expectations with their neglect of explicit interest rates.

The real rate of return on money consists of two parts: the gain or loss in purchasing power due to change in prices, and the nominal or own-rate of return, zero for currency and interest net of service charges for deposits. A similiar real rate of return can be computed for other assets. From a theoretical standpoint it is hard to understand why Friedman and Schwartz are attributing such strategic importance to the first component of real rate of return and so little to the second. Inflationary or deflationary expectations affect the real rate of return on money, but no differently than they affect the real rate of return on a host of other assets fixed in ultimate money value. (Incidentally the authors refer to inflation – presumably unanticipated inflation – as a tax on money. In fact it is a tax on all fixed-money-value assets, and a subsidy on all fixed-money-value debts. The excess of the first over the second is not identical with the stock of money except by accident.) However, these other fixed-money-value assets differ from money in the flexibility of their nominal yields. These can and do rise or fall to compensate at least partially for generally held inflationary or deflationary expectations. Nominal yields on monetary assets, even time deposits, respond more slowly, if at all, because of institutional and legal ceilings.

Consequently, inflationary expectations will affect the demand for money differently, depending on the extent to which nominal yields on other fixed-money-value assets rise to compensate for these expectations.

In 1946-50, for example, interest rates on government bonds did not decline as a result of deflationary expectations. The Fed simply had to make fewer purchases in order to keep rates at the support levels. The public's demand for bonds was greater, and its demand for money less, than if interest rates had been free to adjust downward to expectations of postwar deflation.

2.3. The Stability and Independence of Velocity

The main conclusion of the authors is that although the stock of money has been determined by a variety of forces in the nine decades they review, its relationship to other economic variables has been stable. Has this been so? The annual percentage change in the money supply explains only 31 per cent of the variation in the annual percentage change in money income. [7]

Has velocity been stable and predictable? Friedman and Schwartz point out (p. 682) that the year-to-year change in velocity was less than 10 per cent in 78 of the 91 years and that velocity fell within 90 to 110 per cent of trend in 53 of 92 years. Since a 10 per cent difference in money income is the difference between inflation and recession, these figures are not very reassuring. I have regressed Friedman and Schwartz velocity against the factors they use to explain it: time trend, and percentage increase in money income, the latter representing a cyclical variable. The residual standard deviation of velocity is 42, one-sixth of its mean value (regression 1.2, Table 23.1).

But no one, even the most skeptical of the importance of monetary factors, is surprised to find a fairly close statistical relationship between the course of economic activity and the money stock. The direction of influence in this correlation is something else again. For example, the authors cite the contractions of money stock that have accompanied major business contractions. We know, however, that some events — e.g., loss of foreign demand for U.S. products — could contribute both to business contraction and to monetary contraction. Furthermore, business contractions themselves set in motion forces which reduce the money stock — banks, business borrowers, and depositors all become more cautious. The same may be true historically of the monetary authorities, reacting, however mistakenly, in response to "needs of trade" or defending the dollar against external drain. An inspection of the authors' own figures will show that it is adverse changes in the two ratios, deposit/reserves and deposit/currency, more than changes in high-powered money, which are proximately responsible for contracting the money stock. So the sins of the monetary authorities are generally ones of omission rather than commission.

Of course, the authors are aware of the two-way nature of the relationship between money and economic activity. They say:

Apparently, the forces determining the long-run rate of growth of real income are largely independent of the long-run rate of growth of the stock of money, so long as both proceed smoothly. But marked instability of money is accompanied by instability of economic growth [p. 678].

Changes in the money stock are therefore a consequence as well as an independent source of change in money income and prices, though, once they occur, they produce still further effects on income and prices. Mutual interaction, but with money rather clearly the senior partner in longer-run movements and in major cyclical movements, and more nearly an equal partner with money income and prices in shorter-run and milder movements — this is the generalization supported by our evidence [p. 695]. [8]

Friedman and Schwartz's monetary interpretation of history requires not simply that monetary contractions and major business contractions are statistically associated, but two further propositions: Preventing monetary contraction would have prevented these business contractions, and nothing else would have done so. The authors require also, of course, the corresponding propositions regarding marked expansions of money income.

I believe that this amounts to saying that velocity is independent of autonomous, policy-engineered alterations in stock of money. For if such an increase in the stock of money would, by lowering interest rates or otherwise, result in a systematic reduction of velocity, then the linkage of money and business activity is much weaker than the authors think. And the historically observed correlation is much less comfort to the monetary authorities. Results like those of Latané, already cited, relating velocity to interest rates are therefore of the greatest importance.

I do not wish to be misunderstood. Friedman and Schwartz cite some convincing examples of monetary changes that were clearly independent of contemporary or immediately preceding economic events: the increased gold production in 1897-1914 and the sharp increases in the Federal Reserve discount rate in 1920 and again in 1931. I am willing to agree that these monetary events contributed in important degree to the economic events which followed.

Consider the following three propositions: Money does not matter. It does too matter. Money is all that matters. It is all too easy to slip from the second proposition to the third, to use reasoning and evidence which support the second to claim the third. In this book Friedman and Schwartz have ably and convincingly marshalled evidence for the proposition that money matters. They have put to rout the neo-Keynesian, if he exists, who regards monetary events as mere epiphenomena, postscripts added as afterthoughts to the non-monetary factors that completely determine income, employment, and even prices. But in their zeal and exuberance Friedman and his followers often seem to go — though perhaps less in this book than elsewhere — beyond their own logic and statistics to the other extreme, where the stock of money becomes the necessary and sufficient determinant of money income. Much as I admire their work, I cannot follow them there.

Remember that the difference between the propositions "Money matters" and "Money is all that matters" is also the difference between the propositions "Fiscal policy matters" and "Fiscal policy doesn't matter." If there is a tight linkage, at any moment of time, between money income and the stock of money, then pure fiscal policy – e.g., bond-financed government spending – cannot raise money income. But if the income-velocity of money is flexible in response to interest rates, the stock of money itself, or other variables, then expansionary fiscal policy can raise both velocity and money income. [9] When the authors minimize or blur the distinction between the weak and strong porpositions concerning the importance of money, they do not warn the reader how crucial are the issues of policy involved.

3. Judgments on Monetary Policy

Enough of the parochial disputes of monetary theorists. The notorious disagreements among economists are a source of great comfort to practical men in business, finance, and government. When the experts differ the policy-maker can in better conscience do what he would have done anyway. By reputation monetary economists are especially prone to mutually cancelling differences of opinion. Many controversies on monetary theory and policy pit Friedman and his followers against the rest of the profession. But consensus among Friedman's opponents generally extends no farther than the proposition that Friedman is wrong. In the course of their narrative the authors frequently pause to point out error and to allege harm resulting from Keynesian ways of thinking.

But as Friedman and Schwartz led me through the major decisions of monetary politics and monetary policy of the past century, I did not find their Monday morning quarterbacking very controversial. I think that economists today – though they differ sharply in theoretical approach and political color – would agree very widely on the major practical and operational issues of these nine decades.

I prefer to end with this note of operational agreement rather than with theoretical discord. Laymen should not be too disheartened, or heartened, by strife among academic monetary theorists. Economists are likely to show a united front when the occasion arises to second guess the decisions of men of affairs. Friedman and Schwartz – believing so strongly in the powers of good or evil of monetary policy – are even more critical of the use of these powers than other economists.

I will give some examples, working more or less backward in time.

1. As already noted, the authors condemn the Federal Reserve and the Treasury for restrictive policy from 1933 to 1941. Many economists would assign to monetary factors much less weight than Friedman and Schwartz do in explaining the course of economic activity in those years, in particular the recession of 1937. But few would, I think, dispute the authors' retrospective practical conclusions. The monetary authorities should have tried harder to promote expansion in 1933-36 and 1937-40 – nothing would have been lost and something might have been gained. The 1936-37 increases in reserve requirements, whether or not they caused the recession, were too drastic. Throughout the period the authorities were too little concerned with deflationary risks immediately at hand and too much concerned to forestall the hypothetical future dangers of excess liquidity. Incidentally I note with some dismay that at least some members of the central banking fraternity wished to use monetary policy to keep a rein on fiscal policy. One of the reasons given for immobilizing reserves in a Federal Reserve Bank of New York memorandum (quoted by the authors, p. 523) was to remove the temptation easy money gives national, state, and local governments to "overborrow." The same memorandum offers as another reason for restrictive policy the danger that "large excess reserves may, by causing foreign expectation of favorable conditions for speculative investment, accentuate the gold *inflow*" (my italics). It appears that no matter which gold problem we may have, tighter money is the remedy.

2. Economists will differ also in the weights they assign monetary factors in the origins, severity, and length of the Great Contraction of 1929-33. But from today's vantage point no one will defend the passive acquiescence of the Fed in the monetary contraction and banking collapse. The Fed's failure to undertake an aggressive policy of open market purchases seems incredible. Even when open market purchases were finally carried out in the spring and summer of 1932, it was less for economic reasons than to forestall unsound inflationary actions by the Congress. The System's indifference to domestic crisis stands in contrast to its classic reflex to the U.K. devaluation in 1931; the Fed raised the discount rate two points. Even so French balances didn't stay in New York very much longer.

The traditional excuse for Federal Reserve passivity in this period has been a technical one, the alleged shortage of "free gold." The Federal Reserve Banks were required to hold gold reserves of 35 per cent against their deposit liabilities and 40 per cent against their note liabilities. The other 60 per cent of Federal Reserve Notes had to be backed either by "eligible paper" or by gold. When banks stopped discounting during the contraction, the Federal Reserve Banks ran short of eligible paper; correspondingly Federal Reserve Notes had to be covered by gold more than 40 per cent. The problem was finally resolved by the Glass-Steagall Act of February 1932, which permitted government securities to serve in place of eligible paper as collateral for notes.

Friedman and Schwartz find no evidence that free gold was in fact an important constraint on Federal Reserve action or a central consideration in discussions within the System at the time. If it had been an effective constraint, they point out, there were several avenues of escape that could have been tried, including earlier request for corrective legislation. In fact the Administration rather than the Fed asked for the legislation, and its enactment was not followed by a change in Federal Reserve policy until six weeks later. [10]

3. Perhaps there would be less agreement among economists with the authors' verdict that monetary policy was too tight in 1928-29. A speculative stock market boom during a period of stable noninflationary economic growth presented the System with a difficult and cruel dilemma. A policy tight enough to curb the stock market would inevitably make credit costly or unavailable to ordinary business and agricultural borrowers. In a sense, of course, inflated stock prices themselves spelled easy money and encouraged real investment, but only for business legally and institutionally prepared to issue new equities. There were not enough of these, in the short run at least, to offset the restrictive effects of tight bank credit on business dependent on debt finance. Personally I agree with the judgment of Friedman and Schwartz that in 1928-29 the System should have ignored the stock market in arriving at its general credit policy and concentrated instead on easing money sufficiently to promote the continued expansion of the economy. But given this judgment, the authors are unduly doctrinaire in rejecting out of hand the use of moral suasion or selective controls against stock market credit.

4. Economists of all schools would, I think, agree with the authors that the Fed was too slow to raise the discount rate after World War I and then contributed to a drastic deflation in 1920 by raising the rate from 4 to 7 per cent in six months.

5. Preservation or restoration of the gold value of the dollar has on several occasions been accorded undeserved primacy as a goal of monetary policy, at severe cost to the domestic economy. Concerning the 1879 resumption of gold dollar convertibility at the pre-Civil War rate, the authors' judgment in retrospect is that, given that a gold standard was to be reestablished, it would have been preferable to have resumed at a parity that gave a dollar-pound

exhange rate somewhere between the pre-Civil War rate and the rate at the end of the war. However, they point out that the progress of real output does not appear to have been set back by the severe and painful price deflations which preceded and followed resumption.

Similarly, Friedman and Schwartz have some sympathy for the silver agitation prior to 1897. But they are not, of course, for bimetallism; and they recognize also that silver agitation, so long as it led to uncertainty about the country's commitment to gold, made the gold standard even more deflationary than it would have been otherwise. The dilemma between gold standard and internal stability recurred in 1932-33, and the authors clearly would have put internal stability first. They point out that the Fed and Treasury played the gold standard game asymmetrically; gold inflows were sterilized before 1929 and after 1933, but gold outflows were not sterilized in the intervening years. To a certain extent they think this has also happened during the most recent decade.

6. I have left until last the authors' views on recent monetary policies and controversies. Federal Reserve policy since World War II gets fairly good marks from Friedman and Schwartz. They condemn the continuation of the bond price support policy after the war, but find that it did little harm until the Korean inflation. They also condemn the 4 1/4 per cent interest rate ceiling on government bonds. They cannot get excited about the "bills only" controversy, partly because they agree with the policy's advocates in stressing "monetary" rather than "credit" effects, partly because such policy need not prevent the Treasury-cum-Federal Reserve from achieving any desired maturity distribution of debt held outside the government. They applaud the Fed's discovery of the quantity of money and of the principle that it should keep pace with the real growth of the economy. The period as a whole has been one of unusual stability in the rate of change of the stock of money, but the authors detect a growing variability and attribute it in part to increased self-assurance on the part of the monetary managers. So far as month-to-month anticyclical policy is concerned, the authors find little to criticize. They feel the Fed reacted too late and too strongly at times, but they praise the shifts to ease that occurred before the cyclical peaks of 1953 and 1960.

4. Conclusions

I have not done justice to the scope of this book. History presents the theoretically-minded scholar with one challenge after another. Here these are met with the brilliance and finesse one would expect. Examples are: the determination of the exchange rate and gold premium during the greenback era, the economics of the 1879 resumption; the silver question; balance-of-payments pressure and adjustments in the 1890's; FDR's gold purchase policy; the mechanics of Federal Reserve bond support policy during and after World War II. The reader is advised in no event to omit the footnotes, which contain may gems of monetary theory: on Gresham's law; purchasing power parity; the prohibition and regulation of interest on commercial bank deposits; the significance of the "free reserve" position of member banks; the monetary mechanics of shifts among currency, demand deposits, time deposits, and other thrift accounts.

This is one of those rare books that leave their mark on all future research on the subject.

Notes

[1] Milton Friedman and Anna Jacobson Schwartz, *A Monetary History of the United States 1879-1960*. National Bureau of Economic Research, Studies in Business Cycles, No. 12 (Princeton: Princeton University Press, 1963). Pp. xxiv, 860.

[2] "The support program converted all securities into the equivalent of money" (p. 563). The authors are more cautious in discussing, on page 598 and page 625, the consequences of the Accord.

[3] In an interesting statistical study of the period, George Horwich has compared the responsiveness of bank earning assets to external loan demand, represented by personal income, on the one hand, and to effective reserves, on the other. His results, which are the more convincing because a similar test comes out the other way round for the 'fifties. support the "Keynesian" rather than the Friedman and Schwartz interpretation of the 'thirties. "Effective Reserves, Credit, and Causality in the Banking System of the Thirties." in D. Carson, ed., *Banking and Monetary Studies*, Homewood, Ill.: Irwin, 1963), pp. 80-100.

[4] Friedman and Schwartz recognize that this interpretation must be "highly tentative" and "await further evidence" (p. 675).

[5] H.A. Latané, "Income Velocity and Interest Rates – A Pragmatic Approach," *Review of Economics and Statistics* (Nov. 1960) 445-49.

[6] In this correlation for 1869-1914, the velocity series is from Friedman and Schwartz (Table A-5, p. 774). The series for D/C is given in Table B-3, pp. 799-801. For years after 1907, where monthly observations are given, the observation for the year is the average of the twelve months. For previous years, for which observations are available for only one or two months a year, estimates were made for missing months by linear interpolation, and yearly estimates by averaging the resulting monthly series.

[7] Regression of $\Delta Y/Y$ on $\Delta M/M$, 1869-1959, where Y is Friedman and Schwartz money income series (derivation described p. 775), and M is Friedman and Schwartz money (series given in Table A-1, pp. 704-20). Annual observations of M are averages of monthly figures. Monthly figures are not provided for all months prior to May 1907.

They were estimated by linear interpolation between the months for which observations are given.

[8] Elsewhere the authors have summarized their position as follows: "For major movements in |money| income, we concluded that there is an extremely strong case for the proposition that sizable changes in the rate of change in the money stock are a necessary and sufficient condition for sizable-changes in the rate of change in money income. For minor movements, we concluded that, while the evidence was far less strong, it is plausible to suppose that changes in the stock of money played an important independent role, though certainly the evidence for these minor movements does not rule out other interpretations." Friedman and Schwartz, "Money and Business Cycles," *Review of Economics and Statistics* (Feb. 1963), Supplement, p. 63.

[9] This is a well-understood point of macroeconomic theory, explained among other places in my article "Liquidity Preference and Monetary Policy," *Review of Economics and Statistics* (May 1947), 124-31 (Chapter 3 above).

[10] In their historical research on Federal Reserve policy-making in this and other eras, the authors were limited to the materials available in the private papers of Federal Reserve officials, principally those of George L. Harrison (an official of the New York Bank 1920-40 and its governor or president 1928-40), Charles L. Hamlin (a member of the Board 1914-36), and E.A. Goldenweiser (director of research and statistics for the Board 1926-45). Now, thanks to the constructive action of the present Board of Governors in making available past minutes of the Board and the Open Market Committee, scholars will be able to provide a more definitive history of Federal Reserve policy-making. It is entirely possible that future research will alter the interpretations to which the available evidence led Friedman and Schwartz.

CHAPTER 24

MONEY AND INCOME: POST HOC ERGO PROPTER HOC?

Milton Friedman asserts that changes in the supply of money M (defined to include time deposits) are the principal cause of changes in money income Y. In his less guarded and more popular expositions, he comes close to asserting that they are the unique cause. [1] In support of this position Friedman and his associates and followers have marshaled an imposing volume of evidence, of several kinds.

Historical case studies are one kind of evidence. For example, in their monumental *Monetary History of the United States 1867-1960,* [2] Friedman and Anna Schwartz carefully analyze and interpret the role of money and monetary policy in the important episodes of American economic history since the Civil War. Summary regressions of time series of economic aggregates are a second type of evidence. Presumed effects are simply regressed on presumed causes; the single equations estimated are something like the econometrician's "reduced forms." In a study with David Meiselman, [3] Friedman concluded that his monetary explanation of variations in money incomes fits the data better than a simple Keynesian multiplier model. More recent studies in the same vein claim that monetary policy does better than fiscal policy in explaining postwar fluctuations of money income. [4]

A third type of evidence relates to timing, specifically to leads and lags at cylindrical turning points. Much of the work of Friedman and his associates at the National Bureau of Economic Research has been devoted to this subject. [5] Turning points in the rate of change of money supply, $\dot{M}$, [6] show a long lead, and turning points in the money stock, M, itself (relative to trend) a shorter lead, over turning points in money income, Y. A great deal of the

Reprinted from *Quarterly Journal of Economics*, 84 (May 1970), 301-17. Also Cowles Foundation Paper No. 323. Part 4 reprinted from *Quarterly Journal of Economics,* 84 (May 1970), 328–29. Footnotes, figures, and tables have been renumbered.

The research described in this paper was carried out under grants from the National Science Foundation and from the Ford Foundation. I am grateful to Milton Friedman for helpful comments on an earlier draft of this paper.

popular and semiprofessional appeal of the modern quantity theory can be attributed to these often repeated facts.

However, the relevance of timing evidence has been seriously questioned. [7] Friedman himself says, "These regular and sizable leads of the money series are themselves suggestive of an influence running from money to business but they are by no means decisive." [8] The apparent leads may "really" be lagged responses — either positive or negative ("inverted") — of money to previous changes in business activity. Friedman cautiously rejects this possibility. He finds that the M series conforms more closely to the NBER reference cycle on a positive basis with money leading than on an inverted basis with money lagging, and he regards the business-money causal nexus as very likely to be inverted. Having satisfied himself that the dominant association of $\dot{M}$ and business activity is positive, Friedman concludes, "... it is not easy to rationalize positive conformity with a lead as reflecting supply response," [9] i.e., response of the supply of money to changes in business activity.

The purpose of the present paper is to spell out the lead-lag timing implications of alternative theoretical models of the relation between money and money income. In one model, a version of the ultra-Keynesian theory that Friedman is so often attacking, monetary developments are just a sideshow to the main events. In the other model, one of Friedman's own, monetary developments are of decisive causal significance. What kinds of observed relations between money and money income and their rates of change do the opposing models generate? Do they imply different lead-lag patterns?

In the ultra-Keynesian model, changes in the money supply are a passive response to income changes generated, via the multiplier mechanism, by autonomous investment and government expenditure. This makes it possible to see what kinds of observations of money stock M and its rate of change $\dot{M}$ would be generated in an ultra-Keynesian world. These can then be compared with the observations that would be generated by a Friedman economy. Here it is necessary to express Friedman's hypothesis with more precision and simplicity than it is usually expounded. However, this can be done with the help of the model of the demand for money set forth in his article with Anna Schwartz, "Money and Business Cycles." [10]

I hasten to say that I do not believe the ultra-Keynesian model to be exhibited (nor would Keynes), any more than I believe Friedman's. I do think, nevertheless, that the exercise points up the dangers of accepting timing evidence as empirical proof of propositions about causation. [11] I shall show that the ultra-Keynesian model — in which money has no causal importance whatever — throws up observations which a superficial believer in *post hoc ergo propter hoc* would regard as more favorable to the idea that money is causally important than does Friedman's own model. What is even more striking and surprising is that the ultra-Keynesian model implies cyclical timing patterns just like the empirical patterns that Friedman reports, while the Friedman model does not.

1. An Ultra-Keynesian Model

The ultra-Keynesian multiplier model has

$$Y = m(G + \dot{K}) \tag{1}$$

where Y is net national product, G is the current rate of government expenditure, and $\dot{K}$ is net capital accumulation, all in nominal units. (The division of cyclical fluctuations in income between real output and prices is inessential to the argument of the paper and is ignored throughout.) The multiplier m is derived routinely from the identity:

Saving + Taxes = Government Expenditure + Net Investment

$$s(1-t)Y + tY = G + \dot{K} \tag{2}$$

where s is the marginal propensity to save from income after taxes and t is the constant tax rate (net of transfers). Therefore the multiplier,

$$m = \frac{1}{s(1-t) + t} . \tag{3}$$

The determination of income by equation (2) is illustrated in the familiar textbook diagram, Figure 24.1.

Private wealth W is the capital stock K plus the government debt D (whether monetized or not), the cumulative total of past deficits, $G-tY$. Saving, the change in private wealth, is

$$s(1-t)Y = \dot{W} = \dot{K} + G - tY = (\dot{K} + G)(1 - tm) . \tag{4}$$

In Figure 24.1 government deficit is AB, and net capital accumulation is BC.

The public's balance sheet is

$$W = K + D = K - L + M + B \tag{5}$$

where B is the public's holdings of the nonmonetary debt (bonds) of the government, L is the debt of the public to the banking system, and M is the public's holdings of the monetary liabilities of the government and the

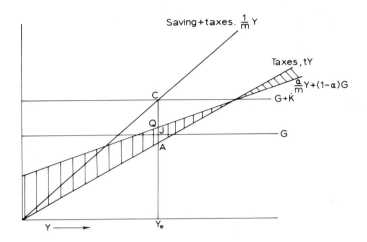

Fig. 24.1.

banking system. To be consistent with Friedman's model and his empirical findings, M includes time deposits as well as demand deposits.

The portfolio behavior of the public in this ultra-Keynesian world is very primitive. Real investment is autonomous; indeed, exogenous fluctuations in the pace of capital formation are the source of the business cycle. This implies that there are autonomous shifts in the proportions in which the public wishes to allocate its wealth among the available assets. During investment booms, capital becomes more attractive relative to money and bonds; during investment recessions, the reverse occurs. [12] By the same token, borrowing from banks rises in booms and falls in recessions. Specifically, the public's debt to the banking system is taken to be a fixed proportion of the capital stock:

$$L = \alpha K \qquad (0 < \alpha < 1) . \qquad (6)$$

The only portfolio decision left is the allocation of the remainder of the public's net worth – $(W-K+L)$, which is equal to $(D + \alpha K)$ – among the two remaining assets, money (currency and bank deposits) and bonds (interest-bearing government debt). This is the choice of Keynesian liquidity preference theory. The demand for money can be written as the sum of two components, an asset demand related to the interest rate and to allocable wealth and a transactions demand proportional to income:

$$M = a_0(r)(D + \alpha K) + a_1 Y \tag{7}$$

where r is the interest rate on bonds and the derivative $a_0'(r)$ is negative. By subtraction, public demand for bonds is

$$(1 - a_0(r))(D + \alpha K) - a_1 Y.$$

The main point of the exercise can be made by assuming that the monetary authority provides bank reserves as necessary to keep r constant, so that a_0 is a constant. The monetary system responds to the "needs of trade." With the help of the monetary authority, banks are able and willing to meet the fluctuating demand of their borrowing customers for credit and of their depositors for money. In Friedman's terms, this is a "supply response" with "positive conformity" of money to business activity. It is indeed a response which he regards as all too common in central banking, one for which he has severely criticized the Federal Reserve. If these criticisms are justified, then this endogenous response must have played an important role in generating monetary time series.

The relation among flows corresponding to (7) is

$$\dot{M} = a_0(\dot{D} + \alpha \dot{K}) + a_1 \dot{Y}$$
$$= a_0(G - tY + \alpha \dot{K}) + a_1 \dot{Y}. \tag{8}$$

Using (1) converts (8) into

$$\dot{M} = a_0 [G(1 - \alpha) + Y \frac{\alpha}{m} - t)] + a_1 \dot{Y}. \tag{9}$$

Thus, for given G, $\dot{M}$ is a linear function of Y and $\dot{Y}$, and these vary in response to autonomous changes in investment $\dot{K}$. The relationship to $\dot{Y}$ is, of course, positive. Consider now the relationship to Y. In Figure 24.1 at income level Y_e, $\dot{D}$ is represented by AJ. Let JQ equal αJC, the amount of real investment covered by new indebtedness to banks. Then AQ represents $\dot{D} + \alpha \dot{K}$, the quantity which the public divides between accumulations of money and of bonds. Imagine that G is held constant, while $\dot{K}$ varies autonomously and carries Y with it. Then the vertical distance through the shaded area, of which AQ is an example, is $\dot{D} + \alpha \dot{K}$. This declines with Y, as illustrated, provided the line through Q has a slope smaller than t, i.e., that α/m is smaller than t. (For example, if the multiplier is $2-1/2$ and the tax ratio is $1/5$, the loan-to-investment ratio α must be smaller than $1/2$. In this case $\dot{D} + \alpha \dot{K}$ will become negative, as illustrated, at sufficiently high values of Y, where the government budget is in large surplus.

The financial operations of the government and the banks are as follows: The government and the monetary authority divided the increase of debt $\dot{D}$ between "high-powered money" and bonds in such manner as to keep the interest rate on target. If we assume no change in currency holdings by the public, the increase $\dot{M}$ in money requires an increase of $k\dot{M}$, where k is the required reserve ratio, in bank reserves. Banks' loan assets increase by $\dot{L} = \alpha\dot{K}$. The difference $[\dot{M}(1-k)-\dot{L}]$ the banks allocate between excess reserves and bond holdings, in proportions that depend on the interest rate. Thus the monetary authority provides enough new high-powered money to meet increased reserve requirements and any new demand for excess reserves. The remainder of the increase in public debt $\dot{D}$ takes the form of bonds, and it is just enough to satisfy the demands of the banks and the public. This can be seen as follows: The increase in public demand for the bonds is $\dot{W} + \dot{L} - \dot{K} - \dot{M}$ $= \dot{D} + \alpha\dot{K} - \dot{M}$. The increase in the banks' demand for bonds is $\dot{M} - \dot{L} - \dot{H}$ $= \dot{M} - \alpha\dot{K} - \dot{H}$, where $\dot{H}$ is the increase in required and excess reserves. Adding the two together, we see that the increase in demand for bonds is $\dot{D} - \dot{H}$, just equal to the supply. In short, Walras' law guarantees that if the money market is cleared, the bond market is also cleared.

A dollar increase in government spending has the same effect in raising income and tax receipts as a dollar increase in private investment. Both raise income Y by the multiplier m, and taxes by tm. However, they have different effects on $\dot{D} + \alpha\dot{K}$ and thus on $\dot{M}$. An increase in government expenditures raises $\dot{D} + \alpha\dot{K}$ by $1-tm$; an increase in private investment, by $\alpha - tm$. Since α is less than 1, the demand for money is raised more by an increase of government expenditure. This fact is clear from (9). For given Y, a dollar increase in G (replacing a dollar of $\dot{K}$) increases $\dot{M}$ by $1-\alpha$.

A tax cut sufficient to create the same increase in income would entail an even larger rise in $\dot{D} + \alpha\dot{K}$ and in the demand for additional money. Our ultra-Keynesian would not be surprised to find the money supply rising especially fast in an income expansion propelled by deficit spending. He would not even be surprised if some observers of the accelerated pace of monetary expansion in the wake of a tax cut conclude that monetary rather than fiscal policy caused the boom. [13]

Let us return, however, to a model cycle generated by fluctuation in private investment $\dot{K}$, with government expenditure and the tax rate constant. The model abstracts from trends in Y and its components. However, private wealth grows over the model cycle, and this growth is responsible for an upward trend in M. What will be the cyclical behavior of the money supply M and of its rate of change $\dot{M}$, in reference to the cycles in money income Y and its rate of change $\dot{Y}$?

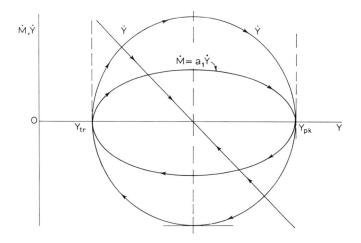

Fig. 24.2. Ultra-Keynesian Cycle.

There are two components of $\dot{M}$, one related to Y and one to $\dot{Y}$. The Y-component has already been discussed. Its relationship to Y is shown in Figure 24.2, as the downward sloping line. Y_{tr} and Y_{pk} are the trough and peak of the cycle. In the illustration, $\dot{M}$ for stationary Y does not become negative, even at Y_{pk}. The second or transactions component is simply proportional to $\dot{Y}$: $\alpha_1 \dot{Y}$ in equation (8) or (9) above. This can be added to Figure 24.2, provided we know the relation of $\dot{Y}$ to Y. That relation is illustrated in Figure 24.3, on the assumption that the cycle in $\dot{K}$ and Y is a sine wave. The circle, with arrows, shows $\dot{Y}$ zero at the trough of Y, $\dot{Y}$ at its own peak, Y at its peak with $\dot{Y}$ again zero, $\dot{Y}$ at its trough, and so on. The ellipse within the circle represents the corresponding cycle in the second component of $\dot{M}$.

In Figure 24.2 this component is added vertically to the line representing the first component. The squashed ellipse in Figure 24.2 shows the cycle of $\dot{M}$ as income moves from Y_{tr} to Y_{pk} and back. The order of events in the cycle can be read by following the perimeter of the squashed ellipse clockwise. In Figure 24.2 there is a brief period of the cycle when $\dot{M}$ is negative. Thus M has a late peak and early trough, and grows on balance over the cycle. It can easily be imagined, however, that the ellipse in Figure 24.2 lies entirely above the axis, so that M grows continuously but at varying rates. Or, if the first or level component of $\dot{M}$ became negative before Y reached its peak, then M would lead Y at the peak as well as at the trough. In any case, it is clear that

$\dot{M}$ not only has a long lead over Y, more than a quarter of a cycle, but also leads $\dot{Y}$.

The horizontal line through the squashed ellipse represents the average value of $\dot{M}$. The stock of money M, corrected for trend, will reach its peak and trough when actual $\dot{M}$ is equal to average $\dot{M}$. These points are also indicated in Figure 24.2. They precede turning points in Y but not in $\dot{Y}$.

It is easy to modify Figure 24.2 to allow for a rise in interest rates during expansions of money income and a decline in contractions. In an ultra-Keynesian world this "leaning against the wind" by the monetary authorities would be irrelevant to stabilization. But it might occur nonetheless, because the monetary authorities mistakenly believe in their *own* powers or are just operationally conservative in changing the supply of high-powered money, or because they worry about the balance of payments. Anyway, it would be represented in Figure 24.2 by a steepening of the central line. This would result in a still longer lead of $\dot{M}$ with respect to $\dot{Y}$ and Y.

Equation (8) would read

$$\dot{M} = a_0(r) \, (\dot{D} + \alpha \dot{K}) + a_0'(r) \, (D + \alpha K) \, \dot{r} + a_1 \dot{Y} . \qquad (8')$$

As r rises with Y, the decline in α_0 reinforces the decline in $\dot{D} + \alpha \dot{K}$. Assuming that $\dot{r}$ is positively related to $\dot{Y}$, and given that $\alpha_0'(r)$ is negative, the second term contributes a negative relation of $\dot{M}$ to $\dot{Y}$. This would make the ellipse of Figure 24.3 flatter, as well as distorting its shape. Indeed, it could conceivably reverse the net effect of $\dot{Y}$ on $\dot{M}$ and therefore reverse the order of events in the cycle. But the central bank surely does not lean against the wind so hard as that, especially in an ultra-Keynesian world.

The results would also be reinforced if a term in $\dot{Y}$, with a positive coefficient, were added to the basic demand for money equation (7). The logic of such a term would be that changes in wealth are in the first instance absorbed in cash balances, with more permanent portfolio allocations following later. Thus demand for money would be especially high when income and saving are rapidly increasing. This, after all, is what one would expect of money as "a temporary abode of purchasing power," to use Professor Friedman's famous phrase.

A $\dot{Y}$ term in expression (7) for M means a $\ddot{Y}$ term in expression (8) for $\dot{M}$. In a cycle of the type illustrated in Figure 24.3, $\ddot{Y}$ is inversely related to Y. Therefore a $\ddot{Y}$ component of $\dot{M}$ will be high at low levels of Y and low at peak levels. Like the interest rate effect, this will increase the slope of the central line in Figure 24.2 and accentuate the lead-lag pattern there depicted.

There is nothing sacred about sine waves, and neither is a sine-curve cycle crucial for the timing pattern shown in Figure 24.2. The reader is invited to

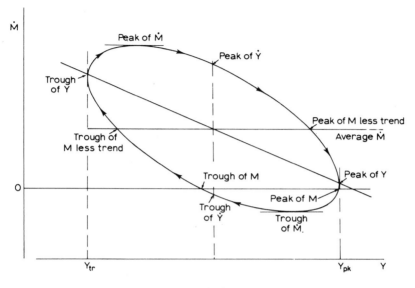

Fig. 24.3.

experiment with noncircular shapes of the relation of $\dot{Y}$ to Y in Figure 24.3. He will find it easy to change the lengths of the lags and leads, and in extreme cases to produce some coincidences and ambiguities. But the essential message to Figure 24.2 comes through, provided that $\dot{M}$ is related negatively to Y and positively to $\dot{Y}$.

2. A Friedman Model

I turn now to the cyclical pattern implied by Friedman's own "permanent income" theory of the demand for money. For present purposes this may be expressed as follows:

$$1nM = A + \delta \ 1nY_p^* . \qquad (10)$$

Here M is the same quantity of money as in the ultra-Keynesian model; Y_p^* is permanent income; δ is the elasticity of the demand for money with respect to permanent income, estimated by Friedman to be of the order of 1.8. Income and permanent income grow secularly at an exponential rate β. As above, we abstract from this trend of income and consider the deviations from trend, Y_p and Y. Since $\ln Y_p = \ln Y_p^* - \beta t - C$, equation (10) can be restated as

$$\ln M = B + \delta \ln Y_p + \delta \beta t . \tag{11}$$

For rates of change, (11) implies

$$\dot{M}/M = \delta(\dot{Y}_p/Y_p) + \delta\beta . \tag{12}$$

Permanent income, corrected for trend, is a weighted geometric average of current and past actual incomes, also corrected for trend, with the weights receding exponentially. Thus when actual and permanent income differ, the public changes its estimate of permanent income by some fraction of their relative difference. Specifically,

$$\dot{Y}_p/Y_p = w(\ln Y - \ln Y_p) , \text{ or}$$

$$\ln Y = \frac{1}{w}(\dot{Y}_p/Y_p) + \ln Y_p . \tag{13}$$

Friedman has estimated, mainly in connection with his work on the consumption function, that revision of permanent income eliminates about one-third of its deviation from actual income within a year. In other words, the weight of the current year's income is one-third, and the weights of past years' incomes two-thirds, in the calculation of permanent income. If the revision is taken to be continuous, as in (13), rather than discrete, these weights imply a value of 0.40 for w.

In this model the supply of money and its rate of change are autonomous. The demand for money must adjust to the supply at every point of time. Permanent income is the only variable involved in the demand for money; so it must do the adjusting. But much of permanent income is past history; the only part that can adjust is current income. Roughly speaking, Friedman's numerical estimates imply that permanent income must rise 0.55 per cent to absorb a 1 per cent increment in the supply of money. But in the short run money is much more powerful. Current year's income must rise by 1.65 per cent to make permanent income rise 0.55 per cent. Thus in a cyclical boom, in which the supply of money keeps rising, current income must rise even faster. In this way the theory explains why the velocity of money moves up and down with income in business cycles and reconciles this observation with Friedman's finding that secularly velocity declines as income rises.

An explicit relation of income to money supply can be obtained from (13) by using (11) to express $\ln Y_p$ in terms of $\ln M$ and (12) to express $\dot{Y}_p/Y_p$ in terms of $\dot{M}/M$:

$$1nY = \frac{\dot{M}/M}{\delta w} + \frac{1nM}{\delta} - \beta t - \frac{\beta}{w} - \frac{A}{\delta}, \tag{14}$$

$$\dot{Y}/Y = \frac{\dot{g}_M}{\delta w} + \frac{g_M}{\delta} - \beta, \tag{15}$$

for convenience letting g_M denote $\dot{M}/M$ and $\dot{g}_M$, its time derivative. Equation (15) will be used for the analysis of cyclical timing patterns. It relates the rate of change of income, abstracting from trend, to the rate of change of the money stock and to the change in that rate. Note that if g_M is held steady at $\delta\beta$ then $\dot{Y}/Y$ will be zero and income will be on trend.

This exposition is based on Friedman's theory as set forth in his article with Anna Schwartz. [14] I have used continuous rather than discrete time, and I have related money demand to money income, ignoring the complication that real income and price level enter Friedman's formula somewhat differently. These simplifications do not impair the essential message of the theory for the present purpose. [15]

Consider a business cycle generated by a sine wave in g_M. What will be the resulting movement of $\dot{Y}/Y$? This is, according to (15), the sum of two components, one linear in g_M itself, the other proportional to $\dot{g}_M$. The first is indicated by the positively sloped line in Figure 24.4. The trough and peak of g_M are indicated by g_{Mtr} and g_{Mpk}. The average value of g_M over the cycle is positive, specifically $\delta\beta$, while the average value of $\dot{Y}/Y$ is, of course, zero. These average values are shown as point Q in Figure 24.4. To show the second component on the same diagram, we must use the relationship between $\dot{g}_M$ and g_M; depicted by the circle in Figure 24.5. The large ellipse in which the

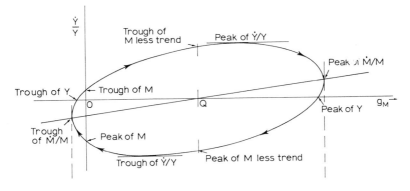

Fig. 24.4. Friedman Cycle.

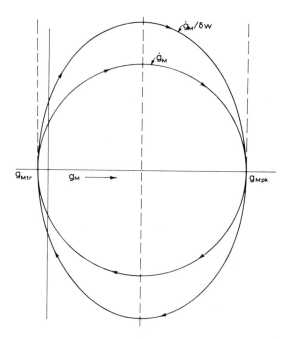

Fig. 24.5.

circle is inscribed is $\dot{g}_M/\delta w$, where $1/\delta w$ exceeds one, in keeping with Friedman's theory and numerical estimates. It is this which must be added vertically to the line of Figure 24.4 to exhibit the total change in income $\dot{Y}/Y$. As in the case of Figure 24.2, the order of events in the cycle may be read by following the perimeter of the misshapen ellipse in Figure 24.4 clockwise.

In this monetary model of business fluctuations, $\dot{M}/M$ *lags* $\dot{Y}/Y$ and has only a short lead over Y itself. The money stock itself lags Y at peak and trough. However, as in the other model, there might be no cycle in M at all: $\dot{M}/M$ might never be negative. This would be shown in Figure 24.4 by moving the vertical axis entirely to the left of the ellipse. If it were moved part way, the trough in M might precede the trough in Y. But the major conclusions remain.

As in Figure 24.2, it is also possible to indicate in Figure 24.4 the peak and trough in the deviation of the money stock from trend. The average level of $\dot{M}/M$ is shown by the dashed vertical line through Q. When actual $\dot{M}/M$

equals this average, trend-corrected M reaches its peak and trough. Figure 24.4 shows that these turning points lag the corresponding turning points in Y.

As is the case of the ultra-Keynesian model, the cycle does not need to be a sine wave in order to produce the basic order of events over the cycle.

3. Comparisons of Timing Implications

In Table 24.1, I have summarized the timing implications of the two models, as indicated in Figures 24.2 and 24.4.

Clearly the monetary-causal model implies a much less impressive lead of money over business activity than its opposite.

Consider now the empirical evidence. The cyclical timing patterns reported by Friedman and Schwartz are as follows: [16]

(a) For "mild depression cycles" they find no cycle in M.

(b) For "deep depression cycles" they find a cycle in M, mildly lagging the NBER reference cycle, with which money income is roughly coincident, at peaks.

(c) They find that the rate of change of the money stock leads at peaks and troughs. This lead is dramatically long, so much so "as to suggest the possibility of interpreting the rate of change series as inverted, *i.e.*, as generally declining during reference expansion and rising during reference contraction."

Table 24.1.
Order of Events in Model Cycles

Ultra-Keynesian	Friedman
trough of Y	trough of Y or [trough of M]
peak of $\dot{M}$	[trough of M] or [trough of Y]
peak of $\dot{Y}$	trough of M corrected for trend
peak of M corrected for trend	peak of $\dot{Y}/Y$
peak of Y or [peak of M]	peak of $\dot{M}/M$
[peak of M] or peak of Y	peak of Y
trough of $\dot{M}$	peak of M corrected for trend
trough of $\dot{Y}$ or [trough of M]	trough of $\dot{Y}/Y$ or [peak of M]
[trough of M] or trough of $\dot{Y}$	[peak of M] or trough of $\dot{Y}/Y$
trough of M corrected for trend	trough of $\dot{M}/M$
trough of Y	trough of Y or [trough of M]

Note: events in brackets [ ] need not occur at all.

(d) They show a generally procyclical behavior of velocity Y/M, but with some tendency for velocity to start declining before the reference peak.

Friedman has also summarized the evidence in an earlier article, as follows:

> ... peaks in the rate of change of the money stock precede reference cycle peaks by 16 months (on the average) ... peaks in the deviation of money stock from its trend do so by five months ... such absolute peaks as occur in the money stock precede reference cycle peaks by less than five months and may even lag ... peaks in the rate of change of income precede such peaks as occur in the stock of money ... they probably also precede peaks in the deviation of the money stock from its trend ... they probably also follow peaks in the rate of change of money. [17]

In comparing these findings with the patterns of Figures 24.2 and 24.4, it is helpful to recall that sixteen months is roughly three-eighths and five months roughly one-eighth of a complete cycle. Figure 24.2 agrees with the empirical summary not only in order of events but also in the lengths of these leads or lags.

Every single piece of observed evidence that Friedman reports on timing is consistent with the timing implications of the ultra-Keynesian model, as depicted in Figure 24.2. This evidence actually contradicts his own "permanent income" theory and lends support to the ultra-Keynesian model.

As the quotation in (c) above indicates, Friedman himself has worried whether the very long lead of $\dot{M}$ over Y and the reference cycle may not prove altogether too much. It might be a lag instead of a lead. "An inverse relation", he says elsewhere, "with money lagging would be much easier to rationalize in terms of business influencing money than of money influencing business ..." [18]

It is only fair to notice, however, that there are two Friedmans when it comes to describing the causal mechanism from money to money income. One is the Friedman of the permanent income hypothesis, with the implications set forth above. The logic is that the demand for money is quite insensitive to current income, because current income has only a fractional weight in permanent income. This has the virtue of explaining why the monetary multiplier in the cyclical short run is so large and why velocity varies procyclically. But the cost of this explanation, as we have seen, is that it implies an immediate response as well as a powerful response. What is gained from the hypothesis in explaining amplitude is lost in explaining timing.

Friedman recognizes some of the limitations of the permanent income model. He sees that it cannot be applied without modification to quarterly as well as annual data. Since the current quarter of income experience has presumably even less weight in determining permanent income, and thus the demand for money, than the current year of income experience, the money multiplier should be much larger (three or four times as large) on a quarter-to-quarter application of (15) than on a year-to-year application. [19]

Faced by this sort of *reductio ad absurdum*, Friedman says:

> In generalizing to a quarterly basis, it will no longer be satisfactory to suppose that actual and desired money balances are always equal. It will be desirable to allow instead for a discrepancy between these two totals, which the holders of balances seek to eliminate at a rate depending on the size of the discrepancy. This will introduce past money balances into the estimated demand equation not only as a proxy for prior permanent incomes [as in (14) and (15)] but also as a determinant of the discrepancies in the process of being correct. [20]

The second Friedman explains the money-income causal nexus, and the reason that it takes some time to operate, in much more conventional and less controversial terms. This description relies heavily on discrepancies of the type just discussed. Excessive money balances, for example, are not immediately absorbed by mammoth spurts of money income. They are gradually worked off – affecting interest rates, prices of financial and physical assets, and eventually investment and consumption spending. [21] This account, though not yet expressed with the precision of the permanent income hypothesis, can doubtless be formulated so as to be consistent with the observed evidence on timing. But at a cost. It cannot attribute to money a large short-run multiplier or explain the procyclical movement of velocity. Indeed it leaves room for interest rates and other variables to affect velocity. Therefore it cannot have those clearcut implications regarding monetary and fiscal policy with which Professor Friedman has so confidently identified himself.

4. Rejoinder to a Comment by Professor Milton Friedman on the Foregoing Paper [22]

Professor Friedman's tone of pained indignation obscures his essential agreement with the main points of my paper. Indeed, much of his reply says that this agreement should already have been clear to any reader of his work. Nevertheless I am glad to have his current stipulations.

He agrees that cyclical leads of money over money income say virtually nothing about direction of causation; he says that he studies and reports these timing sequences for quite other reasons. He agrees that, while consistency with timing observations is not decisive evidence for a hypothesis, inconsistency with those observations requires rejection of the hypothesis. He agrees that his permanent income theory of money demand "does not yield the observed timing relations between money and business." Therefore, he says, it is "only an element" of a complete theory, an element "designed to account for the observed tendency of cyclical fluctuations in income to be wider in amplitude than cyclical fluctuations in money."

That was my concluding point: The element of Friedman's monetary theory that accounts for his amplitude evidence — that is, the procyclical movement of velocity — is not consistent with his timing evidence. Likewise, as well as I can understand other "elements" of his theory, they may be consistent with timing evidence but cannot account for the amplitude observations. [23] Perhaps Friedman can provide a formulation of the money-income nexus that is consistent with both kinds of evidence, so that it is not necessary to vary the model with the evidence to be explained. Recognizing the shortcomings of the permanent income theory, he may wish to consider whether the observed procyclical movement of velocity might be related, via "liquidity preference" considerations, to procyclical fluctuation of interest rates.

My ultra-Keynesian model exemplifies the fact that timing sequences consistent with observations, and superficially favorable to hypotheses stressing the causal importance of money, can be generated by a structure in which money has no causal role. Friedman doesn't like the structure, but I believe he accepts the methodological point. Whether the particular model I used to illustrate the point deserves the label I gave it is not a question of great moment. [24]

Milton Friedman's work on money is important and influential; it commands the attention of economists, policy makers, journalists, and men of affairs throughout the world. That is why it deserves and receives serious critical discussion. I am continually perplexed by Friedman's propensity in professional debate to evade by verbal quibbling the responsibility and the credit for the characteristic propositions of "monetarism" associated with his name.

Notes

[1] See, for example, his column in *Newsweek*, Jan. 30, 1967, p. 86, "Higher Taxes? No." He says, "To have a significant impact on the economy, a tax increase must somehow affect monetary policy — the quantity of money and its rate of growth. . . . The Federal Reserve can increase the quantity of money by precisely the same amount with or without a tax rise. The tax reduction of 1964 . . . encouraged the Fed to follow a more expansionary policy. This monetary expansion explains the long-continued

economic expansion. And it is the turnabout in monetary policy since April 1966 that explains the growing signs of recession."

[2] National Bureau of Economic Research, *Studies in Business Cycles*, No. 12 (Princeton: Princeton University Press, 1963).

[3] Friedman and David Meiselman, "The Relative Stability of Monetary Velocity and the Investment Multiplier in the United States 1897–1958". Commission on Money and Credit, *Stabilization Polices* (Englewood Cliffs, N.J.: Prentice-Hall, Inc., 1963), 165-268.

[4] Leonall Anderson and Jerry Jordan, "Monetary and Fiscal Actions: A Test of their Relative Importance in Economic Stabilization," *Federal Reserve Bank of St. Louis Review* (Nov. 1968), 11-24.

[5] See Friedman, "The Lag in the Effect of Monetary Policy," *Journal of Political Economy*, 69 (Oct. 1961), 447-66; Friedman and Schwartz, "Money and Business Cycles," *Review of Economics and Statistics*, Feb. 1963 Supplement, 32-64; Friedman, "The Monetary Studies of the National Bureau," *Annual Report of the National Bureau of Economic Research 1964.*

[6] Throughout this paper x' will denote the time derivative of x, dx/dt, and x', the second derivative of x with respect to time.

[7] By, among others, J. Kareken and R. Solow, "Lags in Monetary Policy," Commission on Money and Credit, *Stabilization Policies* (Englewood Cliffs, N.J.: Prentice-Hall, Inc., 1963), 14-25. They pointed out that a rate of change like $\dot{M}$ will generally lead a level like Y, in the manner that a cosine series "leads" a sine series. Friedman replied in "The Lag in the Effect of Monetary Policy", *loc. cit.*, that both $\dot{M}$ and Y have the dimension of a flow and that in any case he finds $\dot{M}$ leading $\dot{Y}$ and trend-corrected M leading Y. Kareken and Solow found little lead, if any, of $\dot{M}$ over the rate of change of the industrial production index, but they should have used a monetary rather than a real measure of business activity.

[8] In "The Monetary Studies of the National Bureau," *loc. cit.*, 13.

[9] *Ibid.*, 14.

[10] *Loc. cit.*

[11] The same methodological lesson is given by the simulations of more complicated models in William C. Brainard and James Tobin, "Pitfalls of Financial Model Building," *American Economic Review (Papers and Proceedings)*, May 1968, 19-122 (chapter 20 above).

[12] It might seem more Keynesian to let bonds alone bear the brunt of the autonomous shifts to and from capital. But "money" here includes time deposits.

[13] Note Friedman's comment in *Newsweek* quoted in note 1.

[14] "Money and Business Cycles", *loc. cit.*, 56-59.

[15] Elsewhere, with Craig Swan, I have considered the permanent income theory in full detail and tested the model and Friedman's numerical estimates of the parameters against postwar U.S. data. See J. Tobin and Craig Swan, "Money and Permanent Income: Some Empirical Tests," *American Economic Review*, 59 (May 1969), 285-95.

[16] Friedman and Schwartz, "Money and Business Cycles," *loc. cit.*, especially Charts 2, 4, and 6, and p. 36.

[17] "The Lag in the Effect of Monetary Policy," *loc. cit.*, 456.

[18] *Ibid.*, 458.

[19] When the model is formulated in discrete rather than continuous time, equation (14) becomes (here interpreting M, as well as Y, as trend-corrected)

$$\ln Y(t) = \frac{1}{\delta w} \ln M(t) - \frac{(1-w)}{\delta w} \ln M(t-1) - \text{const.}$$

Since w, the weight of current period income, varies inversely with the length of the period, the multiplier of $\ln M(t)$ is larger the shorter the period.

A formulation free of this paradox would relate trend-corrected "permanent money balances" to trend-corrected "permanent income":

$$\ln M_p(t) = \sum_{-\infty}^{t} v(1-v)^{t-\tau} \ln M(\tau)$$

$$= \delta \sum_{-\infty}^{t} w(1-w)^{t-\tau} \ln Y(\tau) = \delta Y_p(t)$$

$$v \ln M(t) + (1-v) \ln M_p(t-1) = \delta w \ln Y(t) \\ + \delta(1-w) \ln Y_p(t-1)$$

$$\ln Y(t) = \frac{v}{\delta w} \ln M(t) + \frac{w-v}{\delta w} \ln M_p(t-1) .$$

Since v/w is presumably independent of the time period chosen, this formulation avoids the *reductio ad absurdum*. But it also has different implications both for policy and for estimation.

[20] "Money and Business Cycles", *loc. cit.*, 59.

[21] Passages describing this mechanism may be found in each of the Friedman articles previously cited.

[22] Both his comment and this rejoinder appeared in *Quarterly Journal of Economics* 84 (May 1970).

[23] Consider, for example, the distributed lag equation

$$\frac{\Delta Y_t}{Y_t} = \sum_{i=0}^{s} b_i \frac{\Delta M_{t-i}}{M_{t-i}}$$

where all

$$b_i > 0 \qquad \text{and} \qquad \sum_{i=0}^{s} b_i = 1 .$$

This has the "right" timing implications; cyclical fluctuations in the rate of growth of the money supply will precede those in the rate of change of income. But what about amplitudes? Velocity is increasing, zero, or decreasing as the following expression is positive, zero, or negative:

$$\frac{\Delta Y_t}{Y_t} - \frac{\Delta M_t}{M_t} = \sum_{i=0}^{s} b_i \frac{\Delta M_{t-i}}{M_{t-i}} - \frac{\Delta M_t}{M_t}$$

when $\Delta M/M$ is rising, the expression is negative — money income is growing more slowly than money, and velocity is declining.

[24] Friedman objects that the money demand function is neither Keynesian nor plausible. But his objection is based not on the relation of money to income in the money demand equation taken by itself but on the relation of money to income in the model as a whole. The fact that model-wide implications differ from single-equation impacts is, of course, the basic point of my paper.

INDEX

Adjustment: behavior, 361–363; cross, 360; dynamics of, 359; speeds, 371
Administrative costs, 291, 301
Advertising, 285
Affluent Society, The (Galbraith), 180
Age, old, 440
Agents, natural, 20
Aggregate: consumption, 180–182; demand for cash, 246; supply, 60, 62, 66; wealth, 222, 325–326
Aggregation: errors of, 220; function, 242; model, 47–48, 115, 128; system and theory, 28, 75
Alhadeff, David and Charlotte, 282n
American Bankers Association, 471n
American Economic Association, 194n
American Economic Review, cited, 10–11n, 25n, 80n, 83n, 98–99n, 107–108n, 132n, 173–174n, 194n, 217n, 282n–283n, 322n, 338n, 352n, 469n, 471n, 513n
Anarchic systems and models, 48–54, 62
Anderson, Leonall, 513n
Angell, J. W., cited, 46n
Annuity, 442–443
Anti-inflationary policies and programs, 2, 73, 99, 102, 104, 107, 341, 446, 457, 466–468
Arndt, H. W., 45n
Arrow, Kenneth, 188, 194n, 199
Assets: accumulation of, 107, 325; earning, 56, 229, 243, 278–279, 389; bank, 277, 475; capital, 334; disposable, 356, 452n; exchange of, 219–220; financial, 218, 274, 299–300, 323–324; fixed, 221; holdings of, 83–85, 90, 399; liquid, 86–90, 96, 343, 388, 396, 410, 419–420, 487; monetary, 138, 244, 260, 283–287, 291; physical, 87, 264–265, 275, 328, 334, 338, 352–353, 356–357; preferences of, 116–117; and prices, 97, 322, 326; private, 87; reserve value of, 53, 302, 312; reversibility of, 219; safe, 116, 172n, 215;

short-term, 481; and stocks, 83, 274–275, 330; substitutes for, 106, 337; swapping effects of, 349–350; yields of, 150, 157, 161, 230, 274
Atlantic Community, output of, 174
Authority, use of, 284, 501–504

Bach, G. L., 460
Balance equations, 336; sheets, 129, 226, 283, 300, 322–325, 384, 386, 390–391, 403, 407, 429, 447, 454, 473
Balance of payments, 445, 495
Balance of trade, 14, 23, 450n
Balanced growth, 120–121, 148, 189, 205, 207, 209, 212–213
Balances: budget, 50, 54, 72–73, 118, 140, 142–144, 185, 468; idle, 39, 41; precautionary, 36; private, 87; working, 29, 34, 46n
Bank of England, 449
Bank: borrowing from, 500; credit, 100, 272, 421, 423; crisis, 467, 479; debits, 39, 41, 43; deposits, 68, 107, 132n, 171, 221, 227, 269–281, 292, 297, 335, 337, 389, 392, 420–422, 451n, 484, 495, 500; discount rates, 225, 335, 353, 407; earnings, 421, 495n; liabilities, 51, 277, 279, 281, 452; loan rates, 272, 274, 292, 344, 365, 385, 420–421, 465, 475; notes and obligations, 86, 441, 476; regulations, 298; reserves, 32, 68, 221, 224, 273, 284, 287, 292, 341, 353, 355, 365, 367–370, 377n, 389 392, 407, 435, 451n, 462, 464, 466, 469n, 502; securities, 372–373
"Banker's fountain pens," 273, 278
Banking industry and system of, 88, 272, 276–281, 284, 292, 322, 335, 368, 417, 419, 433, 452n, 473–474
Banking and Monetary Statistics, 46n
Banking and Monetary Studies (Carson), 272n, 495n
Bankruptcy law, 166
Banks: 223, 293, 304, 363, 387–391,

524 INDEX

Price Index, Consumer, 440, 444, 449
Production and productivity, 54, 58, 71, 116–117, 120, 136–137, 187, 196, 209, 216, 218, 220, 225
Profit, gross and net, 57, 135, 138, 139, 211, 213, 217, 418
Promissory notes, 274
Property: income, 49–51, 60, 68, 70–71; private, 68–69; owners, 3, 17
Pseudo-opportunity locus, 163–170
Purchasing power, 95, 104, 171, 324, 345, 399, 416, 439, 441, 443, 449, 472, 487–488, 495, 504

"Q" Regulation ceiling rates, 321n, 339–340, 343, 358
Quarterly Journal of Economics, 4n, 11n, 25n, 81n, 194n, 228n, 240n, 282n, 497n
Quasi rents, 203, 209–211, 214

Rate-of-return equations, 189–190, 285–290, 295, 297, 299, 326–328, 332, 336, 338, 385–386, 398–399, 447
"Rational" behavior, 18–19
Ratios, reserve, 279, 311, 319, 339, 389, 410, 447
Readings in Monetary Theory, 228n
Real estate, 244, 274, 358, 384
Recession, 408, 489, 500
Reconstruction Finance Corp., 456
Redemptions, 449, 466
Reforms, 347
Refunding operations, 431, 460
Regulatory measures, 284, 358
Rent: of capital, 117, 119–121, 124; quasi, 203, 209–211, 214
Replies to Questions and Other Material for the Use of the Subcommittee on General Credit Control and Debt Management, 469n
Report of the Subcommittee on General Credit Control and Debt Management, 457–459, 468
Reserve: balances, 387; borrowed, 426; earnings, 421; free, 281, 396, 409–410; funds, 390; ratios, 279, 311, 319, 339, 389, 410, 447; requirements, 276, 279, 281, 291, 295–298, 310, 318, 321n, 341–342, 363, 433, 458; unborrowed, 367
Retirement program, 103, 180, 249–251, 285, 394, 441–443

Review of Economics and Statistics 27n, 45–46n, 79n, 107n, 173n, 229n, 270n, 456n, 495–496n, 513
Review of Economic Studies, 109n, 111n, 194–195n, 215, 228n, 242n, 270n
Richardson, J. H., 25n
Risk: aversion, 119, 164, 249, 254–257; free, 440–444; portfolio, 161, 251; private, 169, 171, 187–188; reduction, 274, 399; taking of, 80n, 166, 215, 219, 251, 260, 263, 269, 398, 400–402, 412, 449
Risk Aversion and Portfolio Choice (Tobin and Hester), 242n
Roosa, Robert V., 462
Ruggles, R., 25n

S function (*See* Saving, function)
Salant, Walter, 242n
Salary, 8, 269n
Samuelson, Paul A., 75, 168, 173n, 217, 228n, 269n, 462, 464, 467
Savage, L. J., 271n
Saving and savings; accounts, 159, 281, 344; accumulated; 22–23; behavior, 3, 136–137, 148; collective, 183; compulsory, 106–107; current, 20–21, 28–29; decisions, 160, 184; function, 28–29, 33–34, 51, 53, 62, 76, 78, 116, 122, 125; gross, 189, 202, 206, 213; incentive, 73; interest on, 51, 65, 113; normal, 100–101, 103–104, 144; private, 99, 140, 169, 185, 220, 277, 345; public, 273, 281; ratio rates, 94, 180, 182, 189, 192, 206–207, 213; types of, 9, 14, 34, 108n, 154, 188
Savings and loan associations, 85, 275–277, 326, 339–342, 346, 421–422, 443, 472, 484
Say's Law, 196
Schelling, T. C., 98n
Schwartz, Anna, 471–476, 479–498, 507, 509
Securities: holding, 33, 277, 370–375; long-term, 343, 395–398, 401, 404; markets, 29, 269n, 293, 473, 484; return rates, 334, 337, 364–365, 377; sales, 107, 368; issues, 449; short-term, 226, 280, 378, 395–396, 429, 481; Treasury, 54, 353–355, 361, 368
Separation theorem, 215
Shaw, E. S., 227–228n, 282n